DATE DUE

DEMCO 38-296

Encyclopedia of
International Peacekeeping Operations

Encyclopedia of
International Peacekeeping Operations

Oliver Ramsbotham
and Tom Woodhouse

ABC-CLIO

Santa Barbara, California
Denver, Colorado
Oxford, England

United Nations maps reprinted courtesy of the United Nations Department of Public Information

Library of Congress Cataloging-in-Publication Data
Ramsbotham, Oliver.
    Encyclopedia of international peacekeeping operations / Oliver
Ramsbotham and Tom Woodhouse.
        p.   cm.
    Includes bibliographical references and index.
    ISBN 0-87436-892-8 (alk. paper)
    1. United Nations—Armed Forces.   2. Security, International.
I. Woodhouse, Tom.   II. Title.
JZ6374.R36   1999
355.3'57—dc21

                                                                    98-49834
                                                                         CIP

04 03 02 01 00 99   9 8 7 6 5 4 3 2 1

ABC-CLIO, Inc.
130 Cremona Drive, P.O. Box 1911
Santa Barbara, California 93116-1911

Typesetting by Letra Libre

This book is printed on acid-free paper ∞.

Manufactured in the United States of America

Contents

Preface   vii

Acknowledgments and List of Contributors   ix

Introduction   xi

Acronyms and Abbreviations Used in

     Peacekeeping   xxvii

Encyclopedia of International Peacekeeping Operations   1

Appendixes   307

Bibliography   323

Index   335

Preface

This encyclopedia was produced in order to respond to the remarkable growth of peacekeeping as a method of international conflict management and resolution, particularly during the 1990s. United Nations peacekeeping has a history that dates back over forty years and peacekeeping now affects many countries of the world, either as providers of peacekeeping forces or as conflict-prone states where peacekeepers are serving. The literature on peacekeeping is now extensive, and includes specialized journals, manuals, and handbooks produced by military colleges; biographies and autobiographies on prominent personalities; and dedicated Internet sites and many other sources of information. It is hoped that this work will provide a comprehensive and accessible reference source for information on all aspects of the theory and practice of peacekeeping in the contemporary world. We must acknowledge our debt to all those whose research has provided the bedrock of knowledge that has made this enterprise possible. Readers of the encyclopedia will see that entries acknowledge information sources as appropriate, and that the lengthy bibliography provides a comprehensive guide to further sources, for those who wish to deepen their knowledge of the field. The value of the Internet as a rich source of information is also reflected here, and World Wide Web sites are indicated in the text as a means of enabling readers to access updated information.

There will inevitably be omissions, for which we apologize; and while we have endeavored to be as accurate as possible, we hope that we have not made too many errors. Readers who may wish to comment on matters of omission, or who may have ideas on how to improve future versions of this work, are welcome to contact the authors via the homepage of the Centre for Conflict Resolution at the University of Bradford (http://www.brad.ac.uk/acad/confres/crchome.html).

Dr. Oliver Ramsbotham
Dr. Tom Woodhouse
Bradford, West Yorkshire
July 1998

It is not possible to produce a book of this nature without the help of a large number of people. In addition to those who wrote specific contributions (listed below), we are very grateful for the help and support of a special group of people whose generosity in giving time, energy, and care to this project enabled us to complete it. We wish to thank Angela Kane and her colleagues in the United Nations Department of Public Information and the Dag Hammarskjöld Library for help, especially with material for biographies. Alexander Austen, Wibke Hansen, and Laina Reynolds provided magnificent support in the final stages of producing the book and helped especially with general research assistance, searching for photographs, computer support and virus protection, cross-referencing, and acronym hunting. Alexander Ramsbotham and Tamara Duffey wrote a number of entries, acknowledged below, and were always available for deployment on urgent missions. Laura Beaumont provided skilled and patient support in the production of the bibliography. Toby Feakin helped with the collection of maps and produced the tables that appear in the appendixes. Gerrard Quille and Marta Martinelli researched and drafted material for the biographical entries. We also wish to thank Bernard Stinson, who was both our "force commander" and "special representative," coordinating our efforts, providing research assistance, being an Internet wizard, and drawing material together for word processing. Finally we wish to thank our families, who have suffered much in the cause of peacekeeping.

Contributors

Alexander Austen and Wibke Hansen: Central African Republic

Laura Beaumont: U.S. Sinai Support Mission/Sinai Field Mission

Andrew Cottey: Conflict prevention

Acknowledgments and List of Contributors

Tamara Duffey: Culture and peacekeeping; Haiti; Somalia; Training for peacekeeping; Women and peacekeeping

Tamara Duffey and Richard Jones: Regional organizations and peacekeeping

Jeannie Grussendorf: Organization for Security and Cooperation in Europe (OSCE)

Yuka Hasegawa: World Wide Web

Nick Lewer: Sri Lanka

Nick Lewer and Steve Schofield: Nonlethal weapons and peacekeeping

Ananda Millard: Child soldiers

Michael Pugh: Naval peacekeeping; New Zealand; Parsons, Anthony

Alexander Ramsbotham: Congo; Middle East conflict; Organization of African Unity; UNDOF; UNEF I and II; UNTSO. Also research assistance and collaboration in writing Dominican Republic; ONUCA; UNASOG; UNGOMAP; UNIIMOG; UNIKOM; UNMOT; UNSCOP.

Laina Reynolds: Civilian component in peacekeeping operations; Civilian police (United Nations Civilian Police [CIVPOL]); Guatemala; Human rights

Martin Rupiya: Zimbabwe

Anders Sandberg: Intelligence support and peacekeeping operations

Martin Smith: North Atlantic Treaty Organization (NATO)

Defining Peacekeeping

The official United Nations account of peacekeeping, *The Blue Helmets,* defines peacekeeping as follows: "A peacekeeping operation has come to be defined as an operation involving military personnel, but without enforcement powers, undertaken by the United Nations to help maintain or restore international peace and security in areas of conflict." It is generally accepted that peacekeeping is a function of the United Nations, but there are occasions when international and regional organizations other than the United Nations have performed peacekeeping functions, and there are operations that can be seen as early peacekeeping efforts that predated the formation of the United Nations in 1945. After World War I, for example, multinational military bodies were used to establish and administer the new European frontiers that had been agreed upon in peace treaties after the war. Also after World War I, the League of Nations conducted activities that were comparable in some respects to peacekeeping. However, since 1945 peacekeeping has been the technique most frequently used by and associated with the United Nations to terminate conflicts and establish peace, so much so that the organization was awarded the Nobel Peace Prize for its peacekeeping activities in 1988.

Peacekeeping is not mentioned in the UN Charter, and peacekeeping operations are often described as falling between chapter 6 and chapter 7 of the charter. Chapter 6 refers to the techniques that the Security Council can adopt in pursuit of the peaceful settlement of disputes, such as mediation, arbitration, negotiation, and fact-finding. Chapter 7 gives the Security Council power to enforce decisions, including through the use of armed forces if necessary, to maintain or restore international peace and security. Article 99 gives the secretary-general power to carry out "good offices missions," including fact-finding and inquiry, to encourage hostile parties to seek a negotiated settlement. Peacekeeping is thus not explicitly provided for in the UN Charter, and therefore peacekeeping operations were once described by Dag Hammarskjöld as "chapter six-and-a-half" initiatives. The first full-fledged peacekeeping mission, and the first to be called a peacekeeping mission,

Introduction

came in 1956, when the United Nations Emergency Force I (UNEF I) was established in response to British and French forces' invasion of Egypt during the Suez Canal crisis. UNEF I served as a precedent for all subsequent missions. It established a set of principles that still define the essence of peacekeeping. Secretary-General Dag Hammarskjöld and Lester B. Pearson (General Assembly president, 1952–1953) defined the principles as follows:

- The principle of the consent of the parties to the dispute for the establishment of the mission
- The principle of nonuse of force except in self-defense
- The principle of voluntary contributions of contingents from small, neutral countries to participate in the force
- The principle of impartiality
- The principle of control of peacekeeping operations by the secretary-general

Although a number of these principles have been contested and challenged, particularly in the debate about the nature and efficacy of peacekeeping in post–Cold War conflicts, they proved durable enough over a period of 30 years for Brian Urquhart to describe the document in which they are defined as "a conceptual masterpiece in a completely new field, the blue print for a non-violent, international military operation" (Fetherston, 1994a). During the Cold War period, 13 peacekeeping operations were established, and for most of these years and in most of these missions peacekeeping was restricted to the monitoring of borders and buffer zones after cease-fires had been agreed upon. Typically, these operations were composed of lightly armed national troop contingents from UN member states.

The History of Peacekeeping, 1945–1988

Since 1945 there have been 42 UN peacekeeping operations. The first initiative contributing to the development of the United Nations' peacekeeping framework was the United Nations Special Committee on the Balkans (UNSCOB) established in 1947 in response to the civil war in Greece. The next operation, the United Nations Truce Supervision Organization (UNTSO), was established in June 1948 to supervise Arab-Israel conflict in Palestine and was composed of a UN mediator and military observers. UNTSO has been in constant operation since its establishment, and as of 1998 it was still reporting on the situation in the Middle East as well as providing personnel and support to the two other Middle East observer missions (UNDOF and UNIFIL). UNTSO's pioneering experience helped to establish several other peacekeeping operations in the Middle East. The third initiative was established in the context of the Indo-Pakistani conflict over Kashmir when, in January 1948, the Security Council created a United Nations Commission for India and Pakistan (UNCIP) with the task of investigating the situation and providing a mediatory influence. When a cease-fire went into effect in September 1949, UNCIP was withdrawn, and the military observers were integrated into the United Nations Military Observer Group in India and Pakistan (UNMOGIP). UNMOGIP continues to monitor the cease-fire agreement.

As already noted, the first mission explicitly labeled "peacekeeping" was UNEF I. It was dispatched to the Sinai peninsula in response to the 1956 Suez Canal crisis to observe the cease-fire and the withdrawal of British, French, and Israeli forces from Egyptian territory. Although UNEF helped to keep the peace in the Sinai for over a

decade, the operation was withdrawn in 1967 after a period of rising tension. As the first armed UN peacekeeping operation, UNEF was important as a precedent for other UN forces, as well as a test case for the value of armed, neutral forces in restraining conflict. The United Nations Disengagement Observer Force (UNDOF) was established in May 1974 following the outbreak of war between Israel and Egypt (around the Sinai and Suez Canal) and between Israel and Syria (on the Golan Heights). It was created to supervise the implementation of an agreement on disengagement signed between Israel and Syria, and it continues to inspect armaments and force levels in the area of separation. The United Nations Interim Force in Lebanon (UNIFIL) was established in March 1978 following the invasion of southern Lebanon by Israeli forces. UNIFIL was created to confirm the withdrawal of Israeli forces from Lebanon and to assist the Lebanese government in reinstating its authority. UNIFIL, viewed as a "quasi-permanent fixture," is still deployed to prevent hostile activities and to protect the civilian population.

After UNEF I, the second major early operation to shape both the practice and normative framework for UN peacekeeping operations was the United Nations Operation in the Congo (ONUC). Established in 1960 in an attempt to calm the former Belgian Congo, where civil war erupted during the process of decolonization, it was the UN's second armed peacekeeping operation and, for 30 years, the largest. The initial mandate simply called for the withdrawal of Belgian troops. In 1961 the Security Council revised its mandate, creating a far stronger intervention policy. In 1964, once its mandate was fulfilled, the force withdrew, having no expectations of solving the country's broader political problems. The operation in the former Congo was an important landmark in UN peacekeeping for several reasons. First, the United Nations was operating on unfamiliar ground (previous missions had involved monitoring border zones in the Middle East) and in an environment where the institutions of the state were collapsing. Second, ONUC was the first peacekeeping operation to include a substantial civilian component. Third, it raised the first questions about action under chapter 7 of the UN Charter and the use of force in UN peacekeeping. Initially, ONUC was deployed as a peacekeeping operation, but when it became clear that ONUC would not otherwise achieve its objectives, the Security Council authorized the use of force. This was the first and, until the peacekeeping efforts in Somalia in the early 1990s, the only case of a transition from peacekeeping to peace enforcement. Hence, ONUC is frequently seen as a formidable example in the UN's development of peacekeeping of what not to do. The struggles that ONUC faced helped to ensure that the United Nations supported no new peacekeeping operations for a decade.

In 1964, prior to the withdrawal of troops from the Republic of the Congo and following the outbreak of violence between Greek and Turkish Cypriot communities after Cyprus became independent from Britain, the United Nations Peacekeeping Force in Cyprus (UNFICYP) was established. Its original mandate was to prevent a recurrence of the violence between the two communities and to restore law and order to the island. Because of recurring hostilities, UNFICYP continues to patrol and monitor a cease-fire line and buffer zone that extends across the island.

Several additional operations were established during the Cold War period, but their influence on the development of peacekeeping has been limited. These included the United Nations Observation Group in Lebanon (UNOGIL), the United Nations Temporary Executive Authority in West Irian and the United Nations Security Force in West New Guinea (UNTEA/UNSF), the United Nations Yemen Observer Mission (UNYOM), the Representative of the Secretary-General in the Dominican Republic (DOMREP), the United Nations India-Pakistan

Observer Mission (UNIPOM), and the second United Nations Emergency Force (UNEF II), also deployed for conflict between Egypt and Israel.

The 13 operations established during the Cold War, 5 of which are still deployed today, gradually nurtured the development of a body of principles, procedures, and practices that have been applied to contemporary peacekeeping.

The History of Peacekeeping since 1988

Since 1988 there has been a dramatic increase in the number of peacekeeping operations. As of 31 January 1988, when the Cold War was coming to an end, there were only five operations in the field: three in the Middle East, a small observer mission in Kashmir, and UNFICYP in Cyprus.

However, as of 31 January 1992, the date of the first Security Council Summit, 11 peacekeeping operations were deployed (7 were traditional missions and 4 were multifunctional). As of 16 December 1994, the eve of the fiftieth anniversary of the United Nations, 17 operations were deployed (9 were traditional missions and 8 were multifunctional) (see Table 1).

Between 1988, when the Cold War was winding down and UN peacekeeping operations were awarded the Nobel Peace Prize, and 1996, 29 operations were created, compared to 13 operations between 1948 and 1978 and none in the decade that followed. The dramatic increase in the number of peacekeeping operations has been accompanied by a change in their very nature, specifically, in their *function* (the single function associated with traditional operations has evolved

Table 1 The Growth of UN Peacekeeping, 1988–1994

	January 1988	January 1992	December 1994
Number of active missions	5	11	17
Number of troop-contributing countries	26	56	76
Military personnel	9,570	11,495	73,393
Civilian police personnel	35	155	2,130
International civilian personnel	1,516	2,206	2,260
Annual UN peacekeeping budget	US$230.4 million	US$1,689.6 million	US$3,610 million

United Nations peace-keeping operations as of June 1996

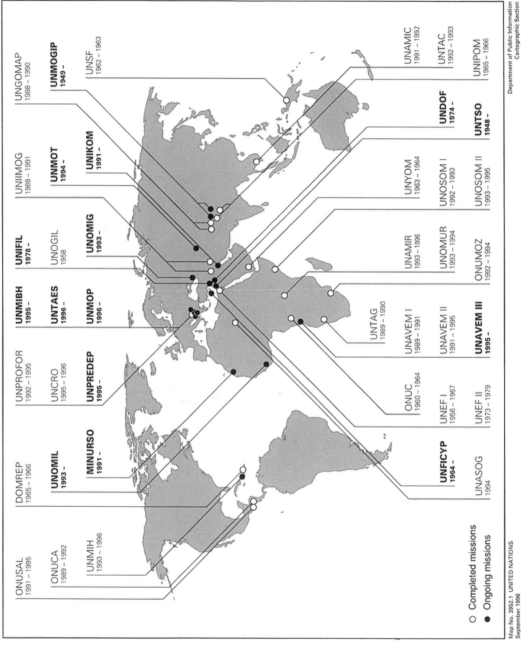

ONUSAL
1991 – 1995

ONUCA
1989 – 1992

UNMIH
1993 – 1996

DOMREP
1965 – 1966

**UNOMIL
1993 –**

**MINURSO
1991 –**

UNPROFOR
1992 – 1995

UNCRO
1995 – 1996

**UNPREDEP
1995 –**

UNMIBH
1995 –

UNTAES
1996 –

UNMOP
1996 –

UNIFIL
1978 –

UNOGIL
1958

UNOMIG
1993 –

UNIIMOG
1988 – 1991

**UNMOT
1994 –**

**UNIKOM
1991 –**

UNGOMAP
1988 – 1990

**UNMOGIP
1949 –**

UNSF
1962 – 1963

UNAMIC
1991 – 1992

UNTAC
1992 – 1993

UNIPOM
1965 – 1966

**UNDOF
1974 –**

**UNTSO
1948 –**

UNYOM
1963 – 1964

UNOSOM I
1992 – 1993

UNOSOM II
1993 – 1995

UNAMIR
1993 – 1996

UNOMUR
1993 – 1994

ONUMOZ
1992 – 1994

UNTAG
1989 – 1990

UNAVEM I
1989 – 1991

UNAVEM II
1991 – 1995

**UNAVEM III
1995 –**

ONUC
1960 – 1964

UNEF I
1956 – 1967

UNEF II
1973 – 1979

**UNFICYP
1964 –**

UNASOG
1994

○ Completed missions

● Ongoing missions

Map No. 3962.1 UNITED NATIONS
September 1996

Department of Public Information
Cartographic Section

xiv

into a multiplicity of tasks), in their *application* (operations have been established to respond to the new breed of conflict in areas not previously recognized), and in their *composition* (peacekeepers now come from a variety of sources—military, civilian police, and diplomatic—and from many nations and cultures).

Contemporary peacekeeping can be appropriately characterized as multilateral, multidimensional, and multinational/multicultural.

Multilateralism refers to the several levels of actors that may be involved in an operation. First, the operation consists of the parties to the conflict; there may be as few as two identifiable parties (for example, Frente da Libertaçao do Mozambique [FRELIMO] and Resistencia Nacional Mocambicana [RENAMO] in Mozambique) or as many as 15 (for example, in Somalia, where a throng of clans vied for power). Second, the operation includes peacekeepers themselves, the UN and other international participants.

Furthermore, the operation is multidimensional, having military, civilian police, and civilian components. The military component—the land, naval, and air forces contributed by UN member states—includes both armed and unarmed soldiers (the latter are referred to as military observers). The military component is responsible for such tasks as the monitoring and verification of cease-fires; the cantonment (or containment), disarmament, and demobilization of combatants; the overseeing of the withdrawal of foreign forces; mine awareness education and mine clearance; and the provision of security for UN and other international activities in support of a peace process. Essentially, the military component serves in a supporting role, maintaining a secure environment in which the civilian components can work.

Third, a civilian police component has become increasingly involved in peacekeeping operations, playing an important role somewhere between the military and civilian actors. Operating under authority from the UN Security Council, international police monitors assist in the creation of secure environments and the maintenance of public order. Their public security responsibilities range from crowd control to the establishment and maintenance of a judicial system to actual law enforcement. In addition, civilian police monitor, train, and advise local law enforcement authorities on organizational, administrative, and human rights issues.

Fourth, there is a sizable civilian component, sometimes outnumbering the military component. The civilian component can be subdivided into two main groupings. First, there are intergovernmental organizations (IGOs), that is, organizations that are mandated by agreements drawn up between two or more states. This includes all UN agencies (e.g., the United Nations High Commissioner for Refugees [UNHCR], the World Food Program [WFP], the United Nations Children's Fund [UNICEF], and the United Nations Development Program [UNDP]); it includes regional organizations (e.g., the Organization of African Unity [OAU], the Organization of American States [OAS], and the Organization for Security and Cooperation in Europe [OSCE]); and it includes the International Committee of the Red Cross/Red Crescent (ICRC). Second, there are nongovernmental organizations (NGOs), that is, national and international organizations that are constituted separately from the government of the country in which they are founded. In addition, there is a UN civilian chief of mission (a special representative of the secretary-general). In contrast to the military component's strength, which lies in the effective coercive influence it can exercise over belligerents, the civilian component's strength may be diplomatic, economic, ideological, scientific and technical, humanitarian, or legal areas.

The civilian component can be further analyzed into several important subcomponents: a political element responsible for the political guidance of the overall peace process, including assisting in the rehabilitation of existing political institutions and promoting national reconciliation; a police element responsible for restoring public law and order; an electoral element that monitors and verifies all aspects and stages of an electoral process, coordinates the technical assistance of the process, educates the public about electoral processes, and helps to develop grassroots democratic institutions; a human rights element that monitors the human rights situation, investigates specific cases of alleged human rights violations, and promotes human rights; and a humanitarian element responsible for the delivery of humanitarian aid (food and other emergency relief supplies), implementing refugee repatriation programs, resettling displaced persons, and reintegration of ex-combatants.

Multinationalism and *multiculturalism* mean that a peacekeeping force is assembled by a multiplicity of troop-contributing nations, from Australia to Guinea Bissau, France to Nepal, the United States to Uruguay, and that the civilian component is derived from a diverse range of nations. Each nation or agency comes to the operation with its own political and cultural background, its varied understandings of the conflict situation, and its own diverse approaches and techniques.

The following section is a brief overview of the multilateral, multinational/multicultural, and multidimensional peacekeeping operations established between 1988 and 1995. Of the 29 operations established since 1988, 12 clearly exhibit these three characteristics.

The first multidimensional operation to be established at the end of the Cold War was the United Nations Transitional Assistance Group (UNTAG), which was implemented in February 1989 for Namibia. With essentially a political mandate, UNTAG was the first mission to prepare a nation for elections and independence, making the Namibian conflict one of the few examples of a successful peaceful solution to a long-term conflict. The UNTAG operation moved the United Nation beyond the traditional role of peacekeeping, breaking new ground and encouraging similar UN intervention in other long-term conflicts.

In November 1989, the United Nations Observer Mission in Central America (ONUCA) was established to support the regional peace process. ONUCA is unique in that it began as an observation mission, grew into a security force that assisted in the demobilization of the Contras in Nicaragua, and supported the establishment of the more ambitious operation in El Salvador. With its highly visible civilian component successfully overseeing a national electoral process, it became the second post–Cold War mission exemplifying the changing nature of peacekeeping. As a contin-

uation of the Central American peace process, the United Nations Observer Mission in El Salvador (ONUSAL) was established in May 1991. It was mandated to monitor the human rights situation and to supervise the electoral process, again illustrating the effective multidimensional character of contemporary peacekeeping.

The second United Nations Angola Verification Mission (UNAVEM II), an extension and expansion of the limited UNAVEM I, was established in May 1991 and was succeeded by UNAVEM III in February 1995. Although setbacks were experienced by UNAVEM II and III, UNAVEM is a paradigmatic example of the second generation of peacekeeping. It took on the more complex responsibilities characteristically faced by post–Cold War peacekeeping. Its tasks have not only involved the traditional peacekeeping function of monitoring a cease-fire (performed by its military component) but have also included the supervision of the Angolan police force, the monitoring of the electoral process, and humanitarian efforts to alleviate the suffering of the Angolan population (carried out by police and civilian components).

The United Nations Mission for the Referendum in Western Sahara (MINURSO) was mandated in April 1991 to carry out a number of tasks, including refugee repatriation and registration of voters for a referendum of self-determination. However, the parties involved have failed to cooperate, and MINURSO has been unable to achieve its aims. MINURSO's difficulties illustrate the challenges of intervening in protracted and complex conflicts. The chain of conflicts in the former Yugoslavia presented UN peacekeeping with unprecedented challenges, illustrating yet again the complexities involved in responding to post–Cold War conflict. The United Nations Protection Force in Former Yugoslavia (UNPROFOR I)—initially authorized in February 1992 to monitor a cease-fire, to provide support for a political peace process, and to support the provision of humanitarian aid in Croatia—found itself drawn into an ever-worsening, complex, and volatile situation as it oversaw the disintegration of a state and the emergence of stable new states. Its mandate was first extended to Bosnia and Herzegovina (UNPROFOR II), under chapter 7 arrangements, to monitor the humanitarian situation. The United Nations then took the innovative step of deploying a preventive peacekeeping force in Macedonia (initially called UNPROFOR III, then called the United Nations Preventive Deployment Force Macedonia [UNPREDEP]). With its constantly changing and often ambiguous mandate, UNPROFOR is a classic example of an effort in which the line between second-generation (peacekeeping) and peace-enforcement operations has become blurred. UNPROFOR was, in the early 1990s, the largest and most expensive peacekeeping mission deployed by the United Nations. UNPROFOR has also been one of the most controversial peacekeeping operations. The continuation and escalation of the conflict led to severe criticism of peacekeeping, aimed at, among other things, the role of third-party intervention in civil wars (e.g., issues of impartiality, consent) and the availability of resources.

The United Nations Transitional Authority in Cambodia (UNTAC) was established in February 1992 to help rebuild the country and oversee its transition to democratic rule. UNTAC is significant in that in 1992 it was the largest and most ambitious UN peacekeeping operation in the UN's history, with significant multidimensional, multilateral, and multicultural features. Furthermore, it was seen, along with the operation in Namibia, as a major achievement for the United Nations and a model for the study of post–Cold War peacekeeping.

The United Nations Operation in Somalia (UNOSOM), however, like UNPROFOR, presented the United Nations with one of the greatest challenges of its history. Established in April 1992, the United Nations Operation in Somalia (UNOSOM) represented an ambitious plan to rebuild the institutions of a collapsed state. It provided important lessons about the changing nature of conflict and about the theory and practice of multidimensional peacekeeping in the post–Cold War era. Additionally, UNOSOM's chapter 7 mandate has raised serious questions about the role of peace enforcement, consent, and impartiality.

The United Nations Operation in Mozambique (ONUMOZ), established in December 1992, was based on an operational concept with four fully integrated and coordinated components: political, military, electoral, and humanitarian. It successfully verified the cease-fire arrangements, demobilized troops, and initiated a reintegration program; assisted in the formation of a new army; verified the activities of the national police force (assisted by one of the largest civilian police components in history); coordinated humanitarian assistance for millions of people; assisted in the return of more than four million people; and assisted in a free and fair election process. Although ONUMOZ was deployed for 12 months longer than initially planned, the accomplishment of the mandate was described by the UN secretary-general as a "remarkable achievement" in contemporary peacekeeping.

In September 1993, the United Nations Observer Mission in Liberia (UNOMIL) was established to work with the Economic Organization of West African States (ECOWAS) Military Observer Group (ECOMOG). UNOMIL was the first UN peacekeeping operation undertaken in cooperation with a mission already established by another organization. Although UNOMIL has highlighted many of the difficulties of regional peacekeeping (e.g., lack of troops and equipment), it illustrates the fundamental relationship between the United Nations and regional organizations as envisaged in chapter 8 of the UN Charter, as well as the diversification and flexibility of post–Cold War peacekeeping.

The United Nations Mission in Haiti (UNMIH) was authorized in September 1993 to help modernize the Haitian armed forces, establish a new police force, and assist with the electoral process. Though it suffered some initial setbacks, UNMIH is regarded as a successful peacekeeping operation, enabling the return of democracy and the gradual reinforcement of democratic institutions in Haiti. UNMIH has been a unique peacekeeping experience in that it has worked with a U.S.-led multinational force (MNF) mandated under chapter 7, the Organization of American States (OAS)–UN Joint International Civilian Mission in Haiti (MICIVIH), and has evolved into a development-related mission, the United Nations Support Mission for Haiti (UNSMIH). UNMIH has demonstrated the ability of UN peacekeeping to diversify its functions and operate on various levels.

In response to the extreme violence between the Hutu and Tutsis in Rwanda, the United Nations Assistance Mission in Rwanda (UNAMIR) was established in October 1993 to assume command of the small traditional mission, the United Nations Observer Mission in Uganda/Rwanda (UNOMUR), already deployed in the region. UNAMIR's responsibilities included: monitoring the security situation, assisting in the coordination of humanitarian activities, and the repatriation of Rwandan refugees and displaced persons. However, according to the secretary-general, the international community's delayed reaction to the genocide in Rwanda in 1994 dramatically demonstrated the community's inadequacy to respond with prompt and decisive action to humanitarian crises entwined with armed conflict. The ineffectiveness of the UNAMIR mission has been attributed to an increasing feeling of "Africa fatigue" among the UN powers, a feeling that, in turn, produced a failure of political will to provide the resources necessary for a successful peacekeeping operation. Following the UN's experiences in Somalia and the former Yugoslavia, a more cautious and limited response was taken by the international community in Rwanda. As a result of the UN's and humanitarian agencies' failure to respond effectively to the Rwandan crisis, widespread reforms have been called for by many commentators.

The launching of large-scale operations in 1992 in Cambodia, Somalia, and the former Yugoslavia and the general expansion of the missions led to a qualitative change in the functions of peacekeeping, so that they are now best described as multidimensional. Multidimensionality has pulled some missions toward enforcement responsibilities under chapter 7. In addition, peacekeeping mandates frequently have political and humanitarian components, with civilian and civil police staffs to carry them out. In many operations, mandates that began with a limited responsibility to monitor cease-fires have grown, de facto, as the cease-fires have failed and the missions have found themselves drawn into the protection of civilian populations.

The post-1988 deployments are currently being redefined under new forms of military doctrine that seek to elaborate the principles under which they should operate. These deployments are called variously "multidimensional operations," "second-generation peacekeeping operations," "wider peacekeeping," "second-generation multinational forces," or "peace-support operations." Although different authorities classify their roles in a variety of ways, many current peacekeeping operations now have military, political, and humanitarian functions. These functions are described in Table 2.

Peacekeeping forces still carry out the interposition responsibilities of classical peacekeeping

Table 2 Functions of Post–Cold War Peacekeeping

Military	Political	Humanitarian
Cease-fires observation and monitoring.	Upholding law and order.	Protecting aid convoys.
Maintaining buffer zones.	Helping to establish viable government.	Protecting relief/delivery workers.
Disarming warring factions.	Helping to maintain independent status.	Providing humanitarian aid.
Regulating the disposition of forces.	Coping/negotiating with nongovernment entities.	Establishing, supporting, and protecting regional safe havens and other protected areas.
Preventing infiltration.		
Preventing civil war.	Election administration.	
Verifying security agreements.	Exercising temporary authority.	Assisting in refugee repatriation.
Supervising cantonment.	Providing security and helping to re-establish economic life for the local populace.	Monitoring refugee flow.
Clearing mines.		Logistical support for humanitarian projects including transport, medical, and engineering.
Training/re-forming military units.	Management and arbitration of local disputes.	
	Confidence-building measures.	Verifying human rights agreements.
	Training police forces.	

missions, that is, cease-fire observation, buffer-zone control, and so on. In addition, they now also serve in support roles such as providing security for a variety of nonmilitary operations, including assisting with the repatriation of refugees and monitoring elections and the distribution of humanitarian relief supplies by civilian agencies.

While functions have diversified, the contexts and environments in which the missions are deployed have become more complex. Although there have been exceptions (ONUC in the Congo, and UNIFIL in Lebanon, for example), peacekeeping operations set up since 1956 (under the Hammarskjöld-Pearson principles summarized above) have generally operated in permissive environments where they have the consent and support of host governments for their presence. Increasingly, however, they have been deployed in internal wars or complex political emergencies, defined as situations of civil and international war. In these situations consent may be partial, and conditions of lawlessness and violence in which militias and paramilitary groups act autonomously mean that UN agencies are often confronted and opposed.

Defining Post–Cold War Peacekeeping

During the period 1989 to 1994 peacekeeping became the most visible activity of the United Nations. By the end of this period peacekeeping was also the most controversial activity that the United Nations engaged in. Throughout the early and mid-1990s there has been a barrage of criticism of the United Nations, sometimes on practical grounds but mainly, and more fundamentally, questioning the nature and viability of peacekeeping itself. These critiques suggest that military, political, and humanitarian objectives should not necessarily be inextricably combined and that peacekeeping should go "back to basics," that is, that it should undertake only the relatively simple roles of classical peacekeeping. Other critics have suggested that to survive and to be relevant in the future, peacekeeping must be strengthened and redefined so that it can operate beyond the constraints of classical or first-generation peacekeeping, in a new mode of second-generation capabili-

ties suitable for the challenges of internal conflicts and civil wars. Most recently these new capabilities are described as "peace-support operations." Terminologies can be precise and confusing. The following sections provides definitions of key terms.

Definitions of Peacekeeping and Related Terms

Military Operations Other Than War (MOOTW) This term is used in the military doctrine of the United States. These are military operations that have the objectives of deterring war, resolving conflict and promoting peace, and supporting the civil power in domestic crises. A wide range of activities are defined as forms of MOOTW, including arms control; combating of terrorism; enforcement of sanctions; narcotics interdiction and control; humanitarian assistance; protection of shipping, ensuring of freedom of navigation, and oversight. Peace operations, including peacekeeping, are usually categorized in U.S. doctrine within MOOTW.

Peace Operations An overall term that includes peacekeeping operations, peace-enforcement operations, and other military operations conducted within the context of political and diplomatic efforts to establish and maintain peace.

Peace Support Operations After several decades, peacekeeping activities took on a greater diversity and began to involve larger and more powerful forces, including greater numbers of nonmilitary organizations. Terms like "peace building," "peacemaking," and "peace enforcement" were added to the language of the peacekeepers to describe each additional category of response. "Peace support operations" (PSO) describes the operations and activities of all civil and military organizations deployed to restore peace and/or relieve human suffering. Peace support operations may include diplomatic actions, traditional peacekeeping, and the more forceful military actions required to establish peaceful conditions. In this context, a multinational response comprises several elements, including humanitarian, military, civil administration, and infrastructure development agencies and teams of political negotiators. The civil and military assets for peace support operations can be provided by different sources: collectively by the UN and regional organizations, or individually by nations and nongovernmental organizations. Although divided by outlook, status, and political orientation, each element involved in a PSO is, or should be, working toward the same long-term outcome. (Mackinlay 1996)

Peacekeeping Military operations undertaken with the consent of all major parties to a conflict, intended to facilitate the implementation of a cease-fire or peace agreement, and to support political efforts to reach a long-term solution. (U.S. Army 1994)

A peacekeeping operation has come to be defined as an operation involving military personnel, but without enforcement powers, undertaken by the United Nations to help maintain or restore international peace and security in areas of conflict. (United Nations Blue Helmets, 1996)

Peacekeeping is the deployment of a United Nations presence in the field, hitherto with the consent of all parties concerned, normally involving United Nations military and/or police personnel and frequently civilians as well. Peacekeeping is a technique that expands the possibilities for both the prevention of conflict and making of peace. (Boutros-Ghali 1992)

Field operations established by the United Nations, with the consent of the parties concerned, to help control and resolve conflicts between them, under United Nations command and control, at the expense collectively of the member states, and with military and other personnel and equipment provided voluntarily by them, acting impartially between the parties and using force to the minimum extent necessary. (Goulding 1993)

The prevention, containment, moderation, and termination of hostilities between or within states, through the medium of a peaceful third-party intervention organized and directed internationally, using multinational forces of soldiers, police, and civilians to restore and maintain peace. (International Peace Academy 1994)

Actions designed to enhance international peace, security, and stability which are authorized by competent national and international organizations and which are undertaken cooperatively and individually by military, humanitarian, good governance, civilian police, and other interested agencies and groups. (Pearson Peacekeeping Center 1996)

Peacemaking Peacemaking is a process of diplomacy, mediation, negotiation, or other forms of peaceful settlement that end disputes and resolve the issues that led to conflict. Military activities that support peacemaking include military-to-military relations and security assistance operations. Other military activities, such as exercises and peacetime deployments, may enhance the diplomatic process by demonstrating the engagement of the U.S. abroad. These activities contribute to an atmosphere of cooperation and assistance with allies and friends, thus demonstrating the resolve of the U.S. with regard to its commitments. Such demonstrations of resolve may assist diplomatic efforts at conflict resolution. Military-to-military contacts and security assistance programs also serve to enhance diplomacy by influencing important groups in regions of conflict and by promoting the stable environment necessary for the success of diplomacy. (U.S. Army 1994, p. 2)

Peace Building Peace building consists of postconflict actions, primarily diplomatic, that strengthen and rebuild civil infrastructures and institutions in order to avoid a return to conflict. It also includes mechanisms that advance a sense of confidence and well-being and support economic reconstruction. Military as well as civilian involvement is normally required. Peace-building activities include restoring civil authority, rebuilding physical infrastructures, and reestablishing commerce, schools, and medical facilities. The most extensive peace-building effort in history took place in Europe and Asia in the post–World War II era when the U.S. and its allies assisted nations on those continents devastated by a decade of war. Military support to diplomacy also includes assistance in selected areas such as the conduct of elections and plebiscites and demobilization of former belligerent parties. (U.S. Army 1994, p. 2)

Preventive Diplomacy   Preventive diplomacy involves actions that are taken before an anticipated crisis in order to prevent violence. These actions can include using military forces in preventive deployment, that is, deploying military forces in zones of potential conflict where tensions are rising but where violence has not become acute. These preventive deployments resemble peacekeeping forces in terms of force structures and activities. Preventive deployments can be used in internal or national crises at the request of the government or the parties concerned. The force is deployed on the principle that its presence may provide a symbol that will act as a restraining influence. The objective is to put parties to the conflict under the scrutiny of the international community; they are thereby put under pressure to negotiate a solution before resorting to violence. Specific tasks of a preventive force include acting as an interpositional force to forestall violence, protecting the local delivery of humanitarian relief, assisting local authorities to protect and offer security to threatened minorities, securing and maintaining essential services, and maintaining law and order. The most significant example of a currently deployed preventive force is UNPREDEP in Macedonia.

Peace Enforcement   Peace enforcement is the application or threat of military force, normally following authorization by the international community (through a resolution of the UN Security Council) to enforce compliance with generally accepted resolutions. The purpose of peace enforcement is to restore peace and to support diplomatic efforts for a long-term political solution, particularly in areas where competent civil authorities have ceased to function because of civil war. Peace enforcement may include combat action, which calls for the use of war-fighting capabilities, but combat and noncombat actions may take place simultaneously. Forces may be involved in the separation of belligerents, or they may be engaged in combat against some of them. In U.S. doctrine peace operations are conducted in several phases: The deployment of rapid-reaction combat forces to establish a visible military presence should be followed by a transition from a purely military presence to support for the development of the civil authority. The specific objectives of the mission can include the restoration of order and stability, the protection of humanitarian assistance, the enforcement of sanctions, guarantee and denial of movement, establishment and supervision of protected zones, and the forcible separation of belligerent parties.

The operation in Somalia from 1992 to 1995 is an example of peace enforcement and was authorized under chapter 7 of the UN Charter. Earlier examples include the UN operations in Korea (1950–1953), the operation in the Congo in 1960, and the war against Iraq in Kuwait, all of which were authorized under chapter 7.

War   War is large-scale combat operations in pursuit of national objectives or to protect national interests or the interests of a coalition or alliance of nations. The goal is to win a conflict in terms favorable to the state or states engaging in the conflict and to defeat the opponent.

Practical Critiques

The Department of Peacekeeping Operations (DPKO) is responsible for the day-to-day management of peacekeeping operations and for communications between the United Nations and the field operation. The Department of Humanitarian Affairs (DHA) is responsible for the coordination of humanitarian operations, especially for organizing the delivery of assistance by UN relief organizations and for liaison with NGOs in the field. The Department of Political Affairs (DPA) advises the secretary-general on issues of international peace and security and on the control and resolution of conflicts within and between states. The Department of Administration and Management (DAM) is responsible for the administration and financial support of peacekeeping operations.

Many authorities have pointed to a need to reform the organization of UN operations. Some have distinguished between readiness problems (having to do with mounting and deployment of the force) and operational problems (having to do with continuous support in the field). At both levels peacekeeping poses complex logistical problems. For example, at its height UNOSOM II took troops from 35 different nations. Command and control of military forces become highly complicated when forces from so many nations are involved. Operations suffer from unclear and ambiguous chains of command both within missions and between the mission and the Secretariat in New York, which has overall responsibility for the management of peacekeeping operations. It is well known that national contingents frequently refer to their capitals for orders rather than to the UN force commander or to New York. This failure to establish effective communication with New York is at least in part the result of the lack of direction from the center in New York and of the failure to coordinate the activities of the four main UN bodies involved in managing peacekeeping operations (the DPKO, the DPA, the DHA, and the DAM). Communications between the military, the civil and political, and the humanitarian components of an operation are also a problem, and there is a serious inadequacy in the training of many units sent on peacekeeping operations. Reforms to improve the central management of UN peacekeeping, to improve coordination between New York and the field operations, and to develop central training guidance and standards have been considered and to some degree implemented since 1993.

While some critics have pointed to organizational inefficiency, others have provided damning accounts of the inefficiency and corruption of aspects of UN peacekeeping. In Cambodia and Somalia, for example, there were complaints about lack of accountability when UN personnel were themselves guilty of breaches of local or international law and of abuse of the human rights of local people. These criticisms should be set beside the more positive accounts offered by contributing governments and by the United Nations Secretariat.

Responses to Critiques: New Thinking about Peacekeeping in the 1990s

A number of publications have defined the new challenges for peacekeeping in the 1990s. British doctrine defines peacekeeping as "operations carried out with the consent of the belligerent parties in support of efforts to achieve or maintain peace in order to promote security and sustain life in areas of potential or actual conflict" (British Army, 1995, p. 1-2). The term "wider peacekeeping" is used by the British to describe "the wider aspects of peacekeeping operations carried out with the consent of the belligerent parties but in an environment that may be volatile" (British Army, 1995, p. 2-9). Despite the post–Cold War conflict experience of Somalia and Bosnia especially, the *Field Manual on Wider Peacekeeping* insists on the retention of the principle of consent and on a clear separation between peacekeeping and peace enforcement. Peacekeeping requires consent; peace enforcement does not. A distinction is made between the level of tactical and field operations, where consent may be partial, subject to change, and poorly defined, and the operational (theater) level, where consent comes from formal agreements by recognized parties and is relatively stable. Particularly at the tactical level, consent does not mean seeking universal approval for every action taken, but it does involve "a general public attitude that tolerates a peacekeeping presence and represents a quorum of co-operation." This definition has implications for the degree to which force can be used in an operation that is essentially nonviolent. Force can be used where local opinion supports its use—against banditry or looting, for example. John Mackinlay, who pioneered much of the rethinking, refers to second-generation multinational operations to distinguish the expanded tasks of peacekeepers in creating "the conditions for others [the civil and humanitarian components] to succeed" (Mackinlay 1994, 158). He argues that in semiconsensual and turbulent conflict environments, new concepts and training methods are needed. In the United States, Presidential Decision Directive 25 uses the terms "peace operations" and "peace-support operations" to cover the entire spectrum of activities from traditional peacekeeping to peace enforcement. In *An Agenda for Peace* (1992), UN Secretary-General Boutros Boutros-Ghali introduced the idea of forming "peace enforcement units" that would be more heavily armed than traditional peacekeeping forces and that would be on call from member states, equipped and prepared to monitor and enforce cease-fires and even peace agreements. In order to achieve rapid deployment, Secretary-General Boutros-Ghali requested in 1992 that troops and resources be made available by governments to the UN peace operations at short notice, when necessary. These standby forces were not to be used for peace-enforcement actions but simply for chapter 6–type operations. However, after consultation with member states in 1993 and 1994, the idea of the standby forces was limited to what is now called the United Nations Standby Arrangements System (UNSAS). The Nordic countries, the Netherlands, and Canada have been particularly active in their support for improving the rapid deployment of UN forces through better standby arrangements of this kind.

The Future of Peacekeeping

Disillusionment with the experience of UN peace-keeping has led others to advocate abandoning peacekeeping, except in its limited and classical pre-1988 form, in favor of regional and great power conflict management in which peacekeeping is contracted out to regional organizations and coalitions of states. One example of this kind of conflict management is the use of NATO in Bosnia. Though the number of UN operations has remained at its 1994 peak of 16, the number of personnel involved has been reduced significantly. By March 1997 there were 24,000 UN forces, compared to 76,000 in September 1994. In effect, the United Nations began to opt out of operations that were likely to involve combat risks. By 1997 UN military personnel in peacekeeping operations were outnumbered by forces engaged in coercion and enforcement missions. The Dayton Peace Agreement Implementation Force (IFOR) in Bosnia numbered 60,000 troops, mostly from NATO, whereas its successor, the Stabilization Force (SFOR) numbered 35,000 troops. In 1998, in Georgia and Tajikistan there were 18,000 troops of the Russian-dominated Commonwealth of Independent States (CIS); in Liberia, as part of the ECOMOG operation, there were 7,500 West African troops; and 6,500 troops from southern European states, led by Italy, served in Albania.

These operations are not following a clear peacekeeping mandate, and contracting out is unlikely to replace UN peacekeeping. Most states, despite the difficulties, continue to regard the United Nations as the most appropriate body to safeguard international peace and security because all states are represented through the General Assembly and the Security Council, and many have seen active and valuable service on UN peacekeeping missions. For the future, UN peacekeeping missions may be smaller, but they are likely to be more professionally organized, more efficiently deployed, and better prepared, trained, and equipped. At the national level troop-contributing countries made significant improvements in the 1990s, and international training centers and programs emerged, raising standards of training and producing codes of conduct. In New York a Situation Center was established within the DPKO in 1993, an important improvement: Previously, UN headquarters had only been accessible to peacekeepers in the field between 9:00 A.M. and 5:00 P.M. on normal working days. The Situation Center now functions continuously, with a staff of 24 that reports on the major operations to the UN secretary-general. A Lessons Learned Unit was also established in order to record and analyze the experience gained on UN missions in order to help build institutional memory and to improve performance in future operations. The move toward improving deployment efficiency and speed through a better organized UN Standby Arrangements System (UNSAS) will also strengthen peacekeeping in the future.

UN Secretary-General Kofi Annan pointed to the need for peacekeeping forces to find new capabilities for what he referred to as positive inducements to gain support for peacekeeping mandates among populations in conflict zones. He argued that future peacekeeping forces will need to have a greater coercive capacity, but that reliance on coercion alone will be insufficient, partly because the effect of coercion will erode over time and partly because it is better to attempt to influence the behavior of people in conflict situations by the use of the carrot rather than the stick. Thus, though coercion can restrain violence temporarily, it cannot promote lasting peace; a durable peace and a lasting solution require not only stopping the violence but, crucially, "taking the next step." For Annan, taking the next step means offering positive incentives or induce-

Table 3 United Nations Peacekeeping Missions Deployed at Mid-1998

Mission	Duration	Contributing Countries	Military Personnel	Civilian Police
UNTSO	Jun 1948	20	163 military observers	
UNMOGIP	Jan 1949	8	43 military observers	
UNFICYP	Mar 1964	9	1,212 troops	35
UNDOF	Jun 1974	4	1,064 troops 80 military observers	
UNIFIL	Mar 1978	9	4,520 troops 60 military observers	
MINURSO	Apr 1991	34	123 troops 203 military observers	78
UNIKOM	Apr 1991	33	903 troops 194 military observers	
UNOMIG	Aug 1993	22	82 military observers	
UNMOT	Dec 1994	13	81 military observers	
UNPREDEP	Mar 1995	27	763 troops 35 military observers	26
UNMIBH	Dec 1995	42	3 troops	2,019
UNMOP	Jan 1996	25	28 military observers	
MONUA	Jul 1997	31	903 military contingents 90 military observers	335
MIPONUH	Dec 1997	11		300
UNCIVPOL	Jan 1998	20	31 troops	178
MINURCA	Apr 1998	10	1,350 troops	

Source: United Nations Department of Peacekeeping Operations

ments. Peacekeeping forces, in other words, need to be able to make available rewards in the mission area. This concept of peacekeeping, which Annan sees as absolutely essential for the future effectiveness of peacekeeping operations, brings peacekeeping squarely into the realm of conflict resolution.

The term "peace support operations" is now used to cover a wide range of potential operations, from conflict prevention to peacemaking, and to provide a doctrine that is relevant to the post–Cold War geostrategic environment. It is intended to define a modus operandi for commanders and staff of all services in the future conduct of peacekeeping. In emerging doctrines of peacekeeping, peace enforcement is significantly redefined to have a place within a broader framework of intervention options that nevertheless sees consent and peace building (not victory) as end goals. In the latest British doctrine, the vital division is between peace enforcement and war. Peacekeeping and peace enforcement are to operate on the correct side of the impartiality line and with the ob-

jective of sustaining or restoring consent in the interests of the long-term demands of peace building. However, what defines the essence of peace support here is the need to preserve not so much consent as impartiality.

It is evident from this approach that peace enforcement has to contain within it two dimensions of activity. One of the dimensions brings those who enforce peace close to a state of war (i.e., they must be prepared for combat and have an enforcement capability). At the same time, in order not to breach the impartiality principle, the peace enforcement process must be genuinely capable of building consent so as to limit the necessity of enforcing compliance. If consent cannot be won, the risk of being drawn into prolonged military enforcement actions will increase, as will the danger of "crossing the Mogadishu line," that is, of taking sides and being drawn into the conflict directly. It is clear that unless serious attempts are made to win the belligerents' consent to conflict resolution and postconflict peace building, the new peacekeeping doctrine is fraught with danger of becoming embroiled in warfare.

In order to reduce the chances of this undesirable escalation, British and American doctrines recognize the importance of consent-promoting techniques in peacekeeping, and these techniques are also very similar to Kofi Annan's idea of building and strengthening positive inducements in PSOs. Operationally, there are two categories of techniques that are relevant to PSO doctrine. The first category is composed of techniques to promote cooperation and consent. The second refers to control techniques, where "in particular circumstances the selective use of C2W may be appropriate." C2W is command and control warfare incorporating military activity. It includes psychological operations (PSYOPS), electronic warfare (EW), and operational security (OPSEC). Since it is aimed at influencing communications, information, and perception rather than at physical destruction, command and control warfare may have a key part in PSOs. It may even extend to combat techniques appropriate to war. The likelihood of using combat techniques will be reduced significantly if consent and cooperation techniques are commensurably developed.

The following consent-promoting areas and techniques are defined in PSO doctrine: community information, media operations, civil affairs, and negotiation and mediation. Negotiation and mediation are described as skills required at all stages of a PSO. They are relevant at every level of the operation. All service personnel may be involved, from senior commanders meeting with faction leaders to soldiers at isolated observation points who may become involved in trying to control an incident or arbitrate a dispute. At the wider level, and in a critical sense linking PSO objectives to the goals of conflict resolution, the doctrine includes the objective of making parties to the conflict "stakeholders in the peace process" by providing opportunities to cooperate and through incentives, rewards, and penalties. Within this broader development of the idea of peace support operations there is a likelihood that civilian staff will be more widely used in peacekeeping missions, including the use of white helmets (civilian specialists and staff) to balance and complement the use of military blue helmets (UN peacekeeping personnel), and there will also be a great need to coordinate civil and military aspects of peacekeeping (see Table 3; Map 1) (Boutros-Ghali 1992; Daniel and Hayes 1995; Diehl 1993; Durch 1994; Fetherston 1994b; Findlay 1996; Fisas 1995; James 1990; Moxon-Browne 1998; Ramsbotham and Woodhouse 1996a; Ratner 1997; White 1993).

Scope and Organization of the Book

The book is intended to provide both information and analysis about peacekeeping and its role in the resolution of contemporary conflict. For the most part, peacekeeping since 1945 has been conducted under the direction of the United Nations, and the greater part of this book provides an account of UN operations. However, missions that were not mandated by the United Nations, such as those conducted by Russia and the CIS in the territories of the former Soviet Union, are included, as are other important missions that have been granted legitimacy and approval by the United Nations but that are not under UN control, such as the NATO-led operations in the former Yugoslavia. There are also regional organizations that are beginning to develop policy and capability in peacekeeping, such as the Organization of African Unity (OAU), the Organization for Security and Cooperation in Europe (OSCE), and the Western European Union (WEU).

In most cases some context about the nature of the relevant conflict is provided to introduce the description of the operations. Much of the information for the book came from UN sources, such as the excellent book *The Blue Helmets,* and from other sources of information from the UN Department of Public Information and the UN Department of Peacekeeping Operations. However, a good critical, evaluative, and analytical academic literature has also developed on peacekeeping, and we have drawn upon this, too. Academics such as Rosalyn Higgins pioneered work in the study of peacekeeping, and more recently very good accounts have been written by Alan James and William Durch. There are now also specialized journals dedicated to the study of peacekeeping in international politics. The book also provides analyses and accounts of the broader policy, organizational, national, regional, international, and cultural contexts within which peacekeeping operates. We have also made every effort to include issues and debates that relate to the ways in which peacekeeping is currently being defined and developed in training programs and in the development of national policies toward peacekeeping. Critical thinking about the problems facing peacekeeping in relation to contemporary conflict is also covered by including debates about human rights, conflict resolution theory, postconflict peace building, peace building from below, civilians in peacekeeping, gender critiques and the role of women in peacekeeping, and so on. There are bound to be omissions, and readers are invited to bring these to our attention by contacting the World Wide Web homepage of the Centre for Conflict Resolution, University of Bradford, at http://www.brad.ac.uk/acad/confres/crchome. html. The Internet and the World Wide Web have

been a useful resource in researching this book and will be useful also for readers wishing to find out more about peacekeeping and international conflict and its resolution. The World Wide Web entry guides readers to the relevant Web sites, and throughout the book Web site addresses are given where relevant. Readers wishing to gain a general introduction might look at the main mission entries, covering conflicts in the Middle East, Asia, Africa, Europe, and Central America.

Readers wanting to find particular entries may adopt three routes. First, they may look up the country name for major missions (for example, Mozambique). Second, they may look up the name of the mission under its UN designation (for example, UNAVEM, or the United Nations Angola Verification Mission). Third, they may use the index, which provides comprehensive cross-referencing among mission, country, and mission acronym. A guide to acronyms appears on pages xxvii–xxviii.

DOMREP	Mission of the Representative of the Secretary-General in the Dominican Republic, 1965–1966
ECMM	European Community Monitoring Mission, 1991–
ECOMOG	Military Observer Group of the Economic Organization of West African States, 1990–
IFOR	UN Implementation Force (Bosnia), 1995
MICIVIH	Joint International Civilian Mission in Haiti, OAS-UN, 1993–
MINUGUA	United Nations Verification Mission in Guatemala, 1997
MINURCA	United Nations Mission in the Central African Republic, 1998–
MINURSO	United Nations Mission for the Referendum in Western Sahara, 1991–
MIPONUH	United Nations Civilian Police Mission in Haiti, 1997–
MNF I, II	Multinational Forces I, II, 1982–1984
MONUA	United Nations Observer Mission in Angola, 1997–
ONUC	United Nations Operation in the Congo, 1960–1964
ONUCA	United Nations Observer Group in Central America, 1989–1992
ONUMOZ	United Nations Operation in Mozambique, 1992–1994
ONUSAL	United Nations Observer Mission in El Salvador, 1991–1995
ONUVEH	United Nations Observer Group for the Verification of Elections in Haiti, 1990–1991
ONUVEN	United Nations Observation Mission for the Verification of Elections in Nicaragua, 1989–1990
SFOR	Stabilization Force
UNAMIC	United Nations Advance Mission in Cambodia, 1991–1992
UNAMIR	United Nations Assistance Mission in Rwanda, 1993–1996

Acronyms and Abbreviations Used in Peacekeeping

UNASOG	United Nations Aouzou Strip Observer Group, 1994
UNAVEM I–III	United Nations Angola Verification Missions, 1989–1997
UNCRO	United Nations Confidence Restoration Organization, 1995–1996
UNDOF	United Nations Disengagement Observer Force, 1974–
UNEF I, II	United Nations Emergency Forces I, 1956–1967, and II, 1973–1979
UNFICYP	United Nations Peacekeeping Force in Cyprus, 1964–
UNGCI	United Nations Guards Contingent in Iraq, 1991
UNGOMAP	United Nations Good Offices Mission in Afghanistan and Pakistan, 1988–1990
UNIFIL	United Nations Interim Force in Lebanon, 1978–
UNIIMOG	United Nations Iran-Iraq Military Observer Group, 1988–1991
UNIKOM	United Nations Iraq-Kuwait Military Observation Mission, 1991–
UNIPOM	United Nations India-Pakistan Observation Mission, 1965–1966
UNIPTF	United Nations International Police Task Force, 1995–

UNITAF	Unified Task Force, Somalia, 1992–1993
UNMIBH	United Nations Mission in Bosnia and Herzegovina, 1995–
UNMIH	United Nations Mission in Haiti, 1993–1996
UNMOGIP	United Nations Military Observer Group in India and Pakistan, 1949–
UNMOP	United Nations Mission of Observers in Prevlaka, 1996–
UNMOT	United Nations Mission of Observers in Tajikistan, 1994–
UNOGIL	United Nations Observation Group in Lebanon, 1958
UNOMIG	United Nations Observer Mission in Georgia, 1993–
UNOMIL	United Nations Observer Mission in Liberia, 1993–1997
UNOMSA	United Nations Observer Mission to South Africa, 1992
UNOMSIL	United Nations Observer Mission in Sierra Leone, 1998–
UNOMUR	United Nations Observer Mission in Uganda/Rwanda, 1993–1994
UNOSOM I–II	United Nations Operations in Somalia, 1992–1995
UNPREDEP	United Nations Preventive Deployment Force Macedonia, 1995–

UNPROFOR I–III	United Nations Protection Force in Former Yugoslavia, 1992–1995
UNSCOB	United Nations Special Committee on the Balkans, 1947
UNSCOP	United Nations Special Committee on Palestine, 1947
UNSF	United Nations Security Force in West New Guinea (West Irian), 1962–1963
UNSMIH	United Nations Support Mission for Haiti, 1996–1997
UNTAC	United Nations Transitional Authority in Cambodia, 1992–1993
UNTAES	United Nations Transitional Administration for Eastern Slavonia, Baranja, and Western Sirmium, 1996–1998
UNTAG	United Nations Transitional Assistance Group (Namibia), 1989–1990
UNTEA	United Nations Temporary Executive Authority, 1962–1963
UNTSO	United Nations Truce Supervision Organization, 1948–
UNYOM	United Nations Yemen Observation Mission, 1963–1964

A full list of general acronyms appears in Appendix 3.

Acheson Plan
See Uniting for Peace Resolution

Afghanistan
See UNGOMAP

An Agenda for Peace

On 31 January 1992, the Security Council of the United Nations met for the first time as a Summit of Heads of State or Government. In the context of the end of the Cold War, Secretary-General Boutros Boutros-Ghali was asked by the members of the Security Council to prepare an analysis and recommendations on ways of strengthening and streamlining (within the framework and provisions of the UN Charter) the UN's capacity for preventive diplomacy, peacemaking, and peacekeeping. The report was commissioned in a new and optimistic atmosphere in international politics. There was a conviction that the United Nations had regained an opportunity to achieve the original objectives of the charter, an objective that had been lost in the period of the Cold War: that is, the objective of promoting "social progress and better standards of life in larger freedom."

The resulting report, *An Agenda for Peace: Preventive Diplomacy, Peacemaking, and Peacekeeping,* was published in June 1992. In the report Boutros-Ghali pointed out that since the creation of the United Nations in 1945, over 100 major conflicts around the world had left some 20 million dead. Yet the United Nations had been prevented from dealing with many of these crises by the vetoes cast in the Security Council by one superpower or the other. Because UN action was not seen to be in their interest, the superpowers had cast 279 vetoes. This situation changed with the end of the Cold War, and there were no such vetoes between 31 May 1990 and the end of 1998.

In this changed context the agenda set out broad aims for the United Nations: to identify situations that could produce conflict and to try through diplomacy to remove the sources of danger before violence occurred; where conflict erupts, to engage in peacemaking aimed at resolving the issues that led to conflict; through peace-keeping, to work to preserve peace where fighting has been halted and to assist in implementing agreements achieved by the peacemakers. The United Nations was also to assist in peace building, including the rebuilding of institutions and infrastructures of nations torn by civil war and strife. Underlying all these objectives was the need to address the deepest causes of conflict: economic despair, social injustice, and political oppression.

Key terms were defined. "Preventive diplomacy" is action to prevent disputes from arising between parties, to prevent existing disputes from escalating into conflicts, and to limit the spread of conflicts when they occur. "Peacemaking" is action to bring hostile parties to agreement, essentially through such peaceful means as those foreseen in chapter 6 of the UN Charter. "Peacekeeping" is the deployment of a UN presence in the field, hitherto with the consent of all the parties concerned, normally involving UN military or police personnel and frequently civilians as well. Peacekeeping is a technique that expands the possibilities for both the prevention of conflict and the making of peace. The agenda also defines the concept of postconflict peace building as action to identify and support structures that will tend to strengthen and solidify peace in order to avoid a relapse into conflict.

The agenda is a comprehensive report that considers both nonmilitary and military threats to peace and security and makes 48 recommendations on ways to strengthen the UN's capabilities in the areas of international peace and security.

Most of these recommendations deal with the UN's established peacekeeping and enforcement roles, but the agenda also makes some important and specific innovative recommendations for preventive diplomacy (or conflict prevention) and "postconflict peace building." These include measures to increase the role of regional organizations in conflict prevention, to increase the number of UN fact-finding missions, and to introduce measures to facilitate the free flow of information between member states and the United Nations. The most innovative and contentious proposal under preventive diplomacy concerns the preventive deployment of troops to areas of tension to stop conflict spreading or erupting, including the positioning of troops inside the frontiers of countries threatened by their neighbors. While acknowledging the need to respect national sovereignty, the secretary-general also suggested preventive deployment in cases of national crisis as a means of alleviating suffering by providing humanitarian assistance, limiting or controlling violence, and helping in conciliation efforts. Thus a historically unique preventive deployment to Macedonia was authorized by the Security Council in 1993, though because of the issue of sovereignty and the nonintervention norm governing international relations, such deployments are sensitive and are unlikely to be resorted to frequently.

On peacekeeping, the agenda reiterates proposals made by the Special Committee on Peacekeeping Operations to improve the overall efficiency of peacekeeping, including proposals for the stockpiling of equipment, for better training for peacekeepers, and for securing adequate funding for an expanded role for peacekeeping in the post–Cold War world. The *Agenda for Peace,* under the heading "Peacemaking," also made some innovative and ambitious proposals for strengthening the UN's enforcement capability under chapter 7 of the charter. It proposed, first, that the Security Council should explore with member states the feasibility of making special agreements, as mentioned in article 43 of the charter (this article allows member states to make armed forces, assistance, and facilities available to the Security Council for enforcement action). Second, it recommended that the Security Council consider the establishment of a standby UN force to carry out peace-enforcement operations. As a way of addressing this proposal, the secretary-general has encouraged member states to develop standby forces for peacekeeping rather than for peace enforcement. A Supplement to the *Agenda for Peace* was published in 1995.

See also Boutros-Ghali, Boutros; Conflict prevention; Postconflict reconstruction; Regional organizations and peacekeeping

Ahtisaari, Martti (1937–)

Born 23 June 1937, Martti Ahtisaari began his career in the diplomatic service of the Finnish Ministry of Foreign Affairs. He was Finnish ambassador to Tanzania from 1973 to 1976 and was accredited to Zambia, Somalia, and Mozambique. He specialized particularly in development issues. Among his most senior UN appointments was his role as UN Commissioner for Namibia (1977–1981) and as the special representative of the secretary-general between 1988 and 1990, supervising Namibia's successful transition to independence between 1989 and 1990. His expertise and competency were soon in demand again, and he was senior envoy to the crisis zone of Yugoslavia during 1992 and 1993. The pinnacle of his diplomatic and political career was achieved in 1994, when he became president of the Republic of Finland.

See also Namibia; Special representatives of the secretary-general

Air support

Air operations, which are seen to be of increasing significance in peace support operations, includes the use of fixed-wing aircraft, helicopters, and satellites. The term "air support" refers to any kind of aerial activity that helps a mission, and there are several general or strategic ways in which air power can be used:

- in intelligence gathering or general reconnaissance
- in moving personnel, equipment, casualties, or noncombatants

- for monitoring or policing duties, such as sanctions control or protection of civilians
- for coercive purposes, either as a threat or in actual combat

Air deployment is more powerful, more flexible, and less vulnerable than other kinds of military deployment. At the same time, it is limited by weather, by fuel, by the relatively limited payload of aircraft, and by their need for a greater level of support personnel and equipment. The two most graphic examples of the use of air power in recent mission history are the UN action in Kuwait and the NATO action in Bosnia. In the former, the international forces, acting under a chapter 7 mandate, waged an almost exclusively aerial campaign to force Iraq out of the territory it had invaded. The aerial bombardment and harassment lasted 40 days, after which the conflict on the ground (Operation Desert Storm) lasted for only 4 days. After the surrender of Iraq, aircraft were again used to police the "safe havens" in the north. In Bosnia the United Nations had established six "safe areas" to try to protect the Muslim civilian population, but these were still subject to shelling and other forms of military attack, including attacks on UN peacekeeping personnel themselves. This prompted intervention by NATO, which used air power to support the mission on the ground. The use of NATO aircraft contributed significantly to the process by which negotiations were established to end the conflict. However, in most cases air support operations are based outside the peacekeeping mission's area of operation. Air crews are more removed from the local situation in the conflict zone, and they must therefore rely on local ground forces and on civilian agencies for reliable information and intelligence. Air power can be used for a number of purposes: providing surveillance and early warning, sending signals of intent, supporting allies through medical evacuation and combat search and rescue, carrying out the emergency withdrawal of peacekeeping mission personnel, monitoring weapons and troop movements through high-resolution surveillance systems, and airlifting supplies and personnel to relieve communities following natural disasters such as flood or famine.

See also Intelligence support and peacekeeping operations; Logistics
References and further reading Mackinlay (1996)

Akashi, Yasushi (1931–)

Born 19 January 1931, Yasushi Akashi graduated from the University of Tokyo and went on to complete his master's degree as a Fulbright Scholar at the University of Virginia. He also attended the Fletcher School of Law and Diplomacy and Columbia University. His early career at the United Nations began with a posting as a political affairs officer in 1957. He then served in various positions within the Department of Political and Security Council Affairs, the Department of Under Secretary-General for Special Political Affairs, and the Executive Office of the Secretary-General and as principal officer in the Office for Inter-Agency Affairs and Coordination.

His early experiences at the United Nations also included two committee positions, first as secretary of the Committee on the Financial Emergency of the United Nations and then on the Founding Committee of the United Nations University. In those early years he also served in three missions, in Malaysia, Cambodia, and Thailand.

In 1974 his work was rewarded with an official post from his government as ambassador in the Japanese Mission to the United Nations. Also in 1974 and again in 1977 he was elected by the UN General Assembly to the Advisory Committee on Administrative and Budgetary Questions (ACABQ). In 1978 he was appointed chairman of the Budget and Finance Committee of the Governing Council of the United Nations Development Program (UNDP). His skills and experience were then drawn upon in his senior posting as undersecretary-general for public information (May 1979– March 1987). He then served as undersecretary-general for disarmament affairs (1987–1992) before being called upon by Secretary-General Boutros Boutros-Ghali to serve as his special representative in Cambodia in 1992. He was then made special representative of the secretary-general in the former Yugoslavia.

Akashi has remained active in his academic interests and has served on the Board of Directors of the International Peace Academy and of the Better World Society. His publications include *The United Nations* (1965, 1975), *From the Windows of the United Nations* (1984), and *The Lights and Shadows of the United Nations* (1985). He has also contributed to a number of academic journals and international conferences.

See also   Cambodia; Liberia; Macedonia; Special representatives of the secretary-general; UNPROFOR I–III

Albania

After war broke out in Yugoslavia, there were good grounds for fearing that it would spread to the southern Balkans. This was an area of mixed peoples, weak states, and contested governments. The Kosovo conflict, which had triggered the disintegration of Yugoslavia in 1987, remained acute, and Albania's chaotic transition from communism gave many grounds for concern.

In Kosovo, a formerly autonomous area of Yugoslavia, the Albanian community (90 percent of the population) had been living under Serbian police rule since the revocation of autonomy in 1989. Observers feared that an ignition of the ethnonational conflict would lead to a domino effect, destabilizing Macedonia, drawing in Albania, and in the worst-case scenario starting a new Balkan war in which Greece and Turkey might enter on opposite sides. The situation was taken so seriously that in 1992 President George Bush warned the Yugoslavian president, Slobodan Milosevic, that the United States was prepared to use force against Serbian troops in the event of any conflict caused by Serbian action, and President Bill Clinton repeated the warning in 1993. In response to the danger signals from Yugoslavia, in Macedonia in January 1995 the United Nations deployed its first-ever preventive peacekeeping operation, the United Nations Preventive Deployment Force Macedonia (UNPREDEP). The operation consisted initially of 500 Canadians, who were later replaced by 700 Scandinavians.

Albania emerged from the harshest communist regime in eastern Europe in a state of poverty and distress. In 1995 it was possible to identify a number of important cleavages in Albanian society.

There was a deep political polarization between the Democratic Party that won the 1992 elections and the Socialist Party. The transition to a market economy had resulted in a rapid process of social stratification, with "winners" and "losers" emerging from the transition. There were also potential conflicts between Albania's government and its ethnic minorities and between the regional (Gheg and Tosk) and religious (Orthodox, Catholic, and Muslim) identity groups. The prospects for preventing or managing conflict seemed poor, although a number of bodies including the Soros Foundation, the Council of Europe, development agencies, and the churches were making efforts to improve it. Although small-scale conflicts were rife, it did not seem likely that the major cleavages would lead to a civil war. Yet in early 1997 the Albanian state partly collapsed, armed rebels ransacked the government armories in the south of the country, and 1,800 people were killed in the ensuing anarchy. It was the coincidence of two unexpected events that caused the rebellion: Albanian president Sali Berisha's decision to conduct the 1996 elections in a manner that international observers condemned as neither fair nor free, and the extraordinary growth and collapse of the Albanian "pyramid" schemes. The result was that Berisha, who had removed almost all legitimate sources of opposition, faced a revolt that was directed against him personally and found his army and police force melting away. Nevertheless, the intervention of Operation Alba that followed, directed by the Italian government on the basis of a UN mandate, was a remarkable success. It halted the slide into further violence, it laid the way for fresh elections, and it provided a path out of the crisis that gained international and domestic legitimacy. Franz Vranitzky, the personal representative of the Organization for Security and Cooperation in Europe (OSCE) chair-in-office, played an important role by mediating between Albanian politicians on several occasions, and the Community Sant' Egidio (an Italian nongovernmental organization) in Rome helped broker an agreement on a transitional government. The new Albanian government was more broadly based and began to undertake some measures to reduce political polarization and stabilize the economy. However, it still faced widespread disorder and crime and was not wholly in control of all parts of the country. Albanian politics remain highly charged, and violence in Kosovo during 1998 threatened to spill over into Albania.

See also   Bosnia and Herzegovina; European Community Monitoring Mission; Georgia; Macedonia; Organization for Security and Cooperation in Europe (OSCE); Troop-contributing countries; UNPROFOR I–III

Angola

United Nations Angola Verification Missions (UNAVEM I–III), 1989–1997; United Nations Observer Mission in Angola (MONUA), 1997–

Conflict Profile

Angola is a large, mineral-rich country of approximately 11.2 million inhabitants strategically situated along the southern Atlantic coast of Africa. It covers an area of over 480,000 square miles, roughly the size of Texas, California, and Florida combined, and larger than the total area of Spain, Portugal, France, and the Benelux countries. The capital, Luanda, on the northern end of the country's coastline, has a population of about 1.5 million, but the country is overwhelmingly rural, with 75 percent of the population living in small towns and villages of less than 2,000 people.

Angola has rich mineral reserves, including diamonds, petroleum, and iron ore. The main export crop is coffee, which is cultivated in the north, and subsistence farming is the main economic activity in the more densely populated areas of the country, that is, in the north and central west. The majority of the population follow traditional African religions, 38 percent are Catholic, and 15 percent are Protestant. The official language is Portuguese, but the majority speak African languages derived from Bantu.

War has ravaged Angola since the mid-1960s: first a war for independence, and then a bloody civil war that was fought from 1975 until November 1994 with only one brief respite. This civil war caused more than half-a-million deaths, displaced 3.5 million persons, and left a devastating legacy of land mines that continue to kill and maim innocent civilians. Consequently, Angola's needs are

great. Angola has been the site of the world's largest relief effort. The United Nations estimated that as of 1996, more than a year after the end of the war, 2.2 million Angolans inside the country still needed emergency assistance. Another 325,000 Angolans were still refugees in neighboring countries. Three decades of civil war in Angola left the economy devastated and the vast majority of the population in poverty. The annual inflation rate spiraled into four-digit figures. Despite a wealth of natural resources, gross domestic product per capita declined from an average of $820 between 1986 and 1988 to $410 in 1995. More than 70 percent of Angola's population is considered to be "food insecure." The Ministry of Health estimates that at least 20 percent of infants have been malnourished every year since the mid-1980s. Most indicators of social and economic performance rank Angola among the poorest countries in the world, a ranking that is largely explained by three factors: (1) incessant warfare, which has claimed more than 500,000 lives, has made life in the countryside too insecure for agricultural production, and has destroyed the economic and physical infrastructure; (2) severe human resources constraints because of a massive exodus by educated Angolans at independence and resulting skill shortages that the country has not been able to recoup; and (3) highly inefficient economic management, with excessive reliance on central planning and pervasive administrative controls. According to a UN Security Council report, up to 70 percent of the basic health system has been destroyed, only 18 percent of the population has access to sanitation, only 34 percent has access to safe water, and approximately 70,000 people have been maimed by weapons or land mines.

The United States is the largest provider of bilateral assistance to Angola. Other major contributors include the European Commission, the UN World Food Program, the UN Development Program (UNDP), other UN agencies, the World Bank, the African Development Bank, the International Fund for Agricultural Development, France, the Netherlands, Sweden, Italy, Norway, Portugal, and Germany.

Portugal was the first colonial power to send a fleet to the region. The fleet arrived at the mouth of the Congo River in 1492. All the kingdoms in the region fiercely resisted Portuguese rule and occupation well into the eighteenth century, and the effective conquest of the territory took place in the course of 30 years of military campaigns over the period 1890–1920. By 1974, the year before independence, 350,000 Portuguese lived in Angola, and most of the benefits of the exploitation of the country's mineral and agricultural wealth went to Portuguese middlemen.

Three nationalist groups emerged to organize the fight for independence from Portuguese rule in the 1950s and 1960s: the Movimento Popular de Libertaçao de Angola (MPLA), led by Agostinho Neto; the Frente Nacional de Libertaçao de Angola (FNLA), led by Holden Roberto; and Uniao Nacional para la Independencia Total de Angola (UNITA), led by Jonas Savimbi. However, these anticolonial movements were divided along both ideological and ethnic lines and had different regional origins. These differences served to prolong the conflict, since once independence was achieved, the parties continued to fight among themselves for power. When in April 1974 young officers in the Portuguese army seized power in Portugal in a bloodless coup, they announced that they would give all of the Portuguese colonies their independence. On 15 January 1975 Roberto, Savimbi, and Neto signed the Alvor Agreements, in which they agreed to set up a coalition government for an independent Angola. The new government took office on 31 January 1975, but the agreement broke down immediately as fighting erupted among the MPLA, the FNLA, and UNITA. The MPLA received support from two socialist countries, the USSR and Cuba; the FNLA was directly assisted by the U.S. intelligence services, received arms and advisers from China, and received military aid from Zaire; and UNITA received backing from South Africa (and later from the United States), from Portuguese settlers (until the bulk of them fled in the course of the civil wars), and from Tanzania and Zambia. These Cold War ideological and geostrategic cleavages were compounded by the ethnic divisions that also divided the parties: The MPLA had the support of the Kimbundu tribe, which dominated the capital, Luanda, and its hinterland. This advantage effectively ensured that

the MPLA controlled the capital early in the civil war. FNLA support was primarily among the Bakongo in northern Angola, and Savimbi's UNITA had the support of the largest tribal/ethnic grouping, the Ovimbundu in the south and southeastern parts of the country. With significant Cuban support and Soviet guidance, the MPLA (which declared itself a Marxist-Leninist party in 1977) defeated the forces of the FNLA and UNITA and formed a government that in 1976 was recognized by the United Nations as the legitimate representative of Angola. The country's first president, Agostinho Neto, died in 1979 and was succeeded by José Eduardo dos Santos.

Though defeated, Savimbi turned for support to the white regimes in Rhodesia and in South Africa. He established a base at Jamba near the Namibian border. There, under the protection of the South Africans, he was able to build up a military force numbering over 60,000 troops. From this base he was also able to control a large part of the country, especially some of Angola's diamond mines. However, the situation through the 1980s was in effect a stalemate. The MPLA, though backed by Cuba, was unable to take Jamba, where UNITA had the backing of South Africa. Under the administration of President Ronald Reagan, beginning in 1981, the United States stated once again that it actively supported UNITA and would provide weapons to UNITA, which was countered by large levels of Russian military aid to the MPLA. The war for the control of southern Angola escalated dramatically in 1987 and 1988, with the Cubans building major military bases in southern Angola directed at South African bases in Namibia. However, the series of summit meetings between President Mikhail Gorbachev of the Soviet Union and President Reagan that were to end the Cold War between the two power blocs led to agreements that were to end this phase of the conflict in Angola. Following a change of policy in the United States, the issues of reform in South Africa and independence for Namibia (South West Africa) were to be linked to the removal of Cuban troops from Angola. In June 1988 an outline agreement was reached in New York that provided that Cuba would withdraw its troops from Angola and that South Africa would also withdraw from

Namibia. This agreement, which laid down a timetable for ending the wars in Angola and Namibia, was ratified by the governments of Angola, Cuba, and South Africa on 8 August 1988 in Geneva.

The Deployment of UNAVEM

Following the Geneva agreement, South Africa withdrew all its troops by the end of August 1988, and Cuban troops pulled back from the Namibian border. The diplomatic process that led to the end of South African aid to UNITA and the granting of Namibian independence was advanced further at an agreement at the United Nations in New York on 22 December 1988 that contained a bilateral agreement between Cuba and Angola for the withdrawal of Cuban troops from Angola. As part of this agreement both parties requested that the UN Security Council should verify the withdrawal of the Cuban troops. UN Security Council Resolution (SCR) 626 of 20 December 1988 created the first United Nations Angola Verification Mission (UNAVEM I) with a mandate to oversee and verify the withdrawal of the 50,000 Cuban troops in Angola in stages over the period from April 1989 to July 1991. An advance team arrived in Angola on 3 January 1989. At its peak, UNAVEM I consisted of 70 military observers under the command of Chief Military Observer (CMO) Brig. Gen. Pericles Ferrera Gomes of Brazil. There were also 22 international and 15 local civilian staff members. Although the process of withdrawal was temporarily suspended late in January 1993 in response to an attack by UNITA forces that killed four Cubans, the mandate was achieved with the full pullout of Cuban troops by 25 May 1991, more than a month ahead of schedule.

Although UNAVEM I was limited in its objectives and served to supervise the withdrawal of the troops rather than to enforce their withdrawal, it had a significant impact as a part of the broader peace process in southern Africa. The removal of Cuban troops was important for the United States and for South Africa, and once these troops had departed and the situation in Namibia had improved it was possible to turn attention toward the promotion of a peace process within Angola itself. This process was initiated in the form of talks between the Angolan government and UNITA, mediated by the Portuguese (principally Jose Durao Barroso, the foreign minister of Portugal), with both the United States and the Soviet Union lending their support and encouraging compromise from their respective clients. In May 1991 a de facto cease-fire became official when the two leaders, dos Santos of the MPLA and Savimbi of UNITA, formally signed the Angola Peace Accords (the Bicesse Accords), thus bringing to an end 16 years of civil war. The accords provided for a cease-fire to be monitored by the United Nations, for elections under international monitoring to be held between September and November 1992, and for the integration of a single national army.

When the accords were signed the Angolan government formally requested that the United Nations keep the UNAVEM mission in place in order to verify the implementation of the accords. UNAVEM II was given more comprehensive responsibilities than UNAVEM I, taking on the characteristics that were to become common in post–Cold War peacekeeping operations, covering military, political, and humanitarian issues. However, with the Cold War over and other priorities dominating international affairs, the will to fund a large peacekeeping operation to support the peace process in Angola was lacking, and UNAVEM II was in reality given a limited role, the assumption being that the parties themselves would take responsibility for ensuring its success. This was to be achieved by the work of a Joint Political-Military Commission (CCPM). The committee was made up of representatives of the government of Angola and of UNITA, and representatives from Portugal, the United States, and Russia acted as observers. A Joint Verification and Monitoring Commission (CMVF) and a Joint Commission for the Formation of the Armed Forces (CCFA) created by UN SCR 696 of 30 May 1991 extended the original mission (now UNAVEM II) to cover Angola's internal peace plan until the end of 1992. UNAVEM's role was to ensure that these bodies applied the political and military agreements made in the accords. In November 1991 the task of observing and providing technical help for the elections, to be held in September 1992, was added to the mandate, and an election division, modeled on observation missions conducted in Nicaragua and Haiti, was formed.

UNAVEM II was composed of 350 military observers, 126 police observers, a medical unit of 1,454 international civilian staff, and 41 locally recruited civilian support staff. In addition the election division numbered 100, with a further 300 needed as observers of the polling process. The force commander was Major General Edward Ushie Unimna of Nigeria. In February 1992 Margaret Joan Anstee of the United Kingdom was appointed as the special representative of the secretary-general (SRSG), the first woman appointed as special representative of a peacekeeping mission. Anstee was responsible for both the civilian and military components of the mission. She was replaced in June 1993 by Alioune Blondin Beye (former minister for foreign affairs of Mali). Delays in the deployment of UNAVEM presented problems from the beginning. These delays were in part caused by the delay in approving UNAVEM's budget within the United Nations and in part by the slowness in setting up the meetings of the CCPM. The original timetable envisaged that all troops would have assembled at agreed assembly points by 1 August 1991, but it was clear that the logistical complexity of organizing the assembly made this impossible. A fundamental problem was the lack of adequate food, medical supplies, and clothing at the assembly points, and this, combined with the caution of commanders and leaders on both sides, meant that the assembly and demobilization process was considerably behind schedule by early 1992. The United States flew in food, tents, and other supplies from stockpiles in Europe and the Persian Gulf, and a $27.5 million UN relief program began in October 1991 to deliver food and other material to the assembly points.

When the elections were held in September 1992, UNITA still had about 30,000 fighters, and the MPLA about 10,000. Although the elections gave dos Santos a near majority (49 percent to Savimbi's 40 percent) as president and his party, the MPLA, a clear majority in parliament, the results were contested by Savimbi, despite the fact that they were declared to have been free and fair by the SRSG. Since neither candidate for the presi-

dency had achieved 50 percent, a second round of elections was required. However, the war erupted again in November, with government forces summarily executing UNITA supporters and UNITA forces massacring about 15,000 civilians in the city of Huambo. As part of the peace process the MPLA declared itself a social democratic party and introduced a series of reforms that allowed multiparty democracy. In May 1993 the government of dos Santos was recognized by the United States.

Amid severely escalating violence in the early part of 1993, UNAVEM II remained deployed in an effort to persuade the two parties to resume dialogue and commit themselves to implementing the accords. The original mandate became irrelevant as the joint monitoring mechanisms collapsed and fighting engulfed large numbers of towns. A massive humanitarian crisis was created as thousands fled their homes. It was estimated that during 1993 about 1,000 people died every day from the direct or indirect effects of the war, and the populations of besieged cities such as Kuito and Huambo were cut off, out of the reach of international relief agencies. There were over 250,000 Angolan refugees in the Congo, Namibia, Zaire, and Zambia. By early 1995 some 3.5 million people living in accessible areas were receiving humanitarian aid, and the whole process of aid delivery was made difficult because of the prevailing insecurity and the fact that Angola, with a population of over 11 million people, was also the most land mine–polluted country in the world, with an estimated 10 million unexploded land mines.

UNAVEM II, now confined principally to the capital, Luanda, served to support the mediating efforts of the SRSG and the humanitarian work of the United Nations Humanitarian Assistance Coordination Unit, set up in Luanda in April 1993. In September 1993 the UN Security Council imposed an embargo on the supply of arms and petroleum to UNITA and reiterated its willingness to expand UNAVEM should there be a renewed commitment to the peace process. A breakthrough was achieved late in 1994 in Zambia when the Lusaka Protocol was signed by both parties. The protocol covered agreements on the reestablishment of a cease-fire, the demobilization of UNITA forces, the formation of a national army and a national police force, the completion of the election process, national reconciliation, and an expanded mandate for the United Nations. The cease-fire that followed, beginning on 22 November, and the reconstitution of the CCFA provided the context for a new, expanded mandate for UNAVEM III, which was to take over from UNAVEM II. Beye remained the SRSG; the force commander was Maj. Gen. Chris Abutu Garuba of Nigeria, who was succeeded by Maj. Gen. Phillip Valerio Sibanda of Zimbabwe in October 1995. The mandate of UNAVEM III under UN SCR 976 of 9 February 1995 had five main aspects: to assist in the implementation of the Lusaka Protocol; to supervise, control, and verify the disengagement of forces and to monitor the cease-fire; to monitor the neutrality of the national police and the security arrangements for UNITA leaders; to facilitate humanitarian activities related to the peace process (e.g., the reintegration of demobilized troops into civilian life); and to support, verify, and monitor arrangements for the second round of the electoral process. An advance party of the logistics battalion provided by the United Kingdom arrived to arrange for the deployment in May of UNAVEM III infantry units, and by the end of March 1996 mission strength stood at 7,138, including 6,576 troops, 210 civilian police officers, and 336 military observers.

In late June 1995 a comprehensive working document on the implementation of the Lusaka Protocol was signed by both parties, and a timetable was agreed upon to make up for the delays that were already occurring. Nevertheless, by early 1996 many elements of the protocol agreements were still behind schedule, including the crucial issue of quartering and demobilizing UNITA troops. Also, UNAVEM observers reported numerous violations of basic human rights throughout the country. In response the European Union and the Center for Human Rights of the UN Secretariat agreed to support a UNAVEM project to train Angolans in human rights education. In the humanitarian work of UNAVEM priority was given to reopening roads and assisting in the return of refugees. By August 1995 emphasis was shifting toward social and economic development and reconciliation projects. Following a conference

of donors held in Brussels in September, at which both dos Santos and Savimbi participated, over $900 million was pledged to support a program of community reconciliation and development. However, despite a generally improving situation, conditions were volatile and hostilities were renewed in December 1995, though tensions eased again early in 1996. Demobilization and efforts at creating a government of national unity proceeded in fits and starts through 1996, with frequent allegations of obstructive behavior leveled at UNITA and its leader Savimbi. During that year South African President Nelson Mandela became involved in a mediatory role between dos Santos and Savimbi, and by January 1997 reports indicated that Savimbi was prepared to join a government of national unity, though there were still suggestions of some prevarication. Agreement was reached whereby UNITA would have 70 deputies in the national parliament and 11 ministers in the cabinet, with responsibility for commerce, geology and mines, health, and tourism. At the end of February 1997 UNAVEM was still deployed, and the formal inauguration of the new government of national unity was in abeyance because of UNITA leaders' continued reluctance to participate. However, a Government of Unity and National Reconciliation was formed. On 30 June 1997 under SCR 1118, UNAVEM III was replaced by the United Nations Observer Mission in Angola (MONUA), which was to become operational on 1 July 1997. Its mandate was to help with the completion of the demobilization process and to incorporate UNITA ex-combatants into the new national army.

In a reflection on the role of UN peacekeeping in Angola, SRSG Margaret Anstee referred to Angola as a "forgotten tragedy" because although media attention was focused on Bosnia and Somalia, the level of suffering in Angola was just as severe as in those more media-fashionable conflicts. Anstee identified a number of problems with the UNAVEM mandate. First, the monitoring and verification role given to UNAVEM II was limited, and the consequent reliance on the two parties themselves to carry out the terms of the Bicesse Accords depended on a level of trust between them that did not exist. Second, the resources given to UNAVEM II were inadequate even for its limited monitoring role. At the highest point of deployment, UNAVEM II personnel numbered only 1,000. The resource problem was further compounded for Anstee when electoral monitoring was added to the mandate of UNAVEM II without adequate personnel and resources to support the task; she expressed the opinion that "we have been asked to fly a 747 but had been given the fuel only for a DC3." Third, she argued that in certain vital aspects the Bicesse Accords were flawed. For example, the timetable agreed upon under the accords was too tight and inelastic, requiring a great deal to be done before the elections were scheduled to be held, including the cantonment, demobilization, and disarmament of both armies; the formation of a new national army of forces from both sides; the extension of the central administration to a country whose infrastructure was destroyed; and the development of a neutral national police force. All of these objectives were supposed to have been achieved before the election, but the reality fell short of this. A second weakness in the accords was that they were based on a "winner takes all" concept; that is, there was no provision for compensating or offering guarantees of a role for the losing side. In the prevailing climate of mistrust this was likely to lead the loser in an election to renege on agreements, particularly because the planned demobilization of forces had not occurred. Overall, in Anstee's judgment the preference for a "small but manageable" operation such as UNAVEM II was a false economy, since the country relapsed into civil war, requiring a longer commitment of personnel and resources in the deployment of UNAVEM III. This mission was replaced on 1 July 1997, under SCR 1118, by the smaller MONUA (UN Observer Mission in Angola). In the conditions of renewed civil war as of late 1998, MONUA itself may well be withdrawn.

Expenditures for UNAVEM I amounted to $16,404,200; costs for UNAVEM II amounted to $175,802,600; costs for UNAVEM III by May 1996 amounted to $366,523,999.

See also Child soldiers; Mozambique; Namibia; Postconflict reconstruction; Zimbabwe

References and further reading Anstee (1996); Fortna (1995); Krska (1997); Malaquias (1996); United Nations (1996)

Annan, Kofi (1938–)

Born in 1938 in Ghana, Kofi Annan was elected secretary-general of the United Nations for a five-year term from 1 January 1997 to 31 December 2001. He graduated from the University of Science and Technology at Kumasi, Ghana, and continued his study of economics at Macalester College, St. Paul, Minnesota, in the United States. Continuing to study economics, he undertook a graduate studies program at the Institut des Hautes Etudes Internationales, in Geneva, Switzerland. Between 1971 and 1972 he studied at the Massachusetts Institute of Technology as an Alfred P. Sloan Fellow and received a master of science degree in management. Finally in June 1996, the Cedar Crest College in Allentown, Pennsylvania, awarded him an honorary doctorate of public service.

His distinguished academic career has been matched by his devoted service to the United Nations for over 30 years. His early career between 1962 and 1971 included postings to Addis Ababa, New York, the World Health Organization (WHO), and Geneva. He was also administration officer at the United Nations, Geneva (1972–1974); chief civilian personnel officer, United Nations Emergency Forces (UNEF), Cairo (1974); deputy chief of staff services (1976–1980); deputy director, Division of Administration and head of personnel service, United Nations High Commissioner for Refugees (UNHCR), Geneva (1980–1983); director of administration management services, then director of budget, United Nations, New York (1984–1987); assistant secretary-general, human resources management, United Nations, New York (1987–1990); and controller, program planning, budget, and finance, United Nations, New York (1990–1992).

Annan's career at the United Nations reflected his dedication to both education and economics. His many posts gave him an expert understanding of how the organization worked. This expertise was complemented and rewarded by his appointment at the increasingly active Department of Peacekeeping Operations, which has become a major focus of operational demand and attention in the post–Cold War era. He was appointed undersecretary-general at this post (1993–1995). He then briefly left that post (1995–1996) when he went to serve as special representative of the secretary-general to the former Yugoslavia and as special envoy to the North Atlantic Treaty Organization (NATO).

In March 1996 he returned to the position of United Nations undersecretary-general for peacekeeping operations, from which he was recommended by the Security Council (13 December 1996) and subsequently elected by the General Assembly (17 December 1996) to serve as secretary-general of the United Nations. He began his period in office with a series of reforms within the Secretariat and with the replacement of the Department of Humanitarian Assistance with the Office for Coordination of Humanitarian Assistance.

See also Organization of African Unity; United Nations: organization; United Nations Special Committee on Peacekeeping Operations (C-34)
References and further reading Annan (1997a, 1997b); *Who's Who 1998*

Anstee, Margaret Joan (1926–)

Born 25 June 1926, Margaret Anstee was educated at Newnham College, Oxford, and has degrees in modern and medieval languages. She also has a degree in economics from the University of London and has served as adviser to the president and government of Bolivia and former undersecretary-general of the United Nations (1987–1993). A short spell as lecturer in Spanish at Queen's University Belfast (1947–1948) was followed by the position of third secretary, Foreign Office (1948–1952). Her aptitude for languages proved useful for her next post as administrative officer for the United Nations Technical Assistance Board in Manila, Philippines (1952–1954). She then returned to an academic environment with a spell as Spanish supervisor, Cambridge University (1955–1956). She served with the United Nations between 1952 and 1993, except for a period between 1967 and 1968 when she was senior economic adviser in the prime minister's office. In 1987 she was appointed as undersecretary-general and was director-general of the UN Office in Vienna. She became the first woman ever to head a peacekeeping mission when she was appointed as the special representative of the secretary-general in Angola.

Throughout her career she was a pioneer in posts that had not previously been held by a woman: the first woman field officer for the United Nations, the first woman resident representative of the United Nations Development Program (in Chile), and the first to be appointed assistant secretary-general and undersecretary-general. Her book *Orphan of the Cold War*, published in 1996, gives one of the most insightful and detailed accounts of the work of a UN official and an excellent account of the conflict in Angola.

See also Angola; Special representatives of the secretary-general; Women and peacekeeping
References and further reading Anstee (1996)

Arab League
See League of Arab States

Arab League Force
See League of Arab States

Arab-Israeli conflict
See Lebanon; Multinational Force and Observers; UNDOF; UNEF I; UNEF II; UNTSO

Arms control and disarmament

Although they are often confused, there is a difference between the terms "arms control" and "disarmament." "Arms control" is used more often in an international context and refers to the limiting of military capability to wage war and to the preservation of feelings of national security. In peacekeeping situations, "disarmament" is more often used at a national or theater level and describes postconflict situations such as policing cease-fire agreements or demobilizing armed forces.

The argument for arms control starts from the assumption that states will not voluntarily abandon all their military capability and that it is unrealistic to propose that they should. Furthermore, the argument continues, there are positive aspects to the existence of military weapons. Some national economies, for example, would be in difficulty without the foreign exchange and employment that the arms trade brings. Therefore, it is better to try to control the amount and type of armaments, which stands a chance of success, than to pursue an unrealistic goal of general and complete disarmament, which is bound to fail.

Proponents of disarmament, on the other hand, argue that the existence of weapons makes it not only likely but sometimes necessary that they be used, that their presence creates increased political and military vested interests, that arms are financially too expensive for the global economy, and that the increased power of weapons is a threat to the world itself. There is a further argument that even defensive weapons systems can contribute to increased levels of international insecurity and tension by making neighbors or political rivals uneasy and forcing them to maintain similar systems themselves. Therefore, there should be a coordinated drive to remove all weapons.

Arms Control and Peacekeeping

Arms control measures can include a number of different ways to try to limit offensive capability, such as the prevention of proliferation, the banning of chemical weapons, the banning of biological weapons, the establishment of so-called nuclear-free zones, and control of smaller-scale "battlefield" nuclear weaponry as well as of intercontinental strategic weapons. These measures are often initiated via bilateral or multilateral treaties, but occasionally a state will issue a unilateral declaration of arms limitation or announce that it is actually scrapping weapons.

Disarmament and Peacekeeping

In peacekeeping, disarmament techniques are most often used in localized, postconflict situations. There are a number of situations that require disarmament, such as after a cease-fire when one side (or both) is not a statutory force and is in possession of illegal weapons. The two most common problems for all agencies after a conflict are, first, the large numbers of small arms that find their way into nonmilitary, nonpolice hands, and second, the huge number of land mines that are now used in almost every

conflict because they are cheap and effective. The scale of this particular problem is now referred to as "microdisarmament."

Microdisarmament

Although small arms and light weapons are not major items of interstate warfare, the majority of conflicts in recent years have been intrastate, and the role of smaller weapons in such situations is disproportionately large. In 1993, for example, there were 90 armed conflicts within states, and light weapons accounted for over 90 percent of the deaths and injuries that resulted. Small arms are weapons that are light enough to be carried by an individual or on a light vehicle; they are extremely portable and do not require the same level of maintenance and replenishment as larger weapons. They are also very easy to hide and so can escape the attention of normal surveillance techniques. The term "small arms" is often interpreted to mean handheld, projectile-firing weapons such as handguns and rifles, but included in the category are assault rifles, submachine guns, machine guns, grenades, mines, and antitank and antiaircraft weapons. This means that they have a wide range of offensive capability, and their use is not limited to conflict between individuals. Besides their portability and relative invisibility, the other major problem with small arms is the vast number that are in circulation. Supplying arms to combatants is not a new phenomenon, but the proliferation of this kind of weapon has been most marked since the end of World War II, for various reasons. One important reason for their proliferation is the fact that during the Cold War era the major powers saw fit to arm client groups and nations with small arms. Another rich source of weaponry has been the plundered arsenals of collapsed regimes or legitimate authorities. Some countries suffer frequent raids on military or police arsenals by criminal gangs or political insurgents. And, in addition to these clandestine sources, in 1995 there were almost 300 companies spread throughout more than 50 countries legitimately making and selling small arms on the world market, and the global stock of these weapons is now beyond accurate estimation.

The changes in the nature of military conflicts, from interstate to intrastate conflict and to conflict among groups rather than between central governments and rebels, mean that there are often no clearly identifiable front lines, and it is often no longer feasible to use large-scale weapons in the same way as formerly. Small arms are therefore becoming the weapon of choice for the future, and investment in this sector is expanding rapidly.

Land Mines

Land mines are the other major problem (in terms of the amount of ordnance in existence) after a conflict. As with many handguns, they are light, portable, and easy to make, deploy, and hide. Unlike handguns and other weaponry, once land mines have been deployed it is extremely difficult to recover them intact. This presents a long-term problem in the postconflict reconstruction phase, and civilians are in most danger when trying to resettle an area that has been sown with these weapons. In 1994 there were 20 mines laid for each 1 that was cleared, and 200 people per month are injured or killed by stepping on mines. In 1998 the United Nations estimated that there were then more than 110 million mines planted in 70 countries and that it would take approximately $33 billion and 1,100 years to clear them all at then-current rates of expenditure and progress, even if no more are ever laid. The sheer number of mines and the level of difficulty in recovering them present a major problem for the United Nations and other agencies in peacekeeping and humanitarian assistance programs. The clearing of an area is subject to specific mandate by the Security Council, and such mandates have had to be given with increasing frequency in recent years. Phase 1 is to clear an area to make it safe for military and civilian personnel. Once this initial area has been declared safe for occupation, Phase 2 is to help the affected nation establish its own system for longer-term mine clearance, which may include general education on mine awareness, instruction by specialists in mine marking and clearance, and detailed work on the safe disposal of unexploded weapons.

See also Liberia; Naval peacekeeping; Nonlethal weapons and peacekeeping; Organization for Security and Cooperation in Europe (OSCE)

References and further reading Berdal (1996); Poole and Guthrie (1996); UNIDIR (1995)

Article 19 Crisis
See Financing peacekeeping

ASEAN (Association of Southeast Asian Nations)

The Association of Southeast Asian Nations (ASEAN) was established in 1967 as the successor to the Association of Southeast Asia, and its members at that time were Indonesia, Singapore, Malaysia, Thailand, and the Philippines. One of the main intentions behind the formation of the group was to promote a peaceful region, even though conflict was common in that part of the world at that time. The Vietnam War, for example, was still in full swing, and two other conflicts between ASEAN member states had just been concluded. The organization was also intended to function as a channel of communication among member states and as a collective voice on regional issues (but without replacing any member's individual sovereign rights). Its work is conducted through intergovernmental committees. It has a small secretariat located in Indonesia.

Although peace was one of the main objectives behind the establishment of ASEAN, the regional political agenda was equally important. It was hoped that peace could be attained not just through treaties but through economic, social, and political cooperation. A further political aspect was the need to position the organization within the global context of the Cold War as a nonpartisan organization and to avoid being labeled as "another SEATO." (The Southeast Asia Treaty Organization [SEATO] was one of a series of U.S.-inspired organizations established with the aim of containing communism.)

After four years of tentative steps toward cooperation, the concept of the Zone of Peace, Freedom, and Neutrality (ZOPFAN) was floated. This was a corollary to the concept of the Southeast Asian Nuclear Weapon–Free Zone (SEA-NWFZ). All of these developments were part of a general movement toward regional independent status and an attempt to be free of superpower hegemony. Another regional strategic step forward was taken in 1976 when the ASEAN countries held their first summit meeting, which led to the signing of the ASEAN Concord and the Treaty of Amity and Cooperation. However, the persistence of intraregional disputes such as the Vietnamese invasion of Cambodia (although ASEAN played a major role in the attempted resolution) meant that real progress on the ground was very slow. Full agreement on regional goals was not achieved until 1992—after the end of the Cold War.

The 1992 summit also marks the beginning of a regional relationship with the United Nations on "peace and security," which is directly promoted through the ASEAN Regional Forum (ARF) and enables a whole network of interrelationships at ministerial and civil service levels to function. ASEAN is normally regarded as the most successful regional organization among Third World countries and is best known within the United Nations because of its positive role in ending the Vietnamese occupation of Cambodia, which lasted from 1979 to 1989. Although ASEAN does not have a peacekeeping mechanism, ASEAN countries are becoming actively involved in UN peacekeeping. For example, in January 1996 Malaysia officially opened the Malaysian Peacekeeping Training Center. This center is managed by the Ministry of Defence. Its role is to prepare personnel of the armed forces, police, and civil departments, including nongovernmental organizations, for operational duties in peacekeeping missions. Its objectives are to promote peacekeeping efficiency and professionalism among candidates selected for UN peacekeeping missions; to provide better understanding of the planning and conduct of UN operations; to provide working knowledge and understanding of observers' duties and of the operational, logistical, and administrative procedures of UN operations; and to conduct seminars and forums on selected subjects to enhance the knowledge and understanding of UN peacekeeping efforts.

See also Cambodia; Regional organizations and peacekeeping
References and further reading Krieger (1993); Smith and Jones (1997)

Australia

As a founding member of collective security organizations such as the United Nations and the Commonwealth, Australia has always supported multinational peacekeeping. However, Australia's strategic circumstances in the 1950–1972 period, especially collective defense commitments in Southeast Asia, limited the ability of the Australian Defence Forces (ADF) to contribute to peacekeeping operations during the 1960s and early 1970s. In the 40 years from the end of World War II to the mid-1980s, Australia participated in only ten UN peacekeeping missions, and no more than 44 people were ever deployed at any one time. In the six years from 1988 to 1994, the ADF sent personnel to ten more missions, three of which (the UN Transitional Assistance Group [UNTAG], the UN Transitional Authority in Cambodia [UNTAC], and the UN Assistance Mission in Rwanda [UNAMIR]) had 300 or more ADF personnel. In late March 1992 UNTAC was established under the 1991 Paris Agreements to supervise a cease-fire and general election in Cambodia. The successful conclusion of the agreements themselves was strongly influenced by Australian diplomacy over the 1989–1991 period. The force commander of this highly demanding and complex operation from the beginning has been Australia's Lt. Gen. J. M. Sanderson. In October 1991, prior to the formal establishment of UNTAC, Australia contributed a 65-member communications unit to its precursor, the UN Advance Mission in Cambodia (UNAMIC). On UNTAC's establishment, the ADF contingent increased to 502 persons, comprising the 488-strong Force Communications Unit (FCU) and 14 staff members of HQ UNTAC. Under UN Security Council Resolution (SCR) 794, which established the Unified Task Force (UNITAF) for operations in Somalia, Australia contributed a 937-strong battalion group. Other elements of the Australian contingent included a command and liaison group, a field engineers group, and communications personnel. From 19 January to 14 May 1993, the battalion group operated the 17,000-square-kilometer Baidoa Humanitarian Relief Sector (HRS) in southwestern Somalia. The battalion group was very successful at fostering and protecting humanitarian relief efforts and won widespread international praise for its efforts toward restoring law and order and reestablishing functioning legal, social, and economic systems.

Australia considers its contribution to the UN Commission for Indonesia (UNCI), 1947–1951, to be its first experience with peacekeeping, though it feels that UNCI has not been properly recognized by UN historians. Many UN peacekeeping references do not include UNCI in their list of UN missions, though it may be claimed to be the first UN peacekeeping operation involving military observers (MOs). However, unlike in subsequent MO missions, the MOs were drawn from diplomatic missions within the country, and the personnel were not directly posted to the UN. UNCI was formed when the UN established a Good Offices Commission (GOC) to supervise a cease-fire in the then Dutch East Indies between the Dutch and the self-proclaimed Indonesian Republic. Australia's contribution began in early August 1947, when locally based diplomatic staff were seconded to the GOC. They were joined by four military observers later that month. When the GOC was reorganized

and renamed UNCI in January 1949, the Australian contingent increased to 15. It stayed at that strength until UNCI's task ended in April 1951.

Australian policy toward peacekeeping was clarified in a series of reviews throughout the 1990s. In 1993 the Ministry of Defence issued *Peacekeeping Policy: The Future Australian Defence Force Role,* which argued that there was a strong case for increasing Australian participation in the 1990s, although it was argued that peacekeeping should be seen as a supplement to and not a substitute for a strong national defense force.

See also Cambodia; Training for peacekeeping; Troop-contributing countries
References and further reading Cheeseman (1998)

Austrian Study Center for Peace and Conflict Resolution (International Civilian Peacekeeping and Peacebuilding Training Program: IPT)
See Training for peacekeeping

Balkans
See Albania; Bosnia and Herzegovina; Croatia; Greece; Macedonia; UNPROFOR I–III

Blue Helmets

This has become a common term for UN peace-keeping personnel over the past 40 years because of the (intentionally) distinctive color of their headgear. They were first used in Egypt during the Suez Canal crisis of 1956 to avoid the confusion caused by the similarity between the helmets used by the peacekeeping forces and those used by the invading British army. These first blue helmets were normal equipment painted blue and were intended at the time to be a temporary expedient, but blue helmets and berets are now standard issue to all peacekeeping personnel. The standard reference work on peacekeeping published by the UN is accordingly entitled *The Blue Helmets*.

Bosnia and Herzegovina

United Nations Mission in Bosnia and Herzegovina (UNMIBH), 1995– ; United Nations International Police Task Force (UNIPTF), 1995– ; Implementation Force (IFOR), 1995; Stabilization Force (SFOR), 1996

The Deployment of the United Nations Mission in Bosnia and Herzegovina (UNMIBH) and United Nations International Police Task Force (UNIPTF)
A U.S. peace initiative in the former Yugoslavia led by Assistant Secretary of State Richard Holbrooke, which had begun on 9 August 1995, allowed President Bill Clinton to announce a cease-fire in Bosnia and Herzegovina on 5 October. Peace talks held in Dayton, Ohio, in November 1995 resulted in a detailed agreement (the General Framework Agreement for Peace [GFAP]) that was officially signed in Paris on 14 December 1995.

The agreement provided for the presence of 60,000 North Atlantic Treaty Organization (NATO) troops (including 20,000 from the United States) for one year to supervise its implementation. The International Monetary Fund admitted Bosnia and Herzegovina on the same day and approved a

$45 million emergency loan. Within the peace agreement the various parties (the Republic of Bosnia and Herzegovina, the Republic of Croatia, the Federal Republic of Yugoslavia, the Federation of Bosnia and Herzegovina, and the Republika Srpska) requested that the Security Council establish a UN International Police Task Force (IPTF). The mandate of the UN Protection Force in Former Yugoslavia (UNPROFOR) in Bosnia was extended until 31 January 1996 to facilitate the transfer of authority to the new Implementation Force (IFOR). The IPTF was established under UN Security Council Resolution (SCR) 1035 of 21 December 1995. It was headquartered in Sarajevo along with a UN civilian office. This operation became known as the United Nations Mission in Bosnia and Herzegovina (UNMIBH), which replaced United Nations Peace Forces Headquarters (UNPF-HQ). The coordinator of UNMIBH and the special representative of the secretary-general is Iqbal Riza (Pakistan), who succeeded the interim coordinator, Antonio Pedauye, on 1 February 1996. The commissioner of the IPTF is Peter Fitzgerald (Ireland). With the main responsibility for the peace process passing to IFOR and the Stabilization Force (SFOR) and to the Office of the High Representative (OHR, discussed later), UNMIBH represented a considerable scaling down of UN operations in Bosnia compared with the force levels of UNPROFOR and UNPF-HQ. The tasks of IPTF include monitoring and inspecting law enforcement activities, including judicial organizations and proceedings; advising law enforcement personnel; assisting law enforcement activities; training personnel; assessing threats to public order; and advising government authorities in Bosnia and Herzegovina on effective civilian law enforcement agencies. The UN coordinator, in addition to exercising authority over the commissioner of the IPTF, also has responsibility for other UN activities in Bosnia and Herzegovina, including humanitarian relief, the removal of land mines, the safeguarding of human rights, the promotion of elections, and economic reconstruction. The coordinator also liaises with the NATO-led multinational force and with the high representative appointed by the Peace Implementation Conference to oversee the civilian aspects of the peace process in Bosnia.

By April 1996 the IPTF numbered 1,197 civilian police, supported by international and locally recruited staff. Estimated costs from 1 January 1996 to 30 June 1997 were $201,649,300, which included the costs of the United Nations Mission of Observers in Prevlaka (UNMOP).

The Deployment of IFOR
The main task of supervising the peace process in Bosnia Herzegovina has been assigned to NATO. Following the Dayton Agreement of November 1995 and the signing of the peace agreement (that is, the GFAP) in Paris on 14 December 1995, NATO was given a mandate by the United Nations, on the basis of SCR 1031, to implement the military aspects of the agreement. The NATO-led multinational force is called the Implementation Force (IFOR), and the operation that began on 16 December 1995 was code-named Joint Endeavor.

The political basis for the alliance's role in the former Yugoslavia was established at the North Atlantic Council meeting in Oslo in June 1992. In December 1992, NATO foreign ministers stated that the alliance was also ready to support peacekeeping operations under the authority of the UN Security Council, which has the primary responsibility for international peace and security. Ministers reviewed peacekeeping, sanctions, and embargo enforcement measures already being undertaken by NATO countries, individually and as an alliance, to support the implementation of UN Security Council resolutions relating to the conflict in the former Yugoslavia. They indicated that the alliance was ready to respond positively to further initiatives that the UN secretary-general might take in seeking alliance assistance in this field.

Between 1992 and 1995, the alliance made several key decisions, leading to operations by NATO naval and air forces. The NATO naval forces, in conjunction with the Western European Union, monitored and subsequently enforced the UN embargo and sanctions in the Adriatic. NATO air forces first monitored and then enforced the UN no-fly zone over Bosnia and Herzegovina. The alliance also provided close air support to UNPROFOR in Bosnia and Herzegovina and authorized air strikes to relieve the strangulation of Sarajevo and other threatened safe areas. Decisive action by the alliance in support of the United Nations in the former Yugoslavia, together with a determined diplomatic effort, broke the siege of Sarajevo, led to a genuine cease-fire, and made a negotiated solution to the conflict possible in autumn 1995.

Under the authority of UN SCR 1031 of 15 December 1995, NATO is responsible for the implementation of the military aspects of the Dayton Agreement. IFOR has the following tasks: ensuring continued compliance with the cease-fire; ensuring the withdrawal of forces from the agreed cease-fire zone of separation back to their respective territories; ensuring the separation of forces; ensuring the collection of heavy weapons into cantonment sites and barracks and the demobilization of remaining forces; creating conditions for the safe, orderly, and speedy withdrawal of UN forces that have not transferred to the NATO-led IFOR; and controlling the airspace over Bosnia and Herzegovina.

IFOR has a unified command and is NATO-led, under the political direction and control of the alliance's North Atlantic Council. Overall military authority is in the hands of NATO's supreme allied commander Europe (SACEUR), Gen. George Joulwan. General Joulwan designated Adm. Leighton Smith (NATO's commander in chief southern command [CINCSOUTH]) as the first commander in theater of IFOR (COMIFOR). In July 1996 Admiral Smith retired and Adm. Joseph Lopez was appointed as CINCSOUTH and COMIFOR. COMIFOR is based in Sarajevo.

The IFOR is operating under chapter 7 (peace enforcement) provisions of the UN Charter. Its rules of engagement and its configuration provide for the robust use of force if necessary, both to accomplish its mission and to protect itself. IFOR consists of personnel sent to the theater by participating nations and members of UN peacekeeping forces already in place who have been transferred to NATO command and control.

Every NATO nation with armed forces has committed troops to IFOR. In addition a number of other nations are participating in IFOR. As of September 1996, non-NATO participating nations included Albania, Austria, Czech Republic, Estonia, Finland, Hungary, Latvia, Lithuania, Poland, Romania, Russia, Sweden, and Ukraine—all of which are Partnership for Peace countries—plus Egypt, Jordan, Malaysia, and Morocco. Russian forces joined IFOR in January 1996.

The advance enabling force of 2,600 troops began deploying to Bosnia and Croatia on 2 December 1995. Their task was to establish the headquarters, communications, and logistics necessary to receive the main body of 60,000 IFOR troops being deployed to the area. The deployment of the main body of troops was activated on 16 December, after final approval by the North Atlantic Council of the Operational Plan (OPLAN) and the passing of UN SCR 1031 of 15 December authorizing IFOR's mission.

The transfer of authority from the commander of UN Peace Forces to the commander of IFOR took place on 20 December, when all NATO and non-NATO forces participating in the operation came under the command of the IFOR commander. IFOR secured conditions for the safe, orderly, and timely withdrawal of remaining UN forces not coming under NATO command or control.

By 19 January 1996 the parties to the agreement had withdrawn their forces from the zone of separation on either side of the agreed cease-fire line. By 3 February all forces had been withdrawn from the areas to be transferred. The transfer of territory between Bosnian entities was completed by 19 March, and a new zone of separation was established along the interentity boundary line.

In assessing the situation in Bosnia and Herzegovina four months after the beginning of the IFOR deployment, the North Atlantic Council concluded that IFOR had been successful in bringing about a more secure environment. The parties continue to respect the cessation of hostilities and have generally complied with the major milestones in the Dayton Agreement.

All heavy weapons and forces were to be in cantonments or demobilized by 18 April, which represented the last milestone in the military annex to the peace agreement. This was secured by 27 June 1996. In some areas compliance has fallen short of peace agreement requirements. The parties have released most prisoners of war but not all. The clearance of land mines from the zones of separation and areas being transferred has fallen behind schedule.

In response to the general compliance, the international community has responded by suspending sanctions. After the agreement was initialed, the UN Security Council suspended economic sanctions against the Federal Republic of Yugoslavia (Serbia and Montenegro) and began phasing out the arms embargo.

The United Nations terminated the arms embargo on the former Yugoslavia on 18 June 1996 but indicated that sanctions against the Federal Republic of Yugoslavia (Serbia and Montenegro) or the Bosnian Serbian authorities could be reimposed if they failed significantly to meet their obligations under the peace agreement.

The role of IFOR in implementing the military aspects of the peace agreement helped to create a secure environment within which civil and political reconstruction could take place.

The civilian aspects of the agreement are being carried out by appropriate international and nongovernmental organizations. The London Peace Implementation Conference of 8–9 December 1995 set out the framework for these efforts. The high representative named at the London Conference, Carl Bildt, is charged with monitoring the implementation of the peace agreement and with coordinating the activities of the organizations and agencies involved in civilian implementation.

In view of the importance of the civilian aspects of the peace agreement, IFOR supported working with agencies involved in the civilian elements of the peace process, such as the Office of the High Representative, the IPTF, the International Committee of the Red Cross (ICRC), the UN High Commissioner for Refugees (UNHCR), the Organization for Security and Cooperation in Europe (OSCE), the International Criminal Tribunal for the former Yugoslavia (ICTY), and more than 400 nongovernmental organizations.

IFOR military engineers repaired and opened more than 50 percent of the roads in Bosnia and Herzegovina and rebuilt more than 60 bridges, including those linking the country with Croatia. They have also been involved in removing land mines; repairing railroads; opening airports to civilian traffic; restoring gas, water, and electrical supplies; rebuilding schools and hospitals; and restoring key telecommunication assets. Finally, IFOR includes a specialized group of about 350 specialists such as lawyers, educators, public transportation specialists, engineers, agricultural experts, economists, public health officials, veterinarians, communications experts, and many others. These are part of the Civil-Military Team (CIMIC), which provides technical advice and assistance to various commissions and working groups, civilian organizations, nongovernmental organizations, and IFOR units as well as to the parties to the agreement and to local authorities.

The Deployment of SFOR

The mandate of IFOR expired on 20 December 1996. On 10 December 1996 the North Atlantic Council, meeting in ministerial session, issued a statement on Bosnia and Herzegovina announcing that NATO was prepared to organize and lead SFOR Operation Joint Guard to take the place of IFOR, authorized by a UN SCR under chapter 7 of the UN Charter. On 12 December 1996 the UN Security Council adopted SCR 1088 authorizing the establishment of SFOR as the legal successor to IFOR for a planned period of 18 months. SFOR was activated on 20 December 1996. Its mission was to deter fresh hostilities and to stabilize peace. The size of the force, at the end of 1998 about half the size of IFOR, was to be periodically reviewed by the North Atlantic Council. SFOR's role, like IFOR's, was to maintain a secure environment and

freedom of movement. It also supported the work of other organizations concerned with the civil aspects of the peace. Thus SFOR worked with High Representative Carl Bildt, IPTF, the UN High Commission for Refugees, OSCE, and ICTY. The force commander of SFOR (COMSFOR) was Gen. William W. Crouch, of the U.S. Army.

Whereas IFOR and SFOR were responsible for military aspects of the peace process, responsibility for civilian aspects and the broader processes of political, social, and economic reconstruction and reconciliation was assigned to the high representative, Carl Bildt. The mandate of the high representative is to oversee the implementation of the Bosnian Peace Agreement, initialed in Dayton Ohio on 21 November 1995 and signed in Paris on 14 December. According to the agreement, the tasks of civilian implementation include the establishment of political and constitutional institutions, economic reconstruction and the rehabilitation of infrastructure, promotion of respect for human rights, encouragement of return of displaced persons and refugees, continuation of humanitarian aid, and support for and assistance with the election process being supervised by the OSCE.

Further guidance came at the London Peace Implementation Conference in December 1995, which established a Peace Implementation Council that included all of the signatories to the Paris Agreement and a Steering Board that included the United States, Russia, France, Germany, the United Kingdom, Japan, Canada, Italy, the European Union Presidency, the European Commission, and Turkey on behalf of the Organization of Islamic Countries. The London Conference also confirmed the role of the OSCE in supervising the elections and directed the high representative to establish a Human Rights Task Force. UN SCR 1031 directed UN agencies to cooperate with the high representative and accept general guidance.

The Paris and London Peace Implementation Conferences at the end of 1996 reinforced the powers of the high representative, particularly in the area of economic coordination and in the coordination of independent media projects. In 1996 the OHR had a lead role in running a number of joint bodies that brought together the representatives of the three political entities in Bosnia (the Federation, the Republika Srpska, and the government of Bosnia and Herzegovina) to discuss practical questions of mutual concern in advance of the establishment of the common institutions, which were set up after the elections held in September 1996.

The OHR's principal concerns at its main office in Sarajevo included political affairs, humanitarian and refugee assistance, freedom of movement questions, economic and reconstruction coordination, legal affairs, UN liaison, and human rights—the OHR housed the Human Rights Coordination Center. There was also a cell for military liaison. There were three regional offices within Bosnia and Herzegovina—in Banja Luka, Tuzla, and Mostar—and an international Secretariat in Brussels that deals with planning and strategic issues.

The OHR employed about 85 international staff and 105 local support staff, the majority based in Sarajevo.

See also Croatia; European Community Monitoring Mission; Macedonia; No-fly zones; North Atlantic Treaty Organization (NATO); Organization for Security and Cooperation in Europe (OSCE); Rose, Michael; Safe areas; Stewart, Robert; UNPROFOR I–III
References and further reading Eide and Solli (1995); International Peacekeeping (1994–); Shear (1996); Stewart (1993); United Nations (1996)

Boutros-Ghali, Boutros (1922–)

Born 14 November 1922 in Cairo, Boutros Boutros-Ghali was secretary-general of the United Nations from 1 January 1992 to 31 December 1996. His academic career began with an undergraduate degree in law at Cairo University (1946). He completed his doctoral studies at the University of Paris in 1949. He was professor of international law and international relations in the Department of Political Science at the University of Cairo from 1949 to 1977.

He also embarked on a political career and served as a member of Parliament between 1987 and 1992. He served as minister of state for foreign affairs (1977–1991) and was deputy prime minister (foreign affairs). He was a key protagonist in the Egypt-Israeli "rapprochement" between President Anwar Sadat of Egypt and President Menachem Begin of Israel, which culminated in Sadat's historic visit to Israel.

Boutros-Ghali's exceptional diplomatic and political career, involving difficult negotiations in some of the world's most complicated conflict environments, and his deep academic insight into the issues surrounding such international relations prepared him well for his post as secretary-general of the United Nations. Boutros-Ghali was the first UN secretary-general to come from the African continent.

Concurrent with his successful political and diplomatic career, Boutros-Ghali continued to be well respected in the academic community. He was a member of such forums as the United Nations Commission of International Law (1979–1992). He also distributed his publications on Egyptian foreign affairs as founder and editor of the journal *Al Ahram Iktisadi* (1960–1975). Boutros-Ghali has an impressive (and ongoing) publications list, including major books and numerous contributions to periodicals. The *Agenda for Peace* published in 1992 was one of the most comprehensive statements on the role of the UN in the post–Cold War period.

See also *An Agenda for Peace;* Conflict prevention; Humanitarian intervention; Peace enforcement; Pérez de Cuéllar, Javier; Regional organizations and peacekeeeping; Somalia; UNPROFOR I–III
References and further reading Boutros-Ghali (1992); *Who's Who 1998*

British peacekeeping

The development of British peacekeeping policy and practice can best be explained in the context of 40 years of experience in "low intensity operations" in which Britain gradually pulled out of her colonies, though in many cases in the face of violent unrest and conflict. In the attempt to withdraw in some kind of orderly and controlled fashion, Britain became involved in a succession of counterinsurgency operations in, for example, Cyprus, Kenya, Palestine, Malaysia, and Aden. The approach of British peacekeeping was defined in *Keeping the Peace,* published in 1963 by the British Ministry of Defence, which drew on experiences in the campaigns in Cyprus, Malaya, and Kenya. During the 1970s and 1980s the British approach was determined by experiences in the conflict in Northern Ireland, and during the 1990s by experiences in the wars in the former Yugoslavia. The essence of British doctrine, going back to *Keeping the Peace* in the early 1960s, was that the use of force was only a means to an end. Military force in peacekeeping was necessary to create the conditions from which economic, diplomatic, and political initiatives could achieve an overall solution to the conflict. There was, however, a subtle difference between the concept of self-defense characteristic of classic UN peacekeeping and British thinking on the subject. British doctrine allowed the use of force for more than reactive self-defense. However, the use of force had to be positively justified in that each act must be constructive and not punitive. It was seen as vital that the use of force be credible and impartial in order to fulfill another criterion of the British approach, winning the "hearts and minds" among the local population and isolating insurgents and extremists. British doctrine also placed great emphasis on decentralization and the delegation of command to the lowest level.

British military doctrine is being updated in light of the changed environment in the post–Cold War era, particularly the experiences of UN peacekeeping deployments in Bosnia, Somalia, and Rwanda.

One of the most comprehensive statements about the new peacekeeping is based on British Army experience and appears in its *Field Manual on Wider Peacekeeping* (1995). The manual defines peacekeeping as "operations carried out with the consent of the belligerent parties in support of efforts to achieve or maintain peace in order to promote security and sustain life in areas of potential or actual conflict." The term "wider peacekeeping" is used to describe "the wider aspects of peacekeeping operations carried out with the consent of the belligerent parties but in an environment that may be volatile."

Despite post–Cold War conflict experience, especially of Somalia and Bosnia, the manual insists on the retention of the principle of consent and on a clear separation between peacekeeping and peace enforcement. Peacekeeping requires consent; peace enforcement does not. A distinction is made between the level of tactical and field operations, where consent may be partial, subject to change, and poorly defined, and the operational (theater) level, where consent comes from formal agreements by recognized parties and is relatively stable. Particularly at the tactical level, consent does not mean seeking universal approval for every action taken, but it does involve "a general public attitude that tolerates a peacekeeping presence and represents a quorum of co-operation." This definition has implications for the degree to which force can be used in an operation that is essentially nonviolent. Force can be used where local opinion supports its use—against banditry or looting, for example.

The concept of wider peacekeeping was constructed not just from theory but from postoperational reports and observations, particularly from the United Nations Protection Force in Former Yugoslavia (UNPROFOR) in Bosnia, but also from contrasting experiences in Somalia, where a distinction in overall approach was observed between the armies of Europe and the Commonwealth, on the one hand, and U.S. units, on the other. In general the "lessons learned" here were that "avoidance of escalation, impartiality, negotiation, patience, trust, confidence, the developing of relationships, mediation and restraint do not constitute a disparate collection of useful characteristics and principles. They each serve to develop co-operation by protecting and supporting consent. The requirement for consent is the parent of the principles and techniques."

After September 1997 Joint Warfare Publication (JWP) 3-01 (*Peace Support Operations*) replaced the British Army's field manual volume 5 (*Field Manual on Wider Peacekeeping*) as the British doctrine for peacekeeping and peace-enforcement operations. The term "peace support operations" is now used to cover a wide range of potential operations, from conflict prevention to peacemaking, and to provide a doctrine that is relevant to the post–Cold War geostrategic environment. It is intended to define a modus operandi for commanders and staff of all services in the conduct of peacekeeping. "Wider peacekeeping," as it was defined in the army's field manual volume 5, was the first centrally endorsed doctrinal statement to cover post–Cold War situations in which peacekeeping would be deployed. It was intended to be an interim position only because of the complex and dynamic nature of the conflict experiences in Somalia, Bosnia, and Rwanda. Similarly, JWP 3-01 is regarded as an interim manual, first, because it has not been tested operationally, and second, because it will need further development in order to integrate single-service approaches to joint doctrine.

See also Mackinlay, John; Second-generation peace-keeping

References and further reading British Army (1995); Dobbie (1994); Joint Warfare Publication 3-01 (1997)

Bunche, Ralph (1904–1971)

Ralph Bunche was born in Detroit, Michigan, in the United States on 7 August 1904. His parents both died while he was a child. Though he was brought up in poverty, he became the first black American to receive a doctorate in political science. He earned a bachelor's degree from the University of California, Los Angeles, and a master's degree (1928) and a Ph.D. (1934) from Harvard University. This was followed by postdoctoral studies at Northwestern University, the London School of Economics, and the University of Cape Town (1936–1938). He was appointed head of the Department of Political Science at Howard University in Washington, D.C., and resigned in 1950, when he had risen to the position of professor. He was a member of the U.S. delegation to the Dumbarton Oaks Conference in 1944 and to the UN founding conference in 1945, and he was the only black American to serve on the U.S. delegation to the first meeting of the new General Assembly of the UN in 1946. His successful academic career was mirrored by his career in the diplomatic field at the United Nations after 1946, when he attended the first meeting of the General Assembly. He was made director of the Trusteeship Department of the United Nations in 1947 and rose to the position of undersecretary-general. He worked closely with the first three UN secretaries-general (Trygve Lie, Dag Hammarskjöld, and U Thant). He was appointed by the UN Security Council as acting United Nations mediator in Palestine (1948), which resulted in the mediation of four Armistice Agreements between Israel and the Arab states. He was awarded the Nobel Peace Prize in 1950, the first black American to gain this distinction. His understanding of the role of peacekeeping played an important part in the evolution of the UN's peacekeeping operations. He served, among other posts, in the Middle East, Kashmir, the Congo, Yemen, and Cyprus. His expertise on the Middle East led to a number of senior positions, including as a member of the United Nations Special Commission on Palestine (1947), and to the role of supervisor of the first United Nations Emergency Force (UNEF I) during the 1956 Suez Canal crisis.

He was special representative of the secretary-general in the Congo (1960–1964), which included directing the UN force of about 20,000 military and civilian personnel. In 1964 he similarly supervised the UN Peacekeeping Force in Cyprus.

See also Special representatives of the secretary-general

Cambodia

**United Nations Advance Mission in Cambodia
(UNAMIC), 1991–1992; United Nations
Transitional Authority in Cambodia (UNTAC),
1992–1993**

Conflict Profile

Two key events framed UN involvement in Cambodia. First, on 23 October 1991 the "Agreements on a Comprehensive Political Settlement of the Cambodian Conflict" (the Paris Agreements or the Paris Peace Accords), which paved the way for large-scale UN intervention, were signed. The four hitherto warring factions agreed to UN Security Council plans (initiated by Australia) to cede unprecedented powers to the United Nations Transitional Authority in Cambodia (UNTAC) as the main means of implementing a comprehensive settlement after more than 20 years of war. Second, a year and a half later, elections were held 23–28 May 1993 and were followed by the establishment of a democratically legitimated Constituent Assembly and Provisional Government. The foundations were thus laid for the possibility of an enduring independent, democratic, and pluralistic Cambodian state, and the political space was provided for UNTAC to withdraw. The fact that the elections took place at all, against all the odds, was widely seen to vindicate the huge international effort that had been made by more than 100 countries (34 troop providers). These nations had contributed 15,000 troops and 7,000 civilian personnel over an 18-month period at a cost of $2.8 billion ($1.6 billion for the United Nations Advance Mission in Cambodia [UNAMIC] and UNTAC, the rest for repatriation, rehabilitation, and other programs) and the lives of 20 UN personnel. This was the biggest UN operation since the United Nations Operation in the Congo (ONUC) in the early 1960s, with a number of countries contributing military personnel to UN peacekeeping for the first time, including Brunei, Bulgaria, Germany (a medical team), Japan (an engineering battalion), Namibia, and Uruguay. Despite only qualified success or outright failure in a number of components of UNTAC's mission (and despite the difficulties and setbacks encountered after the withdrawal of UNTAC), this has been

counted a "successful" peacekeeping operation, particularly in comparison with other large UN peacekeeping missions such as the United Nations Operation in Somalia (UNOSOM). Certainly, there could have been no register of electors or remarkable 89.5 percent turnout of voters without UNTAC, and for Yasushi Akashi, the UN secretary-general's special representative and head of UNTAC, the experience of the election itself was highly emotional:

> If people ask me what was the best day of my life, I would say, without hesitation, that it was 23 May 1993. . . . Only people who have experienced more than two decades of incessant fighting and the ravages of war can show this degree of thirst for peace. I remember the tears in the eyes of soldiers at the ceremonies of cantoning and demobilising troops of three factions in June 1992. Voters of both sexes and of all ages at the polling stations told me, in simple words, that they were voting because of their interest in the future of their country or just for peace.

Cambodia is the smallest country in mainland Indochina. It is bordered by Thailand to the west and northwest, Laos to the northeast, and Vietnam to the east and southeast. It has a coastline on the Gulf of Thailand. It is relatively homogeneous ethnically, with Khmers (Cambodians) constituting some 85 percent of the population. Minorities include Vietnamese (the largest minority), Chinese, Cham-Malay Muslims, tribal Khmer Loeus, and a few thousand Thais and Laotians. Cultural unity is derived from a common Khmer language, a historically based sense of national identity, and the predominance of Theravada Buddhism. Relatively few Muslims and Christians survived the 1975–1978 massacres. Although the Khmer name for the country is better rendered "Kampuchea," this name has been discredited by association with the Khmer Rouge period, when the country was called "Democratic Kampuchea." The government reverted to "Cambodia" (French "Cambodge") in 1989; this is also the name used in the Paris Agreements and by the new government thereafter. The population of Cambodia was estimated by the United Nations at nearly 8 million in 1974 and 6 million in 1980, a decrease that reflects the fact that some two million people, 25 percent of the population, were murdered in the "killing fields" of Pol Pot's Kampuchea. The population is estimated to have recovered to nearly 9 million by 1994. The economy has also suffered severely during the long years of civil war. In 1969 the per capita gross domestic product in Cambodia was higher than in Thailand, whereas in 1994 it was only one-sixth that of Thailand—indeed, the lowest in Asia. Pol Pot forced urban dwellers to move to rural areas, and agriculture in the 1980s still employed about 80 percent of the labor force. Chief crops are rice (80 percent of cultivated land), corn, palm sugar, sugarcane, and tobacco. Drought and the withdrawal of Soviet aid severely affected the economy in the early 1990s, and the country suffered 300-percent inflation triggered by the issuing of paper currency to meet government expenses. Timber, gem, and precious metal exports, particularly along the border with Thailand, made a lucrative trade for the peoples in those regions and went some way toward sustaining Khmer Rouge activities.

Cambodia is the remnant of the former Khmer kingdom, which once included the Mekong delta and achieved a cultural magnificence captured in the ruins at Angkor Wat. In recent centuries it has tended to be dominated by more powerful neighbors, particularly Vietnam. The Cambodian-Vietnamese border is not easily defended, and there has been traditional enmity between the two. Increasing pressure from Siam (now Thailand) and Vietnam threatened to eliminate Khmer

independence when King Ang Duong requested a French protectorate in 1863. In the 1940s Japan included Cambodia in its "Greater East Asia Coprosperity Sphere." In 1949 Cambodia joined the French Union as an associated state, but in 1953, as part of the subsequent general collapse of French rule in Indochina, King Norodom Sihanouk negotiated independence for Cambodia, which was confirmed in the 1954 Geneva Agreement. Sihanouk later resigned as king in favor of his father, reverted to the title prince, and organized his own political party, winning 82 percent of the popular vote in 1955 and taking all the seats in the National Assembly against Communist opposition in 1966. Cambodian politics were further destabilized by a subsequent split in the ruling party and by increased involvement in the Vietnam War as North Vietnam used Cambodian territory to supply the south via the Ho Chi Minh trail, prompting heavy U.S. bombing of Cambodia. In 1970 in a right-wing coup, Lt. Col. Lon Nol deposed Sihanouk, abolished the monarchy, and proclaimed the Khmer Republic. This initiated 20 years of civil war as the Khmers Rouges (Sihanouk's name for the Communist Party, usually given in English in the singular: "Khmer Rouge") challenged the U.S.-backed Lon Nol regime. By 1975 the Khmer Rouge took Phnom Penh, and Lon Nol fled. Sihanouk, who had temporarily sided with the Khmer Rouge, resigned; Khieu Samphan became chairman of the State Presidium; and Pol Pot became prime minister. From 1975 to 1978 the Khmer Rouge instigated one of the worst holocausts in human history. In late 1978 the recently united Communist Vietnam, having already gained effective control of Laos, invaded Cambodia with dissident Khmers. They took Phnom Penh in January 1979, driving the Khmer Rouge, still supported by China, into opposition. A new Communist regime under Vietnamese control and with Soviet backing was set up under Heng Samrin and (later) Hun Sen, both former Khmer Rouge members. Under the new regime the country was known at first as the People's Republic of Kampuchea (PRK), but after May 1989 it was known as the State of Cambodia (SOC), and its armed forces were called the Cambodian People's Armed Forces (CPAF). In the ensuing years an anti-Vietnamese alliance was formed from the three former ruling groups: Sihanouk's Front Uni National pour un Cambodge Indépendent, Neutre, Pacifique, et Cooperatif (FUNCINPEC), whose armed forces were called the Armée Nationale pour un Kampuchea Indépendent (ANKI); the right-wing Khmer People's National Liberation Front (KPNLF), whose armed forces were called the KPNL Armed Forces (KPNLAF) and were under the command of Son Sann (Lon Nol's former prime minister); and the Khmer Rouge Party of Democratic Kampuchea (PDK, often abbreviated to DK), whose armed forces were called the National Army of Democratic Kampuchea (NADK), nominally under the command of Khieu Samphan but actually under the command of Pol Pot. In 1982 the three opposition groupings formed the Coalition Government of Democratic Kampuchea (CGDK), which was supported by the United States, China, and the Association of Southeast Asian Nations (ASEAN), who recognized CGDK as the official occupant of Cambodia's UN seat.

During the 1980s, from unpromising beginnings, national, regional, and global conditions changed, so that a peace process that began with the failed New York International Conference on Kampuchea in 1981 and progressed through the partially successful Paris International Conference on Cambodia in July and August 1989 finally succeeded in the Paris Agreements at the reconvened meeting in October 1991. At the national level a "mutually hurting stalemate" eventually induced the SOC and the three factions in the CGDK to be more amenable to outside pressure for a settlement. The SOC, with reasonably effective administrative control over 80 percent of the territory and whose armed forces were some 100,000 to 150,000 strong, was progressively weakened by the withdrawal of Vietnamese military support in 1989 and the shutting off of Soviet aid. FUNCINPEC and the KPNLF had weak military forces, and the PDK, which controlled perhaps 15 percent of the country in the northwest along the Thai border and had some 10,000 to 20,000 seasoned fighters and perhaps another 35,000 "operators," perhaps decided that negotiation and outside intervention that included China would be the best way to

weaken the SOC. At the regional level the ASEAN countries, particularly Indonesia, played a major role, as also in different ways did Japan and Australia. Cambodian leaders may also have been induced to go along with a peace process in order to participate in the Asian "economic miracle" taking place in the region, which now included China and even potentially Vietnam. Above all, perhaps, the rapprochement between China and Vietnam put increasing pressure on their clients, the Khmer Rouge and the SOC, while Soviet-American (and subsequent Russian-American) cooperation ensured that the UN Security Council would remain unified in driving the process through (China only abstained on one Security Council resolution on Cambodia in the period).

The 23 October 1991 Paris Agreements consisted of a Final Act and three instruments: the Agreement on a Comprehensive Political Settlement of the Cambodian Conflict; the Agreement Concerning the Sovereignty, Independence, Territorial Integrity and Inviolability, Neutrality, and National Unity of Cambodia; and the Declaration on the Rehabilitation and Reconstruction of Cambodia. The two agreements had treaty status; the declaration was not legally binding. The agreements were remarkable in two main ways. First, the settlement plan was comprehensive, as was subsequently reflected in the structure of UNTAC, which included military, civil administration, civilian police, electoral, human rights, repatriation, and rehabilitation components, as well as an information and education division. Second, a unique relationship was established between the Supreme National Council (SNC) (the "unique legitimate body and source of authority" in which "the sovereignty, independence and unity of Cambodia are enshrined") and UNTAC during the transitional period, until a Constituent Assembly was elected and could approve a new Cambodian constitution, transform itself into a legislative assembly, and create a new Cambodian government. The 12-member SNC was made up of 6 SOC members and 2 members each from the other three factions, with Sihanouk eventually as a thirteenth member and chairman (his son, Prince Norodom Ranariddh, took over as leader of FUNCINPEC). SNC would advise UNTAC, which would comply so long as there was consensus and the advice was consistent with the Paris Agreements. If there was a lack of consensus the chairman could advise. The secretary-general's special representative (SGSR) would attend SNC meetings. In addition a considerable influence on SNC decision making was exercised by local diplomatic representatives of the great powers. Although the SNC was the legitimate sovereign authority of Cambodia during the transition period and signed two binding international human rights conventions as such, effective control in many areas still rested with SOC, and UNTAC, through the SGSR, had wide supervisory rights, discretion for final decision making when the SNC was deadlocked or was seen to be contravening the spirit of the agreement, and a capacity for independent action in a number of areas.

The Deployment of UNAMIC

Before the arrival of UNTAC, ad hoc arrangements not envisaged in the Paris Agreements were made on the UN secretary-general's suggestion in the shape of what was termed a "good offices" mission—the United Nations Advance Mission in Cambodia (UNAMIC), authorized by Security Council Resolution (SCR) 717 of 16 October 1991. UNAMIC became operational from 9 November 1991 under Mission Commander Ataul Karim (Bangladesh), the civilian chief liaison officer, and Brig. Gen. Jean-Michel Loridan (France), senior military liaison officer. UNAMIC was made up of 8 civilian and 50 military liaison officers, 20 military personnel in the mine awareness unit, and some 75 international and 75 local civilian support staff. France contributed an air operations unit, and Australia contributed a 40-strong military communications unit. Military personnel were contributed by Algeria, Argentina, Australia, Austria, Belgium, Canada, China, France, Germany, Ghana, India, Indonesia, Ireland, Malaysia, New Zealand, Pakistan, Poland, Senegal, Tunisia, Soviet Union, United Kingdom, United States, and Uruguay. The estimated cost of the initial six-month operation was $19.9 million. Halfway through the interim phase, SCR 728 of 8 January 1992 accepted UN Secretary-General Boutros Boutros-Ghali's recommendation to expand UNAMIC's mandate to undertake a major effort to remove land mines, with the addition of 1,440 military personnel to gather information on minefields and to train Cambodians in mine detection and clearance, and a field engineer battalion of 700 to begin clearing repatriation routes.

UNAMIC's task was modest: to enhance the mine-awareness program, train civilian populations on how to avoid injury from mines or booby traps, deploy military liaison units to the military headquarters of the four Cambodian parties, and facilitate communications and maintain contact with the SNC in preparation for the deployment of UNTAC. Critics claim that, distracted by events in Croatia and lulled into a false sense of security by the dispatch of UNAMIC, the Security Council and UN staff in New York somewhat neglected UNAMIC and failed to speed up the deployment of UNTAC. When the first peacekeepers arrived, at the same time as Sihanouk's return on 15 November, they were initially greeted with euphoria. But the absence of UNTAC left a dangerous hiatus in which the four Cambodian factions jockeyed for position without an effective neutral mediator, leading to unchecked cease-fire violations, a selling off of state assets by corrupt officials, lawlessness, and a growing cynicism about the peace process and the UN's role in it. Early on Sihanouk sought but failed to achieve a coalition between FUNCINPEC and the SOC, threatening to cut out the other parties. On 27 November there were violent demonstrations in Phnom Penh on the arrival of the PDK (Khmer Rouge) leader Khieu Samphan; the PDK thought the demonstrations had been engineered by the SOC. On 17 December there were demonstrations in Phnom Penh against government corruption. Although the mixed military working group (MMWG) of the four factions stipulated in the Paris Agreements eventually met on 28 December, in January 1992 the cease-fire was broken by serious clashes between SOC and PDK forces. On 28 February came the first attack against UN peacekeepers in the Kompong Thom area when a UN helicopter came under fire and an Australian peacekeeper was wounded.

The Deployment of UNTAC

The SGSR and the head of mission, Yasushi Akashi (Japan), and Force Commander John Sanderson

(Australia) initiated UNTAC deployment when they arrived in Phnom Penh on 15 March 1992. SCR 745 of 28 February 1992 established UNTAC for an 18-month period with a mandate as set out in one of the annexes to the Paris Agreements. Five meetings of the SNC had been held by the end of April on agendas drawn up by the SGSR in consultation with SNC Chairman Sihanouk, using a "hot line" service to each of the four Cambodian parties in addition to the SNC secretariat.

UNTAC's Action Plan comprised seven distinct but interlocking components:

1. The largest was the military component, which numbered some 15,900 personnel of all ranks and was tasked
   a. to verify withdrawal and nonreturn of foreign forces;
   b. to supervise the cease-fire and organize the regrouping, cantonment, disarming, and demobilizing (70 percent of the cantoned forces) of the four factional armies;
   c. to control and monitor weapons (including monitoring the cessation of outside military assistance); and
   d. to assist the mine-clearing and training process.

   This was a daunting prospect, since Cambodian factional armies were an estimated 200,000 strong (mainly SOC and PDK) in some 650 locations and had a further 250,000 militia whose members were active in almost every village. There were an estimated 6 to 10 million land mines in thousands of square kilometers of minefields. In addition, the infrastructure of roads, airfields, and fuel supplies needed upgrading to make the operation possible. An added time constraint was the onset of the rainy season in May. Eventually 95 regrouping areas and 55 cantonment areas were agreed on (33 for CPAF, 14 for NADK, 5 for KPNLF, and 3 for ANKI). The secretary-general recommended full deployment of the military component during Phase 1 by June 1992. After that, from 13 June on, Phase 2 of UNTAC's mission, that is, the entire regrouping and cantonment process, including demobilization, was to be complete by the end of September 1992. Unfortunately, there were delays and logistical problems in the arrival of a number of national contingents (by the end of April, only 3,694 troops had arrived), only 3 of the 24 checkpoints planned to monitor withdrawal of foreign forces was in place by the end of April, and there was a general lack of clarity about how robustly UNTAC's mandate to use "all necessary means" would be interpreted. This emboldened the Khmer Rouge to turn back a Dutch battalion near Paulin and then to halt a follow-up convoy accompanied by Akashi and Sanderson at a bamboo-pole checkpoint between Paulin and the Thai border on 30 May. This is widely seen to have been a turning point in Cambodian perceptions of UNTAC's effectiveness. On 9 June the Khmer Rouge told the SGSR that UNTAC could not deploy in its areas.

2. The electoral component under a chief electoral officer was made up of 72 international personnel operating from headquarters and 126 international personnel from 21 provincial and municipal centers. In addition, more than 400 UN Volunteers (UNVs) would act as district electoral supervisors in 200 districts, supervising some 4,000 Cambodian personnel during the registration process. During polling itself there would be an extra 1,000 international supervisors and 56,000 Cambodian personnel organized in 8,000 polling teams. A separate advance electoral planning unit (AEPU) was to conduct a demographic survey from March 1992, followed by voter registration during a three-month period beginning in October 1992. The electoral component was further tasked with drafting an electoral law, which was submitted to SNC on 1 April. AEPU is widely regarded as having prepared expertly for the electoral process.

3. The human rights component was tasked with initiating human rights education and training programs, securing the signing of the two Human Rights Conventions by the

SNC, overseeing the human rights record of Cambodian administrative structures, and instituting a quick response mechanism for alleged human rights violations.

4. The repatriation component was tasked to repatriate some 360,000 refugees under the direction of the United Nations High Commissioner for Refugees (UNHCR). Half the refugees were under the age of 15, and 60 percent were from long-standing camps across the Cambodian-Thai border, traditional recruiting grounds for the armed factions, in particular the Khmer Rouge. Repatriation began on 30 March 1992, and by the end of April, 5,763 had returned.

5. The civil administration component was assigned the challenging task of supervising what was effectively an SOC-controlled administration in order to ensure a reasonably neutral environment for the electoral process. Following China's suggestion, the main focus was to be on foreign affairs, national defense, finance, public security, and information. The tasks of the human rights component and the civil administration component were to be accomplished by some 224 specialists and 84 international support staff from UNTAC headquarters and the 21 provincial and municipal centers. This proved one of the most contentious aspects of UNTAC's mission, with the Khmer Rouge perhaps having accepted UNTAC in the first place in the hope that it would effectively emasculate SOC's administrative structures, and SOC circumventing UNTAC supervision by operating through alternative channels.

6. The civilian police component, made up of 3,600 civilian police (CIVPOL) monitors operating centrally and in the 21 provinces and 200 districts, was tasked to supervise the 50,000 local civil police in administering law and order effectively and impartially. By the end of April only 193 CIVPOLs had arrived.

7. The rehabilitation component, under an UNTAC coordinator, was tasked to see to immediate food, health, and housing needs and to make a start on the essential restoration of Cambodia's basic infrastructure and public utilities. In his 1 May Report to the Security Council the UN secretary-general announced that UNTAC had made a "generally good start."

A further stage was marked by Phase 2 of the peace plan, involving the attempted cantonment, disarming, and demobilization of faction forces between 13 June and 15 November 1992. Despite PDK (Khmer Rouge) noncooperation, SOC attempts to hijack the operation, and mounting security problems, UNTAC launched the ambitious cantonment, disarming, and demobilization phase on 13 June 1992. A Ministerial Conference on the Rehabilitation and Reconstruction of Cambodia met in Tokyo between 20 and 22 June 1992, and the 33 participating countries pledged $880 million in aid, well in excess of what had been a $593 million appeal. By 10 September UNTAC had cantoned more than 52,000 troops from the three cooperating parties (50 percent of ANKI, almost all KPNLAF, and 25 percent of CPAF) and impounded about 50,000 weapons. But only some 200 NADK forces turned up. The PDK claimed that Vietnamese forces were still operating in Cambodia and demanded the dissolution of the main institutions and structures in SOC-controlled zones. UNTAC kept the door open to PDK participation and investigated PDK claims but, supported by the UN Security Council, including China, refused to accede to other demands. Despite representations, first by France and Indonesia as cochairs of the Paris Conference and then by Thailand and Japan, the PDK refused to cooperate, claiming that UNTAC was working with the SOC and Vietnam. The PDK leadership was originally internally split on the issue, but once it realized that UNTAC would not dissolve SOC administrative structures and realized that electoral politics would probably go against it, it became increasingly antagonistic, launching attacks on Vietnamese minorities, trying to gain territorial advantage, disrupting UNTAC operations, and playing a cat-and-mouse game with UNTAC forces. Meanwhile the SOC was using intimidatory tactics to support its electoral party (the Cambodian People's Party [CPP]). The situation was worsened by what is widely acknowledged to have been the ineptness of UNTAC's civilian police component, including abuse of local populations by some UNTAC contingents. Only a small number of the military forces seem to have been equally ill-disciplined, but in some quarters peacekeepers were described as "mercenaries" who "come here only to collect their salaries."

In the face of these setbacks, the secretary-general reported to the Security Council the suspension of Phase 2 of the cantonment and demobilization process on 15 November 1992 and released some 40,000 cantoned troops on "agricultural leave," subject to recall by UNTAC, relinquishing to UNTAC impounded weaponry at the same time. The question was raised whether the election process could continue in a deteriorating security situation in which, as Sihanouk noted, "none of the conditions for the election have been met." Nevertheless, encouraged by the remarkable progress made in electoral registration and repatriation, the solidity of the international community, the suggestion that the PDK was intent on doing no more than disrupting the election, and perhaps the desire to extricate itself as soon as possible (UNTAC was costing $100 million a month), the Security Council had accepted the secretary-general's suggestion to press on with the election in SCR 783 of 13 October 1992. For the first time it named the PDK as the main obstacle to peace in Cambodia. A moratorium was placed on the export of uncut logs, minerals, and gems, a move that was described as a "natural resource conservation measure" but that was aimed at shutting off a main PDK resource, and a nonmandatory embargo was placed on petroleum supplies to the PDK. Neither of these was effective, however, because a number of Thai generals had a financial interest in continuing the supplies. Akashi and Sanderson resisted calls for UNTAC to mount a full-scale offensive against the PDK forces, arguing that this would be "a failure, a bankruptcy, of a peacekeeping operation." Instead, the disposition of the military component was adapted to provide protection for the election process with, among other things, the organization of 12 local armed mobile reserve units and a force commander's mobile reserve. In addition, steps were taken to re-

duce political intimidation and violence, and a concerted media effort was coordinated through the Information/Education Division of the SGSR's office. UNTAC's own radio station began broadcasting on 9 November 1992.

A further distinct stage was made up of the electoral process between 30 November 1992 and 28 May 1993. On 30 November 1992 SCR 792 confirmed that elections for a constituent assembly for Cambodia would be held not later than May 1993. In January and February cease-fire violations continued between the CPAF and the NADK. In late March 1993 an UNTAC Bangladeshi soldier was killed, the first UNTAC death; several more deaths followed in April and May in a series of separate attacks. The death of a Japanese UNV in April had serious repercussions in Japan. Nevertheless, between 5 October 1992 and 31 January 1993 more than 4.7 million people, some 96 percent of the eligible voters, had been registered, including returnees, scrutinized by representatives of the political parties, who had the right to challenge those they considered unqualified. Voter lists were entered on UNTAC's computer support system. On 4 April the PDK announced that it would not participate on the grounds that "Vietnamese forces of aggression" continued to occupy Cambodia and a neutral political environment did not exist. The electoral campaign ran from 7 April to 19 May. Twenty political parties successfully submitted the list of 5,000 registered voters required to be eligible to field a candidate. Teams of military observers worked with civilian police to monitor political gatherings and assisted electoral staff in the civil education program. No polling was to be conducted in PDK-controlled areas. At a meeting of the SNC on 21 April the SGSR said that the freeness and fairness of the election would be judged (1) on the extent to which it was free of intimidation and violence, (2) on the extent to which the SOC enjoyed unfair advantages through its military strength and control of administrative structures, and (3) on the technical conduct of the poll. During the first three days of the 23–28 May election some 1,400 fixed polling stations operated throughout the country, including 200 mobile teams for remote areas. Reinforced mobile teams continued for the full six-day period. When counting began on 29 May, the SGSR announced to the SNC that the election had been free and fair, a judgment endorsed in SCR 835 of 2 June 1993. The ballot included 89.5 percent of the registered voters, with 45.47 voting for FUNCINPEC and 38.23 percent for CPP, the SOC party. In the 120-seat Constituent Assembly FUNCINPEC gained 58 seats; CPP, 51; the KPNLF party, the Buddhist Liberal Democratic Party (BLDP), 10; and a fourth party, 1. The Constituent Assembly was to "draw up a constitution and then transform itself into a legislative assembly to establish a new government for all Cambodians."

Finally, it is possible to identify a post-electoral period, from the elections up to the time of the withdrawal of UNTAC, between June and November 1993. Despite the success of the election, difficulties continued (for example, the CPP complained of irregularities, which UNTAC investigated, and in June three eastern provinces declared a temporary "secession" that was overcome after an appeal by Sihanouk). Nevertheless, in September the Constituent Assembly adopted the new Constitution and converted itself into a legislative assembly. Sihanouk was elected king of Cambodia and FUNCINPEC leader Prince Ranariddh and CPP leader Hun Sen were appointed first and second prime ministers. The Security Council set 15 November as the date for completion of the withdrawal of UNTAC (although, acceding to a Cambodian government request, a separate 20-man United Nations Military Liaison Team was established in Phnom Penh for six months).

The budget for UNTAC included provisions for up to 15,547 troops, 893 military observers, and 3,500 civilian police and for up to 1,149 international civilian staff, 465 UNVs, and 4,830 local staff, supplemented by international contractual staff. During the electoral period, more than 50,000 Cambodians served as electoral staff, and some 900 international polling station officers were seconded from 44 countries.

Military personnel were provided by Algeria, Argentina, Australia, Austria, Bangladesh, Belgium, Brunei Darussalam, Bulgaria, Cameroon, Canada, Chile, China, France, Germany, Ghana, India, Indonesia, Ireland, Japan, Malaysia,

Namibia, the Netherlands, New Zealand, Pakistan, the Philippines, Poland, Russian Federation, Senegal, Singapore, Thailand, Tunisia, United Kingdom, United States, and Uruguay.

Civilian police personnel were provided by Algeria, Australia, Austria, Bangladesh, Brunei Darussalam, Bulgaria, Cameroon, Colombia, Egypt, Fiji, France, Germany, Ghana, Hungary, India, Indonesia, Ireland, Italy, Japan, Jordan, Kenya, Malaysia, Morocco, Nepal, the Netherlands, Nigeria, Norway, Pakistan, the Philippines, Singapore, Sweden, and Tunisia.

Expenditures for UNAMIC and UNTAC amounted to $1,620,963,300. The repatriation and resettlement program and the rehabilitation program were funded from voluntary contributions.

See also ASEAN; Codes of conduct; Japan; Liberia; Postconflict reconstruction
References and further reading Chandler (1991); Doyle (1995); Doyle, Johnstone, and Orr (1997); Fetherston (1996); Findlay (1995), Schear (1995); United Nations (1996)

Camp David Accords
See Multinational Force and Observers; UNEF II

Canada
Canada's enduring significance to peacekeeping lies in the seminal contribution made by Lester B. Pearson, secretary of state at Canada's Department for External Affairs between 1948 and 1957. Along with Swedish UN Secretary-General Dag Hammarskjöld, Pearson enunciated the principles under which the first force-level peacekeeping operation was established in 1956 (the United Nations Emergency Force [UNEF] I). The Pearson-Hammarskjöld model of interpositional peacekeeping deployments dominated the international scene from 1956 until the early 1990s. Peacekeeping operations in these environments involved truce stabilization operations between belligerent parties who had agreed to stop fighting and who at the same time were able to exercise a real and effective control over most elements of their population and over subordinate military commanders. Canada has the longest history of in-

volvement with peacekeeping, having had personnel in more than 30 missions since 1956. In 1992 Canada provided 10 percent of the world's peacekeepers. In 1957, in recognition of his work, Lester Pearson was awarded the Nobel Peace Prize. More recently, in 1994, the Canadian government named its new training center the Lester B. Pearson Canadian International Peacekeeping Training Centre.

As of late 1998 more than 3,000 Canadians are deployed in 12 missions, making Canada the fifth-largest troop contributor (after the United Kingdom, France, Bangladesh, and the United States) (see Table 4).

Beginning in March 1992, Canada contributed one of the largest contingents to the UN forces in the former Yugoslavia. In 1995 some 1,300 Canadian troops served with the United Nations Peace Forces (UNPF), under the United Nations Protection Force in Former Yugoslavia (UNPROFOR) at the United Nations Confidence Restoration Operation in Croatia (UNCRO).

In March 1995 Canada contributed 100 police officers and 450 military personnel in Haiti to assist the government of Haiti in sustaining a secure and stable environment, to professionalize the Haitian army, and to create a separate police force.

Since 1974 when the United Nations Disengagement Observer Force (UNDOF) was established to supervise the cease-fire in the Golan Heights and the redeployment of Israeli and Syrian forces, the Canadian contingent has provided logistical, technical, and communications support.

The United Nations Assistance Mission in Rwanda (UNAMIR) was established in September 1993 to assist the interim government with transition measures leading to elections. A Canadian, Maj. Gen. Romeo Dallaire, led the force during the violence in early 1994.

In the Sinai a non-UN mission, the Multinational Force and Observers (MFO), is charged with monitoring adherence to the 1979 Camp David Accords, a tripartite agreement among Egypt, Israel, and the United States. Since 1986 Canada has participated in the MFO, whose mandate is of indefinite duration. Also in the Middle East Canada joined the United Nations Truce Supervision Organization (UNTSO) in 1954; it has a team of military observers with the United Nations Iraq-Kuwait Observation Mission (UNIKOM) and has three staff members deployed with the United Nations Special Commission (UNSCOM) formed in 1991 to inspect and destroy Iraq's chemical and biological weapons.

In Cambodia Canada provided 12 persons to train Cambodians in techniques for removing land mines, as part of the work of the Cambodian Mine Action Center.

Canada rarely sends large, fully formed military units on peacekeeping operations (the deployments in the former Yugoslavia being an ex-

Table 4 Canadian Peacekeeping Deployments

Country	Operation	Number of Canadians	Commenced
Former Yugoslavia	UNPROFOR	1,160	1992
	UNPREDEP UNCRO	1	
	UNMIH	140	
Haiti	UNDOF	558	1993
Golan	UNAMIR	216	1974
Rwanda	MFO (non-UN)	110	1993
Sinai	UNTSO	28	1986
Middle East Cambodia	CMAC	13	1954
Iraq/Kuwait	UNSCOM	12	1992
Cyprus	UNFICYP	3	1991
Guatemala	MINUGUA	2	1964
Kashmir	UNMOGIP	2	1994
	Transportation		1949

ception). Instead, Canada has tended to concentrate its support on assisting the "front end" of peacekeeping missions. This takes the form of offering personnel to the United Nations for planning functions, helping the United Nations to coordinate the initial phases of operations, and offering senior officers to provide leadership on the ground. Canada tends, therefore, to offer specialized skills, such as providing communications, logistics, and medical support in Rwanda and assistance removing land mines in Cambodia.

Canada has also been at the forefront of efforts to develop rapid response capabilities. The Canadian study, *Toward a Rapid Reaction Capability for the United Nations Report,* on building a rapid reaction capability was launched at the forty-ninth General Assembly of the United Nations in September 1994 with the broad objective of reforming peacekeeping operations to make them more effective in responding to global crises. The report made the following recommendations among others: In order to build upon current practice and institutionalize a formal consultative process involving nations contributing to an operation, the UN Secretariat, Security Council members, and member states should establish a troop contributors committee for each peace operation. There should also be a Troop Contributors' Forum, composed of leading troop-contributing nations, that would meet periodically to review general peacekeeping issues. The United Nations should move toward the creation of a unified budget for peace operations, which would place the financing of operations on a more coherent, predictable, and reliable basis. The funding of the revolving Peacekeeping Reserve Fund for operations should be increased to $300 million from the current $150 million, by way of assessed contributions from member states, and interest revenue should be retained in the fund. Member states and the secretary-general should work toward the development of an "early-warning alert" system, which would draw potential crisis situations to the attention of the secretary-general and the Security Council and initiate contingency planning, or at least initial "contingency thinking," within the Secretariat.

The secretary-general should continue the process of strengthening the Department of Peacekeeping Operations, including through loans and secondments from member states, with the objective of establishing an effective political and military central staff for peace operations. In conjunction with member states, the secretary-general should develop rosters of senior military commanders who might serve as force commanders in UN operations and should bring these officers to UN headquarters for periodic discussions about contingency planning, mandates, operational guidance, the integration of humanitarian and human rights concerns into peacekeeping operations, and lessons learned from past operations. The United Nations should also develop packages of equipment for generic missions, including equipment necessary for support of humanitarian assistance and disaster relief, and should either work toward the acquisition or lease and prepositioning of appropriate types and quantities of such equipment or enter into a supply agreement with member states for the provision of this equipment from national reserves. The secretary-general and member states should continue to refine and strengthen the Standby Arrangements System, with special emphasis on the ability of member states to meet specific readiness targets for potential service in rapid-reaction operations. The secretary-general, in conjunction with interested member states, should establish a permanent UN operational-level headquarters, which would be a standing, fully deployable, integrated, multinational group of approximately 30 to 50 persons, augmented in times of crisis, who would conduct contingency planning and rapid deployment as authorized by the Security Council. To ensure multidimensionality, the headquarters should contain a significant civil affairs branch with linkages to the key humanitarian and other agencies and to the nongovernmental sectors.

See also Mackenzie, Lewis; Pearson, Lester B.; Troop-contributing countries; United Nations Standby Arrangements System

References and further reading Canada (1995); Canada. Parliament. Senate Standing Committee on Foreign Affairs (1993); Pearson (1983); Gaffen (1987)

Canadian International Peacekeeping Training Center (Lester B. Pearson Center)
See Training for peacekeeping

Cease-fire

The term "cease-fire" is relatively new. It is not mentioned in the Hague Regulations of 1907, and it does not appear in major works on international law. One authority contends that the term was first used within the United Nations in 1947 in relation to the conflict in Indonesia and that around the time of the creation of the United Nations the terms "cease-fire," "truce," and "armistice" came to mean a chronological sequence in the transition from war to peace. A cease-fire is that part of the process of conflict resolution in which open hostilities are suspended while negotiations take place toward a more lasting solution. The cease-fire precedes demobilization, disarmament, and dispersal of the combatants. Traditionally a cease-fire was organized along geographical lines; a cease-fire line marked the permitted forward positions for each side. A cease-fire agreement could also include the provision of a buffer zone and control zones for the maintenance and monitoring of nonaggressive activity. Where it is not possible for a clear geographical arrangement to be made (e.g., where the combatants live in the same locality) an area cease-fire may be possible. This forbids acts of aggression within an agreed area and requires different approaches and techniques for its implementation and monitoring.

> **References and further reading** Smith (1995)

Central African Republic

In 1996 three mutinies, originating in the nonpayment of salary arrears, took place within the armed forces of the Central African Republic. President Ange-Félix Patassé asked the presidents of Burkina Faso, Chad, Gabon, and Mali to provide mediation for the drawing up of a truce between forces loyal to the president and the rebels. This truce (the Bangui Agreements) was signed on 25 January 1997. It established an international committee to monitor the implementation of the agreements. Under the agreements, on 8 February 1997, an Inter-African force was deployed. This force was the Inter-Africa Mission to Monitor the Implementation of the Bangui Agreements (MISAB).

The mission contributed to security and stability in the area, particularly by supervising and monitoring the surrendering of arms. The total strength of MISAB amounted to 800 troops comprising troops from Burkina Faso, Chad, Gabon, and Mali. Both Senegal and Togo contributed later in the mission. In addition, France provided logistical and financial support. Each of the participating states had the Security Council's authorization under chapter 7 of the UN Charter to ensure the safety of the UN personnel. This authorization was extended twice. However, France was preparing to withdraw its troops from MISAB in April 1998. The only way to maintain stability and security was to make the operation an international peacekeeping operation under the United Nations, and a third and final extension, ending on 15 April 1998, was necessary to ensure a smooth transition to the United Nations Mission in the Central African Republic (MINURCA).

The establishment of MINURCA was recommended by the secretary-general and was established on 27 March 1998 under Security Council Resolution 1159. The mission was planned to run for an initial three-month period, with decisions about extensions thereafter to be made on the basis of assessments made by the secretary-general.

The main function of the multidimensional mission was to maintain stability and to ensure security. This was realized primarily through the monitoring of the disarmament and final disposition of weapons. On a nonmilitary level, short-term police training programs were established and 24 civilian police experts and observers were provided to assist and monitor the neutrality of the gendarmerie. Electoral officers were also provided for forthcoming legislative elections.

Even though MISAB's efforts in supervising the surrender of arms had improved the overall security within the region, security was still an issue of concern when MINURCA started. For example, light weapons were still available within the country and in the nearby vicinity. The secretary-general pointed out in his report that national reconciliation was both fragile and unstable.

MINURCA is intended to provided security and stability in order to sustain and further develop the achievements of MISAB.

MINURCA had its headquarters in Bangui and was authorized to have a military component of up to 1,350 persons. The troops were drawn from Burkina Faso, Canada, Chad, Côte d'Ivoire, Egypt, France, Gabon, Mali, Senegal, and Togo. Furthermore, the secretary-general appointed Oluyemi Adeniji (Nigeria) as special representative and chief of mission.

See also Organization of African Unity
References and further reading "Report of the Secretary-General of the 23rd February 1998: Concerning the Situation in the Central African Republic." (United Nations Department for Public Information)

Central America
See Contadora Group; Dominican Republic; El Salvador; Haiti; Nicaragua; ONUCA

Chad
See Organization of African Unity

Chain of command
UN peacekeeping operations are established by the Security Council and come under its authority. One of the original intentions of the founders of the United Nations was that military deployment would be under the overall control of a Military Staff Committee (MSC), which would either have supreme control of a UN standing army or field control of national troop contingents. Because the MSC never achieved its aims and the standing army plan never came to fruition, the secretary-general is responsible to the Security Council for the direction of the operation. The secretary-general normally appoints a special representative of the secretary-general (SRSG) to be head of mission in the field. Below the SRSG the command in the field can be either a force commander, a chief military observer, or a chief

of staff. Nominally the commander in the field has complete day-to-day control of the operational aspects of the mission, but this can be misleading because there are constraints from several sources. First, the commander has to abide by the terms of the mandate, and this will only have been agreed on, in the majority of missions, with the consent of the "host country." This consent in turn may have conditions attached—such as limitations upon the freedom of movement of armed personnel or weaponry. Second, the commander does not have total control over the military personnel of the mission. There can be as many as 30 different nations represented, and each one may exercise their right to retain control over some aspects of military organization, such as promotion, discipline, or reporting back to national capitals the findings of intelligence-gathering operations. Third, the commander has to take into account the local situation, where there may be competing elements that all require attention, such as the need to offer some protection to thousands of refugees (the humanitarian imperative) while at the same time keeping apart combatant factions (the security imperative). Fourth, the commander needs to deal at an appropriate level with representatives from national government or nongovernmental organizations. Fifth, after dealing with all of these external agents and forces the commander has to establish a good working relationship with the local representatives from other parts of the UN system. Finally, once all of those different relationships are established and working, the commander can turn her or his attention to the command of the military corps—which may contain a number of equally complex relationships within itself, depending upon the ranks of the various officers, the ways in which deployment is to take place, the number of countries represented (with their differing levels of responsibility, experience, and preparation), and the reliance upon personnel outside of the mission for items such as intelligence or transport. In the face of this entire series of multilevel, multidimensional networks, the military understanding of "command and control" has to be revised, and, especially given the drive to improve rapid-deployment capabilities as well, the UN is investigating ways of improving command and control arrangements.

See also Chief military observer; Force commanders; Special representatives of the secretary-general

Charter of the United Nations

The Charter of the United Nations is the legal source of all authority for UN organization and action. A UN peacekeeping mission is only legitimate if it has gone through all the necessary procedures and received a mandate from the Security Council, and the Security Council can only operate within the parameters of the UN Charter. However, the charter does not mention the term "peacekeeping" anywhere within its 111 articles, and so it is difficult to directly relate any peacekeeping action to any relevant chapter or paragraph. Chapter 6 of the UN Charter deals with the pacific settlement of disputes, and article 33 states that "the parties to any dispute, the continuance of which is likely to endanger the maintenance of international peace and security, shall, first of all, seek a solution by negotiation, enquiry, mediation, conciliation, arbitration, judicial settlement, resort to regional agencies or arrangements, or other peaceful means of their own choice." Chapter 7 deals with actions to be taken in response to threats to peace, breaches of peace, and acts of aggression. Under article 39 it is stated that "the Security Council shall determine the existence of any threat to the peace, breach of the peace, or act of aggression and shall make recommendation, or decide what measures shall be taken, in accordance with Articles 41 and 42, to maintain or restore international peace and security." Under article 41 it is stated that "the Security Council may decide what measures not involving the use of armed force are to be employed to give effect to its decisions, and it may call upon the Members of the United Nations to apply such measures. These may include complete or partial interruption of economic relations and of rail, sea, air, postal, telegraphic, radio, and other means of communication, and the severance of diplomatic relations." Article 42 then states that "should the Security Council consider that measures provided for in Article 41 would be inadequate or have proved to be inadequate, it may take

such action by air, sea, or land forces as may be necessary to maintain or restore international peace and security. Such action may include demonstrations, blockade, and other operations by air, sea, or land forces of the United Nations." Neither chapter 6 nor chapter 7 explicitly refers to peacekeeping; rather, it was Secretary-General Dag Hammarskjöld who identified the need for a new section of the charter that would bridge chapters 6 (pacific settlement) and 7 (coercive action), coining the term "Chapter Six-and-a-Half" to identify where peacekeeping should be located within the charter. Because there is no absolute authority contained within the charter, the settlement of disputes via peacekeeping missions has been largely pragmatic. Since the first force-level mission in 1956 (the United Nations Emergency Force [UNEF] I), most peacekeeping missions have been authorized under chapter 6 and are therefore recognized as noncoercive in nature, even though they are composed of military forces. Early missions under chapter 6 are also known as "first-generation peacekeeping."

In certain situations all attempts to settle disputes peacefully have failed, and, in these circumstances chapter 7 is available to allow the Security Council to use stronger action, which can range from economic sanctions to the use of military power for "peace enforcement." Chapter 7 sanctions have been used only against the then Rhodesia, South Africa, and Iraq in the 50 years of the UN's existence, and military action only in Korea, Somalia, and Kuwait.

See also *An Agenda for Peace;* United Nations: organization
References and further reading Bailey and Daws (1995); Fisas (1994)

Chief military observer

Chief military observer (CMO) is the title given to the officer commanding an observation mission. The CMO is part of a three-tier structure of command. The first level is that of overall political direction, which is vested in the Security Council. The second level is that of executive command and is the prerogative of the secretary-general. The third level is that of commander in the field, who can be either the chief of mission, the force commander, or the chief military observer. The observer group that the CMO leads has a wider role than just observing and reporting back. The group monitors cease-fire maintenance, reports on violations, intercedes or negotiates with local commanders, receives complaints about the operation of the cease-fire, and provides some humanitarian assistance. The earliest UN missions in the field, and the longest established, were military observer missions such as those in the Middle East and in Asia (the United Nations Truce Supervision Organization [UNTSO] and the United Nations Military Observer Group in India and Pakistan [UNMOGIP]).

See also Chain of command; Force commanders; Special representatives of the secretary-general

Child soldiers

Under international law (the 1977 Protocol I Additional to the Geneva Convention of 12 August 1949, and Relating to the Protection of Victims of International Armed Conflict, Article 77 [2]; the 1977 Geneva Protocol II Additional to the Geneva Conventions of 12 August 1949, and Relating to the Protection of Victims of Non-International Armed Conflicts, Article 4 [3a], and the Convention on the Rights of the Child 1989, Article 38), a person under the age of 15 who takes part in armed conflict is categorized as a child soldier. However, the Convention on the Rights of the Child defines a child as anyone under the age of 18, and therefore one could extend the definition of a "child soldier" to encompass anyone under 18 years of age taking part in armed combat. It should be noted that to date the Convention on the Rights of the Child is the most ratified international legal document in the history of the United Nations; by 1998, 191 countries had accepted this convention. Currently a protocol additional to the Convention on the Rights of the Child is being drafted that would increase the age of recruitment to 18. Some regional documents have already increased the minimum age for legal recruitment into armed forces to 18 years of age.

It is estimated that there were 200,000 child soldiers from the late 1980s to the late 1990s, although it is impossible to determine the exact numbers worldwide. In 1995–1996, 33 countries were thought to employ child soldiers, but even this information is not definite. Because it is illegal to employ child soldiers, their use is commonly not recorded and it is difficult to monitor them.

Between 1960 and 1994 the following conflicts have officially been reported as having children below the age of 15 participating in active fighting either in governmental forces or as part of rebel groups: (1) wars of independence: Angola (1960–1975); Mozambique (1967–1975); Bangladesh (1971); Eritrea (1961–1981); Guinea-Bissau (1963–1975); Laos (1960–1975); Namibia (1967–1989); Vietnam (1945–1975); Zimbabwe (1972–1980); Kurdistan/Iran (1979–1980, 1980–1980); Kurdistan/Iraq (1961–1970, 1975, 1987–1988, 1991–); Kurdistan/Turkey (1978–1980, 1983–1988, 1990); and Palestine (1948–); (2) civil wars and strife: Cambodia (1970–1975, 1975–1979, 1979–1989); Chad (1968–1976, 1982, 1983–1984, 1986–1987); Cyprus (1984); Djibouti (1981, 1991–1994); Lebanon (1975–1976, 1977–1991); Nicaragua (1978, 1981–1989); Rwanda (1990–1993); Sudan (1983–1986); El Salvador (1980–1992); Vietnam (1962–1975); Afghanistan (1989–); Angola (1976–1991, 1993–); Azerbaijan–Upper Karaboakh (1989–); Burma (1945–); Burundi (1994–); Cambodia (1989–); Chechnya (1994–); Colombia (1970–1984, 1984); Guatemala (1962–); Indonesia/East Timor (1975–); Indonesia/West Papua (1963–); Iran (1979–); Liberia (1990–); Peru (1980–); Philippines (1969–); Rwanda (1994–); Sierra Leone (1992–); Sri Lanka (1983–); Sudan (1983–); and Tajikistan (1993–); (3) international wars and civil wars with foreign intervention: Afghanistan-USSR (1979–1989); Cambodia-Vietnam (1979–1989); Croatia-Serbia (1991); Ecuador-Peru (1995); Iraq/Coalition (1991); Iraq-Iran (1980–1988); Libya-Chad (1982–1984, 1986–1987); Somalia-Ethiopia (1961–1964, 1977–1978); Uganda-Tanzania (1978); United Kingdom–Argentina (1982); United Kingdom–Northern Ireland (1969–); United States–Vietnam (1960–1972); Bosnia and Herzegovina–Serbia (1991–); Kashmir-India-Pakistan (1985–); Lebanon-Israel (1982–); Western Sahara Republic–Morocco (1979–); South Yemen–North Yemen (1994, 1995). The following countries employed children under the age of 18 in conflicts that either ended or were ongoing during 1994–1996: Algeria, Azerbaijan/Armenia, Azerbaijan/Nagorno-Karabakh, Chad, Djibouti, Ecuador/Peru, Mexico/Chiapas, Papua New Guinea, Russian Federation/Chechnya, Tajikistan.

The reasons for recruitment are varied. Some children volunteer after witnessing acts of violence against family members and decide to join an armed force either as a result of fear or revenge. Other children volunteer because the military or guerrilla movement can offer food or clothing. In some cases children become increasingly aware of their political surroundings and choose to become politically active, at times playing a major role in the initiation of the conflict. The messages that are sent to children by their parents, communities, churches, and peer groups can have a great bearing on the child's actions. Although some children are forced into armed groups or institutions, others are simply exposed to skillful manipulation that may lead them toward participation in armed conflict. Militarized groups and government forces have been known to coerce children into leaving their homes under the pretext of gaining an education. Furthermore, children have become child soldiers as a result of being kidnapped by a militarized force or have been required to join the military by their governments. At times armed groups prefer to use child soldiers because children can more easily be turned into fighters: They can be brave, amenable, and nonquestioning and can be easily disciplined. In some cases they are indoctrinated, drugged, forced to participate in cannibalistic rituals, or forced to injure or kill friends or family members as a right of passage or preparation for combat.

Technology has revolutionized warfare. Physical strength and stamina are no longer as necessary as they once were to active participation in an armed conflict. The modern versions of Soviet AK-47 and U.S. M-16 weapons are capable of firing 600 rounds per minute, weigh little more than three kilograms each, and can be used without ex-

tensive training. These types of weapons can therefore be easily used by children.

In addition to the evolution of weaponry, the twentieth century has embraced concepts such as "total war" and "people's war," concepts that essentially erase the long-held distinction between civilians and combatants. Furthermore, the end of the Cold War has accelerated the rate at which children are being employed as soldiers. As Washington and Moscow reduced the funding to their regional military proxies, some military and guerrilla groups have resorted to employing children as active participants in conflicts. A child soldier is less expensive than an adult counterpart.

There are both short-term and long-term consequences of children's participation in war. Detention is one of the possible repercussions of being a child soldier. Child soldier detention can take the following forms: Children can be held as prisoners of war (POWs), may be accused of terrorist actions, and may be accused of desertion. Some POW camps offer education and training. Whether children benefit from being POWs can depend on the type of conflict they participated in and on the stage the conflict is at during their imprisonment. Additionally, it is not uncommon for children who have been detained to lack adequate legal protection or to be subject to abusive interrogation, torture, psychological trauma, inadequate detention facilities, disregard for visitation rights, inadequate explanation of legal procedure, translation problems, inaccessibility to counsel, unreachable bail cost, inconsistent sentencing, or delays and postponements of legal procedure.

From the point of view of the child soldier there may also be positive aspects. A child may find that his or her armed group provides social support, empowerment, validation, and respect from family, teachers, and peers, from which consequently they gain at least a feeling of security and value and a sense of identity.

Just as the causes of the conflict are important to an understanding of a child's reasons for becoming a soldier, the process by which the conflict is brought to an end is important to an understanding of how former child soldiers will cope with their war experiences. In some cases the amount of time spent as part of a militarized group will determine the child's capacity to reintegrate into peacetime society. Children who have been active participants during a conflict may fear retribution or punishment for their actions. Furthermore, their families or communities may reject them, either because of the crimes they have committed, because their communities believe they cannot be trusted, or because they did not fulfill their duty to society as soldiers. Fear of rejection or of losing respect and a lack of means to survive economically can be a deterrent to demobilization. Lack of means for survival, lack of employment, discipline problems, fear and mistrust, and an inability to relate to peace are some of the causal factors for delinquency among former child soldiers. The inability of many former child soldiers to survive outside the environment of conflict presents a significant challenge in peacemaking and in the rehabilitation of war-torn communities.

See also Geneva Conventions and the laws of war; United Nations: organization
References and further reading Brett and McCallin (1996); Goodwin-Gill and Cohn (1997); Grant (1992); UNICEF (1996)

Childers, Erskine (1928–1997)

Born in 1928, Erskine Childers was a leading Irish academic and diplomat. He contributed over 22 years of diplomatic service to the United Nations. His father was a president of the Republic of Ireland. His diplomatic career gave him wide experience in most UN departments before he was rewarded with the appointment of senior advisor to the UN secretary-general. On retiring from this post in 1989, he continued serving the international community as secretary-general of the World Federation of United Nations Associations (WFUNA). While taking part in the fiftieth-anniversary celebrations of the WFUNA in Luxembourg, Childers died from a heart attack. He contributed widely to academic and policy discussions through major publications of studies, which were often coauthored with Sir Brian Urquhart.

References and further reading Childers and Urquhart (1994a)

China

From 1950 to 1971 China was excluded from the United Nations, and throughout that time China was emphatically opposed to peacekeeping. Chinese attitudes to peacekeeping have evolved through four phases, from active opposition and disruption (1950–1971) to nondisruption (1971–1981) to cooperation (1981–1988) to active participation, albeit on a small scale, in field operations (since 1988).

Initially Chinese opposition both to the United Nations and to peacekeeping was based on its view that the United Nations was simply a tool of U.S. imperialism and a place where the United States and the Soviet Union manipulated affairs in their own interests. The UN operation in the Congo was thus seen as a U.S.-manipulated effort to suppress the national liberation movement. Peacekeeping in general, in China's view, was designed to protect the interests of imperialism and to undermine efforts to win independence and freedom. This view was born both out of the revolutionary ideology of Mao Ze-dong's People's Republic and out of the specific experience of the Korean War, in which multinational forces under U.S. command acted under a UN mandate and following a UN resolution that condemned China and North Korea as aggressors. Chinese resentment of this was to color her view of peacekeeping for years. The Special Committee on Peacekeeping Operations was seen as "a notorious international gendarmerie" whose objective was to stamp out the revolutionary struggle. China entered the UN Security Council in 1971 and refused to support or contribute to the costs of peacekeeping operations.

By the late 1970s, however, this attitude was changing as Chinese foreign policy was revised, and a more positive attitude to international cooperation was evident. By the mid-1980s this change was manifested in a supportive policy toward peacekeeping, which was now seen as part of the international community's obligation to preserve and promote peace and security. In 1988 China applied for membership on the Special Committee on Peacekeeping Operations and was accepted as the thirty-fourth member in November of that year. In 1989 China sent its first contingent to participate in a peacekeeping mission, in the form of five military observers who joined the United Nations Disengagement Observer Force (UNDOF) in the Middle East and 20 nonmilitary personnel who joined the United Nations Transitional Assistance Group (UNTAG) in Namibia as electoral observers. In 1992 an engineering battalion formed part of United Nations Transitional Authority in Cambodia (UNTAC). Though China has become positively involved in such traditional "first-generation" peacekeeping missions, it has remained cautious about the authorization of chapter 7 operations involving the use of force. China abstained from voting on Security Council Resolution 678, which authorized the use of "all necessary means" to expel Iraqi troops from Kuwait. China has also emphatically held that peacekeeping should not breach the nonintervention norm in international relations, that the sovereignty of nations should be respected, and that any intervention should be based on the consent of the host government.

See also Cambodia; United Nations: organization
References and further reading Kim (1979); Zhang (1996)

Civil military teams (CIMICs)
See Military-humanitarian relations

Civilian component in peacekeeping operations

Peacekeeping in the traditional, cease-fire monitoring sense has little need for civilian personnel. In contrast, civilians and civil agencies have formed a major, perhaps the most important, element of recent missions. The complex mandates of new, multidisciplinary peacekeeping operations can include a variety of tasks for which military forces are unsuited, such as administering a transitional period in the country, monitoring an election, and supervising government officials or police. Civilian peacekeepers can be deployed alongside military peacekeepers as one component of a comprehensive settlement strategy, or the mission can consist entirely of civilians. The first case is exemplified by missions like the United Nations Transitional Authority in Cambodia (UNTAC) and the United Nations Observer Mission in El Salvador (ONUSAL), the second by the Mision de los Naciones Unidas en Guatemala (MINUGUA) and the Joint International Civilian Mission in Haiti (MICIVIH). In some definitions human rights verification missions such as the latter two are not peacekeeping operations, and indeed the UN Department of Peacekeeping Operations does not have responsibility for them, but they are generally understood as a variety of peace support operation.

Civilians also play an increasingly important role in peacekeeping operations through nongovernmental organizations (NGOs). These organizations, whether engaged in humanitarian relief or development work, can complement the work of military peacekeepers. For example, the United Nations High Commission on Refugees (UNHCR) may contract with one or more humanitarian aid agencies to run refugee camps and resettlement programs. The on-the-ground expertise and local knowledge that NGO workers provide make them invaluable for an effective peacekeeping operation. There can be problems in the relationship between military peacekeepers and civilian NGOs, most particularly a lack of coordination between them. This is at least wasteful and can even be a liability to the continued efficacy of the mission as a whole.

Civilian peacekeeping has certain advantages. In cases like MICIVIH, it can be easier to obtain consent for the operation because an unarmed, international civilian presence is less confrontational than a military presence. Especially in regard to the reestablishment of the rule of law in countries that have experienced repressive military rule, civilian peacekeeping operations will have more legitimacy and be more able to help build sustainable democratic institutions. Whereas military forces are usually deployed in order to separate the parties to a conflict, civilian operations attempt to establish an atmosphere of reconciliation so that the parties can learn to live together.

The disadvantages of civilian peacekeeping stem from two sources: the lack of necessary speed in response and the disjunction between ambitious mandates and limited means. First, most civilian agencies emphasize consultation and consensus building over the directive command structure that characterizes military units. Although this is important for forging democratically acceptable solutions, it takes time, and speed of response is at a premium in most peacekeeping operations. Second, the mandates of civilian peacekeeping operations often include very ambitious goals that amount to creating a democratic culture in countries that have little, if any, experience of democratic governance and the rule of law. The means and resources allocated to these operations and the time frame envisaged for the attainment of their mandated goals are often insufficient to effect changes of this magnitude.

See also Civilian police; Civilians in conflict zones; Congo; Croatia; Demilitarized zone; El Salvador; Guatemala; Haiti; Namibia; UNPROFOR I–III; White Helmets

References and further reading Fisas (1995); Kamarotos (1995); Mackinlay (1996); Ratner (1997)

Civilian police (United Nations Civilian Police [CIVPOL])

The United Nations Civilian Police (CIVPOL) form an important component of many peacekeeping operations. Member states are usually approached to provide small national police contingents at the same time as the military forces for a mission are being recruited. CIVPOL's activities normally fall into three categories, from the most to the least intrusive: the performance of police functions when the host country's police have ceased functioning or been so discredited that they cannot function effectively in an area; monitoring and reporting on officers in the field; and providing training and technical advice to new or revitalized police services. Their activities are to ensure public security, encourage local police to respect human rights through training and monitoring, and build confidence between local communities and the police or between adversarial groups. CIVPOL are regarded as more appropriate for these roles than military troops because their presence is less confrontational and their professional experience is more conducive to the development of an accountable and community-based police force.

The first UN mission to make use of CIVPOL units was the UN Peacekeeping Force in Cyprus (UNFICYP), which was deployed in 1964. The force consisted of 174 police officers from Australia, Austria, Denmark, New Zealand, and Sweden. Since then CIVPOL has been used in many peacekeeping operations, including the United Nations Mission for the Referendum in Western Sahara (MINURSO), the United Nations Preventive Deployment Force Macedonia (UNPREDEP), the United Nations Mission in Bosnia and Herzegovina (UNMIBH), the United Nations Observer Mission in Angola (MONUA), the United Nations Civilian Police Mission in Haiti (MIPONUH), the Civilian Police Support Group, the United Nations Mission in the Central African Republic (MINURCA), the United Nations Transitional Assistance Group (UNTAG), the second and third United Nations Angola Verification Missions (UNAVEM II and III), the United Nations Observer Mission in El Salvador (ONUSAL), the United Nations Protection Force in Former Yugoslavia (UNPROFOR), the United Nations Transitional Authority in Cambodia (UNTAC), the United Nations Operation in Mozambique (ONUMOZ), the second United Nations Operation in Somalia (UNOSOM II), the United Nations Support Mission for Haiti (UNSMIH), the United Nations Assistance Mission in Rwanda (UNAMIR), the United Nations Confidence Restoration Operation in Croatia (UNCRO), the United Nations Transitional Administration for Eastern Slavonia, Baranja, and Western Sirmium (UNTAES), the United Nations Transition Mission in Haiti (UNTMIH), the United Nations Mission in Haiti (UNMIH), and the Mision de los Naciones Unidas en Guatemala (MINUGUA).

The CIVPOL element of the United Nations Transitional Authority in Cambodia (UNTAC), consisting of 3,600 officers, has been criticized for incompetence, corruption, and poor behavior toward the Cambodian population. Since CIVPOL officers are likely to be in close contact with local communities, it is vital to the overall reputation and success of the mission that the officers provide an example of professionalism and respect for human rights. The growing importance of CIVPOL is illustrated by the fact that two current UN missions consist primarily of CIVPOL functions: the Civilian Police Support Group in Croatia and MIPONUH. Both operations are mandated to monitor the performance of local police forces, who have previously received training under various UN-sponsored schemes. Training local police officers is increasingly seen as one of CIVPOL's most important functions. For example, in El Salvador the small CIVPOL contingent did not have the resources to conduct the initial training of the new National Civil Police, but the CIVPOL monitors who accompanied the inexperienced new officers on patrol provided valuable on-the-job training and backup.

In many of the conflicts in which the United Nations is now involved, police forces have been a primary source of human rights violations. Progress in controlling abuses by the police and in developing a force that protects law and order without terrorizing the population is therefore a central part of building a sustainable and democratic peace.

See also Cambodia; Croatia; El Salvador; Guatemala; Haiti
References and further reading
Mackinlay (1996); Ratner (1997)

Civilian-Military Operations Center (CMOC)
See Military-humanitarian relations

Civilians in conflict zones
Civilians and noncombatants often suffer most in any modern conflict. Civilians are the targets in these wars, not the accidental victims of it. In World War I over 80 percent of battlefield deaths were combatants; by the 1990s over 90 percent of war-related deaths are civilians, killed in their own homes and communities, which have become the battlefields of international and civil wars. As a consequence it has been observed that the least dangerous place to be in most contemporary wars is in the military, and "dirty war" strategies, originally identified with state-sponsored terrorism, are now a feature of a widening band of militias, paramilitaries, warlords, and armies seeking control of resources through depredation, terror, and force. Military commanders are regarded under

the Geneva Conventions as having a duty to try to ensure that civilian casualties are minimized and that nonmilitary property is not damaged or destroyed unnecessarily. However, it is also the case that these tenets were propounded at a time when noncombatants could be easily distinguished from military personnel, and in modern conflicts such a simple distinction is not always possible. First, for example, in areas of guerrilla warfare combatants mix with the civilian population as a form of military strategy. Second, recent conflicts in Europe and Africa have seen large-scale population movements within a country or a military theater, which makes it difficult to identify and protect purely civilian areas or property. Third, as standing armies are scaled down, modern conflicts have seen the rise of intensive conscription of large numbers of civilians into military duties. This means that the population at large can be a mélange of service personnel and civilians. And, most seriously, in contemporary civil wars scorched-earth tactics are common; livestock are seized, grain stores are attacked and looted, and wells and watering places are poisoned. Although this does not apply to all internal conflicts, there are war zone economies where civilians are seen as legitimate targets for militias, to be plundered, exploited, or forcibly moved. Humanitarian and development aid is captured, and humanitarian workers are kidnapped, held hostage, and killed.

See also Civilian component in peacekeeping operations; Civilian police; Conflicts: patterns and occurrences; UNPROFOR I–III; White Helmets
References and further reading Cairns (1997); Macrae, Zwi, and Duffield (1994)

Codes of conduct
The International Red Cross and Red Crescent Movement has defined a set of principles governing the activities of nongovernment organizations (NGOs) in disaster response programs. They are summarized as follows:

1. The humanitarian imperative comes first (the right to receive and to offer humanitarian assistance is a fundamental humanitarian principle).

2. Aid is given regardless of race, creed, or nationality of the recipients and without adverse distinction of any kind. Aid priorities are calculated on the basis of need alone (the principle of impartiality; human suffering must be alleviated wherever it is found).

3. Aid will not be used to further a particular political or religious standpoint (the principle of neutrality).

4. Participants shall endeavor not to act as instruments of government foreign policy. (Agencies will not seek to implement the policy of any government except where it coincides with the agencies' own independent policy and will not gather political, military, or economically sensitive information for governments that may serve purposes other than those that are strictly humanitarian.)

5. Participants shall respect the culture, structures, and customs of the host society.

6. Participants will attempt to build disaster response on local capacities. (All people and communities, even in disasters, possess capabilities as well as vulnerabilities, and these capacities should be strengthened by working with local NGOs, employing local staff, and using local economic resources.)

7. Ways shall be found to involve program beneficiaries in the management of relief aid in order to achieve full community participation in the management and implementation of relief and assistance.

8. Relief aid must strive to reduce future vulnerabilities to disaster as well as to meet basic needs and help create sustainable lifestyles.

9. Participants are accountable both to those who require assistance and to those from whom they accept resources.

10. In information, publicity, and advertising activities, aid givers shall recognize disaster victims as dignified humans, not hopeless objects, respecting disaster victims as equal partners in action and using images that portray not only the victims' vulnerabilities and fears but also their capacities and aspirations.

A ten-point code of conduct for blue helmet troops has been issued by the United Nations Department of Peacekeeping Operations (UNDPKO), summarized as follows:

1. Dress, think, talk, act, and behave in a manner befitting the dignity of a disciplined and trusted soldier, displaying the highest integrity and impartiality.

2. Respect the law and culture of the host country.

3. Treat the inhabitants with respect and courtesy; do not solicit material rewards or gifts.

4. Do not indulge in immoral acts of sexual, physical, or psychological abuse.

5. Respect and regard the human rights of all.

6. Properly care and account for all UN property and equipment.

7. Show military courtesy to all members of the mission, including other UN contingents.

8. Show respect for the environment.

9. Do not engage in excessive consumption of alcohol or traffic in drugs.

10. Exercise discretion in handling confidential information and in conducting official business.

The need for such codes of conduct has been dramatically demonstrated in a number of recent missions. In Cambodia there was a marked increase in prostitution, including child prostitution, following the arrival of military personnel under the UN flag between 1991 and 1992, and in Mozambique some UN troops were expelled following allegations of racism, violence, and sexual abuse. In Somalia a UN Canadian battalion was sent home following incidents involving violence against local people, and similar allegations were made against members of the Italian contingent.

See also Human rights
References and further reading
Mackinlay (1996); Moxon-Browne (1998)

Cold War

The "Cold War" is the common term given to the struggle between Communist states and Western liberal democracies for political hegemony that became the dominant feature of world politics after 1945. It is called "cold" to differentiate it from the "hot" war that would be waged with nuclear weapons. The main military alliances of this political struggle were, on the Western side, the North Atlantic Treaty Organization (NATO) and, on the Communist side, the Warsaw Pact, which was a treaty organization comprising the Communist bloc countries, led by the Soviet Union. One of the main effects of the Cold War on the peacekeeping role of the United Nations was that it was difficult to respond or to mount an operation when members of the Security Council were politically opposed and used their power of veto to further their political views. Another difficulty was that the "superpowers" (the United States and the USSR) were both unwilling to allow the United Nations any leeway to act in regional conflicts in which either had a political or military interest. In November 1956, for example, although the United Nations was launching its major United Nations Emergency Force (UNEF) initiative in the Middle East, the USSR successfully blocked any real discussion of its own invasion of Hungary several weeks earlier. The United States, for its part, made sure that the situation in Vietnam (in which it was a major player) was never the subject of substantive Security Council discussions in the late 1960s and early 1970s, although other important peacekeeping missions were launched in other parts of the globe at the same time. Throughout the 1970s and 1980s the three Security Council members from the Western bloc used their power of veto to prevent discussion or action on issues relating to the Middle East and southern Africa in particular. In the first 44 years of the United Nations, for example, the USSR exercised its veto on 114 resolutions; the United States vetoed 67, the United Kingdom 30, France 18, and China 3. The end of the Cold War, following upon the seismic changes to the regimes in the USSR and eastern European countries, has meant that the Security Council is no longer automatically divided or is necessarily locked into an "us and them" set of responses. In the growth in recent years of situations requiring UN action or intervention, peacekeeping has played a central role in the collective response of the international community to international conflict. The opti-

mism surrounding the potential post–Cold War role of the United Nations, and its peacekeeping arm, was most clearly expressed in the *Agenda for Peace* (1992).

See also United Nations: organization
References and further reading Crocker, Hampson, and Aall (1996); Parsons (1995); Rogers and Dando (1992)

Command and control in peacekeeping operations
See Chain of command

Committee of Thirty-Four
See United Nations Special Committee on Peacekeeping Operations (C-34)

The Commonwealth
The Commonwealth has 50 members, 46 of them located in the developing world, and has evolved from the British Empire as an international association of former British colonies that elected to become members after having achieved independence. The Commonwealth Secretariat was established in 1965 and is headed by a secretary-general.

In December 1979 the Commonwealth Monitoring Force (CMF) was established by the Commonwealth to supervise the Lancaster House Agreement between the government of the then Southern Rhodesia (itself in rebellion against the United Kingdom since 1965) and the African guerrilla forces of the Patriotic Front. Under the agreement, UK authority was restored over its rebellious colony, a cease-fire was implemented, a general election was held, and independence was achieved by the new republic of Zimbabwe. The CMF was tasked with monitoring the agreement and resembled a United Nations observer mission, except that its duties were more extensive and its personnel were armed. There was also an attached 11-nation Commonwealth Observer Group (COG) tasked with verifying the conduct of the general elections held in February 1980. The CMF comprised a headquarters and three groups. The first group was tasked with monitoring the Rhodesian security forces. The second group comprised 23 teams of one officer and nine other ranks deployed in remote areas to supervise the rendezvous points where the Patriotic Front guerrillas were concentrated and to organize cantonment at agreed-upon assembly points. The third group comprised seven border-crossing teams monitoring the return of civilian refugees from neighboring countries.

The Commonwealth Heads of Government Meeting in 1989 agreed on an agenda for action that included the reinforcement of democracy and human rights, a concern for the security of small states, and a concern for the political and economic development in southern Africa. The Commonwealth Mission to South Africa provided an important role in providing support for the peace process there, and although the Commonwealth does not have a formal peacekeeping mechanism one calculation suggests that 70 percent of UN peacekeepers are provided by countries that are Commonwealth members and that the Commonwealth should therefore take a more proactive role in peacekeeping and international conflict resolution.

See also British peacekeeping
References and further reading Verrier (1994)

Commonwealth of Independent States

The Commonwealth of Independent States (CIS) was established in December 1991 to coordinate intercommonwealth relations and to provide a mechanism for the orderly dissolution of the USSR. The members of the CIS are Armenia, Azerbaijan, Belarus, Georgia, Kazakhstan, Kyrgyzstan, Moldova, Russia, Tajikistan, Turkmenistan, Ukraine, and Uzbekistan. The framework for peacekeeping in the "near abroad" (the term used by Russia to describe the republics of the former Soviet Union) has been established through the CIS. The Kiev Agreement on Collective Security Forces of March 1992 and the Tashkent Protocol on Collective Peacekeeping Forces of July 1992 in theory laid down the ground rules for peacekeeping. However, a CIS peacekeeping force was not estab-

lished. Instead, CIS member states set up their own national armies, and peacekeeping took the form of bilateral and regional arrangements between Russia and the parties to the particular conflict being addressed. The first deployment on a territory of the former Soviet Union, in 1992, established this format when a combined Russian, Georgian, and Ossetian force was sent to South Ossetia in Georgia. Its mission was to separate Ossetians and Georgian militias. The former were fighting for unification with Ossetians in Russia, the latter to prevent their secession and the breakup of Georgia. The decision to deploy the force was made not by the CIS but by the presidents of Russia and of Georgia. A similar model was used in Moldova when a Russian-dominated trilateral peacekeeping contingent (with Russian, Dniester, and Moldovan forces), described as a CIS peacekeeping force, was deployed in Moldova, also in 1992. The purpose of the deployment was to stop the fighting between Moldovan military forces and the militias of the ethnic Russian minority seeking independence for a "Dniester Republic." The Bishkek Summit of the CIS in the autumn of 1992 agreed upon a further protocol on peacekeeping, a protocol that linked it to the CIS collective security system and that gave responsibility for command, preparation, and training of peacekeepers to the high command of the CIS Joint Armed Forces. However, disagreements about the composition of the CIS Joint Armed Forces command system suggested that such a combined system was unworkable, and plans to create it were abandoned. As of late 1998, peacekeeping in the territories of the former Soviet Union continued to be dominated by Russian forces and Russian interests.

See also Regional organizations and peacekeeping; Russian peacekeeping
References and further reading Allison (1994); Greene (1993); Shaashenkov (1994)

Complex emergency

Since the end of the Cold War the number of UN organizations and peacekeeping forces involved in conflict resolution has increased dramatically. The nature of conflict has changed, and the international community is now increasingly involved in civil wars and intercommunal violence. In the post–Cold War period, in a reinforcement of trends that had been apparent for most of this century, the civilian population has not been so much the victim of what was called collateral damage as, in many areas, the primary target of violence. Warlords and militias may establish their power by the level of control they exercise over civilian populations, and this power is demonstrated by conducting what in the Yugoslav wars became known as "ethnic cleansing," the forced and violent exodus of populations in order to achieve war aims. In modern war there is little recognition of the distinction between combatant and civilian, and those traditionally regarded as the innocent—women, children, and the elderly—have become victims. Humanitarian relief to the victims itself becomes a target of the militias, and its implementation can be impeded or its contents may be plundered or extorted in order to add to the resources of the militias. "Complex emergencies" and "complex political emergencies" are the terms used to describe this phenomenon. They are distinct from traditional interstate territorial conflicts and resource conflict in several respects. The following definition is useful in describing the complex emergencies that characterize so many contemporary war zones:

> A complex emergency is a humanitarian disaster that occurs in a conflict zone and is complicated by, or results from, the conflicting interests of warring parties. Its causes are seldom exclusively natural or military: in many cases a marginally subsistent population is precipitated toward disaster by the consequences of militia action or a natural occurrence such as earthquake or drought. The presence of militias and their interest in controlling and extorting the local population will impede and in some cases seriously threaten relief efforts. In addition to violence against the civilian populations, civilian installations such as hospitals, schools, refugee centers, and cultural sites will become war objectives and may be looted frequently or destroyed.

In the 1990s the response to humanitarian crises has been a large-scale expansion of humanitarian action, and a wide network of agencies have been mobilized to enter war zones with the minimal objective of mitigating the effects of the conflict by providing relief aid. However, it has become increasingly clear that emergency relief, though obviously essential, has limited value in the face of the increasing wave of population displacement and violation of basic human rights in conflict zones. Given this, the objective of providing humanitarian assistance to those in need has increasingly been linked to the imperatives of supporting sustainable peace processes in areas of conflict. In these situations peacekeeping forces have been tasked with fulfilling complex mandates and have needed to find ways of coordinating their efforts with the wide range of international and local humanitarian agencies that respond to civilian need.

See also Conflict resolution theory and peacekeeping; Conflicts: patterns and occurrences; Humanitarian assistance; Humanitarian intervention
References and further reading
Mackinlay (1996); Mackinlay and Kent (1997)

Conference on Security and Cooperation in Europe
See Organization for Security and Cooperation in Europe (OSCE)

Conflict prevention

Conflict prevention (or preventive diplomacy) is the idea that action should be taken to prevent violent conflicts rather than responding only after violence has broken out. After the end of the Cold War, the combination of a growing number of complex conflicts and improved prospects for great power cooperation led to new interest in conflict prevention. In his 1992 report *An Agenda for Peace*, UN Secretary-General Boutros Boutros-Ghali argued that one of the UN's central aims must be "to seek to identify at the earliest possible stage situations that could produce conflict, and try through diplomacy to remove sources of danger before violence results." The report defined preventive diplomacy as "action to prevent disputes from arising between parties, to prevent existing disputes from escalating into conflicts and to limit the spread of the latter when they occur." It suggested that preventive diplomacy could involve measures to build confidence, fact-finding missions, early warning of potential conflicts, the preventive deployment of peacekeeping or deterrent military forces, and the establishment of demilitarized zones. Various efforts have been made to put conflict prevention into practice. The UN secretary-general sends special representatives to potential conflict zones to gather facts, explore options for preventive diplomacy, and mediate between parties. In the first example of its kind, the UN Security Council authorized the deployment of the United Nations Preventive Deployment Force Macedonia (UNPREDEP) before any violence had broken out. Many regional organizations are involved in conflict-prevention activities. The Organization for Security and Cooperation in Europe (OSCE), for example, has deployed missions to various potential conflict areas in Europe and the former Soviet Union and has established a High Commission on National Minorities (HCNM) to prevent violent interethnic conflict. Nongovernmental organizations have also been involved in conflict-prevention activities, often seeking to support grassroots peace organizations and conflict-resolution processes.

Critics of conflict prevention argue that although preventive diplomacy may be a good idea, it is much more difficult to put into practice. Such critics have argued that the causes of violent conflicts are multiple and highly complex, that our understanding of these causes is limited, and that it is therefore not possible to predict with any certainty where and when conflicts might be likely. They have also argued that there are simply too many potential conflicts and that the major powers and international organizations are likely to be overwhelmed by the scale of the effort required for meaningful conflict prevention. Early intervention in potential conflicts within states, further, raises the sensitive issue of state sovereignty, making many governments reluctant to set precedents for international interference in the internal affairs of states. Critics also point out that the most powerful states may not have the interest or the political will to intervene in potential conflicts in faraway countries that have little direct impact on them.

See also *Agenda for Peace;* Macedonia; Organization for Security and Cooperation in Europe (OSCE); United Nations: organization
References and further reading Bauwens and Reychler (1994); Carnegie Commission on Preventing Deadly Conflict (1997); Stedman (1995)

Conflict resolution theory and peacekeeping

The academic study and practice of conflict resolution has much in common with the role of peacekeeping in international conflict management. UN peacekeeping and conflict resolution as a field of academic research have much in common conceptually, and both emerged as distinct areas of theory and practice at about the same historical period. Although there is a longer gestation period in efforts to justify and define a "science of peace," evident in a number of initiatives after World War I, the formation of modern conflict resolution can be dated to developments at the University of Michigan in the mid-1950s, including the founding of the Journal of Conflict Resolution in 1957. At about the same time that conflict resolution was emerging, the basic principles of peacekeeping were defined by Dag Hammarskjöld and Lester Pearson. These were defined to guide the work of the first United Nations Emergency Force (UNEF I), created in response to the Suez Canal crisis in the Middle East in 1956.

It has recently become more common for conflict resolution theorists to refer to peacekeeping as an important instrument of positive conflict transformation, where peacekeepers may use psychological and communication strategies more than military force. In the same way, one of the striking features of recent analyses by practitioners of peacekeeping has been the frequency with which they refer to the relevance of aspects of conflict resolution. Canadian Gen. Clayton Beattie argued that training for peacekeeping would have to be considerably different from conventional combat training because peacekeeping "involves the psychological change from an adversarial to a pacific role; from confrontation to third party interposition. In peacekeeping there is no enemy: the objective is to avoid hostilities, to improve communications between the parties, and to advance the process of reconciliation. This necessitates a full understanding of the causes of the conflict—political, military, and economic—as well as the social and cultural environment. It demands a fair-minded and impartial approach while operating within an atmosphere of distrust and suspicion among the protagonists, often under difficult and provocative conditions."

Thus, although its end goals and objectives may be defined militarily (controlling and ending violence, securing the environment), politically (restoring legitimate government), and economically (assisting efforts for development), peacekeeping on the ground is an essentially psychological process requiring great sensitivity to local perceptions and culture. This is because the original principles of peacekeeping (consent, impartiality, minimum use of force, legitimate conduct, and mutual respect) can only be observed by a closer integration of the communication and problem-solving strategies associated with conflict resolution into the doctrine and practice of peacekeeping. It is noticeable how much of the peacekeeping doctrine of the British Army, elaborated in its Field Manual on Wider Peacekeeping, is suffused with the language of conflict resolution. The same approach is taken in the U.S. doctrine covering peace support operations. Here, the management of consent (based on the principles of impartiality, legitimacy, mutual respect, minimum force, credibility, and transparency) is also related to the techniques of promoting good communication, of negotiation and mediation, and of positive approaches to community relations through an active and well-funded civil affairs program. These consent-promoting techniques constitute the "soft" skills and processes of peacekeeping (as opposed to the "hard," or technical and military skills) designed to win hearts and minds. Much of the objective of these kinds of activity is to provide good information in order to counter rumor, uncertainty, and prejudice, on the one hand, and to foster trust and stability in the area of conflict and positive perceptions of the role of peacekeepers and the nature of the peace process, on the other.

See also Nongovernmental organizations (NGOs); Peace building from below; Postconflict reconstruction

References and further reading
Fetherston (1996); Last (1997); Miall, Ramsbotham, and Woodhouse (forthcoming); Ramsbotham and Woodhouse (1996a)

Conflicts: patterns and occurrences
Some 28 million people may have been killed in more than 150 major armed conflicts, fought mainly in the Third World, since 1945. Only 5 percent of the casualties in World War I were civilians. By World War II the proportion had risen to 50 percent. And, as the century ends, the civilian share may be as high as 90 percent. To this must be added the estimate made by the United Nations High Commission on Refugees (UNHCR) of the primary role played by vicious internal conflict in generating 18.2 million refugees and 24 million internally displaced people in 1993. In African countries like Angola, Eritrea, Liberia, Mozambique, Rwanda, Somalia, and Sudan, up to half or more of the total population have been forced to flee at some point. According to the authoritative *World Military and Social Expenditures* the number of people killed in wars since 1945 has been twice the number of deaths in the nineteenth century and seven times the war-related deaths of the eighteenth century.

The causes, nature, and types of violent armed conflict can be classified in various ways.

For example, in its annual review of international conflict, the Interdisciplinary Research Program on Causes of Human Rights Violations (PIOOM) at Leiden University includes five "stages of conflict": (1) "Peaceful stable situations" are situations with a "high degree of political stability and regime legitimacy." (2) In "political tension situations" there are "growing levels of systemic strain and increasing social and political cleavages, often along factional lines." (3) At this stage, "violent political conflict," tension has escalated to "political crisis" inasmuch as there has been "an erosion of political legitimacy of the national government" or a "rising acceptance of violent factional politics." This is roughly quantified as being conflicts in which fewer than 100 people are killed in any one calendar year (in 1996 PIOOM listed 74 such conflicts). (4) At the next stage, "low-intensity conflict," there is "open hostility and armed conflict among factional groups, regime repression and insurgency" with 100 to 999 people killed in any one year (42 such conflicts were listed for 1996). (5) At this stage, "high-intensity conflict," there is "open warfare among rival groups and/or mass destruction and displacement of sectors of the civilian population" with 1,000 or more people killed (19 such conflicts were listed for 1996). Peter Wallensteen and others of the Conflict Data Project of the Department of Peace and Conflict Research at Uppsala University define "major armed conflicts" as "prolonged combat between the military forces of two or more governments, or of one government and at least one organized armed group," thus ruling out spontaneous violence and massacres of unarmed civilians, and incurring the battle-related deaths of at least 1,000 people for the duration of the conflict (not just for one calendar year, as in the PIOOM figures). Major armed conflicts are subdivided into "intermediate conflicts" and "wars." A "minor armed conflict" is one in which overall deaths are fewer than 1,000. On the other hand, the Minorities at Risk Project at Maryland University, initiated in 1986, compares data on the political aspirations of 233 minority communal groups worldwide and includes measures taken short of the use of armed force. Within this brief is drawn up a list of 29 "ethno-nationalist peoples" who have fought "sustained or recurrent campaigns of armed force aimed at least in part at securing national independence for a communal group, or their unification with kindred groups in adjoining states" between 1945 and the 1990s. Terrorist and guerrilla strategies are counted, with a criterion for inclusion that campaigns must have lasted five years or more. Most of these conflict are occurring in the Third World and result from severe economic inequality and insecurity and from religious, ethnic, and ideologically rooted persecution and animosity.

The striking assumption here is that contemporary conflict will be mainly "internally" generated and that interstate war of the classic kind can be virtually ignored. There has been a relative increase in recent years in the incidence of "identity conflict" (including secessionist movements), "revolutionary conflict" (particularly in the guise of attempts to impose religious ideologies on states), and "factional conflict" (including challenges to state control by criminal factions), all three of which may lead to state fragmentation and collapse.

One major trend, however, shows through in almost all accounts: a decline in the number of interstate wars. Over a longer-term time frame, the number of interstate wars per year per state has decreased from 0.036 for the period 1918–1941 to 0.005 for the period 1945–1995. Since 1989 the decline in the number of interstate wars has approached its limit, to the point where there were no interstate wars in 1993 and 1994, only a minor border altercation between Peru and Ecuador in 1995, and a flare-up in the long-running dispute between India and Pakistan over Kashmir in 1996. This pattern and type of conflict places considerable demands on peacekeeping, and UN peacekeeping operations covered 25 of the 90 conflicts active between 1989 and 1993.

See also Conflict resolution theory and peacekeeping; Internal conflict
References and further reading
European Platform for Conflict Prevention and Transformation (1998); Leger Sivard (annually); Rogers and Dando (1992)

Congo

United Nations Operation in the Congo (ONUC), 1960–1964

Conflict Profile
During the 1950s the European powers adopted various approaches to deal with the pressure for independence that was sweeping across the African continent while simultaneously attempting to maintain some kind of influence in the region. Belgium had employed a policy of paternalism in its government of the large, nearly landlocked territory of the Belgian Congo—the third-largest African country, covering an area roughly the size of western Europe—and had made only meager, preparatory arrangements for the indigenous Congolese elite to assume power once it had left. Of a population of around 14 million, only half were literate, and fewer than 20 per-

cent had been educated to college level. All senior civil servants and military officers were Belgian. The Belgian Congo comprised 70 major ethnic groups, which were subdivided into several hundred tribes. It boasted considerable natural resources, although these were unevenly distributed. The lion's share of exploitable minerals were concentrated in the southern Katanga (now Shaba) Province, which covered roughly a fifth of the country. Katanga generated 80 percent of the Belgian Congo's export income and half the country's overall income, and in 1906 the Belgian mining company Union Minière du Haut Katanga had been given the exclusive mineral rights to the province until 1999. By January 1959 impatience for independence led to riots in the capital, Léopoldville (now Kinshasa). By November the riots had spread to Stanleyville (now Kisangani).

In January 1960 the Belgian government attempted to convene a Round Table conference in Brussels to introduce a four-year timetable for the implementation of the Belgian Congo's independence. However, a conference of Congolese leaders managed to secure a six-month timetable, leading to independence on 30 June of that year. On 30 March, an Executive College of six Congolese political leaders was created to serve as a transitional regime for the country and to draw up a draft constitution to be adopted by the new government. Included within the college were Joseph Kasavubu, leader of the Bakuvu People's Political Party, whose territory included Léopoldville but who had little political loyalty beyond his ethnic and territorial base; Patrice Lumumba, who led the Mouvement National Congolaise (MNC), a left-wing, nationalist party based around Stanleyville; and Moise Tshombe, who headed a coalition of Katangese tribes. The MNC won a majority in both the provincial assemblies and the national parliament during elections in May, and the parliament subsequently elected Kasavubu as head of state, Tshombe as provincial president, and Lumumba as prime minister. Belgium, keen to safeguard its mineral interests in the Congo, was convinced that its nationals would be required to run the country after independence, preserving its influence there. It assumed that the Congolese national security force—the Armée Nationale Congolaise (ANC), as

it was named after independence—which was then under the command of 1,000 Belgian officers, would maintain order in the country and in particular would protect the 100,000 Belgian expatriates living there.

The deficiencies in the Congo's preparation for independence soon became glaringly apparent when, within a week, ANC troops rebelled against their officers. Lumumba, in an attempt to appease the ANC, appointed former medical warrant officer Victor Lundula as force commander and journalist Joseph Mobutu, who had served as a quartermaster's clerk, as chief of staff. The Belgian government was unable to persuade the Congolese government to allow it to employ locally based troops to restore order, and so, on 10 July, on the pretext of protecting its nationals, the Belgian government began a series of unilateral interventions. Belgian troops were deployed in the Katangese capital, Elisabethville (now Lubumbashi), and also in Léopoldville. Tshombe announced the secession of Katanga on 11 July; he appointed Belgians to run its civil administration and Belgian officers to control its military. Northern parts of Katanga comprised a federation of tribes called the Baluba. The Baluba federation was not part of Tshombe's federation and opposed Katanga's secession. Another group of Baluba lived in neighboring Kasai Province, which, one month after Katanga seceded, announced its own secession. The complicated and confusing conflicts of interest within the Congo were soon mirrored by the intense and diverse international interest in the situation.

The potential mineral wealth and strategic importance of the Congo meant that it threatened to become a theater for the enactment of the Cold War. The Soviet Union saw decolonization in general as an opportunity to promote communist ideology throughout the developing world, and, more specifically, many Eastern bloc and nonaligned states opposed Belgian support of the Katangese secession as an attempt to preserve European control in Africa. The West, especially the United States, was concerned by the "domino theory"—the theory that the fall of one country to communism would increase the risk that others would fall—and so sought to limit Soviet influence wherever possible. Western fears were compounded by subsequent Soviet offers of military and other assistance to the Congolese government. French and British attitudes differed from that of most Western countries, since France maintained close ties with Belgium and Britain had a substantial financial stake in the Union Minière du Haut Katanga (see Map 2).

The Deployment of ONUC

Following the unilateral Belgian intervention, various Congolese officials sent out contradictory appeals for international assistance. The resulting confusion was exacerbated by the Congo's divided leadership and the poor state of its communications. Eventually, UN Secretary-General Dag Hammarskjöld officially informed the Security Council that the deteriorating situation in the Congo was likely to present a threat to international peace and security, as authorized by article 99 of the UN Charter. Lumumba and Kasavubu then made a series of direct requests to the Security Council to provide assistance to halt external aggression. On 14 July they asked for help from Moscow, to which Soviet President Nikita Khrushchev agreed. However, by this time, the Security Council had already authorized the secretary-general to provide military assistance to the Congo.

The international, especially superpower, interest in the Congo both ensured Soviet and U.S. support for a peacekeeping mission and also meant that the Security Council was able to demonstrate relatively easily that the situation presented a serious threat to international security. Moreover, Hammarskjöld was an enthusiastic advocate of the concept of peacekeeping. Conversely, it was also the extensive and diverse political interests in the Congo, at local, regional, and superpower levels, that impeded the development of a mandate with precise objectives. On 14 July the Security Council adopted Security Council Resolution 143 authorizing the deployment of the United Nations Operation in the Congo (ONUC) "to provide the [Congolese] government with such military assistance as may be necessary until, through the efforts of the Congolese government with the technical assistance of the United Nations, the national security forces may be able, in the opinion of the government, to fully meet

their tasks." However, the aforementioned political differences among the Security Council member states caused disagreements over the force's character and objectives. ONUC was eventually dispatched under the Uniting for Peace resolution—a controversial resolution that had initially been employed to overcome a similar stalemate during the Korean crisis in the 1950s. The only explicit part of the ONUC mandate was that foreign (i.e., Belgian) troops should withdraw from Congolese territory. It did not provide a specific timetable for withdrawal, authorize the use of force, or define the objectives that Congolese security forces had to meet for ONUC to consider that its mandate had been fulfilled.

By the end of 1960 over 15,000 UN troops had arrived in the Congo. This number had risen to 18,825 by mid-1961 and reached its peak of 19,400 in January 1963, making ONUC easily the largest UN peacekeeping operation to date. India contributed between a third and a quarter of ONUC's personnel between March 1962 and March 1963; the next heaviest contributors were Canada, Ethiopia, Ghana, Indonesia, Ireland, Malaysia, Morocco, Nigeria, Pakistan, Sweden, and Tunisia. Denmark, Holland, and Norway supplied support units, while facilities for internal supply lift were provided by Argentina, Brazil, Italy, and Yugoslavia. The United States supplied a large proportion of the airlift.

The sheer size of the ONUC operation meant that it was extremely expensive. At its peak it cost $210 million per annum, when the annual UN budget only reached $75 million overall. In total, the ONUC mission cost $408 million. As a result, it encountered severe financial difficulties, difficulties that were potentially extremely damaging to the organization as a whole. The political disagreements over the eventual mandate of the mission exacerbated these difficulties. By late 1962 the UN's arrears for peacekeeping, which included ONUC and the United Nations Emergency Force (UNEF) in the Suez, came to $117 million, while only a quarter of the UN member states had paid their assessments. The ONUC mission had been dispatched without receiving funding approval from the General Assembly, and the resultant financial trouble that it experienced ensured a change in this

ONUC deployment as of June 1961

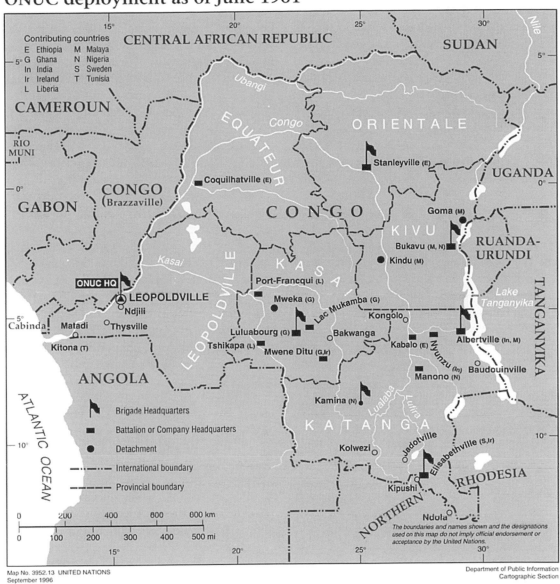

Contributing countries
E Ethiopia   M Malaya
G Ghana   N Nigeria
In India   S Sweden
Ir Ireland   T Tunisia
L Liberia

CENTRAL AFRICAN REPUBLIC

SUDAN

CAMEROUN

RIO MUNI

GABON

CONGO (Brazzaville)

EQUATEUR

Ubangi

Congo

Coquilhatville (E)

ORIENTALE

Stanleyville (E)

UGANDA

C O N G O

Goma (M)

KIVU

Bukavu (M, N)

Kindu (M)

RUANDA-URUNDI

K A S A I

Kasai

Port-Francqui (L)

Mweka (G)

Lac Mukamba (G)

Kongolo

Lake Tanganyika

ONUC HQ

LEOPOLDVILLE

Ndjili

Luluabourg (G)

Bakwanga

Kabalo (E)

Albertville (In, M)

TANGANYIKA

Cabinda

Matadi

Thysville

Tshikapa (L)

Mwene Ditu (G,Ir)

Nyunzu (In)

Baudouinville

Kitona (T)

Manono (N)

ANGOLA

LEOPOLDVILLE

Lualaba

Lufira

Kamina (N)

Brigade Headquarters

Battalion or Company Headquarters

Detachment

International boundary

Provincial boundary

K A T A N G A

Jadotville

Elisabethville (S,Ir)

RHODESIA

Kolwezi

Kipushi

NORTHERN

Ndola

ATLANTIC OCEAN

0   200   400   600   800 km

0   100   200   300   400   500 mi

The boundaries and names shown and the designations used on this map do not imply official endorsement or acceptance by the United Nations.

Map No. 3952.13 UNITED NATIONS
September 1996

Department of Public Information
Cartographic Section

53

procedure. The General Assembly proposed in December 1960 that the ONUC mission be categorized as expenses of the United Nations and so be paid for through compulsory assessments under article 17(2) of the UN Charter. The Soviet Union opposed this idea, however, and it, France, and other Eastern bloc states continually refused to pay their assessments. By December 1961 the General Assembly was forced to issue $200 million in UN bonds to cover expenses amassed by ONUC and UNEF, to be repaid over 25 years through regular UN assessments. This move was again opposed, this time by Belgium, France, the USSR, and 24 developing states. ONUC was eventually funded solely by means of the bonds from mid-1962 through mid-1963. By the end of 1965, the USSR and France owed over two years' worth of regular UN assessments, and a U.S.-forwarded proposal demanded that under article 19 of the UN Charter those two countries be deprived of their vote in the General Assembly. However, the United States ultimately backed down and an exceedingly dangerous situation for the United Nations was thus narrowly avoided, although its repercussions would be felt for a long while after.

It was not long after ONUC's initial deployment that the force found itself in the middle of a political crisis. Although by the first week of September 1962, UN contingents had successfully overseen the withdrawal of Belgian troops and Belgian officers serving with the ANC, they had not been able to stem Belgian support of Tshombe's attempted secession in Katanga. Lumumba became frustrated with the UN's refusal to employ force against Tshombe, and with the help of aircraft and ground support from Moscow, he attempted to quell the secession himself. This prompted Kasavubu to dismiss Lumumba and replace him with Senate President Joseph Ileo. Subsequently, Lumumba himself dismissed the president. In response to the threat to the Congo's internal security that this situation presented, the United Nations closed the country's airports to prevent the movement of Congolese troops and shut down the radio station in Léopoldville. However, Kasavubu was based locally and had no need to fly in extra support, whereas Lumumba was based in the remote Orientale Province. On 16 September, with

suspected U.S. assistance, Mobutu staged an armed coup in support of Kasavubu, dissolving the government. This brought accusations from several states, especially the USSR, that the United Nations had intentionally ousted Lumumba.

The political crisis within the Congo continued to be reflected internationally, in this case at UN headquarters in New York. Pro-Lumumba African states—such as Egypt and Ghana—most non-aligned states, and the Soviet Union were in favor of replacing Mobutu with Lumumba, whereas the West and the majority of francophone African countries supported Mobutu. The eventual murder of Lumumba in Katanga and the threat of all-out civil war spurred the Security Council on 21 February 1961 to authorize the first expansion of the ONUC mandate to allow the use of force beyond self-defense, if necessary, to prevent civil war. This engendered further division among UN member states. Ceylon, Egypt, Ghana, Guinea, Indonesia, and Libya agreed in April that a deadline should be put in place after which enforcement should follow. However, the majority of francophone African nations preferred reliance on the Conciliation Commission, which had been dispatched by the General Assembly in an attempt to reconvene the Congolese Parliament. A similar split also appeared among non-African member states. Dissatisfaction with the United Nations was deeply felt. Ghana, Guinea, Mali, Morocco, the United Arab Republic, and the National Liberation Front in Algeria provided one-third of all ONUC's troops, but by mid-March 1961 all but Ghana had withdrawn their forces, and Ghana reduced its contribution by a third.

Eventually ONUC succeeded in facilitating some degree of political reconciliation, and a formal government of national unity was established in August 1961. The government was led by the moderate Cyril Adoula, and Kasavubu remained head of state. Only Tshombe withheld support for the government. This allowed ONUC to concentrate more on other aspects of its mandate, namely, the removal of mercenaries from Congolese soil. ONUC launched a surprise initiative on 28 August, called Operation Rum Punch, in which 338 of 442 Europeans serving with the Katangese military and occupying senior posts in Elisabethville were captured. Tshombe initially endorsed the move, but his support was misleading because the same Europeans soon reappeared in the ranks of his gendarmerie. ONUC launched a second offensive, Operation Morthor, two weeks later to secure the major radio and telegraph installations, as well as the offices of the security services and the Ministry of Information, in Elisabethville. The operation was unsuccessful, merely resulting in eight days of severe fighting, and it coincided with attempts by the central government to arrest Tshombe. In this, ONUC distinctly veered away from its mandate, which had not provided for the positive use of force to end Katanga's secession. There is evidence to suggest that both initiatives were the result of a certain amount of confusion between UN headquarters in New York, and ONUC's leaders on the ground and had not been authorized by Hammarskjöld. It was not surprising that supporters of Katanga were aggrieved by the direction that the United Nations appeared to be taking, and many Western countries were also critical of the UN's handling of events. The situation was exacerbated by Hammarskjöld's death in an air crash on 18 September while he was on his way to attempt to facilitate negotiations between Tshombe and the central government. Hammarskjöld's replacement as secretary-general, U Thant, was obviously more disposed to use force than his predecessor had been.

International interest in the situation in the Congo was maintained by a number of factors. UN member states desired Congolese unity, as sovereignty and the inviolability of national borders were principles to which all states subscribed; the West was eager to reinforce the new, moderate Congolese government; and the Soviet Union and the nonaligned states remained suspicious of what they perceived to be "neocolonialist" interest in supporting Katanga's de facto secession. The political stability that had been created in Léopoldville and the combined Eastern and Western interest in seeing an end to the Katangese secession enabled the Security Council on 24 November 1961—with France and Great Britain abstaining—to again expand the ONUC mandate. This time it included supporting the central government and ending Katanga's secession. It also authorized the secre-

tary-general to use whatever force was necessary to expel foreign mercenaries from Congolese territory and prevent their return and to halt the influx of weaponry to aid the Katangese secession. The expansion of the ONUC mandate inevitably steered the force in a new direction, away from the traditional peacekeeping values of impartiality and the use of force only in self-defense. Although the international community recognized the authority of the new government, this was not the case throughout the Congo itself, as it continued to experience serious internal disputes. Therefore, in assisting the government to exert its authority, ONUC would be supporting a particular side in a major internal conflict, which would almost certainly involve the positive use of force.

The situation in the Congo continued to deteriorate, however, until in December 1961 ONUC launched another initiative with the same aims as the first. This operation went on for twice as long as its predecessor, and it incurred substantial casualties on both sides. Six non-Congolese and 206 Katangan troops were killed, as were 50 civilians; there were 27 UN fatalities. There has been much debate over whether the action was justified within the Security Council's mandate and the secretary-general's original terms of engagement on the use of force only in self-defense. Analysts have pointed out that ONUC's actions came in response to prolonged periods of violence against UN personnel and positions. On 21 December Tshombe signed the Kitona Accord, which recognized Kasavubu as head of state and the central government's authority. The accord acknowledged the unity of the Congo as a whole and agreed to cede control of the Katangan gendarmerie to Kasavubu. However, in only 24 hours the situation had returned to antagonism, as the Katangese Parliament claimed that it did not possess the necessary authority to ratify Tshombe's agreement, and within a few days violence reemerged between ONUC and Katangese armed forces.

The resulting stalemate between Adoula's government and Tshombe lasted throughout the whole of 1962. In August of that year, U Thant attempted to facilitate reconciliation with the Plan for National Reconciliation, which sought to introduce a more equitable division of revenues between central and provincial government, broader representation within the central government, and the unification of the Congo's defense forces. The plan also threatened economic sanctions if deadlines failed to be met. Adoula agreed in principle to the plan, and Tshombe appeared to capitulate. However, Tshombe again reneged on his agreement, making no attempt to prevent the Katangan armed forces from attacking ONUC and ANC troops. The Cuban missile crisis diverted the international community's attention from the Congo in October and November, but on 10 December U Thant declared that sanctions would be placed on Katanga. The United Nations decided that force would be used, in Operation Grandslam, to end Katanga's secession, and during December ONUC built up its forces in Katanga to 13,500 troops, while Katanga also reinforced its military. A major incentive for the United Nations to speed up the process was the fact that 6,000 Indian troops were scheduled to be withdrawn in March 1963 to fight a border war with China.

The Katangan gendarmerie attacked ONUC positions around Elisabethville on 24 December. The first phase of Operation Grandslam included enlarging ONUC controlled areas in Katanga by eliminating positions and roadblocks of the gendarmerie and thereby enhancing ONUC's freedom of movement in the province. ONUC encountered little resistance, gaining control of Elisabethville and disabling the Katangese air force very quickly. Phase 2 of the operation sought to advance UN control to Jadotville, intending to continue from there to include the mining center of Kolwezi. Mercenaries in the area initially threatened to blow up the Kolwezi mining installations; however, determined pressure from ONUC succeeded in dispersing them across the border into Angola and Rhodesia, leaving the Katangese military without its foreign leaders. Faced with this prospect, the Katangese civil authorities in Kolwezi sought UN protection for their mining installations, which ONUC duly provided. Tshombe subsequently announced the end of Katanga's secession, and on 23 January 1963 the United Nations declared that its operations in Katanga were finished, that the secession was officially over, and that the major centers in the province were under UN control.

The end of Katanga's secession effectively meant that the United Nations was able to judge that its military commitment in the Congo had also come to an end. On 23 January U Thant announced that UN troops would immediately begin a gradual withdrawal. The reintegration of the Katanga Province and the gendarmerie was implemented by the central government, and Adoula requested that 3,000 UN peacekeepers remain in the country to assist with reorganizing and training the ANC. However, once it had become apparent that Kasavubu and Mobutu were continuing with bilateral arrangements for security assistance, the political necessity for a UN presence in the Congo ceased to exist. U Thant then announced the withdrawal of all UN troops, leaving behind a substantial civilian component to facilitate the Congo's return to some kind of normality. ONUC finally withdrew from the Congo on 30 June 1964, although Mobutu seized power in October 1965.

In considering the ONUC operation, it should be remembered that at the time the concept of UN peacekeeping was still very much in its nascent stage. Furthermore, the unusually high level of internal disorder and anarchy in the Congo, combined with the vastness of the country itself, affected the responsibilities that the force had to assume, the size of the area in which it had to operate, and the number of personnel involved. The high level of international interest in the situation placed limitations on the ONUC mandate. It can therefore be argued that ONUC did achieve its objectives of removing foreign mercenaries from the Congo and holding the country together, and under extremely difficult circumstances. However, ONUC considerably stretched the parameters of what had come to be known as UN peacekeeping, and as a result the very principle of peacekeeping itself was put into question. ONUC came very close to becoming an enforcement operation, employing the positive use of force in favor of a particular party to a dispute. The Cold War political context in which the operation was conducted meant that Eastern bloc countries were continually suspicious of the Western-dominated UN's motives. The severe financial difficulties the mission experienced, the continual expansion of the mandate, and the fact that some 200 peacekeepers lost their lives during the operation made member states wary of becoming involved in anything similar, especially in sub-Saharan Africa. Conversely, some analysts have pointed out that the ONUC mission and the circumstances surrounding Lumumba's death worried many nations. Especially concerned were nations in Africa that might have been considering inviting a force onto their soil but feared that UN peacekeepers might ultimately become their hosts' enemies. It is also widely held that after the ONUC operation many countries saw the United Nations merely as a vehicle for U.S. foreign policy. What is certainly evident is that UN peacekeeping entered a period of dormancy following the ONUC mission from which it did not wake until 1973, in response to the Arab-Israeli conflict. Other outcomes of the UN's involvement in the Congo have been that the financial difficulties the organization ran into have troubled it ever since, the role of the secretary-general in subsequent missions has been increasingly limited, and subsequent missions have been provided with only a very short mandate in order to ensure that the Security Council would have to constantly update the mandate, enabling the Permanent Five members to veto an extension if desired.

See also Internal conflict; Organization of African Unity
References and further reading Durch (1994); James (1994); United Nations (1996)

Contadora Group

Like its counterpart in Southeast Asia (the Association of Southeast Asian Nations [ASEAN]), the Contadora Group was an attempt to develop regional identity and self-determination in the face of the struggle between the United States and the USSR for worldwide political hegemony during the Cold War. The group was established in 1983 at a meeting on the island of Contadora by four countries: Colombia, Mexico, Panama, and Venezuela. Their action was prompted by the series of conflicts in the region that showed no signs of abating and that were in danger of provoking superpower intervention. In July 1983 the four countries signed the Declaration of Cancun about Central American Peace. In 1985 four South American countries—Argentina, Brazil, Peru, and Uruguay—organized

themselves as the Contadora Support Group in an attempt to show and to generate solidarity with the group's aims of promoting peaceful coexistence in the region. Although the various wars in the region were in danger of bankrupting some of the combatant countries, one of the fruits of the Contadora Group's work was the meeting in 1987 of the presidents of the countries most involved in the armed disputes—El Salvador, Guatemala, Honduras, and Nicaragua—plus Costa Rica to sign the agreement known as Esquipulas II (after the town in which they met) but formally entitled the Procedure for the Establishment of a Firm and Lasting Peace in Central America. The signatories agreed to the principles of dialogue, amnesty, reconciliation, and democratization and committed themselves to not assisting irregular forces fighting in neighboring countries. Despite the fact that the various regional initiatives had significant anti-U.S. elements, the work of the Contadora Group also paved the way for joint cooperation between the United Nations and the Organization of American States (OAS) and for the agreement known as the Costa del Sol Declaration.

See also ONUCA; Organization of American States (OAS)

Costa del Sol Declaration
See ONUCA

Costs of peacekeeping

For the past 40 years peacekeeping operations have cost the United Nations an average of $75 million each year. Before 1991 mission costs tended to be relatively low. However, the large-scale operations in Somalia and in the former Yugoslavia each had annual budgets of over $1 billion, and the operation in Cambodia cost more than $700 million. In 1990 the peacekeeping budget was $379 million. It rose to a record $3.8 billion in 1994, fell back to $3.2 billion in 1995, and fell again to $1.4 billion in 1996 as the large operations were wound down. The expenses for 1994 exceeded the combined costs of all the 16 peacekeeping operations between 1948 and 1990. Meeting the costs of peacekeeping has been enormously difficult for the United Nations, partly because member states have failed to pay their assessments promptly. For 1994, for example, the United Nations was owed $526 million in unpaid arrears by member states. The largest single defaulter is the United States, which in 1997 owed more than $1.3 billion to the UN's regular and peacekeeping budget. In 1994 Russia was the largest defaulter in its liability to its peacekeeping assessment, owing $317 million. As a result both of the ad hoc financing method and the high level of defaulted payment, the United Nations owes over $1 billion to the 81 member states that contributed peacekeeping forces in 1997. One of the largest contributors, India, is owed more than $58 million; Pakistan, another major contributor, is owed $67 million. Despite the difficult financial situation, peacekeeping has been described as "the bargain of the century" when compared to the costs of conflict and to the costs of maintaining the world's military systems. Put in this context the resources available to the United Nations are very limited. For example, UN figures show that the main UN funds and programs amount to $4.6 billion annually on economic and social development in such areas as population policy, children's welfare, agriculture, food distribution, and so on. This is the equivalent of 80 cents for every person. In contrast, in 1994 the world's governments spent a combined $778 billion on military expenditures, or the equivalent of $134 for every person. The total cost of all peacekeeping operations in 1996 ($1.4 billion) was the equivalent of less than 1 percent of the U.S. military budget, and less than 0.2 percent of global military spending (see Tables 5, 6).

See also Financing peacekeeping; Troop-contributing countries

References and further reading Renner (1993); UNDPKO

Cotonou Peace Agreement
See Liberia

Croatia

United Nations Confidence Restoration Organization (UNCRO), 1995–1996; United

Nations Mission of Observers in Prevlaka (UNMOP), 1996– ; United Nations Transitional Administration for Eastern Slavonia, Baranja, and Western Sirmium (UNTAES), 1996–1998 ; United Nations Civilian Police Support Group, 1998

UNCRO and UNMOP: Conflict Profile
Following the recognition of Croatia as an independent state, initially by Germany on 23 December 1991 and then by the European Union and its member states on 15 January 1992, the refusal of Serbian-dominated areas of Croatia to accept the new state and their place in it led to a bitter armed conflict between the forces of the new state and the Serbs. The president of the new state was Franjo Tudjman, leader of the Croatian Nationalist Party (HDZ). In December 1991 the "Serbian Autonomous Regions" of Krajina and of Slavonia, Baranja, and Western Srem proclaimed themselves as the Serbian Republic of Krajina (Republika Srpska Krajina [RSK]). In June 1992 the RSK held a referendum on the issue of unification with the Serbs in Bosnia (who had styled themselves the "Serbian Republic of Bosnia Herzegovina") with the ultimate aim of establishing a unitary and sovereign Serbian state. A large majority of the approximately 300,000 voters favored this.

Croatian government attacks on these Serb-dominated areas began early in 1992 and continued throughout the year, with particularly strong offensives against the Serbs in Krajina, where a UN report found evidence of a scorched-earth policy against Serbian villages. At the same time Croatia became involved in the conflict in Bosnia, where the Tudjman government became militarily involved in protecting Croat communities. This situation was resolved in March 1994 when, under U.S. influence, Croatia and Bosnia Herzegovina signed an accord agreeing to the creation within Bosnia of a Muslim Croat Federation and to a Croatian-Bosnian Confederation between the countries.

Fighting between Croatian forces and the RSK continued throughout 1993, though a cease-fire was agreed on in March 1994. However, Croats displaced from the United Nations Protected Areas (UNPAs) were becoming increasingly dissatisfied

Table 5 UN Peacekeeping Costs Compared with Military Expenditures

Country	Military Expenditures (A)	Peacekeeping Assessments (B)	Ratio (A to B)
Japan	32,100	55.9	574:1
Germany	39,900	46.0	868:1
France	41,400	37.8	1,096:1
Nigeria	234	0.2	1,191:1
United Kingdom	42,300	29.4	1,441:1
United States	304,500	151.0	2,016:1
China	12,000	4.8	2,520:1
Russia	224,100	60.3	3,714:1
India	7,200	0.4	19,816:1
Pakistan	2,800	0.6	47,522:1

Table 6 Costs of UN Peacekeeping at Peak, 1994 (in millions of $US)

Mission	Personnel	Annual Cost ($ million)
UNPROFOR	36,337	1,900
UNOSOM	19,224	1,000
ONUMOZ	5,413	327
UNIFIL	5,219	138
UNAMIR/UNOMUR	707	98
UNIKOM	1,149	70
UNOMIL	368	65
UNFICYP	1,221	47
MINURSO	268	40
UNDOF	1,061	35
UNTSO	219	30
UNAVEM II	76	25
ONUSAL	222	24
UNMOGIP	40	5
UNMIII	1,267[a]	1
Total	71,546[b]	3,812

[a]Authorized for deployment
[b]Excluding UNMIH

with what they regarded as UN inaction toward helping Croatian refugees return to their homes in the UNPAs. In January 1995 President Tudjman wrote to the secretary-general insisting that the United Nations Protection Force in Former Yugoslavia (UNPROFOR), the peacekeeping force in Croatia, was now unacceptable to the Croatian government and demanding its withdrawal by June 1995. There were suggestions that Tudjman had grown impatient with the United Nations,

which he saw as acting as an obstacle to the reintegration of the UNPAs into Croatia, and that Croatia was prepared to retake the territories by force if necessary. The secretary-general feared that the withdrawal of UNPROFOR would result in a resumption of hostilities, and after talks between President Tudjman and U.S. Vice President Al Gore, the Croatian government decided to agree to a renewal of the mandate, although on radically different terms. The peacekeeping force was to be renamed the United Nations Confidence Restoration Organization (UNCRO), and its troop strength was to be reduced to 5,000.

UNCRO

The UNCRO was set up on 31 March 1995 to replace UNPROFOR in Croatia. Three separate Security Council resolutions had established three distinct operations for Croatia, Bosnia and Herzegovina, and the former Yugoslav republic of Macedonia, referred to collectively as the UN Peace Forces (UNPF). The Croatian regions of Western Slavonia, the Krajina region, and Eastern Slavonia had been seized by Serbian forces after Croatia's unilateral declaration of independence in 1991. Peacekeeping troops and military observers serving with UNCRO were dispatched to these Serb-controlled regions, as well as to the strategically important Prevlaka peninsula.

The UNCRO mandate provided that the force would: fulfill the functions determined in the 29 March 1994 cease-fire agreement signed by the Croatian government and local Serb authorities; facilitate implementation of the 2 December economic agreement (which was created to build confidence between the opposing parties to supplement the cease-fire) and of all relevant Security Council resolutions; help control the cross-border passage of military personnel and matériel over the frontiers between Croatia, Bosnia and Herzegovina, and the Federal Republic of Yugoslavia by monitoring activities and reporting them to the relevant authorities; facilitate the conveyance of humanitarian aid into Bosnia and Herzegovina via Croatian territory; and supervise the demilitarization of the Prevlaka peninsula.

The UNCRO operation was envisaged from the outset as a temporary arrangement and was intended to establish the necessary conditions for the successful completion of a political agreement that both respected Croatia's territorial integrity and ensured individual safety and rights for all Croatians. A Croatian military offensive in May and August 1995 forcibly reintegrated the territories of Western Slavonia and Krajina. Therefore, there was no further need for UN peacekeepers in those areas, and they were subsequently withdrawn.

However, Serbian forces remained in control of Eastern Slavonia, and so the UNCRO mandate remained essentially unaltered. An agreement was then reached between the Croatian government and the Croatian Serb leadership to work toward a negotiated settlement to the future status of Eastern Slavonia. Under the aegis of the United Nations, discussions commenced between the opposing parties. These discussions ultimately resulted on 12 November in the signing of the Basic Agreement on the Region of Eastern Slavonia, Baranja, and Western Sirmium. This included provisions for the peaceful reintegration of Eastern Slavonia into Croatia and sought to set up a UN transitional administration to act as an interim authority in the region. The establishment of the United Nations Transitional Administration for Eastern Slavonia, Baranja, and Western Sirmium (UNTAES) by the Security Council on 15 January 1996 (see the UNTAES: Conflict Profile section in this entry) enabled the termination of the UNCRO mandate on the same day.

UNCRO's headquarters were in Zagreb, and the mission lasted from March 1995 to January 1996.

As of mid-November 1995, UNCRO comprised 581 troops, 194 military observers, and 296 civilian police, supported by international and locally recruited civilian staff. There were 16 military personnel fatalities during the deployment.

UNMOP

In October 1992 UN military observers were deployed to supervise the demilitarization of the strategically significant Prevlaka peninsula in Croatia as part of the UNPROFOR mission in the former Yugoslavia. Then, in March 1995, the Security Council established follow-up missions for UNPROFOR to cover the territories of Croatia, Bosnia and Herzegovina, and the Former Yugoslav Republic of Macedonia (FYROM), known respectively as the UNCRO, UNPROFOR, and the United Nations Preventive Deployment Force Macedonia (UNPREDEP). These were collectively referred to as the United Nations Peace Forces (UNPF).

During the latter part of 1995, the UNCRO and UNPROFOR missions were replaced by two new operations, the United Nations Mission in Bosnia and Herzegovina (UNMIBH) and UNTAES, and the UNPREDEP mandate was extended. However, as the UN military observers and civilian police monitors serving with UNCRO were to be withdrawn, Secretary-General Boutros Boutros-Ghali recommended in a report to the Security Council that a UN presence remain in the Prevlaka peninsula to oversee the demilitarization of the area, in accordance with Security Council Resolution (SCR) 779 (1992). This UN presence was to be known as the United Nations Mission of Observers in Prevlaka (UNMOP).

Boutros-Ghali further suggested that the overall number of military observers to carry out the demilitarization process be expanded from 14 to 28. This expansion was intended to enable the mission to be self-reliant, to monitor the relevant areas more effectively, and also to maintain liaison teams in Dubrovnik and Herzeg Novi. Therefore the Security Council adopted SCR 1038 (1996), by which it authorized the establishment of UNMOP to continue to supervise the demilitarization process in Prevlaka in the interests of reducing tension in the area. UNMOP was mandated for an initial three-month period, which if the secretary-general verified that the mission was effectively reducing tension in the area, could subsequently be extended for an additional three months. The UNMOP operation became independent on 1 February 1996, and the UNMOP mandate has since been extended on 15 July 1996 (SCR 1066), 14 January 1997 (SCR 1093), 14 July 1997 (SCR 1119), and 13 January 1998 (SCR 1147).

UNMOP headquarters are in Dubrovnik, and as of 31 March 1998 UNMOP comprised 28 military observers contributed by 25 countries: Argentina, Bangladesh, Belgium, Brazil, Canada, Czech Republic, Denmark, Egypt, Finland, Ghana, Indonesia, Ireland, Jordan, Kenya, Nepal, New Zealand, Nigeria, Norway, Pakistan, Poland, Portugal, Russian Federation, Sweden, Switzerland, and Ukraine. As of 31 March 1998, the chief military observer was Col. Harold Mwakio Tangai (Kenya).

UNTAES: Conflict Profile

The dispute in Eastern Slavonia formed part of the general disintegration of Yugoslavia, which itself took place within the context of the breakup of the Soviet Union after the late 1980s. In June 1991 Croatia declared independence from the Socialist Federal Republic of Yugoslavia. This prompted Serbian forces to seize about one-third of Croatian land, including the territories of Western Slavonia, Krajina, Eastern Slavonia, and Baranja and Western Sirmium (hereafter referred to as Eastern Slavonia).

Deployment of UNTAES

Several factors furthered international interest in Eastern Slavonia. The continued existence of the Serb enclave of Eastern Slavonia within Croatia meant that the international community still perceived the territory as a potential flash point for the rekindling of violent conflict between Serbs and Croats. Furthermore, the general international consensus that had facilitated the signing of the Dayton Peace Agreement in December 1995, signifying the end of the Bosnian War, was reflected in international attitudes toward Eastern Slavonia.

The situation in Eastern Slavonia also had a serious humanitarian dimension. The conflict in Croatia had a substantial impact on the population of Eastern Slavonia. Since 1991 the demography of the territory has been forcibly altered: An

estimated 70,000 inhabitants of Croat and other ethnic origins left the region, to be replaced by 75,000 Serbs, who were primarily refugees from different areas of Croatia. The United Nations High Commissioner for Refugees (UNHCR) estimated a total population of around 160,000 in the region, including refugees and internally displaced persons.

Thus, to a certain extent through international pressure, on 12 November 1995 the president of Croatia, Franjo Tudjman, and the local Croatian Serb authorities in Eastern Slavonia signed the Basic Agreement on the Region of Eastern Slavonia, Baranja, and Western Sirmium, which foresaw the reintegration of the territory into Croatia. Then, on 15 January 1996, acting under chapter 7 of the UN Charter, the Security Council was able to adopt SCR 1037, by which it sanctioned the establishment of UNTAES to verify compliance with the terms of the basic agreement. The UNTAES operation was authorized for an initial twelve-month period, with an option to extend for an additional twelve months on the request of either of the opposing parties.

UNTAES was provided with both a military and civilian component. The military component was authorized to comprise, initially, some 5,000 troops, who were mandated to oversee the demilitarization of Eastern Slavonia within 30 days of deployment, including all military and police forces, with the exception of police operating under the authorization of UNTAES; to observe the return of refugees and internally displaced people to their places of origin; and to facilitate the maintenance of stability throughout the territory. The civilian component was intended to set up a temporary police force for the transitional period, including assisting in its structural organization, implementing a training program, and generally supervising the judicial system; to facilitate functioning civil administration and public services; to assist in the return of refugees and displaced people; to assist in the organization and supervision of the electoral process for all local government bodies, including municipalities, districts, councils, and a joint council of municipalities for the Serbian community elections, to be completed no later than 30 days before the end of the transitional period; to facilitate development and economic reconstruction of Eastern Slavonia; to observe respect for basic human rights; and to facilitate a mine-removal program throughout the territory.

UNTAES was fully deployed by 20 May 1996. The mission commenced the demilitarization process on 21 May. The transitional administrator, Jacques Paul Klein, was then able to announce the successful conclusion of the demilitarization process within the 30-day limit on 20 June. The demilitarization process included the removal of some 93 tanks, 11 armored personnel carriers, 35 antitank systems, 107 artillery pieces, 123 mortars, and 42 antiaircraft guns.

Several programs were implemented to facilitate the fulfillment of the terms of the basic agreement and hence the peaceful return of Eastern Slavonia to Croatian authority. For instance, on 20 September 1996 the Croatian government passed a general amnesty law covering all actions perpetrated in relation to armed conflicts, with the exception of the most serious violations of humanitarian law characterized as war crimes. Also, on 20 October 1996, a program to buy weapons back from inhabitants of Eastern Slavonia began, a program that was financed by the Croatian government and organized by the military component of UNTAES. By 24 February 1997, Secretary-General Boutros Boutros-Ghali was able to report to the Security Council that the program had successfully collected over 15,000 weapons and 435,000 rounds of ammunition. The successive achievement of UNTAES's mandated objectives meant that on 15 November 1996 the Security Council adopted SCR 1079 extending the UNTAES mandate beyond its first year, for six more months (through 15 July 1997).

Not all aspects of the mission ran smoothly, however. For example, the United Nations complained that the Croatian amnesty law was flawed, since it excluded all Serbs not resident in Eastern Slavonia in 1991 as well as Serbs who had fled the Croatian army's recapture of Krajina and Western Slavonia in 1995. Furthermore, in March 1997 the Security Council voiced concern over the lack of progress in returning displaced and refugee Croatian Serbs. It felt compelled to demand that the Croatian government speed up initiatives to improve conditions of personal and economic security, distribute documentation to Serbs, and resolve property issues. The Security Council also requested that Croatian authorities cease arbitrary arrests of Serbian returnees to Croatia.

On 13–14 April 1997 UNTAES successfully conducted elections in Eastern Slavonia, marking the first occasion since the conflict began that the population of the territory had enjoyed legitimate constitutional representation in Croatia. The elections also facilitated the return of displaced people to the area. An unexpectedly high turnout of voters saw 72,000 votes cast, although technical difficulties meant that one polling station had to be kept open until 15 April. The lack of security incidents or evidence of notable fraud allowed the transitional administrator to certify the results of the elections on 22 April, which were duly accepted by all the major parties involved, with the Independent Democratic Serb Party (SDSS) securing an overall majority in 11 out of 28 municipalities. More than 56,000 displaced people throughout Croatia voted with absentee ballots. More than 150 UNTAES observers were deployed to all polling stations within the UNTAES area of operations, as were 30 observation teams from the Organization for Security and Cooperation in Europe (OSCE) and observers from the Council of Europe (COE).

The successful implementation of the election process allowed UNTAES to begin the initial phase of its withdrawal, so that its strength stood at some 2,385 troops, 412 civilian police, and 101 military observers at the end of August 1997. By 15 November UNTAES had completed the second phase, leaving fewer than 800 military personnel in the area. Meanwhile, during October, the secretary-general reported to the Security Council that around 146,000 citizenship documents, 130,000 Croatian identity cards, and 126,000 passports had been issued. He further announced that between April and October more than 5,200 Serbs had returned to their homes in Croatia, 965 of them in the UN-organized weekly convoys.

However, again, not everything had gone according to plan. The secretary-general reported to the Security Council on 2 October that over the previous 20 months the Croatian government had fulfilled many of the objectives of basic agreement, including successfully addressing the majority of technical issues relating to reintegration. But he added that Croatia had recently been attempting to go back on earlier commitments. For instance, the Croatian government had ignored the results of the municipal elections by using a 1991 census as the basis for deciding the proportional representation of Croats and Serbs in local institutions. Such a move openly contradicted the clear terms of the basic agreement, which unequivocally asserted that everybody who had left Eastern Slavonia or who had entered the territory with prior Croatian permanent resident status would enjoy equal rights with other inhabitants. Similarly, the secretary-general noted that power-sharing agreements between Croat and Serb political parties were not functioning adequately, re vealing a demonstrable lack of commitment on the part of Croatian authorities to the establishment of effective local government administrations. Municipalities in Eastern Slavonia were not provided with sufficient financial resources, and only the tax and customs authorities operated on a full-time basis.

Despite such setbacks, in December 1997 the Security Council adopted SCR 1145, by which it concluded that UNTAES had successfully accomplished the key objectives of the basic agreement. Therefore the Security Council decided that the UNTAES mandate would be allowed to expire on 15 January 1998. SCR 1145 also established the UN Civilian Police Support Group of 180 civilian police monitors. The support group was mandated for a single period of up to nine months and was tasked with continuing UNTAES's function of observing the performance of the Croatian police, especially in relation to the return of displaced people.

UNTAES headquarters were in Vukovar, and the mission had an authorized strength of 5,000 troops, 100 military observers, and 600 civilian police, supported by 317 international civilian staff and 686 local staff. As of 30 September 1997 the total strength of UNTAES military and police personnel stood at 2,847. Thirty countries—Argentina, Austria, Bangladesh, Belgium, Brazil, Czech Republic, Denmark, Egypt, Fiji, Finland, Ghana, Indonesia, Ireland, Jordan, Kenya, Lithuania, Nepal, Netherlands, New Zealand, Nigeria, Norway, Pakistan, Poland, Russian Federation, Slovak Republic, Sweden, Switzerland, Tunisia, Ukraine, and the United States—contributed 2,346 troops, 404 civilian police, and 97 military observers. Also as of 30 September 1997, the transitional administrator was Jacques Paul Klein (United States); Maj. Gen. Willy Hanset (Belgium) was serving as UNTAES force commander, succeeding Maj. Gen. Jozef Schoups (Belgium); Brig. Gen. Purwadi (Indonesia) was the chief military observer; and Brig. Walter Fallmann (Austria) was UNTAES police commissioner. UNTAES suffered four military fatalities during its deployment.

On 7 June 1996 the General Assembly appropriated some $94,269,700 for UNTAES for the period 15 January through 30 June 1996 and an additional $64,769,700 for the same time period as an ad hoc arrangement. The secretary-general, on 4 December 1996, estimated that the cost for the maintenance of UNTAES for the period 1 July 1997 to 30 June 1998 would be $274,993,600. In resolution 51/153 of 20 January 1997, the General Assembly decided to appropriate $140,484,350 for maintaining UNTAES from 1 July 1996 through 30 June 1997.

Upon the termination of UNTAES, 178 police and 31 troops were deployed as the United Nations Civilian Police Support Group, Croatia, to monitor the performance of the Croatian police in the Danube region, especially in relation to the return of displaced persons to the area.

See also European Community Monitoring Mission; Internal conflict; UNPROFOR I–III
References and further reading Berdal (1995); Fetherston, Ramsbotham, and Woodhouse (1994); Schultz (1994)

Culture and peacekeeping

Peacekeeping operations employ an international military force that is composed of troops and personnel, male and female, from a multitude of nations, each with its own culture, religion, politics, and peacekeeping policy, operating under the command of the United Nations (or under the command of a single nation, e.g., the United States in the Unified Task Force [UNITAF], or under the command of a regional organization, e.g., the North Atlantic Treaty Organization [NATO], which commanded a multinational task force in the Implementation Force [IFOR] in Bosnia). Traditionally, UN peacekeeping relied on a handful of member states to provide the majority of the personnel and equipment required to execute a mission. In 1988 only 26 countries were involved in peacekeeping. However, by November 1994 there were 76 troop-contributing countries and with 49 new peacekeepers; as of December 1997 more than 80 countries had participated in a UN peacekeeping mission. There are a multiplicity of inevitable inefficiencies in the strategic and operational conduct of any multinational peacekeeping operation. Many of these inefficiencies can be viewed from a cultural perspective. That is, they arise from occasional variances in the objectives of troop-contributing states (which affect, among other things, the chain of command); in the diverse mix of military capability; in national differences in staff procedures, standards, and equipment; in language difficulties; and in cultural custom and ethos.

There are few studies on the cultural interactions among the national contingents participating in UN peacekeeping operations. However, C. C. Moskos collected information on the United Nations Peacekeeping Force in Cyprus (UNFICYP) through cross-cultural research. Unlike most studies, which tend to focus on the political or legal aspects of peacekeeping or detailed case studies of particular missions, this innovative study sought "to understand the social factors that favour or hinder the peacekeeping role among the actual soldiers of a United Nations military force" (Moskos 1976, p. 1) through a systematic analysis of the military force itself. The aim of the study was primarily to examine the adjustment of military forces to the peacekeeping role (defined by the development of a "constabulary ethic"), or as Fetherston pointed out, adjustment from one "culture" to another (i.e., from a military culture to a third-party culture) (Fetherston, 1994a). The significant aspect of the study, however, is Moskos's cross-cultural analysis. For example, although all the national contingents participating in UNFI-

CYP were recruited from Western parliamentary democracies and broadly shared a common Northern European culture, Moskos notes that there were major differences between the contingents in their recruitment and formation, differences that affected the attitudes of the soldiers toward peacekeeping duties. Moskos shows how differences between the national contingents were at times sources of conflict within UNFICYP and how negative stereotypes were acquired.

In a more recent study, Heiberg (1990) focused on the disparate cultures that characterize the variety of nations participating in a mission. In her study of the relations between UN contingents deployed with the United Nations Interim Force in Lebanon (UNIFIL), she summarized the dilemma: "Language issues aside, each national battalion brings with it its own particular cultural complex and set of assumptions, the distinctiveness of which is not erased by a UN uniform" (p. 148). Heiberg noted that the differences between the various national battalions stem from a wide array of factors. Her observation that motivation for peacekeeping duty was significantly different in units in which service in Lebanon was voluntary (e.g., the Irish, Norwegian, and Finnish units) from motivation among those who were ordered to UNIFIL (e.g., the Ghanaians and Nepalese) confirms Moskos's findings in Cyprus. The nations' historical experiences and military cultures also account for differences between the troops. According to Heiberg, the most obvious cultural differences between the battalions stemmed from the diversity of religious affiliation—secular Lutheranism (Nordic battalions), Catholicism (Irish), fundamental Methodism (Fijians), Hinduism and Buddhism (Nepalese), and Muhammadan (Ghanaians and Senegalese). Another factor cited by Heiberg for understanding the dissimilarities between the battalions and the tensions placed on the internal solidarity of the force was the varying levels of economic development of the troop-contributing countries. Most notably, however, Heiberg argued that cultural diversity served as a source of frequent misunderstandings inside UNIFIL and illustrated this claim through a detailed example involving the Nepalese battalion. She concluded that the discontinuities within

UNIFIL significantly influenced local perceptions of the credibility and legitimacy of the peacekeeping force and limited the force's ability to operate in a coordinated military manner.

See also Codes of conduct; Peace building from below; Women and peacekeeping
References and further reading Duffey (1998); Fetherston (1994a); Heiberg (1986, 1990); Moskos (1976)

Cyprus

United Nations Peacekeeping Force in Cyprus (UNFICYP), 1964–

Conflict Profile
Cyprus, with a population of approximately 700,000, primarily Greek nationals (80 percent) but with a significant Turkish minority (18 percent), had traditionally maintained firm links with Greece until both countries became part of the Ottoman Empire in 1571. Throughout Ottoman occupation the Greek Orthodox church remained the primary political force in Cyprus. In 1878 Cyprus was ceded to Britain as part of a peace deal between Russia and Turkey, a deal that was brokered by British Prime Minister Benjamin Disraeli. During the nineteenth and twentieth centuries, the concept of "enosis," or reunification with Greece, became increasingly prevalent within the Greek Cypriot community, particularly in response to British attempts to secularize the state. After the end of World War II, Britain declined to return responsibility for Cyprus to Athens, initially on the grounds of the Greek civil war. Britain claimed that in the context of Cold War international relations, the internal unrest and political instability in Greece further risked Soviet intervention. However, after the civil war the British government still refused to transfer power to the Greek government.

During the 1950s Greek Cypriots began a terrorist campaign against British occupation through the Greek Cypriot Paramilitary Organization (EOKA), which demanded the right to self-determination. Meanwhile, Turkey, fearful that its traditional enemy, Greece, would gain strategic territory close to Turkey—Cyprus is approxi-

mately 80 kilometers off the southern coast of Turkey—began to take increasing interest in Cyprus's politics. In 1955 Turkish leader Adnan Menderes attempted to rid Istanbul of its ethnic Greek inhabitants by murdering 2,000 of them and driving out the rest—a crime for which he was ultimately hanged in 1961. Since the end of World War II Ankara had developed diplomatic ties with London, primarily through membership in the North Atlantic Treaty Organization (NATO). However, by 1959 EOKA had succeeded in convincing British, Greek, and Turkish representatives to meet in Zurich to negotiate a peace settlement, during which Britain supported Turkish opposition to Cypriot unification with Greece.

The 1959 settlement foresaw Cyprus as a republic; the constitution was designed to cater to both Greek and Turkish communities, while recognizing the former's numerical superiority, and to safeguard the territorial integrity and sovereignty of the island. The settlement also established the special relationship between Cyprus itself and Britain, Greece, and Turkey, who were to guarantee the fundamental principles of the constitution. In the event that guarantees were violated and that no agreement could subsequently be reached between the guarantors over concerted responsive action, the three powers were legally entitled to take unilateral measures to reestablish the original conditions of the settlement. The settlement also granted Britain two Sovereign Base Areas on Cyprus, while Greece and Turkey were allowed to position armed battalions on the island, numbering 950 and 650 respectively. On 16 August 1960 the Cypriot Constitution was signed; Cyprus became an independent, sovereign state; and the island was admitted to the United Nations one month later. A Greek Cypriot president, Archbishop Makarios III, and a Turkish Cypriot vice president, Rauf Denktash, were each elected by their respective communities, and both leaders retained certain legislative veto powers.

Implementation of the conditions of the Constitution experienced difficulties from the outset, exacerbating tension between the communities on the island. Greek Cypriots resented having to abandon the ambitions of enosis, and their Turkish compatriots mistrusted the provisions intended to protect their constitutional security. Tensions intensified during 1963, prompting Makarios, on 23 November, to propose statutory revisions that he claimed would consolidate accord between the two communities by removing Turkish Cypriots' special status. The Turkish community, however, suspected that the amendments were intended to undermine its authority and ultimately realize the Greek Cypriot ambition of enosis. On 21 December open hostilities broke out between the two communities in Nicosia. In response, Ankara made military gestures in support of Turkish Cypriots, and it has been suggested that it was only the influence of Turkey's allies in NATO that prevented the Turks from following through with actual military action.

The government of Cyprus feared that Turkey would forcibly support Turks on the island. At the time, the international community in general believed that such action was very likely to precipitate an armed response from Athens, despite Turkey's military superiority over Greece. The United Kingdom, as constitutional guarantor, and with significant numbers of troops already stationed on the island, was determined to avoid such an outcome, in which it would be expected to intervene. The fact that both Greece and Turkey were members of NATO added extra significance and urgency to matters: The alliance could not afford to have two of its members taking part in open hostilities. On 24 December, the Cypriot government accepted the guarantors' offer to deploy a UK-led peacekeeping force, comprising troops already present on the island, to attempt to defuse the situation. A settlement was brokered between the warring parties, and on 26 December the force was established to patrol a cease-fire "green line" that separated the opposing forces in Nicosia.

Britain was not keen to extend its peacekeeping role indefinitely in the face of a rapidly deteriorating security situation. When the five parties involved in the dispute—the two Cypriot communities, Greece, Turkey, and the United Kingdom—met in London on 15 January 1964 to discuss the situation, the UK representative proposed that the peacekeeping force be expanded to include troops from other NATO member states. However, the Cypriot government rejected the idea out of hand, suspecting a Turkish

bias to any NATO-led operation and with the support of the Soviet Union, suggested instead a UN force. The United Kingdom and the United States, as the paramount NATO member state, were eventually obliged to bring the matter before the UN Security Council. On 4 March 1964 the Security Council agreed that the situation in Cyprus represented a threat to international peace and security. With the consent of the Cypriot government, the Security Council unanimously adopted Security Council Resolution (SCR) 186 authorizing the establishment of the United Nations Peacekeeping Force in Cyprus (UNFICYP) in order to "prevent a recurrence of fighting and, as necessary, to contribute to the maintenance and restoration of law and order and a return to normal conditions."

UNFICYP succeeded in abating open hostilities on Cyprus. However, the force was largely unsuccessful in addressing underlying tensions between the two communities, as evidenced by the crisis that developed in 1967. In November 1967 fighting broke out between the Cypriot National Guard and Turkish Cypriot forces at Ayios Theodhoros, and eventually the National Guard captured the town. The UN secretary-general, in response to a complaint from Ankara, requested that the Cypriot and Greek governments arrange a withdrawal of the Greek Cypriot forces, which was duly carried out on 16 November. However, on 18 and 19 November, the Turkish government authorized overflights of Cyprus's airspace, and violence subsequently spread to Kokkina and Kyrenia. The serious political situation that threatened to develop persuaded the secretary-general to appeal to the leaders of Cyprus, Greece, and Turkey, asking that Greek and Turkish forces that were not part of their UN contingents in Cyprus be withdrawn immediately. Greece and Turkey accordingly agreed that withdrawals would take place between 8 December 1967 and 16 January 1968.

On 15 July 1974 the situation in Cyprus suddenly and dramatically changed. The Cypriot National Guard, at the instigation of the military regime that had seized power in Athens seven years earlier, mounted an attempted coup d'état against the Makarios government in Nicosia. On 20 July, in response to what it perceived to be a revived threat of enosis in Cyprus and a violation of the 1960 Constitution, Turkey forcibly intervened, claiming its jurisdictional right as constitutional guarantor to do so, and occupied an area in the north of the country. The two sides eventually arrived at a cease-fire, and the junta in Athens fell soon after.

The foreign ministers of Greece, Turkey, and the United Kingdom reached a tripartite agreement in Geneva on 30 July 1974. However, in response to the formation of a new government in Nicosia on 14 August by the former speaker of the Cypriot House, Glafcos Clerides, Turkish troops continued their advance through Cyprus and within two days had taken control of the northern third of the island. Around 200,000 Greek Cypriots immediately moved from the north of the country to the south, and around 40,000 Turkish Cypriots moved in the opposite direction; over the next few years, the vast majority of Cypriots relocated to their relevant communities, thereby establishing the effective ethnic and political division of the island. In 1983 the Turkish section of Cyprus declared itself the Turkish Republic of Northern Cyprus (RNC). However, as of 1998 only Turkey recognized the RNC as a sovereign state, and the (Greek) government of the Republic of Cyprus claimed, with broad international support, to represent the entire Cypriot community. Denktash and Clerides continued to lead their respective Cypriot communities, and the island remained divided along the same lines. Periodic outbreaks of violence have continued to occur between the two communities, encouraged by political and military moves by the Greek and Turkish governments. For example, early in 1997 tension rose on the island over the intention of the (Greek) government of the Republic of Cyprus to purchase S-300 antiaircraft missiles from Russia.

The Deployment of UNFICYP

During UNFICYP's inception, both potential troop-contributing countries and parties to the dispute attempted to impose various political and practical conditions on the force's composition. For instance, Ireland, because of its domestic political situation, was wary of becoming involved in a partitioning exercise, and Sweden did not wish to be the only neutral country involved in the operation. The Cypriot government, on the other hand, in order to maintain equilibrium between NATO and non-NATO contributors, demanded the exclusion of either Norway or Denmark. It also proscribed the inclusion of black or colored troops, principally those from Africa, and Turkey similarly excluded troops from Third World countries.

The Soviet Union was in favor of a UN, as opposed to a NATO, force, as a means of preventing NATO from extending its influence to include the newly formed, nonaligned state of Cyprus. However, together with France, Moscow was concerned over the extent of the powers given to the secretary-general in relation to the composition, strength, and mandate of UNFICYP. Although somewhat appeased by the temporary nature of the mandate—UNFICYP was initially authorized for only three months—both countries abstained from voting on the relevant paragraph of the resolution. Traditional peacekeeping forces did not, in general, accept troops from permanent members of the Security Council. However, the United Kingdom's special interest in Cyprus meant that it did contribute personnel to UNFICYP.

UNFICYP was deployed at the end of March 1964, and at its peak its total strength reached in excess of 6,000, provided by Austria, Canada, Denmark, Finland, Ireland, Sweden, and the United Kingdom (see Map 3). Personnel were further provided by Australia, Austria, Denmark, and New Zealand for the civilian police unit (CIVPOL) attached to UNFICYP, which arrived in April. An air unit and a field hospital were also supplied by Britain and Austria respectively. On 6 March 1964 UN Secretary-General U Thant had appointed Lt. Gen. P. S. Gyani (India) as UNFICYP force commander. The force commander is responsible to the secretary-general, and his or her status is commensurate with that of the special representative, a political position responsible for facilitating the secretary-general's mediation duties. Immediately below the force commander are both the chief of staff and the police adviser, who supervise CIVPOL. UNFICYP receives the majority of its logistical support from the two British Sovereign Base Areas and consequently has experienced few logistical problems. The United Kingdom has sup-

UNFICYP deployment as of June 1975

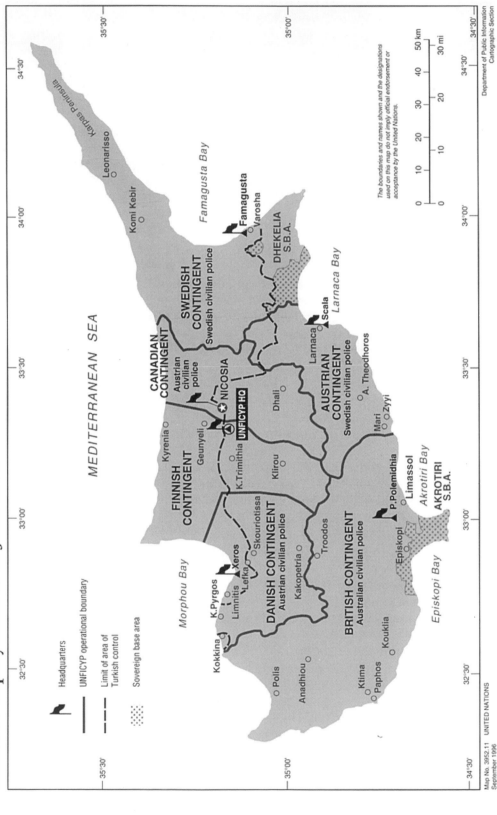

Headquarters

UNFICYP operational boundary

Limit of area of Turkish control

Sovereign base area

MEDITERRANEAN SEA

Karpas Peninsula

Leonarisso

Komi Kebir

Famagusta Bay

Famagusta
Varosha

SWEDISH CONTINGENT
Swedish civilian police

DHEKELIA S.B.A.

Larnaca Bay

CANADIAN CONTINGENT
Austrian civilian police

NICOSIA

Scala

Larnaca

UNFICYP HQ

Dhali

AUSTRIAN CONTINGENT
Swedish civilian police

A. Theodhoros

Kyrenia

Geunyeli

FINNISH CONTINGENT

K.Trimithia

Klirou

Zyyi

Mari

Skouriotissa

Troodos

P.Polemidhia

Limassol

Akrotiri Bay

AKROTIRI S.B.A.

Xeros

Lefka

DANISH CONTINGENT
Austrian civilian police

Kakopetria

BRITISH CONTINGENT
Australian civilian police

Episkopi

Episkopi Bay

K.Pyrgos

Limnitis

Kokkina

Kouklia

Morphou Bay

Polis

Anadhiou

Ktima
Paphos

0   10   20   30   40   50 km
0   10   20   30 mi

The boundaries and names shown and the designations used on this map do not imply official endorsement or acceptance by the United Nations.

Map No. 3952.11   UNITED NATIONS
September 1996

Department of Public Information
Cartographic Section

plied food, fuel, maintenance organization, ordnance stores, and troop vehicles; each national contingent is responsible for other matériel.

The UNFICYP mandate to "use its best efforts to prevent a recurrence of fighting and, as necessary, to contribute to the maintenance and restoration of law and order and a return to normal conditions" was decidedly vague, and UNFICYP personnel relied exclusively on persuasion and negotiation. Though the mandate incorporated certain humanitarian aspects, the political element was largely restricted to maintaining stability. As has been mentioned already, the security situation on the island had persuaded many Cypriots from both communities to abandon their homes in mixed towns and villages in favor of more ethnically homogeneous environments. Where front lines could, thus, be distinguished, UNFICYP interposed itself between the opposing forces. This was particularly evident along the green line in Nicosia, but it was also apparent in the districts of Kyrenia, Lafka, Larnaca, Limassol, and Paphos. UNFICYP also took the initiative in low-level demilitarization duties, as well as in negotiating strategic positions that it might subsequently occupy and in patrolling sensitive areas. The force was quickly able to establish multilevel communications with both communities, and CIVPOL facilitated stability through working with and observing local police. At this stage, therefore, UNFICYP's role was primarily preventive. Though this undoubtedly improved security on the island, it did little to address the underlying causes of the conflict. Indeed, it has been suggested that the reduction in tension caused by the presence of UNFICYP removed the incentive to resolve the conflict, thereby prolonging the conflict.

The incidents of 1974 created a number of problems for UNFICYP. The UNFICYP mandate had not been designed to address military action between the armed forces of the guarantor powers. Indeed, avoiding direct confrontation between Greece and Turkey had been a primary motivation for creating UNFICYP. In accordance with the principles of traditional peacekeeping, the force was restricted from influencing the military situation on the island. The secretary-general, with the tacit support of the Security Council and the British government, recommended that the force attempt to stabilize Cyprus within its present mandate. Britain, as a guarantor of the Cypriot Constitution, had an obligation to uphold its principles. Furthermore, the still-imminent threat of direct conflict between Greece and Turkey, and its potential repercussions, convinced the majority of the international community of UNFICYP's value.

Between 24 July and 14 August 1974, reinforcements of 2,078 personnel increased the overall strength of UNFICYP to 4,444. Also during this period the Security Council adopted a number of resolutions requiring UNFICYP to carry out additional functions in relation to the new security developments. On 16 August a cease-fire was reached, and a de facto cease-fire line was drawn up between the advanced positions of the Cypriot National Guard and the Turkish forces, stretching 180 kilometers from Kato Pyrgos on the northwest coast to Dherinia on the east coast. An official UN buffer zone was established between the opposing sides along this line, ranging from 20 meters wide at its narrowest in Nicosia to 7 kilometers wide near Atheniou. From 1974 onward, preserving this status quo has become UNFICYP's primary function, and patrolling the buffer zone, therefore, forms its central task. To this end, a number of UN observation posts, with night-observation equipment, have been set up along the line. Regular patrols are also carried out along an all-weather track that travels the length of the zone.

The majority of violent incidents on Cyprus have occurred in the capital because the two sides are in close proximity there. UNFICYP has periodically attempted to persuade each side to relinquish its positions along the green line, and in 1989 a limited withdrawal was secured. However, the United Nations has repeatedly failed to achieve agreement over official investigations into levels of troops and matériel. Consequently, tension continues, as each side regularly accuses the other of receiving military reinforcements. Other areas of the buffer zone incorporate some of the island's most fertile land. In the interests of stability, UNFICYP has encouraged farming in these areas and has made considerable efforts to provide an environment secure enough to enable such activities to take place. UNFICYP investigates temporary advances into the buffer zone, supervises the dismantling of military positions within it, and counters attempts to improve frontline positions. It also supervises the transfer of mail and medical supplies between the two communities, provides its good offices—that is, acts as mediator—in relation to water and electricity supplies across the zone, and carries out various humanitarian duties within both communities.

At the time of UNFICYP's original deployment the United Nations had been experiencing financial difficulties, primarily as a result of overextension through the United Nations Operation in the Congo (ONUC) and the first United Nations Emergency Force (UNEF I) operations. Furthermore, just as they had for both ONUC and UNEF I, France and the Soviet Union refused to pay assessments for the operation. Consequently, UNFICYP became the only UN peacekeeping operation to have been funded voluntarily. Financial responsibilities were principally passed on to the contributing countries, although the United Nations was responsible for administrative and logistical costs, for which the secretary-general sought voluntary contributions. The effect of this funding system was that UNFICYP experienced severe financial difficulties. These difficulties, combined with the fact that the security situation in Cyprus had generally improved over the first ten years of the force's deployment, meant that the number of personnel serving with UNFICYP progressively declined during this period until it was less than half its initial strength. During its deployment, several countries have withdrawn or reduced the size of their contingents serving with UNFICYP. These reductions are primarily in response to financial considerations, but they are also the result of concerns over the lack of progress in addressing the country's underlying problems. In 1977 the secretary-general decided not to replace the Finnish contingent, which had withdrawn that year; in February 1987 Sweden withdrew its infantry battalion; and during 1992 the overall strength of the force was diminished by approximately 28 percent following the withdrawal of the Danish battalion and reductions in the size of the Austrian, British, and Canadian contingents. In response to these continued difficulties, in 1993 the Security Council adopted SCR 831, which determined that expenditures that were not covered by voluntary contributions would be treated as UN expenses and that the force should be restructured to comprise three infantry battalions of around 350 persons each. By June 1993 the Special UN Account for UNFICYP was short by some $200 million.

The overall evaluation of UNFICYP's experiences has ultimately been mixed. It has undoubtedly succeeded in limiting overt hostilities between the Greek and Turkish communities on Cyprus and hence has restricted the number of casualties resulting directly from the violence there. Thus, apart from the major transgression in 1974, the force has successfully created suitable conditions for a truce and has maintained the fundamental aspects of the cease-fire under often precarious conditions. Without an appropriately supervised buffer zone there would have been a constant risk that minor cease-fire violations and other security crises would escalate into major incidents, with potentially international consequences. Furthermore, the presence of the force in general facilitated the establishment of a sufficiently stable environment to enable the majority of Cypriots, from both communities, to go about their daily lives. Government services, economic activity, and commercial and civilian traffic all functioned to a useful degree. However, UNFICYP did fail to prevent major crises from developing; nor did it make any significant advances toward demilitarizing the population.

The overall effect of these conditions in relation to prospects for resolving the underlying causes of the conflict is open to more than one interpretation. On the positive side, it can be argued that the reduction in casualties as a result of UNFICYP's actions is justification enough for the force's presence on the island. It can further be argued that the more peaceful environment and the functioning society facilitated by UNFICYP's actions have sufficiently defused hostilities to allow negotiations to take place.

However, on the negative side, it has been suggested that the force's continued presence on the island after more than 30 years is in itself proof of its ineffectiveness: The two communities remain bitterly divided, as is evidenced by the sporadic violence across the UN-monitored green line in 1996. Furthermore, countering the point that the stable environment created by the force has encouraged negotiation, it may be that the resolution of the differences between the Cypriot communities was no less likely at the start of the UNFICYP operation, when the terms of the cease-fire were regularly violated, than later, when they were more strictly adhered to. Indeed, the presence of a stable environment may in fact have removed the urgency to negotiate and consequently discouraged settlement, since the two communities have continued to function normally despite the division of the island. UNFICYP has made only minor efforts to address the root causes of the conflict, as is evidenced by the fact that the force has not attempted comprehensive demilitarization programs nor made any significant headway in promoting a durable political settlement. As a result of the outwardly stable environment on the island, the international community too has been inclined to regard the Cyprus problem as sufficiently resolved as to require scant attention.

As of February 1998 UNFICYP headquarters were in Nicosia. As of late 1998, the special adviser to the secretary-general was Diego Cordovez (Ecuador), the deputy special representative of the secretary-general and chief of mission of UNFICYP was Gustave Feissel (United States), and the force commander was Maj. Gen. Evergisto Arturo de Vergara (Argentina). The force strength (mission total) comprised 1,257 uniformed personnel, made up of 1,222 troops and 35 civilian police, supported by some 330 international and local civilian staff. The contributors of military personnel are Argentina, Australia, Austria, Canada, Finland, Hungary, Ireland, Slovenia, and the United Kingdom. The Security Council regularly reaffirms the UNFICYP mandate every six months.

References and further reading

Evriviades and Bourantonis (1994); Fetherston (1994a); James (1990); United Nations (1996)

Dayton Agreement
See Bosnia and Herzegovina

Declaration of San Isidro de Coronado
See ONUCA

Demilitarized zone
Under the Geneva Conventions of 1949, cultural objects, nondefended localities, and demilitarized zones (DMZs) (including safety zones and neutralized zones) are under special protection, and the conventions provide for their appropriate marking and identification. Military commanders also have the option of establishing various zones to protect people from hostilities. In general this includes hospital, safety, neutralized, and demilitarized zones and nondefended localities. The general aim of these zones is to ensure protection from attack and military operations. The process for establishing DMZs is as follows: The force commander in the area obtains approval from higher command and has that approval transmitted to the opposing forces for agreement, if necessary through a neutral intermediary. For example, during the Falklands-Malvinas conflict of 1982—without any special agreement in writing—the parties to the conflict established a neutral zone at sea where hospital ships could be located. The zone was an area approximately 20 nautical miles in diameter located on the high seas to the north of the islands. In Sri Lanka in the late 1990s a safety zone existed on the Jaffna Peninsula. The zone was approximately seven kilometers in diameter and contained Jaffna Hospital, the major medical facility in the area. No military personnel or installations were allowed to be located in the area. Both parties to the conflict agreed to the zone, which is possible under the provisions of the Geneva Conventions applicable to conflicts not of an international character.

The term was also used at the end of the Arab-Israeli conflict in 1948–1949. The establishment of DMZs was part of the Armistice Agreements, and the term refers to the exclusion of military personnel and weapons from either side of the demarcation lines between Israel and Egypt and between Israel and Syria. The agreement allowed civilians and civil police to return to the areas, since it was a military presence that was proscribed. In contrast to buffer zones, demilitarized zones are not normally occupied by a third party. They are patrolled by observer teams or surveyed from observation posts and are created to exclude military occupation and activity from specified areas. They are areas that are claimed by both sides and where control by one could constitute a direct threat to the other. According to the Nordic UN Manual, demilitarized zones, armistice, and cease-fire lines impose restrictions on freedom of movement and rights of access to landowners. Therefore in order to work their land and other enterprises within the disputed area, access and ways of working must be negotiated. Both the original negotiations and subsequent supervision of the workers are a responsibility often delegated to UN battalions and companies. For example, the peacekeeping battalion might set up liaison organizations so that disputes and complaints can be dealt with. The UN civilian police can help transport crops across demarcation lines and can help transport and observe or supervise the sale of produce in marketing centers that would otherwise be inaccessible or denied to the sellers of the produce. Finally, if hostilities break out in demilitarized zones, public service facilities will be withdrawn, and it is the responsibility of the UN force to attempt negotiations directed at the restoration of suspended public services.

UNYOM deployment as of October 1963

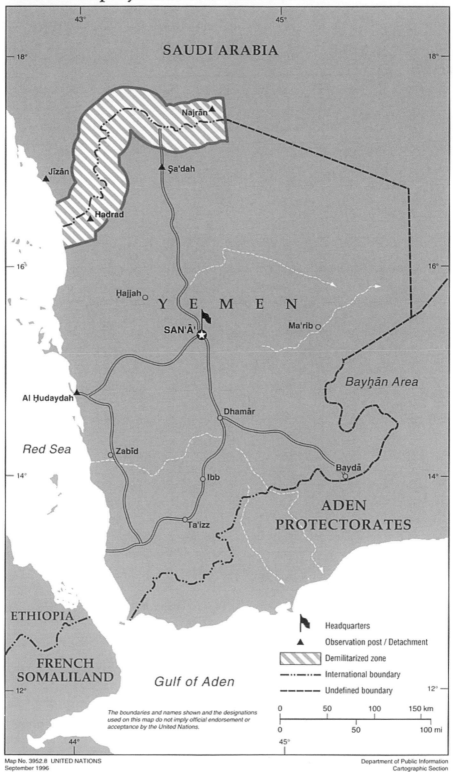

Map No. 3952.8 UNITED NATIONS
September 1996

Department of Public Information
Cartographic Section

Generally demilitarized zones have been established by agreement of the parties at the end of a conflict. However, the establishment of DMZs is now also being regarded as a form of preventive deployment, either on both sides of a border and with the agreement of the two parties as a means of separating potential belligerents, or on one side of the line at the request of one party to remove any pretext for attack. In these cases, demilitarized zones would serve as symbols of the international community's concern that conflict be prevented. At the other end of the spectrum of conflict, DMZs have a place in postconflict peace building as a means of providing a sense of security and encouraging the parties to turn toward the peaceful reconstruction of their societies. (See Map 4.)

See also Conflict prevention; Liberia; Military Observers; ONUCA; Rwanda; UN Truce Supervision Organization; Yemen

De-mining and Peacekeeping
See Arms control and disarmament

Denmark
As one of the four Nordic states, Denmark has been a very active participant in peacekeeping since 1956. Its Defence Act of 1993 defined two mission areas for Danish armed forces: first, a strong commitment to conflict prevention, peacekeeping, and humanitarian missions under UN and Organization for Security and Cooperation in Europe (OSCE) auspices, and second, support for conflict prevention, crisis management, and defense within the North Atlantic Treaty Organization (NATO). During the 1990s the balance of Danish military force structure moved away from preparation for the defense of Denmark toward participation in international missions and in NATO's reaction forces. An expression of this change of emphasis came in 1993 when the Danish Parliament approved the formation of the Danish International Brigade, specifically prepared for participation in peacekeeping, peacemaking, and humanitarian operations. Under the name of the Danish Reaction Brigade (DRB) it

will also be assigned to NATO's Allied Command Europe Rapid Reaction Corps. The International Brigade at full strength has 4,500 personnel, the majority of whom are reservists, and about 1,500 of these are available for UN service. Designed both as a fighting unit and as a peacekeeping unit, the Danish International Brigade is trained and prepared to operate across a broad spectrum of missions, with the capability to escalate from peacekeeping to peace enforcement and war fighting and to de-escalate back to peacekeeping, including humanitarian tasks. In the former Yugoslavia Danish peacekeeping personnel numbered 1,300 in 1995, and the DRB contingent was the most heavily armed contingent within the United Nations Protection Force in Former Yugoslavia (UNPROFOR). Denmark has continued to be an active and enthusiastic supporter of improving the UN's standby forces capacity. In 1995 Denmark proposed a plan for a Multinational UN Standby Forces High Readiness Brigade, to which Denmark would contribute a brigade headquarters element.

See also Cyprus; Logistics; Nordic Countries; Training for Peacekeeping; Troop-contributing countries; UN Standby Arrangements System
References and further reading Karhilo (1996)

Department of Administration and Management
See United Nations: agencies; United Nations: organization

Department of Humanitarian Affairs/Office for the Co-ordination of Humanitarian Affairs
See United Nations: agencies; United Nations: organization

Department of Peacekeeping Operations
See United Nations: agencies; United Nations: organization

Department of Political Affairs
See United Nations: agencies; United Nations: organization

Development
See Peace building from below

Development and Peacekeeping
See Peace building from below

Disarmament
See Arms control and disarmament

Dominican Republic

Mission of the Representative of the Secretary-General in the Dominican Republic (DOMREP), 1965–1966

Conflict Profile
April 1965 witnessed the outbreak of open hostilities in the Dominican Republic between two diametrically opposed factions, one left-wing and the other right-wing. On 24 April the Dominican military regime, headed by Donald Reid Cabral, was ousted by a group of army officers and civilians who were intent on returning to power erstwhile president Juan Bosch. The pro-Bosch group, headed by Col. Francisco Caamaño Deñó, established itself as the self-named Constitutional Government in the Republic. However, it was itself opposed by a combined civilian-military junta called the Government of National Reconstruction, which included high-ranking officers from the Dominican armed forces and was led by Gen. Antonio Imbert Barrera. Each side declared itself the official authority in the Dominican Republic, and fighting broke out between them, primarily in the capital, Santo Domingo.

In response, the United States began to deploy troops to the country, ostensibly to evacuate U.S. citizens and other foreign nationals. However, even after the majority of U.S. nationals had been removed, the number of U.S. troops in the republic continued to increase, reaching 9,500 by 2 May 1965. At this point, U.S. President Lyndon Johnson revealed that the U.S. troops would also help prevent the establishment of a communist state in the Republic, claiming that the U.S. intervention was justified by the communist tendencies of one of the opposing forces. By 5 May the number of U.S. troops in the republic had reached 19,000. Washington sought to legitimize its actions by involving the Organization of American States (OAS). On 6 May the OAS member states narrowly, and somewhat hesitantly, agreed that an OAS-led Inter-American Peace Force (IAPF) should indeed restore peace to the Dominican Republic. It required the vote of the republic itself, represented by the noncommunist faction, to secure OAS involvement. The IAPF enjoyed only scant contributions of personnel from OAS members other than the United States.

Deployment of DOMREP
On 1 May the Soviet Union requested that the Security Council convene urgently to discuss the U.S. intervention in the Dominican Republic. Moscow, unsurprisingly, was opposed to the U.S. actions and wished to see U.S. troops withdrawn immediately. On 14 May Ivory Coast, Jordan, and Malaysia suggested that a UN representative be sent to the area to report on the situation there. The United States successfully fended off such moves until a report from the left-wing group in the Dominican Republic claimed that the violence in the country was threatening the existence of Santo Domingo. Washington, embarrassed to be perceived as so blatantly pursuing its own ends, consequently agreed to the deployment of the Representative of the Secretary-General in the Dominican Republic (DOMREP). Attached to DOMREP was the secretary-general's chief military adviser and two military advisers from Brazil, Chile, or Ecuador. Despite resentment from both the United States and the IAPF, DOMREP played a useful function in making the IAPF accountable to the wider international community. It also made an effective contribution to mediation efforts between the opposing parties.

By the middle of May the United States had begun to question its assumption that it should thwart the political ambitions of the communist-leaning group, realizing that in fact it enjoyed widespread popular support. Therefore, Washington altered its stance of supporting the noncommunist group exclusively in favor of promoting a genuine settlement between the opposing parties. To this end, the IAPF forcibly maintained a cease-fire between the belligerents, while a three-member OAS committee brokered negotiations between them. The accession in August of the opposing parties to the Act of Dominican Reconciliation, which provided for the establishment of a provisional government until national elections were held in 1966, enabled the IAPF to take on new law-and-order duties in support of the provisional authority. Elections in July 1966 returned a new president, Joaquín Balaguer, to office, following which the IAPF began to withdraw. DOMREP was withdrawn in October. Thus, despite its highly partisan origins, IAPF, with the assistance of DOMREP, succeeded in fulfilling a useful peacekeeping function.

DOMREP was headquartered in Santo Domingo, and the mission lasted from May 1965 to October 1966. The mission suffered no fatalities and cost $275,831. However, the IAPF cost considerably more and resulted in 27 dead and approximately 200 wounded.

See also First-generation peacekeeping
References and further reading James (1990); United Nations (1996)

Economic Community of West African States Monitoring Group
See Liberia

Egypt

In 1995 Egypt took the initiative of establishing the Cairo Center for Training on Conflict Resolution and Peacekeeping in Africa (CCPA). This nonprofit center is funded in part and run jointly by the Egyptian Ministries of Foreign Affairs and Defense. It is to be independent in the near future. This center was established in response to African countries' efforts to assume a more active role in dealing with crises and conflicts emanating from within the African continent. This attitude was amply displayed by the decision made by the African Heads of State and Government, meeting in Cairo in June 1993, to establish the Mechanism for Conflict Prevention, Management, and Resolution. It has become clear that to ensure the successful functioning of this mechanism and to assist with Africa's endeavors in this area in general, it is necessary to create and enhance indigenous African capabilities in the fields of conflict management and peacekeeping. The Cairo Center is unique not only because it will ultimately be offering courses in both the mainly civilian field of preventive diplomacy and the military field of peacekeeping under one roof, but also because it will design and present its course material from a primarily African perspective. The center's main objectives are (1) to train African personnel specializing in the prevention, management, and settlement of disputes in Africa; in order to achieve this, the center offers integrated training courses in peacekeeping and civilian-military observation activities involving political and military aspects for African senior officers and civilians; (2) to conduct studies on the most significant problems of the African continent, make recommendations on ways of tackling them, and coordinate, cooperate, and exchange expertise with similar international centers; (3) to work in close coordination with the Organization of African Unity (OAU), with a view to strengthening the role of the OAU Mechanism for Conflict Prevention, Management, and Resolution in the fields of preventive diplomacy and peacekeeping. The Cairo

Center coordinates with other similar centers from within and outside the African continent. It aims to provide simultaneous courses, taught in English and French, in both conflict management and peacekeeping. The center is being geared toward complementing the African indigenous capacity; its activities would be coordinated with the OAU mechanism to ensure that the requirements in these fields are fully met. The courses conducted by the center are Advanced Peacekeeping for Senior Officers, Preventive Diplomacy and Conflict Resolution, and Military Observer and Staff Officer Course in Peacekeeping Operations.

See also Boutros-Ghali, Boutros; Congo; Demilitarized zone; First-generation peacekeeping; Lebanon; Middle East conflict; Multinational Force and Observers; Troop-contributing countries; United Nations Disengagement Observer Force; United Nations Emergency Force I; United Nations Truce Supervision Organization; Yemen
References and further reading
UNDPKO training database at http://www.un.org.dpko/

El Salvador

United Nations Observer Mission in El Salvador (ONUSAL), 1991–1995

Conflict Profile
As has been the case throughout the countries of Central America, El Salvador's political problems in the latter part of the twentieth century stemmed from oligarchic control of economic and political resources, which was a legacy of the colo-

ONUSAL deployment as of April 1992

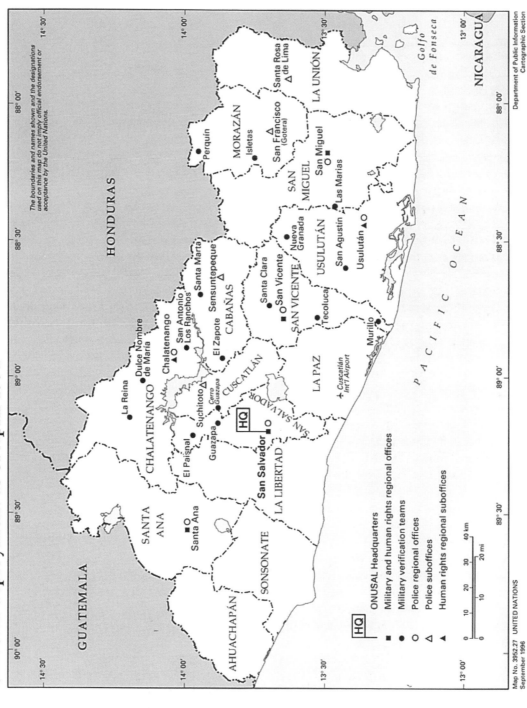

The boundaries and names shown and the designations
used on this map do not imply official endorsement or
acceptance by the United Nations.

GUATEMALA

HONDURAS

NICARAGUA

Golfo de Fonseca

PACIFIC OCEAN

SANTA ANA
Santa Ana

SONSONATE

AHUACHAPÁN

La Reina

CHALATENANGO

Dulce Nombre de María
Chalatenango
San Antonio Los Ranchos
Santa Marta
El Zapote
Sensuntepeque
CABAÑAS
Suchitoto
Cerro Guazapa
Guazapa
El Paisnal

CUSCATLÁN

SAN SALVADOR
HQ
San Salvador
LA LIBERTAD

Perquín
MORAZÁN
Isletas
San Francisco (Gotera)

Santa Rosa de Lima
LA UNIÓN

SAN MIGUEL
San Miguel
Las Marias

Santa Clara
San Vicente
SAN VICENTE
Tecoluca
Murillo

Nueva Granada
USULUTÁN
San Agustín
Usulután

LA PAZ
Cuscatlán Int'l Airport

Legend

HQ	ONUSAL Headquarters
■	Military and human rights regional offices
●	Military verification teams
○	Police regional offices
△	Police suboffices
▲	Human rights regional suboffices

Scale:
0   10   20   30   40 km
0   10   20 mi

nial era of a century before. The El Salvadoran economy is based on coffee, and the few families that owned El Salvador's coffee plantations thereby controlled its politics. Salvadoran political opposition in the twentieth century has tended to be Marxist and extremist, perceiving violent insurgency as the most viable means of dissent. Compromise between such diametrically opposed groups was likely to prove at best problematic.

In the early twentieth century popular dissatisfaction became increasingly apparent to the ruling elites. In response, during the 1920s and 1930s positions of political power were extended to members of the military in order to enlist their help in preserving and reinforcing oligarchic domination. In 1932 Gen. Maximiliano Hernández Martínez took over the presidency of El Salvador, and his 12-year rule established a system of government that, excluding a short interval from 1960 to 1961, lasted until 1979. This system primarily involved supporting military presidents with largely civilian cabinets who would collectively protect the interests of the coffee elites.

The 1930s witnessed severe economic hardship in El Salvador, prompting a combined urban- and agrarian-based uprising against the government, headed by the Communist leader Augustin Farabundo Martí. The government's response was brutal: Martí and his colleagues were executed, and between 10,000 and 30,000 peasants were massacred by the military in what has come to be known as the *Matanza*. El Salvador's economic situation continued to deteriorate throughout the 1940s, 1950s, and 1960s, particularly in rural communities, despite limited industrialization. By 1960, however, organized labor movements had become powerful enough to persuade the army to oust its own military president in favor of a provisional authority that included labor representatives. Nevertheless, a second coup d'état in 1961 returned a military president, Col. Julio Rivera, to power.

In response to their economic plight, many Salvadoran workers migrated to Honduras in search of work. However, in 1969 political disagreements between the two countries persuaded Honduras to renege on an immigration treaty, inducing the repatriation of large numbers of Salvadorans. In the same year, the number of Salvadoran re-turnees increased dramatically following violent incidents that occurred in San Salvador at a football match between the two countries and then on the streets of Tegucigalpa, Honduras. Tension intensified between El Salvador and Honduras, and despite appeals for calm by the Organization of American States (OAS), El Salvadoran air strikes on 14 July precipitated an air war between the two states. After four days of fighting, the OAS negotiated a de facto settlement, although by this time around 2,000 people had died, primarily Honduran civilians.

For El Salvador the principal repercussion from the war with Honduras was the return of between 60,000 and 130,000 expatriate Salvadoran workers to their homeland, which exacerbated the already harsh economic conditions for the majority of Salvadorans. Increasing numbers of opposition movements emerged throughout the 1970s against the ruling military regime. Finally, in October 1979, reformist officers in the Salvadoran military ousted the president, Gen. Carlos Humberto Romero, and installed a junta comprising a combined civilian and military membership. However, despite pledges of social and political reforms, conservative senior officers within the military maintained their firm grip on power, and few changes actually occurred. The following few years witnessed periodic power struggles within the junta and accompanying changes in its composition. José Napoléon Duarte, the leader of the moderate Christian Democratic Party (PDC), which had provided the center of opposition to military government since its inception in 1964, joined the junta in 1980 and became acting president. The regime was thereafter supported by the United States.

As dissatisfaction with the government continued to grow, political opposition groups and disaffected former government officials combined to form the Democratic Revolutionary Front (FDR) to oppose the junta. At the same time, armed opposition groups had also been integrating and, in October 1980, with the incorporation of the military wing of the Communist Party, they established the Frente Farabundo Martí para la Liberación Nacional (FMLN). In January 1981, incited by the murder of the archbishop of San Salvador, Oscar Arnulfo Romero, a longtime opponent of military repression, the FMLN launched a general armed offensive against the government. However, the offensive failed, and the ruling regime took uncompromising revenge on the populace. Death squads had been active in El Salvador since 1975, formed primarily from members of the military and police forces and the national guard, and in the aftermath of the opposition offensive these squads killed many members and potential recruits for the FDR and FMLN. The FMLN retreated to the countryside, where it attempted to build up support among the peasants. Thus, all-out civil war in El Salvador began.

At this time U.S. influence began to play an increasingly important part in Salvadoran politics. Partly because of pressure from the United States, elections were held in El Salvador in March 1982. They were won by the Nationalist Republican Alliance (ARENA), a right-wing group formed in September 1981 from military officers, death squad operatives, and conservative former members of the traditional, ruling oligarchy. ARENA was led by Roberto D'Aubuisson, who was alleged to have been a patron of the death squads. Washington continued to support moderate elements within the government and eventually succeeded in installing Alvaro Magnaña, from the traditional ruling oligarchy, as interim president. In 1984 El Salvador's first democratic, presidential election returned Duarte to power with a substantial majority. Again with considerable U.S. support, Duarte succeeded in suspending the death squads' operations. However, he was ultimately unable to break the grip of the ruling elites and the conservative military, and consequently he was unable to secure peasant support and an end to the conflict. In 1983 Salvadoran opposition fighters launched a second general offensive, which was again ineffectual, although this time U.S. political sway at least succeeded in dissuading the army from uncompromising reprisals.

For the next few years the war continued at relatively low levels, and opposition forces operated primarily in the countryside. However, the FMLN periodically scored more substantial strikes, notably against economic targets such as El Salvador's national electricity grid. During this period, U.S. patronage principally took the form of direct military aid for the Salvadoran government. Between 1982 and 1988 the army had increased its strength from 12,000 to 54,000 persons. Meanwhile, the security situation in the country, combined with a global decline in coffee prices, had had a disastrous effect on the country's economy. In 1988 the FMLN attempted to disrupt congressional elections by intimidating voters. However, the population turned out in large numbers in favor of the right-wing ARENA Party, demonstrating public disaffection with both the FMLN and Duarte's PDC. Thus, despite a few notable military successes, the FMLN had lost a considerable percentage of its popular political support, particularly in urban areas. Soviet and Cuban support of the opposition forces encouraged U.S. patronage of the new government, despite its past and present association with the death squads: Numbers of death squad murders had risen sharply in 1988 from the previous year. Thus, the war in El Salvador was plunged deeper into a Cold War political context.

In the 1989 presidential elections, Duarte, who was ill at the time and died in February the following year, lost to the ARENA candidate, Alfredo Cristiani Burkard, by a significant majority. The East-West détente at the end of the 1980s and declining Soviet support for the FMLN encouraged hopes of an end to the fighting. However, a settlement failed to materialize between the opposing sides, and at the end of 1989 the FMLN, sensing the decline in support, decided to launch another major offensive, their heaviest of the war so far.

Again the offensive was ultimately unsuccessful: It failed to generate popular urban support and was crushed by the Salvadoran military after two weeks. The offensive had deleterious consequences for all parties involved. It revealed that the Salvadoran military had not succeeded in significantly disabling armed opposition. Also, the military had carried out disproportionately severe retaliations in response to the offensive, including indiscriminate air attacks against urban targets suspected of harboring FMLN fighters, as well as the murder by army troops of six Jesuit scholars believed to be opposition sympathizers. Such incidents both damaged the president's moderate reputation and exposed his lack of control over his own armed forces. At the same time, the offensive had also demonstrated the military superiority of the government to the FMLN and had disclosed the limitations of FMLN support, especially in urban areas. During the offensive, a Nicaraguan plane carrying surface-to-air missiles bound for the FMLN had been shot down by the Salvadoran government. This incident reiterated the regional context of the conflict and also compromised the Central American regional peace settlement known as Esquipulas II. It also caused a breakdown in relations between Nicaragua and El Salvador. The FMLN were dealt a further blow when the left-wing Sandinista government lost the Nicaraguan elections in February 1990.

Deployment of ONUSAL

As a result particularly of the end of Nicaraguan support, the FMLN adopted a more conciliatory attitude. It pledged to attack military targets exclusively and also entered into negotiations with the government, under the auspices of the then UN Secretary-General Javier Pérez de Cuéllar, aimed at establishing a political settlement to the conflict. The first substantive agreement between the parties, the Agreement on Human Rights, was reached at San José, Costa Rica, on 26 July 1990. This provided for the establishment of a UN verification mission to monitor compliance, and the guarantees of human rights and fundamental freedoms in El Salvador were determined as part of the agreement. The agreement demanded that the United Nations would: receive reports of human rights violations from all parties to the conflict, would have unopposed opportunity to interview any relevant person in any establishment, would implement an information and educational campaign on human rights both in general and relating to the particular focus of the mission, and would undertake appropriate legal action to defend human rights and fundamental freedoms. It was envisaged that the mission would take up its duties following the cessation of hostilities between the belligerents.

On 29 August 1990 Pérez de Cuéllar obtained Security Council support for an integrated UN operation to verify compliance with the San José Agreement on human rights, with the intention first to establish a cease-fire and then, in the event of an agreed settlement between the parties, to monitor an election process in El Salvador. However, disagreements, primarily over armed forces, prevented the rapid establishment of the operation. A small, preliminary UN mission reported a broad consensus for UN human rights verification from both the government and the FMLN and advised the deployment of the relevant mechanism, despite the relatively unstable security situation that resulted from the lack of a formal cease-fire. Meanwhile, the Mexico City Agreement of 27 April 1991 further encouraged deployment through the establishment of constitutional reforms, including reform of the military.

On 20 May 1991 the Security Council authorized the establishment of the United Nations Observer Mission in El Salvador (ONUSAL), under Security Council Resolution (SCR) 693, and the mission was officially launched on 26 July. The initial phase of the ONUSAL operation took place in two stages. The preparatory stage lasted from July through September, when the mission established regional offices and laid the operational foundations for its future actions. The mission began its second stage on 1 October 1991, when it began to investigate accusations of human rights violations, to establish the veracity of any allegations, to identify and punish those responsible, and to deter future violations. During this phase ONUSAL developed mechanisms to promote coordination with the parties.

During the establishment of ONUSAL fighting continued between the belligerents. For instance, problems developed when the FMLN acquired Soviet surface-to-air missiles, with which it temporarily disabled the Salvadoran air force and gave the opposition fighters with the military the upper hand. However, on 25 September 1991 the opposing sides agreed on a condensed agenda for negotiations, which culminated at the end of December in agreement on all substantive issues in the peace process. This process took place during the final moments of Pérez de Cuéllar's administration as UN secretary-general.

The peace treaty was eventually signed in January 1992. It provided for an almost 50-percent reduction in the strength of the Salvadoran army; the disbanding of the FMLN armed forces and other paramilitary groups; an end to FMLN demands to be included in a coalition government, in deference to participation in the electoral process; a purge of the most extreme members of the military; the establishment of a new National Civil Police (PNC) so that internal security responsibilities could be removed from the military; an FMLN retreat from its extreme Marxist stance; and government agreement to include left-wing parties in Salvadoran politics. An official cease-fire was to commence on 1 February, and it was further agreed that compliance with the above stipulations would be verified by the UN.

Therefore, in addition to ONUSAL's Human Rights Division already stationed in El Salvador, the new UN secretary-general, Boutros Boutros-Ghali, advised that military and police divisions be added. The Security Council duly authorized that the strength of the mission be increased to 1,098. The Human Rights Division of ONUSAL comprised around 30 human rights observers and legal advisers. Its tasks included the objective recording of facts, as well as the exercise of good offices (that is, mediation) in order to assist indigenous efforts to counter violations of human rights agreements. It also helped to reinforce Salvadoran institutions' ability to work in promoting human rights through Cupertino with the National Council for the Defense of Human Rights and with nongovernmental organizations.

From the outset ONUSAL had included 15 military officers from Brazil, Canada, Ecuador, Spain, and Venezuela. These officers provided liaison with the opposing parties' military leaders. They had also, in association with the United Nations Observer Mission in Central America (ONUCA), escorted FMLN commanders in the field from their respective conflict zones to and from peace negotiations in Mexico and New York. When the Military Division of ONUSAL was added, it had an authorized strength of 380 military observers and was responsible for verifying the cessation of hostilities between the opposing forces. It supervised the redeployment of the Salvadoran armed forces to the positions that they were to maintain following the establishment of peace and the demobilization of FMLN forces into agreed areas. It further monitored both parties' troops in these areas,

verified the demobilization of weapons and personnel, supervised movements of both forces, and investigated allegations of violations. On 15 December 1992 the size of the division was reduced following the completion of the cease-fire process, and it was further reduced in May 1993 and December 1994 in response to advances in the peace process.

Sixteen police officials from France, Italy, and Spain had advised ONUSAL in relevant matters from its inception. Since its arrival in El Salvador the Police Division of ONUSAL, which primarily comprised specialists in the organization and operation of civilian police forces, monitored the activities of the PNC throughout the process of transition from armed conflict to national reconciliation. The division had an authorized strength of 631, and the deployment of police observers throughout the country began on 7 February 1992. ONUSAL police observers were also responsible for supervising the Auxiliary Transitory Police (PAT), which maintained public order and security between October 1992 and July 1993, when it was replaced by the new PNC. The police division took on extra duties to facilitate territorial deployment of the PNC from March 1993 onward. It also helped to locate illegal arms caches and provided support for the Human Rights Division and the Electoral Division.

The ONUSAL operation generally ran fairly smoothly, although problems did arise. During the dcmobilization process there were no significant violations of the cease-fire reported. However, the demobilization of the FMLN, in particular, ran late, and there were also suspicions that the FMLN was withholding significant quantities of arms in case of noncompliance by government forces. This culminated in the discovery of an illegal arms cache in a garage in Managua, Nicaragua, in March 1993, after which the FMLN pledged full cooperation with the demilitarization process. On the government side, the removal of discredited members of the Salvadoran armed forces, the establishment of the PNC, and land reforms intended to reintegrate demobilized opposition fighters into the community were all seriously delayed. However, with the help of international political pressure, especially from the United States, these processes were eventually implemented.

On 23 December 1992, following the recognition of the FMLN as a legal political party, the secretary-general reported the official end to the armed conflict in El Salvador. By 30 August 1993 the secretary-general was able to report that the verification and destruction of FMLN weapons had been completed and that its military structure had been dismantled, including the demobilization and reintegration of former combatants into civilian life. This facilitated the start of the democratization process in El Salvador, in the form of national elections set for March 1994. In response to a request by the secretary-general, the Security Council, by its SCR 832 of 27 May 1993, authorized the enlargement of the ONUSAL mandate to include observation of the electoral process.

The Electoral Division of ONUSAL was established in September 1993 to observe the entire electoral process. It was mandated to verify that the provisions made by all electoral authorities were impartial and consistent with the holding of free and fair elections; that all eligible voters were included on electoral rolls; that effective mechanisms were established to prevent duplicate voting, since comprehensive monitoring of the electoral rolls before the elections had proved impossible; that voters had unrestricted freedom of assembly, expression, movement, and organization; and that voters were educated so that they could effectively participate in the election. It was also mandated to listen to complaints over the electoral process, and if required to report them to the Supreme Electoral Tribunal, and to monitor polling stations on election day. The division comprised 36 professional staff and carried out its duties by coordinating with other ONUSAL components.

The election process incorporated four distinct components simultaneously: presidential elections, including provisions for a second round of voting after 28 days in the event that no candidate was returned with an overall majority; parliamentary elections for the National Assembly; municipal elections in 262 mayoral districts; and elections for the Central American Parliament, for which 20 deputies would be elected. From November 1993 to January 1994, the Electoral Division primarily monitored voter registration by observing election campaigns and helping to compose the electoral roll. The presidential election campaign officially opened on 20 November 1993, with the legislative and municipal campaigns beginning on 20 January and 20 February 1994, respectively. Some 900 observers were brought in for election day itself.

On 21 March 1994 it was announced that in spite of serious breaches of electoral procedures or regulations in relation to organization and transparency, the elections had taken place under appropriate conditions of freedom, competitiveness, and security. Around 1.5 million people, representing 55 percent of the eligible Salvadoran voters, took part in the election: a lower figure than had been anticipated. Logistical and structural problems had prevented significant numbers of voters from participating. ARENA won the majority of votes in both the presidential and legislative elections. However, no presidential candidate was returned with an overall majority, requiring a second round to be scheduled for 24 April between the two candidates with the largest percentage of votes: ARENA's Armando Calderón Sol and Rubén Zamora of the Convergencia Democrática (CD)–FMLN–Movimento Nacional Revolucionario (MNR) coalition. In the second round ARENA received 68.35 percent of the vote and the coalition 31.65 percent, with Calderón Sol being returned as president-elect.

Although it had initially been intended that all aspects of the peace settlement would be completed prior to the installation of the new government on 1 June 1994, some major issues remained unresolved. The PNC should have been deployed by 28 July, and the National Police should have been demobilized by 31 October. The land transfer program was also still behind schedule, and so the deadline for the resolution of these problems was extended into 1995. It had also been intended that only a small UN presence would be left in El Salvador after 1 June. However, both Salvadoran parties agreed to a new timetable for the implementation of the salient aspects of the peace agreement, and the Security Council consequently authorized two further extensions to the ONUSAL mandate, first until 30 November 1994 and then 30 April 1995.

On 24 March 1995 the secretary-general reported to the Security Council that the National Police had been successfully demobilized in December the previous year and that thereafter the PNC had taken charge of all security functions in the country. Other aspects of the peace agreement had also been substantially advanced. Since 1 June 1994 there had been a progressive decrease of ONUSAL personnel, during which time the secretary-general had also been preparing other ways to continue UN assistance to El Salvador following the withdrawal of the mission. Thus, on 1 May 1995 a small team of civilian personnel, the United Nations Mission in El Salvador (MINUSAL), stayed on in the country to carry out the UN's remaining observation responsibilities.

The effectiveness of the ONUSAL mission was mixed. The military component of its mandate was completed only after serious setbacks. The armed forces that controlled large parts of the Salvadoran National Police were slow to transfer power to the UN-monitored PNC. Furthermore, although the elections went relatively smoothly on the day, logistical and structural problems prevented a significant proportion of the population from participating. The Human Rights Division did succeed in improving overall observance of human rights through monitoring of the police and judiciary and by reporting violations to the government and international community. However, widespread abuses of human rights continued to occur throughout and after the ONUSAL deployment.

The ONUSAL mission was innovative for a number of reasons. It demonstrated the viability of deploying a UN human rights presence prior to or instead of a military force. The human rights aspect of the mission challenged the very nature of El Salvador's governance and went some way to providing a political voice for Salvadoran citizens. ONUSAL is also an early example of a UN mission operating with the consent of both the government and a substate opposition force (the FMLN); deployment in earlier, more traditional operations had required the consent only of the recognized government. Furthermore, the pursuit of a human rights agenda complicated UN neutrality, since observance of violations often countered

ONUSAL's mediatory role, a problem that affects all missions in circumstances of internal conflict.

The inclusion of human rights issues within the ONUSAL mandate raised their significance to a level meriting a place on the Security Council's agenda, putting them on an equal footing with military issues; prior to the ONUSAL operation, human rights had primarily been the responsibility of the General Assembly.

Last, ONUSAL demonstrated the possibility of sequential deployment dictated by developments on the ground. Even though no cease-fire yet existed in El Salvador, a human rights component was deployed; it was only succeeded by military and police, and then by electoral divisions, as circumstances allowed. Thus, as the opposing parties progressively resolved their differences over specific issues, so relevant UN components were deployed in a series to verify compliance with the relevant agreements, thereby systematically promoting confidence in the peace process as a whole.

ONUSAL's Military Division was headed by Brig. Gen. Victor Suanzes Pardo of Spain. It reached its greatest strength of 368 military observers in February 1992. The authorized strength of the Police Division, headed by Gen. Homero Vaz Bresque, was 631, although this was never actually realized. The strength of both of these divisions was progressively reduced and the peace process was realized. Military observers serving with ONUSAL were provided by Brazil, Canada, Colombia, Ecuador, India, Ireland, Spain, Sweden, and Venezuela, with medical officers also contributed by Argentina and Spain. Police observers were provided by Austria, Brazil, Chile, Colombia, France, Guyana, Italy, Mexico, Spain, and Sweden. The Electoral Division was headed by Rafael López Pintor and normally comprised 36 observers. However, this number increased to 900 during the election periods of 20 March and 24 April 1994. The Human Rights Division was originally led by Philippe Texier, followed by Diego García-Sayán beginning in late 1992, and finally by Reed Broody in 1994. It comprised 30 international civil servants. The ONUSAL operation cost $107,003,650, which was to be met by assessed contributions from UN member states. During the operation there were five UN fatalities: three police observers and two local civilian staff.

See also Child Soldiers; Civilian component in peacekeeping operations; Contadora Group; Human rights; ONUCA; Postconflict reconstruction
References and further reading Costa (1995); International Peacekeeping (1994–); United Nations (1996)

Eliasson, Jan (1940–)

Born in Göteborg, Sweden, on 17 September 1940, Jan Eliasson was a graduate of the Swedish Naval Academy in Stockholm (1962) and earned a master's degree from the School of Economics in Göteborg (1965). He began his diplomatic career in the Foreign Service in 1965, holding positions at the Swedish Ministry for Foreign Affairs as deputy undersecretary for Asian and African affairs (1980–1982), director of the Press and Information Division (1977–1980), executive assistant to the permanent undersecretary of state for foreign affairs (1975–1977), and head of section in the Political Department (1974–1975).

He then served as undersecretary for political affairs in Stockholm (1983–1987), concurrently holding the position of secretary to the Swedish Foreign Policy Advisory Board. Further recognition of his work was followed by appointments as an expert of the Royal Swedish Defence Commission (1984–1986) and as diplomatic adviser in the prime minister's office (1982–1983). His first appointment to the United Nations was as permanent representative to the United Nations (1988), and he also acted as the secretary-general's personal representative (1988–1991) responsible for UN policy concerning the Iran-Iraq war. He has also served as chairman of the General Assembly's working group on emergency relief (1991), vice president of the Economic and Social Council (1991–1992), and chairman of the United Nations Trust Fund for Southern Africa (1988). During the operations to provide humanitarian assistance to Kurds in Iraq, the General Assembly passed Resolution 46/812 of December 1991 seeking to strengthen the coordination of emergency humanitarian assistance within the United Nations. The outcome was the establishment of the new Department of Humanitarian Affairs, headed by Eliasson as undersecretary-general for humanitarian affairs. He is also on the boards of directors of numerous organizations, including the Institute for East-West Security Studies (New York), the International Peace Academy (New York), and the International Association of Permanent Representatives to the United Nations.

See also Special representatives of the secretary-general; United Nations Iran-Iraq Military Observer Group
References and further reading Eliasson (1995); UN Press Release, 14 February 1992

Equipment

Each peacekeeping force needs to be appropriately equipped for its particular task, and the requirements can differ according to the level and objectives of the mission, the location, the terrain, the duration, the time of year, the area to be covered, and so on. Properly equipping its forces is one of the difficulties encountered by the United Nations in launching missions quickly and effectively. The Department of Peacekeeping Operations (DPKO) performs a general assessment of needs at an early stage of a mission, but UN resources do not allow for each mission to be fully and appropriately equipped "off the shelf." Therefore, equipment is provided through one or more of three possible channels:

1. Equipment owned and supplied by the United Nations itself. This kind of equipment usually comprises items such as vehicles, communications, temporary housing, large generators, and so on.
2. Equipment supplied by the contributing country but that will be charged to the United Nations for reimbursement. Such items must be valued when they arrive at mission headquarters and then valued again when the mission ends or the item is scrapped. Payment is usually made over a period of four years, at the end of which time the equipment becomes the outright property of the United Nations.

3. Equipment that is not only owned by the contributing country but that is also necessary for their normal military operations. This equipment is supplied by the contributing country, paid for by their government, and remains their property at the end of the mission.

See also *An Agenda for Peace;* Intelligence support; Logistics; UN Standby Arrangements System

Eritrea

United Nations Observer Mission for the Verification of Elections in Eritrea (ONUVER)

In 1961 Haile Selassie, the then ruler of Ethiopia, annexed the territory of Eritrea and sparked an armed struggle between the central government of Ethiopia and secessionist forces that was to last for 30 years. That war ended in May 1991 with a victory for the independence fighters, and their claim to represent the views of the wider population was put to the test in a referendum in April 1993. The Security Council mandated an Observer Mission to verify the fairness of the elections—which gave an overwhelming vote in favor of independence and which the Observer Mission team adjudged to have been conducted fairly.

Esquipulas II Agreement
See Contadora Group; ONUCA

European Community Monitoring Mission

The European Community Monitoring Mission (ECMM) was established in the very early stages of the war in the former Yugoslavia, which began when Slovenia broke away from Yugoslavia in June 1991. When Slovenia declared its independence, the Yugoslav federal government's military forces, the Yugoslav People's Army (JNA), in Slovenia were surrounded by Slovenian forces in the Ten-Day War that followed the declaration of independence. A series of diplomatic initiatives from the European Community (EC) resulted in the Brioni Talks early in July 1991, which resulted in an agreement calling for a cease-fire and the withdrawal of JNA troops from Slovenia. The task of monitoring the withdrawal of JNA forces was delegated to the EC, which at that time was under the presidency of the Netherlands. The EC put together a mission composed of 150 soldiers, diplomats, and officials from the Conference on Security and Cooperation in Europe (of the CSCE, later the Organization for Security and Cooperation in Europe [OSCE]). In addition, the parties to the conflict insisted on participation by representatives from Canada or the United States, and a Canadian contingent arrived in September 1991.

The terms of the Brioni Agreement led to a Memorandum of Understanding (MOU) signed by Croatia, Slovenia, Yugoslavia, and the EC that established the mandate of the ECMM, which was to secure the cease-fire by lifting the blockade of the JNA, to ensure the return of JNA forces to barracks, and to monitor the suspension of the implementation of independence for three months. The mission area was to be both Slovenia and Croatia, which had also declared independence from Yugoslavia and where fighting had broken out in the summer of 1991 between Croatian forces and Serbian militias with JNA backing. An MOU was then signed between Croatia and Yugoslavia covering the withdrawal of JNA forces from Croatia. ECMM was headquartered in Zagreb, Croatia, with regional centers in Belgrade, Split, and Sarajevo. Although moves were being made late in 1991 to organize the deployment of a UN peacekeeping force, delays and difficulties in organizing this meant that from November 1991 to March 1992 the ECMM was the only peacekeeping or monitoring mission in the disputed areas in Croatia. Following the deployment of the United Nations Protection Force in Former Yugoslavia (UNPROFOR) in the United Nations protected areas (UNPAs) in Croatia, the ECMM became responsible for monitoring the situation in the "pink zones," that is, the areas just outside the UNPAs, which had large Serbian populations and JNA contingents but which were behind Serbian lines. By October 1991 the ECMM was also operating in Bosnia and Herzegovina. By 1994 the ECMM's tasks had evolved to include monitoring and reporting on the political, military, and humanitarian situation; monitoring and reporting violations of the no-fly zone; participating in local confidence-building measures; assisting humanitarian organizations; monitoring the border situations in Hungary, Bulgaria, and Albania; and liaising with the United Nations. There were a number of problems with the organization of the ECMM, including poor communications equipment, especially in the early stages, and confusion over objectives and priorities, especially as direction was prone to change as different European countries took their turns in the European presidency, which rotated every six months. However, there are lessons to be learned from the ECMM's experience: The ECMM teams were small, and the monitoring work they carried out was decentralized and capable of forming an accurate picture of the situation at the local level. However, the coordinating structures to effectively transmit the information gathered were not well developed, and the role of the ECMM in the broader peacekeeping mission was not well understood or well integrated.

See also Croatia; United Nations Protection Force in Former Yugoslavia
References and further reading Maloney (1997)

European Union

The European Union (EU) is slowly developing a role for international conflict management within its foreign policy, which is termed its common foreign and security policy (CFSP). Initially the countries of the European Union did not take a common position on defense and foreign policy, but the beginnings of a common approach can be dated to 1969 when the European Political Cooperation (EPC) was started. This initiative was prompted by the need to reach a common position in responding to conflict in the Middle East, in the hope that a common European view would influence Middle Eastern states involved in conflict. However, EPC was a process of intergovernmental consultation between member states and not an autonomous activity of the European Commission (the EU's administrative and policy arm). The Single European Act provided a recognized legal role for EPC in that it required EU member states to consult each other on foreign policy issues. Under the Treaty of Maastricht (1991) the EU and the Commission were given a stronger role in guiding a collective European foreign policy. EPU was transformed to become the CFSP, and the treaty committed the EU to strengthening peace in Europe and to promoting peacekeeping and peacemaking. The wars in Yugoslavia presented an early and dramatic test of the feasibility and coherence of the new CFSP, and the EU responded firmly in an effort to stop war from breaking out. The EU launched a peacemaking initiative aimed at negotiating peace treaties between the Yugoslav states, and appointed Lord Peter Carrington as their negotiator. The European Community Monitoring Mission (ECMM) was dispatched in July 1991 to assist with negotiations between Croatia and Serbia. It was the first peacekeeping mission deployed to the Balkans and predated UN peacekeeping forces there by ten months. However, none of this prevented the violent breakup of the Yugoslav Federation. Many felt that the European initiative had failed because the EU was unable to back up its position with the capability to use force to maintain cease-fires and enforce a settlement between Serbia and Croatia in the early stages of the war. Britain and France requested the intervention of UN peacekeeping in 1992. In the later stages of the conflict, the roles of the North Atlantic Treaty Organization (NATO), and of U.S. influence, proved decisive in reaching a settlement in the Dayton Accords. The effect of the Yugoslav wars on thinking within the European Commission has been to raise the idea that a common foreign policy for the EU, certainly in relation to Yugoslavia, was hampered by the different interests of the main member states, by the absence of an early warning and early response mechanisms, and by the lack of any credible threat to use military force to back policy. Moves toward the possible future use of force were taken when France and Germany (later joined by Luxembourg, Belgium, and Spain) formed the Eurocorps, a two-division force that was to be put at the disposal of NATO or the Western European Union. The EU has not assembled a peacekeeping force, but the Eurocorps may provide the basis for one in the future. Article J7 of the new Union treaty, signed at Amsterdam in 1997, strengthened the idea of a common defense policy and provided a role for the Western European Union in the so-called Petersburg Tasks (that is, in undertaking humanitarian missions and in peacekeeping and the use of armed forces in crisis management). The Amsterdam Treaty also called for a policy planning and early warning unit to monitor the CFSP, and to provide assessment and early warning of potential crises.

See also Macedonia; Rwanda; United Nations Protection Force in Former Yugoslavia, Western European Union

References and further reading Bryer and Eavis (1996)

Field Administration and Logistics Division, UN
See Logistics; United Nations: organization

Field Manual 100-23
See U.S. peacekeeping

Financing peacekeeping
There are two basic budget levels within the United Nations: the regular budget and the peacekeeping budget. The general budget of the United Nations is approved by the General Assembly, under article 17, paragraphs 1 and 2 of the UN Charter. Member states of the United Nations are billed on 1 January of each year according to a scale of assessment that is based on member states' gross domestic product. However, many states do not pay their dues on time. Article 19 of the UN Charter stipulates that a state that is in arrears for two years in its regular contributions can lose its vote in the General Assembly. This became a crisis over assessments for early operations such as the first United Nations Emergency Force (UNEF I) when some states, including France and the Soviet Union, refused to pay their assessments, and the Soviet Union threatened to withdraw from the United Nations. The crisis was resolved when it was decided that states in arrears could decide not to pay for UN actions in operations with which they disagreed. In 1992, for example, the United Nations was owed $500 million in arrears, which was equivalent to 42 percent of the budget for that year. In general UN peacekeeping operations are not financed from the regular UN budget, though the costs of peacekeeping are considered mandatory expenses of the organization, to be paid by member states. Each peacekeeping operation is funded through its own separate budget. The standard practice for financing peacekeeping was established with the authorization of UNEF I in 1956, when the General Assembly decided that expenses for UNEF I would be provided outside the regular UN budget, and a special account was established. Some missions, however, have been funded through the regular

UN budget because they are military observer missions (such as the United Nations Truce Supervision Organization [UNTSO], the United Nations Observation Group in Lebanon [UNOGIL], the United Nations Military Observer Group in India and Pakistan [UNMOGIP] and India-Pakistan Observer Mission [UNIPOM], and the United Nations Good Offices Mission in Afghanistan and Pakistan [UNGOMAP]), which cost much less than full-scale peacekeeping operations. Other operations, such as the United Nations Yemen Observer Mission (UNYOM) and the United Nations Temporary Executive Authority (UNTEA)/United Nations Security Force in West New Guinea (UNSF), were funded by the parties on whose behalf the mission was deployed (Egypt and Saudi Arabia for UNYOM, and the Netherlands and Indonesia for UNTEA/UNSF).

General Assembly Resolution 1874 (S-IV) of June 1963 defined general principles to serve as guidelines for sharing the financial burden of future peacekeeping operations: The financing of such operations is a collective responsibility of all member states; member states should also be encouraged to make voluntary contributions; and economically less developed countries have a limited capacity to make contributions, whereas the special responsibilities of the permanent members of the Security Council for peace and security imply a fuller responsibility for financing peacekeeping.

In 1973, with the establishment of UNEF II, the financial mechanism that became the model for all subsequent peacekeeping operations was defined. General Assembly Resolution 3101 (XXVIII) requested the secretary-general to open a special account into which the full costs of the force would be appropriated, according to a graded scale of contributions from member states: 63.15 percent was to be paid by the five permanent members of the Security Council (Group A: the United States, the United Kingdom, France, China, and the Soviet Union, now Russia); 34.78 percent was to be paid by economically developed states that were not permanent members of the Security Council (Group B); 2.02 percent was to be paid by states that were economically less developed (Group C); and 0.05 percent was to be paid by the least economically developed states (Group D). This method of assessment means that nearly all peacekeeping expenses are met by the developed states in groups A and B, and in fact differentials in group A mean that the largest contribution (currently 31.73 percent of the total, though reducing to 25 percent) is met by the United States. The combined contribution of the three European members of the Security Council (the United Kingdom, France, and Russia) plus Germany amounts to 31.36 percent of the total assessment for peacekeeping. In most operations established since UNEF II, the UNEF II model of financing is applied, and a special account is established based on article 17, paragraph 2 of the UN Charter; and in each case reference is also made to the principles elaborated in General Assembly Resolution 1874.

The major financial problem for peacekeeping is that there is a large deficit resulting from the very high level of unpaid contributions, and that there are inadequate reserves of working capital. As a result, very few peacekeeping operations can begin after they have been approved by the Security Council. The Secretariat must first prepare a mission budget, which can take many weeks, and the budget must then be submitted to the Advisory Committee on Administrative and Budgetary Questions (ACABQ). When the mission budget is approved by the ACABQ, it then has to be approved by the General Assembly's Fifth Committee and then by the General Assembly, following which an assessment letter is sent to member states. This process adds to the difficulties of mobilizing troops and moving them quickly to the area of operation. Various proposals have been made concerning the reform of financing arrangements for peacekeeping. In 1992 a Peacekeeping Reserve Fund was established by the General Assembly under Resolution 47/217, at a level of $150 million, and there has been a suggestion to establish a United Nations Peace Endowment Fund with an initial target level of $1 billion, to finance the initial costs of authorized peacekeeping operations and other conflict-resolution activities. A report commissioned by the Ford Foundation and published in 1993 criticized the present method of requesting contributions for each individual operation and recommended a unified budget for peacekeeping to which member states would contribute an amount to cover all foreseen operations. The need for more financial resources for peacekeeping is clear and was emphasized by Brian Urquhart, who said that, compared to the costs of war, peacekeeping is inexpensive.

See also Costs of peacekeeping
References and further reading
Cleveland, Henderson, and Kaul (1995); McDermott (1994); Siekman (1993)

Finland

Finland, like the other three Nordic countries (Norway, Denmark, and Sweden), has traditionally seen peacekeeping as a positive element of its security policy, committed to the multilateral management of international conflict. The changes in the security environment in the 1990s have caused important revisions to Finland's policy and to the role of peacekeeping within it. In the 1990s Finland formed links with European security organizations (becoming an observer at the Western European Union [WEU] in 1995), and, in addition to its traditional support for the United Nations, a European dimension has been added to its policy on international conflict management. In 1993 the Ministry of Defense conducted a review in order to consider what changes needed to be made to Finland's peacekeeping law of 1984 in order to accommodate the new demands of the multifunctional missions launched by the United Nations in the 1990s. The result was a proposal to improve the existing UN standby system to prepare for Finnish participation in the new operations. In order to facilitate this, various improvements in training, organization, and equipment were called for. The proposals resulted in considerable controversy within Finland because there was a feeling that Finland did not have the military capability to become involved in complicated conflicts and crises beyond its borders. In the former Yugoslavia, Finland preferred to contribute to the preventive deployment in Macedonia rather than to the joint Nordic battalion attached to the United Nations Protection Force in Former Yugoslavia (UNPROFOR) in Bosnia. However, Finland joined the Partnership for Peace program of the North Atlantic Treaty Organization (NATO) in 1994 and accepted the need for a more robust role for its armed forces within a European security framework. In 1995 there were proposals for a new rapid-deployment force, better trained and better equipped than the existing UN standby force. Once again the idea met with considerable opposition because of fears that the new force would lead Finland into operations beyond traditional peacekeeping, that it would be too costly, that it would result in the emergence of a standing army, and that it was also a move toward NATO membership for Finland. Nevertheless, the Finnish parliament approved the new rapid-reaction force, which is to have both national defense and international peacekeeping tasks, in June 1996.

See also Nordic countries; Training for peacekeeping; Troop-contributing countries
References and further reading Karhilo (1996)

First-generation peacekeeping

The UN-mandated peacekeeping operations that were deployed in the Cold War period, broadly between the deployment of the first United Nations Emergency Force (UNEF I) in 1956 and the deployment of the United Nations Transitional Assistance Group (UNTAG) in Namibia in 1988, are usually described as "traditional," "classical," or "first-generation" peacekeeping. The United Nations defines peacekeeping as "an operation in-

volving military personnel, but without enforcement powers, undertaken by the United Nations to help maintain or restore international peace and security in areas of conflict."

UNEF provided a precedent for other UN forces: the United Nations Disengagement Observer Force (UNDOF) was established in May 1974 following the outbreak of war between Israel and Egypt around the Sinai and the Suez Canal and between Israel and Syria on the Golan Heights. The United Nations Interim Force in Lebanon (UNIFIL) was established in March 1978 to confirm the withdrawal of Israeli forces from Lebanon and to assist the Lebanese government in ensuring the return of effective authority. In 1964, following the outbreak of violence between Greek and Turkish Cypriot communities after Cyprus became independent from Britain, the UN Peacekeeping Force in Cyprus (UNFICYP) was established. UNFICYP continues to patrol and monitor a cease-fire line and buffer zone that extends across the island.

Several additional operations were established during the Cold War period. These included the United Nations Observation Group in Lebanon (UNOGIL), the United Nations Temporary Executive Authority (UNTEA)/United Nations Security Force in West New Guinea (UNSF), the United Nations Yemen Observer Mission (UNYOM), the Representative of the Secretary-General in the Dominican Republic (DOMREP), the United Nations India-Pakistan Observer Mission (UNIPOM), and UNEF II involving Egypt and Israel. With the exception of the United Nations Operation in the Congo (ONUC), all of these were first-generation missions.

Together the 13 operations established during the Cold War (five of which are still deployed today) gradually nurtured the development of a body of principles, procedures, and practices that are still applied to contemporary peacekeeping, although many argue that the missions deployed since 1988 (the so-called second-generation peacekeeping operations) need to operate under modified rules and principles. Secretary-General Dag Hammarskjöld and Lester B. Pearson (General Assembly president, 1952–1953) defined the principles as follows: (1) the principle of the consent of the parties to the dispute for the establishment of the mission; (2) the principle of nonuse of force except in self-defense; (3) the principle of voluntary contributions of contingents from small, neutral countries to participate in the force; (4) the principle of impartiality; (5) the principle of control of peacekeeping operations by the secretary-general. Traditional deployments were usually made of contingents provided by selected countries, normally not from the five permanent members of the Security Council and normally selected to ensure some diversity in geographical representation. They were lightly armed and used force only in self-defense. Their presence is supervisory, and they do not have a mandate or capability to enforce compliance or to restore order. Their military tasks are to observe, monitor, and supervise agreements.

Wiseman has identified five separate phases in the development of traditional peacekeeping: (1) the nascent phase, 1946–1956, during which the foundations were laid; (2) the assertive phase, 1956–1967, when force-level missions were deployed and principles and precedents were established; UN civilian police (CIVPOL) were used for the first time in this period in the UN Peacekeeping Force in Cyprus (UNFICYP); (3) a dormant phase, 1967–1973, during which no new operations were mandated, largely because of the use of the veto and because each superpower dominated its own sphere of interests; (4) a resurgent phase, 1973–1978, when three new force-level operations were established in the Middle East; and (5) a period of maintenance, 1978–1988, when no new operations were established. After 1988 a new period of second-generation operations began to be defined, marked by the cooperation of the superpowers, by an increasing tendency to operate in conflicts with internal dimensions, and by the setting of new precedents that challenged the nonintervention principle and expanded the mandate of peacekeeping operations to undertake political and humanitarian tasks.

See also Second-generation peacekeeping
References and further reading James (1990); Wiseman (1983)

Force commanders

The force commander takes military command of a force-level peacekeeping mission, whereas an observer mission is headed by a chief military observer. The force commander is a key member in the chain of command and is appointed by the secretary-general. The person appointed is normally from a noninvolved nation, and the appointment is subject to agreement by the governments of the combatant states. The force commander may also be designated head of mission, but this post is more often filled by a special representative of the secretary-general.

See also Appendix 1 for a list of UN Force Commanders; Chain of Command

Force Mobile Reserve

The Force Mobile Reserve originated in Lebanon in 1987 as part of the restructuring of the United Nations Interim Force in Lebanon (UNIFIL). Before the restructuring each separate contingent had provided whatever level of reserve support it thought it needed. In 1987 the mission structure was reorganized to supply a permanent core of support troops to provide central reconnaissance and other intelligence and also emergency support for any part of the operation. The Force Mobile Reserve (FMR) is thus charged with maintaining one platoon on instant alert at all times and with being able to reach any location within the UNIFIL area within one hour.

France

France has been an active and influential contributor to UN peacekeeping. Its earliest involvement was with the UN Special Commission on the Balkans, to which military observers were deployed between 1947 and 1954, and with the Commission on Indonesia, deployed from 1947 to 1951. French military observers also served with the United Nations Truce Supervision Organization (UNTSO) in the Middle East beginning in 1948 and with the United Nations Iraq-Kuwait Observer Mission (UNIKOM) in Kuwait. French police units (gendarmes) served with the United Nations Observer Group for the Verification of Elections in Haiti (ONUVEH) and with the United Nations Observer Mission in El Salvador (ONUSAL). A French battalion formed a part of the UN Forces in the Korean War, and military units were subsequently sent to the United Nations Interim Force in Lebanon (UNIFIL), to the United Nations Advance Mission (UNAMIC) and the United Nations Transitional Authority (UNTAC) in Cambodia, to the United Nations Mission for the Referendum in Western Sahara (MINURSO), to the Unified Task Force (UNITAF) in Somalia, and to the United Nations Protection Force in Former Yugoslavia (UNPROFOR) in Croatia and Bosnia. France has also participated in non-UN operations, including the Multinational Force and Observers in the Sinai (from 1982 onward), the Multinational Forces in Beirut (1982–1984), the Military Observers in Beirut (1984–1986), and the Western European Union (WEU) maritime operations in the Persian Gulf (1988 and 1990) and the Adriatic Sea (1993). French, Belgian, and German troops are also integrated in Eurocorps.

French policy toward peacekeeping has been affected in the 1990s by efforts to develop a form of humanitarian diplomacy, which would include a "duty to interfere" in humanitarian emergencies. This idea, in its contemporary form, dates back to the Nigerian Civil War of 1967–1970, when Bernard Kouchner formed the humanitarian organization Médecins sans Frontières to provide humanitarian assistance to victims of conflict. Kouchner was concerned that matters of state sovereignty and the international norm of nonintervention in the internal affairs of states should not impede the delivery of such assistance. France subsequently, in pursuit of this policy of the right to interfere, originated resolutions in the General Assembly in support of establishing humanitarian corridors to provide access to victims of conflict. France contributed the largest contingent—6,300 troops deployed in 1993—to UNPROFOR in Bosnia and Herzegovina and in Croatia. When Gen. Jean Cot took command of UNPROFOR, France became one of the first of the five permanent members of the Security Council (along with the United Kingdom, in the UN Peacekeeping Force in Cyprus [UNFICYP]) to send a general to command a UN Force. France proposed the creation of the "safe areas" in the former Yugoslavia, which were then established in Sarajevo, Bihać, Tuzla, Zepa, Gorazde, and Srebrenica under UN Security Council Resolution (SCR) 824 (of 1993). In 1992 France was the largest overall contributor to UN peacekeeping, and in 1994 it was the second-largest contributor, behind Pakistan. In June 1994, under SCR 929, France initiated a humanitarian operation in Rwanda, Operation Turquoise, that lasted until August 1994. In the 1990s, therefore, France was active in peacekeeping and eager to support its reform and enhancement. In September 1993 it proposed the establishment of a UN standby force and offered to provide a 1,000-strong contingent deployable within 48 hours. The French army has recently considerably improved the training provided for its peacekeeping forces, and France has cooperated with the United Kingdom in a policy to help African countries build up their peacekeeping forces in an Anglo-French Peacekeeping Initiative.

See also European Union; Humanitarian intervention
References and further reading Guillot (1994); McNulty (1997)

General Assembly
See United Nations: organization

Geneva Conventions and the laws of war

The international humanitarian law of armed conflict is part of public international law and is defined by the International Committee of the Red Cross as international rules, established by treaties or custom, that are specifically intended to solve humanitarian problems directly arising from international or noninternational armed conflicts.

A traditional distinction is usually made between the following items:

1. The law of The Hague (the law of war) covers the reciprocal rights and duties of combatants.
2. The law of Geneva (humanitarian law) aims to protect military personnel who are hors de combat (out of combat), such as prisoners or the wounded, and civilian noncombatants. Geneva law, initiated by the 1864 Geneva Convention, is based on universal principles of humanity.

In addition to Hague and Geneva law, two further strands of international humanitarian law are sometimes distinguished:

3. Nuremberg Law embodies judgments from the Nuremberg and Tokyo International Military Tribunals of 1946 and 1947.
4. Humanitarian law may also derive from other sources, including national military field manuals, such as the enlightened Lieber code (1865) in the United States.

The evolution of Geneva law began in 1864, when a diplomatic conference held in Geneva led to 12 European countries signing the first Geneva Convention. In 1899 maritime warfare was brought within the principles of the Geneva Convention. In 1906 the original convention of 1864 was revised, and there was a further revision in 1929. By 1949 Geneva law was expressed in the Four Geneva Conventions (now adopted by 181 states):

Convention I: For the amelioration of the condition of the wounded and sick in armed forces in the field.

Convention II: For the amelioration of the condition of wounded, sick, and shipwrecked members of armed forces at sea.

Convention III: Relative to the treatment of prisoners of war.

Convention IV: Relative to the protection of civilians in time of war.

In 1977 two additional protocols were agreed upon. Protocol I relates to the protection of victims of international armed conflicts. Protocol II relates to the protection of victims of noninternational armed conflicts. The Zagreb Resolution of 1971 dealt with the application of the humanitarian rules of armed conflict to UN forces. Though military forces normally claim to be knowledgeable about the laws of war, few are aware of the implications of Protocols I and II and of associated refugee and human rights law. This issue, and the related issue of the arrest and punishment of war criminals, became of increasing importance for peacekeeping in the light of experiences in the former Yugoslavia and in Rwanda, when International War Crimes tribunals were set up.

See also Child soldiers; Civilians in conflict zones; Demilitarized zone; Humanitarian assistance

References and further reading
MacInnis (1996); McCoubrey and White (1996); Ramsbotham and Woodhouse (1996b); Rogers (1996); Sandoz (1997)

Georgia

United Nations Observer Mission in Georgia (UNOMIG), 1993–

Conflict Profile

The conflict in Georgia developed as a part of the disintegration of the Soviet Union during the late 1980s. Abkhazia is a region of north Georgia, inhabited by a large Abkhazian minority. The lessening of Soviet control of its satellite territories encouraged secessionist ideals among Abkhazians living in Abkhazia, which had always enjoyed a certain degree of autonomy. In April 1991 the Georgian declaration of independence led the Abkhazian leadership to make similar demands, and Abkhazian secessionist ideals were further inflamed by the highly chauvinist attitude of the Georgian leadership of the time, whose motto was "Georgia for the Georgians." However, Tbilisi vehemently repudiated Abkhazian demands, particularly after the nationalist leader Zviad Gamasakhurdia came to power in Georgia in 1990. In March 1992 Gamasakhurdia was replaced as the Georgian head of state by Eduard Shevardnadze, who promoted a more moderate, pluralist policy and attempted to be more accommodating to the requirements of Georgian minority groups. However, by the middle of 1992, Abkhazian dissatisfaction had, with Russian military support, evolved into violent, armed confrontation with the Georgian authorities, and in response, 2,000 government troops were dispatched to subjugate the dissenters. In September the Russian Federation brokered a cease-fire between the opposing parties. The terms of the agreement guaranteed the sovereignty of the Republic of Georgia and covered such issues as demilitarizing illegal armed factions, reducing the strength of the Georgian armed forces in Abkhazia, and exchanging prisoners of war. It also incorporated provisions for the establishment of a Monitoring and Inspection Commission, comprising Abkhazians, Georgian, and Russian representatives, to verify compliance with the terms of the agreement. However, the agreement was never fully realized, and on 1 October 1992 open hostilities between the opposing forces resumed. In 1993, largely because of Russian military assistance, Abkhazian forces defeated the Georgian government forces, and by 27 July a second Russian-brokered settlement had been reached, reestablishing the cease-fire and securing de facto independence for Abkhazia.

Several factors led to international intervention in the Abkhazian conflict. In the first place, there was international concern over the humanitarian element of the conflict, as the instability in Abkhazia had often adopted ethnic dimensions. Both parties to the conflict were pursuing primarily nationalist policies, and it was reported that widespread incidents of ethnic cleansing and human rights abuses had resulted in the creation of considerable numbers of refugees and displaced persons. In terms of international political motivation, Moscow wished to demonstrate its control of its former territories to the international community and wished to bring Georgia back within its sphere of influence, and so it was keen to see secure conditions returned to the country. Similarly, the Georgian authorities sought international respect and approval, and they also wanted to protect the integrity of their state. Furthermore, Georgia desperately needed Russian military and financial aid in order to reverse the country's severe political, economic, and security problems, which the war was worsening. The international community, in general, was wary of further instability within the former Soviet Union, and Abkhazians, who needed Russian support, were to a large extent subject to the authority of Moscow.

Deployment of UNOMIG

On 24 August 1993 the Security Council adopted Security Council Resolution (SCR) 858, by which it established the United Nations Observer Mission in Georgia (UNOMIG). The UN force was to comprise 88 military observers and was mandated to monitor compliance with the cease-fire. However, by 16 September the cease-fire had again broken down, prompting the Security Council to suspend current operations and any further deployment of UNOMIG until agreement could again be reached. Although in May 1994 discussions between the opposing parties again led to the achievement of formal conditions for an agreement on a cease-fire and the separation of forces, insufficient support from UN member states prevented an accord within the Security Council for the establishment of a UN peacekeeping force large enough for the intended operation. Therefore the international community accepted the offer by the Commonwealth of Independent States (CIS) to deploy its own peacekeeping force to monitor compliance with the agreement. The CIS force was deployed in the Gali area of Abkhazia, and a number of CIS peacekeepers were also stationed along the Abkhazian-Georgian border to prevent the outbreak of hostilities. On 21 July 1994 the Security Council adopted SCR 937, by which UNOMIG's strength was increased to 136 military observers and its mandate was expanded to include monitoring the terms of the agreement, monitoring the operation of the CIS peacekeeping force, and investigating and attempting to resolve violations of the agreement.

The deployment of CIS peacekeepers to Abkhazia had a number of effects on political relationships between the protagonists in the Georgian conflict, primarily through securing Tbilisi's compliance with Moscow's wishes and, consequently, marking the end of Russian support for Abkhazia. Such an outcome was potentially disastrous for the Abkhazian cause, and indeed, Abkhazian interests were subsequently largely ignored during negotiations between Moscow and Tbilisi. Russian military bases were established in Georgia, including in the Abkhazian town of Gudauta—a decision in which the Abkhazian authorities were not consulted—and Russian trade routes were reinstated in the country. Georgian accession to Moscow's demands was secured through Russian agreement to recognize central Georgian jurisdiction over the whole of Georgia.

Practical and political measures were also employed to induce Abkhazian compliance with a settlement. Both Georgia and Russia set up a de facto land blockade around Abkhazia, by which Moscow and Tbilisi controlled all traffic in and out of the territory. In 1984 Moscow threatened to withdraw its peacekeepers, a daunting prospect for Abkhazia now that it no longer enjoyed Russian patronage. Moscow further threatened to increase military assistance to Tbilisi in the event of continued Abkhazian intransigence. Meanwhile, the Abkhazian authorities complained that the CIS peacekeeping troops consisted of predominantly Russian Transcaucasus forces, who were estimated to comprise 80 percent Georgian nationals.

Although the parties had largely complied with the terms of the agreement, a severe political setback to peace occurred in November 1994 when the Abkhazian leadership declared Abkhazia to be a sovereign democratic state. In response to a complaint from Tbilisi, the Security Council condemned the proclamation and reaffirmed the territorial integrity of the Republic of Georgia. Despite the resultant impasse in the political process, the Security Council recommended the continued presence of the CIS peacekeeping force in the area and extended the UNOMIG mandate in order to maintain stability in the area in the interest of facilitating negotiations between the two sides.

However, the political stalemate continued, primarily over the status of Abkhazia within the Republic of Georgia. Abkhazia had backed down from its previous demands for total independence and now sought a confederate agreement with Tbilisi that would recognize its sovereign status within a loose but commensurate union between the two entities. Georgia, in return, had offered a certain level of independence to Abkhazia, but disagreements still remained over the details of the relationship. Meanwhile, both Georgia and Abkhazia criticized UNOMIG: Georgia for the lack of progress in the repatriation of Georgian refugees to Abkhazia, and Abkhazia over continued breaches by armed elements into UNOMIG's area of operation.

Presidential and parliamentary elections in Georgia in 1995 returned Shevardnadze to power, and the end of the year witnessed the further cementing of Georgia's relationship with Moscow in the form of mutually beneficial bilateral agreements. At the same time, negotiations between Abkhazia and Georgia under Russian mediation led to a draft outline for a settlement to the conflict, which provided for the establishment of an Abkhaz Republic with its own constitution, legislature, government, military, and budget; a joint Abkhazian-Georgian government and legislature, in which Abkhazia was guaranteed a number of seats and veto powers; a common currency; and a combined defense policy, including provisions for the aggregation of the two entities' military forces.

However, more extreme elements within both parties' leaderships objected to certain aspects of the protocol. Georgians were worried by the continued existence of the Abkhazian army and the potential for further instability that this implied in the event of subsequent disputes between the two parties. They also objected to refusals to guarantee the unopposed return of some 200,000 Georgian refugees to Abkhazia and pushed for the issue to be included as part of the combined CIS/UN peacekeeping mandate. Abkhazians, on the other hand, have complained that the Gali district—where, they claim, large numbers of Georgian refugees have in fact returned unofficially—remains distinctly unstable.

Regional and international involvement in the dispute has had contradictory effects on the potential outcome of the Georgian conflict. On the one hand, CIS intervention has helped to temper the political hegemony of the Russian-Georgian alliance over the Abkhazians. For instance, combined Georgian-Russian demands for sanctions against Abkhazia at the CIS summit in January 1996 were rejected by the other CIS member states. Furthermore, though authorizing the extension of the CIS peacekeeping mandate in Abkhazia, CIS unwillingness to promote Georgian and Russian interests led its members to refuse to broaden the mandate to include provisions for police functions and the verification of refugee returns. Also, in October 1996 the Security Council adopted SCR 1077, by which it authorized the establishment of a human rights office as part of UNOMIG. By mid-1997 a political resolution to the Abkhazian dispute had still not been concluded, although direct negotiations toward this end continued between the two parties.

UNOMIG headquarters are in Sukhumi, Abkhazia. The chief military observer is Maj. Gen. Harun Ar-Rashid (Bangladesh), and Liviu Bota (Romania) is the special representative of the secretary-general. The strength of the mission, as of 31 December 1997, was 106 military observers, supported by international and local civilian staff, and military personnel were contributed by Albania, Austria, Bangladesh, the Czech Republic, Denmark, Egypt, France, Germany, Greece, Hungary, Indonesia, Jordan, Pakistan, Poland, Republic of Korea, Russian Federation, Sweden, Switzerland, Turkey, the United Kingdom, the United States, and Uruguay. UNOMIG costs are met by assessed contributions from member states of the United Nations, and the estimated expenditure for the operation from 7 August 1993 to 30 June 1996 was $30,742,460.

See also   Commonwealth of Independent States; Russian peacekeeping
References and further reading
International Peacekeeping (1994–); United Nations (1996)

Germany

Germany is not a permanent member of the Security Council, but it is the third-largest contributor to the UN budget (providing 8.93 percent of the general budget and 8.87 percent of the peacekeeping budget). Since reunification Germany has wanted a permanent member seat but is aware that this would involve taking on responsibilities for peacekeeping, an issue that Germany has debated since the 1970s. Since the foundation of the modern German state in 1949, and after the inevitable mistrust of German militarism following World War II, there has been a broad consensus both inside and outside Germany that German armed forces should not be deployed abroad. This position was reinforced by interpretations of the German Basic Law, whose article 87 limits the use of the German armed forces. The German constitution was thus interpreted to prevent any deployment of troops outside the North Atlantic Treaty Organization (NATO) area of operation. As in Japan, the ending of the Cold War and the impact of the Gulf War in 1991 changed the situation, and Germany was encouraged by the major powers to participate in peacekeeping, even if this did mean deploying its troops abroad. The German government responded to this encouragement and took the view that there was a legal basis for participation in peacekeeping based on article 24 of the Basic Law, which allowed for the possibility of German participation in systems of collective security. Germany had participated minimally in peacekeeping without attracting political opposition in Germany, as in 1989 when volunteers from the Federal Border Guard served in the United Nations Transitional Assistance Group (UNTAG) mission in Namibia and in 1993 when medical personnel served in Cambodia. However, the German government increased the level of German activity in peacekeeping significantly through its decision to contribute to three missions in the 1990s. The first was the decision to deploy naval units in the NATO/Western European Union (WEU) naval operation that monitored compliance with the UN arms embargo against the Federal Republic of Yugoslavia. The second was German participation in monitoring the ban on flights guaranteed by NATO in the airspace over Bosnia and Herzegovina. Third, the German government decided to approve the participation of 1,700 German troops in the second United Nations Operation in Somalia (UNOSOM II). As a result of these decisions, opposition groups in the German parliament challenged government policy before the Constitutional Court, arguing that the decisions were in breach of the Basic Law and that they violated the right of the parliament to be involved in the decision-making process. On 12 July 1994 the Constitutional Court declared that participation in these three peacekeeping operations was not unconstitutional (adding, however, that the government should have sought the approval of the parliament). A German Army Composite Force served in Somalia under the command of Brig. Gen. H. Harff during 1993. Future German contributions to peacekeeping should take place within a multilateral framework, that is, as a contribution to and with a mandate from international organizations such as the United Nations or the Organization for Security and Cooperation in Europe (OSCE). It is also unlikely that Germany will provide large numbers of troops, but it is well placed to provide support in the form of airlifts, logistical and telecommunications equipment, and generally in the areas of transport, medicine, and police. In the former Yugoslavia, for example, Germany provided the bulk of the equipment for the Pakistani contingent (armored personnel carriers, trucks, ammunition, and winter clothing). Germany also agreed to participate in the Implementation Force under the Dayton Agreement with a military contingent of about 4,000 troops to monitor the peace process in Bosnia.

See also European Union; Financing peacekeeping
References and further reading Asmus (1995); Kummel (1994); Tercinet (1998)

Golan Heights
See UNDOF

Goulding, Marrack (1936–)

Born on 2 September 1936, Marrack Goulding graduated with a first-class honors degree in literature and humanities from Magdalen College, Oxford, in 1959, following which he joined the British Foreign Service. As of 1998 he was patron of the Foreign Policy Center and warden of Saint Anthony's College, Oxford (since 1997). He served as private secretary to the minister of state for foreign and Commonwealth affairs (1972–1975). In 1979 he was counselor and head of Chancery at the UK delegation to the United Nations, while at the same time serving as the alternate representative on the Security Council. He was president of the Trusteeship Council from 1981 to 1982. He was UK ambassador to Angola and São Tomé and Principe between 1983 and 1985. In 1986 he became undersecretary-general of special political affairs and undertook a number of special missions on behalf of the secretary-general in the Middle East, the former Yugoslavia, and Central America. During this period he was in charge of UN peacekeeping, overseeing 13 operations. From 1993 to 1997 he served as undersecretary-general for political affairs.

References and further reading Goulding (1993, 1996); *Who's Who 1998*

Greece

United Nations Special Committee on the Balkans (UNSCOB), 1947

Conflict Profile
During World War II, as a result of the occupation of Greece by the Axis powers, the right-wing Greek

government was forced into exile in Britain. Britain had supported the Greek Communist underground resistance movement, the National Liberation Front (EAM). However, when a rival, non-Communist group emerged in 1943 the British government switched its support to it. In 1944 the opposing parties managed briefly to form a Government of National Unity, but it was not long before the EAM had abandoned the coalition, and British troops arriving in Greece in the same year found themselves fighting both the Germans and the Communists. A series of military defeats forced the Communists into the north of the country, where support from the new Communist regimes in Albania, Bulgaria, and Yugoslavia boosted their campaign.

The Greek conflict presented one of the first cases to be addressed by the newly formed United Nations and helped to establish the bipolar political agenda of the Cold War. The Soviet Union wished to present its own version of events in Greece before the United Nations, and so early in 1946 it complained that the presence of British troops in Greece represented interference in the internal affairs of a sovereign state, in reference to the principle of noninterference, which was one of the mainstays of the UN Charter. The United States and the United Kingdom, on the other hand, were eager to expose the behavior of Greece's Communist neighbors.

Deployment of UNSCOB

The Soviet Union vetoed a U.S. proposal on 24 August to dispatch a UN Commission of Investigation to Greece to look into reports of violent incidents along its northern border. However, a direct complaint from the Greek government later convinced the Soviet Union to accede to the proposal. Unsurprisingly, the subsequent mission early in 1947 confirmed that Greek Communist opposition fighters were indeed receiving Albanian, Bulgarian, and Yugoslavian support. The Soviet Union therefore questioned the validity of the reports and continued to veto further proposed actions by the Security Council. This provided the opportunity for the United States to introduce what became known as the Truman Doctrine, which pledged to provide assistance to any free govern-

ment that was being threatened by external or internal forces. Consequently, the issue was successfully transferred to the General Assembly, which was at the time biased toward the West and in which no nation had veto powers. Thus, on 27 October 1947 the General Assembly authorized the deployment of the United Nations Special Committee on the Balkans (UNSCOB).

UNSCOB was mandated to verify compliance by the four nations involved (Albania, Bulgaria, Yugoslavia, and Greece) to the following conditions: Albania, Bulgaria, and Yugoslavia would cease assistance to the Greek opposition; the four nations would inclusively pursue a peaceful settlement to the dispute; border conventions would be established; and the four nations would cooperate over refugee repatriation. It was intended that personnel contributions for UNSCOB would come from the then eleven members of the Security Council. However, both Poland and the USSR refused, and so UNSCOB actually comprised Australia, Brazil, China, France, Mexico, the Netherlands, Pakistan, the United Kingdom, and the United States. Albania, Bulgaria, and Yugoslavia, for obvious reasons, also opposed a mission that would counter their interests and so refused to allow UNSCOB to operate on their territory. Therefore the commission's area of operation was confined to Greece, severely restricting its ability to fulfill its mandate.

Following the deployment of UNSCOB, opposition activity in the north of Greece progressively declined and relations between the four countries involved steadily improved. However, it is unclear to what extent the commission was responsible for this. Improvement in the Greek economy and armed forces accounted for military victories against the opposition fighters. Furthermore, disagreements with the Soviet Union persuaded Yugoslavia to end its support for the Greek opposition and to open diplomatic relations with Greece. In 1950, commensurate with the decline in opposition activity, UNSCOB was able to scale down from 35 to 24 observers, and late in 1951 the commission was withdrawn. In 1952 the United Nations dispatched the Peace Observer Commission to check on the situation in the area, but a lack of incidents to report on led to its withdrawal in 1953.

The UNSCOB mission was significant for a number of reasons. It was the first UN observer mission to be deployed in a situation of continuing armed conflict. It also helped establish the bipolar context of political relations that was to dictate the actions of the United Nations for the next 45 years. Furthermore, the attitude of Albania, Bulgaria, and Yugoslavia to the mission revealed the importance of consent, while the continued delivery of assistance to the opposition fighters after the deployment of UNSCOB demonstrated the difficulty of preventing movements of matériel and personnel. UNSCOB initially comprised 35 military observers, and the total cost of the operation was around $3 million.

References and further reading Durch (1994); James (1990)

Green Line
See Cyprus

Grenada
See Organization of East Caribbean States (OECS)

Guatemala

Mision de los Naciones Unidas en Guatemala (MINUGUA), 1997–

Conflict Profile

The civil war in Guatemala was the longest running in Central America, lasting from the early 1960s until the 1996 peace agreement between the Guatemalan government and the alliance of rebel groups known as the Unidad Revolucionaria Nacional Guatemalteca (URNG). The roots of the Guatemalan civil war, like the other conflicts in Central America, lie in the inequalities between the small landowning elite and the large majority of poor peasant laborers. The inequalities in Guatemala's case are exaggerated because the indigenous people who make up 60 percent of Guatemala's population are widely discriminated against and poorly integrated into the country's economic and political systems. Over the nearly 40 years of conflict the government engaged in brutal counterinsurgency warfare and massive repression of rebel groups, particularly the indigenous population.

In March 1994 the URNG and the government concluded the Comprehensive Agreement on Human Rights. MINUGUA was established to verify the parties' compliance with the agreement in order to encourage trust and further negotiations. MINUGUA's initial mandate has been expanded to include verification of subsequent agreements between the URNG and the government, such as the accord on the Identity and Rights of Indigenous Peoples signed in 1995 and the formal cease-fire that took effect in December 1996. In early 1997 a group of military observers was attached to the mission by a Security Council decision in order to verify the cease-fire. The name of the mission was changed to the United Nations Verification Mission in Guatemala, but the acronym MINUGUA was retained.

MINUGUA deployed an international staff of over 400, including civilian human rights observers and experts, police observers, and military observers. The mission headquarters was organized into various branches, covering verification, institution building, technical assistance and cooperation, public information, and administration. Fifteen regional and subregional offices were established, with verification teams consisting of police, military, and civilian members. The offices were empowered to receive and investigate allegations of human rights violations and to report on the parties' implementation of the relevant agreements. The second part of MINUGUA's mandate was to strengthen Guatemala's institutional framework for the protection of human rights. This entailed both educational and capacity-building projects.

MINUGUA marks several innovations in peacekeeping operations. First, like the United Nations Observer Mission in El Salvador (ONUSAL) in neighboring El Salvador, it was deployed in advance of a cease-fire because its activities were seen to be crucial to creating an atmosphere in which the conflict could be resolved. The presence of MINUGUA may have been one of the factors encouraging the parties to remain at the negotiating table when the situation threatened to break down. The mission also departed from normal peacekeeping practice by integrating the military observers into the verification teams under civilian supervision. In previous missions the military component had operated separately from the civilian.

Despite considerable success in improving the human rights situation in the country, the international community's efforts to build a sustainable peace have encountered a number of obstacles. Most important, there is a pervasive culture of impunity for human rights abusers. The use of violence has become a habitual part of the exercise of political power, and agents of the state generally have nothing to fear from the weak, politicized judicial and legal systems. Little progress has been made in reforming these institutions. For example, the justice system still uses Spanish exclusively, which means that many non-Spanish-speaking indigenous people are denied access. Another difficulty is that civil society has been nearly destroyed by the war, leaving little space for MINUGUA's educational activities. Also, the peacebuilding process envisioned by the peace accords is, of necessity, a long-term process. The problems that have been encountered in funding the operation reflect the political and financial difficulties of the United Nations and not the continuing need of the Guatemalan people for international support in their efforts to build a peaceful society.

MINUGUA is headquartered in Guatemala City. Its Group of Friends (those countries that have formally agreed to sponsor the peace process) comprises Colombia, Mexico, Norway, Spain, the United States, and Venezuela. As of late 1998, Jean Arnault (France) was special representative and Brig. Gen. Jose B. Rodriguez Rodriguez was chief military observer. The Security Council authorized 155 military observers plus an unspecified number of civilian police and medical personnel to the cease-fire monitoring team, which was attached to the existing human rights monitoring operation. The countries contributing troops were Argentina, Austria, Brazil, Canada, Colombia, Ecuador, Germany, Italy, Norway, the Russian Federation, Singapore, Spain, Sweden, Ukraine, Uruguay, the United States, and Venezuela.

See also ONUCA (United Nations Observer Group in Central America, 1989–1992)
References and further reading
Kamarotos (1995); Louise (1997); information on MINUGUA can be found at the UN's information site at http://www.un.org/Depts/minugua/INDEX.htm

Guatemala Procedure
See Contadora Group; ONUCA

Gulf Wars (Iran-Iraq; Iraq-Kuwait)
The two main conflicts of recent times in the Persian Gulf have been the Iran-Iraq War of 1980–1988 and the Gulf War of 1990–1991 in which Iraq invaded Kuwait. In the Iran-Iraq War efforts by the Security Council to secure a ceasefire were largely unsuccessful, and hostilities continued unabated for several years. In 1984 the two combatant countries agreed to the presence of an observer force that would monitor any attacks on civilians. A cease-fire was agreed to in 1988, and the United Nations Iran-Iraq Military Observer Group (UNIIMOG) was sent to both countries to check on compliance. The second major conflict began with the invasion of Kuwait by Iraq in 1990. There was an immediate response from member states, and a series of motions of increasing severity were made in the Security Council, culminating in a resolution that authorized member states to use "all necessary means" to restore the status quo. The six-week campaign that followed, called Desert Storm, was a classic example of the use of airpower: 40 days of aerial bombardment and harassment were followed by only 4 days of ground combat. Iraq was forced to withdraw and has had to pay reparation damages to Kuwait. The military side of the war was a success, although an expensive one, with total costs to the anti-Iraq allies being estimated at approximately $150 billion. What was less successful in peacekeeping terms was the political outcome. The military defeat of the Iraqi leadership, combined with mixed messages from the West, led to a series of internal upheavals in Iraq, and a number of localized revolts were met by armed repression from the central government. It is estimated, for example, that whereas there were approximately 10,000 civilian

casualties of the war, the number of casualties resulting from the unrest that followed is in the region of 50,000. The suppression of the Kurdish uprising in the north of the country, in which almost two million Kurds were displaced and an unknown number killed, led to a major international humanitarian assistance program and the establishment of safe havens. On 5 April 1991 the Security Council launched Operation Provide Comfort under Security Council Resolution 688 to protect the Kurds. This included airdrops of food and clothing; the imposition of an air exclusion zone north of the thirty-sixth parallel; and the setting up of safe havens for the Kurds in northern Iraq. Six protection zones were established by U.S.,

British, French, and Dutch troops. A second air exclusion zone was imposed in southern Iraq to protect the Shia from Iraqi forces under Operation Southern Watch. Many saw the experience of intervention in Iraq triggered by the events of the Gulf War as a global turning point in which new principles for humanitarian intervention were established around the consensus that the international community would enforce minimum humanitarian standards, even within states.

See also Humanitarian intervention; No-fly zones; Peace enforcement; Safe havens; United Nations Iraq-Kuwait Military Observation Mission (UNIKOM 1991–)
References and further reading Brogan (1992); Hume (1994a); Johnstone (1994)

Haiti

United Nations Observer Group for the Verification of Elections in Haiti (ONUVEH), 1990–1991; United Nations Mission in Haiti (UNMIH), 1993–1996; United Nations Support Mission for Haiti (UNSMIH), 1996–1997

Conflict Profile

From 1957 Haiti was ruled by François Duvalier and, after his death in 1971, by his son, Jean-Claude Duvalier. The regime was responsible for an estimated 40,000 deaths during the 1980s. After a series of protests and strikes, Jean-Claude Duvalier fled, and a government was installed by the military-dominated National Governing Council. A military struggle for power and resulting political instability ensued until, in December 1990, Jean-Bertrand Aristide, leader of the National Front for Change and Democracy, was democratically elected by 67 percent of Haitian voters. The validity of the election was supported by the United Nations, the Organization of American States (OAS), and the Caribbean community. The United Nations Observer Group for the Verification of Elections in Haiti (ONUVEH) was authorized by the UN General Assembly to monitor the country's first free and fair presidential election. At the request of the Haitian government, the mission was not designated a peacekeeping operation. It consisted entirely of civilian observers, although it did have a small component of military officers who advised the Haitian military on conduct during the election.

Hopes of democracy and social and economic progress were shattered in September 1991 when President Aristide was overthrown in a coup d'état, headed by Lt. Gen. Raoul Cedras, and forced into exile. Following the coup, gross and widespread human rights abuses were reported, and the deteriorating political, economic, and humanitarian situation forced thousands of Haitians out of their country.

The international community immediately condemned the violent and unconstitutional actions of the Haitian military forces. With the UN's support, the OAS actively responded to the coup through several initiatives, including a freeze on the financial assets of the state and a trade embargo (except for humanitarian aid). In addition, a civilian mission (OEA/DEMOC) was constituted, at the request of President Aristide, to reestablish democracy in the country. The high-level mission, led by the OAS secretary-general, visited Haiti in August 1992, only to learn that the Haitian parties had failed to cooperate.

On 24 November 1992, General Assembly Resolution 47/20 was adopted, further condemning the actions of the military and demanding the restoration of the legitimate government, as well as declaring the UN's full cooperation with the OAS in finding a solution to the conflict. Following adoption of the resolution, the UN special envoy for Haiti, Dante Caputo, held a series of meetings with President Aristide in Washington, D.C., and with Lieutenant General Cedras and Marc Bazin, the prime minister of the de facto government, in Port-au-Prince, Haiti's capital. In January 1993 Cedras and Bazin agreed, in principle, to an international civilian mission, requested by Aristide, and to dialogue among the Haitian parties.

In March 1993 the OAS and the United Nations deployed the Joint International Civilian Mission in Haiti (MICIVIH). MICIVIH's mandate was to verify respect for human rights as they existed in the Haitian Constitution and in the various international documents. The United Nations component consisted of approximately 200 international staff, including 133 human rights observers.

However, despite efforts by the international community, constitutional order was not reestablished. On 16 June 1993 the Security Council acted under chapter 6 of the UN Charter and adopted Security Council Resolution (SCR) 841, imposing an oil and arms embargo against Haiti. The UN special envoy was to continue to assist in finding a political solution to the crisis through dialogue with Aristide and Cedras. After lengthy discussions, the two leaders signed the Governors Island Agreement in July. The agreement allowed Aristide to return to Haiti as president, created a forum for political dialogue under the guidance of the OAS and the United Nations, and offered hope of finding a solution to the conflict. The agreement also included a request for a UN presence in Haiti.

Deployment of UNMIH

On 23 September 1993, following Aristide's appointment of Robert Malval as prime minister, SCR 867 established the United Nations Mission in Haiti (UNMIH). Its mandate was to help implement the Governors Island Agreement and to assist in modernizing the Haitian armed forces and establishing a new police force. However, when UNMIH's military contingent arrived in Haiti on 11 October, the ship was prevented from docking by armed civilians. This, along with a number of other transgressions, was viewed as a violation of the agreement. The oil and arms embargo, which had been lifted when the agreement was signed, was reimposed by SCR 873. SCR 875 further ensured the strict implementation of the embargo and reaffirmed the UN's commitment to pursue further means of ensuring compliance and cooperation among the Haitian parties.

However, the Haitian military leaders continued to violate the agreement and obstruct the deployment of UNMIH and the return of Aristide. Violence increased dramatically in the country, forcing other members of UNMIH, the majority of MICIVIH staff, and most of the international agencies' personnel to leave. In January 1994 a small group of UN and OAS observers returned to Haiti to begin a gradual buildup. Reports confirmed the excessive violence and extreme human rights abuses.

International efforts continued to search for solutions to the conflict. UNMIH's mandate was extended by SCR 905, adopted on 23 March 1994.

The mandate and financing of MICIVIH were also extended to ensure the continuity of humanitarian assistance. In May SCR 917 imposed a comprehensive set of sanctions against Haiti. Following the refusal of military authorities to comply with the resolutions, additional UNMIH personnel were deployed at sea. Still, no progress was made; tensions increased, the humanitarian crisis worsened, and the human rights situation deteriorated. SCR 933, of 30 June 1994, further extended UNMIH's mandate.

However, difficulties ensued when the de facto authorities in Haiti announced that the staff of MICIVIH were unwanted and had 48 hours to leave the country. The staff were evacuated, following a joint statement by the United Nations and the OAS condemning the actions of the Haitian parties and reaffirming the UN's commitment to finding a solution to the conflict. On 31 July 1994 the Security Council adopted SCR 940 under chapter 7 authorizing the formation of a multinational force (MNF). The resolution also revised and extended UNMIH's mandate. Once a secure and stable environment was established by the MNF, it would be replaced by an expanded and strengthened UNMIH of 6,000 troops. The revised mandate called for UNMIH's assistance in sustaining a secure and stable mandate, to be established by the MNF, and in protecting international personnel and installations; professionalization of the armed forces and creation of a police force; and assistance in establishing and monitoring a free and fair electoral process.

Attempts made by the secretary-general to hold discussions with the Haitian military authorities on peacefully implementing SCR 940 were rebuffed. Consequently, U.S. President Bill Clinton declared that all diplomatic efforts had been expended and that force should therefore be used to remove the military leadership and restore the democratic government. More than 20 countries had agreed to join the MNF. Yet Clinton made one last diplomatic effort: A mission led by former president Jimmy Carter was sent to Haiti. After intensive talks, an agreement was reached. The military leaders would resign after the Haitian parliament granted amnesty, and they would cooperate with the MNF. On 19 September, the 28-

nation MNF (21,000 troops), led by the United States, was deployed to Haiti. Over the ensuing weeks reports indicated that the MNF had made significant progress in reestablishing democracy in the country. MICIVIH was reinstated, and preparations were made for the redeployment of UNMIH.

By the middle of October Cedras and other members of the military leadership had resigned and Aristide returned to Haiti. An UNMIH advance team reported that the MNF was receiving acceptance by the Haitian population and was achieving its objectives. Discussions between the United Nations, Haiti, the United States, and other interested parties were initiated. Despite a still-fragile security situation, conditions in Haiti improved, with violence and human rights abuses declining substantially.

On 30 January 1995 SCR 975 authorized the recruitment and deployment of military contingents, civilian police, and other civilian personnel to resume the UN mission. It also extended UNMIH's mandate. On 31 March the smooth transition from the MNF to UNMIH took place. By April the strength of the military component was 6,017, and the strength of the civilian component was 791, with approximately two-thirds of the military component, one-third of the civilian police component, and a large number of civilian staff coming from the MNF.

Following the transition, UNMIH continued to achieve a relatively secure and stable environment, although there were some cases of politically motivated killings and occasional attacks on humanitarian aid convoys and warehouses. UNMIH's efforts were successful: It helped form and train the Haitian National Police, undertook a number of development projects, and assisted with the electoral process.

The municipal and local elections and the first round of legislative elections were held on 25 June 1995. Although the elections experienced some problems—including organizational problems, allegations of fraud, criticisms of irregularities, and a few incidents of violence—election day was relatively peaceful. Complementary legislative and municipal elections were also held under peaceful conditions

on 13 August, along with a second round and additional reruns on 17 September and runoffs on 8 October. On 17 December, UNMIH, along with 400 international electoral observers, assisted with the free, fair, and peaceful presidential election. The winner was Rene Preval, Aristide's prime minister in 1991.

UNMIH was expected to end on 29 February 1996; however, the secretary-general recommended an extension of UNMIH's mandate to continue its assistance in ensuring the complete functioning of the Haitian government. The Security Council authorized the extension of UNMIH for a final period of four months but decided to significantly reduce the strength of its military and police components, to 1,200 military personnel and 300 civilian police. Canada, however, contributed an additional 700 troops at its own expense.

Remarkable efforts by the MNF and UNMIH enabled the return of democracy and the gradual reinforcement of democratic institutions, which maintained stability in Haiti for two years. This stability led the UN Security Council to adopt SCR 1063 on 28 June 1996, which shifted the operation from one of peacekeeping activity to development-related activity. The United Nations Support Mission for Haiti (UNSMIH) succeeded UNMIH and was given a mandate for the period 1 July 1996 through 30 November 1996. The primary objective of UNSMIH was to establish an effective national police force, and to promote stability and reconciliation. Under SCR 1123 of July 30, 1997, the mission was continued as UNTMIH (UN Transition Mission in Haiti). The current mission is MIPONUH (UN Civilian Police Mission in Haiti) under SCR 1212 of November 15, 1997.

As of October 1996 UNSMIH consisted of 270 international police and 1,250 Canadian and Pakistani peacekeepers. The costs of the UN operations, again as of 1996, have amounted to $336,800,000.

See also Civilian police (United Nations Civilian Police—[CIVPOL]); Regional organizations and peacekeeping
References and further reading Morris (1995); United Nations (1996); UNDPKO

Hammarskjöld, Dag (1905–1961)

Dag Hjalmar Agne Carl Hammarskjöld was born in Jönköping, Sweden, in July 1905. A graduate of the universities of Uppsala and Stockholm, he pursued a career in the Swedish civil service, serving as secretary-general in the Foreign Office between 1949 and 1953. He was appointed as UN secretary-general, succeeding the Norwegian Trygve Lie, in 1953.

Hammarskjöld proved to be one of the most capable and effective to have served in the post, combining great personal integrity with intellectual power, administrative and diplomatic skill, and a commitment to the principles of the United Nations. He continued to develop a strong role for the secretary-general: To the mediating role that Lie had established for the organization in the Middle East, he added a capacity for the secretary-general to intervene in crisis management in major conflicts. With Lester Pearson he created the first force-level peacekeeping mission, deployed to defuse the Suez Canal crisis in 1956, and established the principles under which peacekeeping would operate. The United Nations Operation in the Congo (ONUC) presented Hammarskjöld with enormous difficulties and demonstrated the problems he encountered as he tried to secure the practical development of the UN's supranational power. Some thought his commitment to internationalism and to the independence of the United Nations was too extreme. In the case of ONUC, the USSR supported the initial Security Council decision to deploy a force in the Congo under the assumption that ONUC's mandate reflect Soviet interests in the area. However, they subsequently demanded Hammarskjöld's resignation when Khrushchev addressed the General Assembly in September 1960 and demanded that the office of secretary-general be replaced by a troika of Western, neutral, and pro-Soviet officials (a proposal that would have effectively brought the Secretariat under the direct control of the superpowers). The General Assembly rejected the demand. In 1961 Hammarskjöld was killed when his plane crashed during a flight to meet Moise Tshombe, leader of the secession of Katanga in the Congo conflict. The difficulties and controversy caused by the ONUC mission ensured that the United Nations did not launch another peacekeeping mission for ten years, and no further missions were launched in Africa until the Namibia operation in 1988.

See also Charter of the United Nations; Conflict resolution theory and peacekeeping; Congo (United Nations Operation in the Congo, 1960–1964)
References and further reading Dayal (1976); Gavshon (1962); Lash (1971); Urquhart (1972)

Harbottle, Michael (1917–1997)

Brig. Michael Harbottle served with the British Army and was a former chief of staff of the United Nations Peacekeeping Force in Cyprus. He is author and coauthor of a number of books on international peacekeeping, including the *Peacekeeper's Handbook,* a definitive work that the United Nations and more than 70 countries have used as an instructional manual for peacekeeping operations. He was a senior lecturer in peace studies at universities in England, Canada, and South Africa. In 1983, with his wife Eirwen, he established the Center for International Peacebuilding. He was a founding member of the group of retired senior officers of the North Atlantic Treaty Organization (NATO) armed forces, Generals for Peace and Disarmament, which has been promoting new concepts of security based on cooperation rather than confrontation since 1981.

See also Cyprus; Peace building from below; Training for peacekeeping
References and further reading *The Guardian* (1997); Harbottle (1970, 1971)

Host countries

If a peacekeeping mission is *not* mandated under chapter 7 and is not, therefore, classified as peace *enforcement,* then UN forces can only enter a country after obtaining the express consent of the government of that country. The country is then known as a host country, and certain rights and obligations flow from that status. The host country can, for example, negotiate or impose limitations on the action or geographical movement of the UN forces, or even order their withdrawal. Those forces in turn have duties imposed upon them during their presence in a sovereign state. This principle was first enunciated in 1956 when the Security Council mandated the first United Nations Emergency Force (UNEF I) mission. Once the mandate for the operation is approved, status of forces agreements are signed between the United Nations and the host countries, which may take the form of a treaty or a memorandum of understanding. These agreements detail the rights, privileges, immunities, responsibilities, and obligations of the force in the host country, as well as the services to be provided to the force and its personnel.

Human rights

The first article of the Universal Declaration of Human Rights (1948) states that "all human beings are born free and equal in dignity and rights." Though beyond this basic statement the precise content of human rights has been the subject of controversy, most of the world's countries have, at least on paper, committed themselves to protect and respect the human rights of their citizens. The United Nations is one of the primary bodies responsible for identifying, protecting, and promoting respect for human rights around the world. In the years since the General Assembly passed the Universal Declaration, a substantial number of declarations, conventions, treaties, and monitoring bodies have expanded the definition of human rights and the institutional and legal framework that supports them. The 1990s have seen a reinvigoration of international action in this area, culminating in the establishment of the office of the UN High Commissioner for Human Rights in 1993.

Nevertheless, attention to human rights issues in UN field operations is a relatively new development. Beginning in 1990 with the United Nations Observer Mission in El Salvador (ONUSAL), various UN peacekeeping missions have been mandated to investigate, monitor, and report on the status of human rights in host countries. The establishment of an impartial international human rights operation was seen in El Salvador and other countries as being essential to building an atmosphere of trust in the fragile postconflict sit-

uation. In 1994 the United Nations deployed its largest human rights verification mission to neighboring Guatemala. The Mision de los Naciones Unidas en Guatemala (MINUGUA) was deployed before a final peace agreement had been signed in order to verify compliance with a human rights agreement between the parties. The mission was quite successful in reducing instances of torture, forced disappearance, and arbitrary detention. The tasks of human rights verification units can include, among other things, communicating with local people about how they are treated by authorities; educating judges, police, and citizens about human rights; looking into and reporting on allegations of violations of basic human rights; and institution building, particularly improvements in policing and the administration of justice. Although their mandates do not generally include the power to prosecute past human rights violators, their investigations can provide valuable evidence if criminal proceedings are undertaken. Missions that contained a human rights component or were entirely focused on human rights include the Joint International Civilian Mission in Haiti (MICIVIH), the United Nations Transitional Authority in Cambodia (UNTAC), and Human Rights Field Operation, Rwanda (HRFOR).

The implementation of human rights agreements is often difficult and complex. The very conditions that necessitate the deployment of a UN mission are often the least favorable for effective protection of human rights. This is illustrated by the experience of UNTAC in Cambodia, where the lack of a functioning, impartial court system and the lack of cooperation from the governmental authorities made it nearly impossible for the human rights monitors and special prosecutor to carry out their mandate. Other missions have encountered similar practical difficulties, caused by the government's inability or unwillingness to implement reforms. In some cases peacekeepers themselves have been implicated in the violation of human rights. Secretary-General Kofi Annan has given a high priority to the improvement of the UN's ability to protect human rights worldwide because the United Nations has come to recognize that human rights violations are a root cause of international insecurity and instability. Thus they are not purely internal matters but, rather, the legitimate concern of the international community.

See also Geneva Conventions and the laws of war; Bosnia and Herzegovina (UNMIBH, 1995– ; UNIPTF, 1995– ; IFOR, 1995; SFOR, 1996); Civilian police (United Nations Civilian Police—CIVPOL); Codes of conduct; El Salvador (ONUSAL, 1991–1995); Guatemala (MINUGUA—Mision de los Naciones Unidas en Guatemala, 1997–); Humanitarian Intervention; Organization for Security and Co-operation in Europe; Postconflict reconstruction; Rwanda (UNOMUR, 1993–1994 and UNAMIR, 1993–1996); United Nations (The United Nations Human Rights Center); United Nations Protection Force, Former Yugoslavia, (UNPROFOR I–III)
References and further reading Amnesty International (1994); Fisas (1995); Kamarotos (1995); Kenny (1997); Mackinlay (1996); Ratner (1997); Thornberrry (1995)

Humanitarian assistance

International humanitarian relief or assistance is concerned with relieving the immediate needs of victims of natural or political disasters. According to the United Nations High Commissioner for Refugees (UNHCR), the aim of humanitarian assistance is to sustain dignified life, to strengthen local institutions' efforts to relieve suffering and build self-reliance, and to ensure that the first step is taken toward reconstruction, rehabilitation, and development. The right to this assistance rests on the three legal pillars of international humanitarian law, human rights law, and refugee law. Article 25 of the Universal Declaration of Human Rights recognizes a right to food, clothing, housing, and medical care in crisis situations. The international law of armed conflict is defined by the International Committee of the Red Cross/Red Crescent as "international rules, established by treaties or custom, which are specifically intended to solve humanitarian problems directly arising from international or non-international conflicts, and which, for humanitarian reasons, limit the right of parties to a conflict to use the methods and means of warfare of their choice, or protect persons or property that are, or may be, affected by conflict." The formulation of these international rules began in Geneva in 1863, when Henry Dunant formed the International Committee for the relief of mili-

tary wounded. The first Geneva Convention was signed in 1864, and the first International Conference of the Red Cross held in 1867. A series of revisions of the Geneva Conventions were made, the most significant in recent years being the Four Conventions of 1949 and the Additional Protocols of 1977, which cover (1) the amelioration of conditions of the sick and wounded in armed forces in the field, (2) the amelioration of conditions of the sick and shipwrecked members of armed forces at sea, (3) the treatment of prisoners of war, and (4) the protection of civilians in times of war. This protection applies to victims of international and noninternational armed conflicts. In 1965 the seven fundamental principles of the Red Cross/Red Crescent were promulgated, defining the essence of humanitarianism and humanitarian assistance. These are the principles of humanity, impartiality, neutrality, independence, voluntary service, unity, and universality. These principles embody the heart of humanitarianism, namely, that a concern for the interests and welfare of human beings is paramount and that there is a common humanity that lies beneath political divisions, even in war. The International Committee of the Red Cross/Red Crescent is the only international organization, apart from the UNHCR, with a mandate under international law. A variety of agencies and organizations have emerged to undertake the work of international refugee and humanitarian assistance, principally the UNHCR, established in 1951, and the UN Department of Humanitarian Affairs (DHA), established by the General Assembly in 1991. UN peacekeeping entered the field of humanitarian assistance increasingly during the 1990s, when peacekeepers took on directly humanitarian roles such as protecting aid convoys and providing logistical support for humanitarian assistance (including transport and medical supplies).

See also Codes of conduct; Liberia (UNOMIL, 1993– and ECOMOG, 1990–); Military-humanitarian relations; Mozambique (ONUMOZ, 1992–1994); Somalia (UNOSOM I and II, 1992–1995, and UNITAF, 1992); United Nations Protection Force in Former Yugoslavia, (UNPROFOR I–III)
References and further reading Minear and Weiss (1995); Ramsbotham and Woodhouse (1996a); Steele (1998)

Humanitarian intervention

The primary responsibility for the well-being of a population rests with the lawful government or de facto authorities of the affected state. Where the government or authorities are unable or unwilling to appropriately protect and support their populations, an international humanitarian response may take place. This may take the form of consensual humanitarian assistance to a functioning civil infrastructure, usually with the concurrence of the government of the state concerned, or it may take the form of humanitarian intervention—in a civil war situation, for example—where consent to humanitarian operations is fluid or incomplete. During the Cold War, that is, broadly from the end of World War II to the dissolution of the Soviet Union in the late 1980s, humanitarian intervention was defined as the threat or use of force by a state in order to prevent or stop serious violations of fundamental human rights. Such intervention was carried out without the permission of the legitimate government of the state in which the violations were occurring. An example of this is the 1979 invasion of Uganda by President Nyerere of Tanzania, aimed at ending the brutal regime of President Idi Amin. Since the end of the Cold War, however, the context for humanitarian intervention has changed. During the Cold War most cases of humanitarian intervention involved oppression of populations by overstrong governments. During the 1990s it has generally been in situations where weak governments are facing internal opposition, that is, in civil war situations where human rights are denied and famine, population displacement, ethnic cleansing, and even genocide threaten their civilian populations. Humanitarian intervention is now best understood not as a matter of individual action by states but mainly as a collective response through the United Nations. It is now conceived as combining nonforcible military options such as peacekeeping with the work of nonmilitary agencies to provide assistance to communities in conflict-generated crises. The role of military peacekeeping forces in these situations is to help establish a secure environment for nonmilitary operations, such as the repatriation of refugees and the distribution of humanitarian relief by civilian agencies. Much of the redefinition of humanitarian intervention came about as the result of the events in the Gulf War in 1990–1991. Defeated in the Gulf War, but not removed from power, Iraq's President Saddam Hussein took vengeance on the Kurdish population of Iraq for rebelling against his regime during the war. Four hundred thousand Kurds fled toward the Turkish border, where by late March 1991 up to 1,000 were dying each day. On 5 April 1991 the UN Security Council passed Security Council Resolution (SCR) 688, authorizing the launch of Operation Provide Comfort to protect the Kurds. This involved airdrops of food and other relief supplies and, crucially, the setting up of safe havens in the north of Iraq. Six protection zones were set up by U.S., British, French, and Dutch troops. On 26 August 1991, under Operation Southern Watch, a no-fly zone was set up to protect the Shia in southern Iraq. Furthermore, under the memorandum of understanding that followed SCR 688, it was asserted that there was a right to assistance throughout Iraq. The significance of SCR 688 was that it created a precedent, intervening on humanitarian grounds even though it meant intervening in the internal policies of a nation (in this case, Iraq). Significant advances came in a series of UN General Assembly resolutions (GARs). GAR 43/131 of 8 December 1988 (Humanitarian Assistance to Victims of Natural Disasters and Similar Emergency Situations) declared that access to victims of natural disasters "and similar emergency situations" (widely interpreted to imply "man-made") could be demanded as a right by humanitarian organizations; abandonment of such victims without humanitarian assistance "constitutes a threat to human life and an offence to human dignity." GAR 45/100 of 14 December 1990 mandated that governments should allow unfettered access by accredited agencies, where necessary establishing "relief corridors for the distribution of emergency medical and food aid." Finally, on 19 December 1991, at the same time as the Iraqi relief efforts were going on, the General Assembly passed Resolution 46/182 of 19 December 1991 (Strengthening of the Coordination of Humanitarian Emergency Assistance of the United Nations), which led to the establishment of a new Department of Humanitarian Affairs (DHA) in March 1992. The DHA was charged with coordinating humanitarian assistance efforts, mobilizing the necessary international support and making sure that emergency relief was not an isolated effort but was, rather, coordinated with a proper attention to the root causes of the humanitarian crises. By the early 1990s a new context for humanitarian intervention had been defined. UN Secretary-General Javier Pérez de Cuéllar declared that the principle of nonintervention (that is, that states have a right to govern their own affairs) should not provide a justification for ignoring the massive and systematic violation of human rights. In June 1992 the new UN secretary-general, Boutros Boutros-Ghali, produced his *Agenda for Peace,* in which he argued that peacekeeping also would need to change: Conducted "hitherto with the consent of all parties concerned," peacekeeping might need to be capable of taking enforcement action in responding to humanitarian crises.

See also Gulf Wars (Iran-Iraq; Iraq-Kuwait); Peace enforcement
References and further reading Parsons (1995); Ramsbotham and Woodhouse (1996b)

Implementation Force (IFOR)
See Bosnia and Herzegovina

India

India has been one of the most consistent contributors to UN peacekeeping, having provided members and observers to the very first commissions in Korea and Palestine in 1947 and deploying infantry battalions to the first United Nations Emergency Force (UNEF I), the first full UN peacekeeping mission, in 1956. Since then India has provided forces, commanders, and observers to most of the missions, from missions to the Congo in 1960 to those in Somalia and Angola in the 1990s. During the mid-1990s the Indian contribution to ongoing UN peacekeeping operations totaled 5,340 troops, approximately 8 percent of the total, making India the third-highest troop-contributing country (after Pakistan and France). India, with 1.4 million troops, has the fourth-largest army in the world and has a wide range of conflict experience, qualifying it well in a general sense to provide peacekeeping personnel. India provided troops to UNEF I from 1956 until 1967, when President Gamal Abdel Nasser of Egypt insisted on the withdrawal of UNEF. India also made a major contribution to the United Nations Operation in the Congo (ONUC), providing a quarter of UN personnel between 1960 and 1964. In ONUC 36 Indian troops were killed and 124 were wounded. During the 1990s India provided military observers for many UN missions, including service in the Iran-Iraq and the Iraq-Kuwait border dispute missions and in Namibia, Angola, Central America, and Liberia. In the 1990s military contingents also served in Cambodia, Mozambique, Haiti, Angola, Rwanda, and Somalia, while the first force commander of the United Nations Protection Force in Former Yugoslavia (UNPROFOR) was Indian, Lt. Gen. Satish Nambiar. Indian experience in Somalia (where it contributed close to 5,000 personnel), as for so many other countries who sent contingents to that country, was controversial. On the one hand, the experience of the Indian Peacekeeping Force (IPKF) in Sri Lanka and earlier involvement in the Congo served India well for the

large Somalia operation; others argued that India was ill-prepared for the dangerous conditions that prevailed in Somalia between 1993 and 1995. However, India's service in Somalia was an example of good peacekeeping practices. In particular the Indian peacekeepers are said to have won the respect of Somalis because they made an effort to understand local culture and traditions, and they were active in a range of humanitarian activities, from helping to run schools and orphanages to digging wells and participating in other building projects.

It is not clear what India's future role in peacekeeping will be. It is clear that past participation has served India's national interest, hence its involvement in missions in east and southeast Asia and in the Middle East. India's participation in other missions can be attributed to motivations such as humanitarian concern (as in Rwanda and Somalia). More pragmatically, payment for service in UN peacekeeping has the financial benefit of contributing to the costs of maintaining their own large army. Providing forces for UN peacekeeping does increase international recognition. India desires to take a permanent seat on a reformed Security Council, and its chances would be considerably enhanced by its peacekeeping activities.

See also Sri Lanka (Indian Peacekeeping Force); United Nations India-Pakistan Observation Mission (UNIPOM); United Nations Military Observer Group in India and Pakistan (UNMOGIP)
References and further reading Bullion (1997)

Indonesia

United Nations Temporary Executive Authority (UNTEA), 1962–1963; United Nations Security Force in West New Guinea (UNSF)

Conflict Profile

Disagreements between the Netherlands and Indonesia over ownership of West New Guinea after the end of World War II led, during the 1950s, to a progressive breakdown in relations between the two countries. Two attempts by Indonesia to bring the issue before the Security Council, in 1954 and 1957, proved unsuccessful. As a result, Jakarta resorted to more direct confrontation with the Netherlands, appropriating Netherlands territory in Indonesia and expelling its nationals. In the early 1960s Indonesia also began to reinforce its military capability. They were assisted by the Soviet Union, which, along with China, supported Indonesia's claim to West New Guinea. Meanwhile, the Netherlands realized the increasing trend toward UN recognition of the independence of former colonial states, which was also being endorsed by the United States. Therefore the Netherlands relinquished its imperial ambitions toward West New Guinea and attempted instead to bolster the territory's political and economic development toward independence. However, any moves to incorporate the United Nations in this process were opposed by Jakarta, which claimed that the inhabitants of West New Guinea were, in fact, Indonesians.

Deployment of UNTEA and UNSF

In 1961 the Indonesian president, Sukarno, revealed his intention to take West New Guinea, or West Irian, as he referred to it, by force if necessary, and he began to make various military moves to that end, including activities in West New Guinea itself. Moscow realized the potential political advantages to be gained both from opposing continued imperialism and from establishing its own influence in the area by supporting Indonesia. At this point the United States, although an ally of the Netherlands, was nevertheless, in view of the problems it was already experiencing in Vietnam, wary of being drawn into another war in Southeast Asia, particularly because of Soviet pledges of assistance to Indonesia. The Netherlands sensed this lack of U.S. commit-

ment, and early in 1962 agreed to direct negotiations with Indonesia, and also accepted the involvement in the peace process of an independent mediator. At Indonesian insistence, an American was appointed as the representative of the secretary-general, but he was widely regarded, albeit unofficially, as primarily representing the interests of the U.S. government.

Continuing Indonesian military activity in West New Guinea presented severe problems for the negotiation process, but on 15 August 1962 the opposing parties signed an accord accepting a UN-administered transitional authority for the territory. The parties to the dispute agreed to fund the supervision operation, a pledge they both subsequently upheld. The accord established terms for a UN-supervised cease-fire between the opposing sides, to be followed by three distinct stages: the overall administration of West New Guinea during the seven-month transitional period from October 1962 through April 1963; the subsequent transfer of authority to Indonesia after 1 May; and UN involvement in helping the inhabitants of West New Guinea determine for themselves, by the end of 1969, whether they wanted to be affiliated with Indonesia.

Some 21 military observers were dispatched to fulfill the first objective of the accord, which was to verify compliance with the terms of the cease-fire. A significant proportion of this task involved conveying the news of the cease-fire to the 1,500 Indonesian troops deployed throughout mountainous West New Guinea. A 1,500-strong United Nations Security Force in West New Guinea (West Irian) (UNSF), comprising primarily Pakistani troops as acceptable to both sides, was attached to the United Nations Temporary Executive Authority (UNTEA) to oversee the administrative function. However, as it had not been authorized by the Security Council, UNTEA did not operate under an official mandate. Repeated calls from Indonesia to accelerate the transitional process were resisted by the United Nations until the official end date for the transitional period at the end of April. By this time UNTEA had successfully verified the withdrawal of Dutch personnel, as well as arrangements for the transfer of authority to Indonesian administration. Indonesian demands were then heeded, as transfer took place at 12:30 P.M. on 1 May. UNTEA successfully and expeditiously administered West New Guinea during the seven-month transitional phase.

However, UNTEA was less effective in overseeing the right of the people of West New Guinea to freely determine their future status in relation to Indonesia. Apart from a few UN experts, UNTEA and UNSF withdrew from the area after 1 May 1963. This enabled Indonesia to pursue virtually unopposed the forcible suppression of nationalist or resistance tendencies among the West New Guinean population. In 1968 the UN secretary-general did dispatch a special representative to the area to monitor the process of self-determination. However, the special representative had no authority to manage or intervene in the process in any way. The government-controlled process of self-determination took the form of gathering official representatives of the people into councils that would publicly pronounce their desire to remain affiliated to Indonesia or not. Unsurprisingly, a 100-percent endorsement of continued Indonesian authority was returned, which the UN special representative confirmed as an act of free choice by representatives of the people.

Expenditures for the entire operation came to $26.4 million. Personnel for UNTEA's 21-strong observer group were supplied from the existing United Nations Operation in the Congo (ONUC), the United Nations Emergency Force (UNEF), and the United Nations Truce Supervision Organization (UNTSO), as well as by Sri Lanka. Personnel for UNSF were primarily contributed by Pakistan, although air contingents were provided by the United States and Canada.

See also Association of Southeast Asian Nations (ASEAN); Cambodia; Troop-contributing countries
References and further reading Durch (1994); James (1990); United Nations (1996)

Indo-Pakistan conflict
See UNMOGIP

Intelligence support and peacekeeping operations
During the Cold War period the United Nations did not have any agency of its own gathering intelligence information. It was not seen to be appropriate for the United Nations as an organization that had no enemies and that did not wish generally to be associated with covert information gathering. The gathering of military intelligence was therefore for a long time frowned upon in UN thinking. It was feared that intelligence gathering would compromise the United Nations in the field, since consent from the host government was necessary before peacekeeping forces could be deployed. Intelligence gathering was also seen to jeopardize the impartiality of the force.

The reluctance of many troop-contributing nations to share intelligence information with the United Nations stems from a fear of leaks and a concern about the lack of procedures within the United Nations for handling sensitive information. Peacekeeping cannot easily accommodate itself to the normal principles of military intelligence gathering because, by its nature, peacekeeping is international. Personnel from as many as 40 states participate in a mission, and the loyalty of personnel when faced with sensitive information is likely to be to their own countries rather than to the United Nations. Thus, concern that the United Nations did not have secure procedures for handling sensitive information and fears that the United Nations itself had been infiltrated by members of factions (e.g., by supporters of Aidid in Somalia) are said to have resulted in failures of communication among contingents in Somalia, failures that led to the killing of U.S. soldiers in October 1991. During the post–Cold War period the concept and practice of peacekeeping changed in many ways. One of the lessons learned from the new peacekeeping operations was the need for more information. One important step toward increasing the UN's data was taken in December 1991 in the Fact-Finding Declaration, which stated the need to improve the information-gathering capability of the United Nations, a position supported, for example, by the Nordic countries in their Skagen Document of October 1991.

In 1993 a Situation Room was established within the Department of Peacekeeping Operations to improve daily contacts with missions in the field. The Situation Room functions 24 hours a day, seven days a week, serving the secretary-general, his Secretariat, and the missions. Troop-contributing nations have their own resources for intelligence-information gathering in their battalions, and they all tend to have the same broad approach to organizing and processing intelligence-information gathering. First, it is normally referred to as gathering "military information" instead of "intelligence," giving it a more neutral and less hostile character toward the host nation in a mission area. Second, the military commander has the responsibility to organize military information and to integrate it with the information that civilian elements have. Third, the information-gathering process is much the same as in conventional operations, except that the process is more open. Finally, most national contingents now agree that peacekeeping operations in the future will need broader and complex information-gathering capabilities, focusing especially on better knowledge of the geopolitical situation, on historic and cultural influences in the conflict zone, on the nature of ethnic identity, and on profiles of leading personalities and political leaders.

The organization and collection of information in UN peacekeeping operations can be subdivided all through the mission area of responsibility. Information gathering organized at the mission headquarters, or Force Headquarters, has in some instances been designated as military information offices (MIO). The first office established for gathering intelligence information in a UN peacekeeping operation was the Military Information Branch in the United Nations Operation in the Congo (ONUC), 1960–1964. Offices or cells are also organized at sector and battalion headquarters. Military observers also have their information-gathering office, where information is collated and analyzed. The UN Civilian Police (CIVPOL) and Civil Affairs also have resources to gather and analyze information in the mission areas. However, there is no joint organization to coordinate and analyze the information they collect in the mission.

The collection process at lower levels consists mostly of gathering information from observation posts, patrols, and liaison officers. Other missions have used more advanced information-gathering equipment, such as air reconnaissance, signal intelligence, and prisoner interrogation. When it comes to sharing intelligence, there is some distinction between the troop-contributing nations. The Nordic countries and the British have realized the importance of sharing some intelligence and improving the UN system. The North Atlantic Treaty Organization (NATO), on the other hand, is more reluctant to share intelligence outside the organization. When the Situation Room was established in 1993, the U.S. government installed the Joint Deployable Intelligence Support System (JDISS), which is a database through which the United States shares some of its intelligence information with the United Nations, connecting it with NATO databases. Other intelligence systems, such as Cymbeline artillery and mortar location radar, have been used in Bosnia.

Future peacekeeping operations, therefore, will demand more complex intelligence-gathering capabilities, and there are a variety of sources from which this capability can be developed. A number of sources of information are available for general conflict-monitoring purposes, not least the news provided by news networks such as CNN and established news agencies. Satellite data are also commercially available. Greater use can also be made of new advanced technologies for information gathering. The Synthetic Aperture Radar, ground surveillance technologies, and passive ground sensors can detect arms caches and trace vehicle movements and could improve peacekeepers' efficiency in monitoring cease-fires and disarming factions in internal conflicts. The main issue for the United Nations, however, is the extent to which UN intelligence gathering can be better institutionalized and coordinated. This will also gain greater urgency if the organization is to improve its early warning and conflict-prevention capabilities.

See also Air support; Logistics; No-fly zones; Sri Lanka; U.S. peacekeeping
References and further reading Dorn and Bell (1995); Smith (1994)

Internal conflict

Peacekeeping is said to involve internal conflict when the peacekeeping mission serves within a national jurisdiction or has a primary concern in its mandate with domestic political issues rather than matters relating to a conflict between two states (e.g., over a cease-fire line or a contested border). The majority of missions established since 1988 have been internal peacekeeping missions, and although this is not a new development—some peacekeeping missions before 1988 did involve internal peacekeeping (e.g., in the Congo between 1960 and 1964)—there has been a preponderance of this kind of peacekeeping in the 1990s. Alan James has identified eight different types of internal peacekeeping: First, there is the restoration of order through the deployment of sizable forces, as in the Congo and in the second United Nations Operation in Somalia (UNOSOM II). Second, there is the category of emollience, in which peacekeepers attempt to improve the local situation through goodwill (that is, mediation) missions and efforts to produce agreements that might in turn lead to a more comprehensive settlement (e.g., in Haiti, South Africa, Georgia, Moldova, and Tajikistan). Third, there are operations concerned with preventing a conflict from escalating in a state with internal difficulties, as, for example, the United Nations Interim Force in Lebanon (UNIFIL) did. The fourth type of role served by peacekeepers in internal conflicts is political purgation, that is, the monitoring of the end of a civil war, as when the United Nations Good Offices Mission in Afghanistan and Pakistan (UNGOMAP) force checked the departure of Soviet forces from Afghanistan in 1988. A fifth role in internal conflict is that of reconciliation, in which peacekeepers help to implement postconflict peace agreements, as, for example, in 1992 through the United Nations Transitional Authority in Cambodia (UNTAC). The sixth role is that of supporting quarantine, that is, preventing conflicts from spilling over from one area into an adjacent area, as, for example, with the preventive deployment of the United Nations Preventive Deployment Force Macedonia (UNPREDEP) from 1992. The seventh role is linked to implementing the right to self determination, as the United Nations Mission for the Referendum in Western Sahara (MINURSO) did. Finally, internal conflict has called on peacekeeping missions to become increasingly involved in assisting with the delivery of humanitarian relief.

Internal conflicts, in comparison to border disputes, have proved particularly testing for UN peacekeeping for a number of reasons: Passions will be running high; warlords and guerrilla groups may not wish to uphold agreements made; virtually no matter what peacekeepers do, their actions might be seen to affect the situation and to swing the balance of power one way or another; and finally, the stakes may be much higher in internal conflicts because the issue at stake is not just the division of a piece of territory, as in a border conflict, but the very existence and control of the state itself.

See also Conflicts: patterns and occurrences; Interposition; Regional organizations and peacekeeping **References and further reading** Bratt (1997); Duke (1994); James (1994)

International Association of Peacekeeping Training Centers
See Training for peacekeeping

International Commission for Supervision and Control

U.S. withdrawal from Vietnam, 1973–1975

The International Commission for Supervision and Control was established as part of the Paris Accords that were agreed on in the final stages of the Vietnam War and was thus not a "normal" peacekeeping mission as such. Its members—Canada, Indonesia, Hungary, and Poland—were divided along ideological grounds in their support for the belligerent parties in order to try to maintain parity of treatment. Unfortunately, the cease-fire that the commission was established to oversee did not materialize, and the operation became one of verbal criticism of each side. There were further difficulties in that not all of the combatant parties paid their agreed share of the costs of the commission, and it ceased to operate in 1974.

International Commission for Support and Verification (OAS Mission, 1990–1996)
See Nicaragua; ONUCA

International Committee of the Red Cross/International Committee of the Red Crescent

The International Committee of the Red Cross/Red Crescent (ICRC) is a nongovernmental entity, which, as L. Minear and T. G. Weiss have expressed it, is related to the nongovernmental organization (NGO) "genus" but which has a distinct recognition and place in international law. Formed in the 1860s and based in Geneva, its International Committee was instrumental in formulating the Geneva Conventions in 1949 and the two Additional Protocols of 1977. The Red Crescent was also adapted as a symbol of the movement: The League of Red Cross Societies was formed in 1919, and in 1983 this became the League of Red Cross and Red Crescent Societies. It has exceptionally been granted observer status by the UN General Assembly, and it is one of the only two international relief organizations recognized with a mandate under international law (the other is the United Nations High Commissioner for Refugees [UNHCR]). Its seven humanitarian principles (the principles of humanity, impartiality, neutrality, independence, voluntary service, unity, and universality) provide the most comprehensive definition of the guidelines for humanitarian action in war enunciated by any humanitarian organization. Its generally strict adherence to its principles provides the advantage of a clear understanding of how the ICRC operates; thus, in Yugoslavia it distanced itself from the UN peacekeeping forces, believing that they had become part of the conflict. However, its rigidity of principle has meant that in severe situations it has not been able to make the compromises that other agencies make in order to enlarge humanitarian space. In the former Yugoslavia, it was second only to the UNHCR, the UN's lead agency, in scale of activity and numbers of personnel.

See also   Nobel Peace Prize; Military-humanitarian relations; Somalia
References and further reading
Mackinlay (1996); Minnear and Weiss (1995); Ramsbotham and Woodhouse (1996a)

International Peace Academy
See Training for peacekeeping

International Verification and Follow-Up Commission
See Contadora Group; ONUCA

Internationalization

One of the ways in which the United Nations has tried to settle disputes between nations where there is no clear title to a particular territory is by establishing the disputed area as a form of protectorate under the administration of the United Nations. This happened in Trieste in 1947; in Jerusalem, also in 1947; and was proposed to the two parties in the Falklands-Malvinas dispute in 1982. In none of these cases was the proposal a success, although for different reasons. In Trieste the Cold War and shifting allegiances blocked the appointment of a governor; in Jerusalem the Arab-Israeli conflict settled the matter in a military way; and in the Falklands-Malvinas the disputant countries could not come to an agreement on the terms of the UN guardianship.

Interposition

An important part of the peacekeeping process is the need to keep belligerent parties physically away from each other. Interposition refers to the presence of mission personnel between combatant groups, either to enable cease-fire negotiations to begin or to police an existing cease-fire. In conflicts between countries, the role of the interposition force can be seen relatively clearly. Soldiers serving as peacekeepers in most (though not all) of the peacekeeping missions before 1988 ("first-generation," "classical," or "traditional" peacekeeping) were often serving in interpositional roles, placed between belligerent groups in order to supervise a cease-fire or a peace agreement. However, in conflict among groups within a country (internal conflict), the operation can be more complex and difficult because chains of authority and command may be unclear, cease-fire agreements are disregarded by some militias, and there are no clear demarcation lines or borders between belligerents.

Iraq

United Nations Guards Contingent in Iraq (UNGCI), 1991; United Nations Special Commission (UNSCOM), 1992–

UNGCI

The defeat of Iraq by the UN-authorized Coalition forces did not result in the removal from power of the Iraqi regime of President Saddam Hussein. The regime was powerful enough to conduct a brutal repression of revolts by Kurds in the north and by Shia in the south of the country. Western states responded with airdrops of humanitarian aid and then by establishing safe havens for the Kurds in the north, following intervention by Western troops. In May 1991 Iraq consented to the replacement of these 15,000 Western troops by 500 UN Guards.

UNSCOM

As a condition of the cease-fire agreement between Iraq and the Coalition forces in the Gulf War, the United Nations Special Commission (UNSCOM) was formed under Security Council Resolution 687/91, in April 1991, to supervise, in part, the destruction of Iraq's nuclear, biological, and chemical (NBC) weapons.

UNSCOM's mandate is to carry out immediate on-site inspections and destruction of Iraq's biological, chemical, and missile capability, based on Iraq's declared stockpiles and locations and the designation of any additional locations by the Special Commission itself, there is no termination date for mandate. UNSCOM's tasks are to take position in theater for the destruction, removal, or rendering harmless of all chemical and biological weapons, all stocks of agents, all related subsystems and components, and all research, development, support and manufacturing facility items. UNSCOM is to supervise the destruction by Iraq of all its ballistic missiles with a range greater than 160 kilometers and related major parts and repair and production facilities; and to assist the secretary-general in implementing the plan for the long-term monitoring and verification of Iraq's continued compliance with its undertaking not to use, develop, construct, or acquire prohibited equipment. Finally, UNSCOM is to assist the direc-tor-general of the International Atomic Energy Agency (IAEA) in the following: carrying out immediate on-site inspection of Iraq's nuclear capabilities based on Iraq's declared locations and the designation of any additional locations by UNSCOM itself, and carrying out the plan authorized by the Security Council calling for the destruction, removal, or rendering harmless of all NBC weapons. The headquarters for the Special Commission is located in New York, with Baghdad and Bahrain serving as offices for the Special Commission. Considerable international tension has resulted from the work of the commission, as, for example, in 1998 when the government of Iraq obstructed and prohibited access to sites in Iraq, particularly the presidential palaces, by UNSCOM inspection teams. In December 1998 UNSCOM was withdrawn because of alleged Iraqi noncompliance with UNSCOM's weapons inspection program. As a punishment for this noncompliance, the regime of President Saddam Hussein was subjected to a series of air attacks on military facilities in Iraq by U.S. and British air forces.

See also Air support; Child soldiers; Gulf War; Humanitarian intervention; League of Arab States; Middle East conflict; No-fly zones; Peace enforcement; Safe areas; United Nations Iran-Iraq Military Observer Group; United Nations Iraq-Kuwait Military Observation Mission, 1991–

Irish peacekeeping

The Irish Defence Forces first contributed to UN peacekeeping in 1958 when 50 military observers served with the United Nations Observation Group in Lebanon (UNOGIL). Since 1958 Irish units and military observers have served in 32 UN missions and in 10 other peacekeeping missions with the European Union, the Organization for Security and Cooperation in Europe (OSCE), and various humanitarian agencies. The most significant troop missions to which the Irish have contributed units include the United Nations Operation in the Congo (ONUC), the United Nations Peacekeeping Force in Cyprus (UNFICYP), the second United Nations Emergency Force (UNEF II) in Sinai, the United Nations Interim Force in Lebanon (UNIFIL), and the second United Nations Operation in Somalia (UNOSOM II). In addition, the Irish police have been active contributors to several missions of the civilian police component (CIVPOL). The Irish Defence Forces numbered about 12,000 in 1997, and approximately 65 percent of these had served on UN peacekeeping missions, an illustration of the importance of peacekeeping in Irish defense and foreign policy. Irish commitment to peacekeeping in the future was emphasized in a 1996 white paper on foreign policy that recognized the important role played by UN peacekeeping in the containment of international conflict. In response to the call of the UN secretary-general that member states should indicate the forces that they were able to make available for use in peacekeeping (under the United Nations Standby Arrangements System [UNSAS] intended to reduce deployment time in the event of emergencies), the Irish government agreed to make available up to 850 personnel and up to 2 military officers to a standby component at UN headquarters in New York. However, Irish agreement to contribute to UN peacekeeping is influenced by clearly identified factors, including consideration of how the mission relates to Irish foreign policy and whether the mandate requirements are appropriate to Irish skills and capabilities. The Irish army is a professional force, but Irish military personnel serving as peacekeepers have volunteered for such service. Irish policy has been progressive especially in its development of expertise and professionalism in its forces through a comprehensive dedicated training program. The United Nations Training School Ireland (UNTSI) was established in 1993 as a part of the Irish Military College, devoted exclusively to teaching peacekeeping principles and practice. In addition to training Irish personnel, UNTSI has trained officers from over 20 nations in military observer skills and is also beginning to develop joint training programs to reflect the multifunctional tasks, combining military, police, and civilian roles, that contemporary peacekeeping demands.

See also Childers, Erskine; Training for peacekeeping; Troop-contributing countries
References and further reading
Macdonald (1997); Murphy (1998)

Israel
See Middle East conflict

Italy
Italy first participated in a peacekeeping mission in 1958, when Italian armed forces provided military observers to the United Nations Truce Supervision Organization (UNTSO) in Lebanon and the Sinai. Since then Italy has been a significant participant in most of the peacekeeping operations, for example in Lebanon, Cambodia, Mozambique, and Somalia. In Albania in 1997 a UN-mandated multinational operation, Operation Alba, was directed by the Italian government and succeeded in stabilizing the political situation and stemming the violence there.

In 1994 the Italian Joint Chiefs of Staff issued the document *Joint Forces Handbook for Peace Operations*, which defined six different categories of activity under the term "peace support": humanitarian missions, preventive diplomacy operations, peacemaking operations, peacekeeping operations, peace-enforcing operations, and peacebuilding operations. The 1994 *Handbook* provides guidelines for conducting peace operations, guidelines for multinational operations conducted within the United Nations or within regional organizations, and guidelines on organizational and logistical matters. Other relevant handbooks adopted by the Italian armed forces include the *Manual for Peacekeeping Operations and Humanitarian Missions*, November 1994; the *Logistics Manual for Out of Area Operations*, 1994; and the *Training Programme for Peace Operations*, 1993. The Italian armed forces provide training for their members at the Institute of War of the Italian Army in Civitavecchia. Additional training on international humanitarian law is supplied by the armed forces and the Italian Red Cross. Italy also is the location of one of the first centers specializing in the training of civilian peacekeepers. The Training Program for Civilian Personnel of Peacekeeping/Humanitarian Operations was established within the Scoula Superiore di Studi Universitari e Di Perfezionamento S. Anna, in Pisa. The program was created because of the multifunctional development of peacekeeping, which includes tasks such as refugee and humanitarian assistance, reforming police and judicial systems, human rights monitoring, and the supervision and organization of elections. As a result there are now large numbers of civilians involved in peacekeeping and related missions, and a real need has emerged for training and preparation of civilian peacekeepers. The Training Program at Pisa provides training in skills and procedures related to election monitoring; human rights monitoring; humanitarian and refugee assistance; international humanitarian law; communication, negotiation, and conflict-resolution skills; and rules of conduct, personal safety, and health.

The first worldwide logistics base for peacekeeping, the UN Logistics Base in Brindisi, was provided by the Italian government for the United Nations in 1994.

See also Logistics; Somalia; Training for peacekeeping
References and further reading Guttry (1996)

Jammu and Kashmir
See UNMOGIP and UNIPOM

Japan

In 1992, 600 Japanese troops, serving as UN peacekeepers, were deployed to Cambodia as part of the United Nations Transitional Authority in Cambodia (UNTAC). This decision by the Japanese government to allow its first military overseas ground presence since 1945 was controversial both domestically and internationally, particularly because of the legacy of Japanese Imperial Army aggression during World War II. However, initial doubts were overcome by the general view, promoted by the United States, for example, that Japan has a positive role to play in collective security activities and that Japanese military and economic power in Asia can and should be harnessed to foster security and economic and political development, especially in Asia.

The main obstacles to Japanese military participation in peacekeeping operations, however, came from within Japan itself. Following World War II Japan represented its national security concerns through its Peace Constitution and prescribed a nonoffensive role for its army, the Japanese Self Defence Force (JSDF). The first signs of changing this postwar policy were seen during the Gulf War in 1991, when Japan came under intense pressure to support the war. The Japanese government offered an aid package of $13 billion. In April 1991, after the successful conclusion of Operation Desert Storm and the defeat of Iraq, the administration of Prime Minister Toshiki Kaifu ordered the deployment of four Maritime Self-Defence Force (MSDF) minesweepers to the Persian Gulf. The deployment returned to Japan in October 1991 and was regarded as a success. This experience enabled the Kaifu administration to prepare the ground for peacekeeping legislation, the Peacekeeping Operations Law. The law restricted participation by Japanese personnel to UN-sponsored peacekeeping operations only and also specified a number of further restrictions. At the same time the Disaster Relief Law was amended to allow the Ground Self-Defence Force (GSDF) to be deployed

overseas for disaster relief work. During intense debates about the Peacekeeping Operations Law the Liberal Democrats replaced Kaifu with Kiichi Miyazawa as prime minister. Though Japanese public opinion still had deep reservations about Japan's wartime legacy, there was also a growing national consensus that Japan had obligations to the international community, and the Peacekeeping Law was passed by the Japanese legislature on 15 June 1992.

See also ASEAN; Cambodia (United Nations Advance Mission in Cambodia, 1991–1992; United Nations Transitional Authority in Cambodia, 1992–1993); Financing peacekeeping; Troop-contributing countries
References and further reading Harrison and Nishihara (1995)

Jerusalem: internationalization proposals

In 1947 the British mandate in Palestine was coming to an end, and discussions took place about the political system that would succeed it. At the same time the city of Jerusalem was being claimed by both Arabs and Jews, who each regarded it as sacred territory. To try to resolve this situation the General Assembly decided that Jerusalem and its surrounding territory (including the equally sacred village of Bethlehem) should be given international status, and the Trusteeship Council was asked to draft a statute for the city. The Trusteeship Council recommended that there should be a governor to administer the city on behalf of the

United Nations, that the police force should be recruited from outside of Palestine and be responsible to the governor, and that the city should be completely demilitarized. The concept of internationalization never became a reality. In 1948 during the Arab-Israeli fighting, parts of Jerusalem were captured by Jordan and the remainder by Israel. Both states refused to relinquish what they held, and Jerusalem remained divided until the war of 1967, when the Israelis took control of the whole city.

See also Internationalization; Middle East conflict
References and further reading James (1990)

Jordan
See Middle East conflict; UNTSO

Kampuchea
See Cambodia

Kashmir
See UNMOGIP and UNIPOM

Katanga
See Congo

Korean War (1950–1953)

The Korean War began in 1950, and although an armistice was not signed until 1953, the main body of the fighting took place within the first 12 months. The ostensible cause of the war was an invasion of South Korea by the North Koreans, but this act followed upon two years' tension between the two countries (since their foundation in 1948), and this tension in turn has to be seen within the wider context of the ideological split of the Cold War. After the initial North Korean advance, pushing back the U.S. and South Korean forces, the United Nations asked member states to support the South. (This was only possible at the time because of the temporary absence of the USSR from the Security Council, another episode of the Cold War.) The resulting participation by UN troops can be seen as an early example of UN peace enforcement, although, strictly speaking, this was not a UN mission because the personnel were not under the overall command of the Security Council. After the UN forces began their support of the South Koreans and were beginning to gain ground, the Chinese came to the aid of the North, which again pushed southward. The fighting came to a stalemate around the thirty-eighth parallel (which was approximately the original border), and peace negotiations began in July 1951, with an armistice being signed in 1953 at Panmunjom that accepted the thirty-eighth parallel as the border. An observer presence has been in place at Panmunjom since that date.

> **See also** China; Lie, Trygve (1896–1968); Peace enforcement
> **References and further reading**
> Gordenker (1959); James (1990)

Kuwait
See Gulf Wars (Iran-Iraq; Iraq-Kuwait); UNIKOM

Lancaster House Agreement (1979)
See The Commonwealth

League of Arab States

The League of Arab States was established in 1945 with a membership of seven Arab states: Egypt, Iraq, Lebanon, Saudi Arabia, Syria, Transjordan (later Jordan), and Yemen. Between 1945 and 1993 the membership was increased to 23 states, with a headquarters in Cairo. The league was the forerunner of later regional organizations such as the Association of Southeast Asian Nations (ASEAN) in that the intention was to work together cooperatively on political, social, economic, and security issues and that there is a central body (the Council of the League of Arab States) to coordinate league affairs, but it differs from other regional bodies in that one of the geographically central Semitic countries—Israel—is excluded. League members have contributed troops to UN peacekeeping missions, but the league itself has acted militarily in concert on only two occasions: in Kuwait in 1961 and in Lebanon in 1975. In the first case, in a situation that had echoes 30 years later, the newly independent Kuwait was threatened with invasion by Iraq and had only a small British force as protection. The league was in some political difficulty because Iraq was also a member, but a resolution was passed in July 1961 pledging league support for Kuwait's independence, and the organization, mirroring UN procedures, signed an agreement with the government of Kuwait setting out the legal status of the proposed force. Despite a number of other political problems within the league, a force was finally assembled and arrived during September and October 1961. The force was called the Arab League Force and was still in place in 1963 when a coup in Iraq brought about a change of government, one that had no designs (at that time) on Kuwait. The force was withdrawn in February 1963. The second major peacekeeping initiative was the establishment of the Symbolic Arab Security Force (ASF) in 1976. At that time there was a civil war in Lebanon that was having destabilizing effects throughout the region, and Syria was expanding its own forces inside the country. The league mandated a peacekeeping force in June 1976, which, even though it would have to deal with a problem partly inspired by Syria, would also have Syrian troops within the contingent. Just as they had in the Kuwaiti operation in 1961, the league procedures mirrored those of the United Nations, and a multinational force was assembled. There was a series of intergovernment disputes about the presence and composition of the force, but it was eventually deployed beginning in June 1976. The ASF found it difficult to fulfill its own mandate because it was small, because the Christian sections of the Lebanese conflict refused to accept an Arab force, and because the Syrians, while still part of the peacekeeping deployment, actually went on the offensive inside Lebanon. The situation became so grave that an Arab Summit meeting had to be called—at Riyadh in October 1976—which agreed to increase the peacekeeping force, to alter its terms of reference to make it more assertive and powerful in character, to rename it the Arab Deterrent Force, and to put the contingent under the command of the president of Lebanon. The brief for the new force was similar to that of a UN mission: to oversee the cease-fire and to act as an interposition force between the combatants. Once again the size, composition, and deployment of an Arab League Peacekeeping Force was the subject of disagreement. The Palestinians objected to the Syrian presence, the Syrians objected to the inclusion of the Palestinians, and Egypt walked out on the whole mission. Deployment was eventually agreed on but, once again, the initiative was blocked, this time by the Israelis as well as the Christians. The

UN mandate for the United Nations Interim Force in Lebanon (UNIFIL) (which had a similar brief) raised Arab hackles because of the implication that they could not cope with the situation.

Throughout the late 1970s the troop contingents were gradually reduced as member states withdrew from the operation. In April 1979 the only nation still militarily supporting the mission was Syria—which was in an unofficial state of war with Israel at the same time as it was nominally operating the peacekeeping mission. The mandate for the Arab force expired in 1982 and was not renewed, but Syria maintained a force on Lebanese territory nevertheless.

See also Lebanon
References and further reading Zacher (1979)

League of Nations

As World War I drew to a close there was widespread concern to ensure that such a devastating conflict could never be repeated. The League of Nations was established in 1919 as part of one of the postwar treaties—the Versailles Peace Settlement—and set out operating principles concerned with promoting collective security, arbitrating in international disputes, arms reduction, and open diplomacy. Germany joined the league in 1926, but the U.S. Congress never ratified U.S. membership. Although the league carried out many "good works" in the aftermath of the war—mainly in overseeing peaceful territorial reorganization—it failed to achieve its stated aims. One reason was that the member countries found it very difficult to subordinate national interests to international ones. Another reason was that the majority of the league's missions were not genuinely "international"; rather, they were carried out by representatives of the victorious Allies and were thus open to the criticism that they were neither disinterested nor neutral. The league never had any real power in international terms and was impotent in the face of German and Japanese expansion and the concomitant arms buildup during the 1930s. Of the missions carried out by the league, two stand out as attempts to be genuinely neutral:

1. The Vilna International Force, planned in 1920 but not operative because of the lack of consent from the conflicting parties—Poland and Lithuania—both of which claimed sovereignty over Vilna. The Soviet Union also objected to the presence of an international force near its border.

2. The Saar International Force (1934–1935) was in some respects a forerunner of later UN operations, such as the United Nations Transitional Assistance Group (UNTAG) in Namibia. After a fifteen-year rule by the Governing Commission appointed by the League of Nations, a 3,300-strong International Force successfully oversaw the plebiscite that resulted in the return of the Saar region to Germany.

Although it failed to prevent the return to militarism in the 1930s, the League of Nations represents an important step forward in international diplomacy and conflict resolution, and the analysis of shortcomings in the powers and organizations of the league helped in the establishment of the United Nations in 1945.

See also United Nations: organization; World War I and history of peacekeeping
References and further reading James (1990); Walters (1960)

Lebanon

United Nations Observation Group in Lebanon (UNOGIL), 1958; United Nations Interim Force in Lebanon (UNIFIL), 1978; Multinational Forces (MNF) I and II, 1982–1984

UNOGIL: Conflict Profile
The security problems for the state of Lebanon stem from at least as far back as its artificial expansion by its colonial administrator, France, which hoped to make the country more economically viable as a single entity. However, this expansion incorporated a large Muslim minority into what had essentially been a Maronite Christian community. In anticipation of associated problems on the achievement of independence, an un-

written National Covenant of 1943 decreed that Christians would no longer look to France or other Western states for support, and the Muslim community would not attempt to join with Syria or any other Arab state. Furthermore, the state administration would reflect the national ethnic balance of six Christians to five Muslims. Thus, there would be a Christian president, a Sunni Muslim prime minister, a Shia Muslim parliamentary speaker, and a Christian-to-Muslim ratio of 6 to 5 within Parliament.

The National Covenant failed, however, to acknowledge the fact that the societal balance was changing, and by 1991 a demographic estimate revealed a 4 to 6 Christian-to-Muslim ratio. It was also unlikely either that Christians would view Muslims as political equals or that Muslims would accept their position of political inferiority. Furthermore, the Christian community's political advantage gave them an economic advantage, further exacerbating already tense societal divisions. Intra-community discrimination also occurred, as Shia Muslims in the south were more politically marginalized than their northern Sunni counterparts.

Therefore, the intended stability in Lebanon did not materialize, as internal divisions within the country became increasingly entangled in regional and international politics. Two opposing trends in the 1950s served to compound societal stratification. On the one hand, the threat felt by the Lebanese Christian community from the Muslim-Arab world in general, particularly in relation to the Palestinian struggle, was heightened by the overtly pan-Arab nationalist stance of the Egyptian president, Gamal Abdel Nasser. On the other hand, in response to Nasserism, Lebanon's Christian president, Camille Chamoun, had been leaning toward both the West and conservative Arab monarchies. Such bias had been particularly evident during the recent Suez Canal crisis, when Chamoun had refused to support pan-Arab calls to cut diplomatic relations with Britain and France. The situation was further compounded in 1958, when Chamoun attempted to introduce constitutional amendments that would secure him a second presidential term and Nasser succeeded in combining the Egyptian and Syrian states as the United Arab Republic (UAR).

Deployment of the United Nations Observation Group in Lebanon (UNOGIL)

Overt hostilities between the Lebanese communities were sparked in May 1958 by the murder of a Christian newspaper editor. Deployment of the Lebanese Army, which was equitably divided between Christians and Muslims, to defuse the situation was delayed for fear that the army itself would become split along ethnic lines and therefore exacerbate tensions. Consequently, Muslim fighters were able to occupy part of Beirut and a large area along the Lebanese-Syrian border. Chamoun attributed responsibility for the violence to UAR interference in Lebanese domestic affairs. On these grounds, he sought U.S. assistance, and complained to both the Arab League and the United Nations. However, Chamoun rejected both the terms of the U.S. offer of assistance and the Arab League's conciliatory proposal, and so the problem was left to the United Nations.

The appeal to the international community fully immersed the Lebanese conflict in Cold War politics. At that time, the UN Security Council demonstrated a noticeable Western bias and the Soviet Union was also allied to both Egypt and Syria, so Moscow rejected the Lebanese government's claim of UAR interference. However, fear that the matter might be transferred to the even more Western-oriented General Assembly prevented the Soviet Union from using its Security Council veto. Ultimately, on 11 June 1958, a compromise was reached at the United Nations. By adopting Security Council Resolution (SCR) 128, the Security Council authorized the deployment of a 100-strong, unarmed observer group, the United Nations Observation Group in Lebanon (UNOGIL), to investigate the situation, primarily in relation to illegal, cross-border transfers of arms or personnel into the country.

Although the group was not allowed full access to the boundary area between Lebanon and Syria, the most likely area for potential cross-border activity, UNOGIL nevertheless reported that the majority of the opposition forces operating in the country were in fact Lebanese. However, the Lebanese government continued to request U.S. intervention for its own protection. This request was finally answered, as 14,000 U.S. marines were deployed to Lebanon in response to the 14 July overthrow of the pro-Western government in Iraq and to the threat that this represented to Western allies in the Middle East. King Hussein also successfully requested British military assistance in Jordan for the same reason. However, U.S. demands that UNOGIL be armed were rejected, and the situation subsequently died down as the new Iraqi regime demonstrated moderate tendencies. During this period events in the Lebanon itself also began to stabilize, finally allowing UNOGIL observers increased access to the Syrian border area. U.S. assistance then facilitated the selection of the Lebanese Army commander, General Chehab, as a universally acceptable replacement for President Chamoun, and so the dispute was effectively defused. However, the problem remained of how to remove the U.S. and UK troops from Lebanon and Jordan, respectively. Therefore, as circumstances in Lebanon reached their most stable point, UNOGIL was expanded to 500 observers to oversee the withdrawal of foreign troops. UNOGIL itself was withdrawn soon after.

The value of the UNOGIL mission is questionable. On the one hand, it can be argued that events in Lebanon never presented a serious enough risk to international peace and security to warrant international intervention. Furthermore, only after the situation had already been stabilized did the force reach a strength sufficient to fulfill its mandate of monitoring cross-border movements of troops and arms. On the other hand, however, the combined effects in the Middle East of both rising Arab nationalism and competing Cold War rivalry added increased regional and international significance to events. Therefore, UNOGIL can be seen to have delayed U.S. intervention long enough, and sufficiently dampened its repercussions, to avoid an escalation of the situation to a regionwide, or even bipolar, context.

UNIFIL: Conflict Profile

The Lebanese security problems just described did not evaporate following the settlement of the 1958 conflict. Societal divisions continued to be susceptible to the strains of regional politics, as Lebanon periodically became the theater for the enactment of the Israeli-Palestinian conflict. The 1948 Israeli War of Independence between the new state of Israel and her Arab neighbors had witnessed the relocation of around 100,000 Palestinians to southern Lebanon. A further, and much larger, influx of around 400,000 Palestinians into southern Lebanon occurred after the 1967 Arab-Israeli war (the Six-Day War), which significantly altered the ethnic balance in the country. Soon after this, King Hussein of Jordan declared that Palestinian fighters would no longer be allowed to use Jordanian territory as a base for operations, and so the Palestinians saw southern Lebanon as a viable alternative. On 3 November 1969 the leader of the Palestinian Liberation Organization (PLO), Yasser Arafat, signed the Cairo Agreement, which was designed to regulate the Palestinian armed presence in southern Lebanon. In reality, however, the agreement merely served to ratify the establishment of southern Lebanon as the principal site from which to launch Palestinian armed attacks against Israel.

Lebanon's sociopolitical situation facilitated such developments. Lebanese politics had become fragmented, and state control was sufficiently parochial and weak to allow Palestinian fighters to act with relative impunity in the south of the country. Furthermore, many Shia Muslims in the south, in response to their political marginalization by both the Maronite Christian and Sunni Muslim communities, had embraced the radical philosophies of Imam Musa Sadr and consequently were sympathetic to the Palestinian cause. Conversely, the Maronite community resented the freedom of movement afforded to PLO fighters.

Open hostilities broke out in 1975. The leaders of neighboring Syria sensed the potential regional repercussions of such a situation, primarily on the relations between Arabs and Israelis: If Lebanese society became formally split between Christians and Muslims, Israel was the natural regional defender of the Christian community; at the same time, a Palestinian military victory in Lebanon was also likely to prompt Israeli intervention.

As a result, the Syrian president, Hafiz al-Assad, dispatched 3,000 troops to the area to guarantee a recently agreed-on cease-fire between the opposing Lebanese parties. This deployment also became part of the confusion surrounding the changes to the Arab League Force that established the Arab Deterrent Force following upon the Riyadh Summit. Syria was not only part of the peacekeeping force but was also pursuing her own anti-Israel interests, and there were other issues of internal dissent within the Arab regional body. In addition, the UN mandate for UNIFIL was regarded by the League of Arab States as undermining their own efforts at peacekeeping. Syria's actions aroused Israeli fears, since Syria was not only her most implacable Arab rival but also maintained close Soviet ties, in opposition to Tel Aviv's links with the United States. Syria thus had to provide guarantees to Israel that its troops would not progress farther south than the "red line" that traversed Lebanon from east to west along the Litani River. However, this, in turn, meant that the Palestinians were still allowed freedom of movement in southern Lebanon below the red line, and so the opportunities for tension across the Israel-Lebanon border remained. On 14–15 March 1978, in response to a Palestinian attack on a tourist bus in Israel on 11 March, Israeli Prime Minister Menachem Begin authorized the invasion of southern Lebanon by the Israeli Defence Force (IDF).

Deployment of UNIFIL

The IDF quickly established control of a six-mile-wide "security zone" along the Lebanese border, much to the annoyance of U.S. President Jimmy Carter, who was in the process of negotiating an Israeli-Egyptian peace settlement. In order to avoid accusations of bias in favor of its ally, Israel, especially in view of the considerable Soviet military presence in the region in support of more radical Arab states and in view of the escalatory dangers that such a situation represented, Washington referred the problem to the United Nations, suggesting that a UN force be deployed to assist in the withdrawal of Israeli forces. Moscow and its allies concurred that Israeli troops should withdraw. However, they emphasized Israeli culpability in the situation and demanded that Tel Aviv be solely responsible for the force's expenditures. Eventually both the Soviet Union and Czechoslovakia were to abstain from the vote that authorized the establishment of UNIFIL, and Moscow and other members of the Warsaw Pact would also refuse to pay

their assessments for the operation until the East-West détente in the latter 1980s. France, as Lebanon's former colonial power, had a particular responsibility for events there and so was a strong supporter of Israeli withdrawal under UN supervision. A pan-Arab consensus also existed in favor of UN intervention. Israel, on the other hand, was against interference in its affairs and was only persuaded to accede to UN involvement under severe U.S. political pressure.

On 19 March 1978 the Security Council adopted SCR 425, by which it demanded respect for Lebanon's territorial integrity and national sovereignty, the restoration of Lebanese governmental authority, a cessation of Israeli military action against Lebanon's territorial integrity and a withdrawal of Israeli forces, and the establishment of UNIFIL to supervise the accomplishment of these provisions. However, in order to accommodate the contradictory requirements of the interested parties, the UNIFIL mandate deliberately contained equivocal language, and such vagaries led to disagreement over the force's area of operation and responsibilities. It was suggested that the UNIFIL area of operation should comprise the territory evacuated by the IDF. Meanwhile, in anticipation of this, the IDF in southern Lebanon had advanced northward as far as the Litani River in order to make the UN buffer zone between Israel and the PLO as wide as possible. This area, except for a Palestinian-controlled region around Tyre known as the "Tyre pocket," was eventually agreed upon as UNIFIL operational territory. The Israelis and Palestinians also disagreed over what UNIFIL's objectives should be within that area. Tel Aviv believed that the area should be cleared of all Palestinians, whereas Arafat referred to the Cairo Agreement as legitimization for a continued Palestinian presence there.

It was originally planned that UNIFIL would comprise some 4,000 personnel. However, the secretary-general recommended increasing the strength to 6,000 to cover the Israeli withdrawal, and this was duly achieved by June 1975. Troops were contributed by Fiji, France, Iran, Ireland, Nepal, Nigeria, Norway, and Senegal; logistical units arrived from Canada, France, and Norway; and 42 military observers from the United Nations Truce Supervision Organization (UNTSO) were also deployed to assist with the force's establishment. Although it was not normal practice to involve troops from permanent members of the Security Council in peacekeeping operations, French troops were included in UNIFIL in view of France's particular interest in Lebanon, as had previously been done with British troops in Cyprus. The strength of UNIFIL was again increased in 1982, to 7,000, with the inclusion of Canadian, Fijian, Ghanaian, Dutch, and Swedish troops.

The UNIFIL operation was planned in three distinct phases: First, the force would monitor the withdrawal of Israeli troops from southern Lebanon; second, an atmosphere of security and stability was to be achieved in the UNIFIL area of operation; and last, the territory would be returned to Lebanese authority. However, observers have pointed out that, as has already been mentioned, the Lebanese authority's jurisdiction had not in reality stretched as far as the south of the country for a number of years.

The first phase began smoothly. Israeli forces progressively withdrew from the buffer zone and transferred evacuated territory to the United Nations. However, in withdrawing from the southernmost region of the zone in June, an area that has since come to be known as "the enclave," the IDF handed authority over to the local Christian militia, under the command of Maj. Saad Haddad, known as the De Facto Forces (DFF), who were closely allied with Tel Aviv. Although UNIFIL did succeed in establishing several positions within the enclave, and in fact had its headquarters within the enclave, at En Naqura, it never achieved full control or even freedom of movement in the area, whereas IDF troops were granted unimpeded access.

Neither was UNIFIL able to establish full authority over the rest of the buffer zone. The situation was exacerbated by the presence of PLO troops to the north of the zone and Syrians to the east. UNIFIL personnel regularly became targets for Palestinian and Lebanese fighters from the north, and hostilities broke out between those fighters and the DFF across the buffer zone. These latter skirmishes often involved Israeli forces, who

regularly retaliated with strikes north of the red line. In April 1979 UNIFIL headquarters themselves were shelled, and Lebanese troops were prevented from deploying in the zone. Despite various UN-brokered cease-fires, tensions continued over the next few years, primarily between the IDF and DFF and the PLO.

In July 1981 the Security Council adopted SCR 490, which formalized international support for a recent cease-fire and for the reinstitution of Lebanese authority throughout its territory. The cease-fire held until April 1982, although PLO infiltration and DFF harassment continued within the buffer zone. During this period UNIFIL did achieve some successes. It had managed to increase security in the zone by means of checkpoints at points of entry, observation posts, regular foot and motorized patrols, and deployment of guards along its perimeter. Large numbers of civilians had been able to return to the area, and UNIFIL accomplished a vital humanitarian function by periodically providing emergency food and medical supplies when required, implementing various community projects, and carrying out mine-clearance operations. Furthermore, the conflict had been restricted from escalating either to a regional level in the form of a direct confrontation between Israel and Syria or to an international level in the form of superpower involvement.

On 6 June 1982 Israel launched a second major offensive into southern Lebanon. The preceding months had witnessed increased tension between Israelis and Palestinians. Israeli officials were attacked abroad, and Tel Aviv launched retaliatory air strikes against suspected Palestinian targets in southern Lebanon. UNIFIL was able to offer no real resistance to the invading army. The Israeli forces quickly reached the outskirts of Beirut, and PLO fighters were effectively expelled from the occupied territory. UNIFIL continued to operate in the buffer zone under its original mandate and maintained its force strength of 6,000. The UN force carried on with its various humanitarian activities and again managed to maintain some kind of stability in the area by limiting the activities of IDF and DFF troops. However, the UN presence as a peacekeeping force became essentially titular, serving primarily as a demonstration of international disapproval of Israel's actions but incapable of directly influencing them.

The emergence of various political groups complicated the situation in Lebanon during the period up to 1985. Sections of the disaffected Lebanese Shia population had formed an armed group, the Amal movement, which received support from Syria and worked in opposition to the PLO. Following the expulsion of the PLO forces in 1982, the Amal had become a type of de facto authority in southern Lebanon. Furthermore, following the death of Haddad in 1984, the DFF had reformed as the South Lebanon Army (SLA).

In September 1983 the IDF, under international supervision, withdrew from the outskirts of Beirut (see the MNF I section in this entry). A further redeployment in February 1985 followed an announcement from Tel Aviv that Israeli troops would have evacuated the whole of southern Lebanon by the middle of the year. The Israeli withdrawal prompted increased armed Shia action against the IDF, in the face of which UNIFIL was again impotent. However, the ensuing phased withdrawal of IDF troops stopped before the Israeli border, as Tel Aviv refused to completely abandon southern Lebanon. Indeed, the new Israeli "security zone," which has come to be known as the "Israeli-controlled area" (ICA), proved to be more extensive than the pre-1982 version had been.

The SLA were left nominally in charge of the ICA, with only a small IDF presence, although there were no illusions as to the availability of Israeli support whenever required. This situation left UNIFIL in a precarious predicament, since its area of operation encroached into the ICA. To continue operations in occupied territory transgressed traditional peacekeeping philosophy. However, to withdraw would have appeared to sanction illegal Israeli actions, which would have seriously damaged the UN's reputation of impartiality, particularly among Arab states. In response, UNIFIL divided the security zone into three primary sections, one of which was the ICA. The United Nations retained a token presence within the ICA and a more substantial deployment in the other zones. Within the ICA, UNIFIL has not been in a position to take any action against illegal activities, and the force has been severely restricted in other zones, where security action has been limited to checkpoints, observation posts, and patrols.

Continued factionalization of political groups during the 1980s served to further complicate the situation in southern Lebanon. Amal remained popular in the area, but a new, more extreme Shia group, Hezbollah, emerged. Hezbollah was patronized by the Iranian regime. Whereas Amal had been primarily intent on removing the Israeli presence from southern Lebanon, Hezbollah harbored wider ambitions of pan-Arab unity and radical Islamism. Hezbollah's increasing popularity prompted more extremist attitudes from Amal, further heightening tension in the area. For instance, in 1986 the death of a local Amal leader at the hands of a French peacekeeper precipitated violent attacks against French positions from both Amal and, subsequently, Hezbollah. Events were exacerbated by France's colonial history in Lebanon and contemporaneous French links with Iraq during the Iran-Iraq War. But for the diplomatic intervention of Syria and Iran and expressions of support for UNIFIL from both Israel and Amal, the situation might have developed to international proportions. The 1985 Israeli redeployment also prompted renewed PLO activity between the ICA and the Litani River, and serious tension remains in the area at the end of the century. For instance, in spring 1996 Hezbollah fighters launched mortar attacks from near the UN camp at Qana. In response Israeli fighter planes initiated air strikes against the suspected targets, killing many civilians within the camps in the process.

The UN mission in Lebanon can be evaluated both positively and negatively, depending on the analytical perspective. On the one hand, it is evident that UNIFIL has failed to realize its mandate as a peacekeeping force. The authority of the Lebanese government has not been restored throughout the country, the armed forces of a neighboring country continue to occupy a significant proportion of Lebanese territory within the UN area of operations, and armed factions also continue to operate within that area. However, the authority of the Lebanese government had been eroded long before the arrival of the Israeli armed forces, and so its restoration was not solely contingent on the removal of the IDF from Lebanon. Furthermore, the Israelis had only grudgingly consented to the UNIFIL deployment in the first place, offering limited cooperation with the UN force, and it seems likely that the establishment of a permanent Israeli security zone had been planned from the start. Nor had other armed factions operating in the area, mostly contrary to the UNIFIL mandate, consented to the UN presence.

At the same time, it is likely that UNIFIL's buffer role between Israel and its enemies in southern Lebanon, although by no means hermetic, has prevented more frequent and more serious outbreaks of violence between the opposing parties. The UN presence has also helped prevent Syria and Israel from coming to blows. In turn, both of these functions have prevented any cross-border violence from developing to regional, and possibly international, dimensions. UNIFIL has also served in an invaluable humanitarian capacity. The provision of basic facilities such as health care and water supplies and the atmosphere of relative stability that the force has helped to establish have enabled civilians to return to southern Lebanon and to attempt to pursue a normal life. The international significance of UNIFIL is reflected in the continuing renewal of its mandate and regular payment of assessments for the operation by UN member states.

As of 31 December 1997 the force commander of UNIFIL was Maj. Gen. Jioje Konouse Konrote (Fiji), and the force strength was 4,470 troops, assisted by approximately 60 military observers serving with UNTSO and supported by international and local civilian staff. Military personnel have been contributed by Fiji, Finland, France, Ghana, Ireland, Italy, Nepal, Norway, and Poland.

MNF I

The second Israeli invasion of Lebanon, launched as a result of increasing tension between Israel and the members of the PLO stationed in southern Lebanon, quickly reached as far north as the outskirts of Beirut. An estimated 6,000–8,000 PLO fighters had infiltrated the Beirut population, and the IDF placed the city under siege for a period of two months. Israeli raids often took the form of air attacks against suspected PLO urban positions, and during the siege some 10,000 people, mainly Lebanese civilians, were killed. The IDF rural offensive was more discriminating in directly targeting Palestinian fighters, significantly reducing PLO numbers in the countryside. The first Israeli invasion of 1978 had precipitated the entry of Syrian troops into Lebanon, and these troops still maintained positions in West Beirut, causing fighting to break out between the Syrians and the IDF.

The likelihood that the violence in Beirut would escalate domestically, regionally, and internationally, coupled with diplomatic embarrassment over the behavior of its ally, Israel, encouraged the United States to promote a negotiated settlement to the dispute. Various factors persuaded the belligerents to accede to U.S. wishes. In military terms, although Israel had enjoyed considerable success against the PLO in the countryside, its urban offensive had failed to significantly damage Palestinian positions in Beirut, and the Israelis were reluctant to get involved in difficult and costly urban warfare. Political considerations, both domestic and international, also affected Israel's stance. Domestic opinion did not approve of the numerous Israeli casualties being reported from the conflict, and Israel's actions in Lebanon had prompted severe international criticism, including from the United States. Thus Tel Aviv was ready to accept U.S. proposals, provided assurances were given that PLO fighters had left Lebanon and that Syrians had evacuated West Beirut. The defeat of Palestinians in rural areas convinced the PLO leadership to agree to withdraw from Lebanon, on condition that face-saving measures and a safe exit were guaranteed. Meanwhile heavy losses had already persuaded the Syrians to agree to a cease-fire with Israel on 11 June, and so President Assad was amenable to a peaceful solution.

There was a general consensus amongst the protagonists that some kind of supervisory force would be required to facilitate the above provisions. However, Israel was wary of a pro-Palestinian bias within the United Nations and so opposed a UN operation. Although Israel was not the host nation and therefore had no legal say over any prospective operation, in reality Tel Aviv's central and influential position in the conflict provided it with de facto veto powers. Following the example of the U.S.-led Multinational Force and Observers (MFO) that had recently been deployed to the Sinai and encouraged by its historical ties with Washington, Israel suggested the establishment of a similar U.S.-led, non-UN peacekeeping force to supervise the peace settlement in Lebanon. The Christian-dominated Lebanese government was also in favor of such a move, while the PLO was reassured by the involvement of a nation as powerful as the United States in the process.

Thus, on 21 August, following the establishment of a cease-fire between the opposing parties, the first members of the first Multinational Force (MNF I) began to deploy to Beirut. The force comprised 800 U.S., 800 French, and 400 Italian troops and operated under a very strict peacekeeping mandate. The operation was to be completed within 30 days, the troops were forbidden to use any force except in self-defense, and any deviation from the timetable for the evacuation of PLO fighters would precipitate the force's immediate withdrawal. The operation ran smoothly. By 9 September all Palestinian and Syrian troops had been removed from Beirut, and the MNF left the city on 12 September. Thus an extremely volatile situation, with potentially far-reaching consequences, had been effectively defused. However, as the next section, MNF II, reveals, the underlying problems in Lebanon were far from over.

MNF II

On 14 September 1982, two days after MNF I had withdrawn from Beirut, the recently elected Lebanese president, Bashir Gemayel, was assassinated. On 15 September the Israeli Defense Force (IDF) entered West Beirut, a predominantly Muslim sector of the capital that is separated from the Maronite Christian side by a "green line" that bisects the city. Then the Christian-dominated Lebanese Army, under Israeli instigation, entered Palestinian refugee camps at Sabra and Shatila in search of PLO fighters, killing between 800 and 2,000 refugees in the process. This prompted widespread international condemnation and convinced the countries that had participated in MNF I, France, Italy, and in particular the United States, to hastily announce the force's reestablishment.

Brief delays followed Israeli prevarication, but by the end of September the international presence, as Multinational Force II (MNF II), had been redeployed in Beirut, and the IDF had withdrawn from the western part of the city.

At its peak, the United States contributed 1,400 troops, the Italians 2,200, and the United Kingdom a small contingent of 100 to MNF II. Thus the second force was larger, and more heavily armed, than the first had been and was not subject to the same time restrictions—no date was set for its withdrawal. However, it was still mandated under strict traditional peacekeeping principles. MNF II was initially to deploy between Israeli troops and Muslim fighters in Beirut in order to promote stability and to establish an atmosphere of security throughout the capital. It would then assist the Lebanese Army in its law-and-order duties in the city, thereby facilitating the return of authority to the Lebanese government.

At first the operation went according to plan. MNF joined the Lebanese Army at checkpoints and during patrols around Beirut, successfully establishing a more stable environment in the city, and also helped to train Lebanese troops. However, a poorly brokered agreement between Israel and the Lebanese government created significant difficulties for the peacekeeping force. Both the Palestinians and the Lebanese Muslim community were suspicious of the predominantly pro-Christian Lebanese Army, with its strong links to Israel, and these suspicions transferred directly onto MNF. MNF was further mistrusted because of traditional U.S. ties with Israel, while French colonial associations with the Lebanese Christian Maronite community were still widely remembered. During this period PLO fighters began to operate again within Palestinian refugee camps, while Sunni militias were able to launch periodic attacks against Israeli positions.

Meanwhile, in May 1983 Washington brokered the terms for an Israeli withdrawal. However, the terms of the agreement protected Israeli security objectives in southern Lebanon, and this was perceived throughout the Arab community as Lebanese accession to Israeli interests. Syria also resented having been excluded from the negotiations. In September Israeli forces withdrew from

West Beirut and handed their positions over to the Lebanese Army, which attempted to arrest suspected PLO and Muslim fighters. Hostilities between Syrian-backed Muslim militia and Lebanese government forces then dramatically increased. MNF II personnel, particularly U.S. and French positions, were regularly involved in these hostilities. Consequently, MNF II became increasingly proactive in the conflict, fighting on the side of the Lebanese Army, until the death of 241 U.S. and 58 French troops at the hands of suicide bombers in October prompted forcible retaliation from the relevant peacekeeping contingents. MNF II's deviation into combat ultimately prompted its withdrawal, as it had ceased to act within traditional peacekeeping principles. Therefore, from early 1984 on, the Americans, Italians, and finally the French progressively pulled out of Beirut. French proposals that a UN force replace MNF II were vetoed by the Soviet Union, which, as an ally of Syria, did not wish to counter Syrian-backed Muslim advances in Lebanon.

The failure of the MNF II operation resulted from a number of primary factors. Like its predecessor, MNF I, MNF II was required to support a government that had long since lost authority and legitimacy in the eyes of the people it was supposed to serve. Furthermore, the police duties that MNF II was asked to perform inevitably made its supposed impartiality seem suspect, and the perception that MNF II might not be impartial was heightened by the political associations of the force's contributors, particularly in respect to the status of the Lebanese government. MNF II's involvement in military activity in favor of one side in the dispute confirmed such suspicions of bias and therefore precipitated the force's failure and withdrawal.

See also League of Arab States; United Nations Truce Supervision Organization, 1948–
References and further reading Boerma (1979); Durch (1993, 1994); Erskine (1989); Heiberg (1986); James (1990); Rabinovich (1985); Thakur (1987); United Nations (1966)

Liberia

Military Observer Group of the Economic Organization of West African States

(ECOMOG), 1990– ; United Nations Observer Mission in Liberia (UNOMIL), 1993–1997

Conflict Profile
Liberia has been described as the first country since the end of the Cold War "to commit national suicide." The vicious civil war initiated by the insurrection of Charles Taylor's National Patriotic Front of Liberia (NPFL) against the regime of Samuel K. Doe on Christmas Eve 1989 has resulted in the deaths of up to 150,000 Liberians, mass displacement of a majority of the population, and almost complete national breakdown. In terms of peacekeeping two features have been particularly noteworthy. First is the remarkable experiment in regional peacekeeping by armed forces of the Economic Organization of West African States (ECOWAS) from 25 August 1990. Second is the fact that the United Nations Observer Mission in Liberia (UNOMIL), established on 22 September 1993 by UN Security Council Resolution (SCR) 866, was "the first United Nations peace-keeping mission undertaken in cooperation with a peace-keeping operation already set up by another organization."

With an Atlantic seaboard along the west African Guinea coast, Liberia is a country of tropical rain forests and broken plateaus. Founded in the 1820s as a U.S.-sponsored settlement of freed slaves, Liberia has been an independent republic since 1847, over a century before its west African neighbors began to gain independence from Britain, France, Portugal, and Spain beginning in 1957. Liberia was dependent upon U.S. political protection and economic aid. In the 1920s the U.S. Firestone company became the dominant investor in Liberia's rubber plantations. Iron ore now accounts for more than 50 percent of export revenue, although the industry employs only 2 percent of the workforce. The economy also benefits from Liberia's status as a "flag of convenience" for nearly 2,500 ships, about one-fifth of world maritime tonnage. Three-quarters of the labor force is employed in agriculture, although more than half the country's grain has to be imported. In the 1980s the economy suffered from a fall in world commodity prices, the burden of payments on an external debt of £1.7 billion ($2.7 billion U.S.), and

International Monetary Fund suspension of aid after 1986 in response to nonpayment of debts.

Political power before 1980 was in the hands of a few leading families within the small "Americo-Liberian" elite that made up between 2 percent and 4 percent of the population. The rest of the population is made up of members of some 16 main indigenous tribes speaking 28 native languages and largely adhering to traditional religions. About 10 percent of the population are Christian, and 10–20 percent are Muslim. After the presidency of William Tubman (1944–1971) the status quo was increasingly challenged under his successor, William Tolbert, whose regime was finally overthrown in a bloody coup led by Samuel Doe in 1980, when the long period of Americo-Liberian hegemony came to an end. After an initial period of euphoria, the Doe regime, attempting to cling to power against international pressure to democratize, progressively succumbed to economic failure, political corruption, increasingly blatant dependence upon Doe's own ethnic group (the Krahn) and another ethnic group (the Mandingo), and a decline in U.S. support as the Cold War came to an end. When Taylor's NPFL invaded Nimba County, on the northeastern border, from the Ivory Coast at the end of 1989, the tribal dimension of the conflict was shown by the fact that his forces were largely recruited from the Mano and Gio tribes. Doe's Armed Forces of Liberia (AFL) responded ferociously, but by July 1990 the NPFL had seized control of 95 percent of the country and 12 of the 13 counties and was advancing on the capital, Monrovia. The war was brutal, including massacres, rapes, and other atrocities; by the end of the year more than 10,000 had been killed, there were 600,000 refugees in neighboring countries, and perhaps half the population of some 2.3 million was internally displaced.

The Deployment of ECOMOG

The international community was slow to respond. The United States did not intervene to support the Doe regime. The Organization of African Unity (OAU) stayed clear, perhaps remembering earlier failure in Chad. The UN secretary-general tried to raise the issue of Liberia in the Security

Council on 28 May 1990, but this was blocked by African governments led by Nigeria, which was keen to keep external interference out of the region. Instead, in response to an appeal to Nigeria and Togo by Doe on 7 May 1990, Nigeria took the lead in suggesting an intervention by the ECOWAS states, despite the fact that francophone members such as Côte d'Ivoire and Burkina Faso supported the Taylor insurrection. ECOWAS set up a Standing Mediation Committee (SMC) made up of Nigeria, Gambia, Ghana, Mali, and Togo on 28 May to mediate in the conflict, and on 6 July the committee presented a Peace Plan providing for a cease-fire, the establishment of a peacekeeping force, the encampment and disarmament of fighters, the establishment of an interim government, and free and fair elections to be held under international supervision within 12 months. This was the first of a series of similar plans proposed over the ensuing years. Taylor, believing that he would win an outright military victory, rejected the plan. ECOWAS nevertheless pressed ahead, forming the Military Observer Group of the Economic Organization of West African States (ECOMOG) on 6 August. ECOMOG was made up of military units from the SMC countries together with Sierra Leone and Guinea under the command of Gen. Arnold Quainoo (Ghana); it had a voluntarily raised operational budget of £50 million. Nigeria contributed the bulk of the 4,000 ECOMOG forces, which landed in Monrovia beginning 25 August 1990. The fact that ECOMOG was opposed by Taylor from the beginning conditioned much of the peacekeeping effort that followed. On 30 August an Interim Government of National Unity (IGNU) was set up with Dr. Amos Sawyer, former political opponent of Doe, as interim president. On 10 September Doe was killed at an ECOMOG compound, despite the fact that he had gone there under guarantee of safety from the ECOMOG commander. On 27 November 1990, in the face of a military stalemate between Taylor's forces, which controlled most of the nation, and ECOMOG's forces, which maintained a 20-kilometer "security perimeter" around Monrovia, a cease-fire was eventually negotiated that held, on and off, until 15 October 1992.

By the beginning of 1991 there were four contenders for power: (1) Taylor's NPFL, with a fighting force of about 3,000; control of 90 percent of Liberian territory and most of the timber, mineral, and rubber-producing wealth; and a 24-member interim government with headquarters at Gbarnga; (2) the IGNU in Monrovia, dependent upon protection by ECOMOG forces and supplies from the United Nations and relief agencies, which were consequently seen to be partisan by the NPFL; (3) a breakaway from NPFL since February 1990, the Independent National Patriotic Front of Liberia (INPFL) led by Prince Johnson, centered to the southwest of Monrovia with some 500 fighters; and (4) after May 1990, the 3,000-strong forces of the United Liberation Movement for Democracy in Liberia (ULIMO), founded by three exiled anti-Taylor groups in Guinea (including the Liberian Peace Council [LPC]), which was seen to be made up largely of members of the Krahn tribe and former Doe officials. Doe's original AFL also survived in skeletal form.

Between November 1990 and October 1991 several attempts to mediate peace were made, including conferences at Bamako (November 1990), Lomé (February 1991), and Monrovia (March 1991). Meanwhile internal tensions within ECOWAS were reflected by shifts in initiative from the anglophone-dominated SMC to the francophone-dominated Committee of Five (Ghana, Senegal, Guinea-Bissau, Togo, Côte d'Ivoire). Whereas Nigeria tended to favor imposition of a solution by force despite Taylor's objections, Côte d'Ivoire favored negotiation. In particular, President Houphouet-Boigny of Côte d'Ivoire initiated a series of meetings at Yamoussoukro, the fourth of which (Yamoussoukro IV) finally seemed to cement an agreement between Sawyer and Taylor on 30 October 1991. The main provisions were that (1) ECOMOG would establish a demilitarized zone between the combatants, in particular NPFL and ULIMO, and all combatants would be disarmed and encamped within 60 days, both under the supervision of ECOMOG; (2) IGNU and NPFL would appoint a special electoral commission to prepare for national elections under international supervision; (3) both sides would cooperate in establishing appropriate institutions to oversee the transitional arrangements; and (4) all roads would be opened. A United Nations Special Coordinator's

Office (UNSCOL) had opened in December 1990 and was expanded to help coordinate the peace process and humanitarian assistance through the United Nations Development Program (UNDP), the Food and Agriculture Organization (FAO), the United Nations Children's Fund (UNICEF), the World Food Program (WFP), and the World Health Organization (WHO). Regional arrangements were made to assist refugees in neighboring countries. On 22 January 1992 the UN Security Council took up the Liberian question for the first time, commending the peacekeeping efforts of ECOWAS and supporting the Yamoussoukro IV measures.

In 1992, however, attempts to implement the peace plan foundered. Details included continuing conflict between ULIMO and NPFL forces, disagreement between IGNU and NPFL about the definition and control of transitional arrangements, and Taylor's refusal to be disarmed by ECOMOG and ECOMOG's refusal to accept Taylor's proposal that his commanders collect and secure weapons. On 15 July the ECOWAS Committee of Five at Dakar resolved to impose comprehensive economic sanctions on NPFL-held areas unless NPFL took part in the disarmament process. On 15 October 1992 the precarious November 1990 cease-fire was comprehensively breached when NPFL launched a full-scale two-month siege of Monrovia. The bizarre ferocity of the Liberian conflict was revealed to the world's media as Taylor's teenage army, drunk and dressed in wigs, wedding dresses, and goggles, indulged in an orgy of bloodshed and drove nearly a quarter of a million people into flight. Having raised the siege of Monrovia, ECOMOG, supported by ULIMO, attempted in January 1993 to defeat the NPFL outright, reinforced by 5,000 fresh troops from Nigeria and Ghana. Despite large initial gains for ECOMOG, by May 1993 a military stalemate had reemerged.

In response to all this and in particular to an ECOWAS request, the UN Security Council was finally stung into imposing a general and complete embargo on weapons and military equipment to Liberia, except supplies to ECOWAS forces, in SCR 788 of 19 November 1992. The secretary-general was asked to send a special representative (SRSG) to evaluate the situation and make recommendations for a possibly expanded UN response. Trevor Livingston Gordon-Somers (Jamaica), appointed SRSG, consulted the parties to the Liberian conflict and the executive secretary and member states of ECOWAS. On 12 March 1993 the secretary-general informed the Security Council that there was a general desire for a larger UN role and recommended coordination with ECOWAS as envisaged under chapter 8 of the UN Charter. The UN could play a role in political reconciliation and in humanitarian and electoral assistance. SCR 813 of 26 March 1993 suggested a meeting of the Liberian factions to affirm the Yamoussoukro IV Accord and recommended discussions with the Liberian parties and ECOWAS about the UN contribution. The upshot was a relaunch of the peace process at a three-day meeting in Cotonou, Benin, cochaired by the ECOWAS executive secretary, the UN SGSR, and Canaan Banana, president of the OAU. On 25 July 1993 the IGNU, NPFL, and ULIMO signed the Cotonou Peace Agreement, which provided the framework for direct UN involvement. By SCR 856 of 10 August 1993 an advance team of 30 UN military observers was sent to Liberia to participate in supervising the new 1 August ceasefire before the arrival of the full UN mission (see Map 6).

The Deployment of UNOMIL

UNOMIL was deployed alongside ECOMOG between September 1993 and August 1994, implementing the Cotonou Peace Agreement. By SCR 866 of 22 September 1993, UNOMIL was initially established for a seven-month period to work with ECOMOG on implementing the agreement. It was made up of a military component under the command of the chief military observer (CMO), Maj. Gen. Daniel Opande (Kenya) (succeeded in November 1995 by Maj. Gen. Mahmoud Talha [Egypt]), and a civilian component made up of an Administrative Division, a Humanitarian and Development Affairs Division, and an Electoral Division. SRSG Gordon-Somers was overall head of mission (succeeded in December 1994 by Anthony Nyakyi [United Republic of Tanzania]). The authorized strength of UNOMIL was 303 military observers, 20 military medical personnel, and 45

military engineers. There was also provision for 89 civilian international personnel, 58 UN Volunteers, and 136 local staff.

Following the lines of the 1979 Lancaster House Agreement for Zimbabwe and, more recently, the 1990 Paris Peace Agreements in Cambodia, the Cotonou Peace Agreement envisaged linked stages leading to nationwide elections in September 1994. Security for returning refugees and displaced people depended upon the disarmament of the factions, which in turn required adequate economic restoration to give a prospect of rehabilitation. Unlike in Cambodia, however, the interim government, the IGNU, was one of the warring parties, and the Liberian National Transitional Government (LNTG) (intended to have a life span of six months) was torn by faction and had scant authority outside Monrovia. Although not officially designated to do so, many Liberians assumed at first that the UN's SRSG would take over a much expanded form of the former UNSCOL coordinating role, along the lines of the influential role played by SGSR Yasushi Akashi in Cambodia. At the time UNOMIL was initiated, the United Nations Transitional Authority in Cambodia (UNTAC) was about to pull out of Cambodia after having successfully supervised the May 1993 elections. In the event, however, UNOMIL was evidently a very small mission compared with UNTAC and was almost entirely dependent upon ECOMOG for its security. UNOMIL deployed to Monrovia and to the four ECOMOG sector headquarters, but it proceeded elsewhere at its own risk—as shown when in June 1994 and again in September 1994 UNOMIL teams were seized and humiliated by the factions. SRSG Gordon-Somers's authority was accordingly severely circumscribed. The ECOMOG commander retained final authority over his forces, whereas UNOMIL vehicles were regularly stopped and searched at ECOMOG roadblocks and UNOMIL was also required to observe the ECOMOG curfew.

Although in the Cotonou Agreement the UN's coordinating role was seen to be complementary to ECOMOG's security role, the relationship was not made clear. The idea was for the two organizations to work in parallel at all levels, but many Liberians saw UNOMIL as subordinate to ECOMOG. It did

UNOMIL deployment as of December 1995

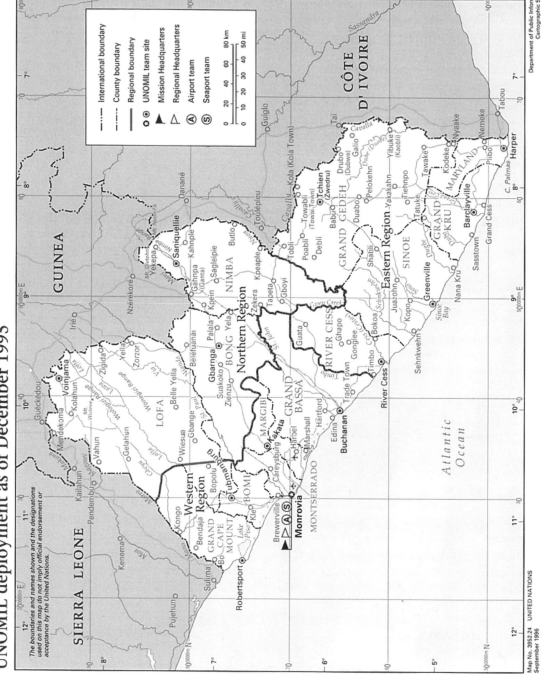

The boundaries and names shown and the designations used on this map do not imply official endorsement or acceptance by the United Nations.

Legend

- ---·---·--- International boundary
- ---··---··--- County boundary
- ——— Regional boundary
- ○ ⊙ UNOMIL team site
- ▲ Mission Headquarters
- △ Regional Headquarters
- Ⓐ Airport team
- Ⓢ Seaport team

Scale:
0 10 20 30 40 60 80 km
0 10 20 30 40 50 mi

Department of Public Information
Cartographic Section

Map No. 3952.24   UNITED NATIONS
September 1996

not seem plausible that ECOMOG's activities would be effectively "monitored and verified by the United Nations observers" as envisaged in the agreement. Other criticisms of the agreement concerned the vagueness of article 15 on procedures for the elections (which were left to LNTG and an Electoral Commission) and the loosely defined goal of "disarming" the factions before alternative means of employment were found, political arrangements for overseeing the process were secure, or plans for creating a composite national army were agreed upon. Between 700,000 and perhaps more than 1 million Liberians were still displaced, and the 1985 electoral boundaries had been rendered obsolete. Finally, aid programs were seen as creating dependency and as being too sophisticated to be sustained by a Liberian government. UNOMIL's plan for demobilization was in many ways well conceived—for example, it recognized the difficulties involved in rehabilitating young Liberians indoctrinated as faction fighters whose home communities had been uprooted or destroyed. But lack of a nationwide political authority, ECOMOG's delays in reaching disarmament and demobilization location sites, and a complex pattern of localized reasons for resisting demobilization meant that by 22 June 1994 only 755 AFL forces, 741 NPFL forces, and 769 ULIMO forces had been disarmed out of what were estimated to be some 60,000 soldiers altogether.

ECOMOG's ambivalent role was a fundamental problem. ECOMOG was now operating in small, lightly armed bands as peacekeepers, but as recently as April 1993 it had mounted a full-scale assault on the NPFL, with rocket launchers, naval gunfire, and ground attack aircraft. The political interests of Nigeria, which provided some 8,000 of what were now 11,500 ECOMOG forces, were seen to favor LPC, whereas francophone ECOWAS states leaned toward NPFL. The addition of two battalions of east African troops (from Tanzania and Uganda) could not transform the situation.

The five-member Council of State was selected by the Liberian parties by 17 August 1993, but delays to the disarmament process held up the swearing-in, and there was no agreement about the final composition of the LNTG, particularly

about the disposition of the ministerial portfolios of defense, foreign affairs, justice, and finance. By January 1994 UNOMIL and the expanded ECOMOG forces had arrived, and ten encampment sites for AFL, NPFL, and ULIMO were identified. The Joint Cease-Fire Monitoring Committee, set up by the warring factions at Cotonou, was replaced by a Violations Committee chaired by the UNOMIL CMO. On 15 February 1994 the Liberian parties agreed to install the LNTG and begin disarmament on 7 March, with a view to holding elections on 7 September. The transitional Legislative Assembly was inducted into office, and the Supreme Court of Liberia opened. The electoral process was estimated to cost $13.7 million. UNOMIL and ECOMOG deployed reasonably successfully in the western (Tubmanburg) and central-northern (Gbarnga) regions, but there was continuing insecurity in the northern (Lofa) and southeastern parts of the country. In the former the Lofa Defence Force (LDF) emerged and in the latter the LPC reemerged; both were armed factions that had not taken part in the Cotonou process. The UN Security Council, meeting in April 1994, applied pressure by making renewal of UNOMIL's mandate dependent upon full installation of the LNTG and substantial progress in the peace process. No sooner were interparty disputes about representation and ministerial briefs on the LNTG finally resolved, however, than the ULIMO leadership split along ethnic lines on the issue of ULIMO nominees, with Chairman Alhaji Kromah representing the Mandingo and Gen. Roosevelt Johnson the Krahn. Fighting broke out between ULIMO-M and ULIMO-K and also between the NPFL and the LPC in the southeast. There were signs of a further split in the NPFL (leading to the emergence of the breakaway Central Revolutionary Council [CRC]) as faction leaders lost control of some of their forces and banditry and civilian harassment increased. The important question was raised whether swift initial disarmament was the wisest strategy in circumstances of national breakdown where there was no alternative source of authority to ensure security. Both ULIMO/LPC and NPFL accused ECOMOG of lacking impartiality and of favoring the other side. The disarmament process stalled (only 3,192 combatants demobilized), ECOMOG and UNOMIL were unable to deploy in a number of areas, Nigerian and Ugandan soldiers were abducted, and a UN Security Council deadline for all-party meetings in July 1994 was ignored. The UN secretary-general sent a special envoy, Lakhdar Brahimi, to assess the situation.

A further stage in the conflict can be identified between September 1994 and July 1995, concerned with implementing the Akosombo and Accra Agreements. On 7 September 1994 President Jerry Rawlings of Ghana, chairman of ECOWAS, succeeded in convening a meeting attended by NPFL, the various wings of ULIMO (ULIMO-J did not sign), and AFL at Akosombo, Ghana, facilitated by UN and OAU representatives. The LDF and the LPC refused to attend. On 12 September a supplementary agreement confirming the Cotonou Agreement was signed. Representation on LNTG was broadened by the addition of representatives from the 13 counties. Elections were envisaged by October 1995. Unfortunately, the situation in Liberia continued to deteriorate into a confusion of factional fighting between rival warlords. A further 200,000 people were displaced, and movement of relief supplies into and around the country became impossible. In September, 43 UNOMIL observers and six representatives of nongovernmental organizations were detained by NPFL forces and mistreated. ULIMO-J also attacked ECOMOG-UNOMIL personnel. As a result UNOMIL numbers were sharply reduced—on the military side down to 90 observers from the authorized strength of 368. By June 1995 it was estimated that 1.1 million out of the 1.5 million in need were receiving humanitarian assistance; 400,000 remained inaccessible. By August the number in need had risen to 1.8 million. The UN secretary-general sent a high-level mission under Lansana Kouyaté to the region. He reported that peace in Liberia lay in the hands of the political and faction leaders and urged the six ECOWAS countries most affected—Burkina Faso, Côte d'Ivoire, Ghana, Guinea, Nigeria, and Sierra Leone—to resolve their differences and harmonize their policies on Liberia.

In December the fragmented Liberian factions were finally brought together to sign the Accra Agreement. The agreement consisted of two instruments, one signed by the Akosombo signatories (NPFL, ULIMO-K, AFL) and one signed by the other factions (ULIMO-J, LPC, LDF, CRC-NPFL, and the Liberian National Conference [LNC]). In the event, however, the AFL and coalition forces (ULIMO-J, LDF, LPC, CRC-NPFL) could not agree on their joint nominee to the new Council of State. A technical team was sent by the UN secretary-general in February 1995 to assess the ECOMOG-UNOMIL requirements for implementation of the Accra Agreement. ECOMOG's current strength was given as 8,430 troops in 10 infantry battalions, and ECOMOG estimated a need for some 12,000 troops altogether to fulfill its mission. At the same time a $65 million interagency consolidated humanitarian appeal was launched. In recommendations to the Security Council in April 1995 the secretary-general described the options as follows: If the Liberian factions showed a willingness to implement the Accra Agreement, then either (1) UNOMIL's authorized strength as determined in 1993 should be restored and ECOMOG should be strengthened together with firmer enforcement of the arms embargo and better harmonization of ECOWAS policies, or (2) a full-scale UN peacekeeping force should be envisaged. But if no progress was made by the Liberian parties, then either (3) UNOMIL should be further scaled down, or (4) it should be withdrawn altogether. The secretary-general recommended option 3. By SCR 1001 of 30 June 1995 the Security Council renewed UNOMIL's mandate until 15 September 1995, but it warned that if no substantial progress toward peace was made the mandate would not be renewed thereafter. ECOWAS heads of state, meeting in Accra in late July, responded by warning that the withdrawal of UNOMIL would gravely compromise ECOMOG efforts to bring peace to Liberia.

The period between July 1995 and August 1996 represents another distinct phase, in which the Abuja Agreement was implemented. A renewed attempt was made to bring the warring factions together, culminating in a meeting at Abuja, Nigeria, from 16 to 19 August 1995, at which leaders of all the Liberian factions, as well as Chief Tamba Taylor, representing the traditional chiefs, signed an agreement confirming the previous Cotonou and Akosombo accords as clarified by the Accra Agreement. A comprehensive cease-fire was scheduled for 26 August 1995, and a six-man Council of State was to be installed on 1 September. The Council of State was to remain in power for a year until elections could be held on 20 August 1996. On 13 September 1995 the UN secretary-general reported that prospects for peace in Liberia were "perhaps better now than they have been at any time since the outbreak of the civil war." He recommended an extension of UNOMIL's mandate but underlined the gravity of the task of implementing the Abuja Agreement: Liberia was suffering from political fragmentation and institutional collapse; the nation contained 50,000 to 60,000 combatants, of whom 25 percent were children; the domestic police were not adequate to maintain law and order; and the economic infrastructure was ruined. A technical team visited Liberia in September 1995 to assess its requirements, and a recommended adjustment of UNOMIL's mandate was endorsed by SCR 1020 of 10 November 1995. Despite limited resources, including some 160 military observers, UNOMIL's function was tasked to exercise good offices—that is, to act as mediator—in support of ECOWAS and the transitional government; to help investigate and report alleged breaches of the cease-fire; to help monitor other military provisions including disarming and demobilization of combatants and to assist in the maintenance of assembly sites; to support humanitarian assistance activities, report human rights violations, and help local human rights groups; and to observe and verify the election process and the scheduled 20 August 1996 presidential and legislative elections in consultation with ECOWAS and OAU. ECOMOG, with troop strength enhanced to 12,000 total, was to monitor borders and entry points to Liberia to enforce the arms embargo, to assemble and disarm the factions, to establish checkpoints to verify movement of arms and assist the return of displaced people, and to carry out intensive patrols to create the confidence necessary for the electoral process. It was depressing to note how similar the program envisaged in the Abuja Agreement was to the original Peace Plan proposed by ECOWAS in May 1990.

In parallel with the political and military plans went an extensive humanitarian effort to sustain some 1.5 million Liberians, about 60 percent of the population. Approximately 700,000 Liberians were refugees in neighboring countries. In November 1995 a UN Humanitarian Coordination Unit was created to dovetail the work of UNICEF, the United Nations High Commission on Refugees (UNHCR), WFP, and other international agencies, including nongovernmental organizations. The unit consisted of a Humanitarian Assistance Coordination Office and a Demobilization and Reintegration Office.

Once again, however, after some initial progress the familiar pattern repeated itself. There were delays in the deployment of ECOMOG forces and renewed fighting between the factions in the early months of 1996. Political leaders on the Council of State, far from resolving the problems, became themselves caught up in them. Conditions for civilians deteriorated again sharply, and in renewed fighting UN staff were forced from homes and offices, robbed, and harassed despite the brave efforts of the local UN staff to help them. In the confusion, 88 of UNOMIL's 93 military observers were relocated to neighboring countries. ECOMOG refused to intervene in the factional fighting on the grounds that this was not part of its mandate, although when reinforcements arrived some protection was given to UN personnel, the mediation team, and the factional representatives involved in consultation. In his 21 May 1996 report the UN secretary-general concluded that there was little UNOMIL could do in the circumstances. Only the Liberian parties themselves could create the conditions that would enable regional or UN peacekeeping forces to assist the peace process.

When originally established, UNOMIL included 303 military observers, 20 medical personnel, and 45 military engineers. In October 1994, given the deteriorating conditions, UNOMIL's strength was reduced to some 90 military personnel, with further reductions coming in May and July 1995. After the Abuja Agreement recommended it, strength was increased to some 160 military observers, although following the subsequent outbreak of fighting the number of observers was reduced to 15 in April 1996. Military personnel were provided by Austria, Bangladesh, China, Czech Republic, Egypt, Guinea-Bissau, Hungary, India, Jordan, Kenya, Malaysia, Pakistan, Slovak Republic, and Uruguay. There was also an original provision for 89 civilian international personnel, 58 UN Volunteers, and 136 local staff. With the expanded mandate of November 1995, these estimates were increased, particularly by an expansion of local staff.

Estimated costs of UNOMIL from its inception in 1993 to 31 March 1996 came to $77,981,100.

References and further reading Ofuatey-Kodjoe (1994); Olonisakin (1996); Outram (1997); United Nations (1996)

Lie, Trygve (1896–1968)

Trygve Halvdan Lie was born on 16 June 1896 in Oslo, Norway. He qualified in law at the University of Oslo, entered Parliament in 1935, served in various ministries of the Norwegian government, and led the Norwegian delegation to the founding conference of the United Nations at San Francisco in 1945. He was the first secretary-general of the United Nations, in which post he served between 1946 and 1953. Lie is credited with having established a positive role for the office of secretary-general, insisting on the right of the head of the new organization to take initiatives in order to bring matters of concern to the Security Council (rather than being seen merely as the passive servant of the Security Council). His first test in office was the issue of the conflict between the emergent state of Israel and the Palestinians. In this conflict he established a mediating and independent role for the United Nations. Lie was also an advocate of establishing a credible military force under the Secretariat and the secretary-general. His "Memorandum for Peace through the United Nations," issued in 1950, was a further attempt to established a strong and positive role for the United Nations and its agencies in the face of growing disagreement among the superpowers that threatened to paralyze the United Nations. The outbreak of the Korean War in 1950, in which the United Nations declared North Korea to be the aggressor, resulted in Lie losing the support of the Soviet Union, which vetoed the renewal of his term of office.

Though no peacekeeping missions were initiated during his period of office, the early UN commissions in the Balkans, in Palestine, in Pakistan, and in Indonesia were first steps in a process that was to result in the formation of peacekeeping forces in 1956.

References and further reading Lie (1954)

Logistics

Mounting a UN mission is a very complex operation, even when the political decisions have been taken expeditiously. The process is managed by the Field Administration and Logistics Division. Each appropriate member state (including some who may be on the periphery of a conflict) is asked to agree to contribute personnel, equipment, or finances, and this can take time to work through each different political or administrative system. Once the individual contributions have been agreed to, the personnel and equipment have to be transported to the theater of operations. The mission also needs adequate supplies of food, fuel, and spare parts, as well as workshop capability and communications systems in order to function properly once in place. This complex process is at the heart of logistics, and it is not therefore surprising to learn that it can take between three and six months (on average) to fully deploy a mission.

In the past the United Nations has tried to overcome some of the logistical problems by building up a resource base of its own, by buying equipment and storing it centrally for mission use (currently located at Brindisi in Italy). But this system also has drawbacks, particularly the time lag between identifying a need, agreeing upon the purchase, and eventually acquiring it.

As of the late 1990s the secretary-general has been seeking to establish a new system to try to improve the organization's response time. Each member state is being asked to contribute resources on a "standby" basis. The agreed-upon resources will be housed in the "home" country but will be permanently available to the United Nations for mission deployment. The secretary-general will, via a series of individual agreements with each member state, have a central database of the resources available at any given time, and the planning and operational processes will thus be accelerated.

In terms of mission operation each contingent will be expected to be self-sufficient until the UN support systems are functioning. The time scale for this self-sufficiency is a *minimum* of 30 days, with 180 days *recommended* for spare parts and 60 days *recommended* for all other aspects.

This new system is still in its early days, and there are some teething problems to be overcome before it can be fully operational. For example, of the 185 member states, only 65 have given a provisional indication of the standby resources they are willing to commit. Of these, only 8 (Austria, Bolivia, Denmark, Ghana, Italy, Jordan, Malaysia, and Singapore) have actually signed the Memorandum of Understanding that formally commits them to participation. As another example, the resources for each mission are divided between those needed for operational functions and those needed for support functions. The majority of member states are equipped to provide the former, but only 36 have the necessary support capacities. The most striking example is the U.S. role in providing significant air transport and air support functions.

Currently, the secretary-general can call upon a theoretical 83,00 personnel under the United Nations Standby Arrangements System (UNSAS), including 880 civilian police and 240 civilian specialists.

See also Italy; Military medicine and peacekeeping

Macedonia

United Nations Preventive Deployment Force Macedonia (UNPREDEP), 1995–

The United Nations Preventive Deployment Force Macedonia (UNPREDEP) was created under Security Council Resolution 983 of 31 March 1995 as part of a general restructuring of UN peacekeeping forces in the former Yugoslavia. During the restructuring UNPREDEP was constituted as a separate peacekeeping force with headquarters in Skopje, Macedonia. The joint theater headquarters for all the peacekeeping operations, based in Zagreb, was known as the United Nations Peace Forces Headquarters (UNPF-HQ), which existed until the end of January 1996. From March 1995 to January 1996 overall command and control of UNPREDEP was under the special representative of the secretary-general (SRSG), Yasushi Akashi (Japan), based in UNPF-HQ in Zagreb (and from November 1995 to January 1996, his successor Kofi Annan) and under the theater force commander Lt. Gen. Bernard Janvier. From February 1996 to the late 1990s the SRSG was Henryk Sokalski (Poland). The military commander from March 1995 to February 1996 was Brig. Gen. Juha Engström (Finland), and the force commander from March 1996 to the late 1990s was Brig. Gen. Bo Lennart Wranker (Sweden).

The total strength of the mission by late 1995 was 1,000 military personnel, in addition to 26 civilian police monitors and 168 civilian peacekeepers. The tasks of UNPREDEP in Macedonia remained the same as they had been for the third United Nations Protection Force in Former Yugoslavia (UNPROFOR III) between 1992 and 1995: that is, to monitor Macedonia's borders with the Federal Republic of Yugoslavia (FRY) and Albania and to work with other agencies to provide humanitarian assistance and to promote reconciliation among ethnic and political groups within Macedonia. There is a significant Albanian minority in Macedonia, and events in Albania impact the situation in Macedonia. The political situation within Albania remained tense, and an assassination attempt was made on the president of the republic of Macedonia, Kiro Gligorov, in October 1995, though he recovered and resumed office in

January 1996. Although a variety of ethnic groups in Macedonia (including Rhomas, Serbs, Turks, and Vlachs) had a series of claims and aspirations that they felt were not being adequately addressed within the existing political system, the main rift was between ethnic Macedonians and ethnic Albanians. According to the census of 1994 these two groups constituted 67 percent and 23 percent of the population respectively. Although the census had been monitored and organized by the Council of Europe and the European Union, these figures were disputed by ethnic Albanian leaders, who felt that the true proportion of Albanians in the population was higher. The results of elections held in October 1994 were also challenged by opposition groups, though these too had been monitored by the Council of Europe and the Organization for Security and Cooperation in Europe (OSCE). These opposition groups refused to participate in the parliament, resulting in a fragile democracy that, in the context of the precarious economic conditions prevailing in the country, felt unable to accommodate the demands of ethnic Albanians. These demands included recognition of distinctive status as a constituent nation, the conduct of university-level education in the Albanian language and the foundation of an Albanian-language university, proportional representation in significant public institutions, and recognition of Albanian as a second language.

Though the ruling coalition under President Gligorov passed a number of reforms supporting democratization, the Albanians' substantial demands have not been met. When the government of Macedonia requested the continuation of UNPREDEP, following the termination of the missions in Bosnia and Croatia, the need was explained primarily in terms of external security concerns, namely, the need for the normalization of relations with FRY, the need for stability and sustainability around the peace process in Bosnia and Herzegovina, and the need for Macedonia to build up its own indigenous defense capabilities. From 1 February 1996 on UNPREDEP became an independent mission reporting directly to New York, and the mandate was renewed. Although the internal situation has not been resolved, it is generally agreed that this experiment in preventive deployment has been successful and that UNPREDEP has made a significant contribution to stability in the region and to the security of Macedonia. Some of the factors that are said to have contributed to the success of UNPROFOR III and UNPREDEP were the presence of a U.S. battalion in the mission, signaling an American military and political interest; the balancing of these troops with Nordic troops, with their long experience of peacekeeping; and the continuing monitoring of the military, political, economic, and social situation, providing an objective knowledge of events. This monitoring enabled a good knowledge of risk and risk assessment to be built up, helping to counter rumor and the potential for conflict escalation that rumor may generate. For example, in 1994 the assessment of the U.S. State Department was that there was a significant risk that the conflict would spread if there was a mass exodus of ethnic Albanians from the Kosovo region of Serbia, through Macedonia, and on to the Greek border. Such a move would create the risk of conflict between Greece and Turkey, but regular monitoring by UNPREDEP suggested that the risk was in fact low. Similarly, some observers believed in March 1995 that military tension in the southern Balkans was high and that a number of Serb units were massed along the border with Macedonia. UNPREDEP was able to authoritatively deny this and thus contributed to de-escalation. UNPREDEP's border identification and verification also contributed significantly to confidence building. Macedonia's border with Serbia has been the subject of long-standing dispute. The UN commander proposed an administrative UN boundary, initially named the Northern Limit of the Area of Operations (NLAOO) but generally called the "UN line." By July 1994 both Serbian and Macedonian patrols had come to respect this boundary, which had become a de facto buffer zone between parties potentially in conflict.

Full costs for UNPREDEP have not been determined as of the late 1990s, but costs for the six-month period from January to June 1996 were estimated at $24,694,800.

See also Albania; Conflict prevention in Former Yugoslavia; United Nations Protection Force
References and further reading Carnegie Commission on Preventing Deadly Conflict (1997); Lund (1997); United Nations (1996)

Mackenzie, Lewis (1940–)

Born 30 April 1940 in Nova Scotia, Canada, Lewis Mackenzie joined the Queen's Own Rifles in 1960 and gained his first experience of peacekeeping on duty in the Gaza Strip in 1963 serving with the Canadian contingent in the first United Nations Emergency Force (UNEF I). In 1965 he was attached to the UN Peacekeeping Force in Cyprus (UNFICYP). In 1971 he was promoted to the rank of major. In 1972 he was selected to serve with the International Committee of Control and Supervision in Vietnam, followed by a return to Cyprus in 1978 and promotion to lieutenant colonel. In 1978 he was promoted to brigadier general, and in 1990 he returned to work under the aegis of the United Nations when he became acting commander of the United Nations Observer Mission to Central America (UNOMCA). In 1992 he held a senior command position in the United Nations Protection Force in Former Yugoslavia (UNPROFOR), where he was the first force commander in Bosnia. He was one of the many commanders who were critical of the mandate of UNPROFOR and the difficulties of implementing it.

See also Canada; UNPROFOR I–III
References and further reading
Mackenzie (1993, 1994)

Mackinlay, John (1944–)

John Mackinlay has been a leading exponent of ideas concerning the nature of post–Cold War peacekeeping. He has extensive experience in the British army, and was commissioned from the Royal Military Academy Sandhurst to the Sixth Gurkhas and has served in Malaya, Brunei, Nepal, Hong Kong, Borneo, and Northern Ireland. He graduated from the Army Staff College and held staff appointments in the North Atlantic Treaty Organization (NATO) and with the UK Ministry of Defense (UK MoD) in London, Washington, and with Multinational Force and Observers in Sinai. His academic career began in 1985 as a Defence Fellow at Churchill College Cambridge, and he has done extensive research on the Arab-Israeli war zones, including Beirut and south Lebanon, for his "Assessment of Peacekeeping Operations at the Arab-Israeli Interface," completed as a Ph.D. dissertation at the Department of War Studies, Kings College London. In 1991 he directed Second Generation Multinational Operations, a Ford Foundation research project on peacekeeping in the post–Cold War era at the Watson Institute, Brown University, Rhode Island. In 1994 he was appointed UK professor at the U.S. European Command's Marshall Center, in the College for Strategic Studies, Garmisch. In 1996 he became a senior research associate of the Center for Defence Studies and a senior lecturer of the War Studies Department, Kings College London, and at the new UK Joint Services Command and Staff College.

See also Second-generation peacekeeping
References and further reading Mackinlay (1996, 1998)

Mandate, mission mandate

In peacekeeping operations the mandate expresses the objectives of a mission and is approved, in the case of the United Nations, by a resolution of the Security Council. The mandate provides the authority for a mission and will normally cover such issues as the role of the peacekeeping force, the tasks to be performed, the size and organization of the force or mission, the appointment of the force commander, the appointment of the official responsible for the mission, usually a special representative of the secretary-general, arrangements for finance and logistics, the terms or conditions imposed by the host nation, and the time scale for the mission (see Box 1).

See also Arms control and disarmament; Civilian component in peacekeeping operations; Human rights; Regional organizations and peacekeeping; Somalia; United Nations: organization; United Nations Protection Force in Former Yugoslavia
References and further reading U.S. Army (1994)

Microdisarmament
See Arms control and disarmament

Middle East conflict

The Middle East has been the scene of much instability and conflict in recent history and remains one of the most volatile regions in the international political system. The United Nations has undertaken numerous peacekeeping operations in the area—indeed, one of the first ever UN peacekeeping mission was deployed to the Middle East in 1948 (the United Nations Truce Supervision Organization [UNTSO]). The Middle East's contemporary problems can to a large extent be traced back to the division of the region by Western powers after World War I. Prior to this, from 1516 to 1918, the majority of the area came under the jurisdiction of the Ottoman Empire. The Ottomans used both dynastic and religious (Islamic) authority to exercise control over the region, which nevertheless remained multiethnic throughout the empire's existence; ethnoreligious factions maintained their independent cultural identities. The decline of the Ottoman Empire culminated with its collapse at the end of World War I, following which the Middle East came under Europe's sphere of influence. By the early 1920s Great Britain had established its authority in Egypt, Iraq, the Sudan, Palestine, and Transjordan (as Jordan was then called), and was the paramount power in the area, although France controlled Syria and Lebanon until 1946. Throughout the period between the two world wars, Britain's principal objective had been to maintain hegemony over the region; it had no interest in promoting or imposing a British way of life or style of

Box 1: Example of a Typical Mandate for a UN Peacekeeping Mission

The UNSC [United Nations Security Council], noting that the present situation with regard to [country or countries] is likely to threaten international peace and security and may further deteriorate unless additional measures are promptly taken to maintain peace and to seek out a durable solution:

Considering the positions taken by the parties in relation to the "peaceful intentions" signed at New York on [date]: Having in mind the relevant provisions of the charter of the UN and its Article 2, paragraph 4, which reads: "All members shall refrain in their international relations from the threat or use of force against the territorial integrity or political independence of any state, or in any manner inconsistent with the purposes of the United Nations":

a. Calls upon all member states, in conformity with their obligations under the charter of the UN, to refrain from any action or threat of action likely to worsen the situation in [   ] and [   ], or to endanger international peace.

b. Asks the governments of [   ], which have the responsibility for the maintenance and restoration of law and order, to take all additional measures necessary to stop violence and bloodshed in their countries.

c. Recommends the creation, with the consent of the governments of [   ], of a UN peacekeeping force in those countries. The composition and size of the force shall be established by the SYG [secretary-general], in consultation with the governments of [   ]. The commander of the force shall be appointed by the SYG and report to him. The SYG, who shall keep the governments providing the force fully informed, shall report periodically to the UNSC on its operation.

d. Recommends that the function of the force should be, in the interest of preserving international peace and security, to use its best efforts to prevent a recurrence of fighting and, as necessary, to contribute to the maintenance and restoration of law and order and a return to normal conditions.

e. Recommends that the stationing of the force shall be for a period of three months, all costs pertaining to it being met in a manner to be agreed upon by the governments providing the contingents and by the governments of [   ]. The SYG may also accept voluntary contributions for that purpose.

f. Recommends further that the SYG designate, in agreement with the governments of [   ], a mediator, who shall use his best endeavors with the representatives of the communities and also with the aforesaid governments for the purpose of promoting a peaceful solution and an agreed-upon settlement to the problem confronting [   ], in accordance with the charter of the UN, having in mind the well-being of the peoples of [   ] as a whole and the preservation of international peace and security. The mediator shall report periodically to the SYG on his efforts.

g. Requests the SYG to provide, from funds of the UN, as appropriate for the remuneration and expenses of the mediator and his staff.

Source: U.S. Army, *Field Manual 100-23: Peace Operations* (Washington, DC: Department of the Army, 1994)

government. A turning point for the Ottomans had been their siding with Germany in World War I, which ultimately brought about the empire's destruction. Furthermore, in the search for allies in the war, Britain promised the French that the two countries would divide the area between them after the war; it promised Hussein, the Sharif of Mecca, that Britain would support Arab independence; and most crucially, it promised British Jews that Britain would support a sovereign homeland for Jews in Palestine.

Following the war the British divided the area under its authority into two states to be ruled by two of Hussein's sons: Iraq, to be ruled by Faisal, and subsequently, Transjordan, to be ruled by Abdullah. This division involved arbitrarily establishing national boundaries designed to enhance British strategic and economic aspirations in the region but paying little respect to social, religious, or ethnic delineations among the native population. It was in the British interest to reduce friction on the Arabian peninsula, which it did by promoting cooperation between leaders, facilitating the use of traditionally established grazing areas by local tribes, and arbitrating in frontier disagreements, and so defining the jurisdictions of neighboring leaders. This meant that ideas of national, territorial sovereignty were introduced into the area, where tribal borders had traditionally prevailed. This foreign imposition of state boundaries and leaders had far-reaching and unforeseen effects in the Middle East and provided the context for a series of conflicts between Israel and its neighbors that led to the original introduction of peacekeeping forces and their continued employment in the region.

See also Lebanon; UNDOF, 1974– ; UNEF I and UNEF II; UNSCOP, 1947; UNTSO, 1948
References and further reading Brogan (1992); Durch (1994); Pelcovits (1993); Smith (1996); Touval (1985)

Military medicine and peacekeeping

Some obvious medical problems face mission personnel, particularly when the force is helping refugees or displaced people who may be suffering from all the diseases and medical problems that come from overcrowding and lack of food and proper sanitation. To an extent these can be anticipated and the necessary precautions taken because the twin processes of logistics and planning for a complex emergency mean that detailed knowledge has been employed to deal with the expected medical problems, and the resources will be on hand to handle those problems. However, one of the most important problems facing a mission commander is not the range of possible clinical conditions but the psychological effects of the huge levels of stress experienced by troops and workers on the ground. A peacekeeping mission is different from other operations in its mixture of military and humanitarian perspectives and can be a severe shock in a number of ways to those who are inexperienced or not properly prepared. Combat-trained troops, for example, have a particular kind of training that equips them to act in situations where a peacekeeper is only allowed to observe or has to adopt a lower profile, and the

peacekeeper's inability to observe and not act sets up patterns of stress. Distress responses are also apparent when military peacekeepers do not have the mandate, the training, or the resources to provide help for the suffering civilians they encounter. Long periods of inaction can also be stressful for those accustomed to an active regime if they are left only to their own devices. The problem of stress is now recognized as a major hazard to mission effectiveness, and force commanders and their senior officers now take steps to provide instruction in stress management. A valuable resource for mission planning and operation is the United Nations Medical Support Unit (MSU), which provides a medical perspective in preparing for a mission, in the logistics of deployment, and in the training of contingent personnel, including headquarters briefings for senior staff as well as on-site briefings for mission medical staff. In addition the MSU will advise on the establishment of a local medical infrastructure and provide a medical perspective on holding and evacuation procedures.

References and further reading Olsson (1996); Internet at http://www.un.org/Depts/dpko/medical/medroles.htm

Military observers

An observer mission has to be mandated by the Security Council and is the subject of a Status of Forces Agreement, but it differs from a peacekeeping mission or a peace enforcement mission in several important ways. First, the role of the mission is, as its name implies, to observe rather than to take action. If an observer group witnesses a breach of an agreement, it is a part of their instructions to report the transgression rather than try to rectify it. Similarly, if belligerents appear to be about to recommence hostilities, it is not the role of observers to act as an interposition force but to report upon developments. Second, observer mission personnel are deployed differently: Observers are deployed in groups composed of individuals from different forces rather than in platoons or brigades from one particular nation. For some tasks—such as liaison—an observer may be deployed individually rather than in a group.

Civilian officials from national governments or from nongovernmental organizations may also be members of observer groups. Third, in general observers are unarmed, although they may carry sidearms for personal protection.

Military observers are recruited for a wide range of tasks, from confidence restoration in immediate postconflict situations to the observation of elections. Their main role has been to monitor combatants' adherence to the terms of a cease-fire or a truce and to observe that agreed-on demilitarized zones are honored, but an observer group may also be deployed to supervise cease-fire lines, buffer zones, enclaves, and so on or to oversee the exchange of prisoners of war, of territory, or of noncombatants. Observer groups may also oversee refugee camps, arms collection points, or the conduct of censuses, plebiscites, or elections. In addition to witnessing and reporting, an observer mission may be called upon to act as mediators or arbitrators if the terms of an agreement are not sufficiently clear. Mission personnel may also be required to investigate complaints about alleged violations of an agreement or to negotiate on behalf of a particular group.

See also Angola; Cambodia; Croatia; El Salvador; Georgia; Guatemala; Indonesia; Lebanon; Liberia; Morocco; Mozambique; Namibia; ONUCA; Rwanda; Tajikistan; United Nations Aouzou Strip Observer Group; United Nations Disengagement Observer Force; United Nations Military Observer Group in India and Pakistan; United Nations Protection Force in Former Yugoslavia; United Nations Truce Supervision Organization; Yemen

Military Staff Committee (MSC)

The formation of a Military Staff Committee (MSC) was part of the original establishment of the United Nations when it was envisaged that the organization could have a "world policing" role via its democratic structure and with the use of a standing army. The MSC, dealt with in chapter 7 of the UN Charter, was to fulfill the role in the UN army that the Joint Chiefs of Staff play in conventional national forces and would be able to command an overwhelming force of arms to quell any threats to world peace. The members of the committee would be the senior post-holders from each of the permanent members of the Security Coun-

cil, who represented at the time the most militarily powerful nations in the world. The concept of the standing army that the MSC was to command was not clearly thought out from its inception. If the force was not to be permanently stationed in any one part of the globe, it would have to be "on call" from each contributing nation for immediate deployment by the MSC, which was an unrealistic assessment of the way that individual countries could or would act. In addition, the establishment of the MSC coincided with the start of the Cold War, and the USSR position on the use of military power was different from that of the other members of the Security Council. The committee began its work by trying in 1947 to establish principles and procedures for the establishment and organization of a UN military force, but this first bout of activity marked the beginning and the end of the committee's active role in shaping UN policy and action. The MSC has continued to meet, but its membership is not at the "Supreme High Command" level that was originally envisaged. However, some recent proposals have recommended the re-formation of a stronger MSC to improve the rapid deployment of peacekeeping operations.

See also Chain of command; Peace enforcement; Second-generation peacekeeping

Military-humanitarian relations

In post–Cold War conflicts peacekeeping deployments became central to the international community's response to armed conflict. Peacekeeping had to become better organized, more capable, and better protected than in traditional Cold War peacekeeping, and civilian agencies involved in humanitarian assistance had to work more closely with military peacekeepers. Humanitarian assistance involves a wide range of activities, from providing humanitarian relief (food, medicine, clothing) and helping resettle displaced populations to restoring the economy and the civilian infrastructure (rebuilding schools and hospitals, for example).

The different groups involved in modern peacekeeping may have different long-term goals; the military peacekeeping mandate, and the goal of the United Nations and its agencies, may be to stabilize the situation by securing a cease-fire and a peace agreement that restores the state government and its institutions, whereas human rights and development nongovernmental organizations may be more interested either in long-term development or in helping create conflict resolution practices that empower communities to peacefully manage future conflicts and that extend political space to constituencies that the traditional state structures may not be comfortable with. The coordination of national, supranational, and nongovernmental organizations with different objectives, different organizational cultures, different interests and motives, and different organizational capabilities is challenging.

In the UN system coordination is organized through the Department of Humanitarian Affairs (DHA), whose undersecretary-general is also the emergency relief coordinator (ERC) and in this role chairs the Interagency Standing Committee (IASC), which is made up of the executive heads of the United Nations High Commissioner for Refugees (UNHCR), the United Nations Children's Fund (UNICEF), the World Food Program (WFP), the Food and Agriculture Organization (FAO), the World Health Organization (WHO), and the United Nations Development Program (UNDP). The International Committee of the Red Cross/Red Crescent (ICRC) and the International Organization on Migration (IOM) are also represented, and other intergovernmental organizations and NGOs are invited to attend as appropriate. At the operational level the special representative of the secretary-general (SRSG) has responsibility for the overall coordination of UN operations in a country and represents the secretary-general to the government of the host country. The ERC and the IASC may also appoint a humanitarian coordinator to facilitate the coordination of humanitarian assistance in the field, and this resident coordinator will also chair the UN Disaster Management Teams that may be set up in the most vulnerable countries. In cases of natural disasters the DHA has set up United Nations disaster assessment and coordination teams (UNDAC) with on-site operations coordination centers.

For NGOs the International Council for Voluntary Agencies (ICVA), based in Geneva, is the primary coordinating organization. It includes a standing Committee on Humanitarian Responses, which alerts northern NGOs to emerging needs, though in reality its coordinating reach and capability is limited. In the United States about 160 agencies have joined an organization called Inter-Action, which represents their interests at the national level. This representation has included holding coordinating meetings with the U.S. Department of State, with the United States Agency for International Development (US-AID), and with the Department of Defense, through which U.S. NGOs have participated in preparatory training at the Joint Readiness Training Center (JRTC). In most emergencies, once in the field, coordinating networks or umbrella groupings of NGOs generally develop, as for example LINK in Mozambique and the International NGO Consortium in Somalia. However, despite these mechanisms and codes of conduct, there is still a problem coordinating the efforts of the various actors in conflict-related humanitarian crises. It is now recognized that further coordination between the different types of NGOs and between the civil and military forces assigned to humanitarian missions is a high-priority matter. In a crisis the military peacekeeping forces will normally have the greatest capabilities in terms of communications equipment and transport, in addition to some intelligence capability. Given these powerful communication and information resources, the military tends to become a center for other agencies seeking information. In recent operations an interface for coordination of military and civilian tasks has been provided by the formation of civilian-military operations centers (CMOCs).

See also Humanitarian assistance; Humanitarian intervention

References and further reading Joint Warfighting Center (1995); Mackinlay (1996); Mackinlay and Kent (1997); Minear and Weiss (1995); Slim (1996)

Mission of the Representative of the Secretary General in the Dominican Republic (DOMREP)
See Dominican Republic

Mixed Armistice Commission
See UNTSO

Morocco

United Nations Mission for the Referendum in Western Sahara (MINURSO), 1991–

Conflict Profile

Western Sahara lies on Africa's northwest coast, bordering Algeria, Morocco, and Mauritania. It measures about a quarter-million square kilometers and contains rich mineral deposits. When the colonial Spanish regime withdrew in 1976, it ultimately refused calls by the Organization of African Unity (OAU) and the United Nations for a referendum on Saharan self-determination and instead divided responsibility for the region between the neighboring countries of Mauritania and Morocco. However, such an outcome was not accepted by the Popular Front for the Liberation of Saguia el-Hamra and Rio de Oro (POLISARIO), which acted on behalf of the Saharan Arab Democratic Republic (SADR) for the people of the region. POLISARIO launched an insurgency campaign against the occupying powers, demanding self-determination as its ultimate objective, and as a result of the ensuing violence many of the indigenous Sahrawi people were forced to flee to neighboring Algeria. By 1979 Mauritania had been convinced to withdraw from the territory, prompting Morocco to lay claim to it all. In 1980, in order to protect the part of Western Sahara that it controlled, Morocco began constructing a sand barrier, containing mines and electronic sensors, across the desert. By April 1987 the barrier extended most of the way across the territory.

Regional and international politics complicated the conflict over Western Sahara. The OAU continued to urge both a cease-fire between the opposing parties and a referendum to determine the territory's future status. In 1984 SADR was admitted to the OAU, precipitating Morocco's withdrawal. Algeria, Cuba, and Libya supported POLISARIO, while Saudi Arabia and the United States maintained ties with Morocco. Throughout the 1980s Morocco continued to resist repeated demands for a referendum by both the OAU and the United Nations. However, toward the end of the decade, a détente between Morocco and Algeria, combined with political pressure from Saudi Arabia and the United States, convinced POLISARIO and Morocco respectively to enter negotiations with a view to establishing a peace agreement.

On the opening of negotiations between the opposing parties, the United Nations dispatched a fact-finding mission to the area to determine the parameters a settlement would need to work within. UN Secretary-General Javier Pérez de Cuéllar, on the strength of the mission's results, formulated a peace plan incorporating provisions for a cease-fire and a plebiscite under UN supervision; on 30 August 1988 the two sides provisionally accepted the secretary-general's initiative. The proposed UN mission would set a precedent: The United Nations had earlier, in Namibia, monitored the election process and verified its results, but in this instance it would conduct the election itself. Moreover, the special representative of the secretary-general (SRSG) was provided with extraordinarily inclusive powers over everything to do with the referendum. Thus, on 20 September 1988, the Security Council adopted Security Council Resolution (SCR) 621 authorizing the appointment of Hector Gros Espiell (Uruguay) as special representative to negotiate the terms of the settlement.

Deployment of MINURSO

Various political considerations influenced the establishment of MINURSO. POLISARIO was, in international terms, politically well supported. However, it recognized that it was unlikely to achieve a military victory over Morocco, and the resumption of diplomatic relations between Morocco and POLISARIO's principal ally, Algeria, had also been a serious setback for the POLISARIO cause. Therefore POLISARIO saw the UN-sponsored referendum as the best means of ratifying its claim to self-determination, although defeat would have been likely to have represented an end to its campaign in all forms. Morocco, on the other hand, vehemently maintained its right of authority over Western Sahara and its inhabitants and harbored various plans to ensure success in the referendum. Both France and the United States had links with Morocco and were therefore keen to see an end to the dispute. However, other permanent members of the Security Council did not view the operation as sufficiently important for UN intervention and only authorized its establishment once a reduced budget had been arranged. A Soviet initiative that all five permanent members contribute military observers to MINURSO was eventually accepted.

However, political differences and contradictory objectives between the two sides delayed agreement over certain details in the operation's mandate. King Hassan II of Morocco refused to consider POLISARIO's initial demands that Moroccan troops leave Western Sahara before the plebiscite take place. POLISARIO also insisted on direct negotiations with Morocco, as such contact implied official recognition of the organization by its adversary. Thus various versions of the peace initiative were periodically refused by both sides. At the same time, the relatively low priority given to the conflict by the international community meant that external political pressure on the parties to reach agreement was not exerted as strongly as it might have been.

Nevertheless, Morocco and POLISARIO eventually consented, in principle, to the secretary-general's settlement plan for Western Sahara, and on 27 June 1990 the Security Council approved it, by its SCR 658. The plan suggested a 2,000-strong operation, comprising civilian personnel, police officers, and military observers, that would progressively monitor a cease-fire between the belligerents, a reduction in the number of Moroccan military personnel in Western Sahara, the demobilization of Moroccan and POLISARIO troops to designated areas, the release of Western Saharan political prisoners, an exchange of prisoners of war between the opposing sides, the implementation of a repatriation program for Sahrawi refugees, identification and registration of eligible voters in the referendum, organization of the referendum and verification that it was free and fair, and the announcement of its results.

Continued objections over details in the plan further delayed deployment of the UN force. However, on 29 April 1991 the Security Council adopted SCR 690, by which it established MINURSO to implement a revised version of the 1990 settlement plan. The new version of the plan foresaw a reduction both in the number and duration of Moroccan military personnel remaining in Western Sahara after the cease-fire was in place and in the strength and duration of the UN operation itself. A period of 11 weeks was allowed after the establishment of the cease-fire for the registration of eligible voters, who were to be approved by an Identification Commission as part of MINURSO. Both parties accepted the secretary-general's proposal that the formal cease-fire should be effective from 6 September on.

Since both Morocco and POLISARIO had acceded to the plan for a UN-supervised referendum, they both turned their attention to voter eligibility as the principal remaining manipulable issue. Moroccan conviction that it was the rightful authority in Western Sahara and its determination that things remain that way were exemplified in early 1991, when it presented a list of 120,000 alleged former Sahrawis living in Morocco to be included in the prospective plebiscite—which outnumbered the entire Sahrawi population from a 1974 census. POLISARIO, on the other hand, complained that it had initially agreed with Morocco that the 1974 census would serve as the basis for the electorate and that any expansion beyond this would be incompatible with the relevant provisions of the settlement plan.

Even without manipulation by the opposing parties, the issue of eligibility had already proved problematic. To qualify for the ballot, Saharan refugees in Algeria had had to be repatriated and POLISARIO fighters demobilized. A further problem concerning voter registration derived from the itinerant nature of Saharan society, which meant that the Sahrawi people had little written evidence of citizenship (such as birth certificates). Thus the Identification Commission was forced to rely on the verbal accounts of Sahrawi tribal leaders for a major part of the identification process.

As a result of such discrepancies, violence broke out between the two sides. The secretary-general then suggested that the formal cease-fire should still come into effect 6 September but that the rest of the provisions for the settlement would only begin once the outstanding tasks had been completed. The Security Council approved the proposal, and it was agreed that 228 military observers and certain logistical and administrative support staff would be deployed to monitor the terms of the cease-fire and the cessation of hostilities.

In November 1993, following negotiations with the parties, the chair of the Identification Commission secured the agreement of both Morocco and POLISARIO to initiate the registration process, which subsequently got under way in the Tindouf and Layoune areas of the territory. POLISARIO was assured that under the terms of the compromise agreement, thousands of potential POLISARIO voters from outside the territory would be included in the electorate. However, POLISARIO had still not acceded to the latest version of the peace settlement as a whole. Despite this lack of agreement, the Security Council decided that the Identification Commission should continue its work to register eligible voters for the referendum, while MINURSO continued its efforts to obtain the cooperation of both parties.

Further disagreements over the involvement of OAU observers in the identification process were eventually resolved, and on 28 August 1994 the identification and registration operation finally began. However, this process proved to be even more complicated than had originally been anticipated and in November 1994 the secretary-general informed the Security Council that it would take several months before sufficient progress was made in the identification process to be able to set a date for the referendum and a revised timetable for the settlement plan.

However, the parties to the dispute maintained their commitment, in principle, to the peace plan, so the secretary-general suggested that by enlarging MINURSO the identification process would be sufficiently accelerated that the cease-fire could commence on 1 June 1995 and the referendum could take place in October 1995. On 13 January 1995 the Security Council approved the secretary-general's proposal by adopting SCR 973. However, continued disagreements and logistical complications meant that the identification process remained difficult and slow. As of 18 November 1995, 233,487 applications had been processed, from which 75,794 people had been convoked (gathered together for identification purposes). Some 58,947 of those convoked had been identified, leaving a total of 157,693 applicants outstanding. By the end of the year, the opposing parties had again reached an impasse over the continuation of the identification process.

By May 1996, despite the fact that both parties remained committed to the peace settlement as a whole, substantive progress had still not been made over identification. Therefore the secretary-general recommended that the identification process be suspended until both parties were able to demonstrate a commitment to resuming and completing the identification process without further delays. He reiterated that the United Nations also remained committed to the peace process in Western Sahara and therefore suggested that the MINURSO mandate be extended, although at a reduced strength.

The suspension remained in place until, in March 1997, the secretary-general appointed a personal envoy, James Baker III (United States), to reassess the situation. The personal envoy facilitated direct negotiations between Morocco and POLISARIO that successfully managed to address the principal disagreements over the implementation of the identification process, and by September 1997 the secretary-general was able to recommend that the process be resumed. Accordingly, on 20 October 1997 the Security Council adopted SCR 1133, by which it approved the secretary-general's plan, urging that the identification process be concluded by 31 May 1998. It further recommended that by 15 November 1997 the secretary-general submit a new plan, including a revised timetable and financial implications, for holding the plebiscite for the self-determination of the people of Western Sahara, in accordance with the 1991 settlement plan and the agreements reached between the parties for its implementation.

The political situation in Western Sahara is extremely complicated, and the conflicting demands of two parties involved has made resolution of the dispute particularly difficult. However, certain aspects of the structure of the UN mission have not facilitated an expeditious solution. MINURSO incorporated the formal separation of the peacemaking (i.e., diplomatic) and peacekeeping aspects of the operation, and the lack of communication between the two elements hampered mediation. This deficiency was particularly relevant to the conflict in Western Sahara, since the negotiation process formed such a crucial aspect of the peace initiative.

Furthermore, the relative lack of international interest in the dispute has meant that not enough external political pressure has materialized to alter the opposing parties' behavior. However, recent developments have given hope that some solution may eventually be forthcoming.

MINURSO headquarters are in Layoune. MINURSO was originally intended to reach a full strength of 1,700 military observers, 100 police officers, and 800 to 1,000 civilian personnel. On deployment, military personnel were originally provided by Argentina, Australia, Austria, Bangladesh, Belgium, Canada, China, Egypt, France, Ghana, Greece, Guinea, Honduras, Ireland, Italy, Kenya, Malaysia, Nigeria, Pakistan, Poland, the Russian Federation, Switzerland, Tunisia, the United Kingdom, the United States, and Venezuela. As of 31 January 1998, MINURSO totaled 301 personnel, comprising 202 military observers, 21 military support personnel, and 78 civilian police, supported by a number of international and local civilian staff. Military personnel were contributed by Argentina, Austria, Bangladesh, China, Egypt, El Salvador, France, Ghana, Greece, Guinea, Honduras, Ireland, Italy, Kenya, Malaysia, Nigeria, Pakistan, Poland, Portugal, Republic of Korea, the Russian Federation, the United States, Uruguay, and Venezuela. Civilian police personnel were provided by Canada, Egypt, Ghana, India, Malaysia, Nigeria, Pakistan, Portugal, and Sweden. MINURSO is financed through assessed contributions from UN member states, and the estimated expenditures for the operation from inception in April 1991 to 31 May 1996 were $224,813,800.

See also Child soldiers; Troop-contributing countries
References and further reading Chopra (1994b); Durch (1994); United Nations (1996); Zoubir and Volman (1993)

Mozambique

United Nations Operation in Mozambique (ONUMOZ), 1992–1994

Conflict Profile
Mozambique lies on the southeast coast of Africa and has a 1,500-mile Indian Ocean seaboard. It has a land area the size of Turkey (784,961 square kilometers) and a population of some 17 million (1993 estimate). It is bordered by Tanzania to the north; Malawi, Zambia, and Zimbabwe to the west (these three depend on west-east routes across Mozambique to Nacala in the northern region and Beira in the southern region for access to the sea); and South Africa and Swaziland to the south. The population is mainly Bantu divided into several dozen tribal groups. Most practice traditional religions, but 20 percent of the population are Christian and 10 percent Muslim. Agriculture employs two-thirds of the workforce, with exports of cashew nuts, cotton, and tea. There are deposits of natural gas, bauxite, iron, manganese, and other ores. Since independence in 1975 from Portugal (which had maintained a presence in Mozambique for nearly 500 years), war and drought have wrought devastation, triggered by the precipitate abandonment of the country by almost all the 240,000 Portuguese settlers. By the end of the 1980s the *International Index of Human Suffering* rated Mozambique "the most unhappy nation on earth." Nearly one million had died in the fighting and associated deprivation, a quarter of the population had been displaced, and one-and-a-half million had fled abroad. By the late 1980s some 80 percent of schools had been closed or destroyed, together with more than 600 rural clinics, and much of the infrastructure of railways, bridges, and power lines had been severely damaged. The government controlled little more than the capital in the south (Maputo) and, with military help from Tanzania, Malawi, and Zimbabwe, the five transport corridors of Nacala, Tete, Beira, Route Number 1, and Limpopo. The Resistencia Nacional Mocambicana (RENAMO) rebels, supported by South Africa, ranged sporadically over the rest. Local populations were prey to armed raids and banditry. Thousands of children were commandeered, particularly into the RENAMO forces. The 1988 U.S. State Department Gersony Report condemned atrocities, again mainly by RENAMO. During the 1980s per capita income halved to $95 a year, a third lower even than that in Somalia, a country similarly devastated by war. Probably more than half the population was kept alive by foreign aid agencies, in those areas that

were accessible. The Frente da Libertaçao do Mozambique (FRELIMO) government, led since 1986 by Joaquim Chissano, abandoned Marxist-Leninist economic policies in the late 1980s and undertook liberalizing reforms, thus opening the way to aid from international financial institutions. Nevertheless, continuing fighting prevented significant improvement, so that when the UN survey teams arrived in September 1992 to assess the possibility of a UN mission, the report was extremely bleak.

The General Peace Agreement (GPA) of 4 October 1992 between the FRELIMO government and the rebel RENAMO ended some 30 years of more or less continuous internal war in Mozambique, including FRELIMO's 1962–1974 war of liberation against Portuguese rule and RENAMO's 1977–1992 challenge to the subsequent FRELIMO government. The United Nations, which had only played a role in the latter stages of the four-year peace process leading up to the GPA, was asked to chair the Supervisory and Monitoring Commission (CSC) set up to supervise the implementation of the agreement and to undertake specific functions in relation to the cease-fire, transitional arrangements, the elections, and humanitarian assistance. ONUMOZ carried out this mandate over the two-year period between December 1992 and January 1995—one year longer than originally envisaged in the overambitious timetable determined by the negotiators. Participants were mindful of comparable processes in Cambodia and Angola. Unlike the operation in Angola, ONUMOZ has been called a success because cease-fire arrangements were verified; 75,000 forces from both sides were demobilized and the rest earmarked for incorporation in a new national army; one of the largest UN civilian police (CIVPOL) components was deployed to enhance confidence during the transition period; more than four million people (one-and-a-half million from neighboring countries) were assisted back to their places of origin; millions benefited from the humanitarian program, which also included the reintegration of former soldiers and training in the removal of land mines; and above all, RENAMO was converted from a military faction to a political party to the extent it took part in elections held in

October 1994, which were declared to be "free and fair." Presidential and legislative elections laid the political foundations for normalization and a possible rebuilding of the country. The situation remained precarious, many if not most tasks were left uncompleted, and there were criticisms of specific factors and shortcomings. Nevertheless, in announcing the termination of the mission at the end of 1994, UN Secretary-General Boutros Boutros-Ghali described ONUMOZ's accomplishments as a "remarkable achievement," and it has been repeatedly cited since then in assessments of the potential for UN peacekeeping as an example of "success" to offset "failure" elsewhere. Reasons given for the relative success of ONUMOZ have included the inability of the warring factions to continue fighting with any prospect of victory in conditions of drought and national collapse (unlike the Uniao Nacional para la Independencia Total de Angola [UNITA] in Angola, RENAMO did not control valued economic assets); the withdrawal of Soviet support from the FRELIMO government and of South African support from RENAMO and subsequent concerted pressure from neighboring countries (particularly those wanting safe access across Mozambique to the sea); the subsequent readiness of the warring parties to settle and continue the struggle by political means; the persistence and skill of the mediators in painstakingly bringing the sides together over the years leading up to the October 1992 GPA (including informal channels through the Catholic church; the good offices, that is, mediation, of Zimbabwe and Kenya; and subsequent technical advice from the United States); the clarity of the ONUMOZ mandate; and the sustained support from the UN Security Council, including adequate resources for the mission.

The 4 October 1992 GPA, signed in Rome by Joaquim Chissano, Mozambique's president, and Afonso Dhlakama, president of RENAMO, included seven protocols and incorporated a number of earlier partial agreements. It envisaged a cease-fire on "E-day," 15 October 1992, followed by separation of forces and demobilization within six months of E-day and formation of a new integrated Mozambican Defence Force (FADM), arrangements for government during the transition period, guiding principles for humanitarian assistance, and preparations for national elections to take place no later than 15 October 1993. On 9 October the UN secretary-general submitted a report to the Security Council recommending provisions for the proposed UN role. On 13 October the Security Council approved the appointment of an interim secretary-general's special representative (SGSR) and a preliminary team of military observers. Aldo Ajello (Italy), with 21 observers, arrived in Mozambique on 15 October 1992 (E-day) as interim SGSR (and after March 1993, formal SGSR). Meetings between government and RENAMO representatives were arranged and the CSC, chaired by the United Nations, was established on 4 November to oversee implementation of the GPA, decide disputes, and coordinate the activities of subordinate commissions: the Cease-Fire Commission (CCF), the Reintegration Commission (CORE), and the Joint Commission for the Formation of the Mozambican Defence Force (CCFADM). The CSC was made up of government and RENAMO delegations, together with representatives from Italy, the host of the Rome talks, France, Germany, Portugal, the United Kingdom, the United States, and the Organization of African Unity (OAU).

The Deployment of UNOMOZ
It was not until 3 December 1992 in a report to the Security Council that the UN secretary-general recommended a large-scale peacekeeping mission in Mozambique, arguing that without it the peace process would be unlikely to succeed. Mindful of recent events, he noted the risks involved but concluded that they were nevertheless worth taking. On 16 December 1992 ONUMOZ was mandated, by Security Council Resolution (SCR) 797, until 31 October 1993. Building on past experience, the operational concept was based on four components: a humanitarian/economic provision, military protection, political progress, and an electoral process. These components, to be coordinated by the SRSG, were interdependent: Without sufficient humanitarian/economic provision, security could deteriorate and demobilization fail; without adequate military protection and the demobilization and reintegration of the warring armies, humanitarian aid would not get through and conditions

would not exist for successful elections; without enough political progress in achieving acceptable transitional arrangements, confidence for other components would be lacking; and without a legitimate electoral process, none of the other gains would be secure. The SRSG's office would require 20 international staff members as well as locally recruited staff to give overall direction. The four main elements of the mission were to be as follows: (1) The military component was tasked with verifying the cease-fire; monitoring the withdrawal of foreign forces; providing security in the five transport corridors; verifying the separation and concentration in assembly points of some 100,000 soldiers for demobilization and reintegration into society (or retraining in a new national army); supervising the collection, storage, and destruction of weapons; monitoring the disbanding of other irregular armed groups; and providing security for vital infrastructures and all those involved in international support for the peace process. It was a daunting undertaking. The military component would require a headquarters company and military police platoon; 354 military observers; five infantry battalions; one engineer battalion; three logistics companies; air, communications, medical, and movement control support units; and a civilian technical unit to provide logistical support for the demobilization program. ONUMOZ's general verification duties would be carried out by UN military observer teams at the 49 designated assembly areas and other locations. (2) The political component included UN CIVPOL in monitoring the activities of the Mozambican police, although this was not specifically envisaged in the GPA. One of RENAMO's main concerns was the activity of the government's secret police (the SNASP) and the likelihood that the state apparatus would be used to intimidate opposition parties and pervert the electoral process. The government was reluctant to accept these provisions and was slow to implement provisions for the joint National Commission for Administration, National Information Commission, and Police Commission. (3) The electoral component was focused around ONUMOZ's Electoral Division, whose task was to monitor the electoral process organized by the National Elections Commission (NEC) and to oversee contacts between the government, RENAMO, the main political parties, and the NEC. The SRSG would also organize technical assistance through the United Nations Development Program (UNDP) and other channels. The Electoral Division comprised up to 148 international electoral officers and staff, and some 1,200 international observers were to follow for the elections themselves. (4) The humanitarian component was innovative in the extent to which it was integrated into ONUMOZ through the United Nations Office for Humanitarian Assistance Coordination (UNOHAC), which was based in Maputo and had suboffices at regional and provincial levels. UNOHAC replaced the existing UN Special Coordinator for Emergency Relief Operations, and operational agencies and nongovernmental organizations (NGOs) were asked to send representatives to work with UNOHAC. As well as continuing the provision of emergency aid, UNOHAC's tasks included assistance for displaced people and returning refugees, provision for demobilized soldiers in the assembly areas (identification of training and employment opportunities, provision of vocational kits and a credit scheme, counseling and referral service), training in the removal of land mines, and generally serving as an instrument of reconciliation.

Although the effort to integrate the different components of the mission is generally seen to have been an improvement over some earlier missions, the slowness with which the cumbersome system was put into operation has been criticized. Force Commander Maj. Gen. L. G. Rodrigues da Silva (Brazil) was appointed on 14 February 1993 (to be succeeded on 1 March 1994 by Maj. Gen. Mohammed Abdus Salam [Bangladesh]), there were administrative and logistical delays in the deployment of ONUMOZ forces, and there had been no clear status-of-forces agreement (an agreement on the terms and conditions of deployment of the peacekeepers) with the Mozambican government. These were dangerous shortcomings in view of the political inexperience of RENAMO, the two opponents' conflicting priorities in the peace process, and the continuing deep distrust between them. The Mozambican government wanted an early disarming of RENAMO and

wanted its members reintegrated into society with minimum disturbance to the status quo. RENAMO, on the other hand, wanted all foreign troops out of Mozambique and wanted 65 percent of ONUMOZ deployed before the assembly process began. RENAMO also wanted close international supervision of government police (and secret police) activities, guaranteed freedom of access to the media, and large-scale financial and technical assistance in building a political capacity in order to be able to fight the presidential and Assembly elections on something like equal terms with the government. On 2 April the UN secretary-general reported that the original timetable was not viable. Six months after the Rome GPA was signed the peace process seemed to be in jeopardy. The ominous shadow of the failed peace process in Angola hung over the mission.

Fortunately, despite the delays the cease-fire more or less held, by May 1993 ONUMOZ was finally deployed in all three regions, foreign forces from Malawi and Zimbabwe were largely withdrawn, a voluntary trust fund had been established to help RENAMO establish itself as a political party, the work of the Joint Commissions was resumed, the effort to repatriate and bring home exiled and displaced persons was intensified, and a status-of-forces agreement was signed with the government on 14 May. A revised timetable was drawn up that envisaged concentration and demobilization of government and RENAMO troops in stages, beginning in September 1993, with half the soldiers to be demobilized by January 1994 and the rest by May 1994. A new national army of 30,000 was to be formed. Half were to be in place by May 1994 and the rest by September 1994. Demobilized soldiers would be relocated in time to vote in the elections. Learning from the Angolan disaster, the UN Security Council mandated that all of this was to be completed before the election process. Meanwhile the work of the Joint Commissions would resume on 3 June 1993, voter registration would take place between April and June 1994, and resettled persons were to be back in their home areas by April 1994 so that they could take part in the process. The elections themselves would be held a year later than originally planned, in October 1994. Eventually, after direct talks between President Chissano and RENAMO leader Dhlakama on 23 August 1993, an agreement to the new arrangements was signed on 3 September. RENAMO agreed to the reintegration of areas it formerly controlled into state administration, and the government agreed to UN monitoring of all police activities and the rights and liberties of citizens and to the provision of technical support to the new joint Police Commission. The 128 police observers already authorized under SCR 797 (of 1992) would be deployed at once, and recommendations would be made for a strengthened CIVPOL component. Between 17 and 20 October 1993 the UN secretary-general visited Mozambique, met Chissano, Dhlakama, and other leaders, and announced a breakthrough in the peace process. On 5 November 1993 SCR 879 renewed ONUMOZ's mandate for six months, subject to review within 90 days.

On 30 November the second stage of the five-stage demilitarization process—cantonment, demobilization, and repatriation of soldiers—began (the first stage was the continuing task of monitoring the cease-fire; stages three to five were collection and destruction of weapons, including land mines; integration of opposing forces into a new national military; and integrating demobilized forces into civilian life). Problems here were aggravated by the efforts of both parties to retain control of territory where the GPA had allowed "dual administration" of territory controlled by the government and RENAMO. The SRSG suggested a four-phase introduction of assembly points on the principle of "strategic parity." The first 20 of the 49 assembly areas were opened at the end of November 1993, and the remaining 29 became operational in February 1994. There were also problems over the estimated 155,000-strong government militia that were scattered through the countryside and were often only under nominal official control. It soon turned out that figures for the strength of government forces had been inflated by the Ministry of Defence officials, who then pocketed the subsequently allocated funds. RENAMO was suspicious of this. Eventually, the agreed-upon overall figure for government troops was reduced from 76,405 to 64,466. Conversely, RENAMO clandestinely demobilized the child soldiers (under

the age of 15) it was notorious for using—only 3,632 were discovered at RENAMO bases. There were also severe delays in forming the proposed new national army (FADM). Despite efforts to provide recreation and to sustain the morale of cantoned troops subject to prolonged delays, there were repeated disturbances, including assaults on RENAMO generals. Nevertheless, by mid-April 1994, 55 percent of government and 81 percent of RENAMO soldiers were cantoned, and 20 percent of government and 3 percent of RENAMO soldiers had been demobilized and transported to the districts of their choice. At the end of April the UN secretary-general reported that the mission was on course to establish the main conditions for successful completion on schedule, with a view to withdrawal of ONUMOZ by 31 January 1995. The current strength of ONUMOZ's military component was given as 5,914 of all ranks, including 375 military observers. This would be reduced by some 2,000 by the end of May. By 5 July, 84 percent (41,974) of government troops and 90 percent (17,402) of RENAMO troops were in the assembly areas. Both sides were withholding crack troops and large caches of weapons. By August 15 a sudden influx of government troops to the cantonment areas (ably handled by the administrators) had brought registered figures to 64,130 (government) and 22,637 (RENAMO), leaving an estimated 5,000 government troops and 2,000 RENAMO troops still outside the process. The total number of weapons recovered was 150,000. At the same time the formation of FADM was proceeding much more slowly than envisaged. The United Nations was reluctant to get involved with this process, which was to have been aided by France, Portugal, and the United Kingdom. By 4 July only 3,000 FADM soldiers had been trained, under the joint command of Brig. L. Lidimo (for the government) and Lt. Gen. M. Ngonhamo (for RENAMO). By election time in October 1994 fewer than 10,000 soldiers had completed training, and the target size for FADM was lowered from 30,000 to 15,000. The failure to complete the military provisions of the GPA on time meant, as the UN secretary-general warned, that during the election period there might be three armies potentially in existence. In the event these fears were not realized, but they illustrate the precarious nature of complex peace processes and the narrow line between success and failure in ambitious UN peacekeeping operations such as ONUMOZ.

Meanwhile, at the end of January 1994, the UN secretary-general reported that conditions had evolved in Mozambique to the point where there was a need for an enhanced CIVPOL presence to accommodate a shift of emphasis from monitoring cease-fire arrangements to verification of police activity and human rights. He recommended an additional 1,006 civilian police, bringing the full complement to 1,144, as was subsequently authorized by SCR 898 of 23 February 1994.

On the humanitarian front, UNOHAC played the central role in ONUMOZ's activities. The international community provided more than 78 percent of the $650 million needed for humanitarian assistance during ONUMOZ's mandate period. More than 40 UN organizations and agencies and international public organizations and NGOs, as well as Mozambican bodies, were delivering emergency assistance at more than 300 delivery points, many of them in previously inaccessible areas. These enterprises were coordinated through the Coordinated Program of Assistance developed in cooperation with the two major parties and the donor community. Perhaps the major project was the resettlement of some six million Mozambicans, including those who had fled abroad, the internally displaced, and some 370,000 demobilized soldiers and their dependents. In the attempt to coordinate this ambitious program, UNOHAC's field officers convened humanitarian assistance committees to contact all concerned parties. UNDP implemented the Reintegration Support Scheme for former soldiers. The United Nations High Commissioner for Refugees (UNHCR) estimated that by the end of 1994 nearly 4,300,000 people had been resettled in their original places of residence. With the help of UNHCR and NGOs more than 700 primary schools and 250 health care facilities were opened in rural areas, with another 310 health care posts planned in collaboration with the World Bank and the World Food Program (WFP). In a program assisted by the United Nations Children's Fund (UNICEF), some 2,000 wells were opened to provide one water source per 500 people.

Meanwhile, the electoral process had been negotiating comparable difficulties. A draft electoral law presented by the Mozambican government on 26 March 1993 was contested by RENAMO and other political parties. In August the multiparty consultative conference convened to overcome the differences again broke down over composition of the NEC. The UN secretary-general's visit of 17–20 October 1993 broke the deadlock, but there was subsequent disagreement over voting rights for expatriate Mozambicans, composition of provincial and district electoral commissions, and other issues. Consensus on these matters was finally reached on 26 November. The Electoral Law was approved in the Mozambican National Assembly on 9 December 1993 and the NEC was appointed on 21 January 1994. Voter registration began on 1 June and was extended to 2 September. The initial estimate of eligible voters, based on the 1980 census, was found to be inaccurate and was lowered to 7,894,850, of whom three-quarters had been registered by 22 August. In a report of 26 August the UN secretary-general estimated that about 75 percent of those internally displaced had now been resettled, although there were still some 342,000 refugees in neighboring countries. The humanitarian programs were seen to have contributed to the process of national reconciliation. Security was a major problem, for banditry and crime rose as armed forces on both sides withdrew from many areas. Nevertheless, prospects were reasonable for the electoral campaign, which was scheduled to start on 22 September 1994. The main role for ONUMOZ in September and October, therefore, was to create a stable environment for free and fair elections and to aid in technical assistance for the electoral process. As the election approached, the political stakes increased, the danger of disruption rose, and overshadowing all was the fear that those who thought they would lose out in the election might, as in Angola, reject the whole process. Some candidates were making ominous remarks to that effect. On the eve of the elections some 2,300 electoral observers, including 900 from the United Nations, were deployed to verify the polling and counting of votes. The OAU, the European Union, and other organizations also sent teams of observers. On 26 October, the day before polling started, Afonso Dhlakama, president of RENAMO, alleged irregularities and announced his decision to withdraw. The UN Security Council, the UN secretary-general, the ambassadors of the states' members of the commissions, and other ambassadors in Maputo, as well as the presidents of South Africa, Zimbabwe, and other countries in the region, urged him to reconsider. The voting went ahead, with more than half the registered voters casting their ballots on 27 October, and RENAMO monitors were present at most polling stations. On 28 October Dhlakama reversed his decision, and the voting period was extended by a day, to 29 October, to accommodate this. In some provinces more than 90 percent of the registered electorate voted. The mandate for ONUMOZ was to expire on 15 November, whereas the new government would not be installed before 15 December, so SCR 957 of 15 November 1994 extended the mandate for a month, with residual operations to be completed by 31 January 1995. The NEC announced that the elections had been free and fair on 19 November, after some delays because of, among other things, computerization errors. In the presidential election Chissano won a renewal of office with 2,633,740 votes (53.3 percent) over Dhlakama with 1,666,965 votes (33.7 percent). Of registered voters, 87.9 percent participated. In the legislative election FRELIMO won 129 seats in the new parliament with 44.3 percent of the vote; RENAMO, 109 seats with 37.8 percent; and Uniao Democratica (UD), 12 seats with 5.2 percent. The UN secretary-general congratulated the people and leaders of Mozambique on the success of the elections and called on all Mozambicans to pursue the task of national reconciliation. ONUMOZ's mandate formally came to an end on 9 December, the day the new presidency was inaugurated. Remaining ONUMOZ assets were liquidated by 31 January 1995, although other UN personnel remained on economic and assistance programs. At the end of the ONUMOZ mandate, UNOHAC transferred coordination responsibilities to the UN resident coordinator in Maputo. The ongoing mine clearance program became a joint responsibility of UNDP and the United Nations Department of Humanitarian Affairs (DHA). The ONUMOZ budget contained $11 million for mine clearance, together with $7.5 million for a DHA trust fund. A National Mine-Clearance Plan began to tackle the estimated two million land mines left after the war. By the end of the ONUMOZ mandate 450 Mozambicans had been trained in mine clearance, but no more than a start had been made on mine clearance, with no more than a few hundred mines having been disabled.

The originally authorized strength for ONUMOZ included a 6,625-strong military contingent, a military observer group of 354 officers, some 355 international staff, and 506 local staff. In February 1994 an establishment of 1,144 civilian police was authorized, including the 128 CIVPOL personnel authorized earlier. The following states provided military and CIVPOL personnel: Argentina, Australia, Austria, Bangladesh, Bolivia, Botswana, Brazil, Canada, Cape Verde, China, Czech Republic, Egypt, Finland, Ghana, Guinea-Bissau, Guyana, Hungary, India, Indonesia, Ireland, Italy, Japan, Jordan, Malaysia, Nepal, the Netherlands, New Zealand, Nigeria, Norway, Pakistan, Portugal, Russian Federation, Spain, Sri Lanka, Sweden, Switzerland, Togo, the United States, Uruguay, and Zambia. Costs of ONUMOZ were borne by member states in accordance with UN Charter article 17, paragraph 2. For the period 15 October 1992 to 15 November 1994 expenditures were $471,199,200. A further $39,053,300 was appropriated for the liquidation period from 16 November 1994 to 31 March 1995.

See also Angola; Cambodia; Child soldiers; Codes of conduct; Military-humanitarian relations; Postconflict reconstruction
References and further reading Alden (1995); Durch (1994); Malaquias (1996); Willett (1995); United Nations (1996)

Multinational Force and Observers

After the Yom Kippur War between Israel and Egypt and Syria (Egypt and Syria were supported by Iraqi, Jordanian, and Libyan military units) in 1973 the United Nations mandated the second United Nations Emergency Force (UNEF II) to oversee the cease-fire line and buffer zones between Egypt and Israel. After six years the two sides came together to sign a peace agreement (the Camp David Accords), and UNEF II was to be an integral part of the disengagement process, which would have needed an extension of the force's mandate. However, the USSR had a diplomatic interest in the politics of the region, and when the rest of the Arab world condemned Egypt for signing the treaty and enlisted the support of the Soviet Union, the continued deployment of UNEF II was clearly problematic. The USSR threatened to use its veto power in the Security Council to block an extension of the force's mandate, and it was disbanded. There, was, however, an immediate need for a neutral force of some kind to oversee the implementation phase of the accords. One partial answer was to deploy the Sinai Field Mission, but this still left an operational gap in the observation and supervision process. The United States had promised, as part of the Camp David Accords, to ensure that a neutral force would be forthcoming, even in the face of USSR intransigence in the Security Council. Two years after the Camp David talks, in 1981, Egypt, Israel, and the United States signed a protocol that created the new force: the Multinational Force and Observers (MFO). It was to be based in Rome with a civilian director general and would have its own distinct identity in terms of insignia, budget, and legal status. Thus, although the MFO would be fulfilling all the duties envisaged for the extended UNEF II, it would not need Security Council clearance and mandate. There were a number of political difficulties in actually mustering a force to serve under this new banner because of the difficult international circumstances in which both

Egypt and Israel found themselves. Many countries still did not recognize Israel as a state, a number more had severed ties with Egypt over the Camp David Accords, the regional politics of the Organization of African Unity (OAU) meant that Egypt was reluctant to call upon members of that organization to help, and the European Community nations were wary of being identified too closely with the United States in the Middle East. The force was finally composed of infantry battalions from the United States, Fiji, and Colombia with later contributions from the United Kingdom, France, Italy, Holland, Canada, New Zealand, and Uruguay. The first two force commanders were Norwegian. The role of the MFO is that of an observer mission, but as with most such exercises the work of the contingent goes beyond mere observation. The MFO is seen as an impartial authority and as a diplomatic arbitrator in some cases. Although not strictly present in an interpositional sense, the strategic placements of the force have a similar psychological effect. A further valuable role of the MFO, given the recent history of the region and the surprise attacks that have taken place, is its "early warning" capability.

See also Interposition; Middle East conflict
References and further reading
Hoffman (1983); James (1990); Mackinlay (1989); Pelcovits (1993)

Multinational Forces I and II (Lebanon, 1982–1984)
See Lebanon

Namibia

United Nations Transitional Assistance Group (UNTAG), 1989

Conflict Profile

Covering an area of 825,000 square kilometers (larger than France and Germany combined), Namibia has a population of only 1.5 million. Situated in southwest Africa on the Atlantic coast, it is bordered by Angola to the north, Zambia to the northeast (at the end of the Caprivi Strip), Botswana to the west, and South Africa to the south. From the Namib Desert on the coast, the country rises to a high plateau that merges into the Kalahari Desert in the east. Its capital is Windhoek. Sovereignty over Walvis Bay, its only deepwater port, is still contested by South Africa on the grounds that the port was annexed by Britain in 1878 and subsequently incorporated into South African territory. Most of the population lives in the northern third of the country. The Ovambo people make up about half the population, with a substantial Kavango, Hereo, Damara, and Nama, as well as "colored" and "white," presence. Diamonds constitute half the export earnings, and there are deposits of uranium, copper, lead, zinc, and tin.

The United Nations inherited responsibility for Namibia from the League of Nations. Namibia had become a German colony in 1884 (when it was called German South West Africa), but in 1920 the League of Nations, recognizing South African occupation of the country during World War I, awarded a class "C" mandate to South Africa. This gave South Africa conditional administrative powers but did not permit incorporation. After World War II South Africa refused to accept UN authority and tried to annex the territory. In the 1950s and 1960s the independence of former European African colonies and the extension of apartheid to Namibia exposed South Africa to an increasingly hostile world opinion. In 1966 the UN General Assembly revoked South Africa's mandate, and in 1971 the International Court of Justice ruled its occupation of Namibia illegal. In 1966 the South West African People's Organization (SWAPO) (expanded from the earlier Ovambo People's Organization) began military action through its People's Liberation Army of Namibia (PLAN). In 1973 the

UN General Assembly recognized SWAPO as the sole representative of the Namibian people. After the Portuguese withdrew from Angola and its colonial government was replaced by an indigenous Marxist regime, regional and great power involvement in Namibia intensified. Events in Angola were critical. The ruling Movimento Popular de Libertação de Angola (MPLA) regime in Angola, supported by the Soviet Union and Cuba, backed SWAPO's struggle for independence in Namibia. In response, in 1975, at the Turnhalle building in Windhoek, South Africa attempted to forestall outside interference by launching a constitutional initiative (the "Turnhalle initiative") to give independence to Namibia on its own terms, including separate administrations for different ethnic groups. This was rejected by the international community. Fearing that the UN General Assembly would extend its sanctions and that an escalating war of liberation in Namibia would increase Soviet influence, a "Contact Group" of Western states (Canada, France, the United Kingdom, the United States, and West Germany) was established in January 1976 to mediate a peaceful settlement. In a note to the UN Security Council on 10 April 1978, the Contact Group proposed the creation of the United Nations Transitional Assistance Group (UNTAG) to assist a special representative of the secretary-general (SGSR) in supervising elections that would lead to a new constitution for an independent Namibia. Following recommendations from UN Secretary-General Kurt Waldheim, the plan was adopted in Security Council Resolution (SCR) 435 (of 1978), which envisaged a one-year transition period to the elections. In conception, the Resolution 435 Peace Plan thus anticipated the 1979 Lancaster House Agreement in Zimbabwe as the prototype for a number of later UN-assisted transitions to peace and democracy after prolonged conflict, although in the event it took more than a decade before the plan was finally put into operation.

Ten years later, U.S.-mediated negotiations between Angola, Cuba, and South Africa led to agreement on "Principles for a Peaceful Settlement in South-West Africa" in July 1988 and to the 22 December 1988 Namibia Accords. The accords linked implementation of Resolution 435 to the withdrawal of Cuban troops from Angola, a trade-off of interests on both sides. The fighting in Namibia and Angola was at a stalemate; in Namibia the bloody battle of Cuíto Cuanavale between November 1987 and March 1988 proved to be a watershed in bringing both sides to the negotiating table. On the South African side the economic costs of maintaining a presence in Namibia were becoming prohibitive at a time when sanctions were biting and the tide of liberal opinion was rising domestically. The transformation of Soviet policy under Mikhail Gorbachev gave some scope for compromise on the other side. The prospect of escaping the $20 million–per–year cost of maintaining Cuban troops was also welcomed. By early August 1988 there was a de facto cease-fire. Cooperation between the great powers in the UN Security Council helped to drive the process forward, led by the new U.S. policy of "constructive engagement" in the region. The Soviet Union was able to withdraw from unsustainable commitments with honor, and U.S. prestige and influence were enhanced.

UNTAG's mandate was, therefore, based on the ten-year-old Resolution 435 to assist the SGSR for up to a year "to ensure the early independence of Namibia through free and fair elections under the supervision and control of the United Nations." Subsequent protocols were added, as were details from the 1978 Contact Group note. According to the original plan as envisaged in the "Settlement Proposal," the SGSR would have direct responsibility for administering the territory during the tran-

sition phase. However, in the process of negotiation a compromise was reached with Pretoria, whose administrator-general would remain in charge, with the United Nations exercising a monitoring brief with no powers of enforcement. The secretary-general's recommendations were approved in SCR 632 on 16 February 1989, although disagreements over procurement meant that the budget was not endorsed until 1 March. Given the UN's financial problems, this delay in endorsing the budget contributed to UNTAG's delayed start (see Map 7).

The Deployment of UNTAG

UNTAG, under SGSR Martti Ahtisaari, was operational from "D-day," 1 April 1989, to 21 March 1990, although disputes in New York and logistical delays meant that by the start date fewer than 1,000 of the advance guard of the designated 4,650 troops were in Namibia preparing for the three 850-strong battalions from Kenya, Malaysia, and Finland. At this point the whole enterprise was thrown into confusion by the unexpected incursion of 1,500 to 1,800 SWAPO guerrillas into northern Namibia from Angola on 31 March and 1 April. With UNTAG unable to contain the incursion, the danger was that the South African Defence Force (SADF) troops, who should have been confined to bases by that date, would reenter the fray. It took concerted pressure on all sides and delicate negotiations, only finally completed by 13 May 1989, to persuade SWAPO to retire to the sixteenth parallel and SADF to return to base. Opinions vary as to why SWAPO mounted this incursion, but it is generally agreed that the peace process survived this early setback mainly because by this stage it was in the perceived interest of all principal parties that it should do so. In addition, regional powers as well as both the Soviet Union and the United States exerted coordinated pressure.

Meanwhile, in the second week of April the main body of UNTAG troops began to arrive (albeit unable to speak the local language of Ovamboland and almost none accompanied by interpreters). UNTAG's Irish, Dutch, and Swedish civilian police did not appear until 15 April. Tardiness of deployment was, therefore, already a problem in what was

UNTAG civilian deployment as of November 1989

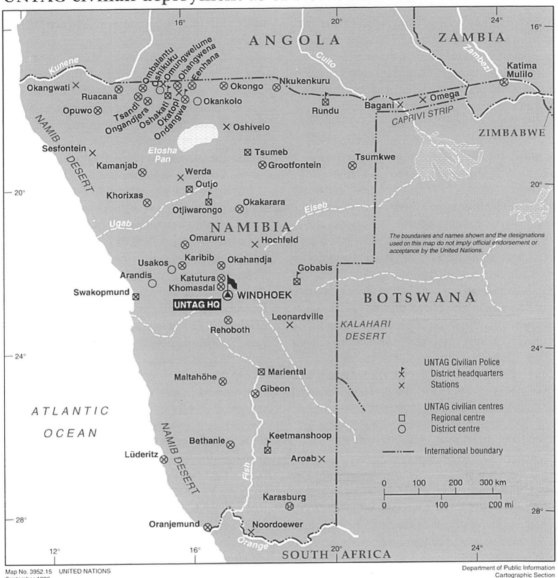

Map No. 3952.15   UNITED NATIONS
September 1996

Department of Public Information
Cartographic Section

later seen as the prototype for other second-generation peace implementation missions of this kind. UNTAG can hardly be blamed for the SWAPO incursion, which began before it was scheduled to arrive, but the fragile state of the peace process in ensuing weeks showed how important prompt deployment was for instilling confidence and setting parameters for subsequent actions.

UNTAG's central task was to "create the political conditions for free and fair elections" in Namibia. All other activities served this end. Five interlocking tasks had to be performed.

First, once South African and SWAPO forces were finally confined to base by 13 May 1989, the South African military presence in Namibia had to be dismantled. All but 1,500 of the SADF troops were withdrawn by 24 June, and the remainder were withdrawn after the elections by 21 November. Several hundred SADF personnel remained, fulfilling civilian functions such as running airfields, and efforts were made to replace them. More problematic was the demobilization of nearly 12,000 "citizen forces" and "commandos" and, above all, the 21,000-strong South West Africa Territorial Force (SWATF). This was largely complete by 1 June, and arms and equipment were gathered in drill halls supervised by UNTAG. SWATF personnel retained their uniforms, however, and continued to report to headquarters to receive pay for several months, causing international concern. Nor was a simple way found to demobilize the bushmen battalions, who were not able to return to their places of origin. UNTAG military observers monitored Namibia's borders with South Africa, but the long northern border posed particular problems in view of the mixed populations living on either side of it, necessitating reinforcements from UNTAG's regular battalions and civilian police (CIVPOL). A Verification Mechanism was established by the Joint Commission to investigate repeated South African allegations that SWAPO was planning to move in the north. An investigation by the SGSR into one accusation that UNTAG was complicit in SWAPO's advances led to the conclusion that some South African elements wanted to disrupt the independence process.

Second, the South West Africa Police (SWAPOL) had to be monitored. This was perhaps the most

sensitive area of all. Throughout the transition phase the South African administrator-general remained responsible for law and order, but UNTAG was charged with ensuring that this did not lead to undue interference with the electoral process. The challenging task was to create a more or less neutral political arena so that campaigning could be carried out free from intimidation. This went against the ingrained culture of control and repression within the security forces. UNTAG's CIVPOL was duly increased from the originally planned 360 (although the initial deployment was in fact 500) to 1,500. Despite initial resistance, CIVPOL increasingly accompanied SWAPOL on its patrols, and it was eventually accepted in many cases that CIVPOL, rather than SWAPOL, would police political gatherings. One of the most serious problems faced in monitoring the police was the fact that about two-thirds (perhaps 2,000) of the notorious *Koevoet* ("crowbar") special counterinsurgency unit had been absorbed into the police force before 1 April 1989. This became one of the most contentious issues between the SGSR and the South African administrator-general, coming high on the list of items discussed when the UN secretary-general visited in July. SCR 640 of 29 August 1989 demanded the disbanding of the *Koevoet*. Eventually the South African foreign minister announced the demobilization of the *Koevoet* members of SWAPOL in September and October.

Third, discriminatory laws that inhibited free and fair elections had to be repealed. After elaborate negotiation 56 pieces of legislation were repealed, although the notorious Law AG-8, governing ethnic administration, remained because the administrator-general argued that it did not interfere with the elections and that local administration could not be reconstructed so swiftly. A full amnesty for political prisoners was laid down as an essential requirement in the Settlement Proposal, but amnesty had been a major bone of contention since Resolution 435 was adopted. South Africa wanted to distinguish between political crimes and common law crimes but was eventually persuaded to proclaim an unqualified amnesty on 6 June 1989. Lists of those detained both by SWAPO and South Africa were compiled with help from nongovernmental organizations

(NGOs), and disputed cases were referred to the independent jurist, Professor Carl Nörgaard. Both sides accused the other of failing to release all prisoners, and the issue became particularly prominent during the election campaign.

Fourth, the peace process opened the way to the return of refugees, a return that was implemented by the United Nations High Commissioner for Refugees (UNHCR) aided by a number of other UN agencies together with the Council of Churches in Namibia. An airlift of refugees followed the June amnesty. Most returnees came from Angola, but they also came from Zambia and 44 other countries. UNTAG military forces provided security at their points of arrival. Returning refugees then passed through secondary reception centers on their way back to their home areas. The repatriation program was largely completed between June and September 1989. In the end 42,736 Namibians were repatriated, contributing positively to the atmosphere of cooperation and trust essential for the election process, despite inevitable problems such as the search for returning SWAPO members by ex-*Koevoet* elements.

Finally, there was the function of voter registration and electoral supervision. Ensuring that electoral arrangements were not subverted was a demanding task. Despite the precautions already described, UNTAG could do little to prevent SWAPOL personnel from firing on unarmed crowds on occasion, and it was later admitted that perhaps $35 million was covertly contributed by the South African authorities to discredit SWAPO and to support political parties opposed to it. The Civil Cooperation Bureau of the South African Army was blamed for the assassination of Anton Lubowski, the only white member of SWAPO leadership.

The electoral process itself had been planned for ten years, and a system of proportional representation had been decided upon. The South African administrator-general produced a draft electoral proclamation, subsequently much modified under pressure from the SGSR. This included a written undertaking that no application for registration could be rejected without UNTAG's explicit concurrence. Registration began on 3 July and closed on 23 September. Seventy registration centers were set up, and 110 mobile registration teams covered 2,200 points throughout Namibia, each supervised by UNTAG officials and CIVPOL. UNTAG also supervised the computerized lists of voters and made them available to the political parties. Altogether, 701,483 voters registered, more than anticipated, reflecting considerable enthusiasm in Namibia for the unprecedented experience. Ten political parties were eventually registered. The process of voting itself was elaborate, given the size of the country and the novelty of the undertaking. There were 358 polling stations set up, and 1,758 UN personnel took part. South Africa's administrator-general for Namibia would run the elections, but "under UN supervision and control"; troops from UNTAG's military component helped police the elections. Electoral supervisors were given training at four-day seminars in four training centers, while senior officials attended sessions in New York and Geneva. In order to induct Namibians into what was largely a novel experience and to encourage participation, UNTAG used all the media available, notably radio, the press, pamphlets, and visual aids. One source of tension was the South African authorities' bringing in by bus 10,000 white South Africans who were technically eligible to vote, even though many of them were not normally resident there. Their aim was to prevent SWAPO from winning the two-thirds majority needed to be able to impose its own constitution.

Nevertheless, despite all difficulties, when polling closed on 1 November over 97 percent of the registered voters had participated. Queues of voters, often more than a kilometer long, waited patiently to exercise democratic rights for the first time. Final results, declared on 14 November, showed that no party had a two-thirds majority. SWAPO had gained 41 of the Assembly's 72 seats; the Democratic Turnhalle Alliance (DTA), 21 seats; and five other parties shared the remaining 10 seats. The elections were declared free and fair. In the words of SGSR Ahtisaari: "Its youngest democracy has given the whole world a shining lesson in democracy, exemplary as to commitment, restraint and tolerance." The Constituent Assembly met on 21 November 1989 and proceeded to draw up a constitution, subsequently adopted on 9 February 1990. During the period between the elections and independence, the South African administrator-general remained responsible for administration, but increasingly UNTAG's CIVPOL took over from SWAPOL in maintaining stability. UNTAG's military component was rapidly wound down, although a Tripartite Military Integration Committee was set up under the chairmanship of UNTAG to develop the concept of an integrated Namibian army. The independence ceremony took place on 21 March 1990.

UNTAG's civilian component included six elements: (1) The Special Representative's Office in Windhoek was responsible for overall coordination and liaison with the South African administrator-general, supported by 42 political offices in 10 regions of Namibia. (2) A quasi-autonomous independent jurist (Professor Carl Nörgaard, first appointed in 1978) was to advise on disputes concerning the release of political detainees. (3) The Office of UNHCR was responsible for the refugee repatriation and resettlement program and was financed separately from the rest of UNTAG. (4) The Electoral Division was run by a relatively small central staff in Windhoek. It was reinforced by 180 additional staff for the electoral registration process and 885 specialist personnel, provided by 27 countries, to supervise the elections themselves. (5) The Division of Administration was responsible for administration and logistics for UNTAG other than that provided by the military component, UNHCR, and CIVPOL. Training seminars for key headquarters and regional or district staff were carried out in New York and Geneva in March 1989. (6) For the reasons already seen, UNTAG's CIVPOL had a relatively more prominent role to play compared to the military component than was envisaged in the 1978 plan. Led by Commissioner Steven Fanning (Ireland), the original 500 officers were reinforced by two further contingents of 500 deployed to 49 police stations. UNTAG's civilian component, therefore, was made up of nearly 2,000 civilians together with some 1,500 CIVPOL from 25 countries.

The military component, under Force Commander Lt. Gen. Prem Chand of India, consisted of (1) 300 military monitors and observers provided by 14 countries, (2) three infantry battalions provided by Finland, Kenya, and Malaysia (with four additional battalions held in reserve), and (3) a number of logistics units provided by the United Kingdom (a signals unit), Australia (an engineer squad), Denmark (an administrative company), Canada and Poland (supply, transport, and maintenance units), Italy (a helicopter squadron), and Spain (a squadron of light aircraft). Germany and Switzerland provided civilian supply and medical units, while the Soviet Union and the United States provided air transport for initial deployments. The total maximum military deployment was 4,493 troops. UNTAG's overall expenditure was $368,584,324.

See also Ahtisaari, Martti; Angola; Postconflict reconstruction; Second-generation peacekeeping
References and further reading Durch (1994); Fetherston (1994a); Fortna (1995); Jaster (1990); United Nations (1996)

Naval peacekeeping

The use of naval and other maritime forces to uphold international mandates can be traced back at least as far the 1920 Schleswig-Holstein plebiscite when British and French naval personnel from ships off the Danish coast formed part of the International Commission to ensure calm during the referendum. The first UN observer mission (the United Nations Truce Supervision Organization [UNTSO] of 1948) was supported by a U.S. aircraft carrier, three U.S. destroyers, and a French minesweeper, all flying the UN pennant below their national flags. Subsequently naval elements played important roles in many peacekeeping and related operations. In 1962–1963 in West New Guinea, as part of the United Nations Temporary Executive Authority (UNTEA), Pakistan supplied crews to operate nine vessels. In 1965–1967, the Royal Navy patrolled off Beira, Mozambique, to enforce UN oil sanctions against Rhodesia. In 1982 multinational naval units gave offshore support to ground troops and protected the evacuation of Palestinians as part of the first Multinational Force (MNF I) in Lebanon. Since 1982 Italian vessels have patrolled the Strait of Tiran as part of the Multinational Force and Observers (MFO) for disengagement in the Sinai. In 1984 navies cooperated in mine clearing in the Gulf of Suez. During the "Tanker War" of 1984–1988, Western European Union (WEU) ships carried out deterrence, convoying, and countermine measures in the Persian Gulf. In 1990–1992 Argentine patrol vessels and crews monitored arms control in the Gulf of Fonseca as part of the United Nations Observer Mission in Central America (ONUCA). Since the 1990s ships have enforced sanctions against Iraq. In 1991 a disaster relief operation in Bangladesh involved U.S. ships. After 1991 ships offshore provided logistical support to multinational forces in Somalia. Since 1991 WEU and North Atlantic Treaty Organization (NATO) forces have monitored the Adriatic coast, enforced sanctions, supported a no-fly zone, and supported multinational forces in the former Yugoslavia. From 1992 to 1994 the United Nations Transitional Authority in Cambodia (UNTAC) naval units provided lake, river, and coastal patrols in Cambodia. In 1992–1994 a U.S.-led blockade of Haiti prevented a refugee exodus and supported foreign troops ashore. In 1994 the multinational force sent to Albania was landed and supplied by naval elements. In reality, the traditional peacekeeping concept of interposition between opposing forces cannot be easily applied at sea. Purely maritime disputes are not usually urgent or likely to trigger a crisis (fishing disputes are an occasional exception). Ocean boundary issues are amenable to conflict resolution because they have little symbolic and emotive content, and territorial squabbles are not reinforced by any inhabitants. In the peacekeeping context, maritime forces are used overwhelmingly to support the management of disputes on land. The great value of maritime forces lies in their flexibility and ability to sustain operations without trespassing into areas of national sovereignty, their global reach, their diplomatic power as signals of international concern or intent, their ability to land and embark large numbers of troops and stocks of material, and their relative safety as havens for evacuees and casualties. Naval deployments can also be increased quickly if required, though this can be construed as, or can become, indistinguishable from "gunboat diplomacy." One potential drawback of a UN naval policy is that it would be dominated by northern naval powers. However, maritime forces benefit from a surprising potential for multinational interoperability and the lack of maritime opposition from factions in civil wars.

See also Bosnia and Herzegovina; Logistics; Second-generation peacekeeping
References and further reading Pugh (1994)

New Zealand

New Zealand has participated in more than 15 UN peacekeeping and similar operations since 1952, when three territorial volunteers went to Kashmir to join the United Nations Military Observer Group in India and Pakistan (UNMOGIP) to monitor a cease-fire. As the number and scope of UN operations increased in the mid-1990s, the New Zealand deployments mirrored global requirements and were less concentrated in the traditional Middle East region or where their allies were stationed. The number of personnel detailed for UN duties increased too, but, except in Bosnia, not dramatically. In fact, many of New Zealand's contributions were made in so-called penny-packets, as befits a country with a small economy whose defense spending is about 1.1 percent of gross domestic product. Virtually any country can provide infantry. By contrast, the specialist skills provided by New Zealand have been highly valued. New Zealand personnel have been especially appreciated for their mine-clearing expertise and for their training skills: in northern Pakistan for Afghan refugees in 1989–1991; in Cambodia, where 20 New Zealanders were the first mine-clearing specialists to arrive in 1991 (followed by 40 communications specialists, technical advisers, and a naval contingent for patrolling coastal and inland waters); and in Mozambique in 1994. New Zealand has provided engineering and policing expertise in Namibia. Military observers (MOs) have been sent to Haiti and Cambodia, and over a dozen MOs participated in the three UN missions to Angola. In Somalia 62 Royal New Zealand Air Force personnel operated Andover transports, and for relief operations in Rwanda a Hercules transport aircraft and 36 staff were deployed. Finally, New Zealanders have often been in headquarters staff, at the heart of administration, operational planning, and negotiations between disputants. Seven were on the staff in Somalia (in the second United Nations Operation in Somalia (UNOSOM II) and others supported the United Nations High Commissioner for Refugees dealing with the exodus from Rwanda. By contrast, the contribution to the United Nations Protection Force in Former Yugoslavia (UNPROFOR) in Bosnia was something of a departure from this pattern, and it may prove to have been an aberration. From the small beginnings of a handful of MOs sent in 1992, the New Zealand involvement escalated considerably in 1994 with the arrival of an infantry contingent of 250 persons. "Kiwi Company," as it was known, was chiefly engaged in local negotiations, humanitarian activities, and the monitoring of compliance with agreements between Muslims and Croats. The New Zealand unit in UNPROFOR did not become part of the Dayton Implementation Force (IFOR) in Bosnia but returned home in early 1996.

See also Troop-contributing countries

Nicaragua

International Commission for Support and Verification (CIAV)–Organization of American States (OAS) Mission in Nicaragua, 1990–1996

Conflict Profile
In August 1996 in the Honduran town of Tela the presidents of the Central American states signed "the Joint Plan for Demobilization, Repatriation or Voluntary resettlement of the members of the armed opposition movement *Resistencia Nicaraguense* and their families either in Nicaragua or other countries." The International Commission for Support and Verification (CIAV) was created for this purpose and is presided over by the secretary-general of the Organization of American States (OAS). The CIAV-OAS Mission consists of a main office in Managua and eight offices in key areas. The personnel comprise 11 international officials and 40 national officials. The mission's geographical coverage extends throughout Nicaragua's zones of conflict, serving a population in

excess of 650,000 people, including demobilized soldiers from the former Nicaraguan Resistance, discharged members of the Sandinista Popular Army (EPS), displaced and repatriated people, and other victims of the war.

Program for Observation and Verification (PSV)
The Program for Observation and Verification (PSV) dealt with activities related to the verification and observation of violations of human rights. Among other tasks, the Tela plan entrusted the CIAV-OAS Mission with guaranteeing the practice of fundamental rights and freedoms for repatriated and demobilized people through the establishment of an Observation Commission and observation offices. The commission enabled all those protected by the plan to report any violation of their rights and security. It appointed security officers to make regular visits to the affected area in order to monitor effectively. Subsequently the OAS General Assembly decided to expand and enhance the CIAV-OAS mandate in Nicaragua so that it covered everyone affected by the conflicts.

To fulfill their mandate, the PSV officers carried out the following tasks: mediation and negotiation in armed conflicts and in landownership and other disputes; verification of human rights compliance; investigation of complaints; negotiations with Nicaraguan authorities (to track complaints); design of reports containing statistics and written information on violence in rural areas; and monitoring in conflict zones.

Program for Institutional Support (PAI)
The Program for Institutional Support (PAI) provided support to state institutions as well as to the civilian population. It made it possible for the CIAV mission to undertake a transition from peacekeeping to peace building. For this purpose, the CIAV-OAS Mission designed a strategy that not only involved the traditional peace-building aspects of support to state institutions but also introduced a significant component for strengthening civil society by creating peace commissions in rural conflict zones.

The network of Peace and Human Rights Commissions is a mechanism for protecting civil society by protecting human rights, resolving conflicts, and decreasing violence. The CIAV-OAS

Mission supported the formation of the network to cover the towns located in the most conflict-prone regions. Not only did these zones have the greatest propensity for conflict, the strongest cultures of violence, and the most problematic economic situations (with extensive poverty), they were also barely furnished with state institutions—and when such institutions were present they lacked credibility. As a result, there were no public or state mechanisms for resolving conflicts or protecting human rights. Moreover, there was no significant nongovernmental organization activity either. Consequently, these zones can be characterized as lacking institutionalization.

The CIAV-OAS role in encouraging respect for human rights and conflict mediation began to operate through these Peace Commissions in the 41 towns that had the highest rates of violence. They were formed by respected leaders, usually *campesinos* (small farmers and peasants). The internal organization of the commissions was flexible, and they were adjusted to the needs and expectations in each place. Generally, they had boards elected democratically by the community, and in some cases they were working commissions. The commissions were tasked to

1. promote and spread human rights through the organization of training workshops aimed at teaching *campesinos* and others civil standards and at stimulating policies for living in peace. The workshops discussed human rights, Nicaragua's constitution, democracy, the electoral system, criminal laws, the agrarian system, community organization, and so on.
2. attend to complaints and investigate them. The commissions received complaints about violations of standards, carried out investigations, and presented the results to the appropriate authority.
3. mediate in conflict resolution. The credibility of the commissions enabled them to act on controversial issues with the purpose of reaching peaceful agreements, not only in conflicts over possession of land but also in problems arising from armed groups. In this way the mission temporarily compensated

for the lack of state mechanisms in conflict resolution and prevented people from taking the law into their own hands or practicing private justice.

See also ONUCA; Organization of African States
References and further reading Rosende and Beltrand (1997)

Nigerian peacekeeping
See Liberia

Nobel Peace Prize
" . . . and one part to the person who shall have done the most or the best work for fraternity between nations, for the abolition or reduction of standing armies and for the holding and promotion of peace congresses." This excerpt from the will of Alfred Nobel provides the only briefing for the committee responsible for the awarding of the Nobel Peace Prize each year. Because of the changes in the nature and conduct of conflicts throughout the twentieth century, it is the responsibility of this committee to interpret the founder's meaning and, where appropriate, to make an award. The committee is drawn from the members of the Norwegian parliament—the Norting. The long-standing question as to why this should be so—since, first, Alfred Nobel was a Swede, and, second, the other four sections of the Nobel awards are all decided in Sweden—remains unanswered. It is possible that because the two countries were united at the time he drew up his will, he wanted to share responsibilities between them. It is also possible that he was influenced by his love of Norwegian literature and culture. A third possibility is that he was impressed by the Norting's record of public interest in mediation, arbitration, and pacific resolution of international disputes. The first woman to be awarded the Peace Prize was Bertha von Suttner in 1905, and the first organization to be recognized was the International Committee of the Red Cross/Red Crescent (ICRC) in 1917. Since the inception of the United Nations the prize has been awarded to individuals connected with the organization—Cordell Hull in 1945, Lester Pearson in 1957, and Dag Hammarskjöld

(posthumously) in 1961. In 1988 the entire corps of Peacekeeping Forces was awarded a collective Nobel Peace Prize.

See also Bunche, Ralph; Pearson, Lester B.; Perez de Cuellar, Javier
References and further reading A complete listing of Nobel Prize winners and their achievements can be found on the World Wide Web at http//www.nobel.se/

No-fly zones

A modern development in peace missions has been the recognition that aircraft can threaten civilians by their very presence, not just when they are in attack mode. They can also gather a great deal of intelligence even when flying high above the civilian population. This has been a particular problem in two recent conflicts: in Iraq after the second of the Gulf Wars, when central government helicopters and planes were used against the civilian population in the north and the south in order to subdue civil unrest, and in Bosnia when the population came under attack by Serbian forces. Because both of these situations were peace enforcement actions the response of the UN Allied Forces (in Iraq) and the North Atlantic Treaty Organization (NATO) (in Bosnia) was to designate areas of airspace where aircraft from the belligerents were forbidden to operate in any form. These areas were formally called "air exclusion zones" and later became known as "no-fly zones."

See also Air support; Bosnia and Herzegovina; Gulf Wars; Regional organizations and peacekeeping; United Nations Protection Force in Former Yugoslavia

Nongovernmental organizations (NGOs)

Nongovernmental organizations (NGOs) are recognized in article 71 of the UN Charter as independent, non–profit-making organizations formed from a variety of religious and humanitarian motives. By the 1990s the global network of NGOs or, in the United States, private voluntary organizations (PVOs), had grown to be vast and diverse. They range from small local operations that function to help individuals in a specific conflict to es-

tablished groups, often well known to the public (for example Médecins sans Frontières [Doctors without Borders], Oxfam-UK, Concern, Save the Children, and so on), with professional administrative and field-based staffs, substantial budgets, and sophisticated communications. Looked at globally, the aggregated power of these NGOs is immense: During the 1980s Africa became the largest recipient of food aid and humanitarian assistance, and NGOs became the main agencies of delivering and managing this aid. In 1993 emergency aid amounted to $5 billion, or 10 percent of total overseas development assistance, and 60 percent of this was disbursed through NGOs. There are over 4,000 development NGOs in the Organization of Economic Cooperation and Development (OECD) countries, NGOs that work mainly overseas, and an estimated 20,000 other national NGOs outside the OECD countries that may become the field-based partners of the larger NGOs (that is, of the international NGOs [INGOs], which can operate in many countries and regions and which, like Oxfam and Save the Children, have multinational organization). Finally, there is a myriad of grassroots and community-based organizations (sometimes called GROs or CBOs) that represent local interests, local opinion, and local cultures and that should not be ignored as part of the humanitarian system. However, despite the variety and diversity of the NGO world, it is estimated that about 30 large INGOs based in the United States and in Europe handle about 75 percent of all NGO-disbursed emergency aid.

In the course of the most extreme emergencies, the number of NGOs in the field can escalate dramatically; in Rwanda, for example, there were over 200 NGOs active at the height of the crisis in 1995. Similarly, the number of NGOs active in the former Yugoslavia went through a remarkable expansion as the crisis unfolded. Between February and September 1993 the number of NGOs virtually doubled from 65 to 127, and although the majority of them, 91, were internationally based and were more or less well known, 36 were indigenous NGOs (that is, the GROs and CBOs), often developed in response to the war. The main UN agencies relied on NGOs as partners: 22 worked for the United Nations High Commissioner for Refugees

(UNHCR), the lead UN agency, and both the World Health Organization (WHO) and the World Food Program (WFP) held regular meetings with NGOs working in the food aid and health aspects of relief.

NGOs are involved in a wide variety of services, including famine early warning, food supply and distribution, emergency feeding, water and sanitation, public health programs, human rights monitoring, conflict early warning, conflict prevention, peace building and conflict resolution, family tracing and reunification, psychosocial care, agricultural projects, income generation, educational activities, and projects related to the development of civic institutions and the building of civil society.

See also Civilian component in peacekeeping operations; Codes of conduct; International Committee of the Red Cross; Military-humanitarian relations; Mozambique; Peace building from below
References and further reading
Mackinlay (1996); Schirch (1995); Weiss and Minear (1995)

Nonlethal weapons and peacekeeping

Rapid technological advances have meant the development of nonlethal weapons (NLWs), which until recently would have been dismissed as being in the realm of science fiction. Such NLWs are now receiving serious consideration by military forces, and some have been deployed by U.S. forces during the Gulf War and in Somalia, Haiti, and the former Yugoslavia. The United Nations will probably be tasked with ever more peace support operations, and NLWs may provide UN force commanders in such operations with options other than lethal force. Deployment of NLWs in these scenarios raises ethical, legal, and humanitarian questions regarding the criteria and guidelines for their use, their impact on international arms control conventions, and the danger of lowering the threshold of international intervention in the affairs of states.

Defining NLWs is no easy matter. The term "nonlethal" has been subject to criticism both as a euphemism and as an oxymoron. Other terms have been suggested that are said to more accurately reflect the true nature of nonlethal weapons:

less-than-lethal, disabling, weapons that do not cross the death barrier, soft-kill, pre-lethal, and worse-than-lethal. Proponents of nonlethal weapons acknowledge that ambiguity exists, since the use of any weapon brings with it the risk of injury and death. But they argue that the term "nonlethal" accurately reflects the intention neither to kill nor to permanently harm. For this reason they reject the terms "disabling" and "less-than-lethal" because they imply permanent effects (such as loss of limbs). Opponents argue that more accurate terms would be either "pre-lethal," to imply temporary incapacitation to make a follow-on attack with conventional weapons easier, or "worse-than-lethal," to highlight the terrible psychological trauma that may affect individuals if these weapons result in severe injuries (e.g., blinding by lasers).

Certainly, the term "nonlethal" has a reassuring connotation. Compared to lethal weapons, which kill and maim not only troops but also civilians, the prospect of a new generation of weapons that could minimize injuries must resonate strongly with a popular opinion that has grown increasingly reluctant to countenance deaths and serious casualties through military action—especially in the era of instant media coverage. Perhaps the most comprehensive definition, in this context, is that provided by Christopher Lamb, the U.S. director of policy and planning in the Office of the Assistant Secretary of Defense for Special Operations: "Non-lethal weapons are discriminate weapons that are explicitly designed and employed so as to incapacitate personnel or material, while minimizing fatalities and undesired damage to property and environment. Unlike weapons that permanently destroy targets through blast, fragmentation, or presentation, non-lethal weapons have relatively reversible effects on targets and/or are able to discriminate between targets and nontargets in the weapon's area of impact."

Nonlethal weapons could be used within the two categories of war fighting and peace support operations. NLWs may be used, for example, to separate combatants and noncombatants; in peacekeeping operations to control crowds and riots; in war fighting to disable or disrupt military logistics and communication systems and to neu-

---

Box 2: Nonlethal Weapons Acquired for U.S. Marines in Somalia

Before any new weapons system is acquired it is reviewed under Department of Defense Instruction 5500.15, which checks the legality of each weapon under international law, to ensure that it does not violate U.S. treaty obligations.

- Sticky foam
- Aqueous foam
- Stinger grenades
- Forty-millimeter munitions: no. 40B stinger cartridges; no. 40W wooden baton rounds; no. 2504 tri-flex beanbag rounds; no. 40F foam rubber round
- Twelve-gauge shotgun munitions: no. 23 beanbag rounds; no. 23 rubber-pellet cartridges; no. 23 wooden baton rounds
- Oleoresin capsicum (OC) aerosol pepper projectors; Mk4, Mk5, Mk46

Source: N. Lewer and S. Schofield, "Non-Lethal Weapons for UN Military Operations," *International Peacekeeping* 4, no. 3 (autumn 1997): 71–93.

---

tralize power supplies, transport, and other aspects of civilian and military infrastructure; to spread propaganda and (mis)information; to disable or destroy weapons of mass destruction; to evacuate noncombatants; to protect humanitarian relief delivery; to help in counterdrug missions; and to enforce economic sanctions by using measures that, for example, rapidly degrade vehicle tires and lines of communication.

In peacekeeping terms the most notable use of NLWs was in Somalia. In January 1995 the UN decided to terminate the second United Nations Operation in Somalia (UNOSOM II) and a request was made to the United States for military forces to help protect its withdrawal. The First U.S. Marine Expeditionary Force (1 MEF), based at Camp Pendleton under the command of Lt. Gen. Anthony Zinni, was ordered to provide the appropriate military elements for what was designated Operation United Shield. During the planning stages it was recognized that much of the marines' task would be engaging with hostile unarmed civilians, such as looters and rioters, so the staff of the Tactical Exercise Control Group of 1 MEF began to look for the best available crowd-control equipment to perform this function.

The rules of engagement (ROE) for United Shield were based on the standard principle of a graduated response, authorizing the use of the "minimum force" necessary to repel attacks or imminent threat of attack and to ensure the safety of the troops. But the ROE also contained specific restrictions on the use of certain "crowd-control" devices.

During United Shield, in which over 2,000 U.S. and Italian marines were deployed, there was only limited use of NLWs such as sticky foam and caltrops (road spikes to deflate tires) to enhance barrier systems at night during the final stages of the withdrawal. There is a clearly identified requirement for NLWs in operations other than war, but at the time of United Shield most NLWs were still under development and few were actually available for operational deployment in sufficient quantities. Lieutenant General Zinni, a supporter of NLWs, said that the flexibility of the new technology allowed him to operate more effectively in environments like Somalia. The Marine Corps commandant, Gen. Charles Krulak, said that an initial concern of some marine commanders, that NLWs would make the troops "soft," did not materialize. The marines did not seem any less ready to use lethal force if required to do so. In the main, NLWs have been subordinate to conventional weapons, being used either to enhance force projection or as the first stage of a graduated response up to and including the use of lethal force. As deployments in Somalia indicate, military planners accept that NLWs may provide troops with more flexibility to deal with the range of new conflict scenarios (see Box 2).

See also Arms control and disarmament
References and further reading Lewer and Schofield (1997)

Nordic countries

During the Suez Canal crisis in 1956 the Canadian external affairs minister Lester Pearson called on governments to provide forces for limited UN duties. In 1959 UN Secretary-General Dag Hammarskjöld called on countries involved in the first peacekeeping mission in the Middle East to include troops for peacekeeping in their normal military planning. This idea has more recently been formalized in the United Nations Standby Arrangements System (UNSAS), but since the 1960s standby forces for use in peacekeeping operations were set up by a small group of countries, in particular by Canada and the Nordic countries. For peacekeeping purposes, the Nordic countries can be defined as Denmark, Norway, Sweden, and Finland. By 1968 each of these countries had established arrangements whereby both regular officers and reserves were available for UN service on very short notice. By the early 1990s Norway had a maximum of 2,022 personnel available; Denmark, 1,500; Finland, 2,000; and Sweden, 3,000. These forces were not available for enforcement operations, and although ready to deploy quickly they were not a permanent standing force. There is a high level of institutionalized coordination between the four countries. Planning for joint participation in a mission is organized through the Nordic Committee for Military United Nations Matters (NORDSAMFN). There is a Nordic Economic Working Committee to cover finance. Combined training is also provided: Norway trains logistics and movement-control personnel, Finland trains the military observers, Sweden trains staff officers, and Denmark, military police. The four countries have unique experience in terms of operational coordination. A combined Danish and Norwegian battalion (DANFOR) served in the first United Nations Emergency Force (UNEF I) between 1956 and 1967. A joint Nordic infantry battalion (NORBATT I) has served in the first UN preventive deployment in Macedonia. During the Cold War period the Nordic countries combined provided approximately one in four of all UN peacekeepers. During the 1990s, when the number of nations providing peacekeeping troops expanded and the size of missions grew, the Nordics provided one in ten of all peacekeepers, second only to France. This combined approach has given the Nordic countries an influence and significance in peacekeeping that are out of proportion to the size of these countries. Changes in European security organizations are also having an impact on peacekeeping and on Nordic participation, as new roles of cooperative conflict management are being defined within both the Western European Union (WEU) and the Organization for Security and Cooperation in Europe (OSCE). In 1993 peacekeeping was incorporated into the North Atlantic Treaty Organization (NATO) planning tasks, and in January 1994 the Partnership for Peace program was initiated. The Nordic approach to peacekeeping is therefore being reviewed in the light of the experience of the 1990s, when multifunctional missions have called for different forms of organization and preparation than that of the traditional missions, and in the light of new approaches to cooperative security in Europe.

The impact of the war in the former Yugoslavia on the evolution of peacekeeping policy has been profound, and the impact has been felt and reflected in Nordic peacekeeping policy. Each of the contributing countries has reviewed its doctrine and organization in different ways. The 1964 standby force model has been abolished in Denmark, which has a new International Brigade. In Norway the standby force model has been retained, but alongside a new Immediate Reaction Force. There is also variation in attitudes to the use of force. The Nordic countries that are NATO members, Norway and Denmark, are more prepared to enter enforcement actions linked to NATO than are the non-NATO Nordic members, Sweden and Finland. Although Sweden is prepared to offer limited symbolic contributions to peace enforcement, Finland has ruled out peace enforcement.

See also Demilitarized zone; Denmark; Finland; Intelligence support and peacekeeping operations; Norwegian peacekeeping; Swedish peacekeeping; Training for peacekeeping
References and further reading Karhilo (1996); Nordic Committee for Military United Nations Matters (NORDSAMFN) (1993)

North Atlantic Treaty Organization (NATO)

During the Cold War period the North Atlantic Treaty Organization (NATO) was not involved in organizing or supporting international peacekeeping and related operations in any way. But since 1990 interest has become increasingly focused on a possible NATO role in this area, for three reasons: First, the view has been growing among NATO supporters in the United States and Western Europe that the institution must either go out of area (that is, be prepared to operate beyond the territory of its member states) or out of business. Second, a tentative institutional relationship between NATO and the United Nations has been evolving since spring 1992, when contacts were first established by then UN Secretary-General Boutros Boutros-Ghali and his NATO counterpart, Manfred Woerner. This was the first time that channels of communication between the two institutions had been established. Third, probably the most important factor has been NATO's involvement in Bosnia, which can be divided into two phases. The first, lasting from summer 1992 to the end of 1995, saw joint NATO military assets, such as multinational headquarters staffs and infrastructure and NATO Airborne Warning and Control System (AWACS) aircraft, being deployed to Bosnia to support the international relief operations being carried out there by the United Nations Protection Force in Former Yugoslavia (UNPROFOR). The second phase commenced after the negotiation of the Dayton Peace Accords under U.S. auspices in autumn 1995. At the end of that year UNPROFOR gave way to a NATO-led multinational Implementation Force (IFOR), which was charged with overseeing and policing the implementation of the accords. IFOR included military units from most NATO nations and contributions from Russia and many of NATO's "cooperation partners" in east-central Europe. At the end of 1996 IFOR gave way to the Stabi-

lization Force (SFOR). SFOR is somewhat smaller than its predecessor but has remained deployed and commanded within a NATO framework.

The Bosnian experience may have left NATO planners needing to put into theory what their forces have been doing there in practice. Conceptual work on peacekeeping did get off to a relatively slow start at SHAPE (Supreme Headquarters Allied Powers in Europe), NATO's top military headquarters, during 1992 and 1993. In 1994 SHAPE planners came up with the concept of international "peace support operations" as a new mission for NATO. Critics have charged that the concept of "peace support operations" is flawed because, they argue, it deliberately blurs established conceptual boundaries between peacekeeping and enforcement operations. Recently, however, there have been indications of more sophisticated thinking on the part of the NATO and SHAPE planners. They accept that traditional peacekeeping norms will continue to be valid and applicable for some contingencies and that it is not likely that an overt NATO contribution to such operations will be appropriate. The planners see NATO as having a specific contribution to make to humanitarian relief operations in deteriorating security environments, similar to the situation in Bosnia between 1992 and 1995. Some NATO planners have referred to such operations as "multifunctional peacekeeping." Although there has undoubtedly been a self-serving element in NATO's interest in contributing to international peace operations since 1992, the planners are right to point out that NATO can offer unique integrated planning, command, and other resources, plus military units from nations well used to working and training together. Such assets are not available to any other international institution, including the United Nations, at present. In view of this, it seems unlikely that NATO's involvement in international peace operations will remain limited to Bosnia over the longer term.

See also Air support; Bosnia and Herzegovina; Cold War; Cyprus; Denmark; European Union; Finland; Germany; Intelligence support and peacekeeping operations; Naval peacekeeping; No-fly zones; Nordic countries; Norwegian peacekeeping; OSCE; Partnership for Peace; Regional organizations and peacekeeping; Safe areas; UNPROFOR I–III

References and further reading British American Security Information Council (1994); Leurdijk (1994); Smith (1995)

Norwegian peacekeeping

Like the other Nordic countries, Norway has for a long time linked its own security policy with its support for and participation in UN peacekeeping. In a Norwegian government white paper of 1994, Norway's extensive participation in peacekeeping was seen to be a means of strengthening Norwegian security. Norway has two levels of capability for using its forces abroad: its UN Standby Force and the Immediate Reaction Force (IRF) units, set up in 1993 specifically for service within the North Atlantic Treaty Organization (NATO) IRF. In 1993 the Norwegian parliament agreed to expand its existing standby force from 1,330 to 2,000. The reorganized standby force comprised units from the army, the navy, and the air force. The standby force is made up of an infantry battalion; an engineer company; military police, transport, and logistics units; a maintenance and medical company; naval vessels; and an air transport unit. Norway's activities in peacekeeping in the 1990s have mostly been with the United Nations Interim Force in Lebanon (UNIFIL) and with the United Nations Protection Force in Former Yugoslavia (UNPROFOR). In 1994 the Norwegian government established guidelines governing the participation of Norwegian armed forces in international operations. Within these guidelines, the UN Standby Force was to be used in traditional peacekeeping operations that did not require large and heavily armed deployments. For enforcement operations or in crisis situations, Norwegian participation with combat troops would be limited to the IRF battalion operating within NATO. An interesting facet of Norwegian policy is its development of a capacity for nonmilitary forms of peacekeeping and peacemaking in order to respond to the humanitarian needs of threatened communities. In the early 1990s the Norwegian government supported the establishment of the Norwegian Emergency Preparedness Systems (NOREPS), a network of nongovernmental organizations (NGOs). From this is provided a standby arrangement (NORSTAFF) whereby specialists in various fields such as health care, mine detection, and construction can be deployed within 72 hours. NORSTAFF deployed a field hospital within the United Nations Assistance Mission in Rwanda (UNAMIR) in 1995, the first time such a civilian structure has been deployed within a peacekeeping mission. Since the 1980s the Norwegian Resource Bank for Democracy and Human Rights (NORDEM) has, at the request of UN agencies or of parties to conflict, sent teams of relief workers, human rights monitors, and mediators to areas of conflict throughout the world.

See also Lie, Trygve; Nordic Countries; North Atlantic Treaty Organization

References and further reading Karhilo (1996); Nordic Committee for Military United Nations Matters (NORDSAMFN) (1993)

Observer groups
See UNTSO

ONUC (United Nations Operation in the Congo), 1960–1964
See Congo

ONUCA (United Nations Observer Group in Central America), 1989–1992

Conflict Profile

The 1970s and 1980s witnessed a proliferation of armed opposition movements throughout Central America, encouraged internally by economic and political disparity and fueled externally by the competing interests of the two superpowers. Oligarchic control of economic and political resources prevailed in those countries, primarily as a legacy of the colonial era. Although independent since the nineteenth century, Central American regimes often resorted to repressive political policies, and postwar insurgency movements increasingly pursued ideals supporting the redistribution of wealth and political power. Successful economic growth during the 1960s enabled many Central American governments to counter domestic instability; however, this process was reversed in the 1970s.

Throughout the 1970s in Nicaragua, the left-wing Sandinista opposition movement—the Sandinista Front for National Liberation (FSLN)—received burgeoning domestic and international support, despite U.S. patronage of the incumbent Somoza regime. The Somoza dynasty had been in power since 1936, extracting large proportions of Nicaragua's revenue for personal gain. The Somoza family relied on its U.S. links, the enduring oligarchic regime, and control of the Nicaraguan National Guard to maintain control. However, as a Sandinista victory became increasingly imminent, U.S. President Jimmy Carter's administration withdrew its support for Somoza, facilitating the accession to power of the Sandinistas on 19 July 1979.

The Sandinista regime quickly began to develop close ties with Cuba and the USSR. It also moved progressively toward single-party rule, prompting unease in Washington. U.S. hostility to the Sandinistas was increased by Sandinista support of the communist Frente Farabundo Martí para la Liberación Nacional (FMLN) opposition forces in El Salvador. The arrival of Ronald Reagan's administration in 1981 consolidated U.S. opposition to the Sandinistas, and in the absence of a credible political alternative to the Sandinistas in Nicaragua, Washington unilaterally attempted to develop an opposition force almost from scratch, the Contras. The Contras were largely based in neighboring Honduras and received the vast majority of their financial and military backing from the United States. With such backing the Contras were soon able to engage in overt hostilities against the Sandinista regime. The ensuing civil war affected disproportionate numbers of the Nicaraguan population, both directly and indirectly: It created widespread casualties and displacement and had devastating consequences for the domestic economy.

The war incorporated national, regional, and international dynamics, which ultimately added urgency to the search for a negotiated settlement. On the national level the Sandinista regime was eager to reverse the economic decline that was resulting from the war. Meanwhile, partly as a consequence of the economic troubles, domestic political opinion was progressively turning away from the government. Furthermore, during the latter 1980s Soviet patronage of the Sandinista regime was dwindling as part of the atmosphere of détente with the West being promoted by President Mikhail Gorbachev. On the regional level, neighboring countries were directly affected by the conflict. For instance, large numbers of Contra fighters resided in Honduras, using it as a base for their political activities, and El Salvador and Guatemala were themselves the victims of internal unrest. Sandinista support of the El Salvadoran opposition in particular helped to regionalize and, especially given the attitude of Washington, which did not wish to see the communist FMLN come to power, to internationalize the conflict. Meanwhile, none of the Central American countries desired military intervention by the United States, which in the existing Cold War atmosphere was intent on opposing communist ideologies anywhere in a region so close to its borders. U.S. interest in Nicaragua, and Central America in general, was further influenced by the strategic importance of the Panama Canal.

Therefore, in 1984 the governments of Colombia, Mexico, Panama, and Venezuela—known collectively as the Contadora Group—launched a peace initiative and were subsequently supported by the presidents of the five Central American states: Costa Rica, El Salvador, Guatemala, Honduras, and Nicaragua. U.S. objections prevented progress on the initial proposal forwarded by these nations. However, the initiative was revised, and Argentina, Brazil, Peru, and Uruguay, who came to be known as the Contadora Support Group, also pledged to uphold the peace process. In February 1986 the foreign ministers of the five Central American states met in Esquipulas in Guatemala and composed a new peace deal: Esquipulas I. However, subsequent objections to the agreement by El Salvador, Honduras, and Costa Rica meant that this deal, too, was ultimately rejected.

In 1987 the president of Costa Rica, Oscar Arias, devised another peace plan, which on 7 August of that year all five Central American presidents agreed to. Arias's plan, known as Esquipulas II, was based on the previous deals, but it incorporated provisions for national reconciliation, including amnesty for political prisoners; negotiated cessation of hostilities, including procedures to secure cease-fires; democratization,

including free and fair elections; cessation of assistance to opposition forces; prevention of opposition movements' use of neighboring territory to develop their military and political capabilities; demilitarization; support for refugees and displaced people; international verification through an International Commission for Verification and Follow-Up (CIVS); and an authorized timetable of events. CIVS comprised the secretaries-general of the UN and the Organization of American States (OAS), the ministers for foreign affairs of the Central American states, and representatives of the Contadora Group and the Contadora Support Group. However, Arias still failed to deter the Reagan administration from supporting the Contras. Reagan remained convinced that this strategy could induce concessions from the Sandinista government.

Deployment of ONUCA

The situation in Nicaragua had been on the agenda of the UN General Assembly since 1983, and on 7 October 1987 the Assembly expressed its support of Esquipulas II in Resolution 42/1. However, regional quarreling again prevented the conclusion of a verification plan. In February 1989 the presidents of the five Central American states met again in El Salvador. Consequently, Nicaragua agreed to bring forward planned national elections from November to February 1990, to allow international observation of those elections, and to initiate provisions for the inclusion of opposition parties in the election process. The Executive Commission of Central American Foreign Ministers, which had replaced CIVS, was entrusted with devising a verification mechanism. Following consultations with the UN Secretariat in New York in March, the commission entreated the secretary-general to prepare an observer mission for Nicaragua. In July 1989, in response to Nicaragua's request that the United Nations observe prospective elections, the secretary-general dispatched the United Nations Observation Mission for the Verification of Elections in Nicaragua (ONUVEN) to monitor the revision of legislation concerning electoral procedure. ONUVEN was a purely civilian mission and therefore cannot independently be considered a peacekeeping force. However, it did represent an invaluable element of the United Nations Observer Group in Central America (ONUCA).

The establishment of the ONUCA peacekeeping operation itself required that the Nicaraguan government agree to postpone legal action against Honduras. Nicaragua had accused Honduras, at the International Court of Justice (ICJ), of harboring Contra fighters. On 7 August in Honduras, the Tela Accord was agreed upon between the Sandinista government and opposition groups. It deferred legal action in return for pledges of demobilization, repatriation, or relocation of Contras living in Honduras, to be accomplished by the end of the year. Although the Contras themselves were not party to the deal, which was also opposed by Washington, a new joint OAS-UN International Commission for Support and Verification (CIAV) was established to observe this process. Following this, on 11 October 1989, UN Secretary-General Pérez de Cuéllar recommended the establishment of ONUCA to the Security Council.

Deployment encountered further obstacles, however. Contra fighters attempted to disrupt the registration of voters for the forthcoming elections, and the related instability convinced the Nicaraguan government to suspend cease-fire arrangements. Consequently, the demilitarization of the Contras had not even begun by the time the deadline for completion of the process had passed. At the same time, a Nicaraguan plane was found to be carrying surface-to-air missiles bound for the FMLN in El Salvador, and as a result the El Salvadoran government broke off diplomatic ties with Nicaragua. The Central American presidents then, on 12 December, released the San Isidro Declaration, which included a further agreement by the Sandinista regime for a 6 to 12-month postponement of their case before the ICJ, as well as an agreement to enable demobilized Contras to vote in the forthcoming elections. These concessions proved sufficient to revive the peace process and finally allow the establishment of ONUCA. The eventual deployment of the operation was also made easier by a change in attitude at the White House. The accession of President George Bush's administration and the increasingly cooperative stance of the Soviet Union led to a change in Washington's stance on the Nicaraguan affair. The United States became less intent on securing the collapse of the Sandinista regime at all costs and consequently withdrew military support for the Contras. Elections were eventually successfully held in February 1990. The Unión Nacional Opositora (UNO) coalition, led by Violeta Barrios de Chamorro, defeated the Sandinistas, although the Sandinistas remained the strongest single party.

The ONUCA mandate was regularly revised in response to changing circumstances on the ground. Initially, as agreement with the Contras over demobilization had yet to be reached, it had been restricted to monitoring the provisions of Esquipulas II, namely, ceasing aid to irregular armed forces and preventing the use of neighboring territory for purposes of aggression, including prohibiting media transmissions in support of irregular military operations in any of the Central American states. However, demobilization remained a problem. Contras still stationed in Honduras were reluctant to disarm outside Nicaragua, while the government did not wish to allow large numbers of armed fighters into the country.

Nevertheless, on 19 April 1990 in Managua, following the San Isidro Declaration and the completion of the Nicaraguan elections, an agreement was finally reached with the Nicaraguan government over provisions for the demobilization of the Contras. The Managua Agreements called for a formal, ONUCA-monitored ccase-fire; the demobilization of Contras in Honduras at their existing camps, followed by their immediate repatriation; the establishment of five "security zones," each measuring 500–600 square kilometers, for the demobilization of Contras within Nicaragua; the withdrawal of government forces to positions no closer than 20 kilometers to these zones (these larger areas were known as "demilitarized zones)"; the provision of humanitarian aid to former Contras in the security zones; and an agreed timetable for demobilization, to be completed by 10 June. ONUCA would monitor the withdrawals, guarantee security in the security zones, and take responsibility for receiving and disposing of weapons and other matériel from the demobilized forces; the CIAV would be responsible for aid and resettlement.

To facilitate implementation of these additional tasks, on 27 March 1990 the Security Council adopted Security Council Resolution (SCR) 650, which included provisions for the addition of armed personnel to ONUCA. It was the first time that a UN operation had included provisions for demilitarization as part of its mandate. The demobilization process got off to a slow start. Although the Sandinista regime had lost the election, it still controlled the Nicaraguan Army. Contra leaders, known as *commandantes,* initially suspended the demobilization process, complaining that minimum conditions for demobilization had not yet been met and accusing the Sandinistas of violating the cease-fire agreement. However, ONUCA investigations revealed no substance to these allegations.

On 30 May President Chamorro, the leaders of the Nicaraguan resistance, and the archbishop of Managua agreed upon terms for the Managua Protocol, whereby the Nicaraguan government pledged to establish "development areas" in which demobilized fighters would be resettled. In return, the resistance reaffirmed its pledge to complete the demobilization process by 10 June. From this point on, the demobilization process, in general, proceeded smoothly. However, a three-week extension, to the end of June, of ONUCA's mandate to oversee the demobilization was required, and on 29 June, the secretary-general informed the Security Council that demobilization had been completed at 1900 hours the previous day. The process had witnessed 19,614 fighters demobilized in Nicaragua, and a further 2,759 in Honduras. Some 15,144 small arms had been handed over to ONUCA, as well as heavy machine guns, grenade launchers, and grenades, mortars, land mines, and various missiles.

The completion of the demobilization process meant that ONUCA could return to its original mandate of monitoring the provisions of the Esquipulas II agreement. Consequently, a large part of ONUCA's military component withdrew in line with the reduced mandate. The overall size of the operation was gradually reduced as the various provisions of Esquipulas II were progressively met. Many UN personnel serving with ONUCA were transferred directly to the United Nations

Observer Mission in El Salvador (ONUSAL), where security conditions were rapidly deteriorating. The ONUCA mandate was finally terminated on 17 January 1992.

The ONUCA mandate had evolved in line with the changing political situation on the ground. The first phase of the ONUCA deployment, to monitor compliance with the Esquipulas II agreement, failed to detect significant violations of that agreement, much to the frustration of ONUCA force commanders. However, the presence of the UN peacekeepers undoubtedly promoted confidence among the parties involved in the peace process. Furthermore, the demobilization process, the first to be undertaken by the United Nations, played an important role in the process of democratization and reconciliation in Nicaragua. Again in the second phase, demobilization was as much a confidence-boosting measure as a physical requirement, since the United Nations could not have accounted for all Contra armaments. However, this is not to denigrate the value of the UN presence. The operation did encounter some problems. Insufficient advance planning and logistical deficiencies hampered its effectiveness; also, instability reemerged in 1991, although a large part of this was the result of criminal rather than political activity, and the Nicaraguan government did attempt to negotiate in response. The presence of the UN force, ultimately, facilitated peaceful change in Nicaragua.

ONUCA had headquarters in Tegucigalpa, Honduras, and the mission lasted from December 1989 to January 1992. The authorized strength of ONUCA was 260 military observers, an infantry battalion of approximately 800 of all ranks, and crews and support personnel for an air wing and naval unit. The operation also included international and locally recruited civilian staff. The chief military observer (CMO) of ONUCA from 21 November 1989 to 20 December 1990 was Maj. Gen. Agustín Queseda Goméz (Spain); then, after the reduction in the strength of the mission, Brig. Gen. Lewis Mackenzie (Canada) served as acting CMO from 18 December 1990 to 13 May 1991, when Brig. Gen. Victor Suanzes Pardo (Spain) assumed command and kept it until withdrawal. Initial contributions of military observers were provided by Canada, Colombia, Ireland, Spain, and Venezuela; they were subsequently joined by military observers from Brazil, Ecuador, India, and Sweden. Four patrol boats and crews were supplied by Argentina, and the Federal Republic of Germany contributed a civilian medical unit and fixed-wing aircraft, also staffed by civilians. Venezuela supplied an infantry battalion to carry out the demobilization process as part of the expansion of the ONUCA mandate. There were no UN fatalities during the deployment. ONUCA costs were considered expenses of the organization and therefore were paid through regular assessments into a special account. Overall expenditures totaled $88,573,157.

See also El Salvador; Guatemala; Nicaragua; Organization of American States
References and further reading Baranyi and North (1992); Durch (1994); Klepak (1994); United Nations (1996)

ONUMOZ (United Nations Operation in Mozambique), 1992–1994
See Mozambique

ONUSAL (United Nations Observer Mission in El Salvador), 1991–1995
See El Salvador

ONUVEH (United Nations Observer Group for the Verification of Elections in Haiti), 1990–1991
See Haiti

Organization of African Unity

Force in Chad I and Chad II, 1980–1982
The first meeting of the leaders of independent African states, which at the time numbered 32, took place in the Ethiopian capital, Addis Ababa, on 25 May 1963. At this meeting, the title "Organization of African Unity (OAU)" was formally agreed upon, and the OAU Charter was also drawn up and signed. Article 2 of the charter summarized the OAU's objectives as being to promote the unity and solidarity of African states; to coordinate and enhance cooperation between African states toward achieving a better life for African people; to uphold the sovereignty, territorial integrity, and independence of OAU member states; to eradicate colonialism from the continent; and to promote international cooperation, respecting the principles of the UN Charter and the Universal Declaration of Human Rights. Toward this end OAU member states committed themselves to coordinate policy on politics, diplomacy, economics, education, culture, health, sanitation, nutritional issues, scientific and technological advancement, and defense and security.

Mutual defense and security, therefore, formed an integral part of the OAU's objectives from its inception. However, the early experiences of OAU member states with UN peacekeeping operations were not auspicious. As a result of the United Nations Operation in the Congo (ONUC), which deployed in 1964, and especially the coincidental death of Congolese president Patrice Lumumba, African leaders widely saw the United Nations as an instrument for the pursuance of Western interests. Thus a tendency emerged among OAU members to "try OAU first" in continental disputes.

However, at the time of the OAU's establishment African heads of state were concerned that artificially and arbitrarily demarcated colonial frontiers in Africa would lead both to border disputes between emerging African independent states and to problems associated with societal groups straddling such frontiers. Thus worries over infringements of their own borders induced African leaders to place particular emphasis on the principles of state sovereignty and the inviolability of national boundaries. Specifically, article 3(2) of the OAU Charter prescribes noninterference and recognizes their territorial integrity, and this article has been used to prohibit continental peacekeeping initiatives by the OAU, since the majority of conflicts in Africa have been internal.

Furthermore, accompanying the principle of noninterference was the implicit assumption that an incumbent African government, by definition, must retain legitimate authority, irrespective of that state's domestic situation. Thus the OAU has been constitutionally bound not only to avoid intervention in the majority of conflicts on the continent but also to habitually uphold the existing status quo within states, notwithstanding the specifics of individual circumstances. For instance, although most African leaders privately approved of Tanzania's President Julius Nyerere's intervention to remove Idi Amin Dada from power in Uganda in the 1970s, Presidents Gaafar Nimeiri of Sudan and Olesegun Obasanjo of Nigeria, nevertheless, publicly criticized Nyerere at the OAU summit in July 1979.

There has been only one example of peacekeeping by the OAU, over Libya's invasion of Chad in December 1980 and the announcement by Libyan President Muammar al-Gadhafi that the two countries would merge. However, although neither the United States nor France wished to see the Soviet-backed, radical Libyan government gain influence in the area, the legacy of the problematic Congo operation discouraged UN involvement. Meanwhile, although the OAU was keen to maintain its stance of "trying the OAU first," the involvement of an external party (Libya) in the dispute meant that the OAU principle of territorial integrity prevailed over that of noninterference.

Thus, in late 1981 the OAU deployed a 3,500-strong peacekeeping force, the Inter-African Force (IAF), to attempt to restore order to Chad, comprising troops from Nigeria (1,587), Senegal (694), and Zaire (845), as well as military observers from Algeria, Kenya, Guinea-Bissau, and Zambia. However, the IAF lacked significant commitment from either the contributing OAU member states or the parties to the dispute. Thus there was no political settlement when the force was deployed, nor was one forthcoming after deployment. The IAF also lacked financial and other resources, and not all the personnel that had been promised to the mission were actually forthcoming. Furthermore, the force's mandate was vague and subject to periodic alterations. The IAF ultimately failed to achieve its objective of returning peace to Chad and was ignominiously withdrawn during 1982. The IAF's principal legacy has been that African nations have been more reluctant to contribute personnel to OAU peacekeeping operations. The OAU did deploy a small Neutral Military Observers Group in Rwanda. Its mandate expired in October 1993,

when the United Nations deployed the United Nations Assistance Mission in Rwanda (UNAMIR).

More recently, however, a continentwide trend away from absolute respect for the principle of noninterference has been emerging, and consequently the OAU has been attempting to expand its conflict management capabilities. Most recently, at the 1997 summit in Harare, the OAU broke new ground and condemned militarism, military governments, and military coups in Africa. At the summit, UN Secretary-General Kofi Annan asserted that Africa could no longer "tolerate or accept as *fait accompli* the illegal seizure of power from elected governments by military cliques. . . . if the use of force becomes the last resort, and inevitable, it may have to come to that."

Perhaps the paramount example of the OAU's appetite to undertake increased conflict management responsibilities was the establishment in 1993 of the Mechanism for Conflict Prevention, Management, and Resolution (MCPMR). The Central Organ, a committee of member states, was established alongside MCPMR to control the conflict resolution process. Like the UN Security Council, the Central Organ directs OAU security considerations. However, unlike the Security Council, the Central Organ has no permanent membership and no veto powers.

However, even with the establishment of the MCPMR the OAU has not completely overcome its interventionist problems. MCPMR still surrenders absolute authority to article 3(2) of the OAU Charter, and it may intervene in conflict internal to a state only with the concurrence of OAU member states, except in extreme cases where the existence of the state is seriously threatened. In establishing MCPMR, OAU members agreed that the emphasis should be on anticipating and preventing conflict, with responses to actual conflict situations predominantly restricted to peacemaking initiatives. It was foreseen that where interventions were ultimately required, the OAU would defer to the United Nations, as defined explicitly in the Declaration of Heads of State and Government on the Establishment, within the OAU, of a Mechanism for Conflict Prevention, Management, and Resolution, which asserted that OAU cooperation with the United Nations "goes beyond mere technical advice and includes financial support, as well as all the necessary logistical assistance."

Other factors have hampered the OAU's ability to undertake peacekeeping activities. Structural immaturity and a weak Secretariat have limited the OAU's organizational capacity. Furthermore, within the OAU Secretariat, the secretary-general has largely been restricted to being an administrator. There have been recent indications of an expansion of the secretary-general's role, since the establishment of MCPMR has theoretically granted the secretary-general extended versatility in the areas of conflict anticipation, conflict prevention, and peacemaking in general. However, the lack of OAU Charter provisions to constitutionalize political initiatives has forced the secretary-general to primarily rely on informal arrangements to play substantive political roles in the management of African crises.

See also Egypt; Liberia; Morocco; Mozambique; Regional organizations and peacekeeping; Rwanda; United Nations Aouzou Strip Observer Group
References and further reading Cilliers and Mills (1995); May and Cleaver (1997); May and Massey (1998); Organization of African Unity (1993)

Organization of American States (OAS)

The Organization of American States (OAS) was originally founded in 1890 with mainly commercial objectives. The current name and charter were adopted in 1948, and by the late 1990s the organization had 35 member states. In addition to the goals of economic development and the promotion of justice, a major objective is to work with the United Nations to ensure a peaceful resolution of disputes. In 1965 the OAS worked in the Dominican Republic on behalf of the international community to restore normality after civil unrest within the country. The multinational force—called the Inter-American Peace Force (IAPF)—was formed with personnel from six North and South American countries and was active for nearly 16 months. The force commander was answerable not to the UN secretary-general but to a committee formed by the troop-contributing countries, an arrangement that mirrored that of the UN's usual peacekeeping missions.

See also Contadora Group; Dominican Republic; El Salvador; Haiti; ONUCA; Regional organizations and peacekeeping

Organization of East Caribbean States (OECS)

The Organization of East Caribbean States (OECS) was founded in 1981 and has seven members. The members of the organization have been active in one international operation that was claimed to be "peace enforcement," although the facts are open to interpretation. In 1983, after an internal coup on the Caribbean island of Grenada, the OECS decided upon an armed invasion to try to restore normality. The complicating factor was that the actual invasion was launched by personnel from the United States—a country from outside the OECS—although the OECS and the British governor-general of Grenada had asked the United States to do so. An invasion force of over 7,000 troops, mostly of U.S. marines but including troops from a number of Caribbean nations, had overwhelmed the coup leaders and the small Grenadian army that supported them by December 1983, when the U.S.-led force withdrew.

Organization for Security and Cooperation in Europe (OSCE)

The Organization for Security and Cooperation in Europe (OSCE) was established in 1975, under the name "Conference on Security and Cooperation in Europe" (CSCE), with the signing of its charter, the Helsinki Final Act. Thirty-five heads of government and state convened to represent all European states (except Albania), the United States, and Canada. The CSCE was based on a comprehensive concept of security. It contained within its charter four dimensions that were to be the cornerstones of a European security framework that brought together countries belonging to the opposing ideological blocs of the East-West conflict.

Designed to foster security through cooperation and trust building, the four dimensions represent the comprehensive concept of security that underlies all CSCE aspects. These four elements (also known as "baskets") are (1) questions relating to security in Europe; (2) cooperation in the fields of economics, of science and technology, and of the environment; (3) cooperation in humanitarian and other fields; and (4) follow-up to the conference.

Today, after a dramatic increase in membership after the breakup of the Soviet Union, the OSCE has 53 members. All members have equal status and are represented on a basis of common rules, norms, and interests, and all decisions are made by consensus. The following states are members of the OSCE: Albania, Armenia, Austria, Azerbaijan, Belarus, Belgium, Bosnia and Herzegovina, Bulgaria, Canada, Croatia, Cyprus, Czech Republic, Denmark, Estonia, Finland, Former Yugoslav Republic of Macedonia, France, Georgia, Germany, Greece, the Holy See, Hungary, Iceland, Ireland, Italy, Kazakhstan, Kyrgyzstan, Latvia, Liechtenstein, Lithuania, Luxembourg, Malta, Moldova, Monaco, Switzerland, the Netherlands, Norway, Poland, Portugal, Romania, Russia, San Marino, Slovak Republic, Slovenia, Spain, Sweden, Tajikistan, Turkey, Turkmenistan, Ukraine, the United Kingdom, the United States, Uzbekistan, and Yugoslavia (Serbia and Montenegro) (suspended).

In its first decade of existence, the CSCE, though emphasizing the human rights component enshrined in its basket 3, was limited in its activities by the bipolar structures of the Cold War. However, although the Helsinki Final Act does not constitute a legally binding treaty, it nevertheless constituted an international arrangement that was the closest Europe was to come to a peace treaty. Furthermore, important steps were initiated through the Helsinki Process, which allowed dissident voices in the Communist bloc countries to speak out against repressive regimes.

The CSCE's constant emphasis on dialogue rather than confrontation provided the European security community with a forum for creative debates within which new perspectives could be discussed. It thus partook in the creation of an optimistic political atmosphere that was more receptive to the reform policies instigated by Mikhail Gorbachev in the mid- to late 1980s than at any time before. Especially conducive to this process was the enlargement of the CSCE's Confidence and Security-Building Measures (CSBM),

with which military security could be strengthened through an open exchange of information on military maneuvers. During this period of renewed détente, three main arms control treaties were signed under the auspices of the CSCE: the Intermediate-Range Nuclear Forces (INF) Treaty in December 1987, the Conventional Armed Forces (CFE) Treaty in November 1990, and the Strategic Arms Reduction Talks (START) in July 1991.

Throughout its early history the CSCE functioned as a multilateral conference where the facilitation of dialogue and negotiations between East and West was paramount. However, with the demise of the Warsaw Pact a new period of institutionalization was inaugurated, reflecting the new challenges Europe faced in the post-Communist era. Since the beginning of the OSCE's restructuring process, member states set priorities and determine the organization's orientation at the highest political level at the Summits of Heads of State or Government.

At a meeting in Paris in 1990 the CSCE received new structures and institutions, including the establishment of a Secretariat to schedule biannual meetings of heads of state and to coordinate regular meetings of a Council of Foreign Ministers. The charter also included provisions for creating a Conflict Prevention Center (CPC) in Vienna and for establishing an Office for Free Elections (OFE) in Warsaw. (At the 1992 Helsinki Follow-Up Meeting [FUM] the OFE was turned into the Office for Democratic Institutions and Human Rights [ODIHR].) Three main political consultative bodies were also established: the Council of Ministers, consisting of foreign ministers from the participating states; a Committee of Senior Officials to assist the council and manage day-to-day business; and regular Summit Meetings of Heads of State or Government.

Based on the realization that future conflicts were likely to take place *within* rather than *between* states, the CSCE developed a range of mechanisms that would allow it to intervene in participating states' affairs. It is considered particularly important to undertake intervention before tensions escalate into violent and often protracted conflict. The main goal established at the Helsinki II Summit in 1992 was thus to act quickly in regard to tensions and to facilitate their transformation. In this respect, the creation of the post for a High Commission on National Minorities (HCNM) was particularly important to the restructuring process. Furthermore, the Helsinki II Document called for the use of peacekeeping operations under the aegis of the CSCE, for which the CSCE could contract out forces from other international organizations, such as the North Atlantic Treaty Organization (NATO), the Western European Union (WEU), or the Commonwealth of Independent States (CIS).

The institutionalization process gained further momentum in the two years between the 1992 Helsinki Summit and the 1994 Budapest Summit. With the inauguration of Max van der Stoel as the first high commissioner on national minorities a new phase of further institutionalization for the management and ultimately the prevention of intrastate conflicts started. Since its inception, the HCNM has investigated a number of cases of ethnic tension and examined the social, economic, and humanitarian problems of the Romany population in some CSCE participating states. In December 1992 the CSCE Council established the new post of secretary-general. The first secretary-general, who served from 1993 to 1996, was Wilhelm Höynck; the secretary-general in 1998 was Giancarlo Aragona. In 1993 the CSCE Council opened a strengthened Secretariat in Vienna with an office in Prague. Throughout 1993 the CSCE expanded its operational profile by dispatching several conflict-prevention and crisis-management missions in areas of potential and actual conflict. Since February 1993 the CSCE has also been coordinating the enforcement of sanctions imposed on Serbia-Montenegro with Sanctions Assistance Missions. In March the CSCE Economic Forum met for the first time, deciding to work toward a favorable business climate and acknowledging the importance of human factors in the economic transition process of central and eastern European countries. The 1992 provisions for Human Dimension Seminars were successfully implemented, and nine seminars took place between 1992 and 1994.

The 1994 Budapest Document not only formalized the transformation of the conference into a regional security organization by changing its name to the OSCE, but it also emphasized the need to strengthen the restructuring process. Within this overall aim, the Budapest Document established the OSCE as the primary instrument for early warning, conflict management, and crisis management in the OSCE region, and it also stressed the need for closer cooperation with existing European institutions. Exceptional cases that could not be dealt with at the regional level should be referred to the United Nations. Furthermore, the Budapest Document authorized the OSCE to send a peacekeeping mission to Nagorno-Karabakh and requested the strengthening of the chairman-in-office, as well as of the secretary-general, the Secretariat, the HCNM, and the ODIHR. It adopted a Code of Conduct on Politico-Military Aspects of Security setting forth principles guiding the role of armed forces in democratic societies and called for a discussion within the OSCE on a model of common and comprehensive security based on CSCE principles and commitments.

Since the Budapest Summit, the OSCE has begun work on a security model for the twenty-first century and has intensified its dialogue and cooperation not only with other international institutions but also with nongovernmental organizations (NGOs). The most recent event, which can be seen as confirming the OSCE's importance as an international organization, is the role the OSCE is to play as part of the General Framework Agreement for Peace in Bosnia and Herzegovina. At the fifth meeting of the OSCE's Council of Ministers (7–8 December 1995), it was decided that the OSCE was to implement the civil side of the Dayton Accords. This includes supervising elections, monitoring human rights, and assisting the parties in their negotiations on arms control and confidence and security building.

The Lisbon document was divided into several parts: the Lisbon Summit Declaration, the Lisbon Declaration on a Common and Comprehensive Security Model for Europe for the Twenty-first Century, a Framework for Arms Control, and a text entitled "Development of the Agenda of the Forum for Security Cooperation." Much less substantial than the preceding summit documents, the main results of the Lisbon Summit centered around issues of arms control. Participants agreed to start revisions on the CFE Treaty, and a new arms control agenda was set, resulting in the separate annex, the A Framework for Arms Control, which aims at mutually reinforcing arms control obligations and commitments. Despite its solemn wording, the Lisbon Summit Declaration merely repeats earlier commitments to general OSCE principles and does not change the institutional character of the OSCE. However, some implicit changes can be found in both the role of the secretary-general, whose political responsibility has been greatly enhanced, and the role of the chairman-in-office, whose importance in OSCE decision making has grown considerably. Despite these slow advances, the major problem encountered at the Lisbon Summit was the dispute concerning Nagorno-Karabakh. Because the delegates were unable to reach consensus on the wording of the text, Armenia effectively blocked the text's incorporation into the declaration. As a way out of this impasse, the text was adopted as a Statement of the OSCE Chairman-in-Office, which included the regret that Armenia could not accept it. Though this episode shows the problems surrounding consensus decision making in a vast organization such as the OSCE, it also indicates a strengthening of the consensus-minus-one principle (a principle introduced in order to overcome the OSCE's inability to vote on the conflict in Yugoslavia), which allows the organization to make decisions even without the consent of the concerned party.

As a consequence of growing demands on the United Nations to carry out peacekeeping operations (PKOs) since the end of the Cold War, regional organizations are under more pressure taking on regional problems. This changed attitude was partly reflected in the decision of OSCE heads of state and government to include in their 1992 Helsinki Summit Document provisions for PKOs to be sent out under the auspices of the OSCE.

In the preparation phase of the Helsinki II Follow-Up Meeting, negotiations were held about the incorporation of PKOs under the aegis of the OSCE. These were finalized in the Helsinki II Document, which states that "peacekeeping constitutes an important operational element of the overall capability of the CSCE for conflict prevention and crisis management intended to comple-

ment the political process of dispute resolution" (chapter 3, page 19, section 17). OSCE PKOs can only be carried out with the consent of the parties concerned and will not entail enforcement action; instead, they will focus on the supervision and maintenance of cease-fires, the monitoring of troop withdrawals, the maintenance of law and order, the provision of humanitarian and medical aid, and the assistance of refugees. Since the CSCE-OSCE does not have a military contingent of its own, it has made provisions for contracting out PKOs to other, more experienced, international institutions, such as the United Nations, NATO, the WEU, or even the CIS.

The provisions made at the Helsinki FUM found some application in 1994 when, after the arrangement of a cease-fire on 12 May 1994, the CSCE began considering the deployment of a multinational peacekeeping mission for the Nagorno-Karabakh conflict. For this peacekeeping mission, the Budapest Review Conference included in its decisions the establishment of a "high level planning group in Vienna to make recommendations on, inter alia, the size and characteristics of the force, command and control, logistics, allocation of units and resources, rules of engagement and arrangements with contributing States" (chapter 2, page 5, section 4). Because of lack of consent by the conflicting parties, an OSCE peacekeeping operation has not yet taken place. However, much of the OSCE's fieldwork consists of monitoring and observation of areas of potential and actual tension. In its long-term involvement in conflict prevention and crisis management, the OSCE currently deploys missions in several OSCE member states, including Bosnia and Herzegovina, Croatia, Estonia, Georgia, Latvia, the former Yugoslav Republic of Macedonia, Moldova, Tajikistan, and Ukraine. It offers an Assistance Group to Chechnya; employs Missions of Long Duration to Kosovo, Sandjak, and Vojvodina; and has a personal representative of the OSCE chairman-in-office on the OSCE Minsk Conference on Nagorno-Karabakh.

See also Albania; Bosnia and Herzegovina; Conflict prevention; European Community Monitoring Mission; Partnership for Peace; Regional organizations and peacekeeping; United Nations Protection Force in Former Yugoslavia

References and further reading Further information can be obtained from the OSCE's homepage on http://www.osceprag.cz/, where major CSCE/OSCE documents can be downloaded and where a detailed contents page offers gates to general information, OSCE News, and an elaborate breakdown of OSCE institutions and mechanisms

Ossetia
See Commonwealth of Independent States

Owen, David, Lord (1938–)

David Owen was educated at Sidney Sussex College, University of Cambridge, and St. Thomas's Hospital London (where he received his master's degree). He served in the medical profession (as a research fellow of the Royal Medical Unit, 1966–1968) before entering politics. A Labour Party MP for Plymouth Sutton (1966–1974), he served as parliamentary private secretary to the minister of defense (1966–1968) before appointment in the senior post as parliamentary undersecretary of state for defense (Royal Navy) (1968–1970). In 1976 he was appointed minister of state at the Foreign Office, and after one year was promoted to secretary of state for Foreign and Commonwealth affairs (1977–1979). Now a member of the House of Lords, he was a member of the Independent Commission on International Humanitarian Issues (1983–1988). His diplomatic and political skills were harnessed for the service of the European Union (August 1992–June 1995), as European Union cochairman of the International Conference on the Former Yugoslavia. He was also a member of the Carnegie Commission on Preventing Deadly Conflict and contributed to its Final Report (December 1997).

See also UNPROFOR I–III
References and further reading Owen (1995)

"Painting a country blue"

This phrase was first used by Douglas Hurd, the then UK foreign secretary (1989–1995). It was intended to illustrate the comprehensive support that a UN mission could provide for a country where all normal institutions and structures had broken down (as in Somalia) or where the United Nations was involved in the support of postconflict reconstruction (as in Namibia and Cambodia). Such support could encompass the provision of peace and security, humanitarian assistance, disarmament and demobilization of combatants, and support for restoring political and social institutions.

Pakistan

Pakistan became a member of the United Nations in September 1947 and has contributed to international peacekeeping operations since 1960. Pakistan exemplifies the general trend toward increasing participation by less developed countries, a trend most evident between 1992 and 1994, and in 1997 Pakistan had the largest number of serving peacekeepers. Pakistan contributed logistical support and military observers to a number of early missions, including the United Nations Operation in the Congo (ONUC) in 1960, the United Nations Yemen Observer Mission (UNYOM) in 1964, and the United Nations Security Force in West New Guinea (UNSF) in 1962. Its participation increased markedly in the 1990s with battalion levels of forces sent to Cambodia, Bosnia, Croatia, Somalia, and Haiti. Its role in the United Nations Operation in Somalia (UNOSOM) between 1992 and 1995 can be used to illustrate Pakistan's contribution to peacekeeping and also to illustrate the complexities that were associated with this operation. In September 1992, when Pakistani troops arrived in Mogadishu, they were the first troops to respond to the UN's request. In addition to the tasks of securing the sea-lanes and airports, they had the further objective of recovering unauthorized arms and providing medical aid. The medical aid comprised 26 doctors and 6 nurses. When UNOSOM I was expanded at the time of the intervention of the Unified Task Force (UNITAF) after December 1992, Pakistan became

a major contributor to the mission. Pakistan's role changed again when the UNITAF operation was handed over to UNOSOM II in May 1993 and the operation in Somalia entered into a four-month period of "humanitarian war" between UNOSOM II and the Somali factional leader General Aidid. UNOSOM II set out to disarm the militias. On 5 June 1993 Pakistani troops were ambushed in southern Mogadishu as some of them were inspecting an arms depot belonging to General Aidid and others were distributing food as part of the humanitarian relief program. In the ambush 25 soldiers were killed and 54 injured. The event triggered a set of responses that led to the closure of the mission. UN Secretary-General Boutros Boutros-Ghali condemned the "treacherous attack on those who were on a mission of peace, reconciliation and reconstruction." On 12 June UNOSOM II launched an attack on Aidid's forces, which resulted in the death of 100 Somalians, but the hunt for Aidid failed. On 3 October 18 U.S. soldiers were killed and a large number wounded. The United States announced that its troops would be withdrawn by March 1994. Belgium, France, and Sweden pulled their troops out by the end of 1993, and Germany, Italy, Norway, and Turkey pulled out in March 1994. On 5 March 1995 the Pakistani peacekeeping troops left, the last of the troops to leave Somalia. Pakistan is likely to continue to contribute to peacekeeping at a high level in the near future. One explanation for this may be that Pakistan is positioning itself for a seat on the Security Council and sees participation in peacekeeping as a means of demonstrating commitment.

See also Troop-contributing countries; United Nations Good Offices Mission in Afghanistan and Pakistan; United Nations India-Pakistan Observer Mission; United Nations Military Observer Group in India and Pakistan

Papua New Guinea

South Pacific Peacekeeping Force

Papua New Guinea's defense forces have confronted secessionist opposition forces in the border province of Bougainville. Since 1988 the Bougainville Interim Government (BIG) and its military arm the Bougainville Revolutionary Army (BRA) have fought for the independence of the 10,660-square-kilometer (4,100-square-mile) island, home to 160,000 people. They also demanded $11.3 billion in compensation for the "environment, social and land destruction and chemical pollution" caused by the Panguna copper mine in the center of the island. An Agreement on Peace, Security, and Development on Bougainville was signed at Lincoln University, New Zealand, on 23 January 1998 (the Lincoln Agreement) by the government of Papua New Guinea, the Bougainville transitional government, the Bougainville Resistance Force, the BIG, the BRA, and the Bougainville leaders. Under the agreement an existing truce was extended and a further and permanent cease-fire was to take effect on 30 April 1998. Under the agreement parties agreed to achieve and maintain peace; to renounce the use of armed force and violence; to resolve any differences by consultation, both at the time and in the future; and to confirm their respect for human rights and the rule of law. A peace-monitoring group (known as the South Pacific Peacekeeping Force) composed of civilian and military personnel from Australia, Fiji, New Zealand, and Vanuatu, was also mandated to monitor the implementation of the agreement. The force of up to 260 soldiers was to be rotated, leaving 150 truce monitors on the island at any one time.

See also Australia; New Zealand

References and further reading
International Peacekeeping (1994–)

Parsons, Anthony (1922–1996)

Anthony Parsons is said to have had an unmatched understanding of the Arab world. His expertise in this area developed from his time spent as a regular army officer in Syria, Palestine, and Baghdad; his studies in Arabic and Persian at Oxford; and his time spent as diplomat in several Middle Eastern capitals. His other area of expertise, at the United Nations, was established when he became a permanent representative to the British mission during the Falklands War. Other posts include his appointments as ambassador to Washington and as a special adviser to British Prime Minister Margaret Thatcher. He became a well-respected figure in the field of international relations, serving as research fellow for the University of Exeter and as an external validator for the international relations degree at the University of Plymouth. Parsons was optimistic about the evolution of international organizations, in particular the United Nations, which he felt held a crucial role as a force against colonialism and racism. Like many others, he felt this to be increasingly so with the end of the Cold War, but he realized that new problems arose for international relations with the demise of the Soviet Union. In his work *From Cold War to Hot Peace* (1995), Parsons outlined several threats to international cooperation. Despite these new problems, Parsons welcomed the growing legitimacy of the United Nations particularly as a forum for developing multilateral approaches to conflict resolution, which he felt would be further enhanced by the increasing feasibility and demand for reform. He criticized the failure to provide proper financing for the United Nations and was concerned about the movement from peacekeeping to peace enforcement. He was also unconvinced about the value of subcontracting peacekeeping to regional organizations.

See also Peace enforcement
References and further reading Parsons (1995)

Partnership for Peace

This initiative is an attempt by the nations represented in the North Atlantic Cooperation Council (NACC) to establish a new kind of international defense structure that will help maintain peace and stability across Europe. The underpinning theory is that cooperation not only maximizes resources but reduces tensions and some possible causes of conflicts. With this emphasis in mind the Partnership for Peace was set up under the aegis of the North Atlantic Treaty Organization (NATO). The spur to action was the breakup of the old Soviet bloc and the resulting push for independence by some of the nations or regional ethnic groupings that had been contained within it. The first stage was an agreement by 38 countries (16 NATO members plus 22 Cooperation Council members) to support the ideals of joint peacekeeping and to contribute (on a case-by-case basis) to peacekeeping missions under the control of the United Nations or the Organization for Security and Cooperation in Europe (OSCE). At the same time there was an outline agreement to pool experience and skills with each other and with the countries of the Conference on Security and Cooperation in Europe (CSCE). The framework for peace enhancement was strengthened in 1994 when the heads of government of the NATO states published their Partnership for Peace plan and the parallel committees of the NACC and NATO were brought together in a more structured way. One outcome was a series of joint simulated peacekeeping exercises in different parts of the continent, as well as some firmer proposals on a collective approach to education, training, appraisal, and logistics for peacekeeping missions in general.

Partnership for Peace initiatives take the form of a series of agreements between NATO and each partner individually. By 1998 27 countries had signed a formal agreement. Included in this number were former Warsaw Pact countries and some neutral or nonaligned states. When an agreement has been signed, an Individual Partnership Program becomes part of its structure. This sets out objectives for each side and the detailed support that will be provided toward their attainment. The Implementation Force (IFOR) (the UN-mandated NATO mission that operated to oversee the Bosnian peace agreement) included within its ranks forces from 12 partnership countries working alongside their NATO counterparts.

See also Finland; Nordic countries; North Atlantic Treaty Organization

Peace building from below

The failure to realize and fulfill the optimistic expectations for peacekeeping, peacemaking, and peace building that UN Secretary-General Boutros Boutros-Ghali proclaimed (in his *Agenda for Peace* in 1992) to be achievable objectives of a post–Cold War UN system has provoked a revision of thinking about ways of managing and resolving conflict and about the roles of peacekeeping forces. Out of this revision of thinking has come a new set of phrases to describe the complex dynamics and processes of conflict resolution, including the idea that effective and sustainable peacemaking processes must be based not merely on manipulating peace agreements made by elites but, more importantly, on empowering the communities torn apart by war to build peace from below. The revision of thinking is relevant to contemporary peacekeeping in three ways: First, it recognizes that embedded cultures and economies of violence provide more formidable barriers to constructive intervention than originally assumed by the earlier research of conflict theory. In these conflicts "simple," one-dimensional interventions, whether by traditional mediators aiming at formal peace agreements or by peacekeepers placed to supervise cease-fires or oversee elections, are unlikely to produce comprehensive or lasting resolution. Second, it emphasizes the significance of postconflict peace building and the idea that formal agreements need to be underpinned by understandings, structures, and long-term development frameworks that will erode cultures of violence and sustain peace processes on the ground. Third, it forwards the related idea that local actors, the nongovernmental sector, and the links with local knowledge and wisdom are significant. This alliance is to enhance sustainable citizen-based peace-building initiatives and to open up participatory public political spaces in order to allow institutions of civil society to flourish. A challenge for the future development of peacekeeping policy is to coordinate the security objectives of the mission with the agendas of humanitarian, human rights, and development agencies working for long-term recovery. John Paul Lederach has stressed the importance of this approach, which he called "indigenous empowerment."

It has been recognized that there is an important role for the United Nations in this process of empowerment and a need to connect the official mandates of the UN agencies, including peacekeeping, and the unofficial roles of the nongovernmental organizations (NGOs) in conflict zones. Lederach's comprehensive approach entails building what he refers to as an infrastructure for peace "that legitimates and integrates multiple levels of the population affected, in terms of both input in the peace process and its implementation." He described the affected population as a triangle, with the key military and political leaders at the apex, at level one. In the middle, at level two, are the national leaders who have significance as leaders in sectors such as health and education and within the military hierarchies. Finally, at the grassroots level, level three, are the vast majority of the affected population: the common people; displaced and refugee populations; local leaders, elders, and church groups; and locally based NGOs. The armed combatants are also represented at this level, as guerrillas and soldiers in militias. Most peacemaking at the level of international diplomacy operates at level one of this triangle, but for conflict resolution to be successful and sustainable peacemaking strategies must be coordinated across all three levels. In this new thinking peace building from below is of decisive importance, for it is the means by which, according to Lederach, a peace constituency can be built within the setting of the conflict itself. Once again this is a departure from conventional practice, in which peacemaking resources from outside the conflict (diplomats, third-party intervenors, peacekeeping forces) are valued more highly than peacemaking assets that may exist within the community. In applying a peace building–from–below approach the way in which a conflict is viewed is transformed; whereas normally people within the conflict are seen as the

problem, with outsiders providing the solution to the conflict, in the perspective of peace building from below solutions are derived and built from local resources. This does not deny a role for outsider third parties, but it does suggest a need for a reorientation of their roles.

See also *An Agenda for Peace;* Guatemala; Nongovernmental organizations, Postconflict reconstruction; Training for peacekeeping
References and further reading Albert (1997); Fetherston (1996); Herbst (1996); Karamotos (1995); Lederach (1995); Schirch (1995); Schultz (1994); Woodhouse (1998)

Peace enforcement

From as early as the discussions in 1944 at Dumbarton Oaks that led to the formation of the United Nations, there have been a number of proposals for creating a standing UN military unit to enforce peace, and in some proposals the Military Staff Committee, set up under the UN Charter, would provide the command center for such a force. Intermittent proposals to create a permanent UN force have been made but not acted upon. Interest strengthened again in the aftermath of the Gulf War and the action of UN-authorized coalition forces against Iraq. A special summit of the Security Council was held in January 1992 that requested UN Secretary-General Boutros Boutros-Ghali to report on ways in which the Security Council could become more effective in maintaining international peace and security.

In his *Agenda for Peace* (1992), Boutros-Ghali introduced the idea of forming "peace enforcement units" that would be more heavily armed than traditional peacekeeping forces and that would be on call from member states, equipped and prepared to monitor and enforce cease-fires and even peace agreements. The Dutch minister of foreign affairs, Hans van Mierlo, argued in the General Assembly in September 1994 that if member states were unwilling to provide peacekeeping forces for particular operations, then it would be necessary to consider establishing a UN Legion, that is, a full-time professional force. He referred to such a force as a "fire brigade" that would be rapidly deployable and that would enable the United Nations to save lives in situations such as occurred in Rwanda in May 1994. At the same time, Canadian Foreign Minister Jean Quellet suggested the need to study the possibility of creating a permanent UN military force. Similarly, the Commission on Global Governance suggested a 10,000-strong United Nations Volunteer Force to be able to provide rapid intervention in the early stages of a conflict. The force would be equipped to take combat risks in the early stages of a conflict; it would not replace traditional peacekeeping forces nor the large-scale enforcement operations mandated under chapter 7 of the UN Charter; rather, it would fill a gap by providing the Security Council with the ability to back up preventive diplomacy with effective peace enforcement units on the ground. Brian Urquhart, former undersecretary-general of the United Nations, has also called for a permanent 5,000-strong UN volunteer military force to provide credible peace enforcement units. Proposals of this kind have tended not to be supported by significant member states or by the Security Council, and the reform of peacekeeping capabilities has tended toward the provision of forces on a standby basis by member states rather than permanent standing forces. Major member states have been concerned about the United Nations acquiring greater autonomy that would enable it to respond robustly to crisis situations. The main problem continues to lie in the United States, where the "Vietnam syndrome," that is, military conservatism about involvement in operations other than war, and the frequent criticism of the United Nations by politicians have prevented peacekeeping from being properly resourced.

See also *An Agenda for Peace;* Bosnia and Herzegovina; British peacekeeping; Charter of the United Nations; Korean War; No-fly zones; Safe areas; Second-generation peacekeeping; Somalia; UN Standby Arrangements System; U.S. peacekeeping

References and further reading Berdal (1993); Conetta and Knight (1995); Daniel and Hayes (1995, 1996); Findlay (1997); Goulding (1996); Johansen (1990); Pugh (1996)

Pearson, Lester B. (1897–1972)

Born in Ontario, Canada, on 23 April 1897, Lester B. Pearson graduated from the University of Toronto in 1919, and after a fellowship at the University of Toronto he taught in its History Department between 1924 and 1928. He was appointed first secretary in the Department of External Affairs between 1928 and 1935; this appointment was followed by a post in London between 1935 and 1941 as secretary in the Canadian High Commission. He joined the Canadian Legation in Washington in 1942 and was Canada's adviser at the Dumbarton Oaks meeting that led to the formation of the United Nations (1944). In 1945 he was appointed ambassador to the United States, and as such he attended the San Francisco Conference (1945) that founded the United Nations.

He was appointed deputy minister of external affairs in September 1946, becoming minister in 1948. He was leader of the Canadian Liberal Party between 1958 and 1968 and prime minister of Canada between 1963 and 1968. He also, as chairman of the UN Political and Security Committee, played a decisive role in mediating the Palestinian crisis in the late 1940s, and he was prominent in the foundation of the UN Relief and Rehabilitation Administration in 1943. He advocated the positive role to be played by smaller nations in protecting international security. During the Suez Canal crisis of 1956 he successfully guided a proposal to establish a peacekeeping force (the first United Nations Emergency Force [UNEF I]) through the United Nations, for which he was awarded the Nobel Peace Prize in 1957. As prime minister of Canada between 1963 and 1968 he was prominent in the decision to send a peacekeeping force to Cyprus (the UN Peacekeeping Force in Cyprus [UNFICYP]) and a second United Nations Emergency Force to Sinai in 1967, both with Canadian participation. He died 27 December 1972. The Canadian government named its peacekeeping center in Nova Scotia the Lester B. Pearson International Peacekeeping Training Center in his honor. Pearson wrote or contributed to a number of works, including his memoirs, *Democracy in World Politics* (1955), *Diplomacy in the Nuclear Age* (1959), *Words and Occasions* (1970), and a study of international aid for the World Bank.

See also Canada; Conflict resolution theory and peacekeeping; First-generation peacekeeping; Nobel Peace Prize; Training for peacekeeping

References and further reading Bothwell (1978); Burns (1975)

Pérez de Cuéllar, Javier (1920–)

Born in Lima, Peru, 19 January 1920, Pérez de Cuéllar served as secretary-general of the United Nations from January 1982 to December 1991. His career as a diplomat began in 1940 when he joined the Peruvian Ministry of Foreign Affairs. He then held positions as secretary at the Peruvian embassies in France, the United Kingdom, Bolivia, and Brazil, as well as counselor and minister counselor at the embassy in Brazil. On his return to Peru he was promoted to ambassador and served in Switzerland, the Soviet Union, Poland, and Venezuela. He was secretary-general (deputy minister) for foreign affairs (1966).

At the first session of the General Assembly (1946) he took part as a member of the Peruvian delegation, becoming Peru's permanent representative to the United Nations between 1971 and 1975. His duties at the United Nations included representing Peru in the Security Council between 1973 and 1974. This included the period of the Cyprus emergency of 1974 when he was president of the Security Council. His handling of the role prompted his appointment as special representative of the secretary-general in Cyprus (18 September 1974–December 1977), after which he returned to Peru's Foreign Service.

He soon returned to the United Nations in a high-profile role as UN undersecretary-general for special political affairs (27 February 1979). Concurrently, he acted as the secretary-general's personal representative to Afghanistan. He continued to act on behalf of the secretary-general on Afghanistan, but he rejoined his country's Ministry of Foreign Affairs (1981). Again, this represented a short departure from the United Nations, which ended with his appointment as secretary-general of the United Nations on January 1 1982. His expertise was recognized with his appointment by the General Assembly to serve for a second term, which ended in December 1991. In 1988 the Nobel Peace Prize was awarded to UN peacekeepers for "demanding and hazardous service in the cause of peace." In accepting the award on their behalf, Javier Pérez de Cuéllar said: "Peacekeeping operations symbolize the world community's will to peace and represent the impartial, practical expression of that will. The award of the Nobel Peace Prize to these operations illustrates the hope and strengthens the promise of this extraordinary concept."

His career included almost 45 years of service at the United Nations, from its inception throughout the Cold War and then at its helm, steering it into the early post–Cold War period. De Cuéllar declared that the principle of nonintervention (i.e., that states have a right to govern their own affairs) should not provide a justification for allowing massive and systematic violation of human rights, a statement that prepared the ground for a more assertive role for the United Nations in the 1990s. Pérez de Cuéllar's service and talents have been recognized on numerous occasions, and he has received decorations from some 25 countries. He has also contributed widely to academic journals, international conferences, and major publications. He was awarded the Olaf Palme Prize for International Understanding and Common Security by the Olaf Palme Memorial Fund (1989) and the Jawaharlal Nehru Award for International Understanding (1989).

References and further reading UN Press Release, 17 January 1990

Persian Gulf
See Gulf Wars (Iran-Iraq; Iraq-Kuwait)

Pink zones
See UNPROFOR I–III

Postconflict reconstruction

In his *Agenda for Peace* published in 1992, UN Secretary-General Boutros Boutros-Ghali defined postconflict peace building as "actions to identify and support structures which will tend to strengthen and solidify peace in order to avoid a relapse into conflict." This was at first largely taken to mean military demobilization and the political transition to participatory electoral democracy, and this remains the core of the UN's postsettlement peace-building procedure. The 1995 *Supplement to An Agenda for Peace* envisaged that postconflict peace building would initially be undertaken by multifunctional UN peacekeeping operations, then be handed over to civilian agencies under a resident coordinator, and finally be transferred entirely to local agents. Since *An Agenda for Peace* was published the concept has been progressively expanded to include a broader agenda aimed at alleviating the worst effects of war on the population and promoting a sustainable development approach that tackles the root causes of conflict-generated emergencies. There are in effect two interlinked tasks in postconflict reconstruction and peace building. The first task is to prevent a relapse into war, and the second task is to construct a self-sustaining peace. UN peacekeeping doctrine has been developed around the idea of peace-support operations, which aimed to link the task of military containment of conflict with the long-term goals of rehabilitation and the rebuilding of communities economically, politically, and socially.

The UN's continuous involvement in postsettlement peace building of this kind goes back at least as far as the 1978 Settlement Proposal in Namibia, devised by the Contact Group of Western States, in which the United Nations Transitional Assistance Group (UNTAG) was mandated under Security Council Resolution (SCR) 435 to assist a special representative appointed by the UN secretary-general "to ensure the early independence of Namibia through free and fair elections under the supervision and control of the United Nations." The transitional phase was to last a year. This formula for expediting the withdrawal of a former colonial master and its replacement by a fledgling independent state, put into practice in the interim in Southern Rhodesia/Zimbabwe, was revived ten years later in very different circumstances and immediately became the main model for the UN's new postsettlement peace-building efforts in a number of long-standing internal wars. In a sharp break with earlier international practice, rebel forces were now to be accorded equal status with governments, and both were to be regarded as proto–political parties deserving of equal access to a new UN-sanctioned, reformed political process. The ending of the Cold War drew a line under what had been an almost automatic backing of rival sides by the superpowers, opened up the possibility of concerted action through the Security Council, and ushered in the apparent global triumph of "liberal internationalism" in its twin manifestations as liberal parliamentary democracy and liberal market capitalism.

The major postsettlement UN peace-building missions between 1988 and 1998 have been in Namibia (UNTAG), Angola (the third United Nations Angola Verification Mission [UNAVEM III]), El Salvador (the United Nations Observer Mission in El Salvador [ONUSAL]), Cambodia (the United Nations Transitional Authority in Cambodia [UNTAC]), Mozambique (the United Nations Operation in Mozambique [ONUMOZ]), and Bosnia (the Implementation Force [IFOR] and the Stabilization Force [SFOR]). The individual elements in the UN's postsettlement peace-building procedure have varied in detail from case to case, but within a recognizable overall pattern. In 1992 the UN secretary-general described the main tasks as "disarming the previously warring parties and the restoration of order, the custody and possible destruction of weapons, repatriating refugees, advisory and training support for security personnel, monitoring elections, advancing efforts to protect human rights, reforming or strengthening governmental institutions and promoting formal and informal processes of political participation." Three years later, in the *Supplement to An Agenda for Peace,* the key elements of peace building were described, in similar if expanded terms, as demilitarization, the control of small arms, institutional reform, improved police and judicial systems, the monitoring of human rights, electoral reform, and social and economic development (paragraph 47), while in 1997 postconflict peace building was seen to involve "the creation or strengthening of national institutions, the monitoring of elections, the promotion of human rights, the provision of reintegration and rehabilitation programs and the creation of conditions for resumed development."

See also Internal conflict; Peace building from below; White Helmets
References and further reading Ball (1996); Ball and Halevy (1996); Kumar (1997)

Presidential decision directives and peacekeeping
See U.S. peacekeeping

Preventive deployment
See Conflict prevention; Macedonia

Procurement
See Logistics

Refugees

In 1951 the United Nations defined a refugee as someone who is outside his or her homeland owing to a well-founded fear of persecution on the basis of race, religion, nationality, membership of a social group, or political opinion. This differentiates the refugee from an internally displaced person (IDP) who may be uprooted but does not fulfill the other criteria. Since 1951 the definition of refugee has undergone some changes in some parts of the world and has been broadened in some countries to cover threats from external aggression or foreign occupation or domination. In the United States, for example, until 1980 foreign nationals were accepted as refugees if they were fleeing communism. Some other countries have instituted degrees of refugeeship to accommodate those who flee their homelands for well-founded reasons other than fear of individual persecution. In 1997 there were an estimated 50 million people who had been uprooted from their homes and who had been forced to move or to flee somewhere else (see Table 7). Of these, just over 13 million people qualified for status as "refugees," the remainder being "internally displaced persons," "returnees," or some other category. Whether the 1951 definition is the only or even the best definition of refugee is increasingly being questioned. Originating in European disputes of the early twentieth century, it is a definition that is too narrow for the circumstances in which many people find themselves today. In some countries or regions, for example, a government may put entire sections of a population at risk by being unable to

maintain law and order or otherwise regulate the state. In peacekeeping terms the need to deal with refugees is often part of the situation assessment that a force commander has to undertake, and their presence may limit the parameters for normal military-based action by, for example, providing cover for combatants. The main agency with responsibility for refugees is the United Nations High Commission for Refugees (UNHCR), which, along with other bodies such as the Red Cross or Red Crescent, may have a significant presence in an area where peacekeeping is needed.

See also Bosnia and Herzegovina (UNMIBH 1995– ; UNIPTF 1995– ; IFOR, 1995; SFOR, 1996); Conflicts: patterns and occurrences; Humanitarian assistance; Military medicine and peacekeeping; United Nations: organization

References and further reading UNHCR (1997)

Table 7 Number of Refugees, Returnees, and IDPs, 1997

	Refugees	Returnees	Internally Displaced People (IDPs)	Others of Concern	Total
Africa	4,341,000	1,693,000	2,058,000		8,091,000
Asia	4,809,000	1,241,100	1,719,000	156,000	7,925,000
Europe	3,166,000	308,000	1,066,000	1,209,000	5,749,000
Latin America	88,000	70,000	11,000		169,000
North America	720,000				720,000
Oceania	75,000				75,000
Total	13,200,000	3,311,000	4,854,000	1,365,000	22,729,000

Source: Data from UNHCR, *The State of the World's Refugees.* Oxford: Oxford University Press, 1997.

Regional organizations and peacekeeping

The UN Charter deliberately provides no precise definition of what constitutes a regional organization, thus allowing flexibility for undertakings by a group of states. The term covers treaty-based organizations, whether created before or after the founding of the United Nations, regional organizations for mutual security and defense, organizations for general regional development or for cooperation on a particular economic topic or function, and groups created to deal with a specific political, economic, or social issue of current concern. Such regional, subregional, and interregional organizations include, for example, the Organization of African Unity (OAU), the Organization of American States (OAS), the Economic Organization of West African States (ECOWAS), the Organization for Security and Cooperation in Europe (OSCE), the North Atlantic Treaty Organization (NATO), and the Commonwealth of Independent States (CIS).

The United Nations Charter devotes chapter 8 to regional arrangements or organizations for dealing with matters relating to the maintenance of international peace and security. Article 52 of the charter stipulates that UN member states "shall make every effort to achieve pacific settlement of local disputes through such regional arrangements or by such regional agencies before referring them to the Security Council." The UN's *Report of the Secretary-General on the Work of the Organization* (1995) distinguishes five different forms of cooperation that are already under way between regional organizations and the United Nations: (1) *Consultation:* For example, an agreement for increased cooperation was signed between the OAS and the United Nations in April 1995. (2) *Diplomatic support:* For example, the OSCE provided technical input to the United Nations on constitutional issues relating to Abkhazia, and the United Nations provided advice and guidance to the OSCE on the deployment of a peacekeeping force to the disputed Azeri enclave of Nagorno-Karabakh. (3) *Operational support:* In support of the United Nations Protection Force in Former Yugoslavia (UNPROFOR) in Bosnia and Herzegovina, NATO conducted widespread air strikes and flew thousands of sorties to enforce the no-fly air exclusion zone; the Western European Union (WEU) also monitored compliance with UN sanctions against Serbia by patrolling ports along the Danube. (4) *Codeployment:* Examples of peacekeeping missions that are working alongside each other include the United Nations Observer Mission in Liberia (UNOMIL) and the Military Observer Group of the Economic Organization of West African States (ECOMOG); the United Nations Observer Mission in Georgia (UNOMIG) and the CIS peacekeeping force; and the United Nations Mission of Observers in Tajikistan (UNMOT) and the CIS peacekeeping force. (5) *Joint operations:* For example, the United Nations Mission in Haiti (UNMIH) and the OAS deployed a 92-member international civilian mission—the Joint International Civilian Mission in Haiti (MICIVIH)—to Haiti to verify the human rights situation according to the Haitian constitution and international agreements.

In January 1993 the UN Security Council invited regional organizations to analyze and outline methods for strengthening cooperation with the world body. The General Assembly further institutionalized the process in its Resolution 48/42, which welcomed the decision of the secretary-general to develop a set of guidelines on cooperation. In his *Supplement to An Agenda for Peace,* Secretary-General Boutros Boutros-Ghali identified four principles governing cooperation: Formal mechanisms for consultation should be agreed upon and established; the primacy of the United Nations in the maintenance of international peace and security, as set out in the charter, must be respected; the division of labor must be clearly defined and agreed upon in order to avoid overlap and institutional rivalry where the United Nations and a regional organization are both working on the same conflict; and consistency by members of regional organizations, which are also member states of the United Nations, is needed in dealing with a common problem of interest to both organizations.

By contracting out some of the responsibilities for conflict intervention to regional agencies the United Nations can more effectively fulfill its duties as enshrined in the charter. Regional support offers both advantages and alternatives to purely UN intervention. These include: (1) *Geopolitics:* Countries in the conflict region are more likely to have an interest in finding solutions to the conflict because of such factors as economic interdependence, political alliances, mutual historical ties, and a closeness and informality of relations. (2) *Proximity to the conflict zone:* Member states of regional organizations are more likely to be aware of an escalation of tensions in a neighboring state and are consequently in a position to prevent an outbreak of conflict or a situation of destabilization. For example, the OAU proposed to station officials in each of the 53 member states to report on internal conflict, signs of tension, and breakdown in communications between groups before they could degenerate into war. The close proximity to a conflict zone also means that the speed of deployment is significantly increased. (3) *Forum for dialogue and cooperation:* Ongoing dialogue enhances stability and trust between and within nations. (4) *Homogeneity of membership and common culture:* Lack of understanding of local and regional cultures by the United Nations has often jeopardized the success of peacekeeping operations and resulted in detrimental effects on local societies (e.g., Somalia). The homogeneity of membership and common culture found in regional organizations can advance consensus, make intervention more acceptable to the disputants, and provide greater insight into local problems and the root causes of conflict.

Though regional organizations have an important role to play, a number of problems still need to be overcome to make cooperation more effective, including financial, logistical, and technical inadequacies; a lack of standardized training and common doctrine; different interpretations of mandates; confusion over command and control and decision making; and different perceptions about the use of enforcement action. Issues of partiality also often complicate and jeopardize regional peacekeeping operations. Similarly, historical tensions, inequalities, and mutual rivalries can prevent regional agencies from dealing effectively with intrastate conflict.

Suggestions for improving the effectiveness of regional peacekeeping include strengthening and creating logistics bases, training centers, and standby arrangements, with political and financial support from UN member states and regional powers (e.g., the Cairo Center for African Crisis Solving was established in 1993 under the OAU Crisis Prevention Mechanism to qualify specialized African corps in predicting, managing, and solving crisis in Africa); closer coordination between the United Nations and regional organizations to establish dialogue and a forum for cooperation; and encouragement by the United Nations for meetings of regional organizations to establish and enlarge their own peacekeeping and peacemaking initiatives.

See also Association of Southeast Asian Nations (ASEAN); Commonwealth of Independent States; Contadora Group; European Union (EU); North Atlantic Treaty Organization (NATO); Organization of African Unity; Organization of American States (OAS); Organization of East Caribbean States (OECS); Organization for Security and Cooperation in Europe (OSCE); Western European Union (WEU)
References and further reading Achayra (1995); Barnett (1995); Pearson Peacekeeping Center (1996); Peck (1998); Zacher (1979)

Rikhye, Indar Jit (1920–)

Born in Lahore, India, on 30 July 1920, Indar Jit Rikhye graduated from the Indian Military Academy (1939) and the Indian Defence Services Staff College (1952). He was commissioned as an officer in 1939 and rose to the rank of major general. His first attachment to the United Nations was as chief of staff in the UN Emergency Force in Gaza, Egypt (1958–1960). He then served as commander in a return to the UN Emergency Force, in Gaza and Sinai, Egypt (1966–1967). He was appointed military adviser to the secretary-general between 1960 and 1969. He formally retired from the Indian Army in 1967 and worked with the International Peace Academy (1970–1989). He was awarded the Medal of Honour from Kyung Hee University in Seoul (1981) and the Prize for Peace Education from the United Nations Educational, Scientific, and Cultural Organization (UNESCO) (1985).

See also India
References and further reading Rikhye (1984, 1992)

Rose, Michael (1940–)

Born on 5 January 1940, Michael Rose graduated from St. Edmund Hall, Oxford. He has been former adjutant general (1995–1997), aide-de-camp general to Her Majesty the Queen (1995–1997), and commander of the United Nations Protection Force in Former Yugoslavia (UNPROFOR) (1994–1995).

In 1964 Rose joined the Coldstream Guards and saw service in Germany, Aden, Malaysia, the Gulf States, Dhofar, Northern Ireland, and the Falkland Islands. He was commanding officer of 22 SAS Regiment (1979–1982), and then commanded the Thirty-Ninth Infantry Brigade (1983–1985). Between 1988 and 1989 he was director of the School of Infantry, he was commander of the Second Infantry Division from 1989 to 1991, and he returned to Staff College as commandant between 1991 and 1993. He then held concurrently the positions of commander UK Field Army and inspector-general of the Territorial Army (1993–1994). This operational and command experience was the background to his posting as force commander to UNPROFOR in Bosnia and Herzegovina in 1994–1995, a time when the war in Bosnia was at its height, when air strikes led by the North Atlantic Treaty Organization (NATO) were targeted against Serbian positions, and when UNPROFOR was trying to defend the safe areas.

See also Bosnia and Herzegovina; British peacekeeping; UNPROFOR I–III
References and further reading Rose (1998)

Rules of engagement

Rules of engagement (ROE) are the guidelines by which a mission is conducted and by which each member of the mission knows how to respond to any given situation. The "Rules of Engagement" is a long, detailed, and comprehensive document that is an integral part of mission planning. The guidelines contained within the document consider the political, legal, moral, and cultural aspects of the mission as well as the purely military responses. Political ends as well as military means are also crucial to the formulation, since each peacekeeping mission is a political endeavor. Logistically the document should also consider every phase of an operation in detail—from the first disembarkation of personnel and equipment to the final withdrawal—and should also take into account "peripheral" factors such as local supply arrangements, the treatment of noncombatants, and the responsibilities of local civilian police. The ROE need also to take into account the different backgrounds and mores of the participating troops, as well as possible differences of interpretation or understanding of supposedly common terms.

The difficult balance that the ROE have to achieve is the use of a military structure to deliver political or humanitarian objectives and the marrying of military priorities in a civilian context. Because a peacekeeping mission is an exercise unlike anything done in training, the use of the ROE has to be instilled through training before a force is deployed.

The following is a summary of the Rules of Engagement Card issued to the U.S. forces deployed under Operation Provide Comfort as part of the exercise to protect the Kurdish population of Iraq after the Gulf War:

- All military operations will be conducted according to the laws of war.
- Forces will not fire unless fired upon, unless there is clear evidence of hostile intent (the threat or imminent use of force by an Iraqi force or other foreign force, terrorist group, or individuals against the United States, U.S. forces, U.S. citizens, or Kurdish or other refugees located above the thirty-eighth parallel or otherwise located within a U.S. or allied save haven refugee area).
- In the event that U.S. forces are attacked or threatened by unarmed hostile elements, mobs, or rioters, the responsibility for the protection of U.S. forces rests with the U.S. commanding officer. The on-scene commander will employ the following measures to overcome the threat:
  - Warning to demonstrators

- Show of force, including the use of riot control formations
- Warning shots fired over the heads of hostile elements
- Other reasonable use of force necessary under the circumstances and proportional to the threat
- Use of the following guidelines when applying these rules:
    - i. use of force only to protect lives
    - ii. use of minimum force necessary.

See also Peace enforcement; Training for peacekeeping

Russian peacekeeping

Russia, a permanent member of the Security Council, makes a significant contribution to the peacekeeping budget of the United Nations (8.5 percent). It has played an important but problematic role in peacekeeping. During the 1990s about 15,000 Russians were serving on peacekeeping operations, but only 1,550 of these were deployed on UN missions (most of these with the United Nations Protection Force in Former Yugoslavia [UNPROFOR]). The majority of Russian peacekeepers were deployed in territories of the former Soviet Union in what was called the "near abroad." Since the breakup of the Soviet Union in late 1991 there has been debate about the nature of Russian peacekeeping: On the one hand, Moscow has been encouraged to stick to classic UN standards of peacekeeping (including adherence to the principles of consent, impartiality, minimum force, and UN control), while, on the other hand, Russia has claimed that there are certain peculiarities or differences in peacekeeping operations in its former territories and in the need for a special role for Russia in these operations.

In March 1992 the 11 members of the Commonwealth of Independent States (CIS) signed an agreement on the formation of collective peacekeeping forces, but a combined command did not come about; instead, several operations, usually dominated by Russians, were launched to respond to conflicts in and around the borders of Russia and the CIS states, where Russia feels obliged to restore and maintain order: a Russian-Georgian-Ossetian force in South Ossetia (Georgia); a Russian-Moldovan force in Moldova in 1992; in 1993 a collective CIS force in Tajikistan in autumn and in Ingush-Ossetia; and in 1994 a 3,000-strong force deployed between Georgia and Abkhazia. Unlike in Western doctrine and in UN practice, the difference between peacekeeping and peace enforcement in these operations is often blurred. Russian specialists use the terms *mirotvorcheskie voiska* (peacemaking forces) and *voiska po podderzhanivu mira* (peacekeeping forces, or forces for the maintenance of peace) interchangeably. Neither the United Nations nor the Organization for Security and Cooperation in Europe (OSCE) has formally recognized Russian and CIS peacekeeping forces in the near abroad, though the United Nations has dispatched relatively small observer missions, such as the United Nations Observer Mission in Georgia (UNOMIG), which was encouraged to cooperate with the CIS peacekeeping force already there. Since Russia's missions lack international recognition, Russia must finance its own missions, which is proving to be very expensive and which is causing Russia to push for international recognition for its peacekeeping role, allowing it to reclaim costs from, for example, the United Nations. Another way to achieve the sharing of costs would be to reopen the original idea of a CIS-wide peacekeeping force. Russia has also considered engaging peacekeeping forces from "acceptable" states from outside the CIS in peacekeeping missions in the former Soviet Union. The use of an Indian military contingent for peacekeeping in Central Asia has been discussed, as has the idea of using forces from neutral European states experienced in peacekeeping, such as Sweden, Finland, and Austria. However, such countries would be wary of joining missions not mandated by the United Nations and would be wary also of the prospect of becoming involved in peace enforcement rather than peacekeeping. The legal and conceptual aspects of Russian and CIS peacekeeping are still being developed, but some principles or guidelines for practice are emerging, including the willingness to use enforcement capability in zones where there is still active fighting; a reliance on specially trained professional soldiers; and the desire to maintain at least the appearance of third-party neutrality. For example, training centers have been established within the Twenty-Seventh and Forty-Fifth Motorized Rifle Divisions, which are to become permanent peacekeeping units. On the issue of neutrality, most Russian experts on peacekeeping agree that military units should not be used for peacekeeping where they are already based, such as the Fourteenth Army in Moldova. However, maintaining neutrality in the deployment of any Russian peacekeepers in the near abroad is problematic because of extensive Russian interests and large Russian minorities throughout the territories of the former Soviet Union. Despite these problems and peculiarities of Russian peacekeeping, interventions in Tajikistan, Georgia, and Moldova have been seen to be relatively successful, and the recent successful negotiations between Moldova and the Dniester Republic, facilitated by missions from the OSCE and Russia, point to a model of regional peacekeeping that may provide the basis for a successful regional peacekeeping mechanism in the future management of conflicts in the Russian near abroad.

See also Commonwealth of Independent States
References and further reading Baev (1994); Raevsky and Vorobbev (1994); Shashenkov (1994)

Rwanda

United Nations Observer Mission in Uganda/Rwanda (UNOMUR), 1993–1994; United Nations Assistance Mission in Rwanda (UNAMIR), 1993–1996

Conflict Profile
During a three-month period in 1994 an estimated 500,000 to 800,000 people, and according to some estimates possibly up to one million people, were killed in the course of a genocidal civil war in Rwanda. Over two million people fled and became refugees in neighboring countries, and up to one million became displaced within Rwanda. The conflict and its aftermath continue to trouble the African Great Lakes Region within which Rwanda is situated.

Rwanda is one of the smallest countries in Africa, similar in size to Burundi to the south and to its former colonial power, Belgium. It is also one of the most densely populated, and the actual area of arable land must support a total population of 7.15 million people (according to the 1991 census), an average of 406 people per square kilometer, the highest population density in mainland Africa. The country is divided into ten prefectures, each headed by a prefect, and the prefectures are divided into 143 communes governed by mayors or *bourgmestres*. Mayors and prefects are appointed by the president. According to the 1991 census, 90.4 percent of the population was Hutu, 8.2 percent Tutsi, and less than 1 percent a marginalized minority of pygmoid Twa. The population is overwhelmingly engaged in peasant farming, with 95 percent living in the countryside; 3 percent are engaged in industry, and 66 percent of the urban population is concentrated in the capital, Kigali. Only 4 percent of the population are economically active within the cash economy, and with an annual average increase in population of 3 percent, neither the farming households nor the small industrial and service sector can absorb the increase in the working population. Most peasant farming households therefore also earn money from working informally in small trades such as brick making or by engaging in the "black economy," including cross-border trade and smuggling. The pressure on rural households to feed families from subsistence farming has become severe; population pressure is forcing the unsustainable use of marginal land, and soil fertility is deteriorating. The material conditions of the population are severe: 2.6 million are without access to potable water, and 3.2 million are without sanitation. The position of women is especially disadvantaged, since although in theory they are given equal status as citizens under the constitution, in effect women can own nothing legally.

The formal economy is built around the two cash crops, tea and coffee. In Rwanda coffee is grown by about 700,000 smallholders, who were obliged to grow some coffee on their land and were in return guaranteed a certain price per kilo from the government. By 1986 coffee exports produced over 80 percent of Rwanda's export earnings. However, these earnings have fallen dramatically in the 1990s, partly as a result of the collapse of world coffee prices and also, since 1990, as a result of the conflict that raged into genocidal slaughter in 1994. The performance of the economy generally worsened dramatically by the end of the 1980s, and with the national debt having increased by 450 percent between 1980 and 1992 (from $189 million to $873 million), a structural adjustment program was introduced by the World Bank and the International Monetary Fund (IMF) between 1990 and 1992, coinciding with the outbreak of the war.

Most of the population live on hill farms, in a *rugo* (a compound or household), and every hill contains a collection of *ingo* (plural for *rugo*), where both Hutu and Tutsi live side by side. These communities form the basic unit of society. The administrative language is French, but the common vernacular language is Kinyarwanda. In 1991 up to 50 percent of the population was illiterate. Ninety percent of the population is Christian, 63 percent of these Catholics who were brought into the church as a result of French missionary activity, which had a vigorous presence beginning in the late nineteenth century. Most of the founders of Hutu nationalism were educated at Catholic schools, and there has been a close relationship between leaders of church and state.

The first inhabitants of Rwanda were hunter-gatherers and forest dwellers whose contemporary descendants are the minority Twa. About A.D. 1000 there began a migration of farmers (Hutu), from what is now Cameroon, who cleared the forests and began settled agriculture. The Tutsi probably arrived in the Great Lakes Region as part of yet another migration, this one southward from the Horn of Africa. They were pastoralists who traded cattle products for agricultural products, but this peaceful trading was followed by Tutsi conquests and military and administrative control. One Tutsi clan, the Nyiginya, initially achieved political dominance in eastern Rwanda, and over a period of several centuries they formed the core of a state that expanded westward. In addition to being distinguished by clear physical differences, Hutu and Tutsi were distinguished largely by occupational categories: Tutsi were cattle herders, soldiers, and administrators, whereas Hutu were farmers. However, Tutsi were assimilated in the sense that they spoke the language used by Hutu (Kinyarwanda), they adopted Hutu traditions and cults, the two groups lived side by side, and a clan system in which Hutu and Tutsi had common membership spanned the whole society. By the end of the nineteenth century Rwanda was united under King (*mwami*) Kigeri IV, who as head of state owned all land and cattle. The *mwami* and all army chiefs were Tutsi, and the provinces were administered by chiefs who were always Tutsi: Thus precolonial Rwandese state formation developed into a Tutsi-dominated structure built to consolidate political power. Hutu participated in the middle and lower levels of the administration.

Initially under German colonial rule and then (as Ruanda-Urundi) occupied by Belgium, Rwanda came under Belgian trusteeship first for the League of Nations and then for the United Nations. The distinction between Hutu and Tutsi was maintained, and in 1933 compulsory identity cards were introduced by the Belgian administrators, after which all Rwandese were decisively categorized into Hutu, Tutsi, or Twa. The Tutsi were given a monopoly of political and administrative power under Belgian trusteeship. This whole system was thrown into reverse when during the 1950s, as part of the process of decolonization, the Belgians shifted support from the minority Tutsi to the majority Hutu. During the three-year period between 1959 and 1961 the Tutsi-dominated monarchy was replaced during the Hutu revolution by a Hutu-dominated independent republic. In July 1962 Rwanda gained independence from Belgium, under the presidency of Gregoire Kayibanda from the Parmehutu Party. The seeds of the modern conflict were sown in this period when tens of thousands of Tutsi, in a series of upheavals, were forced into exile in neighboring countries, and refugee groups began armed attacks across the border into Rwanda. By the early 1990s it has been estimated that there were 600,000 Tutsi refugees in Zaire, Tanzania, Burundi, and Uganda, equivalent to about 9 percent of the total population of the country, or 50 percent of the Tutsi population.

In 1973, following a coup d'état, Maj. Gen. Juvenal Habyarimana took power and formed the Second Republic, backed by a new party, the Mouvement Révolutionnaire National pour le Développement (MRND), which became the only party under the constitution of 1978. The exiled Tutsi became increasingly militant, and in 1988, following a conference on Rwandan refugees held in Washington, D.C., the Rwandese Patriotic Front (RPF) was formed in Kampala, Uganda. Based in and supported by Uganda, the RPF launched an attack on northern Rwanda and demanded the right to resettle large numbers of mainly Tutsi refugees, as well as a series of political reforms, including the formation of a multiparty democracy. The RPF had very close links with the Ugandan army of President Museveni. Despite a series of internal and later international efforts to resolve the conflict between the RPF and the Habyarimana regime, a particular difficulty and obstacle to reform and moderation was caused by the makeup of the regime itself. The Hutu of northern Rwanda had remained independent of the centralizing state under the Tutsi *mwami*. However, in 1911 they were militarily defeated by a combined force of German and southern Rwandan Tutsi troops, leaving a legacy of both resentment and suspicion and reinforcing the memory of a past not dominated by Tutsi. Habyarimana's informal council (*akazu*), composed of his wife and his brothers-in-law, represented this Hutu subculture, and this made the regime amenable to pressure from those suspicious of reconciliatory gestures and hostile to those moderate Hutu who favored dialogue with the RPF. The *akazu* was also implicated in the massacres that occurred beginning in April 1994, building up the Hutu militias (the *interahamwe*, meaning "those who work together"), which carried out much of the killings, and issuing instructions to the mayors. Nonetheless, there was growing internal and international pressure on Habyarimana and the MRND to allow a multiparty system, to respect human rights, and to enable a fair resettlement of refugees.

By late 1992, although the RPF had made significant military advances, there was a stalemate. A series of cease-fires were agreed to, with Belgium, Tanzania, and Uganda involved at various times as mediators. The Organization of African Unity (OAU), after talks in Zaire in 1990, agreed to send a small observer force to oversee a cease-fire (the Groupement des Observateurs Militaires Neutres [GOMN]), and peace negotiations (the Arusha talks, held in Tanzania between the RPF and the Rwandan government) began on 10 August 1992, facilitated especially by Tanzania but with the involvement of Burundi, Zaire, Belgium, France, Germany, the United States, Senegal, and the OAU. Following a year of negotiations, agreement was reached on a set of protocols covering human rights issues, power sharing in a transitional government and parliament, the resettlement of refugees and internally displaced persons (who by February 1993 numbered one million), and the creation of a unified national army. Presidential and parliamentary elections were to be organized at the end of the transitional period, and a commission would be appointed to draft a new constitution that would then be put to a referendum. Nine months after the inauguration of the transitional government, the first groups of refugees would be allowed to resettle in a number of repatriation areas. It was in the military reforms specified in the Arusha Agreements that the role for a peacekeeping force was defined. Under the Arusha Agreements, finally signed in August 1993 by President Habyarimana and the RPF leader Alexis Kanyarengwe, there was provision for a neutral international force, either UN peacekeepers or an enlarged deployment of the OAU's GOMN under UN supervision. This force would provide security in Kigali and in Rwanda overall, supervise the demilitarized zone along the border with Uganda, and supervise the transitional political agreements. Indeed, it was stated that the deployment of such a force was a precondition for the whole process to proceed. However, the implementation of the accords was delayed, partly because of the UN's slowness in deploying troops and partly because of Habyarimana's continued resistance to implementing the changes.

Despite formal agreement to Arusha, part of the strategy of Habyarimana's regime was to promote ethnic and political polarization, and there is considerable evidence of an organized extremism within and around the presidency, which was either linked directly to, or at least did nothing to restrain, the outbreak of a series of massacres and abuses of human rights, mostly directed against Tutsi communities but also against Hutu moderates. The Hutu militias were first seen in action in a massacre of Tutsi at Bugesera in March 1992, and a pattern was emerging in a series of similar events: A massacre would be preceded by intense ethnic propaganda by highly placed officials in the ruling MRND and by local mayors, and *interahamwe* militias across the country would recruit new members, mostly among unemployed young men, loyal to the hard-liners and providing a chain of command from the elite into the rural communes. Thus when the Arusha Agreements were signed in August 1993, polarization within Rwanda itself was increasing rather than diminishing, and political moderates came under increasing pressure because the Habyarimana regime equated opponents of their party with enemies of the Hutu people. To add to the tensions, in July 1993 Radio-Television Libre des Milles Collines (RTLMC) began broadcasting. RTLMC backed the hard-line members of the MRND and the uncompromising Hutu party, the Coalition pour la Défence de la République (CDR), and was opposed to the Arusha process. It provided another powerful element in the incitement of Hutu against Tutsi and moderate politicians.

Despite all this it was generally felt in late 1993 that the Arusha process would move forward, albeit more slowly than had been planned. Formal approval was given by the UN Security Council for the deployment of 2,500 peacekeepers by March 1994, and the first troops arrived in October 1993. However, the foundation on which all other activities depended, the enlarged transitional government that was to be the vehicle of the peace process, never came into existence. Two major trigger events precipitated the outbreak of a total, massively violent civil war. In October 1993 the first democratically elected Hutu president of Burundi, Rwanda's neighbor to the south, whose problems mirrored those of Rwanda, was assassinated by Tutsi soldiers in the Burundian army. Many saw this as the death knell for the Arusha Accords. Thousands died in Burundi in the aftermath of the coup, and about 70,000 Hutu from Burundi fled into southern Rwanda. For those hard-liners in Rwanda who wished to spell out the

lesson of the assassination, the message was clear: Arusha could not work because the Tutsi would never accept Hutu rule even within a government of national unity. If this first event made the failure of the Arusha Accords likely, the second trigger event made their failure certain and plunged the country into a period of violence that is commonly regarded as one of the worst in human history. On the evening of 6 April 1994 the Mystère Falcon aircraft carrying President Habyarimana of Rwanda and President Ntaryamira of Burundi, who were returning from a meeting in Tanzania, was shot down on its approach to Kigali airport, killing all on board. On the same evening what appeared to be a planned program of killing began, directed from the highest level. Prunier's authoritative study published in 1995 identified the main perpetrators of the genocide as the core group of Habyarimana's closest advisers; up to 300 leaders of the local communes; the *interahamwe* militias, possibly numbering up to 30,000, who carried out most of the killing; and members of the military elite and the Presidential Guard, who provided support to local *interahamwe*. The first act was the killing of opposition politicians, mostly Hutu, followed by civilians who supported the peace process, including journalists, civil servants, and human rights activists. One of the first victims was Prime Minister Agathe Uwilingiyimana, who was killed along with the UN peacekeepers from Belgium who were acting as her bodyguards.

After the annihilation of the political opposition the Tutsi community in general became the target. In the three months from April to June 1994 between 500,000 and 800,000 people were killed, two million had fled to neighboring countries, and one million were displaced within Rwanda. In the ensuing humanitarian crisis $1.4 billion was made available by the international community, the largest donors being the European Community's Humanitarian Office (ECHO) and various departments of the U.S. government. The bulk of this aid was channeled through the United Nations High Commissioner for Refugees (UNHCR), the World Food Program (WFP), and the Red Cross movement. In addition up to 200 nongovernmental organizations (NGOs) became involved in humanitarian relief. The United Nations had already been very active in organizing humanitarian relief; Secretary-General Boutros Boutros-Ghali had launched an interagency appeal in March 1993 that raised $78 million to assist the 900,000 displaced by war and living in 30 refugee camps. Because of the severity of the violence and the chaos that broke out after 6 April, humanitarian personnel were evacuated and humanitarian operations were temporarily suspended. However, the UN Disaster Management Team was reestablished with its base in Nairobi, under the direction of the newly created United Nations Rwanda Emergency Office (UNREO).

On 8 April the RPF resumed its offensive from the north, joined by a 600-strong battalion stationed in Kigali under the Arusha Agreements. By the middle of July Kigali, the capital, was taken and a new government installed, with Pasteur Bizimungu as president and Faustin Twagiramungu as prime minister, both Hutu; but effective power rested with the Tutsi Gen. Paul Kagame, commander of the RPF and vice president and minister of defense in the new regime.

The Deployment of the United Nations Observer Mission in Uganda/Rwanda (UNOMUR) and the United Nations Assistance Mission in Rwanda (UNAMIR)

Following incursions into Rwanda from Uganda beginning in 1990, Rwanda accused Uganda of arming and supporting the RPF, an accusation that Uganda denied. In 1993 both countries asked the United Nations to help establish the facts and to deploy military observers along the border, and a small technical mission was dispatched early in April 1993. On 22 June 1993 the Security Council, in Security Council Resolution (SCR) 846, authorized the establishment of a United Nations Observer Mission Uganda/Rwanda (UNOMUR) on the Ugandan side of the border to verify that no military assistance was being provided. The secretary-general appointed Brig. Gen. Romeo Dallaire (Canada) as the chief military observer (CMO) and a status of mission agreement was finalized on 16 August 1993. By the end of September the mission, headquartered in Kabale, Uganda, 20 kilometers north of the border with Rwanda, had reached its authorized strength of 81 military ob-

servers (MOs), provided by Bangladesh, Botswana, Brazil, Hungary, the Netherlands, Senegal, Slovak Republic, and Zimbabwe. Dallaire later served as force commander of UNAMIR until August 1994, when he was replaced by Maj. Gen. Guy Tousignant (Canada), who served until December 1995. Brig. Gen. Shiva Kumar (India) was appointed as acting force commander.

In June 1993 both parties (the RPF and the government of Rwanda) asked the United Nations to be prepared for the quick deployment of a peacekeeping force as soon as the Arusha peace talks were concluded. In August 1993, following the signing of the Arusha Agreements, the small NMOG (Neutral Military Observers Group) I was replaced by an expanded NMOG II with 130 personnel, pending the arrival of an international peacekeeping force. Following a UN reconnaissance mission to Rwanda on 19–31 August, the secretary-general recommended the establishment of a United Nations Assistance Mission in Rwanda (UNAMIR), which was agreed to under SCR 872 of 5 October 1993. Brigadier General Dallaire arrived in Kigali as force commander on 22 October, followed by an advanced party of 21 military personnel. A status of forces agreement was signed by the government on 5 November and agreed to by the RPF. On 12 November the secretary-general appointed Jacques-Roger Booh-Booh, former minister for external relations of Cameroon, as his special representative in Rwanda. In June 1994 he was succeeded by S. M. Khan (Pakistan). The UNAMIR operation was planned in four phases; phase one would end when the transitional government was established (anticipated to be late 1993); phase two would last for 90 days and would involve the demobilization of armed forces and the integration of a new national army; during phase three, planned to last nine months, UNAMIR would establish and monitor a new demilitarized zone (DMZ), and the integration of the armed forces and the gendarmerie would be completed; and in phase four, planned to take four months, the task would be to supervise the final stages of the transitional arrangements in the buildup to the elections agreed on in the Arusha talks. Throughout all four phases the mission would assist in ensuring security in the capital, Kigali, and provide security for the repatriation of refugees and displaced persons. It would also assist in the coordination of humanitarian relief operations. Mission strength would build up to 2,548 in phase two and decline to about 930 by phase four. UNOMUR would come under the command of the new mission, but it would continue its monitoring work along the border. UNAMIR's DMZ sector headquarters was established on 1 November when NMOG II was absorbed into UNAMIR, and deployment of the Kigali battalion, composed of Bangladeshi and Belgian troops, was completed by early December 1993. In January and February the civilian police (CIVPOL) were also established in Kigali.

However, a major obstacle to progress with the plan was the failure to install the transitional government. Despite this, and while expressing concern at the lack of progress, SCR 909 on 5 April 1994 extended the mandate of UNAMIR for a further six months, until July 1994. The next day the presidential aircraft was shot down at Kigali, which, as already discussed, projected the war into a vicious and decisive phase. Following the killing of ten of its peacekeepers in one of the first acts of the ensuing violence, the Belgian government withdrew its battalion from UNAMIR. On 20 April the secretary-general informed the Security Council that in the new situation UNAMIR could not carry out the tasks for which they had been deployed. Three options were offered: to massively reinforce UNAMIR; to reduce it to a small group to remain in the capital under the force commander, acting as an intermediary to secure a cease-fire; or to withdraw altogether. Under SCR 912 of 21 April 1994 the second option was taken. With massacres continuing on a large scale in Kigali and, especially, in the south of the country, the secretary-general urged the Security Council to consider taking more forceful action to restore law and order, though to do so would require a much larger commitment than member states appeared willing to consider. Powerless to stop the massacres, Secretary-General Boutros-Ghali publicly referred to the massacres as genocide.

On 18 May 1994 SCR 918 imposed an arms embargo on Rwanda and expanded UNAMIR's mandate to provide for the security and protection of refugees through the establishment of secure areas and to provide security for relief operations. Authorization was granted to expand the force to 5,500 troops (UNAMIR II). In SCR 935 of 1 July 1994 concern was expressed about reports of continued violations of international humanitarian law, and this resulted in the formation of a Commission of Experts (based in Geneva) to investigate the violations. Because of serious delays in deploying UNAMIR forces under its expanded mandate of May 1994 (by the end of July 1994 less than 500 troops had been deployed) the Security Council, under SCR 929 of 22 June 1994, accepted and authorized a French proposal to deploy a force (Operation Turquoise), under chapter 7 of the charter, tasked to establish a humanitarian protected zone in southwest Rwanda, where there were an estimated two million internally displaced persons. For UNAMIR and for UNREO (now established in Kigali), the priority was to attempt to deal with the unprecedented humanitarian crisis principally in the northwest and southwest of the country. The French troops of Operation Turquoise withdrew as they had planned on 21 August, having done much to stabilize the situation in their zone in the southwest. However, there was much suspicion of France's reasons for intervening, including the beliefs that its intervention was motivated by French domestic and foreign policy interests rather than by purely humanitarian concerns and that the French sought to bolster the forces of the Hutu regime. UNOMUR was withdrawn by 21 September.

Although approved in May, UNAMIR only reached its full operational strength in October, with 5,500 troops deployed in six sectors, including Kigali. Human rights field operations were conducted by 100 officers tasked to investigate violations of international law. On 9 December 1994 the final report of the Commission of Experts concluded that there was overwhelming evidence of acts of genocide against Tutsi by Hutu, and under SCR 955 of 8 November 1994 the Security Council had established an International Tribunal for Rwanda to prosecute those responsible for violations of international law. Early in 1995 the Human Rights Field Operation in Rwanda (HFOR) became fully operational and followed a strategy intended to promote confidence building and national reconciliation by concrete attention to issues of justice and human rights.

Increasing concern was expressed about those who incited people to flee from Rwanda and who threatened those seeking to return home, since it was clear that many of the former political leaders and the militias were determined to prevent people from returning and apparently intended to mount an armed invasion to regain power. There were reports in early 1995 that the forces of the former Rwandese government were rearming, and the RPF tightened its own security policy. This issue caused tension between the new government and UNAMIR, which was accused of doing little to stop arms deliveries to former government forces in the camps in countries surrounding Rwanda, while a general arms embargo continued to apply to Rwanda itself. In April 1995 the government decided to cordon off the eight remaining camps for internally displaced persons in the south of the country. At the largest of these (Kibeho), many died when an estimated 80,000 inhabitants tried to break out of the camp. Outside the country the 1.4 million refugees in eastern Zaire, especially around Lake Kivu in the Goma region, presented both a severe humanitarian challenge and an explosive security situation. A joint technical team of the UN Department of Peacekeeping Operations (DPKO) and UNHCR recommended international supervision of security in the camps, but there was little willingness among member states to supply personnel. The general situation was made more tense because intimidation within the camps and fear of reprisals on return made it very difficult to convince people to return home.

Despite the alarming instability and continuing violence, the context in which UNAMIR was operating had changed. The full-scale war and the genocide had ended with the establishment of a new government of national unity on 19 July 1994, and the new government raised questions about the role and future of UNAMIR. UNAMIR's mandate was extended for six months, from June 1995 to December 1996, but with troop numbers reduced from about 5,000 to 1,800. The government of Rwanda was asserting its sovereignty and responsibility for security, general governance, and

reconciliation, and UNAMIR's role was changed, with more emphasis on supporting the construction of bridges, roads, and schools and providing transport for humanitarian assistance.

Tension was heightening in the border areas, and there were continued fears of infiltration from armed elements of the former government. In a visit to the region in July 1995 Secretary-General Boutros-Ghali emphasized the dangers of instability in the whole of the Great Lakes Region. In August 1995, under SCR 1011, the Security Council decided to lift its arms embargo on Rwanda, a decision that Zaire strongly objected to because it feared an increase of tension and in the flow of refugees. In response, the government of Zaire provoked a new refugee crisis when it decided to begin the forced repatriation of refugees to Rwanda and Burundi, a move that threatened the UNHCR policy of a safe, orderly, and phased repatriation. By late 1995, however, it was evident that the rate of return of refugees was very slow because of continued misinformation and intimidation in the camps spread by the militias of the former regime, who wished to hold power in a community in exile and from this base perhaps ultimately to recapture power in Rwanda. Eventually, in the later part of 1996, this situation was to destabilize neighboring Zaire, when the refugee crisis there, linked to a corrupt and failing government, provoked an armed rebellion in the east of the country.

Despite a general feeling throughout the international community that the mandate of UNAMIR should be renewed in order to support the process of the organized return of refugees, the government of Rwanda officially informed the secretary-general that it did not wish the mandate to be extended because it felt that the country no longer required a peacekeeping mission and that priorities had shifted to the rehabilitation, reconstruction, and development needs of the country. The mandate's renewal for the period from December 1995 to March 1996 was to be for its final period, to enable a phase in which the withdrawal could be organized. UNAMIR completed its withdrawal from Rwanda by 19 April 1996. A reduced Human Rights Field Operation remained, and the government of Rwanda agreed to the establishment of a

United Nations Office in Rwanda that would continue to support the processes of reconciliation, the return of refugees, the strengthening of the judicial system, and the rehabilitation of the country's infrastructure.

The effectiveness of the UNAMIR mission, and of the international community's response in general to the crisis, was inhibited from the beginning by a number of factors. It has been suggested that an increasing feeling of "Africa fatigue" and "compassion fatigue" was beginning to affect the judgments and motivations of the main powers in the UN system, and that this produced a failure of political will to provide the mandate and the resources that an effective peacekeeping operation would require. Particularly after the experience in Somalia, a more cautious attitude to the potential of peacekeeping was coloring the thinking of some politicians and policy makers, especially in the United States, and this was to have paralyzing effects in Rwanda. Belgium withdrew its peacekeepers when ten of them were killed after the assassination of Habyarimana. Just as the killing was escalating to genocide, the Security Council cut the peacekeeping force to fewer than 300 (in fact, over 400 stayed in Kigali), and when a new and larger force was authorized it took up to six months to organize their arrival in the country. Thus, by July 1994, three months after the killings began, none of the UNAMIR II troops had arrived in Rwanda. The failure of the United Nations to react effectively has led to calls for a range of reforms of peacekeeping, including better preparation for early and rapid deployment. The massiveness of the Rwandan humanitarian tragedy (e.g., in Goma, Zaire, one million refugees crossed the border in the space of a few days, the fastest exodus ever witnessed by aid agencies) made it clear that the humanitarian agencies of the international community were also poorly prepared to respond. Here too a series of reforms have been called for, in planning and preparation capabilities in advance of a crisis, in coordination of the efforts of the various agencies, and in achieving a better understanding between the military and civilian humanitarian agencies.

Operating costs for UNAMIR and UNOMUR combined were estimated to be about $450 million.

See also Complex emergency; France; Internal conflict; Military-humanitarian relations; Refugees
References and further reading Eriksson (1996); United Nations (1996); Vassall-Adams (1994); Whitman and Pocock (1996)

Safe areas

In the contested territories of the former Yugoslavia in 1992 the Muslim population of Bosnia and Herzegovina came under frequent attack from Serbian militias. The United Nations responded with the establishment of six "safe areas" policed by units from the United Nations Protection Force in Former Yugoslavia (UNPROFOR). The safe areas were supposed to function as a protective umbrella and a safe zone where the Muslim civilian inhabitants and Muslim civilians from other parts of the country could safely gather. In April and May 1993, Srebrenica, followed by Sarajevo, Tuzla, Zepa, Gorazde, and Bihać, were declared safe areas under UN resolutions. In fact, the presence of these safe areas did very little to stop Serbian attacks, since the localities were subject to repeated shelling by Serbian forces, and the peacekeepers themselves were often the targets. On several occasions UN peacekeepers were held hostage in and around the safe areas. The refusal of Serbian forces to recognize civilian rights (as expressed in the Geneva Conventions) played a large part in the decision of the North Atlantic Treaty Organization (NATO) to deploy airpower against Serbian positions in an exercise that was not directly mandated by the Security Council but that mirrored chapter 7 peace enforcement. At the same time that the safe areas were being established NATO also initiated the policy of air exclusion zones, also known as no-fly zones.

See also United Nations Protection Force in Former Yugoslavia (UNPROFOR I–III), 1992–1995

Safe havens

In 1991, after the defeat of the Iraqi Army in the second Gulf War, there was a period of civil unrest in various parts of Iraq. In the north the Kurdish population had been in conflict with the central government for decades, especially during the Iran-Iraq war of 1980–1988, when over half of their villages were destroyed and chemical weapons were used against both civilians and fighters. In the aftermath of the Iraq-Kuwait conflict trouble erupted once more in the Kurdish part of the country, and the government responded with armed force. Almost two million Kurds were

displaced and a large number were killed. A major humanitarian assistance program was launched, and a number of "safe havens," that is, areas where military action was proscribed, were defined. These areas were called safe "havens" so as not to impugn Iraq's territorial rights over the region. They extended from the northern border of Iraq to the thirty-sixth parallel, and they were guarded by the United Nations Guards Contingent in Iraq (UNGCI).

Sahnoun, Mohammed (1931–)

Born in Chlef, Algeria, in 1931, Mohammed Sahnoun attended the Sorbonne in Paris and New York University, from which he graduated with a bachelor of arts and a master of arts, respectively, in political science. He served as deputy secretary-general of the Organization of African Unity (OAU) (1964–1973) and as deputy secretary-general of the League of Arab States in charge of Arab-Africa dialogue (1973). Among his senior positions he has been counselor to the president of Algeria on diplomatic affairs, a member of the World Commission on Environment and Development (the Brundtland Commission) during the 1980s, and senior adviser to the secretary-general of the United Nations Conference on Environment and Development (UNCED).

He was Algeria's ambassador to the Federal Republic of Germany (1975–1979) and then to France (1979–1982) before going to the United Nations as chief of Algeria's mission (1982–

1984). He served a term as ambassador to the United States (1984–1989). He then held concurrently the positions of ambassador to Morocco and secretary to the Maghreb Union (1989–1990).

He was the special representative of the secretary-general of the United Nations in Somalia (April–November 1992), where he gained respect for his patient and consensual approach. He insisted that problems there had to be solved by negotiation and consent and with sensitivity to and knowledge of clan politics. He then returned to the OAU in the role of special representative of the secretary-general for the Congo. In 1994 he was a Pearson Fellow with the International Development Research Center in Ottawa, Canada. He was a member of the Special Advisory Group of the War-Torn Societies Project, jointly coordinated by the United Nations Research Institute for Social Development (UNRISD) and the Graduate Institute of International Studies in Geneva. Secretary-General Kofi Annan appointed him as both UN/OAU special representative for the Great Lakes Region of Africa in 1997.

See also Somalia (UNOSOM I and II, 1992–1995; UNITAF, 1992)
References and further reading Sahnoun (1994)

Second-generation multinational operations
See Second-generation peacekeeping

Second-generation peacekeeping

As the scale, frequency, and size of peacekeeping deployments increased after 1988 and through the early 1990s, attention turned to ideas for creating a stronger UN military command system and for forming either some kind of UN standing force or a stronger capacity to deploy effectively equipped forces capable of responding to civil wars and internal conflicts. The general expansion of the use of peacekeeping since 1988 has led to several attempts to redefine peacekeeping in new forms of military doctrine that are appropriate for responding to the volatile conditions in which peacekeep-

ing has had to operate in the intrastate wars of the 1990s. These attempts have generally been undertaken because of the recognition that traditional, classical, or first-generation peacekeeping, designed for use in the Cold War period, was used in the 1990s in situations for which it was not designed (i.e., in internal wars or complex political emergencies).

John Mackinlay and Jarat Chopra have been leading thinkers in the formulation of new forms of policy and planning for second-generation peacekeeping. They, along with many others, have argued that the long-standing United Nations Emergency Force (UNEF) rules of peacekeeping are no longer helpful when strictly applied in the situations of intercommunal violence that have presented challenges to peacekeeping in the 1990s. One of the rules of first-generation peacekeeping was that the parties involved must consent before the United Nations could mandate deployment of a force. However, in internal conflicts state authority may have collapsed, and warlords may have little respect for the rule of law or for negotiated agreements and may not be able to exercise control over local factional leaders. In such situations peacekeeping forces find that consent is uncertain and volatile and that the Security Council plans for peace are sabotaged by often small insurgent groups (as in Somalia, Yugoslavia, and Cambodia). In these situations the first-generation peacekeeping formula (lightly armed troops using minimal force in self-defense) is likely to be ineffective, and something more than peacekeeping but short of full-scale enforcement and war fighting is called for.

In the various redefinitions that have resulted, peacekeeping operations intended for future deployment in complex internal conflicts are variously called "multidimensional operations," "second-generation peacekeeping operations," "wider peacekeeping," "second-generation multinational forces," and "peace-support operations." In most of these formulations attention is paid to strengthening the military capabilities of peacekeeping and to securing better coordination between the various agencies, military and civilian, that have become involved in multifunctional peacekeeping. Sir Brian Urquhart, who helped to develop much peacekeeping policy while serving in the office of the secretary-general between 1949 and 1986, was among the first to recognize the need for a more rapidly deployable and stronger form of peacekeeping. The national armies who had been involved in the major deployments of the 1990s also produced their own field manuals in response to their experiences, all of them trying to define an area of operation between peacekeeping and peace enforcement. In terms of force size, Mackinlay has distinguished three possible force levels: At the highest level are the enforcement operations authorized under chapter 7, which employ large numbers of troops (e.g., in Korea, 390,000) equipped with combat aircraft, naval support, and offensive armored units. These operations do not act impartially but set out to defeat a perceived aggressor. Midlevel operations have force levels of around 20,000 to 25,000 (as in Cambodia, Somalia, and Yugoslavia); low-level forces are the traditional interpositional and observer forces, with up to 1,500 troops (as in Cyprus and the Golan Heights), and the transition and verification missions (e.g., in Namibia), with up to 5,000 personnel. The midlevel force is a multifunctional force that is international in command. Unlike low-level forces, it is not simply symbolic and should be organized to respond to violence directed against the mandate of the mission. Force, however, should be used impartially, against all who oppose the mandate, and not selectively or punitively. Even though consent may be in doubt in the sense that it may not be given by local factions or warlords, the forces must remain impartial. However, midlevel multifunctional forces with 20,000 troops cannot sustain a forceful posture for long, and such a force's main function should be to protect civil and humanitarian agencies, also operating under the mandate. Though it needs to use force against local armed factions, the multinational force at midlevel still must work not to alienate the community in which it is based and must see its objective as the cultivation of consent. One major problem that arose in the first midlevel peacekeeping operations of the early 1990s, however, was the tendency for the stamina, responsiveness, and cohesion of the UN force to weaken in the harsh conditions of the conflict. Mackinlay attributed this to certain "drag factors" causing the UN force to degrade in the field, namely, unclear political objectives, insufficient control over the force's support assets, the autonomy of the different national contingents making up the force, and the poor coordination of military and civilian elements of the operation. These problems cannot easily be addressed, but a variety of reforms have been proposed that are intended to make second-generation peacekeeping more effective, including the renewal of the Military Staff Committee, the use of a stronger political tier of command politically and militarily at UN headquarters in New York, and the development of standing and standby forces. However, the reforms suggested are only part of what is necessary if effective second-generation peacekeeping missions are to be developed. On the one hand, it is recognized that military peacekeeping must be integrated with broader and more effective mechanisms of conflict resolution. Furthermore, it is also argued that peacekeeping missions must be more integrated into the tasks and processes of economic and social development; they cannot be solely concerned with short-term security and emergency relief. During the 1990s there has been greater awareness of the role of development and peace building within peacekeeping—the experiences of El Salvador (the United Nations Observer Mission in El Salvador [ONUSAL]) and Mozambique (the United Nations Operation in Mozambique [ONUMOZ]) being important in developing this awareness—but it is also recognized that there is some way to go before security, relief, conflict-resolution, development, and peace-building components are working coherently together in peace operations.

See also First-generation peacekeeping
References and further reading Daniel and Hayes (1995); Fetherston (1994a); Ginifer (1996); Mackinlay (1996); Mackinlay and Chopra (1992)

Secretary-general

See Annan, Kofi; Boutros-Ghali, Boutros; Hammarskjöld, Dag; Lie,

Trygve; Pérez de Cuéllar, Javier; Thant, U; United Nations: agencies; United Nations: organization; Waldheim, Kurt

Security Council, United Nations
See United Nations: agencies; United Nations: organization

SFOR (Stabilization Force), 1997–
See Bosnia and Herzegovina

Sierra Leone (United Nations Observer Mission in Sierra Leone, 1998–)

Conflict Profile
The conflict in Sierra Leone began in 1991 when guerilla fighters of the Revolutionary United Front (RUF) attempted to overthrow the government. In November 1994 the United Nations appointed a Special Envoy to work with representatives of the Organization of African Unity and the Economic Community of West African States (ECOWAS), in an attempt to secure a negotiated settlement. In 1996, with the conflict still continuing, Dr. Ahmed Tejan Kabbah was elected president and subsequent negotiations between Dr. Kabbah and the RUF resulted, in November 1996, in a peace agreement called the Abidjan Accord. The peace process was aborted, however, when a coup d'état resulted in the overthrow of President Kabbah's government, and its replacement by a military junta known as the Armed Forces Revolutionary Council. In February 1998 military forces belonging to the Military Observer Group of ECOWAS entered Sierra Leone from Liberia and overthrew the junta, and the democratically elected president, Dr. Kabbah, was returned to power. In June 1998 the secretary-general, Kofi Annan, reported to the Security Council that the UN should contribute to restoring peace and stability to the country by assisting with the disarming and demobilizing of former combatants.

The Deployment of UNOMSIL
In response to the report of the Secretary General, the Security Council established the United Nations Observer Mission in Sierra Leone (UNOMSIL) under Resolution 1181. UNOMSIL has an authorized strength of 70 unarmed military observers, a medical unit, five civilian police advisors, 48 international civilian personnel, and 48 locally recruited personnel. It is mandated to monitor the security condition of the country as a whole; to monitor the disarmament and demobilization of former combatants; and to monitor respect for international humanitarian law. Since the mission peronnel are unarmed, the monitoring work is only to be attempted in areas where the military situation is safe and secure enough for UNOMSIL to operate.

The headquarters of UNOMSIL are in Freetown, the capital city. The SRSG and Chief of Mission is Mr. Francis Okelo (Uganda). The Chief Military Observer is Brig. Gen. Subhash Joshi (India). Estimated costs for the initial six months are $18.3 million.

References and further reading
UNDPKO website, http://www.un.org/depts/dpko

Sinai
See Multinational Force and Observers; UNEF I; UNEF II; UNTSO

Somalia

United Nations Operation in Somalia I and II (UNOSOM I and II), 1992–1995; Unified Task Force (UNITAF), 1992

Conflict Profile
Until the 1990s the crisis in Somalia was not a priority on the UN Security Council agenda. However, the overthrow of Muhammad Siyad Barre's regime in January 1991 further intensified a violent civil war and perpetuated the anarchy in Somalia. Barre's fall created a power vacuum in which the various clans struggled for control of different parts of the country. Since then, the fighting has resulted in widespread death and destruction, with an estimated 4.5 million people (half the population) needing emergency humanitarian assistance, 1.5 million refugees fleeing into neighboring countries, and over 400,000 deaths.

Until the colonial era the Somali "nation" was not a single political unit; political identity was based on clan affiliation. When the Ethiopian empire and the colonial powers of Britain, Italy, and France divided the Horn of Africa and the lands of the Somali peoples into five states—British Somaliland, Italian Somalia, French Somaliland (Djibouti), the Ethiopian Ogaden, and northern Kenya—the notion of a Somali nation state began to emerge. The present unitary state of Somalia (the territories of the Republic of Somalia, which include the unrecognized Somaliland Republic) came into existence in 1960 when the former British Somaliland Protectorate in northern Somalia and Italian Somaliland merged. The more than six million Somalis form a single ethnic unit in the northeastern tip of the Horn of Africa. They occupy nearly 1,036,000 square kilometers of arid savanna grassland. Two-thirds (approximately four million) live within the boundaries of the Somali state (which covers almost 640,000 square kilometers), two million in Ethiopia's Ogaden region, 240,000 in northern Kenya, and approximately 100,000 in the republic of Djibouti.

As a predominantly semidesert region with limited vegetation cover and water resources, Somalia is essentially a pastoral republic. Between 60 and 70 percent of the population within the Somali state practice pastoralism, making it central to the cultural and economic life of the country. The Somalis raise a variety of animals, including cattle, sheep, goats, and camels, with camel-herding forming the base of Somali material life. The remaining Somalis are cultivators who occupy the area between the Shabelle and Juba Rivers, the most fertile agricultural region in the country.

Dispersed throughout the Horn, the Somali-speaking people form one of the largest ethnic groups in Africa. They are a Cushitic-speaking family belonging to the Hamitic group, which includes the Afar, Oromo, Saho, and Beja peoples of the Horn. The Somali are ethnically, linguistically, and religiously homogeneous: They share a common ancestry, a single language, and an Islamic (Sunni) heritage resulting from their early trading links with the Arabian Peninsula. Yet they are divided by clan, subclan, and family, which explains much of Somalia's past and present troubles.

The clan is the most important factor in Somali society, with clan identity often undercutting national and religious identities. Based on an elaborate genealogy traced to two brothers, Samaale and Sab, the Somali are divided into six clan-families: the Dir, Issaq, Darod, Hawiye (descendants of Samaale who together make up 70 percent of the population), Digil, and Rahanweyne (descendants of Sab). These clan-families are further divided into subsidiary clans or lineage groups.

The clan-families are to some extent geographically and historically distinct. The Digil and Rahanweyne are agropastoralists living in the Shabelle and Juba Valleys and are often looked down upon by the other, primarily nomadic, clans. They also speak their own distinctive dialect (Af-maymay), although they understand the Somali spoken elsewhere. The Dir live in the Harar-Zeila area in the northwest, whose neighbors in the west are the Issaq (in the former British Somali Protectorate). The Issaq are an offshoot of the Dir who, together with the Hawiye, are grouped together as Irir. The Issaq neighbor the Darod, the largest and most widely distributed of all the Somali groups, inhabiting northeastern Somalia, northeastern Kenya, and the Ogaden region of eastern Ethiopia. The Hawiye occupy the Hiran and Mudug regions and Benadir (where Mogadishu is located, although Mogadishu contains representatives of all the Somali groups in addition to its own distinctive Arabicized city populations, known as Reer Hamar, and the Asharaf). The Hawiye clans also exist across the Shabelle River into the Digil and Rahanweyn areas, in the Trans-Juba region along with the Darod clans, and in northeastern Kenya.

The Somali kinship system and the flexible and constantly shifting alliances of clan kinship groups are firmly embedded in the social, political, and economic culture of the Somali people. Power and politics, in particular, are exercised through temporary coalitions of lineages that are created and broken as interest and opportunity arise. Because of the predominantly nomadic lifestyle—and therefore widely dispersed population—there has been no need for a single political unit, kingship, or central authority. In the absence of a centralized political organization, the clan is the most important political unit in the traditional system. Political alliance is determined by agnatic descent (that is, passed down through the male), and political division corresponds to differences in agnatic origin. The clan itself fosters a tenacious sense of community, invariably protecting and supporting its members.

For the first nine years of its independence Somalia experienced a succession of democratically elected governments. However, in 1969 Somali President Abdirashid Sharma'arke was assassinated, and the Soviet-trained army seized power in a coup d'état. Under the leadership of Gen. Muhammad Siyad Barre of the Marehan (Darod), the Supreme Revolutionary Council (SRC) was created as the new force and "Scientific Socialism" was adopted as the guiding ideology for national development. Initially, Barre's regime seemed promising: It emphasized national unity that transcended clannism and implemented numerous legal and administrative reforms and social, political, and economic programs.

First with Soviet assistance and later with U.S. assistance, Barre was able to build Africa's largest army. Somalia's spending on its military, compared to that on social programs, was proportionately the highest in the world—five dollars was spent on its armed forces for every dollar it spent on education and health. During the 1980s the United States gave up to $200 million in military aid to Barre's regime, and in June 1988, a few weeks after the outbreak of war in northern Somalia, the United States delivered $1.4 million in military aid. But the United States and the Soviet Union were not the only suppliers of military equipment. At different times Italy, Romania, East Germany, Iraq, Iran, Libya, South Africa, Saudi Arabia, and China have all contributed to the massive arsenal of weapons that Somali warlords have had at their disposal.

In 1977 war broke out between Somalia and Ethiopia as Barre attempted to reclaim the Somali-inhabited Ogaden region of eastern Ethiopia. The war received widespread support from the Somalis and was a high point of Somali nationalism and Barre's popularity. However, a year later, Somalia's Cuban-backed army was defeated by the Soviet-supported Ethiopian army, adding to the growing political instability. Somalia's defeat led to a large influx of Ogadeni (Darod) refugees into the north, which disturbed the existing clan demography and further eroded any remaining sense of national unity. With his popularity declining, Barre adopted a divide-and-rule policy with the various clans. In response, the clans began to arm themselves, and before 1988 there were numerous attempted coups.

Each of the clans took a turn at challenging the regime and contributing to the beginnings of the civil war. In 1978 an unsuccessful coup by the Majeerteen (Darod) clan led to the formation of the anti-Barre liberation front, the Somali Salvation Democratic Front (SSDF) in northeast Somalia. In 1981 the Issaq in the north—in response to the threat to their land by Ogadeni refugees and the alienating, dictatorial policies of Barre—began a guerrilla war with the founding of the Somali National Movement (SNM). Fighting escalated explosively in 1988 when the SNM captured the northern cities Burao and Hargeysa, the region's largest city. In retribution, the Somali Armed Forces carried out a systematic attack on the Issaq, forcing an estimated 600,000 civilians, primarily women and children, to flee to Ethiopia and killing approximately 50,000 people between May 1988 and March 1989. In the late 1980s disaffection with Barre's regime also set in among the Hawiye in southern Somalia, who formed the United Somali Congress (USC).

Increasingly, Barre's army was fighting on several fronts, and by late 1990 he was only in control of Mogadishu. In January 1991 Barre was forced to flee the city. As his troops moved south they adopted a scorched-earth policy, slaughtering livestock, destroying crops, and killing local cultivators. Following his flight, he reconstituted his army as the Somali National Front (SNF) and twice attempted to recapture Mogadishu. (In April 1992 Barre fled from Somalia to Kenya and then to Nigeria, where he died of natural causes in January 1995.)

Barre's departure created a power vacuum in Somalia. The USC took control of Mogadishu and appointed Ali Mahdi Mohammed of the Abgaal (Hawiye) as interim president of Somalia. However, the USC quickly broke into rival factions based on different subclans of the Hawiye. One of the factions—the Somali National Alliance (SNA)—was headed by Gen. Mohammed Farah

Aidid of the Habre Gedir (Hawiye) (who, ironically, had been army chief of staff when Barre took power). He had led the USC's military operations that successfully overthrew Barre. However, his election as chairman of the USC at a congress held near the Ethiopia-Somalia border in 1990 was not recognized by the Mogadishu-based faction that appointed Ali Mahdi. General Aidid and several other factional leaders scathingly contested the appointment of Ali Mahdi.

Throughout 1991 the entire Somali state was engulfed in fighting. With no central government, rival factions fought for power over different regions. The SSDF gained power in the northeast; rival factions of the USC fought for control of Mogadishu and adjacent regions; the SNM reclaimed the territory of the former British Somaliland and declared the secession of the northwest region as the independent Republic of Somaliland (although it has not been recognized by the international community); and new factions emerged throughout Somalia, each trying to defend its own interests.

Despite a number of mediation efforts, the crisis worsened and Somali civil and political institutions completely collapsed. In November 1991 civil war broke out between Aidid and Ali Mahdi in Mogadishu. The city was littered with more than 500,000 weapons left by the former Somali army; prices for weapons in Mogadishu fell dramatically (e.g., $50 for an AK-47, $100 for a rocket launcher). It is estimated that as many as 25,000 civilians were killed in the fighting up to March 1992.

The situation in Mogadishu was further complicated by the continued warfare in the south of the country, especially around Kismayu and Baidoa, between USC forces and Barre's SNF. Fighting in the agricultural areas was disastrous: Grain stores and livestock were plundered, water supplies were destroyed, and local farming populations—some two million people—were violently displaced. The consequences of war at the time of a serious drought led to the devastating famine crisis that hit Somalia in 1992–1993. Approximately 4.5 million people—more than half of the country's population—were threatened with starvation and severe malnutrition, and the famine cost an estimated 300,000 lives. The humanitarian situation was catastrophic.

Faced with this crisis and despite the total lack of security, the United Nations continued with its relief operations in association with the International Committee of the Red Cross/Red Crescent (ICRC) and other nongovernmental organizations (NGOs). However, under such lawless conditions efforts to deliver humanitarian aid were frequently obstructed and in some areas impossible. On several occasions, the UN agencies had to temporarily evacuate their personnel and work from Djibouti and Kenya.

On 23 January 1992, as a result of increasing violence and looting of relief supplies, Security Council Resolution (SCR) 733 imposed a complete arms embargo on Somalia, finally placing the country on the UN's agenda. The UN secretary-general, Boutros Boutros-Ghali, in cooperation with the Organization of African Unity (OAU), the Organization of the Islamic Conference (OIC), and the League of Arab States (LAS), called for the cessation of hostilities and a political settlement of the conflict. After a series of talks between the organizations' representatives and the two main factional leaders (Ali Mahdi and Aidid), an Agreement on the Implementation of a Cease-Fire was signed on 3 March. Following the cease-fire agreement, SCR 746 was adopted on 17 March 1992 urging the continuation of the UN's humanitarian work in Somalia. On 27 and 28 March, agreements were signed with the rival factions in Mogadishu to deploy UN observers to monitor the cease-fire and UN security personnel to ensure the safe delivery of humanitarian aid. The secretary-general also submitted a 90-Day Plan of Action to provide $23 million in aid to help the Somali population. Mohammed Sahnoun, an Algerian diplomat, was appointed as special representative to consult with the Somali leaders.

Deployment of UNOSOM I

The agreements paved the way for the establishment of the first United Nations Operation in Somalia (UNOSOM I) on 24 April 1992 under SCR 751. The operation was capaciously mandated to facilitate an immediate cessation of hostilities throughout the country, maintain a permanent cease-fire, create a secure environment for humanitarian assistance by disarming and controlling the weapons of warring parties and supervising the indigenous police force, assist in the rehabilitation of existing political institutions and economy, and promote national reconciliation and peaceful settlement. Progress was slow, however; it took three months of intensive negotiations for the first 50 unarmed observers to be sent, and another two months passed before 500 Pakistani troops were deployed.

During this period the humanitarian crisis ascended to alarming levels. Much of the interclan warfare had declined, but it was replaced by armed looting of food aid, which further exacerbated the famine. The famine was killing 1,000 people every day in the south and was responsible for 70 percent of the deaths of children under five years of age. The Pakistani troops found it impossible to secure the ports and safeguard the food shipments. A second 100-Day Action Program for Accelerated Humanitarian Assistance worth $82.7 million was set back as a result of the hostilities. (Eventually, $67.3 million was received.) The Security Council announced that an additional 3,000 troops would be deployed.

A number of significant events were to follow. Aidid gave orders for the withdrawal of Pakistani troops in Mogadishu, as well as any troops in Kismayu and Berbera. The troops' refusal to withdraw increased the fragility of the situation. More food convoys were hijacked, and ships delivering aid were unable to unload. Clashes with the UN secretary-general had forced Sahnoun to resign, and he was replaced by Ismat Kittani, an Iraqi diplomat and senior member of the UN Secretariat, who had a completely different approach to the conflict. After only a short time in Somalia, Kittani reported that little progress was likely amid such a crisis.

Deployment of UNITAF
In response, the Security Council adopted SCR 794 under chapter 7 (3 December 1992), which authorized a deployment of U.S. troops to Somalia, offered by the outgoing U.S. President George Bush. UNOSOM would work with a unified command of member state forces (37,000 troops from more than 20 nations, including, at its peak, 29,000 U.S. troops) and continue with its original mandate after the withdrawal of the unified command. The U.S.-led Unified Task Force (UNITAF), code-named Operation Restore Hope, was deployed to the south of Somalia on 9 December 1992 and was exclusively mandated to provide a secure environment for the urgent delivery of humanitarian assistance. The main warlords in Mogadishu had agreed to the intervention following talks with the U.S. special envoy Robert Oakley, a former U.S. ambassador to Somalia. The mission is probably best remembered for images of television cameras filming U.S. Navy Seals landing on the beach in Mogadishu as though it was a covert operation.

Following the arrival of UNITAF, a reconciliation conference was hastily arranged among the 15 armed political groups. Although the conference resulted in a cease-fire agreement, signed by the warlords on 8 January 1993 in Addis Ababa, the agreement was criticized because the Somali people do not see the warlords as their representatives. However, the United Nations targeted the warlords because the international community saw them as the country's leaders. Cooperation with them was perceived as being essential, yet it only legitimized the warlords' positions.

Remarkable progress was made on the humanitarian front in the south. A civilian-military operation center (CMOC) was established to assist humanitarian-military cooperation, and large supplies of food and other emergency relief supplies were successfully delivered into the neediest areas. In addition, the two main Somali factions and UNITAF set up a security committee that met daily, and UNITAF helped establish an indigenous Somali police force. Although much had been achieved by UNITAF in six months, a secure environment had not been established, and incidents of violence continued. Moreover, the humanitarian and political situation in many parts of the country remained unstable (see Map 8).

Deployment of UNOSOM II
Military command was transferred from UNITAF to UNOSOM on 4 May 1993. The operation became known as UNOSOM II and was endowed with enforcement powers under chapter 7 through

UNOSOM II deployment as of November 1993

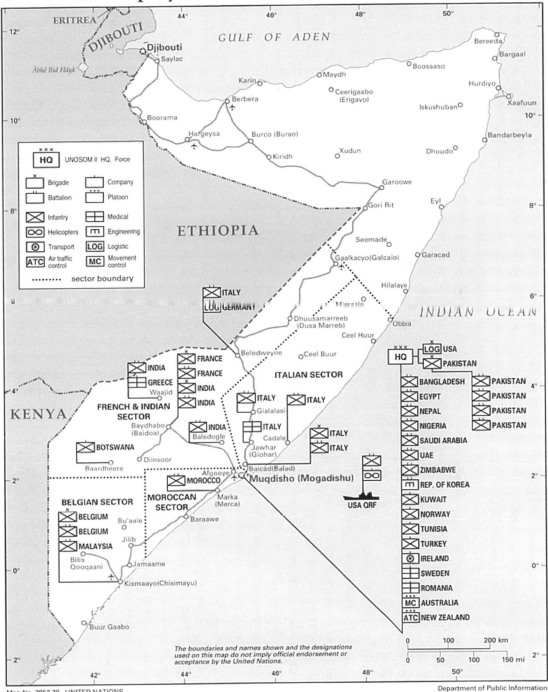

SCR 814 (26 March 1993). The authorized use of force signaled a major change in the UN's approach to Somalia. In contrast to the UNITAF mission, which was confined to the south of the country, UNOSOM troops were deployed throughout Somalia. UNOSOM II's mandate was also broadened to (1) monitor the cease-fire between the warring factions and take action against any faction that violated the cease-fire; (2) supervise the factions after their disarmament and encampment; (3) maintain a register of small arms seized; (4) ensure security of ports, airports, and communications for the delivery of humanitarian aid; (5) protect personnel, installations, and equipment of the humanitarian agencies; (6) establish a program to remove land mines; (7) repatriate refugees and displaced Somalis; (8) reestablish national and regional political and civil administrations; and (9) rehabilitate the economy. Essentially, the ambitious mandate required UNOSOM II to rebuild the state of Somalia.

To deal with the continuing humanitarian crisis, the United Nations, along with assistance from Somalis, UN agencies, ICRC, and NGOs, put together a Relief and Rehabilitation Program and organized a UN Conference on Humanitarian Assistance to Somalia in Addis Ababa (11–13 March 1993). Donors attending the conference pledged over $130 million. The Conference for National Reconciliation in Somalia followed on 15 March with the aim of creating a transitional political and legislative authority for Somalia over a two-year transitional period. The agreement included four basic institutions of authority: a Transitional National Council (TNC), which would act as the main political authority and would include members from each of the regions and from each of the factions; central administrative departments; a regional council in each of the 18 regions of the country; and a district council in each of the 92 districts. Although the conference aimed at including a broader representation than the conference held in January—by involving women, religious leaders, elders, and intellectuals—the warlords were the only signatories to the final agreement on 27 March. The process was nevertheless seen as a significant step. A series of similar reconciliation forums were initiated and supported by

UNOSOM, including a successful peace process in May in Kismayu and the Lower and Middle Juba regions—one of the most conflict-ridden areas of the country.

One of the primary tasks of UNOSOM II was the disarmament of all Somali factions and armed groups. However, these efforts were met with hostility by the factions, especially Aidid's. A series of confrontations evolved between the SNA and Pakistani troops, killing 24 UN Pakistani soldiers and 75 Somalis. Following this fighting, the Security Council adopted SCR 837 on 1 July 1993, strongly condemning the unprovoked armed attacks against UNOSOM II. Humanitarian agencies were encouraged to leave Mogadishu, and the United Nations prepared for military action in order to implement the resolution. On the night of 11 June a three-day air offensive began, targeting areas around Aidid's compound. Aidid refused to surrender. On 18 June a ground offensive was launched in an attempt to take his compound, but by the time the United Nations arrived Aidid had left. A warrant was issued and a $25,000 reward was offered for Aidid's arrest. Many civilians were killed during these confrontations, and the violence further halted any progress achieved in the reconciliation processes. Various UN contingents began to question the UN operation, which seemed to be a war with Aidid and which was almost exclusively being planned by U.S. personnel.

In continuing support of UNOSOM II's mandate, the United States deployed the elite Army Rangers and Delta Force commandos (under U.S., not UN, command). Violent incidents continued, including a disturbing attack in July by U.S. forces on a building in Mogadishu where an SNA meeting was taking place. The attack resulted in a large number of Somali casualties, many of whom were Somali elders trying to find a peaceful solution to the conflict. Following the incident, Somalis from other clans started supporting Aidid, and in retaliation he made a calculated decision to kill U.S. soldiers. Throughout August and September there were fatal attacks on Americans. U.S. forces fought back, killing hundreds of Somalis, many of them innocent civilians.

The final blow came on 3 October when U.S. special forces were trapped by armed SNA members as they attempted to capture senior members in Mogadishu. Fighting broke out, and 18 of the special forces were killed and between 500 and 1,000 Somalis died. The bodies of the U.S. soldiers were subjected to public acts of outrage that were seen on television around the world. Aidid had figured correctly: The systematic attacks on U.S. soldiers powerfully influenced U.S. opinion. President Bill Clinton announced the complete withdrawal of U.S. troops from Somalia by 31 March 1994.

Within days of the attack the USC/SNA declared a unilateral cease-fire of hostilities against UNOSOM II forces. Following a period of relative quiet, the Security Council adopted Resolution 878 (29 October 1993), which extended UNOSOM II's mandate until 18 November 1993. At the forefront of UNOSOM's efforts was the humanitarian issue. At the request of UNOSOM II, a framework for long-term reconstruction and recovery was drafted by a task force (comprised of donors, UN agencies, and NGOs under the coordination of the World Bank). Efforts continued to rebuild political institutions, and 52 out of 81 district councils and 8 out of 13 regional councils were established by December 1993. UNOSOM II continued to support the police and judicial programs. The situation in Somalia was steadily improving.

At this point UNOSOM II was at a crossroads. Although progress had been made in many areas, there was still no effectively functioning government and no national armed force or fully organized police force. There were still incidents of banditry and outbreaks of localized interclan fighting throughout the country, and security continued to be a critical problem for international staff. Furthermore, the incidents in June and October damaged the UN's record of progress and initiated the active rearmament of factions in anticipation of renewed fighting. In reexamining the mandate of UNOSOM II a number of options were considered. The Security Council decided to approve the secretary-general's recommendation for the continuation of UNOSOM II by its Resolution 897 (4 February 1994), yet it authorized a gradual reduction of UNOSOM troops to 22,000. Under this renewal UNOSOM II would refrain from using coercive methods and would rely on the cooperation of the Somali parties in implementing the Addis Ababa

Agreements. The goal was to complete the process by March 1995.

A series of informal consultations were held with the leaders of the Somali political factions regarding the overall political and security situation in the country. In March 1994 a meeting was held in Nairobi with Aidid and Ali Mahdi, the first time they had met since December 1992. After lengthy discussions, Aidid and Ali Mahdi signed a declaration on national reconciliation and committed themselves to finding peaceful means of resolving the conflict. It was also agreed that a National Reconciliation Conference would be convened in order to restore sovereignty to the country. UNOSOM II's mandate was extended for another six months (by SCR 923 of 31 May 1994) in order to ensure the continued commitment of the Somali parties to political reconciliation.

The progress was interrupted in June and July by clashes among clans and subclans, especially in Mogadishu. For several weeks the fighting stopped all humanitarian activities. Progress on national reconciliation also ceased, and new subgroups of factions emerged. In addition, UNOSOM II continued to suffer humiliating attacks. During the Zimbabwean UN unit's withdrawal from Belet Wein in late July, their 150-strong unit was stopped by several hundred members of Aidid's forces. After one week, during which a UN soldier was killed, the Zimbabweans were forced to surrender. Aidid's forces took over $2 million worth of equipment, and, using the white UN armored personnel carriers and dressed as Zimbabwean peacekeepers, Aidid's forces captured two towns in the Bakool region.

Following a special mission sent to Somalia from 28 July to 4 August, the Security Council expressed concern over the increasingly unstable security in the country, as well as the lack of progress toward reconciliation. On 30 September 1994 SCR 946 extended UNOSOM II's mandate until 31 October 1994. Another visit in October, by Undersecretary-General for Peacekeeping Operations Kofi Annan, confirmed the special mission's reports of August. The operation was further extended for an interim period until 4 November in order to complete the review of the mandate. On 4 November 1994 the Security Council, by SCR 954, authorized a phased withdrawal of UNOSOM troops, setting 31 March 1995 as the final date for complete withdrawal. Without full cooperation from the Somali parties there was little the United Nations could do. As the final UNOSOM troops were evacuated in March 1995, hundreds of Somalis descended on the ports and airports to loot what they could.

The authorized strength of UNOSOM II was approximately 28,000 military personnel, from 30 nations, and 54 civilian police. There were also 17,700 troops of the United States Joint Task Force in Somalia that supported UNOSOM II but were not a part of it and remained under U.S. command. There were six main UN organizations at work in Somalia coordinating overall humanitarian efforts: the Food and Agriculture Organization (FAO), the United Nations Development Program (UNDP), the United Nations Children's Fund (UNICEF), the United Nations High Commissioner for Refugees (UNHCR), the World Food Program (WFP), and the World Health Organization (WHO). Additionally, there were some 2,800 civilian staff and more than 30 international organizations and many local NGOs working with the United Nations, with ICRC providing assistance throughout the operation. The operating costs for UNOSOM I amounted to $42,931,700. The operating costs for UNOSOM II amounted to $1,643,485,500.

Intervention in Somalia was one of the most challenging of the UN's undertakings and left a significant historical mark. It was the first time that the United Nations had intervened in a collapsed state without a centralized government and in which it had to deal with severe famine and a multisided civil war. There were a number of other firsts: It was the most expensive UN peacekeeping operation ever staged, the largest multilateral force ever used, and the first time that the United States had placed its troops under the UN flag and command.

The UN's operations in Somalia were extensive and complex, involving attempts at peacemaking, peacekeeping, peace enforcement, and peace building, with a mix of success and failure. The greatest success was in meeting the difficult humanitarian challenge. An estimated quarter of a million lives were saved. A second achievement in Somali was the UN's assistance in bringing about a cease-fire. However, its objective to rebuild a collapsed state, without full cooperation from the Somali factions, proved too ambitious. (Two of the conferences can be said to have been successful: the National Reconciliation Conference in March 1993 and the meeting of all the factions in Nairobi in March 1994. However, some would argue that the UN's approach was ineffectual in that it focused on a top-down approach that was neither impartial nor indigenous.) There was also some success in restoring the Somali police.

Still, the tragic failure in Somalia almost certainly led to the lack of action in Rwanda in 1994 and has inhibited the international community's enthusiasm for large-scale peacekeeping and peace enforcement. The UN's experience in Somalia has certainly provided important lessons for future involvement in violent conflicts and complex humanitarian emergencies. These lessons include drawing a discernible line between peacekeeping and peace enforcement activities; establishing clear, achievable mandates and clear rules of engagement; fully preparing and training the multinational troops; providing for clear channels of command and coordinated civilian-military activity; and eliciting local resources and empowering the indigenous population.

Since the UN's departure from Somalia in March 1995 there have been few improvements in the nation's crisis. Agreements made between the factions have continuously been broken. Aidid was killed in clan fighting in July 1996 only to be replaced by his son, Hussein Aidid. In October Aidid announced his claim to the presidency, which was bitterly contested by other factions, especially Ali Mahdi, who also has claims to the presidency. Somalia remains a fragmented, warring society.

See also Complex emergency; Military-humanitarian relations; Pakistan; Peace enforcement; Sahnoun, Mohammed; Training for peacekeeping

References and further reading Clarke and Herbst (1997); Hirsch and Oakley (1995); UNDPI (1996)

South Africa

United Nations Observer Mission to South Africa (UNOMSA), 1992

Conflict Profile

The first nonracial national elections to be held in South Africa represented the culmination of a protracted and sometimes bloody political struggle, which was widely supported internationally, against the apartheid state regime. The process accelerated during the early 1990s, as February 1990 saw both the release from prison of the leader of the African National Congress (ANC), Nelson Mandela, and the removal of a ban on political organizations by the then South African President F. W. de Klerk. Negotiations between the parties to the dispute ultimately led to an agreement on transitional arrangements that would precede elections for a parliamentary system. It was envisaged that this system would provide both a Constituent Assembly to develop a new national constitution and a Government of National Unity to run the country during the interim transitional period.

Deployment of UNOMSA

Broad international consensus that the apartheid regime in South Africa should be replaced by a democratically elected representative government led to various international initiatives to facilitate the negotiation process between the parties to the dispute. In August 1992 the UN Security Council adopted Security Council Resolution (SCR) 772, by which it authorized assistance to indigenous South African structures that had been established to administer, organize, supervise, and conduct free and fair elections in the country, such as the Independent Electoral Commission (IEC).

On 10 January the UN secretary-general, Boutros Boutros-Ghali, reported to the Security Council, suggesting that around 2,000 UN observers be deployed to South Africa to monitor the first free and fair elections in that country, and on 14 January 1994 the Security Council adopted SCR 894 approving the secretary-general's proposal. By the end of March 1994 some 500 observers had been deployed throughout South Africa, and 1,485 additional international electoral observers joined UNOMSA during the final electoral phase of the operation between 17 and 20 April 1994. A Joint Operations Unit (JOU) developed the electoral deployment plan in consultation with other intergovernmental observer missions that were also contributing to the observation process, comprising in total some 542 international electoral observers from the Organization of African Unity (OAU) (102 observers), the Commonwealth (118 observers), and the European Union (EU) (322 observers). The total number of observers deployed by intergovernmental observer missions working in coordination with UNOMSA totaled 2,527 (including the mission's own 1,985 observers).

In the period just preceding the elections the activities of the international observers included monitoring and reporting on voter education, monitoring the distribution of temporary voter cards, and observing IEC attempts to select sites for and establish balloting and counting stations. Furthermore, UNOMSA's peace-promotion activities facilitated the mission's electoral phase by providing access to grassroots contacts and nongovernmental organization (NGO) networks established during the first 16 months of the mission's deployment.

The UNOMSA mandate to observe the elections required it to monitor the actions of the IEC; the extent of freedom of organization, movement, assembly, and expression during the electoral campaign; compliance by the security forces with the requirements of the laws relating to the electoral process; equitable access to the media; electoral educational initiatives; and the distribution of identification documents and voter's cards to eligible voters. UNOMSA was also mandated to verify that the electoral environment was free and fair, coordinate the activities of non-UN observers, and set up effective coordination with South African and foreign NGOs, which were also observing the electoral process. Despite various complications along the way, the election process was ultimately declared to have been free and fair, and a fully democratic South African government was successfully returned, headed by President Nelson Mandela.

See also Angola (UNAVEM I–III); Mozambique (ONUMOZ, 1992–1994); Namibia (UNTAG, 1989)
References and further reading Boraine, Levy, and Scheffer (1997); International Peacekeeping

(1994–); Lake (1990); Merwe (1989); O'Brien (1994); Zartman (1995)

South Ossetia
See Commonwealth of Independent States

South Pacific Peacekeeping Force
See Papua New Guinea

Special representatives of the secretary-general

The special representative of the secretary-general (SRSG) is usually a civilian and a diplomat. The post of special representative is one of the two key posts appointed by the secretary-general in peacekeeping missions, the other being that of force commander. The SRSG is usually also designated as the head of mission. It is normal for the appointment of the SRSG and the force commander to be agreed upon in advance by the governments of the combatant countries. Appendix 2 lists the SRSGs who have served on UN peacekeeping missions since 1956.

Sri Lanka

Indian Peacekeeping Force, 1987–1990

Conflict Profile

Sri Lanka (whose name means "resplendent island") is situated in the Indian Ocean just off the southeastern end of India. It is separated from the southern Indian state of Tamil Nadu by the 20-mile-wide Palk Strait. Historical and cultural links between the people of the Jaffna Peninsula, at the northern tip of Sri Lanka, and this state of 50 million Tamils have always been close. Sri Lanka measures some 270 miles north to south and 170 miles west to east, an area of 25,300 square miles, about the size of Ireland or Tasmania. Nowhere on the island is more than 80 miles from the sea. The center is mountainous, rising to a maximum height of 8,300 feet, and the climate is tropical with two monsoons, one in the southwest from May to July and one in the north between October and January. It has a population of 18 million made up of Sinhalese (74 percent, mostly Buddhist), Sri Lankan Tamils (12.6 percent, mainly Hindu), Plantation Tamils (5.6 percent, Hindu), Moors (7 percent, Tamil-speaking but of Muslim faith), and Christians from both Sinhalese and Tamil communities. Other groups include Burghers, Malays, and Veddas. The majority of the people (78 percent) live in rural areas.

Compared with that of other parts of the British colonial empire, Ceylon's transition to independence in 1948 was comparatively peaceful, with some consensus between the different ethnic communities. However, policies by successive Sri Lankan (and Sinhalese-dominated) governments and the reactions to these by Tamil people sowed the seeds of what was to become a protracted and vicious conflict. Ceylon became the Republic of Sri Lanka in February 1972.

The conflict, which has been raging at varying intensities since 1983, can be described as being between the largest and most militarily effective Tamil militant group, the Liberation Tigers of Tamil Eelam (LTTE) and the government of Sri Lanka (GOSL). The situation in Sri Lanka has been further inflamed by two violent insurrections, in 1972 and 1989, by the Janatha Vimukht Peramuna (JVP), a group made up mostly of disaffected Sinhalese youth that combined a potent mixture of Marxism and Sinhala nationalism. Although the focus here will be on the conflict between the Indian Peacekeeping Force (IPKF), the LTTE, and the GOSL, the rebellion by the JVP during this time had an important influence on the course of events.

Several general factors can be identified as being root causes of the conflict between the Sinhalese and Tamil communities, which eventually led to the intervention of the IPKF in July 1987. These include political, historical, religious, economic, and cultural factors within the context of what has been described as the double-minority factor: The Sinhalese see themselves as a majority in Sri Lanka but as a minority within the Indian subcontinent, and the Tamils are a minority within Sri Lanka but a majority with respect to the Indian subcontinent.

As for any conflict, there is complex disagreement over historical territorial divisions and spheres of influence. Until 1815 Sri Lanka had never been territorially unified but, rather, had consisted of several kingdoms. The Tamils claim that their ancestors occupied the north and east long before the Sinhalese peoples arrived, and it was the British who "unified" the country through military conquest, imposed colonialism (for administrative and security reasons), and as elsewhere employed the "divide and rule" policy. Arguments about "who has been there the longest" rage between Tamil and Sinhalese academics and advocates. One myth says that the Sinhalese are of Aryan origin, migrants from the Bengal region, who now have an unbroken history 2,500 years old. The land colonization policies of successive GOSL administrations have caused much resentment. It has been Sinhalese policy to establish "colonies" of Sinhalese settlers (mostly farmers) especially in the eastern province, an area traditionally viewed by Tamil nationalists as theirs. The GOSL says that the colonization program is intended to populate uninhabited areas and relieve overpopulation in more crowded areas of the island. Tamils say that its real objective is to dominate Tamil areas and to change their ethnodemography. Views differ over the importance that religion has played in the conflict. Some say that historically there was no "religious" conflict and that the religious element seen in the conflict today is based on a twentieth-century interpretation of Buddhism (as encouraged by Henry Olcot and Dharmapala) that began to explicitly link Sinhala nationalism and Buddhism, giving vent to Buddhist chauvinism. This concept of Buddhism held that Buddha had delegated to Sri Lanka the job of ensuring the continuance of "pure" Buddhism and of saving Buddhism from infidels, that is, non-Buddhists; it held that "there is no Buddhism without the Sinhalese, and no Sinhalese without Buddhism," and that threats to Buddhism must be combated forcefully. In 1956 Tamil-Sinhalese relations took a further turn for the worse when the government of Prime Minister Sirimavo W. Bandaranaike legislated the Official Languages Act (the "Sinhala-Only" Bill). This affected all areas of life, including education, government services, and security forces.

In the view of Tamils there has been a lack of access to economic resources and political power bases because much of the economic wealth remains in the capital, Colombo, and the central and southern regions. Because of the past electoral and representational system, a "minority" group like the Tamils felt that they were excluded from having any real influence on political legislation and decision making. In the Vaddukodai Resolution of 1976 the main Tamil opposition party at the time, the Tamil United Liberation Front (TULF), called for self-determination for the Tamil people of Sri Lanka and for their own "homeland" (Tamil Eelam), where they were to have complete autonomy to ensure their security and prosperity. Since independence Tamils have claimed that they are discriminated against in education and in the police and the armed services. In colonial times Tamils traditionally dominated professional and white-collar positions, and the Sinhalese felt that, in relation to their percentage of the total population, Tamils were overrepresented in the universities and in such professional occupations as medicine, engineering, the police, and the judiciary. After independence various governments introduced legislation to reverse this trend, which Tamils say had the effect of discriminating unfairly against them. For example, Tamil students required higher marks than did Sinhalese students to enter university.

These general factors are fueled by each side's propaganda and demonizing of the other. For example, the Sinhalese accuse the Tigers of being fanatics who murder for no reason and who lack broad support from other Tamils; the Tamils assert that the Sinhalese are determined on the genocide of the Tamil people in Sri Lanka. Both sides have been implicated in acts of brutality, which was exacerbated during the JVP uprisings. Political violence has been commonplace, and state-sponsored violence was responsible for thousands of cases of extrajudicial killings and torture. Political leaders on both sides have manipulated events, exacerbated differences, and massaged facts to maintain and concentrate their own power, and this has played a crucial role in institutionalizing the ethnic conflict. Both the GOSL and the LTTE have extensively used mythology and symbolism in their manipulations. The result over the years has been to create deep mistrust and to allow little meaningful communication between the parties.

In the early 1980s the Indian government saw Sri Lanka's geostrategic and political position as a threat to its security. Several factors influenced this view, including visits by U.S. warships to the deep-water port of Trincomalee (India did not like the idea of another major power occupying this as a naval base), the Voice of America relay station built in Sri Lanka and operated by the United States Information Agency (and widely believed to be used by the CIA for intelligence gathering), close Sri Lankan relationships with Israeli intelligence, and military assistance to Sri Lanka from China and Pakistan. In addition, the possible formation of Tamil Eelam could have created a focal point around which Tamil Nadu politicians could agitate for the creation of a "Dravidian Nation" that might incorporate Tamil Eelam. Despite this last factor and because of internal domestic political pressure, India took an active role in lobbying support for the Tamil cause in the international diplomatic community, which made it difficult for GOSL to buy weapons in the open international market. This was especially so after the anti-Tamil riots of 1983, when the Research and Intelligence Wing (RAW), a specialist unit within Indian intelligence, began training and supplying Sri Lankan militants from bases in Tamil Nadu. Over the years Tamil Nadu has played a crucial role in India's responses to the Sri Lankan conflict. After the 1983 riots tens of thousands of Sri Lankan Tamils fled to Tamil Nadu. This exodus had two main effects: First, it "internationalized" the conflict, and second, it raised strong emotions among the Tamils of Tamil Nadu that put pressure on both Tamil Nadu and Indian national politicians to do something to mitigate the plight of Sri Lankan Tamils. The chief minister of Tamil Nadu, M. G. Ramachandran, had been a great patron of the LTTE during his lifetime.

In summary, the main Indian responses to the Sri Lanka conflict were diplomatic initiatives that included mediation and facilitation of peace talks and proposals between the GOSL and Tamil militant groups, covert operations by RAW and other elements of Indian intelligence in support of Tamil militants, international lobbying on behalf of the Sri Lankan Tamils, sanctuary for refugees, and the direct military intervention of the IPKF in 1987.

In April 1987 two events galvanized the GOSL into action against the LTTE and other militants: The LTTE ambushed some civilian buses and separated out and killed 128 unarmed Sinhalese men, women, and children passengers. Another group placed a bomb at the central bus terminal in Colombo that killed over 100 people. By May fighting between the LTTE and the Sri Lankan Armed Forces (SLAF) in the Jaffna Peninsula had intensified. Tens of thousands of refugees were arriving in Tamil Nadu, and there was a great upsurge of sympathy and support for the Sri Lankan Tamils. In June the SLAF launched Operation Liberation, which President J. R. Jayewardene called "a fight to the finish." The SLAF inflicted a major defeat on the LTTE at Vadamarachi and were poised to capture Jaffna. On 3 June India attempted to send emergency supplies to the peninsula via a convoy of small boats flying Red Cross flags. The convoy was stopped by the Sri Lankan navy and forced to return to Tamil Nadu. On 4 June Indian transport planes escorted by Mirage fighters air-dropped food to the Jaffna peninsula, in a direct violation of Sri Lankan sovereign airspace. India announced that it would not allow Jaffna to fall. Frantic diplomatic activity between the governments of J. R. Jayewardene in Colombo and Rajiv Gandhi in Delhi, in which the Indian high commissioner in Colombo, J. N. Dixit, played a pivotal role, finalized details of the Indo–Sri Lankan Agreement to Establish Peace and Normalcy in Sri Lanka (the accord). It had taken much effort by the Indians to obtain LTTE leader V. Prabhakaran's agreement, and it was later revealed that the LTTE had been offered a considerable amount of money to help persuade them. On 29 July 1987 Gandhi flew to Colombo to sign the accord with President Jayewardene. The signing prompted widespread anti-accord rioting, especially in Colombo and Sinhalese areas of southwest Sri Lanka, and the Sri Lankan prime minister, Ranasinghe Premadasa, refused to attend the ceremony. While Gandhi was inspecting a guard of honor during the signing ceremony, he was attacked by one of the Sri Lankan soldiers.

Since the accord was the instrument for the deployment of Indian Forces in Sri Lanka it is important to briefly review the key points and their general implications. The main provisions of the accord were that the northern and eastern provinces of Sri Lanka would join to form one administrative unit, with an elected Provincial Council, a governor, a chief minister, and a Board of Ministers; that a referendum would be held in the eastern province to allow the people there to decide whether they wished to be linked to the northern province or whether they wanted a separate eastern province; that an interim administration would be established; and that a general amnesty would be granted to Tamil political and other prisoners held under the Prevention of Terrorism Act. The Sri Lankan army would be confined to barracks, and Tamil militant groups would surrender their arms. All of this was to be underwritten and guaranteed by India, who would also provide a peacekeeping force to separate the protagonists and enforce the peace. An Annex to the Accord stated that Trincomalee and other Sri Lankan ports would not be made available for military use by any country in a manner prejudicial to India's interest, that the oil tank farm at Trincomalee would be developed as a joint venture between India and Sri Lanka, and that facilities set up by foreign broadcasting organizations in Sri Lanka would not be used for any military or intelligence purposes.

President Jayewardene's main requirements from the accord were that the LTTE would be disarmed and that they would accept the inherent unity of Sri Lanka, that India would provide the force to disarm the Tigers so that Sri Lankan forces could deal with the JVP uprising in the south, and that India would stop providing aid and sanctuary to the Tamil militants. In return GOSL would promise a degree of autonomy to the Tamils in the north and east and would ensure that no special forces of the United States, Israel, Pakistan, or any other country would be allowed to function from Sri Lankan soil. The accord also included several important guarantees of Indian action should any militant groups operating in Sri Lanka

not accept the proposed framework of proposals for a settlement. Specifically, India guaranteed that it would allow no Indian territory to be used for activities prejudicial to the unity, integrity, and security of Sri Lanka; that the Indian navy and coast guard would cooperate with the Sri Lankan navy in preventing Tamil militant activities from affecting Sri Lanka; that the government of India would give military assistance to the GOSL, if requested, to implement the accord proposals; that the government of India would expedite the repatriation of Indian citizens who were officially "residents" of India from Sri Lanka to India and would also facilitate the repatriation of Sri Lankan refugees from Tamil Nadu to Sri Lanka; and that GOSL and the government of India would cooperate in guaranteeing the physical security of all communities in the northern and eastern provinces.

Several associated factors played a part in leading Jayewardene to agree to the accord. Uppermost in his mind must have been India's warning that it would not allow the SLAF to take control of Jaffna. Jayewardene, along with many in the SLAF, was not sure that even if they did regain control of Jaffna they would be able to retain it. Also, importantly, Jayewardene had been assured that Prabhakaran (whom both Gandhi and Jayewardene considered the main Tamil spokesman) would be flown to Jaffna to order his commanders to comply and to oversee the disarming of the militants, and he had been further assured that if Prabhakaran did not do this properly India would force him to do so.

Prabhakaran and the LTTE viewed the accord with many misgivings. Because the accord supported a Sri Lankan unitary state, their vision of Tamil Eelam was less likely to come about. The accord also denied the Tamils sanctuary in India and threatened LTTE supremacy and dominance in Jaffna, and meant that after giving up their weapons, they would be defenseless against the Sri Lankan Army. Prabhakaran thought that Gandhi's motives had more to do with positioning India as a regional superpower than with promoting the best interests of Sri Lankan Tamils. He felt that the accord was being forced on him to help India establish colonial control over the Tamil areas of Sri Lanka. Prabhakaran was also opposed to the return of the Sri Lankan police to Jaffna and to the requirement that public meetings have IPKF permission. Soon after his return to Jaffna in August 1987, Prabhakaran said he would accept neither the accord, because it did not allow for complete independence, nor the referendum in the eastern province, because Tamils did not have an overall majority there.

Many Sinhalese indulged in several days of rioting, causing widespread damage, when details of the accord were made public. Sinhalese chauvinists claimed that "11 percent of the population would have control over one-third of the island." Buddhist monks went on hunger strikes in protest and the All Ceylon Buddhist Congress (ACBC) strongly condemned the accord. Sinhalese opponents to the accord thought that an IPKF intervention had denied the Sri Lankan army a final victory over the LTTE and that it was an intrusion into Sri Lanka's sovereign affairs. Particularly galling was India's apparent veto on who could or could not use the Trincomalee naval facilities and the power and presence of the IPKF in the eastern provinces. Other Sinhalese were worried that the Sri Lankan army would now have more time to deal with the JVP in the south, where, in consequence, violence would increase. Sinhalese skeptics thought that the Indian presence in support of unified Tamil areas was just a cover for the eventual creation of Eelam.

Most Tamil people initially welcomed the accord and the Indian troops. They saw the IPKF as protecting them from Sri Lankan army atrocities and offering a chance for peace. But they were concerned that if the militants were effectively disarmed and the IPKF then withdrew, they would again be open to abuse from Sri Lankan army and police and from other armed thugs.

The Deployment of IPKF

As a result of the Indo–Sri Lankan accord the IPKF was dispatched to Sri Lanka on 29 July 1987. Its key mission objectives were to

1. supervise a cease-fire between LTTE and the Sri Lankan Army.
2. accept the surrender of LTTE and other Tamil militants' weapons and if they refused

to surrender their weapons to disarm them by force.
3. police the northeast while an interim Tamil administration was established to prepare for elections for a Northeastern Provincial Council (NEPC), which would enable some devolution of power from Colombo to the Tamil people.

The deployment of initial IPKF elements from the Indian Army Fifty-Fourth Division was rapidly carried out so that Sri Lankan troops could be relocated in the south to strengthen security in the GOSL's battle against the JVP, who were violently opposed to the accord. The Indian air force (IAF) ferried over 4,000 SLAF troops within a few days from the peninsula to Colombo. The IPKF hoped that they would be out of Sri Lanka by late 1987 or early 1988. As we shall see, this was overoptimistic, and the force became bogged down in a bitter war with the LTTE, a war that has been referred to as "India's Vietnam." To help the IPKF supervise the surrender of Tamil militants' weapons, the IAF flew Prabhakaran from Delhi to Jaffna on 2 August, and on 4 August, in what is known as his "We love India" speech at Suthumalais, Prabhakaran said that he would not deploy arms against the IPKF. However, he also promised the Tamil people that the LTTE would continue to "fight" for Tamil Eelam. Privately, he said that he thought India had betrayed him, and many LTTE cadres were bitter about surrendering their weapons.

On 5 August an arms-surrender ceremony was held when a token number of arms were handed over to the IPKF at Palaly Air Force Base. Opposition to the accord and to the IPKF from the JVP became more strident, and on 18 August the JVP nearly succeeded in assassinating Jayewardene and other members of his United National Party (UNP) cabinet while they were meeting at the parliament building to discuss the implementation of the accord. During August and September the IPKF established themselves throughout the northern and eastern provinces. At the same time, internecine fighting between the LTTE and other militant groups—such as the Eelam National Democratic Liberation Front (ENDLF), Eelam Peoples Revolutionary Liberation Front (EPRLF),

Peoples Liberation Organization of Tamil Eelam (PLOTE), and the Tamil Eelam Liberation Organization (TELO)—escalated, with the LTTE gaining the upper hand. On 13 September the LTTE attacked and killed dozens of EPRLF, PLOTE, and ENDLF cadres in Batticaloa.

It soon became apparent that the LTTE was not going to disarm, and skirmishes between the IPKF and LTTE escalated. The LTTE were also busy buying and stockpiling weapons, and by 11 August they were openly saying that they would not give up their weapons. As a result other Tamil groups, especially EPRLF, also declared that they would hold on to their arms. Amid increasing anti-Indian protests organized by the LTTE, an LTTE leader, Dharmalingam Thileepan, fasted to death in September. Matters took another turn for the worse when on 3 October the Sri Lankan navy intercepted an LTTE boat smuggling arms to Jaffna. The 17 LTTE cadres captured, including a close aide to Prabhakaran, attempted to commit suicide by swallowing cyanide capsules rather than being taken to Colombo for interrogation, and 13 died. The LTTE responded with a spree of revenge attacks on both military and civilian targets, and this caused a surge of Sinhala refugees, especially from the eastern province. The IPKF was seen to be failing in its role as protector, and this raised the temperature of anti-Indian feeling. Attempting to keep a peace process going, India tried to downplay these incidents, but after the LTTE opened fire on the IPKF in Trincomalee on 7 October, Delhi issued instructions to the IPKF to prepare to crack down on the LTTE, regain control of Jaffna, and generally control LTTE movements and supply routes more rigorously. On 9 October Gandhi and Jayewardene jointly decided to "forcibly disarm the militants" as provided for in the July accord. By this time, and despite increasing conflict, many IPKF officers had developed great respect for the LTTE fighting ability and its commitment to Tamil Eelam, and there was a degree of fraternization between the two, favoring the LTTE over other Tamil groups.

However, by 11 October 1987 the IPKF had abandoned its role as peacekeeper, declared all-out war against the LTTE, and begun operations to dislodge the LTTE from Jaffna. A plan to capture Prabhakaran on 10 October at the LTTE headquarters in Jaffna University ended in disaster, with all the attacking Indian heliborne commandos killed. The IPKF assault on Jaffna (Operation Pawan) was particularly ill prepared: Its intelligence was inaccurate, its troops were equipped with old SLR rifles, it had few armored vehicles, and its maps dated from 1937. The LTTE, whose estimated strength varied between 2,500 and 3,000 cadres, were well armed and motivated, were familiar with the terrain, and knew their enemy well (after all, they had been trained by RAW and specialist forces of the Indian army itself at its bases in Tamil Nadu). At first, because IPKF officers did not remove their badges of rank, they were easy targets for LTTE snipers and suffered heavy casualties. After bitter fighting the LTTE evacuated Jaffna on 24 October, and by 28 October the IPKF was in control. But the cost had been high both in civilian and military casualties and in extensive destruction to buildings and services. As the fighting escalated, so too did reports of human rights abuses by the IPKF, including rape, torture, and killing of civilians. The LTTE relocated to the Vanni jungles, where they had established resupply bases and from where they waged effective guerrilla warfare. Some normalcy returned to Jaffna, as there was a lull in the fighting locally. Major services were restored, and LTTE action was limited to hit-and-run tactics. By this time the IPKF, in the view of many, was no longer an army of liberation but an army of occupation.

On 13 November Jayewardene successfully steered the Provincial Councils Bill and the Thirteenth Amendment through parliament despite minimal help from Prime Minister Premadasa and concerted hostility from the main opposition party, the Sri Lanka Freedom Party (SLFP), and the JVP. Fighting continued between the LTTE and the IPKF throughout November, but on 27 November 1987 the IPKF announced a unilateral ceasefire and demanded the surrender of LTTE weapons. This was rejected by the LTTE.

In 1988 IPKF activity increased in the eastern Batticaloa region. Experienced troops from the Indian Fifty-Seventh Mountain Division conducted search-and-destroy operations and continually harassed LTTE supply routes and bases. As a result the LTTE were considerably weakened, and on 28 February the IPKF ceased all operations for 48 hours and the LTTE agreed to unconditional talks. The cease-fire was short-lived, and hostilities soon began again in earnest when the IPKF moved deeper into the Vanni jungles in search of Prabhakaran. By March 1988 IPKF strength had increased to an estimated 100,000 troops, and it was conducting operations in the Vanni, such as Operation Virat and Operation Viraja. IPKF now worked closely with anti-LTTE Tamil groups, particularly EPRLF, ENDLF, and TELO, who had also been trained by RAW in India and were especially useful in the earlier phases of IPKF operations because, as Rohan Gunaratna has pointed out, they knew the language, they knew the terrain, and they could help IPKF distinguish LTTE cadres from Tamil civilians. However, in several incidents elements of these groups were responsible for the massacre of innocent civilians; there were also cases in which the IPKF killed noncombatants, based on false intelligence that these groups had provided. In April the LTTE offered to begin talks with the IPKF on condition that they pull back to pre–October 1987 positions. The IPKF, of course, refused these terms. The LTTE in turn refused the IPKF demand that they first lay down their weapons before negotiations could begin.

However, pressure was also building to have the IPKF removed from Sri Lanka. Especially vocal in this respect was public and political opinion in Tamil Nadu, where support for the LTTE was growing, and within Sri Lanka from the ultranationalist Sinhalese JVP. In June Gandhi announced a token withdrawal of a few thousand IPKF troops, but it was planned that the bulk of the IPKF was to remain in Sri Lanka until after the provincial elections scheduled for November or until an effective cease-fire was in place.

While the IPKF were busy with the LTTE in the northern and eastern provinces, the SLAF and JVP continued a vicious and bloody struggle in Colombo and the southern provinces. On 10 May 1988 a cease-fire was agreed upon, the GOSL agreed to legalize the JVP and release JVP prisoners (other than those imprisoned for murder), and the JVP agreed to renounce violence. This cessation of hostilities was short-lived, and the situa-

tion with the JVP worsened in September when the IPKF announced the unification of the northern and eastern provinces. The JVP were vehemently opposed to such a move, and from their perspective this further demonstrated that it was India that was really running Sri Lankan affairs. They embarked on another campaign of terror and intimidation, murdering government officials and bombing public buildings, killing police and threatening the families of SLAF personnel, and organizing strikes and protest marches. Some analysts were suggesting that the JVP and the LTTE were cooperating in their anti-IPKF and anti-GOSL activities.

On the political front during 1988, the IPKF and GOSL were trying to push ahead with the implementation of the accord's political elements. The first round of provincial elections for the western, central, and southern provinces took place between 28 April and 9 June 1987. These were boycotted by the SLFP and were violently disrupted by the JVP. Elections for the NEPC took place on 19 November, again amid intimidation and violence from the LTTE and JVP. In the north the EPRLF and ENDLF, who were pro-accord and pro-IPKF, won, and in the east the EPRLF and the Sri Lanka Muslim Congress (SLMC) were elected. The IPKF were accused of helping EPRLF and others, and even of rigging the ballot in their favor. The new chief minister of the NEPC, Annamalai Perumal, was sworn in on 9 December 1988, and the IPKF now had the major task of protecting NEPC members.

In December 1988 the GOSL held presidential elections. Jayewardene, who was then 82, did not stand for reelection. The UNP's candidate, Prime Minister Ranasinghe Premadasa, campaigned on an anti-India platform and defeated the SLFP candidate Sirimavo W. Bandaranaike. Premadasa was officially installed as president on 2 January 1989. Though Premadasa was eager for the IPKF to depart, he wanted them to remain until after the February 1989 parliamentary elections to help maintain security and protect candidates in the northern and eastern areas. In the event, the UNP won 125 seats out of 225.

Meanwhile Premadasa and the LTTE leadership became closer. The two sides met for talks in the Colombo Hilton on 12 May 1989 and on 28 June announced a cessation of hostilities. It was Premadasa's foreign secretary, Ranjan Wijeratne, who was given the delicate job in March 1989 of negotiating the "de-induction" of the IPKF, and a plan was formulated that envisaged the withdrawal of half the IPKF by July 1989, leaving the rest to return to India in batches of about 1,500 per week, so that all the IPKF would be out of Sri Lanka by the end of December of that year. However, on 1 June, the Poya Day of Poson, Premadasa preempted the negotiations and demanded that the IPKF leave Sri Lanka by 29 July, the second anniversary of their arrival. For Gandhi, who was in the middle of an election year, this would have been too humiliating a defeat, and he replied that this timetable was unrealistic and unilateral and that any IPKF withdrawal must be timed so as to ensure that the remaining EPRLF-led administrations could be protected and that the NEPC would be secure. He wanted to ensure that SLAF would quickly fill the vacuum left by departing IPKF troops. By 28 July, the eve of Premadasa's deadline, no troops had left, and once again there was desperate diplomatic activity between Delhi and Colombo.

Bernard Tilakaratna, Premadasa's respected foreign minister and former Sri Lankan high commissioner to India, had been dispatched to Delhi earlier in June to explain to Gandhi the pressure on Premadasa to get things moving. The JVP had called on port workers to refuse to unload Indian ships and had called for a boycott of Indian imports, and some Indian nationals and businesses had been threatened. On 29 July a Sri Lankan delegation, which included A. C. S. Hameed and Wijeratne, met with the Indian leadership in Delhi. They were able to reach some agreement: Six hundred troops were to be withdrawn immediately, and it was proposed that beginning in August 1989 a further 1,500 would depart every week, with the forecast that all would be gone by February 1990. The final agreement reached estimated that the process would, in fact, be completed by the end of March 1990. By September an uneasy truce between the IPKF and LTTE was in force, and by the end of October 1989 all IPKF personnel had withdrawn from the southern Amparai district. But the

security of the pro-Indian EPRLF cadres after IPKF withdrawal was uncertain. The EPRLF and the other pro-Indian Tamil cadres were sure that the LTTE would turn on them. This concern was not shared by the GOSL, which in fact allowed LTTE cadres to occupy areas vacated by departing IPKF soldiers and even helped rearm and resupply LTTE units. In an effort to bolster the NEPC and support the EPRLF and ENDLF, the IPKF set up, armed, and trained the Tamil National Army (TNA), against the wishes of Premadasa, who declared it an illegal force. TNA forces, many of whom had been forcibly conscripted, were no match for the LTTE, and they quickly collapsed under the expected LTTE onslaught.

During November and December 1989 Sri Lankan security forces captured and killed Rohan Wijeweera and other leaders of the JVP, effectively ending their uprising.

Rajiv Gandhi and the Congress (I) Party were defeated in the November 1989 general election in India, and the new National Front Indian Government under Prime Minister V. P. Singh stuck to the staggered-withdrawal "de-induction" timetable. On 24 March 1990 the final IPKF contingents left Sri Lanka. To escape the wrath of the LTTE, several thousand refugees belonging to the EPRLF, ENDLF, TELO, and the remnants of the TNA and NEPC accompanied the IPKF back to India. The IPKF forces had suffered an estimated 1,500 dead and 3,000 wounded, at a cost of about $1.25 billion. At its peak, the IPKF troops represented 10 percent of India's total army of 1.1 million and occupied 30 percent of all her special forces units.

Though the intervention of the IPKF was first seen as a great success—it established India as the dominant regional power, it was welcomed by most of the international community, and for a short time it stopped the violent ethnic conflict—by the time it departed an Indian presence was unwanted by either the GOSL or the Tamils. Perhaps the 2 April 1990 headline "Goodbye and Good Riddance" in *Time* magazine summed up the majority of feelings worldwide. It was ironic that the IPKF, which had intervened to protect the Tamils and to prevent the SLAF from defeating the LTTE, ended up in an all-out war with them. The IPKF intervention was based on an inaccurate intelligence assessment by RAW, who seriously underestimated the LTTE's political and military capabilities. Although RAW trained and armed LTTE cadres in camps in Tamil Nadu, they did not keep records or track of the militant groups. Furthermore, in several respects the accord was flawed from the very beginning. Importantly, the Sri Lankan Tamil groups were not invited into the process of drawing it up, and some felt that Rajiv Gandhi had no moral or legal authority to sign an accord to decide the political future of the Tamils in Sri Lanka. But the Indian army had gained valuable battle experience, particularly in carrying out joint operations between naval, army, and air force elements of the IPKF; in using helicopter gunships in battle conditions; in using naval bombardment to support land operations; and in fighting in built-up areas, including the use of armor in such situations.

The LTTE had been saved twice between 1987 and 1990, first by the IPKF in July 1987 and then by its rapprochement with the GOSL in April 1989, when the IPKF was beginning to get the upper hand. But the honeymoon between the LTTE and GOSL did not last long after the departure of the IPKF, and on 10 June 1990 the LTTE withdrew from peace negotiations with GOSL, and full-scale fighting began again with the outbreak of Eelam War II. It was back to square one. In May 1991 an LTTE suicide bomber assassinated Rajiv Gandhi while he was campaigning in Tamil Nadu, fearing that he might restart Indian intervention in Sri Lanka if he were to be reelected.

See also Child soldiers; Demilitarized zone; India
References and further reading Brogan (1992); Bullion (1992, 1997); O'Ballance (1989)

Status of forces agreement

A peacekeeping operation, as a mandated section of the main organization, has the status, privileges, and immunities of the United Nations organization itself—as provided by the UN Charter in article 105 and the Convention on the Privileges and Immunities of the United Nations. In addition, the peacekeepers are present normally at the invitation of the host nation, and as such their arrival will have been the subject of negotiations and agreements between the secretary-general or the Security Council and the government of that country. This agreement—the status of forces agreement—will explain in detail the position of the operation regarding legal status, responsibility for criminal and civil jurisdiction, premises, taxation, and freedom of movement. It will also cover specific aspects of the deployment such as the use of utilities and infrastructure; settlement of disputes; recruitment of local personnel; displaying of flags and banners; means of identifying vehicles, buildings, and personnel; wearing of uniforms; authority to carry weapons; employment of local labor; liaison arrangements between the force and local authorities; and immunity from search or inspection of force documents, vehicles, or buildings.

See also Host countries; Military observers

Stewart, Robert (1949–)

Born 7 July 1949, Robert Stewart graduated with a first-class honors degree in international politics from the University of Wales, Aberystwyth, and then attended the Royal Military Academy (RMA) at Sandhurst. In 1969 he was appointed commander of the Cheshire Regiment; he then returned briefly to the RMA as an instructor (1979–1980) before moving to the Army Staff College in 1981. In 1986 he was made second in command of the First Battalion of the Cheshire Regiment and was subsequently appointed military adviser to the chairman of the North Atlantic Treaty Organization (NATO) Military Committee at NATO headquarters in Brussels (1989–1991). During 1991–1992 he served with the United Nations Protection Force in Former Yugoslavia (UNPROFOR) in Bosnia and Herzegovina and wrote an account of his experiences there, *Broken Lives* (1993).

See also Bosnia and Herzegovina; British peacekeeping; UNPROFOR I–III
References and further reading Stewart (1993)

Swedish peacekeeping

Sweden has always been an active member of the United Nations and a significant participant in UN peacekeeping, having maintained a standby force since 1964. In Sweden, a new law in peacekeeping was passed in 1992 that enabled the participation of Swedish armed forces in peacekeeping operations not only by the UN but also by the Organization for Security and Cooperation in Europe (OSCE). Although the law envisaged such participation as occurring within traditional deployments, Sweden has participated in a variety of multifunctional deployments, including providing troops as part of the United Nations Operation in the Congo (ONUC) and, most recently, providing a battalion in the United Nations Protection Force in Former Yugoslavia (UNPROFOR). The UNPROFOR battalion was authorized by a special act of Parliament and was the most heavily armed unit ever sent by Sweden on a UN operation. The traditional Swedish standby system to provide UN peacekeeping forces has been strengthened by the formation of the Swedish Armed Forces International Center (SWEDINT), which coordinates training and logistical support. In 1994 Sweden announced its intention to set up a special brigade for international operations, and following the experience of service in UNPROFOR the Ministry of Defence was advocating maintaining preparedness to serve in a wide variety of international operations. A blueprint for the proposed new international force, to be used in peace operations authorized under UN or OSCE mandates, was endorsed in 1995. The force is to be brigade-sized and will contain infantry and special units (including transport, headquarters, medical care, and support for civilian missions); up to 1,400 personnel will be available for service abroad. Although the policy was still being defined as of late 1998, Swedish policy appeared to be sensitive to the wide demands likely to be placed on future peacekeeping. The new force is intended to be prepared for traditional and wider peacekeeping operations: Although the force may have some enforcement capability, the stress is on the need to maintain consent and impartiality and on the need to pursue humanitarian objectives. There is also an emphasis on training, especially to improve civilian-military cooperation and to provide support for civilian initiatives. Participation in international peacekeeping is now defined as one of the principal tasks of and objectives of Swedish defense and foreign policy. The traditional Swedish policy of nonalignment has come under some pressure as Sweden has joined the European Union (EU) and committed itself to an EU common foreign and security policy (CFSP), and this trend will have an impact on future Swedish policy and activities in relation to peacekeeping.

See also Eliasson, Jan (1940–); European Union; Troop-contributing countries
References and further reading Karhilo (1996); Skold (1996)

Symbolic Arab Security Force
See League of Arab States

Syria
See UNDOF

Tajikistan

Conflict Profile

Until the late 1980s, when the decline of the Soviet Union hastened toward collapse, Tajik national identity had been officially defined within the confines of Soviet ideology. Even into the more progressive Gorbachev era, the Soviet regime promoted the issues and ideals of the central authority in Moscow, condemning more local interests as overly nationalist and parochial, and as late as 1989 the Soviet-backed leadership in Dushanbe advocated a corresponding viewpoint. Thus, as had been the case in many Soviet satellite states, the struggle for national identity had long been a prominent feature in Tajik opposition politics. The disintegration of the Soviet Union precipitated a more forceful reaction among many of the Tajik people against the old, Soviet-dominated order as the population attempted to resume control of its own identity.

Although the Moscow-backed Tajik leadership was still in power in 1989, the increasingly nationalist demands of the population were not entirely lost on the leadership in Dushanbe. For example, the Tajik authorities eventually conceded to the establishment of a language law that made Tajik rather than Russian the official state language. However, concessions by the government commonly lagged well behind public demands, and such delays, particularly when conditions in the Soviet Union were changing so rapidly, helped to exacerbate public frustration. At this time, popular requests for political and economic autonomy fell short of demands for total independence. It was not until the collapse of the Soviet Union in 1991 that Tajikistan became fully independent.

Religious and ethnic allegiances played a significant role in the Tajik conflict. As had been the case with Western colonial empires, Soviet demarcation of state borders within the union paid little heed to the wishes or social and ethnic distinctions of their inhabitants. Many ethnic Tajiks lived outside the country's borders (primarily in neighboring Uzbekistan), and around 40 percent of Tajikistan's five million inhabitants were from other ethnic groups. The most significant Tajik minority comprised some 1.1 million Uzbekis (ap-

proximately 21 percent of the population), although the Uzbeki minority was not proportionately represented in senior political positions. The government in Uzbekistan did not concur with the Tajik nationalist movement and encouraged dissent among the Uzbeki population in Tajikistan.

Conversely, the smaller but still significant Russian minority (around 7 percent of the population) enjoyed the political and economic patronage of the government, and the potential for popular resentment that this created was exacerbated by the fact that a significant proportion of the ethnically Russian population could not speak Tajik. Therefore the Russian minority was, for obvious reasons, particularly worried by the thought of severing ties with Moscow, and from its position of relative power it had repeatedly opposed such moves. Islam plays a significant role in the lives of many Tajiks and was a focal point for many dissenting groups in the country. However, when opposition groups combined to promote their causes in a unified fashion, the ruling elites whom they were challenging labeled them collectively as radically Islamist, thereby representing themselves, in contrast, as modern, secular democrats. The ruling elite's position was subsequently strengthened by the fact that a significant proportion of the opposition was later forced to relocate and base its operations in northern Afghanistan.

The Tajik authorities' support for the attempted Communist coup in Moscow in August 1991 prompted the ousting of the Communist Tajik president, Qahhor Mahkamov. However, the Communist Party successfully implemented its own coup in Dushanbe and on 23 September 1991 installed Rahmon Nabiev in power, subsequently consolidating his position in rigged elections in November. Over the coming months the government undertook various actions that revealed an intention to return to the authoritarian order of the 1980s. Therefore, in spring 1992, the leading Tajik opposition movements combined as the United Tajik Opposition (UTO) and demanded political and economic reforms. A violent mass demonstration in Dushanbe in May induced the authorities to concede to the formation of a coalition government, which included more moderate elements of the ruling elite as well as a few members of the opposition. However, significant reforms did not materialize, and violence in Tajikistan intensified, focused primarily on Nabiev as the source of the country's troubles. Armed opposition fighters captured Nabiev in September 1992 and forced him to resign, and he was replaced by Akbarsho Iskandarov as acting president.

Iskandarov did not retain sufficient political power to implement significant reforms, and in November he and the entire government resigned in a last-ditch attempt to stop the fighting. However, this merely served to allow the Supreme Soviet, under the leadership of its speaker, Imomali Rahmonov, to seize power and install a new government in Dushanbe in December (although Rahmonov was not actually appointed president and the post was left vacant). This effectively ended the war in Tajikistan, as the new government embarked on a crackdown on prominent members of the UTO. However, sporadic fighting continued in various regions of the country, and a large proportion of opposition fighters escaped into Afghanistan, from which they launched armed attacks across the border. Victory by the forces of the Tajik government convinced Moscow to provide military and economic assistance to Dushanbe. Russian troops were dispatched to Tajikistan and were stationed along the Afghan border to deter cross-border activity. A smaller number of peacekeeping troops from the Commonwealth of Independent States (CIS) were also deployed to maintain stability throughout the country.

Deployment of UNMOT

The United Nations was involved in various initiatives to facilitate peace in Tajikistan. In October 1992, the secretary-general, Boutros Boutros-Ghali, dispatched a good offices mission to the country, followed in January 1993 by a small unit of political, military, and humanitarian officers. On 26 April the secretary-general appointed a special envoy to Tajikistan, and between April and October 1994, watched by observers from Afghanistan, Iran, Pakistan, and Russia, three rounds of negotiations took place on national reconciliation. By September 1994 the opposing parties had come to the Tehran Agreement, agreeing upon terms for a temporary cease-fire and the establishment of a Joint Commission to verify its implementation, although fighting nevertheless continued. In October 1994 the negotiations also produced agreement on the exchange of prisoners of war: a crucial test of confidence between the two parties. In November presidential elections were held. Rahmonov, with substantial Russian backing, won more than 60 percent of votes cast. The only other candidate, former Prime Minister Abdumalik Abdullojonov, claimed electoral fraud. His allegations were supported both by the Conference on Security and Cooperation in Europe (CSCE), which before the elections had questioned their legitimacy and refused to send observers, and, after the ballot, by Human Rights Watch/Helsinki, who claimed that the elections had been corrupted by intimidation and biased media coverage.

Thus, on 16 December 1994 the Security Council adopted Security Council Resolution (SCR) 968, establishing the United Nations Mission of Observers in Tajikistan (UNMOT). UNMOT was mandated to assist the Joint Commission; to verify the terms of the cease-fire; to monitor the cessation of violence along the Afghan border and throughout the country; to investigate alleged cease-fire violations; to provide good offices; to maintain ties with the belligerents, the CSCE Mission, the CIS peacekeeping forces, and the Russian border forces; to support the efforts of the special envoy of the secretary-general; and to facilitate political cooperation and coordination services. The mission was to be a joint military-civilian operation, comprising a core military contingent of 40 officers supported by civilian staff and additional civilian officers. By the end of January 1995 UNMOT had reached an overall strength of 55, comprising 22 military observers, provided by Austria, Bangladesh, Denmark, Hungary, Jordan, and Uruguay, 11 civilian staff, and 22 local staff.

Despite commitments by both parties to the terms of the cease-fire and to seeking a political settlement, sporadic bouts of violence continued in Tajikistan, although efforts persisted to find an enduring solution to the conflict. For instance, the parties to the dispute regularly acceded to extensions of the cease-fire. On the strength of such efforts the UNMOT mandate was periodically extended, as all sides agreed that the presence of the peacekeeping force advanced the chances for peaceful resolution of the conflict. However, specific factors interfered with the political peace process, notably the presence of 350 Tajik government troops in Gorno-Badakhshan, in contravention of the cease-fire agreement. Consequently, toward the middle of 1995 the level of violence in the country began to increase.

A series of meetings between Rahmonov and the UTO leader, Sayed Abdullo Nuri, ultimately resulted on 17 August 1995 in the signing of a protocol. The protocol established the basic principles for a political solution to the conflict and agreed upon further negotiations aimed at producing a general agreement on the following issues: the basic principles for the establishment of national accord, political and military difficulties, and the repatriation and reintegration into society of refugees and displaced persons. However, delays over agreement as to the venue for negotiations led to further tension and violence, which in turn compromised the talks themselves when they eventually got under way at the end of November. Progress between the two sides remained slow, as further disagreements over various aspects of a political solution continued to make concord elusive. However, it was agreed in principle that members of the opposition must be included in the Tajik government and military and that establishing such a system would require a transitional period that should be supervised by an external body.

In May 1996 the secretary-general appointed Gerd Merrem as his resident special representative and as UNMOT's head of mission. Then, on 27 June 1997 in Moscow, Rakhmonov, Nuri, and Merrem signed the General Agreement on the Establishment of Peace and National Accord in Tajikistan, as well as the Moscow Protocol. Thus, with the signing of the agreement, and combined with the subsequent convocation of the Commission on National Reconciliation, the conditions were met for the initiation of the transitional period. It was envisioned that during transition refugees would be repatriated; UTO fighters would either be demobilized or reintegrated into governmental structures; the military, police, and security apparatus would be reformed; and democratic structures would be improved, leading to national elections and the creation of a new government. UNMOT's military component would also be strengthened from 45 to 120 military observers.

On 14 November 1997, therefore, the Security Council adopted Security Council Resolution (SCR) 1138, by which the UNMOT mandate was extended until 15 May 1998 and expanded to include supplying good offices and expert advice; cooperating with both the Commission on National Reconciliation and the Central Commission on Elections and the Holding of a Referendum; facilitating and coordinating the work of the Contact Group of guarantor states and organizations; investigating allegations of violations of the terms of the cease-fire; verifying the cantonment, demobilization, and reintegration of UTO fighters; facilitating the reintegration of former combatants into government structures; coordinating UN assistance throughout the period of transition; and maintaining links with the opposing parties, the CIS peacekeeping forces, the Russian border forces, and the Organization for Security and Cooperation in Europe (OSCE—formerly CSCE) Mission in Tajikistan.

Thus, although enduring differences between the parties to the Tajik dispute continue to prevent agreement and result in violence, the presence of the Russian, CIS, and UN peacekeeping forces appears to be moving the peace process toward fruition, albeit very gradually. The strong Russian and, to a lesser extent, CIS presence in the process has had the paradoxical effect of adding political weight and commitment, while simultaneously creating suspicion about motivation, especially among the opposition forces. It is therefore hoped that the involvement of the wider international community through the United Nations can temper the more parochial tendencies of the regional initiative without complicating the situation to such an extent the external intervention is disabled.

The UNMOT operation has been deployed since December 1994, and its headquarters are in Dushanbe, the capital of Tajikistan. As of 31 December 1997 the special representative of the secretary-general and head of mission was Gerd Merrem (Germany), and the chief military observer was Brig. Gen. Boleslaw Izydorczyk (Poland). Also as of 31 December 1997, UNMOT's strength comprised 57 military observers, supported by international and local civilian staff. Military personnel were contributed by Austria, Bangladesh, Bulgaria, Denmark, Ghana, Indonesia, Jordan, Nigeria, Poland, Switzerland, Ukraine, and Uruguay. The mission's estimated expenditures from inception to 30 June 1996 were $12,367,337, to be paid by regular assessments from member states.

See also Child soldiers; Commonwealth of Independent States; Russian peacekeeping
References and further reading
International Peacekeeping (1994–); United Nations (1996); UNDPKO

Thant, U (1909–1974)

Born in Pantanaw, Burma, in January 1909, U Thant progressed from being a high school headmaster to holding the post of secretary in the Ministry of Education. He served as permanent representative to the United Nations between 1957 and 1961 and was president of the General Assembly in 1959. Following the death of Dag Hammarskjöld in 1961, U Thant proved to be acceptable to the Soviet Union as a candidate for secretary-general. The Soviet Union had been trying to replace the position of secretary-general with a committee or triumvirate. U Thant was a Buddhist who had a reputation for impartiality and who believed that the United Nations as a world organiza-

tion was uniquely placed to spread values of tolerance. He also saw a positive role for small states in helping to engender values of international democracy and citizenship. He wished to keep the United Nations as much as possible out of the Cold War contest between the East and West power blocs and to develop the role of the secretary-general pragmatically. He played a part in the resolution of the Cuban missile crisis in 1962 and was prominent in securing a cease-fire in the war between India and Pakistan in 1965 and the deployment of the United Nations India-Pakistan Observer Mission (UNIPOM). He failed, however, to persuade the Egyptians to allow the continued deployment of the second United Nations Emergency Force (UNEF II), and the withdrawal of this peacekeeping force was a precipitating factor in the outbreak of the Six-Day War in the Middle East in 1967.

See also Congo (United Nations Operation in the Congo, 1960–1964); United Nations: organization
References and further reading Bingham (1996); Nassif (1988); Thant (1978)

Traditional peacekeeping
See First-generation peacekeeping

Training for peacekeeping

Given the complex multidimensional, multilateral, and multinational nature of contemporary peacekeeping operations, the training received by military and civilian peacekeepers has become a critical factor in the success of a mission. Current training programs aim to adopt a standardized and holistic approach: All military personnel should receive basic military education and training, along with peacekeeping training (e.g., in the nature and history of peacekeeping and in function- and mission-specific training, including immediate military tasks and education in the cultural and political context of the mission) and "contact skills" training (e.g., mediation, negotiation, and cross-cultural communication), and civilian personnel should be given mission- and function-specific training, along with peacemaking and conflict-resolution skills training. Although the training of peacekeepers requires further development—in order to coordinate methods and practices and to enhance the holistic approach—training has improved dramatically over the years, both in the quality and diversity of education and in the number of programs offering such training.

A multitude of centers have undertaken the challenge to train both military and civilian personnel in the various aspects of peacekeeping before they are deployed in the field. This has resulted in a range of training programs that can be divided into the categories UN central (military and civilian), regional military, national military, civilian, and military-civilian.

Though member states are ultimately responsible for the preparation and training of peacekeeping personnel, many nations have appealed to the United Nations to provide support in their training efforts. The United Nations Department of Peacekeeping Operations (DPKO) established a small Training Unit in 1993 to promote standardized peacekeeping training among the many and diverse troop-contributing countries. The core tasks of the Training Unit include advising the DPKO on all training matters, providing expert training assistance, sharing information, coordinating training, and developing training materials and programs that are available to member states to use as guides in national training programs. Instructional materials include the *UN Peacekeeping Training Manual,* the UN Military Observer Course Curriculum, the UN Civilian Police Course Curriculum, and an Instructional Peacekeeping Video Series.

In additional, the Training Unit has established mobile training assistance teams (UNTATs). These teams are composed of experienced peacekeepers provided by member states who have participated in a complicated training program administered by the Training Unit. As of May 1998, 59 member states had contributed a total of 99 officers to UNTATs. The specific aim of the UNTAT program is to provide, on request, a resource pool of peacekeeping-training teams prepared to advise and assist member states in the development and implementation of national peacekeeping training programs. Although not directly involved in train-

ing national units (unless specifically requested by a country and approved by the United Nations through the DPKO Training Unit), UNTATs brief unit commanders and officers concerning tactical techniques and peacekeeping methods. UNTATs can also offer specific premission training, as has been successfully carried out in support of Jordan and Pakistan in preparation for the United Nations Transitional Administration for Eastern Slavonia, Baranja, and Western Sirmium (UNTAES), and in-theater training assistance to an established mission, as demonstrated by the programs in the United Nations Mission in Haiti (UNMIH) in 1995 and the third United Nations Angola Verification Mission (UNAVEM III) in 1995.

The DPKO Training Unit also initiated a series of global peacekeeping-training workshops. The sessions were hosted by the governments of Denmark in February 1995 (Europe), Argentina in April 1995 (Latin America), India in January 1996 (Asia), and Egypt in March 1996 (Africa). The aim of the exercise was to encourage greater regional cooperation and commonality in peacekeeping training and to identify areas where the United Nations could provide assistance to member states' peacekeeping-training programs. To further promote a global network of peacekeeping training, a Peacekeeping Training Courses Database was established by the Training Unit—a collection of information on national peacekeeping-training programs and related activities. The database is updated regularly and organized first by member state and second by type of peacekeeping training/courses (military, police, others, and correspondence).

The United Nations Institute for Training and Research (UNITAR) Program of Correspondence Instruction in Peacekeeping Operations (POCI) offers unique correspondence courses on peacekeeping. The aim of the self-paced training program is to provide standardized common training on a variety of peacekeeping topics and to promote interoperability and a unity of purpose among military officers, civilian employees, and diplomats involved in peacekeeping. The courses—which provide knowledge-based training and adhere to established UN procedures and practices—may be used by member states and resident training centers to supplement their existing training programs. Currently, four courses are offered by UNITAR: Commanding United Nations Peacekeeping Operations: Methods and Techniques for Peacekeeping on the Ground (English and French instruction); History of United Nations Peacekeeping Operations during the Cold War Period: 1945–1987; The Logistical Support of United Nations Peacekeeping Operations (English, French, and Spanish); and The United Nations Peacekeeping Force in the Former Yugoslavia (English and French).

Regional training initiatives have sought to standardize training and promote cooperation among troop-contributing countries. These include the Partnership for Peace (PFP) program of the North Atlantic Treaty Organization (NATO), which has offered a number of bilateral and multilateral joint-training exercises since the program's inception in 1994; the Cairo Peacekeeping Training Center, initiated by Egypt and established in 1995 to train African peacekeeping nations; and the Regional Peacekeeping Training Center in Zimbabwe, mandated by the Interstate Defence and Security Conference (ISDSC) in 1997 to coordinate peacekeeping training in the southern African region (SADC) (participating nations include Angola, Botswana, Lesotho, Malawi, Mozambique, Namibia, South Africa, Swaziland, Tanzania, Zambia, and Zimbabwe). The peacekeeping-training activities of Denmark, Finland, Norway, and Sweden are highly integrated. They are governed by a joint Nordic Committee for Military United Nations Matters (NORDSAMFM). Each Nordic country has taken on the responsibility to run one training event each year; thus, four training centers prepare officers and noncommissioned officers for peacekeeping service: the UN Military Police Course in Denmark, the UN Military Observer Course in Finland, the UN Logistics Course in Norway, and the UN Staff Officer Course in Sweden.

Several member states have been active in cross-national training. The U.S. Office of the Secretary of Defense for Peacekeeping and Peace Enforcement Policy has a notable program for peacekeeping education and training around the world; the Pentagon assists in the establishment of train-ing centers and provides a regular exchange of information and regional training opportunities. Other efforts include the United Kingdom's assistance in establishing the Zimbabwe Staff College, Ireland's support in the development of a peacekeeping-training school in Zambia, and Norway's assistance to training development in South Africa.

Many national troop-contributing countries have established their own peacekeeping training schools. Several well-established centers and programs are noted here: The Argentinean Peacekeeping Academy was created in 1995 to train its national troops in a range of peacekeeping areas. The Australian Defence Force (ADF) Peacekeeping Center was established in 1993, as part of the ADF Warfare Center, to develop and manage peace-operations doctrine and training. The center also conducts regular seminars involving government and nongovernment organizations and academic, military, and civilian personnel from nations in the region. The Austrian Training Center for Peacekeeping Operations was established in 1987. Since its creation the program has been refined, offering specialized courses for both military and civilian personnel, Austrian and non-Austrian. The United Nations Training School Ireland (UNTSI), established in 1993, coordinates the training of Ireland's peacekeepers and liaises with peacekeeping-training schools in other countries. Ireland's training program for the United Nations Interim Force in Lebanon (UNIFIL) is used as a guideline for training Irish personnel for other UN missions. The United Kingdom provides a well-established peacekeeping-training program under the auspices of the Ministry of Defence. This includes mission-specific training packages and specialist training, both open to observation by non-British officers participating at other similar training facilities. Since 1990 the U.S. Department of Defense has offered peacekeeping courses at many levels and at several military institutions and training centers, including the Army Peacekeeping Training Institute (U.S. Army War College), the Navy War College, the Marine Corps Command and Staff College, and the Air University. The U.S. Army Training and Doctrine Command also develops packages that are used worldwide for unit-level, on-station training.

Because civilian peacekeepers are usually recruited individually and are therefore difficult to train on a national basis, international institutions have gradually emerged to provide training. The Austrian Study Center for Peace and Conflict Resolution (ASPR), supported by the Austrian government, trains civilians from a variety of national and professional backgrounds to be available for UN missions. The International Civilian Peacekeeping and Peace Building Training Program offers courses on Civilian Peacekeeping Training, Human Rights Protection, Information Dissemination, Mediation, and Postconflict Reconstruction. In Italy the Scuola Superiore Di Studi Universitari E Perfezionamento S. Anna offers civilian peacekeeping training through its Training Program for the Civilian Personnel of the Peacekeeping/Humanitarian Operations.

The Lester B. Pearson Canadian International Peacekeeping Training Centre (PPC) has established itself as the foremost center for the combined training of international military and civilian personnel. It was created as an independent organization in 1994 by the government of Canada to provide education and training to all members of the "new peacekeeping partnership." The center offers an extensive selection of on-campus courses (taught in English and French), conferences, seminars, and workshops and off-campus training activities (e.g., mobile training teams and electronic distance learning technology). It is also able to provide customized training programs. Course topics include general peacekeeping overview; the legal framework; interdisciplinary cooperation; negotiation and mediation; refugees and displaced persons; demobilization, disarmament, and reintegration; human rights; the maritime dimension; technology and engineering; administration and logistics; personal support; and peacekeeping management command.

Other training initiatives have included seminars and workshops for military and civilian personnel, government and nongovernment organizations, diplomats, policy makers and academics involved in peacekeeping by the International Peace Academy (IPA) in New York and the U.S. Institute for Peace (USIP), and an in-depth project by the Initiative on Conflict Resolution and Ethnicity (INCORE) at the University of Ulster, Northern Ireland, on the Training and Preparation of Military and Civilian Peacekeepers.

To coordinate the increasing number of peacekeeping-training centers and programs worldwide, the International Association of Peacekeeping Training Centres (IAPTC) was created at the Lester B. Pearson Canadian International Peacekeeping Training Centre in July 1995. The aim of the IAPTC is to facilitate communication and information exchange between the various peacekeeping training centers or among people responsible for peacekeeping training to reduce duplication of effort, avoid problems already encountered, promote well-tested practices, enhance specialization, and contribute to cooperation and burden sharing in the training of personnel for contemporary peacekeeping operations.

See also Egypt; Irish peacekeeping; Italy; United Nations organization (DPKO); Zimbabwe
References and further reading Blechman (1994); Haberle-Zemlic, Heje, Moxon-Browne, and Truger (1996); International Peace Academy (1984); Last (1997); the peacekeeping-training database can be found at http://www.un.org/Depts/dpko/training/list1.htm

Troop-contributing countries

Over 90 nations have deployed troops on UN missions, and approximately 80 countries had troops deployed in the late 1990s. Small or medium-sized developed states, and often states that are neutral or nonaligned in their defense policies, have tended to be the most active peacekeepers. Sweden, Canada, Ireland, Austria, and Norway are the countries that have taken part in most operations, and these same counties have a preponderance of officials in command of peacekeeping missions. Sweden, Canada, India, Finland, Norway, and Ireland provided more than half of the 118 military officers who commanded peacekeeping missions up to 1993. Australia, Austria, and New Zealand also have a long history of involvement. A small number of developing states, from large countries like India and Pakistan to smaller developing countries like Fiji, Ghana, Nepal, and Senegal, have also been active. The bulk of the costs of peacekeeping is met by the

United States and European states. Other Third World countries whose contributions to the peacekeeping budget are relatively low nevertheless are significant contributors of troops (e.g., India, Pakistan, Bangladesh, Ghana, and Nigeria). During the 1990s more powerful European nations began to become more heavily involved as troop contributors, particularly in the United Nations Protection Force in Former Yugoslavia (UNPROFOR), the largest mission ever launched by the United Nations, in which France and the United Kingdom had significant numbers deployed (see Table 8).

The overall trend in the 1990s has been toward an increase in peacekeeping contingents from less developed countries. In 1993 the 13 richest coun-

Table 8 Percentage of UN Troop Contributions by Region, 1994

Asia	36.3%
Africa	14.0%
Latin America	3.4%
Europe	39.7%
USA	4.8%
Oceania	1.8%

Source: Data from Fisas, A. V., *Blue Geopolitics: The United Nations Reform and the Future of the Blue Helmets.* London and East Haven, CT: Pluto Press, 1995.

Table 9 First-time Participants in UN Peacekeeping and Observer Missions Since 1989

Country	First Mission	Year	Country	First Mission	Year
Albania	UNOMIG	1994	Honduras	MINURSO	1991
Algeria	UNAMIC	1991	Jamaica	UNTAG	1989
Barbados	UNTAG	1989	Japan	UNTAC	1992
Botswana	ONUMOZ	1993	Jordan	UNAVEM I	1989
Brunei Darussalam	UNTAC	1992	Korea, South	UNOSOM II	1993
Bulgaria	UNTAC	1992	Kuwait	UNOSOM II	1993
Cameroon	UNTAC	1992	Lithuania	UNPROFOR	1994
Cape Verdi	ONUMOZ	1993	Luxembourg	UNPROFOR	1992
Chad	UNAMIR	1994	Malawi	UNAMIR	1993
China	UNTAG	1989	Mali	UNAMIR	1993
Congo	UNAVEM II	1989	Namibia	UNTAC	1992
Costa Rica	UNTAG	1989	Niger	UNAMIR	1994
Cuba	UNOMIG	1994	Romania	UNIKOM	1991
Czechoslovakia	UNAVEM I	1989	Russian Federation	UNIKOM	1991
Czech Republic	UNPROFOR	1993	Saudi Arabia	UNOSOM II	1993
Djibouti	UNMIH	1994	Singapore	UNTAG	1989
Egypt	UNTAG	1989	Slovakia	UNPROFOR	1993
El Salvador	MINURSO	1995	Spain	UNAVEM I	1989
Estonia	UNPROFOR	1995	Switzerland	UNTAG	1989
Germany	UNAMIC	1991	Togo	UNTAG	1989
FRG	UNTAG	1989	Trinidad and Tobago	UNTAG	1989
GDR	UNTAG	1989	Uganda	UNOSOM II	1993
Greece	UNTAG	1989	Ukraine	UNPROFOR	1992
Guatemala	UNMLH	1994	United Arab Emirates	UNOSOM I	1993
Guinea Bissau	UNAVEM II	1991	USA	UNIKOM	1991
Guyana	UNTAG	1989	Zimbabwe	UNAVEM II	1991

Source: Data from T. Findlay, "The New Peacekeepers and the New Peacekeeping." In *Challenges for the New Peacekeepers,* edited by T. Findlay. SIPRI Research Report, no. 12. Oxford and New York: Oxford University Press, 1996.
Note: The USA is listed as a new peacekeeper because during the Cold War period its contribution was largely to provide airlift and logistical support to missions. Post-1989 its role in providing ground troops has been significant, and the USA has also had a leading role in policy debates and development of doctrine.

tries supplied 57 percent of UN Blue Helmets; by 1994 they contributed 36 percent, whereas the poorer countries (those with an average per capita income of less than $700 per year) increased their participation from 28 percent to 42 percent of total troops. Generally speaking, there has been a significant increase in the numbers of troops deployed from Pakistan, India, Bangladesh, Jordan, Malaysia, Egypt, Botswana, Sweden, Zimbabwe, and Ukraine. Among the states in the Association of Southeast Asian Nations (ASEAN) Malaysia was the largest contributor: It had 2,844 troops in UN service in 1994 and had large contingents in both Somalia (1,135) and Bosnia (1,603). Thailand, which has the largest military of all the ASEAN countries, has had only token representation on UN peacekeeping missions. Africa, because of the many civil wars that have raged on that continent, is better known as the largest recipient than as a provider of peacekeeping troops. However, Ghana, Kenya, Nigeria, Senegal, and Tunisia are long-standing troop con-

tributors, while Zimbabwe and Egypt have made significant contributions recently, sending 1,700 personnel to Somalia. In Latin America, only Argentina and Chile have been regular contributors of peacekeeping troops, though recently Brazil has been more active, with 150 troops serving in Angola and Mozambique in 1994.

In general, the enormous expansion of peacekeeping after 1988 resulted in a parallel expansion in the number of countries involved. In 1988, 26 countries were involved in peacekeeping operations; by 1995 more than 80 countries were participating in peacekeeping operations. We can therefore identify a large group of new peacekeepers, that is, the 49 states that participated in peacekeeping for the first time in their history. In addition, 21 states have participated in non-UN peacekeeping missions, also their first experience of peacekeeping.

The motives for participating are varied. Sometimes countries increase their activity when they become nonpermanent members of the Security

Table 10 First-time Participants in Non-UN Peacekeeping Missions Since 1989

Country	First Mission	Year
Antigua and Barbuda	MNF	1994
Armenia	OSCE Skopje	1992
Bahamas	MNF	1994
Belize	MNF	1994
Benin	MNF	1994
Dominica	MNF	1994
Gambia	ECOMOG	1990
Georgia	South Ossetia	1992
Grenada	MNF	1994
Israel	MNF	1994
Kazakhstan	CIS Tajikistan	1993
Kyrgyzstan	CIS Tajikistan	1993
Mauritania	Operation Turquoise	1994
Moldova	Moldova Joint Force	1992
St. Kitts and Nevis	MNF	1994
St. Lucia	MNF	1994
St. Vincent	MNF	1994
Tanzania	ECOMOG	1994
Tonga	SPPKF	1994
Uzbekistan	CIS Tajikistan	1993
Vanuatu	SPPKF[a]	1994

Source: Data from T. Findlay, "The New Peacekeepers and the New Peacekeeping." In *Challenges for the New Peacekeepers,* edited by T. Findlay. SIPRI Research Report, no. 12. Oxford and New York: Oxford University Press, 1996.
[a]SPPKF = South Pacific Peacekeeping Force

Council, as has been the case for Morocco, Spain, Argentina, Pakistan, Nigeria, and the Czech Republic. Isolated for many years until the fall of the Franco regime, Spain first contributed to UN peacekeeping in the United Nations Transitional Assistance Group (UNTAG) in Namibia, and by the end of 1994 it had 1,300 troops deployed in El Salvador, Mozambique, and the former Yugoslavia. Spain has been particularly active in helping to resolve the conflicts in Central America and is significant in providing leadership in Spanish-speaking Latin American states, for which it has provided a training facility specializing in the preparation of police forces for UN service. For some countries the economic incentive is impor-

tant, since participation in peacekeeping can provide income that amounts to a significant proportion of their national defense budget (in the case of Ghana and Nepal, up to 50 percent). Participation also enhances the national image and reputation of an army and provides opportunities for training and upgrading skills within multinational operations. It is also a very tangible form of fulfilling responsibilities for international security and an expression of commitment to the ideals of the United Nations (see Tables 9 and 10).

See also Financing peacekeeping
References and further reading Findlay (1996); Fisas (1995); Kane (1996); Norden (1995); Vogt and Ekoko (1995)

United Nations: agencies

The United Nations Development Program (UNDP)
The United Nations Development Program (UNDP), part of the Secretariat, is the world's largest multilateral technical grant-assistance program. It is the UN's central coordinating organization for development activities. The UNDP, which has its headquarters in New York and has local field offices in 115 countries, was established in 1965 when the General Assembly decided to merge two UN organizations: the Expanded Program of Technical Assistance, set up in 1949, and the Special Fund, which had been set up in 1958 to provide preinvestment assistance to large development projects.

The United Nations High Commissioner for Refugees (UNHCR)
International assistance to refugees was first organized in 1921 with the appointment of a League of Nations High Commissioner for Refugees. In 1943 the United Nations Relief and Rehabilitation Administration was established to bring aid to war-stricken areas of the world. Through its services some six million displaced persons were repatriated at the end of World War II. The International Refugee Organization, whose constitution was approved by the General Assembly in 1946, assumed the functions of the Relief and Rehabilitation Administration. The new agency was also charged with the protection and resettlement of refugees and displaced persons. By the end of 1951 it had assisted in the resettlement of more than a million persons. The Office of the United Nations High Commissioner for Refugees (UNHCR) was established in 1951, with headquarters in Geneva, to replace the International Refugee Organization. The agency's mandate is to provide for the needs of refugees (those who have fled across international borders to escape war and persecution). Although the UNHCR is not normally involved with internally displaced people (those who have not crossed international borders), it has increasingly assumed responsibility for them. The number of internally displaced persons now exceeds the number of international refugees, and the UN secretary-general has designated a special representative with responsibility for monitoring their problems and developing appropriate policies.

The United Nations Human Rights Center
Based in Geneva, the United Nations Human Rights Center is the program arm of the UN Human Rights Commission, a body made up of representatives from 53 member states. The commission sends special rapporteurs to areas where human rights violations are alleged to have occurred, although there has been pressure on the United Nations to monitor human rights more proactively and assertively. Field-based human rights operations are increasing and have included human rights components in UN operations in the United Nations Observer Mission in El Salvador (ONUSAL); in the Joint International Civilian Mission in Haiti (MICIVIH); in the United Nations Transitional Authority in Cambodia (UNTAC); in the Human Rights Field Operation in Rwanda; in the Mision de los Naciones Unidas en Guatemala (MINUGUA); and in the Organization for Security and Cooperation in Europe (OSCE) Mission in Bosnia following the Dayton Peace Agreement. In 1993 the General Assembly approved a UN High Commissioner for Human Rights, a decision that is likely to strengthen this work.

United Nations Children's Fund (UNICEF)
The United Nations International Children's Emergency Fund, headquartered in New York, was created by the General Assembly in 1946 to provide relief to children suffering in the aftermath of World War II. By 1953, when the General Assembly extended UNICEF's mandate indefinitely and the words "International" and "Emer-

gency" were dropped from its name, the fund had begun to focus its attention on the widespread malnutrition, disease, and illiteracy afflicting millions of children throughout the developing world. In 1965 UNICEF was awarded the Nobel Peace Prize. It has continued to provide assistance to women and children in emergencies and promotes programs for longer-term development; it has a tradition of working in civil wars and internal conflicts.

The United Nations Volunteers

Headquartered in Bonn and established by the UN General Assembly in 1970, the United Nations Volunteers (UNV) provides a source of personnel and expertise to all UN agencies and to the International Organization for Migration (IOM). Operating under the UNDP the UNV maintains a register of 5,000 suitably qualified people who may serve on humanitarian relief, rehabilitation, and peace-support missions, typically for periods of 3 to 12 months. Volunteers provide support ranging from food aid distribution, camp construction and management, water and sanitation engineering, and public information and communications technology to human rights monitoring, electoral support work, conflict-resolution training, and psychotherapy and counseling.

The World Food Program

The World Food Program (WFP), headquartered in Rome, was founded in 1963 to provide food aid for relief in war-related emergencies and natural disasters, as well as to promote reconstruction and development. It channels resources from governments and intergovernmental organizations to government ministries in developing countries and has also worked with nongovernmental organizations (NGOs) to provide food aid in civil war–related emergencies. The WFP is responsible for the distribution of most multilateral food aid, but the bulk of international food aid is distributed bilaterally. The WFP operates with the Food and Agriculture Organization (FAO), a global information early warning system on food and agriculture.

The World Health Organization

The World Health Organization (WHO) had its origin in a proposal made at the United Nations Conference on International Organization in San Francisco in 1945, a proposal that envisaged the creation of a specialized institution working in the health field. It came into being in April 1948 after the twenty-sixth United Nations member had ratified WHO's constitution. Its services include the reconstruction of health infrastructures and medical services for the rehabilitation of casualties of war.

See also Civilian component in peacekeeping operations; Human rights; Peace building from below; Postconflict resconstruction; Refugees; White Helmets

United Nations: organization

The failure of the international community through the League of Nations to prevent a second global conflict (World War II, 1939–1945) led to renewed efforts to find a way to avoid such damaging wars in the future. During the course of World War II the leaders of the Allied powers took the steps that were to lead to the formation of the United Nations in 1945. In August 1941 the United States and Great Britain signed the Atlantic Charter, committing themselves to building a new international security system. In January 1942 the term "United Nations" was used for the first time in the Declaration of the United Nations, made by the 26 Allied countries still at war with the Axis powers of Germany and her allies. In October 1943 leaders of Britain, the United States, China, and the Soviet Union signed the Moscow Declaration, reaffirming the commitment to establishing a new international organization. In 1944 the Dumbarton Oaks meeting in the United States resulted in the production of a draft constitution for a postwar international organization. In April 1945 the UN Charter was drafted by 50 participating nations at the Conference on International Organization held in San Francisco, and it was signed during the course of that year by participating states and by the five permanent members of the new Security Council (the United States, Britain, France, China, and the Soviet Union: P-5). The charter came into force on 24 October 1945, the first meeting of the General Assembly was held in London in January 1946, and by the early 1950s the organization had its permanent headquarters on Manhattan Island, New York. In 1996 there were 185 member states.

The stated purpose of the United Nations is to work for peace, security, and cooperation between the nations of the world. Any necessary action in pursuit of this goal is implemented or facilitated by the member states themselves, acting cooperatively through the central body.

The purposes of the organization are resoundingly proclaimed in the preamble to the charter reproduced in Box 3.

General Assembly

The General Assembly is the central organ of the United Nations and is the one forum where every member nation has the right to a seat, the right to speak, and the right to a vote. It is not, however, a world parliament because it has no tax-raising powers and its decisions are not binding on its member states. The power of the assembly resides more in its status as focus of world opinion and in the approval power that it wields over the global budgets for all the work of the United Nations in peacekeeping, humanitarian aid, development, and so on. The General Assembly can also focus world attention on specific issues via special conferences or committees that are able to call upon expert testimony and to command widespread media attention. In the case of peacekeeping, this is done through the Special Committee on Peacekeeping Operations, or the Committee of 34. The General Assembly also is responsible for appointing the secretary-general and for the formal admission of new members. On many issues decisions are made within the General Assembly by a simple majority vote. On more important matters there has to be a two-thirds majority.

The Security Council

The Security Council is responsible for all matters relating to conflicts and conflict resolution, and any member state is entitled to bring any dispute to its attention. The council can be convened at any time—unlike the General Assembly, which normally meets for only three months of each year. Also unlike the General Assembly, decisions of the Security Council are binding on all member states. Once notified of a conflict (or a threat to peace) the council usually attempts to negotiate a pacific conclusion, either by negotiation with the parties concerned or by providing a mediating role. The council can also ask the secretary-general to investigate and report back on the facts of the situation. If fighting is taking place the Security Council will try to broker a cease-fire agreement and may then mandate a mission to police it.

The Security Council is also the body that mandates peace missions, and it has the power under the UN Charter to apply economic sanctions or to organize collective military action in order to enforce peace—or at least a cessation of fighting.

The Security Council has five permanent members—China, France, the Russian Federation, the United Kingdom, and the United States—and ten elected member states, which each serve for two years. Decision making requires nine votes in favor of a motion with the added proviso that, except for purely procedural motions, all five of the permanent members must be in favor. This gives each one of the five a very powerful lever (the power of veto) because one country can prevent the others from taking action. This was a particular problem during the Cold War period, when ideology played a major role in the work of the Security Council.

The Secretary-General

The secretary-general was envisaged as the chief administrator of the United Nations, whose job it would be to carry out the instructions of the General Assembly or the Security Council. But in practice the secretary-general's responsibilities are much deeper and wider, and the officeholder wields more power than is evident from the charter. Legally the secretary-general (SYG in UN terminology) is merely the servant of the major organs, but he or she has the right to take action in two important areas. First, under article 99 of the charter, the SYG can launch a fact-finding mission, which gives the SYG the power to visit a trouble spot or talk to the major actors in person. If the SYG does not do this in person the job can be entrusted to a special representative who reports back directly to the SYG. This kind of action can circumvent the sometimes labyrinthine procedures of the main body and enables the SYG to be a central actor in the resolution of conflicts. The

---

Box 3: From the Preamble to the UN Charter

WE THE PEOPLES OF THE UNITED NATIONS DETERMINED

to save succeeding generations from the scourge of war, which twice in our lifetime has brought untold sorrow to mankind, and

to reaffirm faith in fundamental human rights, in the dignity and worth of the human person, in the equal rights of men and women and of nations large and small, and

to establish conditions under which justice and respect for the obligations arising from treaties and other sources of international law can be maintained, and

to promote social progress and better standards of life in larger freedom,

AND FOR THESE ENDS

to practice tolerance and live together in peace with one another as good neighbours, and

to unite our strength to maintain international peace and security, and

to ensure, by the acceptance of principles and the institution of methods, that armed force shall not be used, save in the common interest, and

to employ international machinery for the promotion of the economic and social advancement of all peoples,

HAVE RESOLVED TO COMBINE OUR EFFORTS TO ACCOMPLISH THESE AIMS

The main body for debate and moving resolutions is the General Assembly, at which every member nation has a vote and the right to speak. The crucial body for implementing action is the Security Council, which has five permanent members and ten time-limited, elected members. To carry-out the decisions of the Assembly and Security Council there is a chief executive—The Secretary General—who heads the Secretariat which in turn has nine departments, each headed by an Under-Secretary.

---

second way that the SYG can exercise personal initiative is via goodwill visits; that is, the SYG can either visit a potential trouble spot and talk to the crucial political actors or establish a useful network of contacts for the future in conflict-prone areas. The Security Council also delegates to the secretary-general responsibility for the day-to-day running of peacekeeping operations.

In addition to the legal rights that accrue to the post, the SYG becomes an important person in global politics because he or she is head of the Secretariat and thus controls the flow of information to and from the major UN bodies. The SYG is also responsible for selecting members of the Secretariat, which provides the officeholder with another source of power as well as a possible constraint. Senior positions are much sought after and are often the subject of intensive lobbying by nations who want one of their own nationals in the post. This serves a dual purpose: It facilitates dialogue between the SYG and senior government officials, but it also constrains her or him in that others can misconstrue the sensitive complexities of the appointments system.

The Secretariat
When the General Assembly or the Security Council debates an issue the Secretariat is the part of the organization that supplies much of the information needed for informed debate and that is then charged with carrying out any decisions that require UN action. The Secretariat is headed by the chief executive—that is, the secretary-general—and comprises nine departments, each one headed by an undersecretary-general (USYG). Although all nine departments of the Secretariat play a role in all external aspects of the work of the United Nations, only four are centrally relevant to the work of the organization in peacekeeping: the Department of Peacekeeping Operations (DPKO);

the Department of Political Affairs (DPA); the Department of Humanitarian Affairs (DHA), now Office for the Coordination of Humanitarian Affairs (OCHA); and the Department of Administration and Management (DAM). In addition the work of a peacekeeping mission often covers the same ground as that of the United Nations High Commissioner for Refugees (UNHCR), since armed conflicts often produce large numbers of displaced people and refugees.

Department of Administration and Management (DAM)

This department is the largest in the whole organization and is responsible for all budgetary administration and other general administrative support. Because a peace mission is a huge undertaking and represents millions of dollars' worth of expenditure in staff and equipment costs, a DAM representative (or team) is present in the field to try to keep track of mission spending. This role is necessary, but it can sometimes create tensions within a mission because budgetary considerations can impinge upon and constrain the force commander's freedom to maneuver.

Department of Humanitarian Affairs/Office for the Coordination of Humanitarian Affairs

The secretary-general established the DHA in early 1992, following the adoption of General Assembly Resolution 46/182 in December 1991. The resolution highlights the UN's leadership and coordination role in ensuring that international efforts provide prompt delivery of relief assistance. The DHA's role is to coordinate the UN response to natural disasters and other emergencies that are beyond the mandate or capacity of any single UN agency (that is, complex emergencies). It assists agencies in reaching agreements on the allocation of responsibilities, conducts consolidated donor appeals, and collects and disseminates relevant information, including appeals for assistance by member states. As part of the UN Secretariat, the DHA works alongside the DPA and the DPKO. The DHA is headed by a USYG, who may also guide the SYG's special representative with respect to the humanitarian aspects of a specific peace operation and the peace operation's interface with private voluntary organizations (PVOs) and nongovern-

mental organizations (NGOs). The undersecretary-general is also appointed as the UN's Emergency Relief Coordinator. The DHA has centers in New York and Geneva. The Geneva office helps coordinate the work of the many humanitarian organizations in the UN system and launches coordinated appeals for specific emergencies. After January 1998 the DHA was reformed and renamed the Office for the Coordination of Humanitarian Affairs as the result of a program of reform initiated by the incoming secretary-general, Kofi Annan. The head of the OCHA is an undersecretary-general who has responsibility for a new Steering Committee to improve the coordination of humanitarian operations. This committee comprises members of UNHCR, the World Food Program (WFP), the United Nations Children's Fund (UNICEF), and the United Nations Development Program (UNDP), as well as the International Committee of the Red Cross/Red Crescent (ICRC) and NGO representatives. The reform of the DHA included halving its staff and redistributing some of its functions to other agencies and departments. For example, its responsibility for disaster mitigation and prevention has been assigned to the UNDP, and its responsibilities for removing land mines have been assigned to the DPKO. The OCHA now has a headquarters staff of 137 and a field staff of 51, covering field coordination arrangements in 16 countries in 1998. In an effort to improve conflict prevention and early warning capabilities, OCHA maintains important on-line information services relevant to peacekeepers and the humanitarian community (see Box 4).

Department of Peacekeeping Operations (DPKO)

The DPKO plans and oversees the operational and political side of UN peacekeeping operations for the secretary-general. Since March 1993 a number of initiatives aimed at upgrading the DPKO in New York have been carried out, including an expansion of staffing levels; the creation of an Office of Planning and Support, with a Planning Division that includes a Civilian Police Unit, a Demining Unit, and a Training Unit; the opening of a Lessons-Learned Unit so that the problems and successes of specific missions can be built into the institutional memory of peacekeeping and made

---

Box 4: Department of Humanitarian Affairs (DHA)/Office for the Coordination of Humanitarian Affairs (OCHA) On-Line Services

Relief Web (www.reliefweb.int): This Internet Web site, managed by the Office for the Coordination of Humanitarian Affairs (OCHA), provides up-to-date information on complex emergencies and natural disasters collected from over 170 sources. Users from over 150 countries access an average of 200,000 documents each month.

Humanitarian Early Warning System (HEWS): This site identifies crises with humanitarian implications. Through long-term and short-term multisectoral analyses of indicators, evaluation of trends, and in-depth field-based information, HEWS informs decisionmakers at headquarters about the likelihood and extent of crises. An extensive database of baseline information for more than 100 countries supports this activity.

Integrated Regional Information Network (IRIN): Since 1995 IRIN (Nairobi) has analyzed and synthesized information on developments in the Great Lakes Region. It issues daily reports as well as thematic studies for over 2,000 primary subscribers in more than 50 countries. IRIN (Abidjan) was set up in 1997 and began providing similar reports covering West Africa. It is envisaged that IRIN will expand its coverage in 1998 to include southern Africa, central Asia, and the Caucasus region as well as the Balkans.

References and further reading OCHA On-Line at http://www.reliefweb.int/dha

---

available for current and future missions; and the establishment of the Situation Center. The Situation Center was set up in April 1993 to monitor the Unified Task Force (UNITAF) and the second United Nations Operation in Somalia (UNOSOM II). It has since been upgraded and now operates in accordance with proper and regularized staff procedures. Steps have also been taken to enhance the flow of information into the UN headquarters from member states through the installation of an intelligence-processing system, known as the Joint Deployable Intelligence Support System (JDISS), in the DPKO. In addition, the Field Administration and Logistics Division (formerly located within the DAM) has been integrated within the DPKO to form the new Office of Planning and Support, thus placing the administrative and logistical aspects of peacekeeping under the same organization as the military planning. The Mission Planning Service (MPS) is responsible for the coordination of short-, medium-, and long-term aspects of mission planning; for the preparation of new missions; and for the revision, planning, and closure of future missions. Its main goal is to ensure preparedness, even in advance of Security Council authorization for a new mission. The MPS is subdivided into a number of units, such as the Generic Planning Unit, which is concerned with a number of issues such as establish-

ing frameworks for coordination with other UN departments and with clarifying UN rules of engagement. However, despite these reforms and mechanisms to improve coordination from the center, mission command on a daily basis is delegated to a field-based force commander, and the UN DPKO is seen as providing mission support rather than mission command.

The Department of Political Affairs (DPA)
The DPA was formed in 1992, absorbing the Office for the Collection of Research and Information set up by Secretary-General Javier Pérez de Cuéllar. The DPA is the political arm of the secretary-general and provides research, analysis, and advice on issues of international peace and security and on the control and resolution of conflicts within member states. It also has executive responsibilities in the fields of preventive diplomacy and peacemaking, including negotiations and other diplomatic activities. Special representatives are appointed to act on behalf of the secretary-general to conduct good offices, fact finding, mediation, and negotiations in specific conflicts. The DPA is thus expected to take the lead in the political side of peace-related work, assisting the secretary-general in any political initiatives aimed at reducing or resolving situations that may be a threat to world peace. This part of its role includes work on

arms reduction or limitation and on actual disarmament, conducted by the Center for Disarmament Affairs. Under reforms instituted by Secretary-General Kofi Annan in 1998, the Center for Disarmament Affairs was replaced by a new Department for Disarmament and Arms Regulation based in New York.

The DPA is also involved in servicing the electoral process of the United Nations, in providing electoral support for any member state that requests it, and in administering the affairs of the General Assembly, the Security Council, and the Trusteeship Council, as well as organizing the Division for Palestinian Rights. Under Kofi Annan's 1998 reforms the DPA, in its capacity as the convener of the Executive Committee on Peace and Security, is also to be a focal point for UN postconflict peace building.

See also Agenda for Peace; Annan, Kofi (1938-); Boutros-Ghali, Boutros; Charter of the United Nations; Financing peacekeeping; First generation peacekeeping; Hammarskjöld, Dag (1905–1961); Humanitarian Assistance; League of Nations; Lie, Trygve (1896–1968); Military-humanitarian relations; Peace enforcement; Perez de Cuellar, Javier; Refugees; Second generation peacekeeping; Status of forces agreement; Thant, U; United Nations Special Committee on Peacekeeping Operations (C-34); Uniting for Peace; Waldheim, Kurt
References and further reading Annan (1997a and 1997b); Bailey (1988); Bailey and Daws (1995); Childers and Urquhart (1994a); Cleveland, Handerson, and Kaul (1995); Coate (1994); Dallen (1992); Evans (1993); Mackinlay (1996); the DPKO maintains an excellent web page at http://www.un.org/dpko/

UNITAF (Unified Task Force), Somalia, 1992
See Somalia

UNAMIC (United Nations Advance Mission in Cambodia), 1991–1992
See Cambodia

UNAVEM (United Nations Angola Verification Missions I–III), 1989–1997
See Angola

UNASOG (United Nations Aouzou Strip Observer Group), 1994

Conflict Profile
The Aouzou Strip is a 45,000-square-meter area of land in the north of the Republic of Chad, on the border with Libya (also called the Socialist People's Libyan Arab Jamahiriya). The strip has been contested between the two countries since it was occupied by Libya in 1973. In 1979 Nigeria dispatched an 800-strong force to the area to monitor compliance with an agreed-upon cease-fire between the opposing parties. However, discord between the host nations and the Nigerian troops led to the Nigerians' withdrawal within a few months. It was then agreed that an Organization of African Unity (OAU) peacekeeping force would replace the Nigerians. The force was intended to comprise troops from Benin, Brazzaville Congo, and Guinea. However, only the Congolese peacekeepers actually arrived in Chad, and the operation was not deployed.

The dispute over the Aouzou Strip continued into the late 1980s. Then in 1988 diplomatic relations were restored between Chad and Libya, and both countries agreed to seek a peaceful solution. In August 1989 the two countries signed a Framework Agreement on the Peaceful Settlement of the Territorial Dispute. They consented to refer the matter to the International Court of Justice (ICJ), and Libya pledged to withdraw its troops from the strip unless a political settlement between Tripoli and N'Djamena permitted them to stay. Both sides presented their respective claims to the Aouzou Strip to the ICJ. Libya's claim was based on the rights of the indigenous inhabitants of the area and of successive sovereign entities, including the Ottoman Empire, Italy, and Libya itself. Chad, on the other hand, primarily cited the Treaty of Friendship and Good Neighborliness, drawn up between France and the United Kingdom of Libya in 1955.

Deployment of UNASOG
On 3 February 1994 the ICJ delivered its verdict that the 1955 Treaty of Friendship demarcated the border between Chad and Libya, and an agreement signed on 4 April that year by the two countries established details of how this verdict would be implemented. The agreement provided for the withdrawal of Libyan troops and the removal of mines

from the strip; the establishment of frontier crossing points; the official demarcation of the border; and an investigation into modalities for monitoring the boundary. It also confirmed that the withdrawal of Libyan forces would be completed by 30 May 1994 and that the process would be supervised by a 50-strong combined Chadian-Libyan team of military officers, supported by UN observers.

The Security Council, on 4 May 1994, adopted Security Council Resolution (SCR) 915, by which it established the United Nations Aouzou Strip Observer Group (UNASOG). UNASOG was authorized to comprise nine military observers, supported by six civilian staff, and was mandated for a period of 40 days to verify the combined Chadian-Libyan supervision of the withdrawal process. On 30 May representatives of the two parties' governments signed a Joint Declaration, witnessed by the chief military observer of UNASOG, agreeing that the Libyan withdrawal from the strip had been satisfactorily completed, and in June UNASOG itself was withdrawn. The nine military observers serving with UNASOG were provided by Bangladesh, Ghana, Honduras, Kenya, Malaysia, and Nigeria, and no fatalities were incurred during the operation. The chief military observer was Col. Mazlan Bahamuddin (Malaysia). Net expenditures for the UNASOG mission amounted to $67,471, appropriated though regular UN assessments.

See also Chad
References and further reading United Nations (1996)

United Nations Assistance Mission in Rwanda, 1993 (UNOMUR 1993–1994/UNAMIR 1993–1996)
See Rwanda

UN Charter and peacekeeping
See Charter of the United Nations

United Nations Children's Fund (UNICEF)
See United Nations: agencies; United Nations: organization

United Nations CIVPOL
See Civilian police (United Nations Civilian Police [CIVPOL])

United Nations Commission for India and Pakistan, 1948
See UNMOGIP

United Nations Commission on Korea
See Korean War

United Nations Conciliation Commission for Palestine, 1947
See UNTSO

UNCRO (United Nations Confidence Restoration Organization), 1995–1996
See Croatia

UNDOF (United Nations Disengagement Observer Force), 1974–

Conflict Profile
The 1973 Arab-Israeli war prompted the creation of another UN peacekeeping force in addition to the second United Nations Emergency Force (UNEF II). The Golan Heights is a stretch of territory situated between Syria and northern Israel that is of crucial strategic importance to both countries. The 1967 Six-Day War had transferred control of the Golan Heights, and therefore the concomitant strategic advantage, to Tel Aviv. The October 1973 Arab attack on Israel allowed Syria to briefly regain some territory in southern Golan. However, the Israeli counteroffensive four days later not only recovered the lost ground but also pushed toward the town of Saassa—in what was termed the "Saassa salient"—moving Israeli forces to within 20 miles of Damascus. On 22 October 1973 a cease-fire demanded by the Security Council under Security Council Resolution (SCR) 338 provided only a brief respite in the fighting between the parties, and from

early March to the end of May 1974 the conflict in the region intensified, involving the use of tanks, artillery, and rockets. The potential implications of the violence aroused considerable concern within the international community. Syria's close diplomatic ties with the Soviet Union and Israel's with the United States meant that the tension was likely to spread beyond the regional level. The fighting also presented a threat to the UN-supervised Israeli disengagement from Egypt that was taking place at the time, and the West had already experienced the hardships of an Arab oil embargo.

Shuttle diplomacy carried out by U.S. Secretary of State Henry Kissinger between Tel Aviv and Damascus eventually brought about, on 29 April, a consensus between Israel and Syria on the principles of a trizonal disengagement proposal. However, it was not until 29 May that the Israeli and Syrian governments finally accepted an Agreement of Disengagement, which called on both parties to observe a cease-fire on land, sea, and air, in implementation of Resolution 338. The agreement asserted that the parties be separated under the terms of the 29 April disengagement proposal, which provided for the interposition of a demilitarized area of separation (AOS), to be occupied by a UN force, between the opposing troops. Either side of the AOS would run areas of limitation of armament and forces (AOLs). The agreement also provided for wounded and prisoners of war to be exchanged between the two sides. Both parties gained by complying with the proposal: Syria would regain the territory that Israel had won back, and a UN-monitored buffer zone improved Tel Aviv's military position. Syrian and Israeli military representatives in the Egyptian Military Working Group of the Geneva Peace Conference were to work out the details of delineating the AOS and AOLs. The agreement was to be signed by the military representatives of the two sides on 31 May. Therefore, on 30 May, the secretary-general transmitted to the Security Council the text of the agreement, as well as the Protocol to the Agreement, which concerned the creation of the United Nations Disengagement Observer Force (UNDOF) (see Map 9).

Deployment of UNDOF

On 31 May 1974 the Security Council also adopted SCR 350 agreeing to immediately estab-

lish UNDOF for an initial period of six months. The UNDOF mandate, described in the Protocol to the Agreement, specified the force's tasks: to supervise compliance with the cease-fire, to monitor the AOS and AOLs, and to facilitate implementation of Resolution 338. The AOS stretched from Mount Hermon in the north to the River Jordan in the south, and on either side of it ran three different AOLs. The first extended 10 kilometers from the AOS, and in it the parties were allowed to deploy no more than 6,000 troops, 75 tanks, and 36 artillery pieces of 122 millimeters or less. The second extended 20 kilometers and allowed for 450 tanks and no more than 162 artillery pieces with a maximum range of 20 kilometers. The third extended 25 kilometers and excluded only surface-to-air missiles. UNDOF was to patrol the AOS and keep checks on the AOLs. Although the five permanent members of the Security Council were precluded from providing personnel for UNDOF, staffing UNDOF was made easier by "borrowing" personnel from other UN operations in the area. Austria, Canada, Peru, and Poland consented to the use of some of their peacekeepers serving with UNEF II, and about 90 military observers from the United Nations Truce Supervision Organization (UNTSO) were also brought in. The considerable territorial gains that Syria had secured during the early stages of the conflict resulted in some disagreement between the parties over the size of the force. Israel favored a 3,000-strong, well-armed force, whereas Syria preferred a small force of observers. A strength of 1,250 was eventually agreed upon. This number was reached by mid-June and has not varied by more than 10 percent since then. The Peruvian contingent was withdrawn after the first year and was replaced by one from Iran. The Iranian troops were themselves withdrawn in March 1979 and were replaced by Finnish forces.

The cease-fire successfully came into effect on 31 May 1974. By 5 June a four-stage disengagement plan and timetable had been agreed upon. It provided for the progressive withdrawal of Israeli forces from areas to the east of the 1967 cease-fire line, to the east of the Sea of Tiberias and northwest of Saassa, to the east and north of Qumeitra,

UNDOF deployment as of November 1995

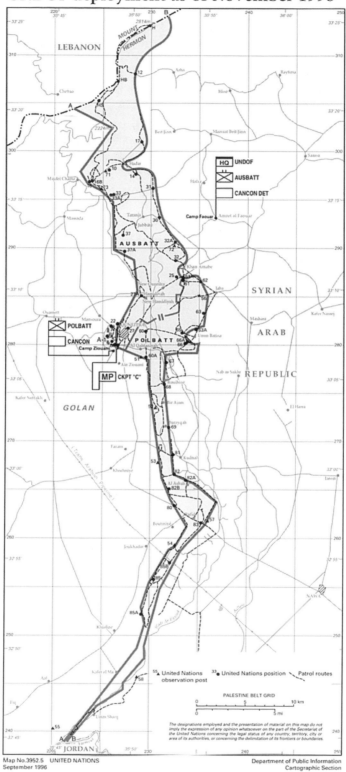

Department of Public Information
Cartographic Section

260

and from the AOS, which would then be occupied by UNDOF. The process began on 14 June and was completed by 27 June. The disengagement process was followed by UNDOF's principal long-term task of supervising the agreement. Observation posts manned 24 hours a day were established, and daily patrols were undertaken by UNDOF personnel in the AOS. Monitoring of the AOLs was carried out by UNTSO military observers from 11 fixed observation posts in each area. The results of their inspections and any violations of the Disengagement Agreements were reported to liaison officers from both parties. There have been no reports of major incidents within the UNDOF area of operation since 1991, when Israel restricted the freedom of movement of the Polish unit serving on the Israeli side of the AOS because of the poor diplomatic relations that existed until then between the two countries.

UNDOF successfully supervised the disengagement of Israeli forces from the Golan Heights and has since maintained peace in the area. This success was to a large extent the result of the propitious political climate. Both parties had agreed to disengage, and both saw the advantage in having an outside force facilitate the disengagement process. The fact that both sides agreed to cease hostilities reflected the international, and especially superpower, interest in reaching a settlement, and the presence of an international peacekeeping force served as a constant reminder of the international interest. This state of affairs allowed the UNDOF mandate to remain simple, precise, and achievable. UNDOF's impartial fulfillment of that mandate undoubtedly encouraged stability in the region and hence facilitated resolution.

UNDOF was paid for through assessments appropriated for UNEF II, whose account was kept open after that mission was terminated in 1979. UNDOF's total expenditure up to 31 May 1996 was estimated at $446,487,000.

See also Middle East conflict
References and further reading Durch (1994); James (1990); Mackinlay (1989); United Nations (1996)

UNEF I (United Nations Emergency Force I), 1956–1967

Conflict Profile

The United Nations Emergency Force that was deployed to the Suez in 1956 was the first force-level UN operation to be characterized, at the time, as peacekeeping. The Suez Canal crisis emerged from an international climate that was dominated by three major trends: the decline of European imperialism, decolonization and the rise of nationalism in the developing world, and the development of the Cold War. Britain and France—at the time the dominant powers in the Middle East—were keen to maintain their influence in the region, especially in view of Britain's recent loss of India and France's of Indochina. The Suez Canal was especially important in maintaining their access to the massive mineral resources that were available in the region. Egyptian President Gamal Abdel Nasser's nationalist, nonaligned ideology, combined with the pan-Arab consensus that this stance engendered, encouraged him to pursue anti-European policies. In 1955 Britain had formed the Baghdad Pact, a security cooperative with Iran, Iraq, Pakistan, and Turkey, ostensibly as a defensive buffer zone against the Soviet Union. However, Nasser perceived the alliance as a threat both to Egypt and to pan-Arab solidarity as a whole and refused to participate. This allowed the West, in the Cold War era of mistrust toward the East, to interpret Nasser's nationalist philosophy as evidence of his inclinations toward communism. The West believed its fears were confirmed when, in 1955, Nasser secured an arms deal with Czechoslovakia that included Soviet aircraft and tanks. The Egyptians' buildup of Soviet weapons was matched by Israeli imports from the United States, which greatly exacerbated the feelings of mistrust in the area. On 19 July the United States withdrew funding for the Aswan Dam project on the Nile, which was to have provided Egypt both with vital electricity and with irrigation for large areas of land. A week later Nasser declared the nationalization of the Suez Canal Company as an alternative means to finance the dam. On 29 October Israeli armed forces, with the tacit support of

Britain and France, crossed the Egyptian border and advanced over the Sinai Desert toward the Suez Canal. On 30 October the British and French, on the pretext of safeguarding the canal but really with the intention of gaining control of it, demanded that the two parties withdraw to positions no closer than ten miles from the canal, threatening to deploy troops if they refused. Egypt rejected the proposal, and so on 31 October British and French aircraft launched a series of strikes against Egyptian air bases and landed troops near Port Said at the northern tip of the canal (see Map 10).

The Deployment of UNEF I

Successive Security Council attempts to require Israeli troops to withdraw were vetoed by the British and French. However, on 2 November 1956, under the terms of the 1950 Uniting for Peace Resolution, the General Assembly passed Security Council Resolution (SCR) 997, proposed by the United States, urging an immediate cease-fire and demanding the reopening of the canal and the withdrawal of forces behind the 1949 armistice lines. SCR 997 was adopted 65 to 5 (Australia, Britain, France, Israel, and New Zealand voted against) with six abstentions (Belgium, Canada, Laos, the Netherlands, Portugal, and South Africa). However, the calls for a cease-fire were ignored, and hostilities continued. On 4 November 1956 the Security Council adopted SCR 998 requesting the secretary-general to submit a proposal for the establishment of a UN force to secure and monitor a cease-fire. The next day the first United Nations Emergency Force (UNEF I) was created by the adoption of SCR 1000, by a vote of 57 to 0 with 19 abstentions (including Britain, Egypt, France, the Soviet Union, and other Eastern bloc states). Then, at midnight on 6–7 November, under political pressure particularly from the United States, Britain finally agreed to a cease-fire.

A number of divergent factors influenced international support for the unprecedented UN policy of deploying a multinational force to Suez. The United States was driven by the Cold War fear that using force to remove Nasser from the canal would engender resentment among other Arab and developing states, which could then be exploited by the Soviet Union. Despite being irritated by the British and French initiative at Suez, Washington was nonetheless eager to help its important allies extricate themselves from the predicament they had driven themselves into. It therefore pursued a policy of defusing the situation by providing Anglo-French forces with a face-saving exit, which would ultimately achieve the objectives that the British and French offensive had ostensibly been trying to secure. The Soviet Union was equally keen to avoid a major confrontation and see the withdrawal of foreign forces from the region. Britain required access to the whole length of the canal for financial reasons. However, for that access it needed Egyptian cooperation, which was itself contingent on the withdrawal of British troops from Egyptian territory. The British and French governments also felt politically isolated, and the French already had plenty of troubles of their own in Algeria. Both countries, therefore, agreed to withdraw by 22 December. The United Nations secured Egyptian compliance by promising that Egypt's national sovereignty would be respected. Israel was persuaded to retreat through political pressure from the United States, but it demonstrated its reluctance to do so by delaying its withdrawal from Gaza and Sharm al-Sheikh at the southernmost tip of the Sinai Peninsula and by refusing to allow UN personnel on its territory.

The UNEF I mandate was fourfold: to secure and then monitor a cease-fire between the opposing parties by creating a buffer zone between them, to monitor the withdrawal of foreign troops, to deter military activity in border areas by means of observation posts and patrols, and to secure the Armistice Agreement between Israel and Egypt. UNEF I comprised units from ten troop-contributing countries: Brazil, Canada, Colombia, Denmark, Finland, India, Indonesia, Norway, Sweden, and Yugoslavia, while offers of assistance from Italy, Switzerland, and the United States were also accepted. Nasser had rejected the involvement of Pakistan because of its participation in the Baghdad Pact and of New Zealand because it was a prominent member of the British Commonwealth. The British and French governments had been insisting that their troops would not withdraw from the Sinai until UNEF I was in position, and so Secretary-General Dag Hammarskjöld attempted to

UNEF I deployment as of August 1957

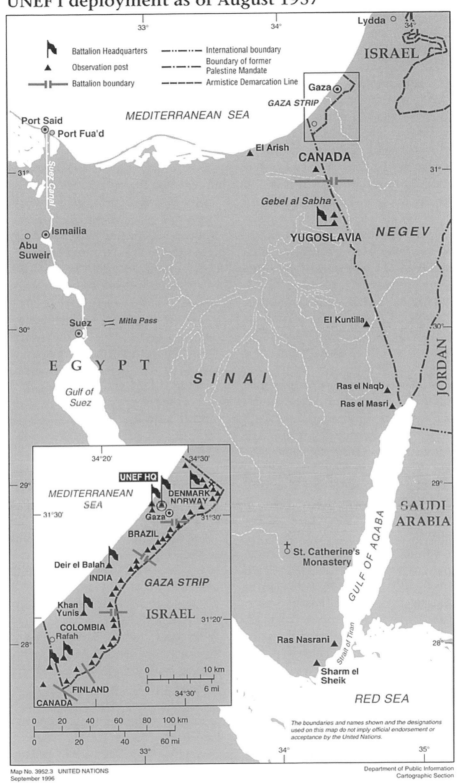

Map No. 3952.3 UNITED NATIONS
September 1996

Department of Public Information
Cartographic Section

get the force's deployment under way as quickly as possible. The first contingents began to arrive on 15 and 16 November, and the arrival of the Brazilian battalion in February 1957 brought the force up to its target strength of around 6,000 troops. This level was maintained until the end of the year, when financial constraints forced a progressive reduction in UNEF I's numbers. By the time it began its withdrawal in May 1967 it had reached 3,378.

After the British and French governments had agreed to withdraw their troops from Egyptian territory, UNEF I was deployed to facilitate this process. The UN force positioned itself between Anglo-French and Egyptian soldiers to deter possible incidents between them as the withdrawal took place. It also assumed responsibility for public services and security from the British and French during the withdrawal, after which it immediately transferred them to the Egyptian authorities. UNEF I was then required to supervise the Israeli withdrawal from the Sinai to behind the Egyptian-Israeli Armistice Demarcation Line (ADL) and the southern border of Gaza. However, Israel refused to withdraw from the peninsula, claiming that the validity of the ADL and ownership of Sharm al-Sheikh remained moot.

U.S. political pressure eventually succeeded in persuading Israel to withdraw its forces from the whole of the Sinai, apart from Gaza, on the grounds that the Israeli occupation was inciting raids by Palestinian fedayeen fighters and from Sharm al-Sheikh in view of its strategic position on the Tiran Strait. The next phase of the UNEF I deployment involved removing Israeli forces from the areas they continued to occupy. The Israeli suggestion that UNEF I personnel be stationed at Sharm al-Sheikh to guarantee Israeli passage through the Tiran Strait was generally accepted. However, Israel continued to question the legality of Egypt's presence in Gaza and proposed a plan in which an Israeli civilian administration would assume authority for the area with the support of the already established United Nations Relief Works Agency for Palestinian Refugees (UNRWA). However, the United Nations refused this proposal in favor of SCR 1125 (1957), which offered to station UNEF I personnel along the ADL that surrounded much of Gaza and promised that Israel's with-

drawal would be followed by action to secure peaceful conditions in the area. After considerable prevarication Israel finally accepted this proposal in the face of U.S. threats of sanctions, and by 12 March 1957 it had withdrawn its troops from both of the disputed areas.

UNEF I had initially been established solely to defuse the precipitant Suez Canal crisis in 1956. However, the United States was eager to maintain stability in such a strategically crucial area and so was highly supportive of a continued UN presence to supervise the cessation of hostilities between Egypt and Israel. On the other hand, the Eastern bloc states, acutely conscious of the Western bias within the UN General Assembly, were not in favor of the idea and voiced concern over Egypt's sovereignty. Egypt, meanwhile, realized the advantages of a multinational military presence between itself and Israel, and so the General Assembly was able to pass Resolution 1125 authorizing UNEF to patrol the Egyptian-Israeli ADL and the international frontier (IF) in the south. However, Israel remained opposed to the Armistice Agreement with Egypt and so refused to allow UNEF troops on its side of the borders. Observation was thus carried out on the Egyptian side only, by means of 72 fixed observation posts and mobile patrols along the ADL, with 8 posts and further patrols along the IF. UNEF air reconnaissance supervised the Sinai coast from the northern end of the Gulf of 'Aqaba to the Tiran Strait. UNEF personnel were lightly armed and were instructed to use force only in self-defense. Anyone it picked up attempting to cross the border would be handed over to the local authorities. Israel assisted the United Nations by prohibiting movement in Gaza within 500 meters of the ADL at night and 50 meters during the day. Even though UNEF was deployed on only one side of the border, the secretary-general reported that the force's presence considerably reduced the number of incidents in its area of operations up to its withdrawal in 1967.

The calm along the Israeli-Egyptian border was in marked contrast to the atmosphere on Israel's borders with Jordan and Syria, where as a result of the creation of the Palestine Liberation Organization (PLO) in 1964, fedayeen raids across the two fronts, followed by Israeli reprisals, became increasingly common occurrences. Tension along the Israeli-Syrian border heightened during the early part of 1967, leading to heavy shelling of Israeli villages on 7 April followed by strikes by Israeli aircraft against Syrian targets. Events came to a head after Egypt received reports from the Soviet Union of a buildup of Israeli troops along the border in anticipation of an invasion of Syria. On 16 May Egypt contacted UNEF I's force commander demanding the withdrawal of all UN troops along Egypt's borders. The force commander forwarded the message to Secretary-General U Thant, who interpreted it as a request for the complete withdrawal of UNEF I from Gaza and Sinai, since the proposed reductions would render UNEF I ineffective. There has since been considerable controversy as to whether UNEF I's total withdrawal had in fact been requested and whether the subsequent complete withdrawal precipitated the ensuing war. Whichever way it was, the Egyptian permanent representative to the United Nations then declared that UNEF I must withdraw from Egypt and Gaza as soon as possible. The secretary-general instructed UNEF I's commander to commence withdrawal on 19 May, to be completed at the end of June. UNEF I troops actually began to leave on 29 May and had virtually all left by 13 June, apart from the force commander and a few staff officers who left on 17 June. The Six-Day War broke out on 5 June. Some UN troops were caught in the fighting in Gaza, and 15 were killed.

Overall, UNEF I achieved its objectives. It successfully supervised the cease-fire, oversaw the withdrawal of foreign military forces from Egypt, and maintained stability along the border with Israel. The success of the mission can be attributable to the support it received in its early stages from the major international powers, Egypt's consent and cooperation in allowing the force on its territory, Israeli acceptance of if not support for the operation, and Secretary-General Hammarskjöld's diplomatic skills. UNEF I was also useful in a number of other ways. It was the first force-level UN peacekeeping operation and established a basic set of principles that have in general served as the basis for all subsequent operations: the principle that impartiality and nonintervention would be maintained; that the parties to the conflict must consent to the mission; that the secretary-general would maintain quotidian control of the operation, as well as of the selection of troop-contributing countries and the force commander; that contingents would be voluntarily recruited from member states other than the Permanent Five; and that the use of force would be prohibited except in self-defense. Secretary-General Hammarskjöld and the Canadian diplomat Lester Pearson are generally credited with devising these principles.

See also First-generation peacekeeping; Hammarskjöld, D.; Middle East conflict; Pearson, Lester B.; UNTSO
References and further reading Burns (1975); Durch (1994); Skold (1996); United Nations (1996)

UNEF II (United Nations Emergency Force II), 1973–1979

Conflict Profile

On 6 October 1973, the Jewish holiday of Yom Kippur, Egyptian troops crossed the Suez Canal and attacked the Israeli armed forces, which had occupied an area to the east of the canal since the Six-Day War in June 1967. Simultaneously, Syrian troops launched a coordinated offensive against Israeli positions on the Golan Heights, which had similarly been seized in June 1967. The initiative caught Israel by surprise, and by 7 October the Egyptians had established defensive positions beyond the United Nations Truce Supervision Organization (UNTSO) observation posts on the east of the canal. Neither side, at this juncture, was prepared to consider a cease-fire: Egypt believed it held the military upper hand, while Israel found it inconceivable that Arabs had penetrated Israeli-held territory. The Security Council convened special sessions between 8 and 12 October to confront the problem. However, a conflict of superpower interests—with the Soviet Union not wishing to intervene against its Arab allies and U.S. support of Israel reinforced by military intelligence reports predicting a swift reversal of events in Israel's favor—meant that it was unable to reach a decision. Bolstered by Soviet arms imports, the Egyptian military forces more than held their own. As Israel began to suffer heavy plane and tank losses, the Israeli government was persuaded to offer a cease-fire on 13 October. However, Egyptian President Anwar Sadat's continued opposition to the idea convinced the United States to provide Israel with enough equipment and supplies to bring about a swift end to the fighting. The arrival of U.S. shipments swung events in Israel's favor. The Israeli Army reached Ismailia and Suez along the canal, almost encircling Egypt's 20,000-strong Third Army; at the same time, Israeli troops were approaching Damascus on the northern front. As an expression of pan-Arab unity at the prospect of Israel gaining the advantage in the war, King Faisal of Saudi Arabia declared an embargo on oil exports to the United States. This persuaded Washington to dispatch Secretary of State Henry Kissinger to Moscow to negotiate with the Soviet Union the terms of a cease-fire, which were subsequently agreed upon. The two superpowers then applied diplomatic pressure to Egypt and Israel to accept the proposal. Sadat was keen to relieve his Third Army, and Israeli Prime Minister Golda Meir relied on the United States for continued arms supplies, and so both accepted the terms.

On 22 October 1973, acting on the Soviet-U.S. joint cease-fire proposal, the Security Council adopted Security Council Resolution (SCR) 338, demanding a cease-fire and requesting the implementation of SCR 242 of 1967, which had called for the withdrawal of Israeli troops from the Egyptian territories they had occupied in the 1967 war. However, on 23 October 1973, as hostilities continued, the Security Council adopted SCR 339 requesting Secretary-General Kurt Waldheim to immediately dispatch UN observers to the region to supervise the cease-fire. On 24 October, with its Third Army still surrounded by Israeli armed forces and so cut off from supplies, Egypt requested that both superpowers deploy troops to the area to enforce a withdrawal of Israeli troops to pre–22 October positions. The U.S. government was not keen on the strategic advantage the Soviet Union would gain from the deployment of its armed forces in Egypt and the Middle East and so opposed the request. The USSR, however, accepted the proposal and threatened unilateral intervention if the United States refused to participate. Washington received intelligence reports of a substantial concentration of Soviet forces in the Mediterranean, possibly in preparation for the deployment of Soviet airborne divisions to Egypt, and that Moscow was preparing to transfer nuclear weapons to Egypt. The United States responded by placing all of its military (including nuclear forces) on a state of alert, precipitating perhaps the most dangerous situation between the superpowers since the Cuban missile crisis of October 1962. Washington then warned Sadat that Soviet intervention would bring about its withdrawal from negotiations with Israel, after which, on 24 October, the Egyptian president submitted a proposal to the Security Council that a multinational UN peacekeeping force be deployed as an alternative.

Deployment of UNEF II

On 25 October 1973 the Security Council adopted Resolution 340, forwarded by its nonaligned members, demanding an immediate cease-fire and a return by the parties to their positions of 22 October. The resolution also called on the secretary-general to increase the number of UNTSO observers in the area and decided to establish a second United Nations Emergency Force (UNEF II), to be composed of personnel from member states excluding the Permanent Five, to act as a buffer between the belligerents. As an emergency measure, while UNEF II's details were being worked out, Waldheim announced that he would immediately dispatch to the area 900 Austrian, Finnish, and Swedish troops serving with the UN Peacekeeping Force in Cyprus (UNFICYP), as well as the UNTSO chief of staff as interim force commander. The force was initially provided with a six-month mandate, until 24 April 1974, and its intended total strength of 7,000 troops was reached by 12 February 1974. Contingents were contributed by 12 countries: Austria, Canada, Finland, Ghana, Indonesia, Ireland, Nepal, Panama, Peru, Senegal, Sweden, and, at the insistence of the Soviet Union and after considerable diplomatic wrangling, Poland, marking the first time an Eastern bloc state was accepted for participation in a peacekeeping force. The USSR's payment of its assessments created another first for UNEF II—it was the first time Moscow had agreed to pay in 20 years—demonstrating the Soviet Union's support of the operation.

UNEF II's original objectives were to monitor the implementation of Resolution 340, to prevent the recrudescence of hostilities between the parties, and to cooperate with the humanitarian activities of the International Committee of the Red Cross/Red Crescent (ICRC). The mandate was eventually renewed eight times. Although a cease-fire was in place when UNEF II was deployed, no disengagement agreement had been reached and so the situation remained volatile. UNEF II troops were therefore sent immediately to the front to interpose themselves wherever possible between the opposing armies, and observation posts and patrols were established in sensitive areas. The speedy dispatch of UN troops had the desired stabilizing effect: The defused atmosphere proved conducive to the creation of successive disengagement agreements, facilitated by political pressure and Kissinger's shuttle diplomacy between Cairo and Tel Aviv. Sadat's Third Army was running dangerously short of supplies, and assurances that a more comprehensive disengagement settlement would be reached at a later date persuaded him to comply with initial disengagement agreements. Meir, on the other hand, was keen to secure the release of Israeli prisoners of war and an end to the naval blockade of the Bab el Mandeb Strait, which afforded access to the Red Sea from the Indian Ocean.

The first of these agreements, signed on 18 January 1974, provided for an Israeli withdrawal from its defensive positions on the canal's west bank to a position 23–32 kilometers from the east bank, the deployment of Egyptian troops along a line 10 kilometers from the east bank, and the establishment of a zone of disengagement between the two, monitored by UNEF II troops. Areas of limited forces and arms were set upon either side of the UN buffer zone. In these areas both parties were allowed a maximum of eight reinforced battalions, 30 tanks, 7,000 troops, and six artillery batteries of up to 120 millimeters. Antiaircraft weapons were prohibited. From 25 January onward, disengagement proceeded by phases. In each phase Israeli forces withdrew from a designated area, which would then be held by UNEF II troops until being handed over to the Egyptians. The operation ran smoothly and was completed by 4 March 1974. As a result of the calm that the disengagement operation brought to the area, from May 1974 UNEF II was able to gradually reduce its strength, until it had reached 3,987 troops by October 1975.

In September 1975 a second agreement was signed providing for further eastward withdrawal of Israeli troops, westward redeployment of Egyptian troops, and the establishment of new, expanded UN buffer zones. Two areas of limited forces and arms were also established on either side of the buffer zones. In these areas the number of military personnel was restricted to 8,000, and armaments were restricted to 75 tanks and 72 artillery pieces, including heavy mortars. Military forces were also prohibited from Ras Sur and Abu Rudeis in the south. Electronic early warning stations were set up within the zones, which were monitored by U.S. civilians known as the Sinai Field Mission (SFM). The agreement also provided for the return of the Gidi and Mitla Passes and the Abu Rudeis oil field to Egyptian administration, and it allowed access to the Suez Canal and Bab el Mandeb to Israeli civilian shipping. The redeployment phase of the second agreement was finished by 22 February 1975, after which UNEF II began the longer-term functions of its mandate. It supervised Egyptian compliance with demilitarization provisions in the south by setting up fixed observation posts and air and land patrols throughout the area. It used similar methods to monitor the buffer zones and, along with UNTSO military observers, carried out fortnightly inspections of the areas of limited armaments and forces. UNEF II's areas of operation remained mostly quiet; the few incidents that did occur were resolved without difficulty and with the cooperation of the parties.

In March 1979 Israel and Egypt concluded a peace treaty that came into effect on 25 April. The treaty provided for a phased Israeli withdrawal from all Egyptian territory over the following three years, after which security arrangements on both sides of the Egyptian-Israeli border would be made; it also provided for the assistance of UN forces and observers for an indefinite period. However, since its peace agreement with Israel, Egypt had become an anathema in the eyes of the rest of the Arab world. The Soviet Union did not wish to jeopardize its good relations with the majority of the Arab states and so made it clear that it would veto any UN involvement in the peace accord and hence any extension of the UNEF II mandate. On 25 July, in accordance with the peace treaty, Israeli forces withdrew from the northern Sinai to the east of El 'Arish, and the Egyptians assumed control of the area. UNEF II assistance was not required during the process, except to provide escorts to the parties. The Security Council allowed the UNEF II mandate to expire when it came up for renewal on 24 July 1979, after which the contingents were swiftly repatriated. Overall expenditures for UNEF II's entire, six-year operation were $446.5 million.

UNEF II undoubtedly assisted in securing the withdrawal of Israeli troops from Egyptian territory and in preventing a recrudescence of hostilities between the two parties. The reasons behind its success lay in the prevailing international political climate, which was highly conducive to a settlement and hence to the creation of a UN peacekeeping force to maintain stability in the region and so facilitate such a settlement. After a tense beginning, both superpowers were keen to see peace returned to such a strategically important part of the world, and both parties to the conflict, for the large part, cooperated with UNEF II, as did local parties. Diplomatic relations between Cairo and Tel Aviv, with the support and assistance of the United States, improved throughout the 1970s, while both the Egyptian and Israeli governments maintained secure authority over their armed forces.

See also Middle East conflict; Multinational force and observers
References and further reading Durch (1994); James (1990); Mackinlay (1989); Quandt (1977); United Nations (1996)

United Nations force commanders
See Force commanders

UNGOMAP (United Nations Good Offices Mission in Afghanistan and Pakistan), 1988–1990

Conflict Profile
The central authority in Afghanistan had, historically, experienced difficulties in extending its con-

trol beyond the capital, Kabul, and the principal cities into the countryside. In 1978 the left-wing People's Democratic Party of Afghanistan (PDPA) took control of the country and attempted to reverse traditional Afghan religious and social structures. However, the new government's attempted reforms experienced increasingly widespread resistance, which spread from rural areas to include the major city of Herat. Popular unrest culminated in the assassination of the president and the subsequent split of the PDPA.

In response, the Soviet Union decided to intervene, dispatching 100,000 troops to support the left-wing government and installing Babrak Karmal, who led one half of the PDPA, as prime minister. However, Moscow had misjudged both the strength and depth of popular opposition to the government, and the lack of cohesion of the Afghan Army, which had ceased to function effectively by the time the Russian troops arrived. The Islamic opposition mujahideen fighters, although not homogeneous, were collectively an effective guerrilla force, scoring periodic victories over the Soviet troops and maintaining ultimate control of the countryside.

However, the mujahideen's lack of cohesion eventually began to tell, as the Soviet and Afghan forces began to enjoy increasing success. Many opposition factions were forced to relocate to Pakistan, where they could base operations, receive assistance from other states, and launch cross-border attacks. The continuing success of the Russian forces in the mid-1980s convinced the United States to step up the level of military aid to the opposition fighters in order to counter the spread of Russian influence into Afghanistan and beyond. Consequently, the mujahideen again began to inflict considerable damage on Soviet and Afghan troops.

Deployment of UNGOMAP
As early as 1980 the issue of Afghanistan appeared on the Security Council's agenda, although, not surprisingly, Soviet opposition to any action forced transfer of the issue to the General Assembly. Interested parties to the dispute in addition to Afghanistan and the Soviet Union included Pakistan and Iran, which were the recipients of some

five million Afghan refugees. On 14 May 1980 the Afghan government announced a possible political solution to the conflict. The solution's four primary provisions would eventually form the basis of the Geneva Accords in the late 1980s. These provisions were the withdrawal of foreign (i.e., Soviet) troops from Afghan territory, noninterference in Afghanistan's internal affairs, international guarantees, and the voluntary repatriation of Afghan refugees. However, attempted negotiations between the interested parties were delayed by the refusal of Iran and Pakistan to recognize the government in Kabul. The personal representative of the secretary-general, Javier Pérez de Cuéllar, persuaded the governments of Afghanistan and Pakistan to attend talks based on the four-point agenda, although Iran would not participate because the mujahideen were excluded. Pérez de Cuéllar's successor, Diego Cordovez, eventually succeeded in getting Afghanistan and Pakistan to sign the Geneva Accords in 1988.

The accords comprised four separate agreements. The first two, between Afghanistan and Pakistan, concerned noninterference and nonintervention and the voluntary repatriation of refugees. The third was an international guarantee of noninterference from the United States and the USSR. Moscow and Washington then witnessed the last agreement, between Afghanistan and Pakistan, which included provisions for the withdrawal of Soviet troops. It was also agreed that the secretary-general would provide a good offices mission, supported by a team of between 10 and 50 unarmed observers, to facilitate implementation of the above tasks. The international community predominantly supported the Geneva Accords. The United States in particular allowed its mistrust of the mujahideen to be overruled by its desire to stem Soviet expansion southward. Washington was successful in preventing smaller states, who were eager to encourage Afghan self-determination, from including the mujahideen in any peace settlement.

However, the next two Soviet leaders, Leonid Brezhnev and Yuri Andropov, had believed that the tenuous maintenance of the left-wing regime in Kabul was worth the number of Soviet casualties from the conflict. The 1985 accession of Mikhail Gorbachev, who favored improved relations with the West, combined with waning domestic support as a result of increasing Soviet losses in Afghanistan, persuaded the Kremlin to alter its policy. Therefore, soon after taking office, Gorbachev announced the Soviet Union's commitment to securing a political solution to the conflict. However, since the USSR did not wish to be perceived as having lost the war, the problem remained of how to organize a withdrawal of Soviet troops without overtly embarrassing Moscow. In February 1988 Gorbachev declared that his country's troops would be withdrawn in the event of a settlement between Afghanistan and Pakistan. Thus, with the provisional agreement of the Security Council, the United Nations Good Offices Mission in Afghanistan and Pakistan (UNGOMAP), comprising 50 military officers, was dispatched to both Afghanistan and Pakistan and was fully operational by 15 May. UNGOMAP was mandated to monitor implementation of the provisions of the Geneva Accord.

The Soviet Union obligingly fulfilled its pledge to withdraw its troops from Afghanistan. Despite increased mujahideen activity in response to the phased withdrawal, UNGOMAP was able to confirm that the entire operation had been completed by 15 February 1989. Thus the peacekeeping force effectively executed its primary task. However, contrary to expectations, the government in Kabul, which had had substantial Soviet support, did not fall following the departure of the Soviet troops, and so the anticipated détente between Afghanistan and Pakistan did not occur. Although there had been no evidence of direct Pakistani interference in Afghanistan's affairs, Pakistan certainly supported the mujahideen. The composition of UNGOMAP was wholly unsuited to addressing the remaining terms of the Geneva Accord under such conditions, as it had no chance of investigating the number of complaints presented to it by the opposing parties. Furthermore, few Afghan refugees were eager to return to the violent situation at home. Therefore, soon after its scheduled completion in January 1990, UNGOMAP was withdrawn and replaced by the Office of the Secretary-General in Afghanistan and Pakistan (OSGAP) to seek a political solution to the conflict. In December 1994, this was replaced by the Office of the Secretary-General in Afghanistan.

UNGOMAP had headquarters in Kabul and Islamabad, and the mission lasted from May 1988 to March 1990. UNGOMAP had a strength of 50 military observers, contributed by Austria, Canada, Denmark, Fiji, Finland, Ghana, Ireland, Nepal, Poland, and Sweden, who were supported by international and locally recruited civilian staff, and it incurred no fatalities.

References and further reading Durch (1994); James (1990); Saikal (1996); Sherry (1996)

United Nations Guards Contingent in Iraq, 1991
See Iraq

United Nations High Commissioner for Refugees
See United Nations: organization

United Nations India-Pakistan Observation Mission (UNIPOM), 1965–1966
See UNMOGIP

United Nations Institute for Training and Research (UNITAR)
See Training for peacekeeping

UNIFIL (United Nations Interim Force in Lebanon), 1978–
See Lebanon

United Nations International Police Task Force (UNIPTF), 1995–
See Bosnia and Herzegovina

UNIIMOG (United Nations Iran-Iraq Military Observer Group), 1988–1991

Conflict Profile
After a prolonged history of instability between Iran and Iraq, relations between the two countries had begun to improve steadily during the 1970s. However, the deposition of the Shah of Iran in 1979 and the subsequent accession to power of the Islamic regime of Ayatollah Ruholla Khomeini caused problems for the secular Ba'ath administration in Baghdad. Deteriorating relations between the two countries eventually developed into violent confrontation in 1980 over disputed territory along the Iran-Iraq border. Iraq had launched attacks against Iranian positions in territory that Baghdad claimed the two sides had agreed should be returned to Iraq.

Subsequent advances by the radical Iranian regime into Iraqi territory caused unease among other Gulf states, prompting them to support the Iraqi cause. Many Western nations also supported Baghdad, although in the mid-1980s military supplies made it through to Tehran from China and from the United States, as part of the Iran-Contra scandal. Neither side was able to achieve a decisive victory, and, fueled by external arms supplies to both countries, the conflict expanded into the Gulf itself as each side attacked the other's tankers and oil installations to damage its economic base. Thus stalemated, the war carried on into the late 1980s.

Deployment of UNIIMOG
As early as 1979 UN Secretary-General Kurt Waldheim had offered his good offices (i.e., services in mediation) to facilitate a negotiated settlement to the Iran-Iraq conflict, and on 28 September 1980 the Security Council adopted Security Council Resolution (SCR) 479, by which it demanded an immediate cessation of violence. In 1982 the Security Council again called for a cease-fire, and in 1983 it also requested the secretary-general to propose terms for a UN observer mission to monitor compliance with the cease-fire. Iraq had miscalculated the strength and commitment of the Iranian people's support for the war and had met with stronger resistance than it had anticipated. Therefore Baghdad tended to be sympathetic to calls for a cease-fire. Tehran, on the other hand, viewed the international community's failure to identify Iraq as the aggressor in the dispute as evidence of its pro-Iraq bias. This perception was reinforced by Iran's international isolation, which

was a result of certain aspects of its behavior, particularly in regard to the taking of hostages.

Up to the mid-1980s the international community had not been overly intent on ending the Gulf conflict because, by preoccupying both sides, it restricted Iran's ability to advance the spread of radical Islam and also limited Iraq's destabilizing behavior. Furthermore, arms sales to both countries provided a welcome boost to many countries' economies. Both superpowers had contradictory interests in the region: The United States opposed the spread of radical Islam but could not be seen to sanction Iraqi aggression, particularly as Iraq was an outspoken opponent of Washington's ally in the region, Israel. And the Soviet Union, although it had welcomed the end to U.S.-Iranian links that had accompanied the 1979 Iranian revolution, still wished to maintain oil supplies from Iraq, and it also became increasingly worried by the rise of radical Islam in Muslim Soviet Central Asia that Tehran was encouraging.

However, the extension of the conflict to shipping in the Gulf and the threat that this represented to Western supplies of oil encouraged the Security Council to adopt SCR 598 in 1987. This reiterated the international community's demands for a UN-supervised end to hostilities in the region, and it enjoyed particular support from both the United Kingdom and the United States. At German insistence, the resolution included provisions for the establishment of an investigative body to assess culpability in the war, which was designed to appease Iranian accusations of UN bias in favor of Iraq. Waning support for the Iranian cause eventually persuaded the Ayatollah to accept, albeit very reluctantly, the terms of Resolution 598 in July 1988.

On 9 August 1998 the Security Council unanimously adopted SCR 619, by which it sanctioned the mandate of UNIIMOG, which was to establish agreed-on cease-fire lines; monitor compliance with the terms of the cease-fire, investigate alleged violations, and restore the situation if violations did occur; prevent alterations to the status quo pending the withdrawal of opposing troops to recognized borders; monitor the withdrawal of those forces; verify the cease-fire along the recognized borders and oversee the exchange of prisoners of war; and facilitate negotiations between the opposing parties toward measures aimed at reducing tension. UNIIMOG was provided with 350 observers from 26 different countries (excluding countries from the Middle East on the grounds that they were interested parties in the dispute) in order to fulfill its mandate.

UNIIMOG undoubtedly helped to maintain the cease-fire along the border between Iran and Iraq, where the situation had remained extremely volatile. Palliative actions by the monitoring body kept successive, relatively minor incidents from escalating into what could easily have amounted to a return to war. UNIIMOG's task was complicated by the opposing parties' conflicting attitudes toward UNIIMOG: Iraq was in general accommodating to the presence of the mission, whereas Iran, who had only accepted the deployment under duress, remained hostile toward it. Some parts of the UNIIMOG mandate, such as the restoration of the situation following verified violations of the cease-fire agreement, were beyond the force's capabilities. Within days of UNIIMOG's deployment, Baghdad had seized several hundred Iranian hostages, who were not released for two years. Similarly, within a month of deployment, Iran had flooded with water the southern region of the frontier in order to disadvantage Iraqi military positions in the area.

Furthermore, UNIIMOG proved unsuccessful in advancing negotiations between the opposing parties toward a more comprehensive political settlement. It was only the overextension of Iraqi resources following its invasion of Kuwait in 1990 (and the allied response) that convinced Baghdad to consolidate the situation along its frontier with Iraq. The subsequent agreement over disputed border territories and the increasing tension in Iraq in the wake of the Gulf crisis convinced the Security Council to progressively reduce UNIIMOG's strength, until its withdrawal was finally completed in February 1991. Thus the effectiveness of the UNIIMOG mission was dependent on the attitude of the host nations. Although it successfully reduced tensions between the two sides, it was only the outbreak of another war involving one of the belligerents that precipitated moves toward a more enduring settlement.

UNIIMOG had headquarters in Tehran and Baghdad, and the mission lasted from August 1988 to February 1991. At its peak, the mission comprised 400 military personnel, supported by international and locally recruited civilian staff. Personnel were contributed by Argentina, Australia, Austria, Bangladesh, Canada, Denmark, Finland, Ghana, Hungary, India, Indonesia, Ireland, Italy, Kenya, Malaysia, New Zealand, Nigeria, Norway, Peru, Poland, Senegal, Sweden, Turkey, Uruguay, Yugoslavia, and Zambia. There was one UNIIMOG fatality during the operation, and UNIIMOG's expenditures amounted to $177,895,000.

See also Gulf Wars
References and further reading Durch (1994); United Nations (1996)

UNIKOM (United Nations Iraq-Kuwait Military Observation Mission), 1991–

Conflict Profile
The United Nations Iraq-Kuwait Observation Mission (UNIKOM) grew out of the international response to Iraq's invasion of Kuwait in August 1990. Following the Iraqi invasion, and primarily at the instigation of the United States, the UN Security Council adopted several resolutions, including one demanding the unconditional withdrawal of Iraqi personnel from Kuwaiti territory. On 29 November, the Security Council presented the Iraqi government with a deadline of 15 January 1991 for the implementation of the relevant resolutions. An inadequate response by the Iraqi government would authorize UN member states to take action under chapter 7 of the UN Charter to enforce their execution. In the meantime, the United States, along with allied states, began to deploy land, sea, and air forces to the area. On 15 January Iraqi troops were still in Kuwait, and so on 16 January air strikes were initiated against Iraq. On 24 February the allied forces launched a ground offensive, which by 27 February had successfully driven Saddam Hussein's forces from Kuwait.

Deployment of UNIKOM
The U.S.-led response to the Iraqi invasion of Kuwait did not follow the pattern of previous international reaction to violence in the area, where conflict had existed for a long time without precipitating such resolute reaction. In particular, until recently Washington had supported Baghdad in its ongoing conflict with Iran. However, the end of the Cold War had engendered a new consensus within the Security Council, allowing it to authorize, for the first time since the Korean conflict in the 1950s, a unified, forcible, collective security response.

Having removed Iraqi personnel from Kuwaiti territory, the Security Council, on 3 April 1991, adopted Security Council Resolution (SCR) 687, by which it established terms for the destruction and future supervision of all Iraqi weapons of mass destruction. Resolution 687 also set down specific terms for a cease-fire and requested that the secretary-general formulate a proposal demarcating a buffer zone along the Iraq-Kuwait border and the Khawr 'Abd Allah waterway to prevent further incidents between the opposing sides. The secretary-general's plan suggested that the buffer zone extend 10 kilometers into Iraq and 5 kilometers into Kuwait. This zone would be monitored by a UN observer unit (UNIKOM) in order to deter violations and to watch for hostile actions mounted in one state that might threaten the other. Implicit within these objectives was the intention to facilitate the withdrawal of allied ground forces from Iraqi territory.

On 9 April 1991 the Security Council adopted SCR 689, authorizing the secretary-general's proposal for the deployment of UNIKOM. UNIKOM was specifically mandated as an observer mission, and so was explicitly restricted from undertaking any forcible action to counter violations of the buffer zone. Nor was it required to fulfill any humanitarian or reconstructive function. Because of the wider international response to Iraq's invasion of Kuwait, of which UNIKOM was a part, the mission enjoyed unprecedented levels of international support. For instance, there was a general consensus that a monitoring force would be required along the Iraq-Kuwait border indefinitely, and UNIKOM's open-ended mandate reflected this commitment. UNIKOM's continued deployment requires only that its mandate be periodically reviewed, rather than extended, although its finances must be extended every six months. The states in the region are ambivalent about the operation, however, as is revealed by the fact that no Persian Gulf countries and no other Arab countries have offered personnel to serve with UNIKOM.

In February 1993, by adopting SCR 806, the Security Council expanded the UNIKOM mandate to authorize the force to undertake physical actions to counter minor breaches of both the buffer zone and the Iraq-Kuwait border, as well as to address difficulties arising from the presence of Iraqi people and structures in the Kuwaiti section of the buffer zone. Accordingly, an additional infantry battalion was attached to UNIKOM. In May 1993 the UN Iraq-Kuwait Boundary Demarcation Commission ratified the Iraq-Kuwait border, and Iraqi citizens living on the Kuwait side of the boundary were returned to Iraqi territory. Since then the situation in the buffer zone has remained calm through the late 1990s.

Despite initial deployment problems, UNIKOM has successfully carried out its traditional peacekeeping role as an interpositional force between two opposing parties, based on a formal agreement—although the consent of one of the parties, Iraq, was secured through coercion. The alterations made by the United Nations in February and May 1993 successfully addressed operational deficiencies that had previously hampered implementation of the UNIKOM mandate.

The UNIKOM force commander as of 1998 was Maj. Gen. Esa Kalervo Tarvainen (Finland). As of 31 December 1997, UNIKOM's strength stood at 1,082 military personnel, comprising 890 troops and support personnel and 192 military observers, supported by 200 international and local civilian staff. Military personnel have been contributed by Argentina, Austria, Bangladesh, Canada, China, Denmark, Fiji, Finland, France, Germany, Ghana, Greece, Hungary, India, Indonesia, Ireland, Italy, Kenya, Malaysia, Nigeria, Pakistan, Poland, Romania, Russian Federation, Senegal, Singapore, Sweden, Thailand, Turkey, the United Kingdom, the United States, Uruguay, and Venezuela.

See also Gulf Wars
References and further reading Durch (1994); United Nations (1996)

UNMOGIP (United Nations Military Observer Group in India and Pakistan), 1949– , and UNIPOM (United Nations India-Pakistan Observer Mission), 1965–1966

Conflict Profile
After India and Pakistan achieved independence from Britain in August 1947, a dispute arose between them over control of the state of Jammu and Kashmir (hereafter referred to as Kashmir). The Indian Independence Act of 1947 partitioned "British India" into two nations, India and Pakistan, whose populations were primarily Hindu and Muslim, respectively. It also provided that Kashmir could determine its own future affiliation with either India or Pakistan. The Kashmiri population was predominantly Muslim, though its ruler, Maharaja Sir Hari Singh, was Hindu. After independence, most people in Kashmir were eager that the province join Pakistan. However, the maharaja delayed any decision on the issue, precipitating violence in the province, including from invading Pathan fighters sent into Kashmir by Pakistan in an attempt to seize the territory from India.

The maharaja complained of Pakistani complicity in the violence, and India offered him assistance on the condition that Kashmir become part of India. The maharaja agreed in October 1947. However, the Indian troops that were dispatched to Kashmir failed to make significant headway against the well-organized Pathan fighters, and the conflict became stalemated, raising the risk of war between India and Pakistan themselves. The Indian government complained to the UN Security Council that Pakistan was behind the invasion of Kashmir; Pakistan retaliated by accusing India of illegally gaining control of the province. Pakistan proposed that the Kashmiris determine their political status in a UN-supervised referendum; India countered that the referendum should be conducted by the Kashmiri government after stability had been returned to the province.

Deployment of UNMOGIP
The international community concurred that it should assist in settling the dispute. Britain wanted its own hasty withdrawal from India to go as

smoothly as possible. Neither India nor Pakistan maintained particularly close links with either superpower, and so Cold War bipolar political relations did not dictate the terms of international involvement in the conflict. Therefore the international community was able to apply collective pressure on both sides to accept UN involvement in pursuing a peaceful settlement. Consequently, on 20 January 1948 the Security Council adopted Security Council Resolution (SCR) 39, by which it authorized the establishment of the United Nations Commission for India and Pakistan (UNCIP) in order to investigate each side's allegations in the dispute and to attempt to mediate a peaceful solution.

Disagreement over the composition of UNCIP delayed its deployment until July, by which time its membership had been expanded to include representatives from Argentina, Belgium, Colombia, Czechoslovakia, and the United States. The Security Council had also broadened its mandate to incorporate the use of observers to end violence in the province and provisions for the appointment of a plebiscite administrator. However, a referendum would only take place after a cease-fire was established and all Pakistani troops had withdrawn from Kashmir. A cease-fire agreement between the opposing parties came into effect in January 1949, and the arrival of the first observers in Kashmir at the end of the same month formed the basis of the United Nations Military Observer Group in India and Pakistan (UNMOGIP).

The observers with UNMOGIP monitored compliance with the terms of the cease-fire, and when, in July 1949, India and Pakistan signed the Karachi Agreement acceding to a cease-fire line, the observers facilitated its demarcation. Kashmir was thus divided between the parties to the dispute, with the intention that the subsequent referendum would determine the future of the territory as a whole. The Karachi Agreement also served as the basis for the UNMOGIP mandate, which provided that the UN mission would monitor the cease-fire line, investigate reported violations, adjudicate disagreements between the two sides, and monitor the composition and strength of each side's forces in designated areas.

UNCIP was withdrawn in 1950 on the premise that its mediatory efforts in relation to the dispute over Kashmir had been exhausted. However, in March 1951 the Security Council decided that UNMOGIP was serving a useful function in supervising the cease-fire and so extended its mandate. It is debatable to what extent the presence of UNMOGIP was responsible for the maintenance of the cease-fire, but apart from minor incidents the mission successfully maintained the terms of the Karachi Agreement until 1965.

Deployment of UNIPOM

In August 1965, in response to Pakistani attempts to foment insurrection in the Indian half of the province, hostilities again broke out between India and Pakistan along the cease-fire line in Kashmir. The fighting spread as India invaded what was then West Pakistan, prompting broad international consensus to attempt to calm the dispute and prevent it from escalating further. The Security Council demanded that India and Pakistan consent to a UN-supervised cease-fire and withdrawal of forces from each other's territory. The two sides agreed, but Pakistan complained that the spread of violence prohibited UNMOGIP from fulfilling its functions.

Thus the secretary-general established the United Nations India-Pakistan Observer Mission (UNIPOM) as a supplement to UNMOGIP. Both UNIPOM and UNMOGIP managed to maintain the cease-fire between the opposing forces, despite regular, often serious, violations. However, the withdrawal of forces proved to be more problematic. It took until January 1966, following negotiations in Tashkent, for a tenuous political settlement to be agreed upon by the belligerents. Five days later, the military aspects of withdrawal had been finalized, and by February of that year Indian and Pakistani troops had been successfully removed from the relevant areas. UNIPOM was itself subsequently withdrawn.

Hostilities between India and Pakistan broke out again toward the end of 1971, primarily over the status of East Pakistan (which as a result became Bangladesh). At independence from Britain, Pakistan was created from two separate Muslim-dominated areas of the British Indian Empire: the Punjab in the west (West Pakistan) and East Bengal in the east (East Pakistan). In December 1971, supported militarily by India, Bangladesh seceded from Pakistan and became an independent state. The war in Bangladesh also affected the situation in the west, with renewed hostilities along the cease-fire line in Kashmir. When stability was restored to the province and the cease-fire was again in place, the demarcation of the cease-fire line had altered since the 1949 Karachi Agreement. And so in July 1972 India and Pakistan agreed on a new Line of Control through Kashmir. India then claimed that the new agreement abrogated the UNMOGIP mandate, because the mission had been deployed specifically in relation to the Karachi Agreement. Pakistan still believed it could claim rightful ownership to Kashmir and therefore advocated the continued presence of UNMOGIP. Thus the UNMOGIP mandate has continued to be extended, and Pakistan has continued to make regular complaints to it about violations. India, on the other hand, has largely ignored the presence of the mission, thereby severely reducing its value as a peacekeeping force.

UNIPOM comprised 96 military observers, supported by international and locally recruited civilian staff, and incurred no fatalities during deployment. Its overall expenditures were $1,713,280. The chief military observer of UNMOGIP as of 28 February 1998 was Maj. Gen. Choung-Jun Ahn (Republic of Korea), and mission strength stood at 44 military observers, contributed by Belgium, Chile, Denmark, Finland, Italy, Republic of Korea, Sweden, and Uruguay. UNMOGIP is financed through regular assessments by UN member states and from its inception to December 1995 had amassed total expenditures of approximately $98,399,102.

References and further reading Dawson (1995); Durch (1994); United Nations (1996)

United Nations Mission of Observers in Prevlaka (UNMOP), 1996–
See Croatia

United Nations Mission for the Referendum in Western Sahara, 1991–
See Morocco

UNMIBH (United Nations Mission in Bosnia and Herzegovina), 1995–
See Bosnia and Herzegovina

UNMIH (United Nations Mission in Haiti), 1993–1996
See Haiti

UNOGIL (United Nations Observation Group in Lebanon), 1958
See Lebanon

United Nations Observation Mission for the Verification of Elections in Nicaragua, 1989–1990
See ONUCA

UNOMIG (United Nations Observer Mission in Georgia), 1993–
See Georgia

UNOMIL (United Nations Observer Mission in Liberia), 1993–1997
See Liberia

UNOMUR (United Nations Observer Mission in Uganda/Rwanda), 1993–1994
See Rwanda

UNOMSA (United Nations Observer Mission to South Africa), 1992
See South Africa

UNOSOM I and II (United Nations Operations in Somalia, I and II), 1992–1995
See Somalia

UNFICYP (United Nations Peacekeeping Force in Cyprus), 1964–
See Cyprus

United Nations peacekeeping forces and self-defense
See Rules of engagement

United Nations personnel privileges and immunities
See Status of forces agreement

UNPREDEP (United Nations Preventive Deployment Force Macedonia), 1995–
See Macedonia

United Nations protected areas
See UNPROFOR I–III

UNPROFOR I–III (United Nations Protection Force in Former Yugoslavia), 1992–1995

Conflict Profile

Before it dissolved violently in a series of civil wars that began in 1991, Yugoslavia was a federal state composed of six republics: Bosnia and Herzegovina, with a population of 3.7 million; Croatia, with a population of 4.3 million; Macedonia, with a population of 1.6 million; Montenegro, with a population of 550,000; Serbia, with a population of 8.4 million; and Slovenia, with a population of 1.6 million. Included in the Serbian republic were two autonomous provinces, Kosovo and Vojvodina. Kosovo, which has a population of nearly 2 million, is 90 percent Albanian and has a strong movement seeking autonomy or independence from Serbia, which by 1998 had become increasingly violent. The country was divided along linguistic, ethnic, and religious lines but was held together under the rule of President Josip Broz Tito and the Communist Party. Tito died in 1980, and after the Communist Parties of the Soviet Union collapsed, by 1990, the separate nationalisms of the Serbs, Slovenes, Croats, and Albanians erupted in a set of conflicts that destabilized the Balkan region. Slovenia and Croatia (led by Franjo Tudj-man) proclaimed independence in June 1991, and the Serbs (led by Slobodan Milosevic), determined to preserve a unitary state that they would dominate, launched military attacks in an effort to prevent secession. The Yugoslav federal troops initially attacked Slovenia, fighting broke out in Croatia as irregular Serb forces began to attack Croatian police and militias, and the Yugoslav Army also launched an attack on Croatia. Knowing that they could not hold Slovenia, the Yugoslav Army concentrated its attacks against Croatia. By November 1991 the town of Vukovar was destroyed, and the army advanced on the town of Osijek. The European Union and the United Nations began a series of mediation and peacekeeping efforts, and Cyrus Vance on behalf of the United Nations succeeded in securing the first of many precarious cease-fires in December 1991.

The conflicts that erupted in the former Yugoslavia from 1991 presented peacekeeping with unparalleled challenges. Deployed into the conflict initially to monitor a cease-fire and to provide support for the political peace process, the peacekeeping force was progressively drawn into a more complex involvement. As the conflict intensified and spread into Bosnia and Herzegovina the humanitarian problems increased: Large numbers of people were displaced or became refugees and there were extensive violations of human rights, particularly associated with "ethnic cleansing." Ethnic cleansing can be defined as the elimination by an ethnic group controlling a territory of members of other ethnic groups. This meant in practice the use of a variety of methods that transgressed domestic and international law, including harassment, torture, rape, summary execution, forced displacement of populations, and confiscation and destruction of homes and buildings, including places of worship and cultural institutions. In response, in August 1992, the Commission on Human Rights convened a special session on the human rights situation in the former Yugoslavia. The commission appointed a special rapporteur to investigate violations, and from March 1993 onward the Center for Human Rights set up field offices in Zagreb and in Skopje, and later in Sarajevo and Mostar. In October 1992 a Commission of Experts was established by the Security Council to examine the evidence of grave breaches of the 1949 Geneva Conventions. This was followed in May 1993 by the decision to establish an International Tribunal to prosecute those responsible for breaches of international humanitarian law in the former Yugoslavia.

In the face of widespread violations of human rights, the number of refugees rose dramatically. Twelve funding appeals for humanitarian assistance were launched between 1991 and 1995. The first appeal anticipated that 500,000 people would need help; by September 1995 it was estimated that humanitarian assistance was needed for 3.5 million people, with a funding need of $823 million. The mandate of the United Nations Protection Force in Former Yugoslavia (UNPROFOR) to intervene in support of providing for humanitarian need began in September 1992, when it was authorized to provide protection for United Nations High Commissioner for Refugees (UNHCR) convoys.

Serious conflict in Yugoslavia first broke out in Croatia. It was initially regarded as an internal affair, and the Security Council did not take any formal action on the Yugoslav crisis until September 1991, when it passed a resolution (Security Council Resolution [SCR] 713) imposing an embargo on the delivery of arms and other military equipment to the area. On 9 November 1991 the Yugoslav presidency (made up of a representative from each of the six Yugoslav republics) asked the Security Council to consider the situation in Croatia and requested the deployment of UN troops to the area. However, the assumption was, based on earlier UN practices, that peacekeeping could not be used unless there were successful negotiations for a cease-fire and a peace agreement.

The initiative on peacemaking in the escalating conflict was taken by the European Community, which called a meeting of the committee of senior officials of the Conference on Security and Cooperation in Europe (CSCE) in July 1991. However, the frequent cease-fires mediated under European auspices were invariably soon broken or completely ignored by the forces on the ground. Overall negotiations were led by Lord Peter Carrington as head of the European Community's Conference on Yugoslavia (ECCY) until mid-1992. Following

moves toward the internationalization of the peacemaking effort, an International Conference on Former Yugoslavia (ICFY) was created in September 1992, cochaired by the EC presidency, represented by Lord David Owen (who succeeded Lord Carrington), and the UN secretary-general, represented by Cyrus Vance (Vance was replaced by Thorvald Stoltenberg in September 1993). Lord Owen was succeeded by Carl Bildt in June 1995. A further negotiation forum was set up in April 1994 in the form of the Contact Group, comprising the foreign ministers of France, Germany, the Russian Federation, and the United Kingdom, a representative of the U.S. secretary of state, the European Union commissioner for foreign affairs, and the two cochairmen of the ICFY. In 1994 the United States took the lead in assisting negotiations to establish a Bosnia-Croat Federation. Efforts were made to negotiate a resolution of the conflict by the ICFY (the Vance-Owen Peace Plan) in January 1993 and by the Contact Group in 1994. The former plan proposed the division of Bosnia and Herzegovina into ten provinces; the latter its division into two, between the Bosnia-Croat Federation and the Bosnian Serbs (who had constituted themselves as the Republika Srpska, under the leadership of Radovan Karadzic). Both plans were rejected by the Bosnian Serbs. The General Agreement negotiated at Dayton that was to lead to peace in the former Yugoslavia was negotiated late in 1995.

On 15 November a meeting of the Security Council was held in which Cyrus Vance, the recently appointed UN special envoy, put forward five conditions for the establishment of a peacekeeping force in Croatia along traditional lines: the agreement of all parties, a clear mandate, the provision of troops and financial backing by UN member states, and the support of the Security Council. Efforts continued toward meeting these guidelines, and on 15 December 1991 SCR 724 approved the concept and plan for a UN peacekeeping operation (dubbed the "Vance Plan" after its chief architect). Even so it was not until two months later, on 21 February 1992, that authorization for deployment was given (under SCR 743), and a further month went by before peacekeepers began to arrive in Croatia.

UNPROFOR was established for an initial one-year period. Its headquarters were initially in Sarajevo, the capital of neighboring Bosnia, but were later moved to Zagreb. From March 1992 until April 1993 UNPROFOR was headed by its force commander. In May 1993 Thorvald Stoltenberg (Norway) was appointed as the special representative of the secretary-general (SRSG) for former Yugoslavia and became the first civilian head of UNPROFOR. He was succeeded by Yasushi Akashi in January 1994. Between March 1992 and March 1995 five military officers served as force commanders: Lt. Gen. Satish Nambiar (India), from March 1992 to March 1993; Lt. Gen. Lars-Eric Wahlgren (Sweden), from March 1993 to June 1993; Lt. Gen. Jean Cot (France), from June 1993 to March 1994; Gen. Bertrand de Lapresle (France), from March 1994 to March 1995; and Gen. Bernard Janvier (France), who took up the post from March 1995. UNPROFOR had three operational commands: UNPROFOR in Croatia (usually referred to as UNPROFOR I, under Force Commander Maj. Gen. Eid Kamel Al-Rodan [Jordan] in March 1995); UNPROFOR in Bosnia and Herzegovina (usually referred to as UNPROFOR II, under Force Commander Lt. Gen. Rupert Smith [United Kingdom] in March 1995); and UNPROFOR in the former Yugoslav Republic of Macedonia (usually referred to as UNPROFOR III, under Force Commander Brig. Gen. Juha Engstrom [Finland] in March 1995). By March 1995 the military component of UNPROFOR amounted to 38,599 persons from 39 countries. There was a civil affairs component that also included over 800 civilian police. There were also over 2,000 international civilian staff and 2,615 local staff.

Deployment of UNPROFOR I (Croatia)

The first signs of a violent conflict breaking out in Yugoslavia appeared in March 1991, when Serbs in Croatia, supported by the Yugoslav People's Army (JNA), opposed Croatian independence from Yugoslavia, which was proclaimed on 25 June 1991. Slovenia also declared its independence in June 1991, as did Macedonia in September and Bosnia and Herzegovina in October, all after popular referenda had been held. On 16 March the self-declared Serbian Autonomous Region of Krajina

took the decision to secede from Croatia, alarmed at the prospects for Serbs in an independent Croatia. Later in the year a second Serbian Autonomous Region was proclaimed in western Slavonia. By the summer of 1991 fighting between the Croatian National Guard on the one hand and Croatian Serbs and units of the JNA on the other had created 90,000 refugees, either Croatian Serbs fleeing to Serbia or Croats moving out of Croatian areas dominated by Serbs. Following heavy fighting around the towns of Vukovar, Vinkovci, and Osijek, by September Croatia had lost one-third of its territory. Vukovar was the key to Serbian control of eastern Slavonia, and it fell to the JNA in November 1991. In the course of fighting the Croatian village of Kijevo, near Knin, was bombarded by Serbian militia and the JNA and became the first case of "cleansing of the ground," or ethnic cleansing, which was soon to become a prominent feature of the conflict, especially as it spread into Bosnia. In December the Serbian Autonomous Regions of Krajina and of Slavonia, Baranja, and Western Srem declared themselves the Serbian Republic of Krajina. Then, on 23 December 1991, Germany formally recognized both Slovenia and Croatia as independent states. Yugoslavia ceased to exist as an internationally recognized state when, on 15 January 1992, the European Union presidency announced that the European Community (EC) and its member states had also chosen to recognize Croatia and Slovenia. After ten months of conflict about 10,000 people had been killed, and at least 5,000 were missing; nearly 500,000 people had become refugees.

In November 1991 a cease-fire agreement was reached that included a proposal for a peacekeeping operation. UNPROFOR was eventually established under SCR 743 of 21 February 1992. The plan initially called for the deployment of just over 13,000 troops (12 battalions), civilian personnel, and civilian police. Its main function was to stabilize the situation in Croatia, creating conditions of peace and security within which negotiations for an overall solution could take place. By 23 March advanced deployments of infantry were under way. UNPROFOR was deployed into four sectors within three United Nations protected areas (UNPAs). Sectors North and South covered the

Krajina region of Croatia, Sector West was in western Slavonia, and Sector East was in eastern Slavonia on the border of the Serbian region of Vojvodina. These UNPAs were areas in Croatia occupied by armed Serbian militias, where fighting had been most intense, and which had a large proportion of Serbs in the civilian populations. Within each UNPA the UN force was mandated to stabilize the situation (which included maintaining an "interim" status quo of existing arrangements for local administration and public order), demilitarize or effect the withdrawal of armed forces, protect the local population, monitor traffic in and out of the UNPAs, monitor local police forces, and assist in the voluntary return of displaced persons and refugees.

The full deployment of UNPROFOR was delayed by several months, so it was not fully operational until late June 1992. The late arrival of some elements of UNPROFOR was caused by financial wrangling in New York as well as by complications created by the outbreak of war in Bosnia. One result of this delay was that ethnic cleansing continued virtually unchecked, and by the time UNPROFOR was operational most of the area's non-Serbian population had already been expelled from the UNPAs. Although UNPROFOR battalions deploying in the UNPAs reported continued violations of the cease fire and were often restricted in their freedom of movement, they did manage to set up regular patrols, checkpoints, and observation posts. They also began the crucial process of establishing liaison networks.

UN military observers (MOs) reported that although elements of the JNA were withdrawing from the UNPAs, as called for in the cease-fire agreement, they were leaving behind arms and equipment for local Serb militias. This problem became significantly worse when, on 27 April 1992, Serbia and Montenegro formed the Federal Republic of Yugoslavia (FRY). In an attempt to establish its credentials, the FRY immediately announced the withdrawal of all individuals from Serbia and Montenegro serving in the JNA in other republics. The intent was to aid the Bosnian Serbs and to counter mounting international pressure on Serbia and Montenegro. This move effectively stranded large numbers of well-armed troops in both Croatia and Bosnia, who had been JNA soldiers who did not live in Serbia or Montenegro, and led to a huge influx of soldiers into existing militias. In Croatia this meant that the peacekeeping mission was faced with a far more militarized situation than had been anticipated and that it would now be responsible for demobilizing a much larger number of militia than expected.

During this initial period of UN activity another unexpected problem arose that would do much to undermine the effectiveness of the operation in Croatia and to increase the complexity of the task. Areas adjacent to the UNPAs (later called the "pink zones") were held by the JNA but did not come under the UN's mandate (which was restricted to the UNPAs) or the cease-fire agreement. UNPROFOR again found itself in a position of having to mediate in a tense and difficult situation.

By the end of May UNPROFOR had moved its headquarters to Belgrade, leaving behind only a skeletal presence of 120 personnel in Sarajevo. Problems persisted in the UNPAs, including increasing militarization and economic hardship created in part by the flood of refugees from Bosnia. The increasing complexity of the situation meant that UNPROFOR's mandate was constantly expanding as experience on the ground brought to light further difficulties in implementing the original mandate. UNPROFOR became involved in interviewing individuals who had been forced from their homes, organizing patrols to protect their homes, and compiling data on those groups believed to be responsible for the expulsions. Based on a laboriously negotiated agreement over the pink zones, UNPROFOR began monitoring both the withdrawal of the JNA from the pink zones and the activities of local police. UNPROFOR's tasks were enlarged again when it was authorized to carry out immigration and customs functions at the international borders of the UNPAs. It became difficult to implement this extension because the Serbian authorities (based in Knin in the southern part of Krajina, Sector South) placed their own controls and checkpoints at all major crossings. The mandate of UNPROFOR was extended again in October 1992 when the operation was given the responsibility of monitoring the demilitarization of the Prevlaka Peninsula near Dubrovnik.

At the beginning of 1993 growing frustration on the part of the Tudjman government over the slow rate of return of displaced persons to the UNPAs led to a major offensive by the Croatian Army in the southern part of Krajina (Sector South). A cease-fire agreement based on an earlier SCR was signed on 6 April 1993. The agreement called for the end of hostilities and the withdrawal of the Croatian Army to positions held prior to the 22 January incursion. Over the following nine months the Croatian Army carried out two more major offensives, and the situation in the pink zones and the UNPAs continued to deteriorate. UNPROFOR continued its efforts to mediate between the two sides and to carry out its mandate. By September 1993 its role had changed from carrying out the Vance Plan and the various extensions of the mandate to a de facto minimalist position: to prevent the resumption or escalation of conflict, to provide a breathing space for the efforts of peacemakers, and to support the provision of humanitarian assistance. Violations of negotiated cease-fires continued through 1994 and 1995, and in March 1995 the secretary-general recognized that UNPROFOR could not be retained in its present role because of the objection of the Croatian government. However, it was also clear that the withdrawal of UNPROFOR from Croatia might lead to the escalation of the war there; nor could the operation in Bosnia be properly supported without the UN support facilities in Zagreb. This was the basis for the restructuring of the force at the end of March 1995.

On 31 March 1995 the Security Council decided to replace UNPROFOR with three separate peacekeeping operations: In Bosnia and Herzegovina the mandate and name of UNPROFOR were retained; in Croatia UNPROFOR was replaced by the United Nations Confidence Restoration Operation in Croatia (UNCRO); and in Macedonia UNPROFOR III was renamed the United Nations Preventive Deployment Force Macedonia (UNPREDEP). The joint headquarters, based in Zagreb, became known as the United Nations Peace Forces Headquarters (UNPF-HQ). Each component was headed by a civilian chief of mission and a military force commander.

Deployment of UNPROFOR II (Bosnia and Herzegovina)

Over the months following the deployment of peacekeepers in Croatia, the attention of the Security Council and the world media shifted away from Croatia toward the troubles of Sarajevo and Bosnia. In response to international pressure and the obvious threat to regional peace and security posed by the conflict, the Security Council progressively stretched UNPROFOR's mandate, which had originally been confined to certain areas of Croatia, to include Sarajevo and eventually to include a large-scale humanitarian relief effort throughout Bosnia. Continued fighting, as well as reports of ethnic cleansing and other atrocities in Bosnia, led the Security Council to pass SCR 757 on 30 May 1992 under the enforcement provisions of chapter 7 of the UN Charter (the peacekeeping force in Croatia was not authorized under enforcement provisions). The UN imposed sanctions against Serbia and Montenegro and demanded that a security zone be formed around Sarajevo airport and that the delivery of humanitarian supplies go unimpeded. At the same time the Security Council began considering a report from the secretary-general that detailed possible alternatives for the protection of humanitarian aid convoys. Secretary-General Boutros Boutros-Ghali argued that such a role for peacekeepers could be problematic and would need to be seriously considered, especially if it involved the use of force. The concern was that the use of force could compromise not only the peacekeeping operation and the ICFY negotiations but also the position of relief agencies operating in the area. Moreover, setting clear and attainable political aims for such enforcement activity was considered virtually impossible. Boutros-Ghali suggested that negotiating agreements for the transport and delivery of aid would be the preferable option and recommended a more limited operation focused on opening Sarajevo's airport to relief flights.

These recommendations foreshadowed what later would evolve into UNPROFOR II, as the Bosnia and Herzegovina command became known. UNPROFOR's mandate was extended on 8 June 1992 under SCR 758. The Security Council voted to deploy military observers in Sarajevo to supervise the withdrawal of heavy weapons from the city and the surrounding area. This was considered the first necessary step in a process that would eventually see the UN take over control of Sarajevo airport and secure it for the delivery of humanitarian aid. A four-part plan recommended the eventual deployment of a battalion that would become "Sector 5" of UNPROFOR. It further stipulated that fulfillment of the mandate was contingent on the continuation of a cease-fire. Progress toward implementation of the new mandate was slow, in large part because of the lack of cooperation from the opposing parties and the resulting fragility of the cease-fire. Nevertheless, after tough negotiations the United Nations took control of Sarajevo airport from the Serbian militias, whereupon the Security Council passed a resolution authorizing the deployment of more peacekeepers to the area. However, despite the arrival of more UN troops in Sarajevo, the war and the humanitarian crisis continued unabated.

The EC peace efforts under Lord Carrington were characterized by a series of brokered and then broken cease-fire agreements, and his tenure as the ECCY's main negotiator finally ended amid some controversy. In the middle of "on and off" peace talks, Lord Carrington negotiated an agreement with the Bosnian factions that called for UN supervision of heavy weaponry in and around Sarajevo. The Security Council quickly agreed to the plan. However, Lord Carrington's nonconsultative approach and the Security Council's rapid response led to a serious dispute with Boutros-Ghali and the Secretariat. Boutros-Ghali complained that the new mandate was not only close to impossible to carry out but that it had been "thrust" upon UNPROFOR without adequate consultation and without financial and other material commitments. Boutros-Ghali argued that the United Nations was already desperately overstretched and that it needed to pay more attention to crises elsewhere in the world. Eventually the dispute was resolved, but it had contributed to a growing feeling in the EC and elsewhere that peacemaking efforts needed to be internationalized and that a new negotiating framework was necessary. Lord Carrington's role was phased out, and a new international conference, the International Conference on Former Yugoslavia, was established and based in Geneva.

The disagreement highlighted several serious problems facing the Secretariat. First, the lack of financial support for UNPROFOR and other peacekeeping operations stood in stark contrast to the international community's enthusiasm for providing peacekeepers with new tasks. Second, there had been no coordination between the peacemaking process led by the EC under Lord Carrington and the peacekeeping process carried out by the Secretariat. The UN was not represented at the London talks that produced the agreement tasking UN peacekeepers with supervising heavy weaponry. The eventual compromise led to a new peace process cochaired by the EC and the United Nations. This new international focus reflected the greater involvement not only of the United Nations but also of the United States and Russia and the increasing interest of the Moslem countries in the Bosnian conflict.

Between March and July 1992 the humanitarian crisis in Bosnia worsened considerably. There were reports of atrocities in prison camps, and widespread ethnic cleansing caused an even greater stream of refugees seeking to escape the war. The work of the international aid agencies became increasingly difficult and dangerous. In one case a UNHCR convoy had to negotiate its way through 90 roadblocks between Zagreb and Sarajevo, many of them manned by undisciplined militias. In view of these difficulties, in mid-May Boutros-Ghali argued that Bosnia "in its present phase" was not "susceptible to the United Nations peacekeeping treatment." An attack on a UN aid convoy heading for the besieged town of Goradze at the end of July 1992, however, shifted international opinion toward more concerted action in Bosnia. The stalemated peacemaking process fanned the flames of increasingly adamant demands for enforcement action.

Under growing international pressure to take action the Security Council adopted two resolutions on 13 August 1992 under the enforcement provisions of chapter 7 of the charter. The first resolution (SCR 770) called upon all states to take "all measures necessary" to facilitate the delivery of humanitarian aid to Sarajevo and other parts of Bosnia. It further stated that all prison camps in the former Yugoslavia must be immediately opened for international inspection. A second resolution (SCR 771) demanded unimpeded and continued access to all camps, prisons, and detention centers within the territory of the former Yugoslavia.

International response was sluggish, however, even after an Italian transport plane bringing humanitarian supplies into Sarajevo was shot down on 3 September 1992, killing the four crew members. The airport was immediately closed and remained so for a month. Five days later, on 8 September, a UN convoy en route from Belgrade to Sarajevo was attacked by Bosnian government forces, and two French soldiers were killed. It was not until 10 September that the Secretariat presented its report on a "concept of operations" for Bosnia based on SCR 770. The proposal suggested that UNPROFOR's mandate be extended and that the military personnel sent to fulfill SCR 770 be placed under the overall direction of the force commander. The Bosnia Command, headquartered just outside Sarajevo in Kiseljak, was subsequently responsible for Sector Sarajevo and four new zones, each with an infantry battalion. Each battalion was responsible for providing protective support to UNHCR-organized convoys inside its own zone.

The plan was approved by the Security Council on 14 September 1992. Although the operation was authorized under chapter 7 of the charter, it did not (to the end of 1993) use force to carry out its mandate. As Boutros-Ghali argued, this new dimension in peacekeeping did not require a revision of the peacekeeping rules of engagement. In this situation peacekeepers were expected to negotiate local agreements and talk their way through the roadblocks that dotted the Bosnian countryside. Eight European countries agreed to contribute to and pay for the new force. By early November 1992 UNPROFOR II comprised 7,000 troops from eight European countries plus an infantry battalion from Canada and a field hospital from the United States. However, the full deployment of peacekeepers was hampered by lack of cooperation from the warring parties and the need to negotiate the specific terms of their deployment. The most persistent and troubling problem obstructing both deployment and operational effectiveness was the existence of numerous roadblocks, controlled by militia groups, that complicated access to many of the areas most in need of humanitarian assistance.

At the beginning of October 1992 the Security Council passed yet another extension of UNPROFOR's mandate. The council authorized the imposition of a ban on military flights in Bosnian airspace and authorized UNPROFOR to monitor compliance with this resolution (SCR 781). The ban lacked the power of enforcement, and by December 1992 the United States confirmed that Serbian planes had flown more than 200 unauthorized flights; by April 1993 the number of flight violations had risen to 500. After a particularly flagrant violation of the ban in March 1993, when Serb fighters bombed two Moslem villages, the United Nations finally authorized NATO to shoot down unauthorized aircraft in the no-fly-zone. However, this order was interpreted as authorizing such an action only as a last resort, and so it had little impact on the situation. Indeed, Human Rights Watch argued that by April 1993 the destruction of civilian populations and targets was being accomplished by ground artillery, not aerial bombardment.

From the beginning of the civil war in Bosnia, Moslem populations were slowly forced back into enclaves and the United Nations and aid agencies were regularly prevented from having access to these areas. In one of the worst cases, in the eastern Bosnian town of Srebrenica, no aid convoys were allowed through for months. Although efforts continued to gain access to Srebrenica and other enclaves, progress was impeded by Serb paramilitary forces. The crisis prompted the Security Council on 16 April 1993 to declare Srebrenica a "safe area" and demand access to the town (SCR 819). Canadian troops were allowed into the town two days later, but they were then subject to the same siege, and Serb forces refused to allow either convoys or troop supplies and reinforcements through.

On 6 May 1993 the Security Council voted to add Sarajevo, Tuzla, Zepa, Gorazde, and Bihać to the list of safe areas. Continued noncompliance by Serb militias led the council to pass a resolution under chapter 7 to "ensure full respect for the safe areas" (SCRs 824 and 836). The secretary-general, responding to the Security Council's request, presented a report detailing the new requirements for troop reinforcements and redeployments based on the new mandate. The report suggested that a troop level of 34,000 would be needed to ensure "deterrence through strength" but advised that the mandate could be implemented, at least initially, with 7,600 new peacekeepers. In establishing and securing the safe areas, UNPROFOR II was tasked with deterring attacks, monitoring a cease-fire, occupying key points in and around the safe areas, and protecting the delivery and distribution of humanitarian relief. In the end the safe areas mandate was not enforced, and by December 1993 only a few thousand troops had arrived—far short of the minimum level needed to do the job. By the end of July 1993 the safe areas were so unsafe that a UN special rapporteur on human rights reported that Gorazde had been bombarded by Bosnian Serb militia artillery for 18 consecutive days in June, which left half its houses destroyed. To complicate matters further, in May 1993 intense fighting broke out between Bosnian Croat forces and the government of Bosnia and Herzegovina, in southern and central Bosnia. In Mostar Croat forces forced Muslims to cross to the east of the city, and fighting there was particularly bitter.

Peacekeepers were increasingly targeted by Bosnian factions, particularly Serb paramilitary groups, adding to the already great frustration of UN personnel on the ground. By the end of 1993 the ICFY was no closer to reaching agreement in either Croatia or Bosnia. The situation was no better on the ground, where, according to the UN mediator Thorvald Stoltenberg, 69 separate cease-fires had been negotiated and broken. In early 1994 fighting around Sarajevo continued; in February 1994 more than 150 civilians were killed when the central market in Sarajevo was shelled. In response the secretary-general requested that NATO be authorized to conduct air strikes against artillery or mortar positions around Sarajevo that might be responsible for attacks on civilians. The area within 20 kilometers of the center of Sarajevo was declared a weapons exclusion zone, enforced by the North Atlantic Treaty Organization (NATO) and monitored by UNPROFOR. However, by the end of March 1994 Bosnian Serb forces launched an attack against the safe area of Gorazde, indiscriminately shelling the city and outlying villages. On 22 April NATO, following a request from the secretary-general, declared a military exclusion zone around Gorazde and threatened air strikes against Bosnian Serbs if they did not withdraw before the 20 April deadline. Similar zones were declared around the other four safe areas.

However, the conflict escalated again in the summer and autumn of 1994 when Sarajevo was hit by a series of attacks by snipers, and NATO warplanes were called in by UNPROFOR to attack Bosnian Serb positions violating the exclusion zone around Sarajevo.

A cease-fire in Bosnia and Herzegovina negotiated by former U.S. President Jimmy Carter, which had come into force on 1 January 1995, failed to last, with violations being committed by both Bosnian Serb and Bosnian government forces. After a military agreement on 20 February between Bosnian and Croatian Serbs, combined Serbian forces tightened their blockade of the Bihać enclave in northwestern Bosnia, one of the UN-designated safe areas. Early in March 1995 the governments of Croatia and Bosnia and Herzegovina concluded a military alliance, and Bosnian government forces started successful offensives against Serb positions on Mount Vlasic near Travnik in central Bosnia, as well as north and east of Tuzla.

Heavy shelling of Sarajevo was resumed by Serbian forces in April 1995, and an assault by Bosnian government forces in May aimed at breaking the siege of Sarajevo failed after heavy government losses. Late in May the UNPROFOR force commander in Bosnia, Lt. Gen. Rupert Smith, issued an ultimatum to the Bosnian Serbs and to the Bosnian government to withdraw their heavy weapons from a 32-kilometer (20-mile) exclusion zone around Sarajevo. The next day Smith ordered bombing raids by NATO aircraft against Serbian weapons stores near their headquarters at Pale, whereupon in retaliation the Serbs took more than 300 UN soldiers hostage. The last of the hostages were all released by 18 June after mediation by President Slobodan Milosevic of Serbia.

With mounting pressure for more decisive and forceful action against Serbian attacks, in early June 1995 defense ministers from NATO countries and other countries decided to create a 14,000-strong rapid deployment force consisting of British, French, and Dutch troops to support UN units and to protect the remaining safe areas. However, the Serbs captured the safe area of Srebrenica in July, having previously disarmed the Dutch UN battalion stationed there. The safe area of Zepa, also in eastern Bosnia, fell to the Serbs that same month.

However, international pressure on the Bosnian Serbs was mounting. On 25 July 1995 the International War Crimes Tribunal for the Former Yugoslavia at The Hague indicted Radovan Karadzic, leader of the Republika Srpska in Bosnia, and his military commander, Gen. Ratko Mladic, on charges of genocide and crimes against humanity.

On 22 July an agreement on political, diplomatic, and military cooperation was signed by Presidents Franjo Tudjman of Croatia and Alija Izetbegovic of Bosnia and Herzegovina. Croatian army forces entered western Bosnia from Croatia to relieve Bihać in a combined operation with Bosnian Croat forces. In August 1995 Serbian forces suffered a series of military defeats at the hands of Croatian and Bosnian government forces in western and central Bosnia and lost a significant amount of territory. Most significantly, the U.S. government began to pressure parties to the conflict in Bosnia to agree to peace talks and on 5 October secured a general cease-fire agreement. On 1 November 1995, under the auspices of the U.S. government, President Izetbegovic of Bosnia and Herzegovina, President Milosevic of Serbia (who also assumed authority to speak for the Bosnian Serbs, thus isolating Karadic and Mladic), and President Tudjman began negotiations in Dayton, Ohio, that were to end the conflict in Bosnia and that also addressed the issue of eastern Slavonia, the last Serb-held area of Croatia. Three weeks later, on 21 November 1995, the General Framework Agreement for Peace (GFAP) in Bosnia and Herzegovina was agreed on and was formally signed by the parties (Croatia, Bosnia and Herzegovina, and the Federal Republic of Yugoslavia [Serbia and Montenegro]) in Paris on 14 December 1995. UNPROFOR ceased to exist on 20 December 1995 when authority was transferred to the Implementation Force (IFOR).

Under the GFAP the parties agreed to respect each other's sovereignty, to settle disputes by peaceful means, and to accept the continued existence of Bosnia and Herzegovina within its existing international borders, but consisting of two democratic entities, the Bosnia-Croat Federation and the Republika Srpska, with the territory divided between them, 51 percent and 49 percent respectively. The GFAP included military aspects, such as the withdrawal of forces and their phased redeployment around Sarajevo, Gorazde, and other locations, and stipulated a multinational Implementation Force to ensure compliance with the GFAP. Civilian aspects of the agreement, to be facilitated by the high representative, Carl Bildt, included the continued delivery of humanitarian aid, economic reconstruction, the establishment of political and constitutional institutions and the holding of free and fair elections, the return of refugees, and the promotion of respect for human rights. Civilian law enforcement was to be provided for by a UN international police task force. While the peace process was being pursued in this way in Bosnia, talks were also conducted about the settlement of remaining issues between Croatia and the Federal Republic of Yugoslavia (Serbia and Montenegro). As a result of these talks, facilitated by the secretary-general's special envoy, Thorvald Stoltenberg, and by Peter Galbraith, the U.S. ambassador to Croatia, Presidents Tudjman of Croatia and Milosevic of Serbia signed the Basic Agreement on the Region of Eastern Slavonia, Baranja, and Western Sirmium on 12 November 1995. The agreement provided for the reintegration into Croatia of these areas, dominated by Serb populations. The agreement provided for a transitional administration under UN auspices to govern the region while the agreement was being implemented.

Deployment of UNPROFOR III (Macedonia)

During the course of the war in both Croatia and Bosnia, the threat was real that violence might spread to other regions in the Balkans, particularly Kosovo and Macedonia. To avert the spread of war to Macedonia the United Nations took the innovative step of deploying a preventive peacekeeping presence into the republic. This peacekeeping presence, which became known as UNPROFOR III, was authorized under SCR 795 of 11 December 1992. The deployment followed a request to the United Nations by the president of the former Yugoslav Republic of Macedonia and a recommendation by the cochairmen of the ICFY. In response, UNPROFOR's mandate and strength were expanded to establish a peacekeeping force on the borders between Macedonia, Albania, and the Federal Republic of Yugoslavia. UNPROFOR III's mandate was preventive, that is, it was to monitor developments on the border that might threaten the stability and territorial integrity of Macedonia. A joint Nordic battalion, headquartered in Skopje, was deployed and was augmented in June 1993 by 300 troops from the United States. By March 1995 force strength stood at 1,069 troops, 24 military observers, and 24 civilian police.

One of the difficulties encountered was that the border between Macedonia and the Federal Republic of Yugoslavia had not been properly demarcated, and there was a series of tense border incidents in early 1994 that were nevertheless stabilized by UNPROFOR working in cooperation with other organizations, principally the Organization for Security and Cooperation in Europe (OSCE).

Probably more threatening to the stability of Macedonia than the prospect of attacks across the border was the internal political situation. Major tension existed between the government and the ethnic Albanian population, who were demanding more recognition of their needs and status. The overall situation was made worse by the poor economic condition of the country, caused in part by an economic blockade imposed by Greece and in part by the UN sanctions on the Federal Republic of Yugoslavia, which was Macedonia's main trading partner. Beginning in March 1994, and working closely with the OSCE monitoring mission in Macedonia, UNPROFOR began to monitor developments within the country, including possible areas of conflict, with the aim of promoting reconciliation between the various groups. As part of this work to promote political and ethnic coopera-

tion, UNPROFOR joined other international institutions in monitoring the parliamentary and presidential elections held in October 1994. Most assessments of the work of UNPROFOR in Macedonia are positive in agreeing that by focusing international attention on Macedonia, internal and international political tensions in the area were lessened. As part of the overall restructuring of UNPROFOR, the mission in Macedonia was changed under SCR 983 of 31 March 1995, which created the United Nations Preventive Deployment Force Macedonia (UNPREDEP) as a separate peacekeeping operation, though the mandate and force level remained the same. The force commander from March 1995 to February 1996 was Brig. Gen. Juha Engstrom (Finland). Beginning in March 1996 Brig. Gen. Bo Lennart Wranker (Sweden) served as force commander.

UN-estimated expenses for the peacekeeping force in the former Yugoslavia between January 1992 and March 1996 were $4,616,725,556 (about $4.7 billion). This figure includes the costs of UNPROFOR from February 1992 to March 1995 and the costs of UNCRO, UNPREDEP, and UNPF-HQ. As of March 1995 the total deployed force strength stood at 38,599 military personnel, including 684 military observers, with contingents from 39 different countries. The force also included 803 civilian police, 2,017 international civilian staff, and 2,615 local staff.

UNPROFOR was the largest and most expensive peacekeeping mission ever deployed by the United Nations. By 1994, because of experiences in the former Yugoslavia and in Somalia, peacekeeping was the most controversial activity in which the United Nations was involved. A series of criticisms was made. Some accounts argued that the whole peacekeeping intervention, especially in Bosnia, was misconstrued and that the peacekeeping force was not only ineffective but that, more seriously, it made matters worse. The criticism is partly directed against third-party intervention in civil wars in general, on the grounds that such interventions cannot be impartial and that their effect is simply to prolong the conflict and therefore, possibly, to prolong suffering. This kind of argument leads to the idea that peacekeeping is an inadequate tool for intervention in active civil wars and that its use should be limited to those conflicts that have been terminated. In these circumstances, where a primarily monitoring presence based on consent is required, the tested principles of classical peacekeeping can be applied.

The alternative argument begins with the claim that peacekeeping forces in the former Yugoslavia were inadequately equipped to carry out the demanding mandates they were given. If this was so, then if peacekeeping is to secure the humanitarian and political objectives that it has acquired in addition to its military roles, it should not be scaled back but significantly strengthened. Thus the need for new doctrines and concepts of peacekeeping has been argued, embodied in terms such as "peace-support operations" and "second-generation peacekeeping."

See also Bosnia and Herzegovina (Implementation Force and Stabilization Force); Croatia; European Community Monitoring Mission; Macedonia; North Atlantic Treaty Organization
References and further reading Berdal (1995); Eide and Solle (1995); Gow and Smith (1992); Woodward (1995); United Nations (1996)

United Nations Special Committee on the Balkans (UNSCOB), 1947
See Greece

UNSCOP (United Nations Special Committee on Palestine), 1947

Until 1947 Palestine, whose population of around two million at that time was approximately two-thirds Arab and one-third Jewish, was administered by the United Kingdom under a mandate from the League of Nations. However, Britain had been unable to reconcile the conflicting claims of the Jewish and Arab inhabitants to the territory. The United Nations became formally involved in the dispute on 2 April 1947, when, as the British mandate over the territory neared its end, the British government brought the matter in front of the General Assembly. During a special session on 15 May, the General Assembly successfully established a fact-finding committee to look into the situation. On Soviet insistence, the strength of the commission was increased from 7 to 11 and the issue of partition of

the territory was included as part of its agenda. Thus the General Assembly established the United Nations Special Committee on Palestine (UNSCOP), which was mandated to make recommendations over the future status of the territory.

UNSCOP was dispatched to the area with broad investigative powers, and based on their findings the majority of the commission proposed that Palestine be partitioned into distinct Arab and Jewish states, connected by a common economic union (this has since become known as the UN Partition Plan). It was further proposed that a UN-administered international regime govern the contested city of Jerusalem, which is an area of crucial religious importance to both parties. A minority of the commission suggested the creation of an independent, binational federal state. On 29 November 1947 the General Assembly passed Resolution 187, by which it ratified the Partition Plan, and also created a UN Palestine Commission to implement the partition process.

However, it was quickly apparent that the Partition Plan would not work: The plan was accepted by the Jewish community, but the Arab community rejected the suggestions both for partition and for a federal state. Thus overt hostilities intensified between the opposing parties, and by 10 April 1948 the commission complained that the unstable situation in Palestine was preventing it from fulfilling its mandate. On 17 April the Security Council called for a cease-fire between the opposing parties, and on 23 April it had established the Truce Commission for Palestine, comprising representatives from Belgium, France, and the United States, to attempt to facilitate the negotiation process. On 14 May 1948, a day before the UK mandate over Palestine expired, the Security Council withdrew the Palestine Commission and appointed in its place a UN Mediator on Palestine. When a cease-fire eventually did come into effect on 11 June 1948, the Security Council authorized the deployment of the United Nations Truce Supervision Organization (UNTSO) to oversee its implementation.

See also Middle East conflict; United Nations Truce Supervision Organization, 1948–
References and further reading Smith (1996)

United Nations Special Committee on Peacekeeping Operations (C-34)

The United Nations Special Committee on Peacekeeping Operations is a committee of the General Assembly of the United Nations, consisting originally of 33 member states and established in 1965 under General Assembly Resolution 2006 (XIX). It became the Committee of 34 when China joined in 1988. The Special Committee on Peacekeeping Operations opened its 1996 session on 1 April 1996. Under the mandate entrusted to it by General Assembly Resolution 50/30 of 22 December 1995, the committee was to "continue its efforts to make a comprehensive review of the whole question of peacekeeping in all its aspects." In adopting its program, the committee decided to hold a maximum of six sessions of general debate between 1 April and 3 April 1996. The Special Committee elected the following individuals to its Bureau: Ibrahim A. Gambari (Nigeria), chair; Emilio J. Cardenas (Argentina), David Karsgaard (Canada), Yukinari Hirose (Japan), and Zbigniew Matuszewski (Poland), vice chairs; and Abderahman S. Abderahman (Egypt), rapporteur. The committee agreed to requests for observer status from delegations of the following member states and organizations: Armenia, Azerbaijan, Bangladesh, Belarus, Belgium, Brazil, Bulgaria, Central African Republic, Chile, Congo, Croatia, Cuba, Cyprus, Czech Republic, Ecuador, Finland, Georgia, Ghana, Greece, Indonesia, Iran, Ireland, Jamaica, Jordan, Kazakhstan, Kenya, Kuwait, Lao People's Democratic Republic, Lebanon, Libya, Lithuania, Luxembourg, Malaysia, Morocco, Namibia, Nepal, New Zealand, Norway, Peru, Philippines, Portugal, Republic of Korea, Slovak Republic, South Africa, Sweden, Tunisia, Turkey, Uganda, Ukraine, Uruguay, Vietnam, Zimbabwe, and the European Commission.

Kofi Annan, at that time undersecretary-general for peacekeeping operations, in his opening address to the committee stressed that "peacekeeping as a primary instrument of the United Nations would not end: many existing operations would continue, and the Security Council might well find it necessary to mandate new ones. In that respect, the Organization would continue to require the capacity to launch, support and manage peacekeeping operations with demanding mandates to carry out multiple tasks, requiring active collaboration with a broad range of international actors. What had been gained in recent years should not be sacrificed."

Annan pointed to a number of internal initiatives that had been implemented to improve the organization's peacekeeping function. The Department of Peacekeeping Operations is now divided into an Office of Operations, responsible for day-to-day executive direction of peacekeeping operations, and an Office of Planning and Support, responsible for all technical matters, including staffing, finance, logistics, and procurement. Annan stated that a Mission Planning Service had been established to design integrated plans for complex, multidimensional operations in coordination with other departments. Also established and developed were the 24-hour Situation Center, communicating with UN missions around the world, as well as the nucleus of a Policy and Analysis Unit, a small Training Unit, and a Lessons Learned Unit.

Upon completion of the 1996 general debate of the Special Committee on Peacekeeping Operations, an open-ended working group met between 9 and 24 April 1996. The final report adopted by the group urged the Secretariat to continue to improve the UN's ability to deploy peacekeeping operations quickly and to further develop the system of standby arrangements. It recommended that member states be invited to consider participating in aspects of these arrangements such as headquarters support, communications, personnel, and logistics.

The committee also suggested that within the Department of Peacekeeping Operations (DPKO) the United Nations should finance posts presently occupied by military officers on loan and that recruitment for those posts should be conducted in accordance with established procedures and the UN Charter. The report also cleared the way for a substantial expansion of the committee's current membership of 34. The 109 member states who have been in the past or are at present contributing personnel to peacekeeping operations and any other member states that were observers at the 1996 session would be eligible for membership at the 1997 session. In the future troop-contributing member states who participate in the committee for three consecutive years as observers could become members at the following session.

The section on enhancing UN peacekeeping capacity contained observations and recommendations regarding planning, organization, and effectiveness; safety and security; training; and cooperation with regional arrangements. The committee encouraged the secretary-general's efforts to improve UN structure and capacity for planning and managing peacekeeping operations, including providing equitable geographical and gender representation. The committee will address the issues raised by the DPKO's use of loaned personnel when the secretary-general has presented his report on the question. The work of the DPKO's Lessons Learned Unit was noted with appreciation. The committee recommended that the secretary-general seek regular financing for the unit.

See also   United Nations: organization (DPKO)

United Nations Standby Arrangements System

Following the events in Rwanda in 1994, when it was suggested that the rapid deployment of sufficiently equipped peacekeeping forces could have prevented the genocide that occurred, interest has increased in the United Nations and in the international community in developing a capacity for the rapid deployment of peacekeeping personnel. The speed of deployment of peacekeeping forces depends on three main factors: Resources must be made available quickly, including political approval and the conclusion of the necessary financial and administrative procedures; the necessary air or sea strategic lift must be rapidly available; and, finally, resources to provide logistical support of the force in the mission area must be available. In order to achieve rapid deployment Secretary-General Boutros Boutros-Ghali requested in 1992 that troops and resources should be made available by governments to the UN peace operations at short notice, when necessary. These Standby Forces were not to be used for peace-enforcement actions but simply for chapter 6–type operations. However,

after consultation with member states in 1993 and 1994, the idea of the Standby Forces was limited to what is now called "the Standby Arrangements System," since a basic prerequisite for the UN Standby Forces could not be met. This prerequisite is defined as an unconditional political commitment of earmarked resources by member states into the UN Standby Forces pool; whereas the Standby Arrangements System is based on conditional pledges by member states to contribute specific resources to the system within an agreed-on response time. The effectiveness and optimization of the Standby Arrangements System are linked to detailed information on resources specified in each of the standby arrangements. By maintaining a comprehensive database, the UN Secretariat is in a better position to determine the resources available to meet peacekeeping mission requirements. It also enables departmental planners to tailor realistic tasks for resources provided by the governments according to their capabilities and to identify any services and materials that should be procured or contracted to fill in any deficiencies.

In the first three years after the system was implemented, 65 member states confirmed their willingness to participate in the Standby Arrangements System, and Austria, Bolivia, Denmark, Ghana, Italy, Jordan, Malaysia, and Singapore signed a Memorandum of Understanding with the United Nations, formalizing the details of their contribution to the Standby Arrangements System. In terms of personnel resources that could be made available to the United Nations, those standby arrangements added up to more than 83,000 personnel; though primarily composed of military, these resources included some 880 civilian police and 240 civilian specialists and experts ranging from surgeons to procurement personnel. In December 1997 seven countries signed an agreement to operationalize standby forces: Canada, Denmark, Sweden, Poland, Norway, Austria, and the Netherlands combined to form the Standby Forces High Readiness Brigade (SHIRBRIG), which will be ready to deploy for traditional peacekeeping operations on a month's notice. SHIRBRIG is intended to be fully operational by January 1999, with a 17-strong multinational brigade staff at Hoevelte Barracks, near Copenhagen. There are nevertheless many questions about whether or not the standby arrangements will be sufficient to deal with future crises. When in May 1994 the United Nations decided to authorize the expansion of the United Nations Assistance Mission in Rwanda (UNAMIR), none of the 19 governments that had undertaken to have forces on standby agreed to provide troops for this mission, fearing the political and financial costs and the danger of getting sucked into the conflict. Because of these limitations there is some argument in favor of a UN standing force, or UN Legion, that does not depend on seeking member state contributions on an ad hoc basis for each new mission, but which is permanently available as a UN military peacekeeping or peace enforcement body.

See also Canada; Nordic countries
References and further reading Canada (1995); Kaysen and Rathgens (1995); Leurdijk (1995); UNDPKO homepage at http://www.un.org/Depts/dpko/

United Nations Standing Army
See Peace enforcement

UNSF and UNTEA (United Nations Security Force and the United Nations Temporary Executive Authority in West Irian), 1962–1963
See Indonesia

United Nations Transitional Administration for Eastern Slavonia, Baranja, and Western Sirmium (UNTAES) 1996–
See UNPROFOR I–III

UNTAG (United Nations Transitional Assistance Group), Namibia, 1989–1990
See Namibia

UNTAC (United Nations Transitional Authority in Cambodia), 1992–1993
See Cambodia

UNTSO (United Nations Truce Supervision Organization), 1948–

Conflict Profile
In 1947 the territory of Palestine had a population of around two million, two-thirds of whom were Arab and the rest Jewish. Until 1947 Palestine was administered by Great Britain under a mandate from the League of Nations, but Britain had been unable to reconcile the conflicting claims of the Jewish and Arab populations. In April 1947 as the end of the British mandate approached, the British government brought the matter before the General Assembly, which in turn set up the United Nations Special Committee on Palestine (UNSCOP) to make recommendations for the territory's future status. In November 1947 UNSCOP proposed an initiative (the UN Partition Plan for Palestine) partitioning Palestine into separate Arab and Jewish states joined by an economic union, with a UN-administered international regime to govern the city of Jerusalem, which both parties claimed. The plan was accepted by the Jewish community but was rejected by the Arabs, and fighting ensued. The Security Council called for a cease-fire and set up the Truce Commission for Palestine on 23 April 1948, comprising representatives from Belgium, France, and the United States, to supervise the cease-fire. On 14 May the General Assembly appointed a UN Mediator for Palestine—Count Folke Bernadotte (Sweden)—charged with finding a peaceful adjustment of the future situation of the territory. Also on 14 May Britain finally relinquished its mandate over the region, and the State of Israel was proclaimed on the territory allotted under the Partition Plan. The Arabs still refused to accept the plan and on 15 May opened hostilities against Israel with the support of other Arab states.

Deployment of UNTSO
The United Nations Truce Supervision Organization (UNTSO) was established in response to the Arab invasion of the new State of Israel and was the first ever UN peacekeeping mission, although it was not referred to as such at the time. In response to the Arab invasion of Palestine, the United States and the USSR were united in support of Israel, the United States for domestic political

reasons and the USSR for ideological ones. Britain, on the other hand, was more intent on assisting the Arab states, for whom it maintained paternalistic feelings of support dating back to the era when it was the colonial power in the area. All Security Council members were in agreement, however, that the violence should be stopped. On 29 May 1948, with Security Council Resolution (SCR) 50, the council called on all parties to cease violent activities for four weeks. It suggested that the Mediator and Truce Commission it had appointed for Palestine should be charged with the task of observing the cease-fire, with the assistance of a sufficient number of military observers. The parties to the conflict complied with the provisions of the cease-fire and the United Nations prepared to deploy observers. In order to overcome problems of the nationality of the observers (that is, to ensure they were from disinterested nations), they were taken from member states of the Mediator and Truce Commission. Soviet objections to its exclusion were ignored, around 100 observers were rapidly dispatched, and so UNTSO was born. The observers were to be unarmed and were to operate strictly with the consent of the opposing parties (Israel and surrounding Arab countries).

The observers were relatively successful in ensuring the success of this first cease-fire, which went into effect on 11 June 1948. The observers wore their own national uniforms, with the addition of a UN armband (the distinctive blue helmets did not appear until November 1956). However, by 9 July hostilities had resumed. In response, on 15 July the Security Council demanded a permanent cease-fire, made provisions for its supervision, and hinted that stronger measures would be taken should the parties fail to comply. The violence was halted, and an additional 300 UN troops from the same countries were sent to the area. However, the truce was regularly broken over the following eight months, and on 17 October Bernadotte, who had been frustrated by UN indecision and lack of resolve, was assassinated by a Jewish terrorist group, along with a senior French observer. It was after this that UNTSO reached its highest strength of 572 observers.

On 16 November, in view of the continued instability in the region, the Security Council called on the parties to agree to an armistice, and on 11 December 1948 the General Assembly passed Resolution 194 establishing the UN Conciliation Commission for Palestine to facilitate a permanent settlement. By July 1949 four separate General Armistice Agreements, each of which relied on UNTSO for at least some of its functions, had been signed between Israel and a neighboring Arab state—Egypt, Jordan, Lebanon, or Syria. Each agreement incorporated a general armistice between the relevant two military forces and set out Armistice Demarcation Lines (ADLs), which were strictly not to be interpreted as fixed or permanent borders between Israel and its Arab neighbors. The Security Council then authorized the continued deployment of UN military personnel to implement the agreements. It reaffirmed the part of its previous truce resolution that had demanded a cessation of hostile acts and provided UNTSO with the authority to attempt to maintain it. The role of the mediator was ended, and UNTSO became an autonomous operation acting on behalf of the Security Council under the command of a chief of staff. The UN Partition Plan for Palestine that had been forwarded by UNSCOP in November 1947 never came to fruition, and the territory was divided up differently: Israel annexed 2,500 square miles; Jordan, 2,200 square miles; and Egypt, the Gaza Strip, which covered an area of 135 square miles. The city of Jerusalem was shared between Israel and Jordan.

UNTSO's role had thus been transformed from observing the truce to maintaining cease-fire lines and supervising compliance with the Armistice Agreements. UNTSO observers were positioned at fixed observation posts, established patrols along the ADLs, and carried out inspections of demilitarized zones. Within each agreement were provisions for the establishment of Mixed Armistice Commissions (MACs). These were designed to investigate complaints about the observance of the agreements and comprised seven members, three from each side with a senior UNTSO member as chair. However, a MAC was only entitled to investigate on condition of full cooperation by both parties and the chair. In view of the political situation, agreement was rare, and so the MACs found it impossible to perform as complete units in the field.

Only the agreement between Israel and Lebanon proved to be in any way stable; complaints abounded from both parties to the other three agreements. Thus the MACs—in the cases of the agreements between Israel and Egypt, Jordan, or Syria—became forums for accusations and allegations rather than for settling disagreements, and they were progressively abandoned.

The commission between Egypt and Israel (EIMAC) was the least secure and experienced four major difficulties: In 1951 Egypt denied Israeli ships access to the Suez Canal, and after 1953 also denied them access to the Strait of Tiran; Israel expelled thousands of Palestinians to the Gaza Strip; Palestinian fedayeen launched increasing numbers of raids into Israeli territory, and there were numerous violations of the Armistice Agreement within the El Auja demilitarized zone. Israeli reprisals to the fedayeen raids culminated in the deaths of 36 Egyptian soldiers in February 1955, resulting in overt hostility between the two nations and ultimately leading to the 1956 Suez Canal crisis. After the outbreak of the crisis, Israel reneged on its agreement with Egypt and refused to cooperate with EIMAC. However, UNTSO maintained its patrols along the Egyptian side of the ADL in Sinai and Gaza, and, with representatives from the United Nations and Egypt, EIMAC continued its investigations. Although in this condition EIMAC was little more than cosmetic, the presence in the area of personnel from the first United Nations Emergency Force (UNEF I) did manage to defuse tension and reduce the level of incidents along Egypt's border with Israel. When UNEF I was withdrawn in 1967, the number of observers serving with EIMAC was increased from 6 to 20, and the number of patrols along the ADLs was correspondingly increased, with no resistance from the Israeli government. However, despite these measures, war was soon to break out again between Israel and the Arab states.

The problems experienced along Israel's border with Syria predominantly centered around the status of Lake Tiberias's eastern shoreline and the demilitarized area to the north and east of the lake. Although the MAC assigned to the Israel-Syria agreement remained intact, it was unable to cope with the sheer volume of complaints it received

(30,000 by Syria and 35,485 by Israel as of 14 October 1966). The lack of progress with the Armistice Agreements meant that their original purpose—preceding more permanent political settlements, to be reached within the first 12 to 18 months—was lost, and both parties looked at them ever more ambivalently. In Jordan the Armistice Agreement created two distinct enclaves for each side around Jerusalem. This, combined with the fact that the West Bank became a haven for the fedayeen, led to substantial problems, which regularly ended in exchanges of fire across the ADLs. Even so, the MAC continued to convene in emergency sessions until June 1967. The MAC for Israel and Lebanon ran smoothly and relatively effectively up to June 1967, aided by the fact that Lebanese authorities made efforts to curb the activities of the fedayeen in Lebanese territory.

In May 1967, in response to a perceived Israeli threat to invade Syria, the Egyptian government demanded that UNEF I withdraw from the Sinai, a demand to which the UN complied. On 5 June Israel, fearing a combined attack from both Egypt and Syria, launched preemptive air and ground strikes and quickly seized the Sinai from Egypt, the West Bank from Jordan, and the Golan Heights from Syria. Since there were no UN observers positioned in the Israeli-Egyptian sector when a cease-fire came into effect on 8 June, there was no impartial presence in the area to confirm or deny either side's allegations of violations. As a result, on 9 July the Security Council authorized the deployment of UNTSO observers along the cease-fire line, which ran along the Suez Canal; the parties agreed to the deployment. By 17 July observation had commenced, with 90 UN personnel from Austria, Burma, Chile, Finland, France, and Sweden stationed at 15 observation posts on the Egyptian and Israeli sides of the line. The observers succeeded in maintaining the cease-fire until early 1969, when hostilities resumed and lasted until August 1970. U.S. diplomatic intervention brought an end to the violence, after which, with UNTSO's assistance, peace reigned until the Yom Kippur War in October 1973.

UNTSO observers, with the consent of Israel and Syria, also demarcated cease-fire lines and a buffer zone between Israeli and Syrian forces on the Golan Heights. By 11 June 1967 seven observation posts had been established on the Israeli side of the line and nine on the Syrian side, and UNTSO personnel conducted patrols in the area. That the two parties consented ensured stability on Golan until 1973. There were an increasing number of Palestinian raids across the Israel-Jordan border after the 1967 war, since many Palestinian fighters were based in Jordan, and Israeli armed forces retaliated. The opposition of the parties involved prohibited a UN presence along the border, despite the Security Council's encouragement. However, tension was considerably reduced between Israel and Jordan in 1970 when the majority of the Palestinian fighters in Jordan moved to Lebanon.

Conversely, subsequent Palestinian raids in 1970 across the Israel-Lebanon border ultimately resulted in Lebanon requesting the deployment of UNTSO observers. Although no fighting had occurred between Israel and Lebanon during the 1967 war, Israel had unilaterally abrogated the Armistice Agreement between them. Increased tension between the two countries in the early 1970s led the Lebanese government, in March 1972, to request a strengthened UN presence in the area. UNTSO observers were subsequently deployed along the Lebanese side of the ADL, although the lack of Israeli cooperation denied the observers any genuine role.

Three new peacekeeping forces (UNEF II, the United Nations Disengagement Observer Force [UNDOF], and the United Nations Interim Force in Lebanon [UNIFIL]) were established in the Middle East as a result of the October 1973 Yom Kippur War and Israel's invasion of southern Lebanon in 1978. All of these forces received initial personnel support from UNTSO, and since the 1973 war UNTSO has largely become a support operation for other peacekeeping missions. It did, however, maintain some individual functions. For example, following the withdrawal of UNEF II in 1979, UNTSO maintained a presence in the Sinai as the Observer Group Egypt (OGE). This was established mainly at the request of the Egyptian government to counterbalance the U.S. presence in non-UN peacekeeping bodies in the area (such as the Multinational Force and Observers [MFO],

which has been deployed since 1982). Up to 1988, when they were allowed to patrol the whole Sinai area, the Soviet Union, as a demonstration of solidarity with the Arab states, had restricted its personnel serving with the OGE to patrolling Cairo and Ismailia. Today most observers serving with the OGE—which in 1996 numbered 16 personnel—are U.S. or Russian nationals, although its role has been reduced to a largely cosmetic one. In Jordan, UNTSO maintained a liaison office in Amman, whose chief was the chair of the Israel-Jordan MAC. A peace treaty was concluded by the parties in 1994, following which, in 1995, the Amman office was closed. On 31 May 1974 the 90 UNTSO observers assigned to the Golan Heights joined UNDOF, becoming the Observer Group Golan (OGG) in 1979. They were stationed at observation posts near the area of operation and conducted inspections of the area of limitation of armaments and forces. UNTSO personnel from the Permanent Five Security Council members are prohibited from serving with UNDOF and so formed a separate unit, the Observation Detachment Damascus (ODD), to provide liaison and support functions for the OGG. The UNTSO detachment in the Israel-Syria sector is the largest in the mission area, comprising, as of early 1996, 85 military observers. Five UNTSO outposts were established in Lebanon in 1972, backed up by Lebanese troops to guarantee the safety of UN personnel. However, the outbreak of internal conflict in Lebanon in 1975 and consequent disintegration of the Lebanese army meant that the unarmed observers had to rely solely on their UN status for their own safety. UNTSO was then assigned to assist UNIFIL, which the Security Council had set up in 1978 following Israel's invasion of Lebanon, forming the Observer Group Lebanon (OGL). OGL personnel were positioned at observation posts, conducted patrols, and performed liaison duties around the UNIFIL area of operation. Israel invaded Lebanon for a second time in June 1982, and in August the Observation Group Beirut (OGB) was established to monitor the situation in and around the city by means of observation posts and mobile patrols. The high number of Palestinian civilian casualties at the Shabra and Shatila refugee camps in September 1982 caused the number of personnel serving with OGB to be increased from 10 to 59. However, the Israeli withdrawal from Beirut in September 1983 allowed the number of OGB personnel to be considerably reduced, and in mid-1992 it was renamed the United Nations Liaison Office in Beirut (UNLOB).

UNTSO has been paid for from the UN's regular budget since its inception in 1948, and so its costs come under the assessment of each biennial program budget. The financial difficulties that the United Nations has progressively experienced have encouraged a series of streamlining measures, which have reduced the number of military observers serving with UNTSO from 298 in 1990 to 178 in 1996.

It is generally perceived that UNTSO failed to fulfill its original objectives of attempting to uphold the cease-fire lines set out in 1948 and preventing incursions across international frontiers. There is also a consensus of opinion that there were three reasons for UNTSO's failure: First, there was no real consent from the parties involved. The parties continuously refused to cooperate with UNTSO, and the frequency and intensity of incidents across the borders increased as the parties perceived that no solution to the conflict was likely to be forthcoming. The parties almost universally refused to cooperate with the MACs, and they also restricted the movements of UNTSO personnel, making UNTSO ineffective. Second, the demarcation lines were indistinct, which provided the parties with endless opportunities for dissent. Third, UNTSO was insufficiently equipped to deal with the situations that developed in the demilitarized zones. Disagreements over ownership of land meant that the zones became the most hotly disputed areas between the parties and hence the most sensitive for the observers. Military forces would therefore have been required to carry out satisfactory inspections of the demilitarized zones.

However, UNTSO has been of considerable use to peacekeeping in general, as the military officers assigned as its observers have regularly been drawn upon as a reserve pool of personnel for new operations. Their ability and readiness to be dispatched at very short notice have made them invaluable to the initial phases of missions in the Middle East and around the world. Military observers serving with UNTSO and its communications system have been deployed to UNEF I in 1956, the United Nations Observation Group in Lebanon (UNOGIL) in 1958, the United Nations Operation in the Congo (ONUC) in 1960, the United Nations Yemen Observer Mission (UNYOM) in 1963, UNEF II in 1973, UNDOF in 1974, UNIFIL in 1978, the United Nations Good Offices Mission in Afghanistan and Pakistan (UNGOMAP) and the United Nations Iran-Iraq Military Observer Group (UNIIMOG) in 1988, the United Nations Angola Verification Mission (UNAVEM) and the United Nations Observer Mission in Central America (ONUCA) in 1989, the United Nations Observer Group for the Verification of Elections in Haiti (ONUVEH) in 1990, the United Nations Iraq-Kuwait Observation Mission (UNIKOM) in 1991, and the United Nations Protection Force in Former Yugoslavia (UNPROFOR) and the United Nations Operation in Mozambique (UNOMOZ) in 1992. UNTSO's total expenditure from its establishment in 1948 through the end of 1995 was $463,667,258.

See also Middle East conflict
References and further reading Durch (1994); James (1990)

UNYOM (United Nations Yemen Observation Mission), 1963–1964
See Yemen

U.S. Multinational Force and Observers
See Lebanon

U.S. peacekeeping

The U.S. approach to peacekeeping has been markedly influenced by U.S. military history and experience and by the role of the United States as a superpower since 1945. U.S. attitudes toward the use of force, as expressed for example during World War II, were governed by a desire to use its large population and technological capability to create the potential for the massive use of military and national force. Once involved in a conflict the United States tended to take an "all or nothing" approach. The Vietnam War demonstrated this and also had a profound impact on U.S. thinking, an impact that is still relevant today. These attitudes were also embodied in the Weinberger Doctrine of 1984, which followed the killing of 239 U.S. Marines in a suicide bomb attack during a peacekeeping mission in Lebanon in 1983. The Weinberger Doctrine formulated major questions that should be addressed by policy makers before U.S. combat troops may be sent abroad. Foremost among the suggestions in the doctrine was the establishment of a number of tightly controlled criteria to be satisfied, including clearly defined political and military objectives, before military force could be engaged wholeheartedly and with the clear intention of winning. The doctrine further stipulated that forces would be engaged only when vital national interests were at stake. This war-fighting doctrine has in turn influenced the attitude of the U.S. public and foreign policy makers to peacekeeping. U.S. military strategy is based on the idea that the primary function of the military is to fight and win wars, and current strategy is designed to cope with the possibility of fighting two nearly simultaneous major regional conflicts (MRCs). The military uses two categories to describe its military role: combat operations, associated with fighting or deterring MRCs, and operations other than war (OOTW). The military gives the former far higher priority. However, it has been argued that following the collapse of the Soviet Union, "fight and win" combat strategies designed to defeat Cold War opponents are insufficient. In the conditions of conflict in the modern, post–Cold War world, efforts have been made to define a doctrine for peacekeeping for the U.S. military under the umbrella term "peace-support operations." Thus Secretary of State George Shultz revised Caspar Weinberger's criteria, arguing that the use of force could be justified not only when vital national interests were at stake but also on moral grounds—for example, when the aim is to bring peace or support peace processes.

Recent U.S. policy for participation in peacekeeping is framed within a wider approach called "peace-support operations." Before the collapse of the Soviet Union U.S. Army doctrine was expressed in FM 100-5, *Operations,* which focused on offense-oriented air-land battle conflict with Warsaw Pact countries. After the fall of the Berlin Wall more attention to activities other than war was clearly needed. This was provided in the updated FM 100-5 in 1993, which had a separate chapter covering the 16 mission categories of OOTW, one of which is peace-support operations (other types of OOTW missions include combating terrorism, counternarcotics operations, sanctions enforcement, and humanitarian assistance). In December 1994 the army then published its peacekeeping doctrine, linked to FM 100-5, as FM 100-23, *Peace Operations.* Here peacekeeping was located within a spectrum of peace-support operations including support to diplomacy (including, for example, the preventive deployment of U.S. troops under UN command in Macedonia), traditional peacekeeping (where classic principles of consent, impartiality, and use of force in self-defense apply), peace enforcement (chapter 7 operations requiring strong force capability), peace-making, and peace building.

Historically the U.S. military has not committed ground forces in significant numbers to peacekeeping operations. U.S. officers have served as members of the Multinational Force and Observers (MFO) with the United Nations Truce Supervision Organization (UNTSO), in the Dominican Republic, and in the Sinai. The United States has provided airlift for other forces (e.g., in the Congo). In the former Yugoslavia the United States, through the North Atlantic Treaty Organization (NATO), has helped to enforce the no-fly zones and the safe areas, and it has also supported the embargo in the Adriatic Sea. In the post–Cold War period the United States has come under increasing pressure to participate in or support peacekeeping operations. In an innovative development in the history of peacekeeping, U.S. ground forces were also deployed to serve in the preventive deployment mission in Macedonia. In the areas of intelligence, communications, and force projection capabilities (strategic airlift and logistics support) the United States has unique resources, and though direct U.S. participation in traditional peacekeeping operations may be kept to a minimum, larger operations involving high levels of risk and complexity will probably not be undertaken without U.S. support. This was true of one of the largest peacekeeping operations ever mounted, when U.S. forces spearheaded the Unified Task Force in Somalia (UNITAF) and also provided, under the follow-on mission, the second United Nations Operation in Somalia (UNOSOM II), the special representative of the secretary-general, and combat units under national command. The role of U.S. forces in Somalia was to a degree controversial. In June and July 1993 the United States launched gunship attacks against Mogadishu in an attempt to capture the Somalian warlord Gen. Mohammed Farah Aidid. The attack failed and worsened the conflict, and 18 U.S. soldiers died in the subsequent withdrawal of U.S. forces. U.S. action was criticized by some of her partners in the UNOSOM operation, and both Italian and Pakistani commanders, for example, expressed their doubts about U.S. strategy, suggesting that the United States was acting independently and without the agreement of her military partners. The first national security strategy document of President Bill Clinton's administration, published in July 1994, declared that multilateral peace operations were an important component of national defense strategy. However bitter, congressional and public criticism after the experience in Somalia resulted in a more cautious attitude toward peacekeeping by the U.S. administration, which still prevails. This was formally expressed in Presidential Decision Directive 25 (PDD 25), which set out a series of questions that had to be addressed before U.S. participation in a mission could be approved (e.g., whether there are clear objectives, whether the means to accomplish the mission are adequate, whether there are clear and realistic criteria for ending the operation, whether involvement in the mission advances U.S. interests, and whether there is an international community of interest for dealing with the problem on a multilateral basis).

See also Cold War; Financing peacekeeping; Troop-contributing countries; United Nations: organization
References and further reading Browne (1995); Joint Warfighting Center (1995); Ruggie (1994); Snow (1993); U.S. Congress Senate Committee on Foreign Relations (1993)

U.S. Sinai Support Mission/ Sinai Field Mission

The 1970s' rapprochement between Egypt and the United States led to important diplomatic openings for the withdrawal of Israel from Egyptian territory. The first Sinai Disengagement Agreement of January 1974 created a UN buffer zone to which a U.S. Sinai Support Mission (SSM) was set to work alongside the UN mission already in existence, the second United Nations Emergency Force (UNEF II). In 1975 the U.S. Sinai Field Mission (SFM), an operation staffed predominantly by civilians and funded by the U.S. government via a commercial contractor, planned to verify through observation that both sides were using their respective observation stations in the Sinai in a nonaggressive and legitimate manner, according to conduct outlined by the United Nations. The SFM was for the most part an accepted neutral channel mediating between the two sides, communicating observations and information on an equal basis. The character of the mission also gave it an important peacekeeping legitimacy: It was civilian-dominated, its upper echelons contained government officials, and each inspection team contained military expertise. With the signing of the Egyptian-Israeli Peace Treaty in 1979 the SFM became more involved in the pacification of the Egyptian-Israeli dispute, particularly after the Soviet Union vetoed the continuation of UNEF II in the face of Arab condemnation. Israel refused to allow the smaller UN subsidiary mission, the United Nations Truce Supervision Organization (UNTSO), to take over, claiming that it lacked adequate equipment and resources. Correspondingly, the SFM continued to work alongside the smaller UN mission, largely because of the positive response the SFM had engendered between the two sides. After 1982 the SFM went on to work within the Multinational Force and Observers in East Sinai.

See also UNEF II
References and further reading James (1990)

Uniting for Peace Resolution

The Uniting for Peace Resolution was passed by the General Assembly on 3 November 1950. It was also known as the Acheson Plan. The resolution had been proposed by the United States to establish a mechanism for UN action in spite of the veto power of the five permanent members of the Security Council. It stipulated that if any aggression occurred and a resolution to deal with it failed in the Security Council because of the veto, an emergency session of the General Assembly might be called on 24 hours' notice by any seven members of the Security Council. The resolution derived its authority from article 10, which enabled the assembly to discuss and make recommendations on any matter within the scope of the UN Charter, and article 11, which gave the General Assembly power to "consider the general principles of cooperation in the maintenance of international peace and security" and the power to "discuss any questions relating to the maintenance of international peace and security." The resolution was first used during the Korean War and was used again in 1956, after Britain and France had used their vetoes to block resolutions calling on them to withdraw their forces from the Suez Canal in Egypt. Following General Assembly Resolution 997 (ES-1), calling for a cease-fire, and the diplomacy of Lester Pearson, the first United Nations Emergency Force (UNEF I) was created to monitor the cease-fire.

See also   United Nations: organization

Urquhart, Brian (1919–)

Born 28 February 1919, Brian Urquhart served in the Dorset Regiment and Airborne Forces of the British Army during World War II, bringing him into active service in both North Africa and Europe. After the war he was personal assistant to Gladwyn Jebb, the executive secretary of the Preparatory Commission of the United Nations in London (1945–1946). In a distinguished 40-year career at the United Nations, he held appointments of various degrees of seniority, including personal assistant to Trygve Lie, the first secretary-general (1954–1971). During Ralph J. Bunche's term of office he held various positions within the Office of the Undersecretary-General for Special Political Affairs, which dealt with peacekeeping and conflict control. In 1974 he was appointed undersecretary-general for special political affairs, which he maintained until his retirement in 1986. That position included such responsibilities as the direction of peacekeeping operations and negotiations in Cyprus, the Middle East, and Namibia. From 1986 to 1996 he was a scholar-in-residence at Ford Foundation's International Affairs Program. As of 1998 he was commissioner on the Carnegie Commission on Preventing Deadly Conflict. He has published extensively on the areas of international relations, peacekeeping, and conflict resolution.

References and further reading   Urquhart (1987)

Vance, Cyrus (1917–)

Cyrus Vance's natural skills as a communicator stood him well in his successful political career, which by 1962 had rewarded him with the position of secretary of the army. This was followed by the position of deputy-secretary of defense (1964–1967). His talent for mediation has been demonstrated by numerous examples during his career, including early posts as special representative of the U.S. president in civil disturbances in Detroit (1967), in the Cyprus crisis (1967), and in Korea (1968) and as negotiator at the Paris Peace Conference on Vietnam (1968–1969). He was appointed in the senior role as U.S. secretary of state in Jimmy Carter's administration (1977–1980). His expertise was also sought by the secretary-general of the United Nations as his personal envoy to Yugoslavia during the unfolding crisis and concurrently as UN cochairman of the International Conference on the Former Yugoslavia. He served again as personal envoy to the secretary-

general in Nagorno-Karabakh and South Africa (1992). Vance's expertise was needed again in the negotiations between Greece and the former Yugoslav Republic of Macedonia (FYROM) (1993). He was also a member of the Carnegie Commission on Preventing Deadly Conflict (1994–1997).

Waldheim, Kurt (1918–)

Born in December 1918, Kurt Waldheim earned a doctorate from the University of Vienna in 1944 and joined the Austrian Foreign Service in 1945. He became permanent Austrian observer to the United Nations in 1955 and was permanent Austrian representative between 1964 and 1968. He served as secretary-general of the United Nations between 1972 and 1981 and presided over what has been described as a "resurgent" period of peacekeeping, following a six-year period when no new missions were launched. During Waldheim's time in office as secretary-general, three new missions were launched in the Middle East (the first United Nations Emergency Force [UNEF II], the United Nations Disengagement Observer Force [UNDOF], and the United Nations Interim Forces in Lebanon [UNIFIL]), and he played a key role in the revision of the mandate of the United Nations Peacekeeping Force in Cyprus (UNFICYP) following the Turkish invasion of the island in 1974.

References and further reading
Waldheim (1985)

West New Guinea/West Irian
See Indonesia

Western European Union (WEU)

The Western European Union (WEU) was formed in 1955 as an alliance of European states to promote and coordinate security and defense. Under the Petersberg Tasks of 1992 the WEU agreed to specify a common role in the areas of humanitarian and rescue assistance and the use of forces in crisis management, including peacekeeping. Meeting in June 1992 in Petersberg Castle near Bonn, Germany, the Council of Ministers of the WEU approved the creation of an Intervention Force capable of intervening outside Europe if necessary, under the auspices of the United Nations. Later in 1992 a "planning cell" was established in Brussels made up of a small group of military and civilian staff. The planning cell would be responsible for

establishing guidelines for the command and direction of potential future operations and for establishing an inventory of forces available. As of 1998 the planning cell was also considering the formation of a Humanitarian Task Force and of a diplomatic planning cell of officials from member states who would be able to respond to areas of potential conflict with the aim of acting early to preempt escalation.

From 1992 onward the WEU was involved in carrying out enforcement actions under UN mandates in the former Yugoslavia, and during the Gulf Wars it was involved in both minesweeping operations and the coordination of actions to enforce compliance with sanctions against Iraq. Originally conceived as a defensive alliance, the WEU has evolved into an organization that can take action where European interests are perceived to be at stake, or where action is called for by the United Nations or the Organization for Security and Cooperation in Europe (OSCE). However, the operational capability of the WEU is still under development. There is a Eurocorps composed of forces from Belgium, France, Germany, Luxembourg, and Spain. A joint rapid reaction force, EUROFOR, with forces from France, Italy, and Spain, was agreed upon in May 1995, as was a European maritime force, EUROMARFOR.

See also France; Naval peacekeeping; Organization for Security and Cooperation in Europe; Regional organizations and peacekeeping
References and further reading Vierruci (1995)

Western Sahara
See Morocco

White Helmets
There have been increasing calls in the 1990s for more civilian specialists and staff in peacekeeping operations in order to deal effectively with the wide range of tasks that the main peacekeeping missions of the 1990s have been called upon to perform (e.g., repatriating refugees, restoring economic and social services, monitoring human rights, organizing elections, and assisting in public administration). Increasing the civilian staff would free the Blue Helmets to conduct the military and security tasks in which they specialize. The idea of the White Helmets has been proposed to address perceived inadequacies, for example in the Bosnian and Rwandan programs. In December 1995 General Assembly Resolution A-50-19, the White Helmets Initiative, was officially passed. The objective of recruiting the White Helmets would be to "make men and women of goodwill available to the United Nations, with the aim of strengthening the reserve capacity of developing countries in support of United Nations activities in the field of emergency humanitarian assistance and the gradual transition from relief to rehabilitation, reconstruction, and development." These White Helmets would form an integral part of the United Nations Volunteers Program, and the UN's Department of Humanitarian Affairs (DHA) would serve as headquarters. The idea was first proposed by the president of Argentina, Carlos Menem, in his speech on the International Day against Hunger in 1993, and the proposal that resulted in the 1995 General Assembly Resolution A-50-19 was brought to the assembly by Argentina, supported by 65 member states. Following the resolution the Dutch representative in the Security Council presented an analysis that recommended the formation of an international brigade of volunteers to be used in emergency situations and natural disasters. In addition to Argentina 22 governments supported the initiative and indicated that they wished to see it implemented, and small contingents have served in Haiti, Armenia, the Gaza Strip, Bolivia, Rwanda, and Jamaica. The Argentinian government has created the Comision Nacional de los Cascos Blancos to support pilot projects and to encourage mechanisms to develop the initiative. However, few governments have made commitments to fund the White Helmets Initiative, and there are other difficulties that need to be resolved. For example, it is not clear operationally whether White Helmets would work alongside Blue Helmets or whether they would become involved only in the postconflict reconstruction phase of a conflict. Second, existing nongovernmental organizations and other UN agencies such as the United Nations Development Program (UNDP) may be concerned that a further corps of volunteers might make coordination of activities even more difficult.

See also Civilian component in peacekeeping operations
References and further reading David (1997)

Women and peacekeeping
The issue of gender has largely been ignored in relation to peacekeeping, but it is likely to become more significant, first, as the civilian component of peacekeeping missions expands, and second, as gender differences in negotiation styles and in the management of conflict become better understood. Despite the expansion of peacekeeping, with its hybrid mixture of military and civilian roles, peacekeeping has continued to be dominated by men, reflecting the traditionally male composition of national armed forces. Of the 17 missions active in 1993, women comprised less than 2 percent of military personnel and less than 1 percent of police. The highest percentage of women in peacekeeping missions was in the United Nations Mission for the Referendum in Western Sahara (MINURSO) and on the Golan Heights in the United Nations Disengagement Observer Force (UNDOF): In MINURSO women made up 9.4 percent of total personnel, and in UNDOF, 4 percent. In Lebanon, 2.3 percent of the 5,247 military peacekeepers were women, and in Somalia 2.1 percent of the 29,703 military personnel were women (all of these from the U.S. contingent, which was 12 percent female).

The percentage of women in the international civilian staff of peacekeeping missions is considerably higher than in military or police contingents. In 1993, 32 percent of the total 2,230 international civilian staff serving in 19 missions were women. The leadership of a peacekeeping mission has been held by a woman only once: Margaret Anstee was the special representative of the secretary-general in Angola.

Edward Moxon-Browne has proposed several reasons for encouraging a higher proportion of women in peacekeeping forces, all of which clearly distinguish the female subculture from the male: If a certain proportion of peacekeepers are female it may help local women in a host country to defuse awkward situations without the need for formal peacekeeper intervention; it may place greater emphasis on "female" attributes such as nonconfrontational approaches in delicate situations, ability to listen and console, and willingness to share responsibilities and to work cooperatively in teams. He has suggested that these characteristics combined could contribute something of added value to the peacekeeping experience. The presence of women soldiers, in contrast to male soldiers, might have a salutary effect in that more female peacekeepers would underline the essentially pacific and nonforce orientation of classic peacekeeping.

References and further reading Moxon-Browne (1998)

World Food Program
See United Nations: organization

World Health Organization
See United Nations: organization

World War I and history of peacekeeping
At the end of World War I (1914–1918) a Conference of Ambassadors was set up in Paris to interpret and apply the provisions of the various treaties that ended the war. The treaties' most significant provisions were the arrangements that changed borders throughout Europe and created a number of new states, particularly in Central Europe. In order to execute these changes, delimitation commissions were also set up, composed of military officers from states represented at the Conference of Ambassadors. Alan James has suggested similarities between the work of these commissions and the role of what was much later (during the 1950s) referred to as peacekeeping, in the sense that the commissioners were military personnel who were impartially conducting the application of provisions of a peace treaty. Provisions were made in the treaties for plebiscites to be held (in Schleswig, Allenstein and Marienwerder, Klagenfurt, Upper Silesia, and Sopron), all of them being territories in Central Europe whose ownership was disputed. Inter-Allied Plebiscite Forces worked between 1920 and 1922 to administer the territories during the plebiscite period, and as international armed forces operating under principles of impartiality and consent, they also provided precedents for modern peacekeeping.

References and further reading James (1990)

World Wide Web
Peacekeeping and related information and databases are widely available on the World Wide Web (WWW) (or the Internet). The United Nations uses its WWW sites as an efficient and cost-effective means of transferring and making available its reports and documents. The UN homepage (http://www.un.org/) offers press briefings, basic information about the United Nations, full text of major documents, and statistical material. The United Nations now distributes most of its major documents on-line, including both the General Assembly and Security Council resolutions and other relevant documents, such as the reports of the Economic and Social Council. Subject-specific documents can be located through the keyword search options. Conference information and reports can also be obtained through this page. The Department of Peacekeeping Operations (DPKO) homepage (http://www.un.org/Depts/dpko/) pro-

vides both general and specialized information. General information includes the World Map of Peacekeeping Operations and Mission Profiles; specialized information includes Lessons Learned and Field Employment with United Nations Peacekeeping. Further databases, such as the National Training for Peacekeeping database and the Glossary of Peacekeeping, are also available through this page.

The Relief Web (http://www.reliefweb.int/) has been developed by the Department of Humanitarian Affairs (DHA) as "the principal repository of information for the humanitarian community in managing the response to humanitarian emergencies." This link offers information on prevention, preparedness, and disaster response and includes sections such as the Emergency Bulletin and country and regional information. Interorganizational networks have also been developed. UN/NGO link (www.un.org/MoreInfo/ngolink/) explores nongovernmental organizations' (NGO) participation and cooperation with the United Nations and offers practical information on the NGO-UN interaction.

The academic on-line network contributes to the enhancement of the current debate on peacekeeping issues. For example, the Project on Peacekeeping Policy of George Mason University (http://ralph.gmu.edu/cfpa/peace/peace.html) consists of peacekeeping documents and research reports as well as policy analysis. Similarly, the Program on Peacekeeping and the United Nations by the Council for a Livable World Education Fund (http://www.clw.org/pub/clud/un/unpeace.html) offers analyses of peacekeeping issues. Moreover, the availability of databases and journals on-line is

also increasing. The Sarajevo On-line project (http://www.axime.com/wm/sarajevo/) is the first on-line journalism project, enabling users to communicate with residents of the city and to have access to the Bosnian media. The Somalia Intervention page (http://www.users.interport.net/~mmaren/intervention.html) includes articles on the UN and U.S. intervention in Somalia and the Somali Archive. These sites also offer links to other peacekeeping-related sites and enable the user to communicate with organizations and individuals. Other sites worth searching for peacekeeping and related information include the Initiative on Conflict Resolution and Ethnicity, a joint initiative of the University of Ulster in Northern Ireland and the United Nations University (http://www.incore.ulst.ac.uk/). The International Relations and Security Network (IRSN), maintained by the Center for Security Studies and Conflict Research (Zurich) and the Euro-Atlantic Foundation (Brussels), provides comprehensive information about security, defense, peace, and conflict at http://www.isn.ethz.ch/. The United States Institute for Peace is at http:/www.usip.org/. Information about training and education in peacekeeping is available at the DPKO homepage already mentioned and at the homepages of the International Association of Peacekeeping Training Centers (http:www.cdnpeacekeeping.ca.iaptc.htm), at the correspondence courses in peacekeeping run by the United Nations Institute for Training and Research (UNITAR) (http://www.wm.edu/unpeacek/index.html), and at the homepage of the Lester B. Pearson Canadian International Peacekeeping Training Center (http://www.cdnpeacekeeping.ns.ca/).

Yemen

United Nations Yemen Observation Mission (UNYOM), 1963–1964

Conflict Profile

A republican revolt in Yemen in September 1962 successfully overthrew the royalist regime. Imam Ahmed bin Yahya died on 19 September and was succeeded by his son, Imam Mohammed Al-Badr, providing the opportunity for the military-led republican opposition forces to overthrow the royal dynasty and proclaim the Yemen Arab Republic. However, the conflict did not end there, and a civil war ensued between the two entities that carried considerable potential for regional and international repercussions. The royalists had traditionally been supported by Saudi Arabia, whereas Egypt favored the new republican authority. Yemen had joined the UAR (United Arab Republic—a union of Egypt and Syria) in 1958 to form the United Arab States, but the alliance was dissolved in 1961 when Syria withdrew. Thus the conflict in Yemen reflected the opposing Arab nationalist and traditionalist trends that were operating both domestically and regionally in the region at the time. Such regional ties also extended internationally, as Saudi Arabia and Egypt were allied to the United States and the Soviet Union, respectively.

Defeated, Imam Al-Badr escaped to the primarily rural northern part of the country, from where he launched a guerrilla campaign against the republican regime. The republicans accused Saudi Arabia of supplying arms for Al-Badr's cause and threatened to extend the fighting into Saudi Arabian territory; the royalists similarly accused Egypt of patronizing the republican regime. In October 1962 Cairo dispatched Egyptian troops to reinforce the republican government against Al-Badr's forces.

Deployment of UNYOM

At the request of the opposing parties, the conflict in Yemen had been taken up in the UN General Assembly. As a result, the then secretary-general, U Thant, sent a fact-finding mission to the area, as did the U.S. government. The result of these missions was an agreement reached in April 1963 be-

tween the governments of Saudi Arabia, UAR, and Yemen that Saudi Arabia would cease providing assistance to the Yemeni royalists and would prohibit the use of Saudi territory for their operations, UAR would withdraw its estimated 15,000–30,000 troops from Yemeni territory, and a 20-kilometer-wide demilitarized zone would be established along the demarcated Saudi-Yemeni border, along which observers would be positioned to verify compliance with the terms of the agreement. A second UN mission to the area suggested that the organization could provide the required observers, who would not number more than 200 nor be deployed for longer than four months. It was also agreed that the governments of UAR and Saudi Arabia would cover the mission's expenses for the first two months.

The United States was eager to improve relations with republican Arab authorities and therefore, in the interests of suppressing the conflict in Yemen, tempered its approval of Saudi support for Al-Badr. The USSR, despite protesting that insufficient pressure had been applied to what it perceived to be the aggressor in the conflict, nevertheless acceded to the mission, having successfully insisted that it required Security Council approval. The United Kingdom was eager to counter Yemeni claims that it was the rightful owner of Aden, which at the time was part of the British-controlled government of the South Arabian Federation. The UAR had realized the limitations of its conventional forces against the royalist guerrillas in the mountainous north of Yemen. The Saudis, meanwhile, had witnessed the defeat of the royal-ist forces in Yemeni urban areas and so were fear-ful of UAR-backed republicans pushing toward their southern frontier. The royalists themselves were not consulted over the deployment.

Therefore, on 11 June 1963 the Security Council adopted Security Council Resolution (SCR) 179, by which it authorized the establishment of the United Nations Yemen Observer Mission (UNYOM) to oversee the terms of the April agreement. Initially the operation went well, for soon after the UNYOM deployment was completed on 4 July, UAR troops began to withdraw, and Saudi Arabia reduced its patronage of the royalists. However, having initially underestimated the extent of rural royalist sup-port, UAR increased its assistance to the republican regime. In response, continued Saudi approval of the UN operation was only secured under U.S. pressure. Effectively, the disengagement agreement was not being upheld, and realizing the futility in regularly verifying such noncompliance, the United Nations altered UNYOM's composition to reflect a more civilian orientation, although its mandate continued to be periodically renewed.

Despite UNYOM's continued presence, violence continued throughout Yemen, and levels of Egyp-tian troops began to increase again. The secretary-general insisted that the presence of the UN force reduced instability in the area. However, the con-sensus remained that, without the genuine com-mitment of the parties to the dispute, UNYOM was making scant contribution to the resolution of the conflict. Therefore, when in August 1964 the Saudi government refused to pay its assessment for the operation, it was agreed that the operation should be terminated, and UNYOM was withdrawn by 4 September.

The UNYOM operation had not maintained sufficient consent or support to be successful. Egypt had underestimated the strength of the royalist movement and so had been forced to ab-rogate its commitment to withdraw its troops. However, popular international sympathy with the Yemeni republican cause, and hence Egyp-tian patronage of it, tempered Cairo's embarrass-ment at having to renege on an internationally sanctioned agreement. International commit-ment to the resolution of the conflict had been insufficient to adopt more drastic measures than had already been agreed upon. Although the United Nations failed to achieve the withdrawal of Egyptian troops, the UNYOM mandate was conceived around the genuine commitment of the parties to the dispute to uphold their pledges. Thus the breakdown of the operation cannot wholly be ascribed to the failure of the original plans.

UNYOM headquarters were in Sana'a, and the operation lasted from July 1963 to September 1964. The operation comprised 25 military ob-servers and 164 military personnel of reconnais-sance and air units, supported by international and locally recruited civilian staff. There were no fatalities during the operation, which cost some $1,840,450.

See also Child soldiers; Financing peacekeeping; First-generation peacekeeping
References and further reading Durch (1994); United Nations (1996)

Yugoslavia (former, 1992–)
See Bosnia and Herzegovina; Croatia; Macedonia; UNPROFOR I–III

Zimbabwe

Elements of the Zimbabwe Defence Force (ZDF) have participated in Somalia in the UN's Unified Task Force (UNITAF), in the second United Nations Operation in Somalia (UNOSOM II), in the second United Nations Angola Verification Mission (UNAVEM II), and in the ongoing UNAVEM III. In all these operations a battalion- or regiment-size unit of just fewer than 1,000 men and women has been deployed for periods of not less than six months. Meanwhile, a smaller Observer Contingent also served in the United Nations Assistance Mission in Rwanda (UNAMIR). Not only has interaction with other national forces at the international level benefited the operational efficiency and preparedness of the ZDF, but its officers have also gained from exercising command of forces beyond national considerations. For example, a Zimbabwean officer, the then Colonel Nyambuya, served as the deputy commander to UNOSOM II and UNAVEM II. It is assumed that it was this initial success that led the United Nations to select a Zimbabwean to serve as commander of UNAVEM III (Maj. Gen. Phillip V. Sibanda).

Furthermore, as a consequence of Zimbabwe's raised profile, Harare was made the host of a UN-recognized peacekeeping training center, the Regional Peacekeeping Training Center, which made Zimbabwe the third center of military-academic peacekeeping training, following the establishment of similar institutions in Accra and Cairo. The course, offered to local and other continental officers, seeks to provide theory and practical skills to senior peacekeeping officers in order to enhance their ability to apply appropriate UN guidelines within a multinational force. The hope is to equip them with a better understanding of wider political, social, and economic linkages in zones of involvement. The Republic of Zimbabwe has been given the mandate by the Interstate Defence and Security Conference (ISDSC) to coordinate and harmonize peacekeeping training in the Southern

African region (SADC). One result of the ISDSC mandate was the signing in August 1997 of the Zimbabwean-Danish Government Agreement. Under this agreement, Zimbabwe continues to play a key role in peacekeeping on the African continent, with the development of the Regional Peacekeeping Training Center in Zimbabwe itself. As of 1998, the members of SADC were Angola, Botswana, Lesotho, Malawi, Mozambique, Namibia, South Africa, Swaziland, Tanzania, Zambia, and Zimbabwe.

It has been recognized in official circles that ZDF forces have gained immensely from serving in an international role both materially and symbolically. The country's profile in humanitarian operations has been raised globally. Finally, it is worth noting that apart from the generous individual allowances that soldiers receive, the UN system allows for a depreciation of the equipment used, calculated at 30 percent in the first two years of use and 20 percent in the third and fourth years. This represents a significant defrayal of military expenses.

See also The Commonwealth; Mozambique; Somalia; Training for peacekeeping; Troop-contributing countries
References and further reading Stedman (1990)

Appendix 1

Force Commanders of UN Peacekeeping Missions, 1948–1998

Peacekeeping Operation	UN Force Commander	Dates
UNTSO (June 1948–)	*	
UNMOGIP (January 1949–)	*	
UNEF I (November 1956–June 1967)	Lt. Gen E. L. M. Burns (Canada)	November 1956–December 1959
	Lt. Gen. P. S. Gyani (India)	December 1959–January 1964
	Maj. Gen. Carlos F. Paiva Chaves (Brazil)	January 1964–August 1964
	Col. Lazar Musicki (Yugoslavia) (Acting)	August 1964–January 1965
	Maj. Gen. Syseno Sarmento (Brazil)	January 1965–January 1966
	Maj. Gen. Indar J. Rikhye (India)	January 1966–June 1967
UNOGIL (June 1958–December 1958)	*	*
ONUC (July 1960–June 1964)	Lt. Gen. Carl C. von Horn (Sweden)	July 1960–December 1960
	Lt. Gen. Sean MacEoin (Ireland)	January 1961–March 1962
	Lt. Gen. Kebbede Guebre (Ethiopia)	April 1962–July 1963
	Maj. Gen. Christian Kaldager (Norway)	August 1963–December 1963
	Maj. Gen. Aguiyu Ironsi (Nigeria)	January 1964–June 1964
UNSF (October 1962–April 1963)	Maj. Gen. Said Uddin Khan (Pakistan)	October 1962–April 1963
UNYOM (July 1963–September 1964)	Lt. Gen. Carl C. von Horn (Sweden)	July 1963–August 1963
	Col. Branko Pavlovic (Yugoslavia) (Acting)	August 1963–September 1963
	Lt. Gen. P. S. Gyani (India)	September 1963–November 1963
UNFICYP (March 1964–)	Lt. Gen. P. S. Gyani (India)	March 1964–June 1964
	Gen. K. S. Thimayya (India)	June 1964–December 1965
	Brig. A. J. Wilson (United Kingdom) (Acting)	December 1965–May 1966
	Lt. Gen. I. A. E. Martola (Finland)	May 1966–December 1969
	Lt. Gen. Dewan Prem Chand (India)	December 1969–December 1976
	Maj. Gen. James J. Quinn (Ireland)	December 1976–February 1981
	Maj. Gen. Günther G. Greindl (Austria)	March 1981–April 1989
	Maj. Gen. Clive Milner (Canada)	April 1989–April 1992

Continues

Force Commanders of UN Peacekeeping Missions, 1948–1998 *(continued)*

Peacekeeping Operation	UN Force Commander	Dates
	Maj. Gen. Michael F. Minehane (Ireland)	April 1992–July 1994
	Brig. Gen. Ahti T. P. Vartianinen (Finland)	August 1994–
DOMREP (May 1965–October 1966)	*	*
UNIPOM (September 1965–March 1966)	*	*
UNEF II (October 1973–July 1979)	Lt. Gen. Ensio P. H. Siilasvuo (Finland):	
	—Interim Commander	October 1973–November 1973
	—Commander	November 1973–August 1975
	Lt. Gen. Bengt Liljestrand (Sweden)	August 1975–November 1976
	Maj. Gen. Rais Abin (Indonesia)	December 1976–September 1979
UNDOF (June 1974–)	Brig. Gen. Gonzalo Briceño Zevallos (Peru) (Interim Commander)	June 1974–December 1974
	Col. Hannes Philipp (Austria)	December 1974–April 1979
	Col. Günther G. Greindl (Austria)	April 1979–February 1981
	Maj. Gen. Erkki R. Kaira (Finland)	February 1981–May 1982
	Maj. Gen. Carl-Gustaf Stahl (Sweden)	June 1982–May 1985
	Maj. Gen. Gustav Hägglund (Finland)	June 1985–May 1986
	Brig. Gen. W. A. Douglas Yuill (Canada) (Acting)	June 1986
	Maj. Gen. N. Gustaf A. Welin (Sweden)	July 1986–September 1988
	Maj. Gen. Adolf Radauer (Austria)	September 1988–September 1991
	Maj. Gen. Roman Misztal (Poland)	September 1991–November 1994
	Col. Jan Kempara (Poland) (Acting)	November 1994–January 1995
	Maj. Gen. Johannes C. Kosters (Netherlands)	January 1995–
UNIFIL (March 1978–)	Lt. Gen. Emmanuel A. Erskine (Ghana):	
	—Interim Commander	March 1978–April 1978
	—Commander	April 1978–February 1981
	Lt. Gen. William Callaghan (Ireland)	February 1981–May 1986
	Maj. Gen. Gustav Hägglund (Finland)	June 1986–June 1988
	Lt. Gen. Lars-Eric Wahlgren (Sweden)	July 1988–February 1993
	Maj. Gen. Trond Furuhovde (Norway)	February 1993–February 1995
	Maj. Gen. Stanislaw Franciszek Woniak (Poland)	April 1995–
UNGOMAP (May 1988–March 1990)	*	*
UNIIMOG (August 1988–February 1990)	*	*
UNAVEM I (January 1989–May 1991)	*	*
UNTAG (April 1989–March 1990)	Maj. Gen. Hannes Philipp (Austria)	September 1978–January 1980
	Lt. Gen. Dewan Prem Chand (India)	January 1980–March 1990
ONUCA (November 1989–January 1992)	*	*

Continues

Force Commanders of UN Peacekeeping Missions, 1948–1998 *(continued)*

Peacekeeping Operation	UN Force Commander	Dates
UNIKOM (April 1991–)	Maj. Gen. Krishna Narayan Singh Thapa (Nepal)	January 1994–December 1995
	Maj. Gen. Gian Giuseppe Santillo (Italy)	December 1995–
MINURSO (April 1991–)	Maj. Gen. Armand Roy (Canada)	June 1991–April 1992
	Brig. Gen. Luis Block Urban (Peru) (Acting)	April 1992–September 1992
	Brig. Gen. André Van Baelen (Belgium)	October 1992–March 1996
	Maj. Gen. José Eduardo Garcia Léandro (Portugal)	March 1996–
UNAVEM III (May 1991– February 1995)	Maj. Gen. Chris Abutu Garuba (Nigeria)	February 1995–September 1995
	Maj. Gen. Phillip Valerio Sibanda (Zimbabwe)	October 1995–
ONUSAL (July 1991–April 1995)	*	*
UNAMIC (October 1991– March 1992)	*	
UNPROFOR (March 1992– December 1995		*
	Lt. Gen. Satish Nambiar (India)	
	Lt. Gen. Lars-Eric Wahlgren (Sweden)	March 1992–March 1993
	Lt. Gen. Jean Cot (France)	March 1993–June 1993
	Gen. Bertrand de Lapresle (France)	June 1993–March 1994
	Gen. Bernard Janvier (France)	March 1994–February 1995
	Lt. Gen. Rupert Smith (United Kingdom)	March 1995–November 1995 March 1995–December 1995
UNTAC (March 1992– September 1993)	Lt. Gen. John Sanderson (Australia)	
UNOSOM I (April 1992–March 1993)	Brig. Gen. Imtiaz Shaheen (Pakistan)	March 1992–September 1993
ONUMOZ (December 1992– December 1994)		June 1992–March 1993
	Maj. Gen. Lélio Gonçalves Rodrigues da Silva (Brazil)	February 1993–February 1994
	Maj. Gen. Mohammad Abdus Salam (Bangladesh)	March 1994–December 1994
UNOSOM II (March 1993– March 1995)	Lt. Gen. Çevik Bir (Turkey)	
	Lt. Gen. Aboo Samah Bin Aboo Bakar (Malaysia)	February 1993–February 1994 March 1994–December 1994
UNOMUR (June 1993– September 1994)	*	*
UNOMIG (August 1993–)	*	*
UNMIH (September 1993–June 1996)	Maj. Gen. Joseph Kinzer (United States)	January 1995–March 1996
	Brig. Gen. J. R. P. Daigle (Canada)	March 1996–June 1996

Continues

Force Commanders of UN Peacekeeping Missions, 1948–1998 (continued)

Peacekeeping Operation	UN Force Commander	Dates
UNOMIL (September 1993–September 1997	Col. David Magomere (Kenya) (Acting)	June 1996–December 1996
	Maj. Gen. Sikander Shani (Pakistan)	December 1996–September 1997
UNAMIR (October 1993–March 1996)	Maj. Gen. Romeo A. Dallaire (Canada)	October 1993–August 1994
	Maj. Gen. Guy Tousignant (Canada)	August 1994–December 1995
	Brig. Gen. Shiva Kumar (India) (Acting)	December 1995–March 1996
UNASOG (May 1994–June 1994)	*	*
UNMOT (December 1994–)	*	*
UNAVEM III (February 1995–June 1997)	Maj. Gen. Chris Abutu Garuba (Nigeria)	February 1995–September 1995
	Maj. Gen. Phillip Valerio Sibanda (Zimbabwe)	October 1995–
UNCRO (March 1995–January 1996)	Maj. Gen. Eid Kamal Al-Rodan (Jordan)	March 1995–December 1995
UNPREDEP (March 1995–)	Brig. Gen. Juha Engström (Finland)	March 1995–February 1996
	Brig. Gen. Bo Lennart Wrankler (Sweden)	February 1996–
UNMIBH (December 1995–)	N/A	N/A
UNTAES (January 1996–January 1998)	Maj. Gen. Jozef Schoups (Belgium)	January 1996–January 1997
	Maj. Gen. William Hanset (Belgium)	January 1997–January 1998
UNMOP (January 1996–)	*	*
MINUGUA (January 1997–May 1997)	Brig. Gen. Jose B. Rodriguez Rodriguez (Spain)	January 1997–May 1997
MONUA (July 1997–)	Maj. Gen. Seth Kofi Obeng (Ghana)	July 1997–
MIPONUH (December 1997–)	*	*
UNCPSG (January 1998–)	*	*
MINURCA (April 1998–)	Brig. Gen. Barthélémy Ralanga (Gabon)	April 1998–

Source: Adapted from United Nations, The Blue Helmets: A Review of United Nations Peacekeeping, 3rd ed. (New York: United Nations Department of Public Information, 1996).

Note: Missions marked with * were military observer missions led by chief military observers.

Appendix 2

Special Representatives of the Secretary-General, 1948–1998

Peacekeeping Operation	Special Representative to the Secretary-General	Dates
UNTSO (June 1948–)	N/A	N/A
UNMOGIP (January 1949–)	N/A	N/A
UNEF I (November 1956–June 1967)	N/A	N/A
UNOGIL (June 1958–December 1958)	N/A	N/A
ONUC (July 1960–June 1964)	Ralph J. Bunche (United States)	July 1960–August 1960
	Andrew W. Cordier (United States)	August 1960–September 1960
	Rajeshwar Dayal (India)	September 1960–May 1961
	Mekki Abbas (Sudan) (Acting)	March 1961–May 1961
UNSF (October 1962–April 1963)	N/A	N/A
UNYOM (July 1963–September 1964)	P. P. Spinelli (Italy)	November 1963–September 1964
UNFICYP (March 1964–)	Galo Plaza Lasso (Ecuador)	May 1964–September 1964
	Carlos A. Bernardes (Brazil)	September 1964–January 1967
	P. P. Spinelli (Italy) (Acting)	January 1967–February 1967
	Bibiano F. Osorio-Tafall (Mexico)	February 1967–June 1974
	Luis Weckmann-Muñoz (Mexico)	July 1974–October 1975
	Javier Pérez de Cuéllar (Peru)	October 1975–December 1977
	Rémy Gorgé (Switzerland) (Acting)	December 1977–April 1978
	Reynaldo Galindo-Phol (El Salvador)	May 1978–April 1980
	Hugo Juan Gobbi (Argentina)	May 1980–December 1984
	James Holger (Chile) (Acting)	January 1985–February 1988
	Oscar Camilión (Argentina)	February 1988–March 1993
	Joe Clark (Canada)	May 1993–April 1996
	Han Sung-Joo (Republic of Korea)	May 1996–
DOMREP (May 1965–October 1966)	José Antonio Maybre (Venezuela)	May 1965–October 1966
UNIPOM (September 1965– March 1966)	N/A	N/A
UNEF II (October 1973–July 1979)	N/A	N/A
UNDOF (June 1974–)	N/A	N/A
UNIFIL (March 1978–)	N/A	N/A

Continues

Special Representatives of the Secretary-General, 1948–1998 *(continued)*

Peacekeeping Operation	Special Representative to the Secretary-General	Dates
UNGOMAP (May 1988–March 1990)	Diego Cordovez (Ecuador)	April 1988–January 1990
	Benon Sevan (Cyprus) (Personal Representative)	May 1989–August 1992
UNIIMOG (August 1988–February 1990)	Jan K. Eliasson (Sweden)	September 1988–February 1991
UNAVEM I (January 1989–May 1991)	N/A	N/A
UNTAG (April 1989–March 1990)	Martti Ahtisaari (Finland)	July 1978–March 1990
ONUCA (November 1989–January 1992)	Alvaro de Soto (Peru)	September 1989–February 1992
UNIKOM (April 1991–)	N/A	N/A
MINURSO (April 1991–)	Hector Gros Espiell (Uruguay)	October 1988–January 1990
	Johannes Manz (Switzerland)	January 1990–March 1992
	Sahabzada Yaqub-Khan (Pakistan)	March 1992–August 1995
	Erik Jensen (Malaysia) (Acting)	August 1995–
UNAVEM III (May 1991–February 1995)	Margaret Joan Anstee (United Kingdom)	February 1992–June 1993
	Alioune Blondin Beye (Mali)	June 1993 to February 1995
ONUSAL (July 1991–April 1995)	Iqbal Riza (Pakistan)	July 1991–March 1993
	Augusto Ramírez-Ocampo (Colombia)	April 1993–March 1994
	Enrique ter Horst (Venezuela)	April 1994–September 1995
UNAMIC (October 1991–March 1992)	N/A	N/A
UNTAC (March 1992–September 1993)	Yasushi Akashi (Japan)	January 1992–September 1993
UNPROFOR (March 1992–December 1995	Cyrus Vance (United States) (Special Envoy)	October 1991–April 1993
	Thorvald Stoltenberg (Norway)	May 1993–December 1994
	Yasushi Akashi (Japan)	January 1994–November 1995
UNOSOM I (April 1992–March 1993)	Mohammed Sahnoun (Algeria)	April 1992–November 1992
	Ismat Kittani (Iraq)	November 1992–March 1993
	Jonathan T. Howe (United States)	after March 1993 (*see* UNOSOM II)
ONUMOZ (December 1992–December 1994)	Aldo Ajello (Italy)	October 1992–December 1994
UNOSOM II (March 1993–March 1995)	Jonathan T. Howe (United States)	March 1993–February 1994
	Lansana Kouyaté (Guinea) (Acting)	February 1994–June 1994
	James Victor Gbeho (Ghana)	July 1994–April 1995
UNOMUR (June 1993–September 1994)	N/A	N/A
UNOMIG (August 1993–)	Edouard Brunner (Switzerland) (Special Envoy)	May 1993–

Continues

Special Representatives of the Secretary-General, 1948–1998 *(continued)*

Peacekeeping Operation	Special Representative to the Secretary-General	Dates
UNMIH (September 1993–June 1996)	Dante Caputo (Argentina):	
	—Special Envoy	December 1992–September 1994
	—Special Representative	September 1993–September 1994
	Lakhdar Brahimi (Algeria)	September 1994–March 1996
	Enrique ter Horst (Venezuela)	March 1996–
UNOMIL (September 1993– September 1997	Trevor Livingston Gordon-Somers (Jamaica)	November 1992–November 1994
	Anthony B. Nyakyi (United Republic of Tanzania)	December 1994–April 1997
	Tuliameni Kalomoh (Namibia)	April 1997–September 1997
UNAMIR (October 1993– March 1996)	Jacques-Roger Booh-Booh (Cameroon)	November 1993–June 1994
	Shaharyar M. Khan (Pakistan)	July 1994–March 1996
UNASOG (May 1994–June 1994)	N/A	N/A
UNMOT (December 1994–)	Ismat Kittani (Iraq) (Special Envoy)	April 1993–December 1993
	Ramiro Píriz-Ballón (Uruguay) (Special Envoy)	December 1993–February 1996
	Gerd Merrem (Germany)	May 1996–
UNAVEM III (February 1995– June 1997)	Alioune Blondin Beye (Mali)	June 1993–
UNCRO (March 1995–January 1996)	N/A	N/A
UNPREDEP (March 1995–)	Henryk J. Sokalski (Poland)	February 1996–
UNMIBH (December 1995–)	Iqbal Riza (Pakistan)	February 1996–
UNTAES (January 1996– January 1998)	N/A	N/A
UNMOP (January 1996–)	N/A	N/A
MINUGUA (January 1997–May 1997)	Jean Arnault (France)	January 1997–May 1997
MONUA (July 1997–)	Alioune Blondin Beye (Mali)	July 1997–
MIPONUH (December 1997–)	Julian Harston (United Kingdom)	December 1997–
UNCPSG (January 1998–)	Souren Seraydarian (Syrian Arab Republic)	January 1998–
MINURCA (April 1998–)	Oluyemi Adeniji (Nigeria)	April 1998–

Source: Adapted from United Nations, *The Blue Helmets: A Review of United Nations Peacekeeping,* 3rd ed. (New York: United Nations Department of Public Information, 1996).

Note: Some missions have a special envoy in addition to or instead of a special representative.

International Peacekeeping: Acronyms

Appendix 3

ACABQ	Advisory Committee on Administrative and Budgetary Questions
ACBC	All Ceylon Buddhist Congress
ACHR	American Convention on Human Rights
ADF	Australian Defence Forces
ADL	Armistice Demarcation Line
AEPU	advance electoral planning unit
AFL	Armed Forces of Liberia
AFM	Army Field Manual
AID	Agency for International Development (United States)
ANC	Armée Nationale Congolaise African National Congress (South Africa)
ANKI	Armée Nationale pour un Kampuchea Indépendent
AOLs	areas of limitation of armament and forces
AOS	area of separation (demilitarized)
ARENA	Nationalist Republican Alliance
ARF	ASEAN Regional Forum
ASEAN	Association of Southeast Asian Nations
ASF	Symbolic Arab Security Force
ASPR	Austrian Study Center for Peace and Conflict Resolution
AWACS	Airborne Warning and Control System
BIG	Bougainville Interim Government
BLDP	Buddhist Liberal Democratic Party (Cambodia)
BRA	Bougainville Revolutionary Army
C2W	command and control warfare
C3I	command, control, communications, and intelligence
CBN	chemical, biological, and nuclear weapons
CBO	community-based organization
CCF	Cease-Fire Commission (Mozambique)
CCFA	Joint Commission for the Formation of the Armed Forces
CCFADM	Joint Commission for the Formation of the Mozambican Defence Force
CCPA	Cairo Center for Training on Conflict Resolution and Peacekeeping in Africa
CCPM	Joint Political-Military Commission (Angola)
CD	Convergencia Democrática Geneva Committee on Disarmament
CDR	Coalition pour la Défense de la République (Rwanda)
CEAO	West African Economic Community
CFE	Conventional Armed Forces Treaty
CFSP	Common Foreign and Security Policy
CGDK	Coalition Government of Democratic Kampuchea
CIAV	International Commission for Support and Verification (Nicaragua)
CIMIC	Civil-Military Team (former Yugoslavia)
CINCSOUTH	NATO's commander in chief southern command
CIS	Commonwealth of Independent States
CIVPOL	civilian police
CIVS	International Commission for Verification and Follow-Up (Central America)
CMF	Commonwealth Monitoring Force
CMO	chief military observer
CMOC	civilian-military operations center
CMVF	Joint Verification and Monitoring Commission
CND	Campaign for Nuclear Disarmament
CNN	Cable News Network
COE	Council of Europe
COG	Commonwealth Observer Group
COMIFOR	force commander in theater of IFOR
COMSFOR	force commander of SFOR

CORE	Reintegration Commission	EPC	European Political Cooperation
CPAF	Cambodian People's Armed Forces	EPRLF	Eelam Peoples Revolutionary Liberation Front
CPC	Conflict Prevention Center (in Vienna)	EPS	Sandinista Popular Army
CPP	Cambodian People's Party	ERC	emergency relief coordinator
CRC	Central Revolutionary Council	EU	European Union
CSBM	Confidence and Security Building Measures	EW	electronic warfare
		FADM	Mozambican Defence Force
CSC	Supervisory and Monitoring Commission	FAO	Food and Agriculture Organization
		FCU	Force Communications Unit
CSCE	Conference on Security and Cooperation in Europe	FDR	Democratic Revolutionary Front
		FMLN	Frente Farabundo Martí para la Liberación Nacional (Farabundo Martí Liberation Front) (El Salvador)
CTBT	Comprehensive Test Ban Treaty		
CWC	Chemical Weapons Convention		
DAM	UN Department of Administration and Management		
		FMR	Force Mobile Reserve
DANFOR	combined Danish and Norwegian Battalion serving in UNEF I	FNLA	Frente Nacional de Libertaçao de Angola
DES	district electoral supervisor	FRELIMO	Frente da Libertaçao do Mozambique
DFF	De Facto Forces		
DHA	United Nations Department of Humanitarian Affairs	FRY	Federal Republic of Yugoslavia
		FSLN	Frente Sandinista (Sandinista Front for National Liberation) (Nicaragua)
DK	Party of Democratic Kampuchea (PDK), often abbreviated to DK		
		FUM	follow-up meeting
DMZ	demilitarized zones	FUNCINPEC	Front Uni National pour un Cambodge Indépendent, Neutre, Pacifique, et Cooperatif (National Front for an Independent, Neutral, Prosperous, and Cooperative Cambodia)
DOMREP	Representative of the Secretary-General in the Dominican Republic		
DOP	Declaration of Principles (Israeli-Palestinian agreement)		
DPA	UN Department of Political Affairs	FYROM	Former Yugoslav Republic of Macedonia
DPKO	UN Department of Peacekeeping Operations		
		GAR	General Assembly resolution
DRB	Danish Reaction Brigade	GATT	General Agreement on Tariffs and Trade
DTA	Democratic Turnhalle Alliance		
EAM	National Liberation Front (Greece)	GCC	Gulf Cooperation Council (Persian Gulf)
EC	European Community		
ECCY	European Community's Conference on Yugoslavia	GDP	gross domestic product
		GFAP	General Framework Agreement for Peace
ECHO	European Community's Humanitarian Office		
		GOC	Good Offices Commission
ECMM	European Community Monitoring Mission	GOI	government of India
		GOMN	Groupement des Observateurs Militaires Neutres (Rwanda)
ECOMOG	Military Observer Group of the Economic Organization of West African States		
		GOSL	government of Sri Lanka
		GPA	General Peace Agreement
ECOWAS	Economic Organization of West African States	GRIT	graduated reduction in international tension
ENDLF	Eelam National Democratic Liberation Front	GRO	grassroots organizations
		GSDF	Ground Self-Defence Force
EOKA	Greek Cypriot Paramilitary Organization	HCNM	High Commissioner on National Minorities

HCRC	High Commission for Human Rights	JDISS	Joint Deployable Intelligence Support System
HDZ	Croatian Nationalist Party	JNA	Yugoslav People's Army
HFOR	Human Rights Field Operation in Rwanda	JOU	Joint Operations Unit (South Africa)
HQ	headquarters	JRTC	Joint Readiness Training Center
HRS	Humanitarian Relief Sector	JSDF	Japanese Self-Defence Force
IAEA	International Atomic Energy Agency	JSTARS	Joint Surveillance and Attack Radar System
IAF	Indian Air Force		
	Inter-African Force (Chad)	JVP	Janatha Vimukht Peramuna
IAPF	Inter-American Peace Force	KPNLAF	Khmer People's National Liberation Armed Forces
IAPTC	International Association of Peacekeeping Training Centers	KPNLF	Khmer People's National Liberation Front
IASC	Interagency Standing Committee	LAS	League of Arab States
ICA	Israeli-controlled area	LDF	Lofa Defence Force
ICFY	International Conference on Former Yugoslavia	LNC	Liberian National Conference
ICJ	International Court of Justice	LNTG	Liberian National Transitional Government
ICRC	International Committee of the Red Cross/Red Crescent	LPC	Liberian Peace Council
ICTY	International Criminal Tribunal for the Former Yugoslavia	LTTE	Liberation Tigers of Tamil Eelam
		MAC	Mixed Armistice Commission
ICVA	International Council for Voluntary Agencies	MCPMR	Mechanism for Conflict Prevention, Management, and Resolution
IDF	Israeli Defence Force	MEF	Marine Expeditionary Force
IDP	internally displaced person	MFO	Multinational Force and Observers
IEC	Independent Electoral Commission	MFO	Multilateral Force and Observers (Sinai)
IFOR	United Nations Implementation Force (Bosnia)	MICIVIH	Joint International Civilian Mission in Haiti, OAS-UN
IGNU	Interim Government of National Unity (Liberia)	MINUGUA	Mision de los Naciones Unidas en Guatemala
IGO	international governmental organization	MINURCA	United Nations Mission in the Central African Republic
IMF	International Monetary Fund	MINURSO	United Nations Mission for the Referendum in Western Sahara
INCOR	Initiative on Conflict Resolution and Ethnicity	MINUSAL	United Nations Mission in El Salvador
INF	intermediate-range nuclear forces	MIO	military information office
INGO	international nongovernmental organization	MIPONUH	United Nations Civilian Police Mission in Haiti
INPFL	Independent National Patriotic Front of Liberia	MISAB	Inter-Africa Mission to Monitor the Implementation of the Bangui Agreements
IOM	International Organization for Migration		
IPA	International Peace Academy	MMWG	mixed military working group
IPKF	Indian Peacekeeping Force	MNC	Mouvement National Congolaise
IPTF	International Police Task Force	MNF	multinational force
IRF	immediate reaction force	MNR	Movimento Nacional Revolucionaria
IRSN	International Relations and Security Network	MO	military observer
		MOD	Ministry of Defence
ISDSC	Interstate Defence and Security Conference	MONUA	United Nations Observer Mission in Angola

MOOTW	military operations other than war		OGB	Observation Group Beirut
MPLA	Movimento Popular de Libertaçao de Angola (Popular Movement for the Liberation of Angola)		OGE	Observer Group Egypt (Sinai)
			OGG	Observer Group Golan
			OGL	Observer Group Lebanon
MPS	Mission Planning Service		OHR	Office of the High Representative
MRC	major regional conflicts		OIC	Organization of the Islamic Conference
MRND	Mouvement Révolutionnaire National pour le Développement			
MSC	Military Staff Committee		ONUC	Operation des Nations Unies au Congo (UN Operation in the Congo)
MSDF	Maritime Self-Defense Force		ONUCA	United Nations Observer Mission in Central America
MSU	United Nations Medical Support Unit			
			ONUMOZ	United Nations Operation in Mozambique
NAC	North Atlantic Council			
NACC	North Atlantic Cooperation Council		ONUSAL	United Nations Observer Mission in El Salvador
NADK	National Army of Democratic Kampuchea		ONUVEH	United Nations Observer Group for the Verification of Elections in Haiti
NATO	North Atlantic Treaty Organization			
NBC	nuclear, biological, and chemical			
NEC	National Elections Commission		ONUVEN	United Nations Observation Mission for the Verification of Elections in Nicaragua
NEPC	Northeastern Provincial Council			
NGO	nongovernmental organization			
NLAOO	Northern Limit of the Area of Operations (former Yugoslavia)		OOTW	operations other than war
NLW	nonlethal weapons		OPLAN	North Atlantic Council of the Operational Plan
NMOG	Neutral Military Observer Group		OPSEC	operational security
NORBATT	joint Nordic infantry battalion		OSCE	Organization for Security and Cooperation in Europe (formerly CSCE)
NORDEM	Norwegian Resource Bank for Democracy and Human Rights			
NORDSAMFN	Nordic Committee for Military United Nations Matters		OSGAP	Office of the Secretary-General in Afghanistan and Pakistan
NOREPS	Norwegian Emergency Preparedness Systems		PAI	Program for Institutional Support
			PAT	Auxiliary Transitory Police
NORSTAFF	network of NGOs coordinated by the Norwegian Refugee Council		PDC	Christian Democratic Party (El Salvador)
NPFL	National Patriotic Front of Liberia		PDD	presidential decision directive (United States)
NPT	Non-Proliferation of Nuclear Weapons Treaty			
			PDK	Party of Democratic Kampuchea
OAN	UN International Civilian Mission (Haiti)		PDPA	People's Democratic Party of Afghanistan
OAS	Organization of American States		PFP	Partnership for Peace
OAU	Organization of African Unity		PIOOM	Interdisciplinary Research Program on Causes of Human Rights Violations
OC	oleoresin capsicum			
OCHA	Office for the Coordination of Humanitarian Affairs			
			PKO	peacekeeping operation
ODD	Observation Detachment Damascus		PLAN	People's Liberation Army of Namibia
ODIHR	Office for Democratic Institutions and Human Rights			
			PLO	Palestine Liberation Organization
OECD	Organization of Economic Cooperation and Development		PLOTE	Peoples Liberation Organization of Tamil Eelam
OECS	Organization of East Caribbean States		PNC	National Civil Police (El Salvador)
			POLISARIO	Popular Front for the Liberation of Saguia el-Hamra and Rio de Oro
OFE	Office for Free Elections			

PPC	Lester B. Pearson Canadian International Peacekeeping Training Centre	SNF	Somali National Front
		SNM	Somali National Movement
		SOC	State of Cambodia
PRC	People's Republic of China	SPPKF	South Pacific Peacekeeping Force
PRK	People's Republic of Kampuchea	SR	special representative
PSO	peace support operations	SRSG	special representative of the secretary-general
PSV	Program for Observation and Verification		
		SSDF	Somali Salvation Democratic Front
PSYOPS	psychological operations	SSM	Sinai Support Mission
PVO	private voluntary organization	START	Strategic Arms Reduction Talks
RAW	Research and Intelligence Wing	SWAPO	South West African People's Organization (Namibia)
RENAMO	Resistencia Nacional Mocambicana (National Mozambican Resistance)		
		SWAPOL	South West Africa Police
		SWATF	South West Africa Territorial Force
RMA	Royal Military Academy (Sandhurst)	SWEDINT	Swedish Armed Forces International Center
RMO	regional multilateral organization		
RNC	Turkish Republic of Northern Cyprus	SYG	secretary-general (UN terminology)
		TELO	Tamil Eelam Liberation Organization
RNZAF	Royal New Zealand Air Force		
ROE	rules of engagement	TNA	Tamil National Army
RPF	Rwandese Patriotic Front	TNC	Transitional National Council
RSK	Republika Srpska Krajina		Transnational Cooperation
RTLMC	Radio-Television Libre des Milles Collines	TULF	Tamil United Liberation Front
		UAR	United Arab Republic
RUF	Revolutionary United Front	UD	Uniao Democratica
SACEUR	NATO's supreme allied commander Europe	ULIMO	United Liberation Movement for Democracy in Liberia
SADC	South Africa Defense Community	UNAMIC	United Nations Advance Mission in Cambodia
SADF	South African Defence Force		
SADR	Saharan Arab Democratic Republic	UNAMIR	United Nations Assistance Mission in Rwanda
SCR	Security Council resolution	UNASOG	United Nations Aouzou Strip Observer Group
SDSS	Independent Democratic Serb Party		
		UNAVEM	United Nations Angola Verification Mission
SEA-NWFZ	Southeast Asian Nuclear Weapon–Free Zone	UNCI	United Nations Commission for Indonesia
SEATO	Southeast Asia Treaty Organization		
SFM	Sinai Field Mission	UNCIP	United Nations Commission for India and Pakistan
SFOR	Stabilization Force		
SG	secretary-general	UNCIVPOL	United Nations Civilian Police
SHIR-BRIG	Standby Forces High Readiness Brigade	UNCRO	United Nations Confidence Restoration Operation
SIPRI	Stockholm International Peace Research Institute	UNDAC	United Nations Disaster Assessment and Coordination Teams
SLA	South Lebanon Army		
SLAF	Sri Lankan Armed Forces	UNDOF	United Nations Disengagement Observer Force
SLMC	Sri Lanka Muslim Congress		
SLPF	Sri Lanka Freedom Party	UNDP	United Nations Development Program
SMC	Standing Mediation Committee		
SNA	Somali National Alliance	UNDPI	United Nations Department of Public Information
SNC	Supreme National Council		

UNDPKO	United Nations Department of Peacekeeping Operations	UNOHAC	United Nations Office for Humanitarian Assistance Coordination
UNEF	United Nations Emergency Forces		
UNESCO	United Nations Educational, Scientific, and Cultural Organization	UNOMCA	United Nations Observer Mission to Central America
UNFICYP	United Nations Peacekeeping Force in Cyprus	UNOMIG	United Nations Observer Mission in Georgia
UNGCI	United Nations Guards Contingent in Iraq	UNOMIL	United Nations Observer Mission in Liberia
UNGOMAP	United Nations Good Offices Mission in Afghanistan and Pakistan	UNOMOZ	United Nations Operation in Mozambique
		UNOMSA	United Nations Observer Mission to South Africa
UNHCR	United Nations High Commissioner for Refugees	UNOMSIL	United Nations Observer Mission in Sierra Leone
UNICEF	United Nations Children's Fund		
UNIFIL	United Nations Interim Force in Lebanon	UNOMUR	United Nations Observer Mission in Uganda/Rwanda
UNIIMOG	United Nations Iran-Iraq Military Observer Group	UNOSAL	United Nations Oberver Mission in El Salvador
UNIKOM	United Nations Iraq-Kuwait Observation Mission	UNOSOM	United Nations Operation in Somalia
UNIPOM	United Nations India Pakistan Observer Mission	UNP	United National Party
		UNPA	United Nations protected areas
UNIPTF	United Nations International Police Task Force	UNPF	United Nations Peace Forces
		UNPF-HQ	United Nations Peace Forces Headquarters
UNITA	Uniao Nacional para la Independencia Total de Angola (National Union for the Total Independence of Angola)	UNPREDEP	United Nations Preventive Deployment Force Macedonia
		UNPROFOR	United Nations Protection Force in Former Yugoslavia
UNITAF	Unified Task Force		
UNITAR	United Nations Institute for Training and Research	UNREO	Rwanda Emergency Office
UNITAR-POCI	United Nations Institute for Training and Research Program of Correspondence Instruction in Peacekeeping Operations	UNRISD	United Nations Research Institute for Social Development
		UNRWA	United Nations Relief Works Agency for Palestinian Refugees
		UNSAS	United Nations Standby Arrangements System
UNLOB	United Nations Liaison Office in Beirut		
		UNSC	United Nations Security Council
UNMIBH	United Nations Mission in Bosnia and Herzegovina	UNSCOB	United Nations Special Committee on the Balkans
UNMIH	United Nations Mission in Haiti	UNSCOL	United Nations Special Coordinator's Office
UNMO	United Nations military observers		
UNMOGIP	United Nations Military Observer Group in India and Pakistan	UNSCOM	United Nations Special Commission
UNMOP	UN Mission of Observers in Prevlaka	UNSCOP	United Nations Special Committee on Palestine
UNMOT	United Nations Mission of Observers in Tajikistan	UNSCR	United Nations Security Council Resolution
UNO	UN organization Unión Nacional Opositora	UNSF	United Nations Security Force in West New Guinea
UNOGIL	United Nations Observation Group in Lebanon	UNSG	United Nations secretary-general

UNSMIH	United Nations Support Mission for Haiti	UNTSO	United Nations Truce Supervision Organization
UNSRSG	United Nations special representative to the secretary-general	UNV	United Nations Volunteers
		UNYOM	United Nations Yemen Observer Mission
UNSYG	United Nations secretary general	URNG	Unidad Revolucionaria Nacional Guatemalteca
UNTAC	United Nations Transitional Authority in Cambodia	US-AID	United States Agency for International Development
UNTAES	United Nations Transitional Administration for Eastern Slavonia, Baranja, and Western Sirmium	USC	United Somali Congress
		USIP	United States Institute for Peace
UNTAG	United Nations Transitional Assistance Group (Namibia)	USYG	undersecretary-general
		UTO	United Tajik Opposition
UNTAT	United Nations training assistance teams	WEU	Western European Union
		WFP	World Food Program
UNTEA	United Nations Temporary Executive Authority	WFUNA	World Federation of United Nations Associations
UNTMIH	United Nations Transition Mission in Haiti	WHO	World Health Organization
		ZDF	Zimbabwe Defence Force
UNTSI	United Nations Training School Ireland	ZOPFAN	Zone of Peace, Freedom, and Neutrality

Abi-Saab, G. 1978. *The United Nations Operations in the Congo, 1960–1964.* Oxford: Oxford University Press.

Achayra, A. 1995. "Regional Organisations and UN Peacekeeping." In *Crisis of Expectations: UN Peacekeeping in the 1990s,* edited by R. Thakur and C. Thayer. Boulder, CO: Westview.

Albert, S. 1997. "The Return of Refugees to Bosnia and Herzegovina: Peacebuilding with People." *International Peacekeeping* 4, no. 3 (autumn): 1–23.

Alden, C. 1995. "Swords into Ploughshares? The United Nations and Demilitarization in Mozambique." *International Peacekeeping* 2, no. 2 (summer): 175–193.

Allard, K. 1995. *Somalia Operations: Lessons Learned.* Washington, DC: National Defense University Press.

Allison, R. 1994. "Peacekeeping in the Soviet Successor States." Chaillot Papers, no. 18. Paris: Institute for Security Studies of Western European Union.

Allsebrook, M. 1986. *Prototypes of Peacemaking: The First Forty Years of the United Nations.* Chicago: St. James Press.

Amate, C. O. C. 1986. *Inside the OAU: Pan-Africanism in Practice.* New York: St. Martin's Press.

Amnesty International. 1994. *Peace-Keeping and Human Rights.* London: International Secretariat.

Annan, K. 1997a. *Renewal amid Transition: Annual Report on the Work of the Organization.* New York: United Nations.

———. 1997b. *UN Secretary-General's Reform Announcement.* New York: United Nations.

Anstee, M. J. 1996. *Orphan of the Cold War: The Inside Story of the Collapse of the Angolan Peace Process, 1992–3.* London: Macmillan Press.

Asmus, R. D. 1995. *Germany's Contribution to Peacekeeping: Issues and Outlook.* Santa Monica, CA: Rand.

Baev, P. 1994. "Russia's Experiments and Experience in Conflict Management and Peacemaking." *International Peacekeeping* 1, no. 3 (autumn): 245–260.

Bailey, S. D. 1982. *How Wars End: The United Nations and the Termination of Armed Conflict, 1946–1964.* 2 vols. Oxford: Clarendon Press.

———. 1988. *The Procedure of the UN Security Council.* 2nd ed. Oxford: Clarendon Press.

Bailey, S. D., and S. Daws. 1995. *The United Nations: A Concise Political Guide.* 3rd ed. London: Macmillan Press.

Ball, N. 1996. "The Challenge of Rebuilding War-Torn Societies." In *Managing Global Chaos: Sources of and Responses to International Conflict.* Edited by

Bibliography

C. A. Crocker, F. O. Hampson, and P. Aall. Washington, DC: United States Institute of Peace Press.

Ball, N., and T. Halevy. 1996. *Making Peace Work: The Role of the International Development Community.* Baltimore: Johns Hopkins University Press.

Baranyi, S., and L. North. 1992. "Stretching the Limits of the Possible: United Nations Peacekeeping in Central America." Aurora Papers, no. 15. Ottawa: Canadian Centre for Global Security.

Barnett, M. 1995. "Partners in Peace? The UN, Regional Organisations, and Peacekeeping." *Review of International Studies* 21, no. 4 (October): 411–433.

Bauwens, W., and L. Reychler, eds. 1994. *The Art of Conflict Prevention.* Brassey's Atlantic Commentaries, no. 7. London: Brassey's.

Benton, B., ed. 1996. *Soldiers of Peace: Fifty Years of United Nations Peacekeeping.* New York: American Historical Publications.

Berdal, M. R. 1993. *Whither UN Peacekeeping? An Analysis of the Changing Military Requirements of UN Peacekeeping with Proposals for Its Enhancement.* London: International Institute for Strategic Studies.

———. 1995. "United Nations Peacekeeping in the Former Yugoslavia." In *Beyond Traditional Peacekeeping,* edited by D. C. F. Daniel and B. C. Hayes. London: Macmillan.

———. 1996. "Disarmament and Demobilisation after Civil Wars." Adelphi Papers, no. 303. London: International Institute for Strategic Studies.

Biermann, W. 1995. *The Evolution of UN Peacekeeping Operations in the Post–Cold War Era.* Copenhagen: Center for Peace and Conflict Research.

Bingham, J. R. 1966. *U Thant of Burma.* London: Victor Gollancz.

Blechman, B. 1994. *Training for Peacekeeping: The United Nations' Role.* 1 vol. Report no. 12.Washington, DC: Henry L. Stimson Center.

Blechman, B., et al. 1993. *The American Military in the 21st Century.* New York: St. Martin's Press.

Boerma, M. 1979. "The United Nations Interim Force in the Lebanon: Peacekeeping in a Domestic Conflict." *Millennium* 8, no. 1: 51–63.

Bolton, J. R. 1994. "Wrong Turn in Somalia." *Foreign Affairs* 73, no. 1: 56–66.

Boraine, A., J. Levy, and R. Scheffer, eds. 1997. *Dealing with the Past: Truth and Reconciliation in South Africa.* Pretoria: IDASA.

Bothwell, B. R. 1978. *Pearson: His Life and World.* Toronto: University of Toronto Press.

Boutros-Ghali, B. 1992. *An Agenda for Peace: Preventive Diplomacy, Peacemaking, and Peace-keeping.* New York: United Nations.

———. 1995. *Supplement to An Agenda for Peace.* New York: United Nations.

Boyd, J. M. 1971. *United Nations Peacekeeping Operations: A Military and Political Appraisal.* Praeger Special Studies in International Politics and Public Affairs. New York: Praeger.

Bratt, D. 1997. "Explaining Peacekeeping Performance: The UN in Internal Conflicts." *International Peacekeeping* 4, no. 3 (autumn): 45–70.

Brecher, M. 1953. *The Struggle for Kashmir.* New York: Oxford University Press.

Brett, R., and M. McCallin. 1996. *Children: The Invisible Soldiers.* Radda Barnen, Sweden: Vaxjo.

British American Security Information Council. 1994. *NATO, Peacekeeping, and the United Nations.* Washington, DC: BASIC.

British Army. 1995. *Field Manual on Wider Peacekeeping.* Vol. 5 of the British Army Field Manual. London: HMSO.

Brogan, P. 1992. *World Conflicts.* London: Bloomsbury.

Browne, M. A. 1990. *United Nations Peacekeeping: Historical Overview and Current Issues. CRS Report to Congress.* Washington, DC: Library of Congress.

———. 1995. *UN Peacekeeping: Issues for Congress.* Congressional Research Service Issue Brief Series. Washington, DC: Library of Congress.

Bryer, D., and P. Eavis, eds. 1996. *Conflict Prevention: A Challenge for Europe.* Oxford: Saferworld, OXFAM.

Bull, H. ed. 1984. *Intervention in World Politics.* Oxford: Clarendon Press.

Bull, O. 1976. *War and Peace in the Middle East: The Experiences and Views of a UN Observer.* London: Leo Cooper.

Bullion, A. 1992. "The Indian Peacekeeping Force in Sri Lanka." *International Peacekeeping* 1, no. 2 (summer): 148–159.

———. 1997. "India and UN Peacekeeping Operations." *International Peacekeeping* 4, no. 1 (spring): 98–114.

Burns, E. L. M. 1975. "Pearson and the Gaza Strip, 1957." In *Freedom and Change: Essays in Honour of Lester B. Pearson,* edited by M. Fry. Toronto: McClelland and Stewart.

Cairns, E. 1997. *A Safer Future: Reducing the Human Costs of War.* Oxford: Oxfam Publications.

Canada. 1995. *Towards a Rapid Reaction Capability for the United Nations Report.* 1 vol.

Canada. Parliament. Senate Standing Committee on Foreign Affairs. 1993. *Meeting New Challenges: Canada's Response to a New Generation of Peacekeeping. Report of the Standing Senate Committee on Foreign Affairs.* Ottawa: Committee on Foreign Affairs.

Carlarne, J. 1997. "Collaborative Action Research and Peacebuilding." *International Peacekeeping* 4, no. 4 (winter): 79–85.

Carnegie Commission on Preventing Deadly Conflict. 1997. *Preventing Deadly Conflict: Final Report.* Washington, DC: Carnegie Commission on Preventing Deadly Conflict.

Cassese, A., ed. 1986. *The Current Legal Regulation of the Use of Force.* Dordrecht, Netherlands, and Boston: Martinus Nijhoff.

Chandler, D. 1991. *The Tragedy of Cambodian History.* London: Yale University Press.

Charters, D. A., ed. 1994. *Peacekeeping and the Challenge of Civil Conflict Resolution.* Fredericton: Centre for Conflict Studies, University of New Brunswick.

Cheeseman, G. 1998. "Structuring the Australian Defence Force for United Nations Operations: Change and Resistance." In *Peacekeeping and Peacemaking: Towards Effective Intervention in Post–Cold War Conflicts,* edited by T. Woodhouse, R. Bruce, and M. Dando. London: Macmillan.

Childers, E., and B. Urquhart. 1994a. *Renewing the United Nations System.* Uppsala, Sweden: Dag Hammarskjöld Foundation.

———. 1994b. *Recommendations Development Dialogue,* no. 2. Uppsala, Sweden: Dag Hammarskjöld Foundation.

———. 1994c. "We, the People of the United Nations." *Development Dialogue,* no. 2. Uppsala, Sweden: Dag Hammarskjöld Foundation.

———. 1994d. "Humanitarian Emergencies." *Development Dialogue,* no. 2. Uppsala, Sweden: Dag Hammarskjöld Foundation.

Chopra, J. 1994a. "United Nations Authority in Cambodia." Thomas J. Watson Jr. Institute of International Studies Occasional Papers, no. 13. Providence, RI: Brown University.

———. 1994b. "Breaking the Stalemate in Western Sahara." *International Peacekeeping* 1, no. 3 (autumn): 303–319.

Cilliers, J., and G. Mills. 1995. *Peacekeeping in Africa.* South Africa: Halfway House.

Clarke, W., and J. Herbst, eds. 1997. *Learning from Somalia: The Lesson of Armed Humanitarian Intervention.* Boulder, CO: Westview.

Clements, K., and C. Wilson, eds. 1994. *UN Peacekeeping at the Crossroads.* Peace Research Centre Monograph, no. 16. Canberra: Australian National University.

Cleveland, H., H. Henderson, and I. Kaul, eds. 1995. *The United Nations: Policy and Financing Alternatives.* Kidlington, Oxford: Elsevier.

Coate, R. A., ed. 1994. *US Policy and the Future of the United Nations.* New York: Twentieth Century Fund Press.

Comprehensive Report on Lessons-Learned from United Nations Operation in Somalia, April 1992–March 1995. 1995. Friedrich Ebert Stiftung, Germany; Life and Peace Institute, Sweden; Norwegian Institute of International Affairs in cooperation with the Lessons-Learned Unit of the Department of Peace-Keeping Operations.

Conetta, C., and C. Knight. 1995. *Vital Force: A Proposal for the Overhaul of the UN Peace Operations System and for the Creation of a UN Legion.* Cambridge, MA: Commonwealth Institute.

Connaughton, R. M. 1993. "Swords and Ploughshares: Coalition Operations, the Nature of Future Conflict, and the United Nations. A Paper." Camberley, England: Strategic and Combat Studies Institute.

Costa, G. 1995. "The United Nations and Reform of the Police in El Salvador." *International Peacekeeping* 2, no. 3 (autumn): 365–390.

Cox, D. 1993. *"An Agenda for Peace" and the Future of Peacekeeping: Report of the Mohonk Mountain House Workshop.* Ottawa: Canadian Centre for Global Security.

Crocker, C. A., F. O. Hampson, and P. Aall. 1996. *Managing Global Chaos: Sources of and Responses to International Conflict.* Washington, DC: United States Institute of Peace Press.

Dallen, R. M. 1992. *A UN Revitalized: A Compilation of UNA-USA Recommendations on Strengthening the Role of the United Nations in Peacemaking, Peacekeeping, and Conflict Prevention.* New York: UNA-USA.

Daniel, D. C. F., and B. C. Hayes. 1996. "Securing Observance of UN Mandates through the Employment of Military Force." *International Peacekeeping* 3, no. 4 (winter): 105–125.

———, eds. 1995. *Beyond Traditional Peacekeeping.* London: Macmillan; New York: St. Martin's Press.

David, C. P. 1997. "After the Blue Helmets Come the White Helmets." *Peacekeeping and International Relations,* January/February.

Dawson, P. 1995. *The Peacekeepers of Kashmir: The UN Military Observer Group in India and Pakistan.* London: Hurst; New York: St. Martin's Press.

Dayal, R. 1976. *Mission for Hammarskjöld: The Congo Crises.* London: Oxford University Press.

de Guttry, A. 1996. *Italian and German Participation in Peacekeeping: From Dual Approaches to Co-operation.* Pisa: University of Santa Anna.

DeLong, K., and S. Tuckey. *Mogadishu! Heroism and Tragedy.* Westport, CT: Praeger.

Diehl, P. F. 1993. *International Peacekeeping.* London: Johns Hopkins University Press.

Dobbie, C. 1994. "A Concept for Post–Cold War Peacekeeping." *Survival* 36, no. 3 (autumn): 121–148.

Doll, W. J., and S. Metz. 1993. *The Army and Multinational Peace Operations: Problems and Solutions.* Carlisle Barracks, PA: Strategic Studies Institute, U.S. Army War College.

Donini, A. 1996. "The Policies of Mercy: UN Coordination in Afghanistan, Mozambique, and Rwanda." Thomas J. Watson Jr. Institute for International Studies Occasional Papers, no. 22. Providence, RI: Brown University.

Dorn, A. W., and D. J. H. Bell. 1995. "Intelligence and Peacekeeping: The UN Operation in the Congo, 1960–64." *International Peacekeeping* 2, no. 1 (spring): 11–33.

Doyle, M. W. 1995. "UN Peacekeeping in Cambodia: UNTAC Civil Mandate." International Peace Academy Occasional Paper Series. London and Boulder, CO: Lynne Rienner.

Doyle, M. W., I. Johnstone, and R. C. Orr, eds. 1997. *Keeping the Peace: Lessons from Multidimensional UN Operations in Cambodia and El Salvador.* Cambridge: Cambridge University Press.

Drysdale, J. 1995. *Whatever Happened to Somalia?* London: HAAN Associates.

Duffey, T. 1998. "Culture, Conflict Resolution, and Peacekeeping." Ph.D. thesis, University of Bradford, England.

Duke, S. 1994. "The United Nations and Intra-State Conflict." *International Peacekeeping* 1, no. 4 (winter): 375–393.

Durch, W. J. 1993. "United Nations Mission for the Referendum in Western Sahara." In *The Evolution of UN Peacekeeping: Case Studies and Comparative Analysis,* edited by W. J. Durch. New York: St. Martin's Press.

———, ed. 1993. *The Evolution of UN Peacekeeping: Case Studies and Comparative Analysis.* New York: St. Martin's Press.

Durch, W. J., and B. M. Blechman. 1992. *Keeping the Peace: The United Nations in the Emerging World Order.* Washington, DC: Henry L. Stimson Center.

Eide, E. B., and P. E. Solle. 1995. "From Blue to Green: The Transition from UNPROFOR to IFOR in Bosnia and Herzegovina." Working Papers, no. 539. Oslo: Norwegian Institute of International Affairs.

Eknes, A. 1989a. "From Scandal to Success: The United Nations and the Iran-Iraq War, 1980–1988." Working Papers, no. 406. Oslo: Norwegian Institute of International Affairs.

———. 1989b. "Revitalizing Peacekeeping: Old Constraints, New Challenges." Working Papers, no. 407. Oslo: Norwegian Institute of International Affairs.

———. 1993. "Blue Helmets in a Blown Mission? UNPROFOR in Former Yugoslavia." Research Reports, no. 174. Oslo: Norwegian Institute of International Affairs.

Elaraby, N. 1983. "UN Peacekeeping: The Egyptian Experience." In *Peacekeeping: Appraisals and Proposals,* edited by H. Wiseman. New York: Pergamon Press.

Eliasson, J. 1995. "Peacekeeping into the 21st Century." *International Peacekeeping* 2, no. 1 (spring): 99–107.

Ennals, D. 1959. *A United Nations Police Force.* London: Fabian.

Eriksson, J. 1996. *The International Response to Conflict and Genocide: Lessons from the Rwanda Experience.* Denmark: Joint Evaluation of Emergency Assistance to Rwanda, Danida.

Erskine, E. A. 1989. *Mission with UNIFIL: An African Soldier's Reflections.* London: Hurst.

European Platform for Conflict Prevention and Transformation. 1998. *Prevention and Management of Violent Conflicts: An International Directory.* Utrecht, Netherlands: European Platform for Conflict Prevention and Transformation.

Evans, G. 1993. *Cooperating for Peace: The Global Agenda for the 1990's and Beyond.* St. Leonards, Australia: Allen and Unwin.

Evriviades, M., and D. Bourantonis. 1994. "Peacekeeping and Peacemaking: Some Lessons from Cyprus." *International Peacekeeping* 1, no. 4 (winter): 394–412.

Fermann, G. 1992. *Bibliography on International Peacekeeping.* Dordrecht, Netherlands, and Boston: Martinus Nijhoff.

Fetherston, A. B. 1994a. *Towards a Theory of United Nations Peacekeeping.* London: Macmillan.

———. 1994b. "Putting the Peace Back into Peacekeeping: Theory Must Inform Practice." *International Peacekeeping* 1, no. 1 (spring): 3–29.

———. 1996. "Peacekeeping as Peacebuilding: Towards a Transformative Agenda." In *Issues in Peace Research 1995–96,* edited by L. Broadhead. Department of Peace Studies. Bradford, England: University of Bradford.

Fetherston, A. B., O. Ramsbotham, and T. Woodhouse. 1994. "UNPROFOR: Some Observations from a Conflict Resolution Perspective." *International Peacekeeping* 1, no. 2 (summer): 170–203.

Findlay, T. 1992. "Conflict Resolution and Peacekeeping in the Post–Cold War Era: Implications for Regional Security." Working Papers, no. 118. Canberra: Australian National University.

———. 1995. *Cambodia: The Legacy and Lessons of UNTAC.* SIPRI Research Reports, no. 9. Oxford: Oxford University Press.

———. 1996. "The New Peacekeepers and the New Peacekeeping." In *Challenges for the New Peacekeepers,* edited by T. Findlay. SIPRI Research Report, no. 12. Oxford and New York: Oxford University Press.

———. 1997. *Fighting for Peace: The Use of Force in Peace Operations.* Oxford: Oxford University Press.

Fisas, A. V. 1995. *Blue Geopolitics: The United Nations Reform and the Future of the Blue Helmets.* London and East Haven, CT: Pluto Press.

Florini, A., and N. Tannenwald. 1984. *On the Front Lines: The United Nations' Role in Preventing and Containing Conflict.* New York: UNA-USA.

Ford Foundation. 1993. *Financing an Effective United Nations: A Report of the Independent Advisory Group on UN Financing.* New York: Ford Foundation.

Fortna, V. P. 1995. "Success and Failure in Southern Africa: Peacekeeping in Namibia and Angola." In *Beyond Traditional Peacekeeping,* edited by D. C. F. Daniel and B. C. Hayes. London: Macmillan.

Franck, T. M. 1988. "The Good Offices Function of the UN Secretary-General." In *United Nations, Divided World: The UN's Roles in International Relations,* edited by A. Roberts and B. Kingsbury. Oxford: Clarendon Press.

Frye, W., ed. 1957. *A United Nations Peace Force.* New York: Oceana.

Funabashi, Y., ed. 1994. *Japan's International Agenda.* London and New York: New York University Press.

Gaffen, F. 1987. *In the Eye of the Storm: A History of Canadian Peacekeeping.* Toronto: Deneau and Wayne.

Galtung, J., and H. Hveem. 1976. "Participants in Peacekeeping Forces." *Cooperation and Conflict,* no. 1: 25–40.

Gavshon, A. L. 1962. *The Mysterious Death of Dag Hammarskjöld.* New York: Walker.

Gibbs, D. N. 1997. "Is Peacekeeping a New Form of Imperialism?" *International Peacekeeping* 4, no. 1 (spring): 122–128.

Ginifer, J. 1996. "Development within UN Peace Missions." *International Peacekeeping,* special issue (summer).

Goldmann, K. 1968. *Peacekeeping and Self-Defence.* Monograph no. 7. Paris: International Information Center on Peace-Keeping Operations.

Goodwin-Gill, G., and I. Cohn. 1997. *Child Soldiers: The Role of Children in Armed Conflict.* New York: Oxford University Press.

Gordenker, L. 1959. *The United Nations and the Peace Unification of Korea: The Politics of Field Operations, 1947–1950.* The Hague: Martinus Nijhoff.

———. 1967. *The UN Secretary-General and the Maintenance of Peace.* New York: Columbia University Press.

Gordenker, L., and T. G. Weiss, eds. 1991. *Soldiers, Peacekeepers, and Disasters.* London: Macmillan.

Goulding, M. 1993. "The Evolution of United Nations Peacekeeping." *International Affairs* 69, no. 3 (summer): 451–464.

———. 1996. "The Use of Force by the United Nations." *International Peacekeeping* 3, no. 1 (spring): 1–18.

Gow, J., and J. D. D. Smith. 1992. *Peace-Making, Peace-Keeping: European Security and the Yugoslav Wars.* London Defence Studies, no. 11. London: Brassey's, for the Centre for Defence Studies.

Grant, J. 1992. *The State of the World's Children.* New York: UNICEF.

Greene, J. M. 1993. "Peacekeeping Doctrines of the CIS." *Jane's Intelligence Review* 5, no. 4: 156–159.

Guillot, P. 1994. "France, Peacekeeping, and Humanitarian Intervention." *International Peacekeeping* 1, no. 1 (spring): 30–43.

Haberle-Zemlec, A., C. Heje, E. Moxon-Browne, and A. Truger. 1996. "The Training and Preparation of Military and Civilian Peacekeepers." Final Report. Derry: INCORE, University of Ulster.

Haglund, D. G., and P. L. Jones. 1989. "Canada, the 'Lessons' of Peacekeeping, and Central America." Occasional Papers, no. 33. Kingston, Ontario: Centre for International Relations, Queen's University.

Handler C. A., and G. T. Raach. 1995. *Peace Operations: Developing an American Strategy.* Washington, DC: National Defense University Press.

Haq, O. ul. 1989. "The Regional Dimension: Pakistan and Afghanistan, the Gulf States, and the Iran-Iraq War." In *Afghanistan, Iran, and Iraq: External Involvement and Multinational Operations,* edited by I. Rikhye. Report no. 31. New York: International Peace Academy.

Harbottle, M. N. 1970. *The Impartial Soldier.* London and Toronto: Oxford Unversity Press.

———. 1971. *The Blue Berets: The Story of the United Nations Peacekeeping Forces.* Harrisburg, PA: Stackpole Books.

Harrison, S. S., and M. Nishihara. 1995. *UN Peacekeeping: Japanese and American Perspectives.* Washington, DC: Carnegie Endowment for International Peace.

Harvey, P. C. 1977. *The Operational Effectiveness of United Nations Peacekeeping Forces, with Particular Reference to the United Nations Emergency Force II, October 1973–September 1975.* Keele, England: University of Keele.

Heiberg, M. 1986. "Peacekeeping in Lebanon: Comparing UNIFIL and the MNF." *Survival* 28, no. 5: 399–421.

———. 1990. "Peacekeepers and Local Populations: Some Comments on UNIFIL." In *The United Nations and Peacekeeping: Results, Limitations, and Prospects,* edited by I. Rikhye and K. Skjelsbaek. London: Macmillan.

Heiberg, M., and J. J. Holst. 1986. "Keeping the Peace in Lebanon: Assessing International and Multinational Peacekeeping." Paper no. 357. Oslo: Norwegian Institute of International Affairs.

Heininger, J. E. 1994. *Peacekeeping in Transition: The United Nations in Cambodia.* New York: Twentieth Century Fund Press.

Herbst, J. 1996. "Introduction: The Everyday Lives of Peacemakers in Somalia." *International Peacekeeping* 33, no. 1 (spring): 39–41.

Higgins, R. 1965. "United Nations Peacekeeping: Political and Financial Problems." *World Today* 21: 324–337.

———. 1969–1981. *United Nations Peacekeeping, 1946–1979: Documents and Commentary.* Vol. 1: *The Middle East.* Vol. 2: *Asia.* Vol. 3: *Africa.* Vol. 4: *Europe.* London: Oxford University Press.

Higgins, R., and M. N. Harbottle. 1971. "United Nations Peacekeeping: Past Lessons and Future Prospects." Annual memorial lecture, David Davies Memorial Institute of International Studies, London.

Hirsch, J. L., and R. B. Oakley. 1995. *Somalia and Operation Restore Hope.* Washington, DC: Institute of Peace Press.

Hoffman, C. 1983. "MFO: Peacekeeping in the Middle East." *Military Review* 63, no. 9: 2–12.

Holt, V. K. 1995. *Briefing Book on Peacekeeping: The U. S. Role in United Nations Peace Operations.* 2nd ed. Washington, DC: Council for a Livable World Education Fund.

Houghton, R. B., and F. G. Trinka. 1985. *Multinational Peacekeeping in the Middle East.* Washington, DC: United States Center for the Study of Foreign Affairs.

House, A. H. 1978. *The UN in the Congo: The Political and Civilian Efforts.* Washington, DC: University Press of America.

Human Rights Watch. 1993. *The Lost Agenda: Human Rights and UN Field Operations.* New York: Human Rights Watch.

Hume, C. 1994a. *The United Nations, Iran, and Iraq: How Peacemaking Changed.* Bloomington: Indiana University Press.

———. 1994b. *Ending Mozambique's War: The Role of Mediation and Good Offices.* Washington, DC: USIP Press.

Hyatt, J. 1993. *Peacekeeping: Selected References.* Special Bibliography, no. 304. Maxwell Air Force Base, Alabama: Air University Library.

Hyde, E. A. 1966. *The United Nations Policy of Non-Intervention in Internal Affairs of the Congo: A Study in the Problem of Peacekeeping with International Force.* Philadelphia: University of Pennsylvania.

International Peace Academy. 1984. *Peacekeeper's Handbook.* 3rd ed. New York: Pergamon Press.

International Peacekeeping. 1994– . M. Pugh, editor. *Mission Digests.* Edited by A. Ramsbotham, O. Ramsbotham, and T. Woodhouse. London: Frank Cass.

James, A. 1969. *The Politics of Peacekeeping.* Studies in International Security, no. 12. New York: Praeger.

———. 1985. "Symbol in Sinai: The Multinational Force and Observers." *Millennium: Journal of International Studies* 14, no. 3: 255–271.

———. 1990. *Peacekeeping in International Politics.* Studies in International Security, no. 20. Basingstoke, England: Macmillan; New York: International Institute for Strategic Studies; St. Martin's Press.

———. 1994. "The Congo Controversies." *International Peacekeeping* 1, no. 1 (spring): 44–58.

Jaster, R. 1990. "The 1998 Peace Accords and the Future of South-Western Africa." Adelphi Papers, no. 253. London: IIS.

Jockel, J. T. 1994. *Canada and International Peacekeeping.* Significant Issues Series. Toronto and Washington, DC: Canadian Institute of Strategic Studies; Center for Strategic and International Studies.

Johansen, R. C. 1990. "UN Peacekeeping: The Changing Utility of Military Force." *Third World Quarterly* 12, no. 2 (spring): 53.

Johnstone, I. 1994. *Aftermath of the Gulf War: An Assessment of UN Action.* Boulder, CO: Lynne Rienner.

Joint Nordic Committee for Military UN Matters. 1986. *Nordic UN Stand-by Forces.* 3rd ed. Stockholm: NORDSAMFN, in cooperation with Forsvaret Laromedelscentral.

Joint Warfare Publication (JWP) 3-01. 1997. *Peace Support Operations.* UK Joint Chiefs of Staff.

Joint Warfighting Center. 1995. *Joint Task Force Commander's Handbook for Peace Operations.* Fort Monroe, VA: Joint Warfighting Center.

Jones, P. 1989. *Peacekeeping: An Annotated Bibliography.* East Kingston, Ontario: Frye.

Jonson, L., and C. Archer, eds. 1996. *Peacekeeping and the Role of Russia in Euroasia.* Boulder, CO: Westview Press.

Kamarotos, A. S. 1995. "Building Peace, Democracy, and Human Rights: International Civilian Missions at the End of the Millennium." *International Peacekeeping* 2, no. 4 (winter): 483–509.

Kane, A. 1996. "Other New and Emerging Peacekeepers." In *Challenges for the New Peacekeepers,* edited by T. Findlay. SIPRI Research Report, no. 12. Oxford and New York: Oxford University Press.

Karhilo, J. 1996. "New Requirements for Multilateral Conflict Management by UN and Other Forces: Nordic Responses." Working Papers, no. 301. Canberra: Strategic and Defence Studies Centre, Australian National University.

Karns, M., and K. A. Mingst. 1990. "Peacekeeping Efforts: Some Fly, Some Flop." *Bulletin of the Atomic Scientists* 46, no. 4: 43–47.

Kaysen, C., and G. Rathjens. 1995. *Peace Operations by the United Nations: The Case for a Volunteer UN Military Force.* Cambridge, MA: Amercan Academy of Arts and Sciences.

Kennedy, K. M. 1996. "The Relationship between the Military and Humanitarian Organisations in Operation *Restore Hope.*" *International Peacekeeping* 3, no. 3 (spring): 92–112.

Kenny, K. 1997. "Introducing the Sustainability Principle to Human Rights Operations." *International Peacekeeping* 4, no. 4 (winter): 61–78.

Kim. S. 1979. *China, the United Nations, and World Order.* Princeton: Princeton University Press.

Klepak, H. P. 1994. "Peacekeeping in Central America." In *Peacekeeping and the Challenge of Civil Conflict Resolution,* edited by D. A. Charters. Fredericton: Centre for Conflict Studies, University of New Brunswick.

Krieger, J. 1993. *The Oxford Companion to Politics of the World.* New York: Oxford University Press.

Kroef, Van der, J. M. 1963. "The West New Guinea Settlement: Its Origins and Implications." *ORBIS* 7, no. 1: 120–149.

Krska, V. 1997. "Peacekeeping in Angola (UNAVEM I and II)." *International Peacekeeping* 4, no. 1 (spring): 75–97.

Kumar, K. 1997. *Rebuilding Societies after Civil War: Critical Roles for International Assistance.* Boulder, CO: Lynne Rienner.

Kummel, G. 1994. "UN Overstretch: A German Perspective." *International Peacekeeping* 1, no. 2 (summer): 160–178.

Lake, A., ed. 1990. *After the Wars: Reconstruction in Afghanistan, Indochina, Central America, South Africa, and the Horn of Africa.* New Brunswick, NJ: Transaction Publishers.

Lash, J. P. 1971. *Dag Hammarskjöld, Custodian of the Bushfire.* New York: Doubleday.

Last, D. M. 1997. *Theory, Doctrine, and Practice of Conflict De-Escalation in Peacekeeping Operations.* Clementsport, Nova Scotia: Canadian Peacekeeping Press.

Lederach, J. P. 1995. "Conflict Transformation in Protracted Internal Conflicts: The Case for a Comprehensive Framework." In *Conflict Transformation,* edited by K. Rupesinghe. Basingstoke, England: Macmillan.

Lefever, E. W. 1964. *United Nations Peacekeeping in the Congo: An Appraisal.* Washington, DC: Brookings Institution.

Leger Sivard, R. Annually. *World Military and Social Expenditures, 1997.* Washington, DC: World Priorities.

Legum, C. 1961. *Congo Disaster.* Baltimore: Penguin.

Leurdijk, D. A. 1994. *The United Nations and NATO in Former Yugoslavia: Partners in International Cooperation.* The Hague: Netherlands Atlantic Commission and Netherlands Institute of International Relations "Clingendael."

———. 1995. "Proposals for Increasing Rapid Deployment Capacity: A Survey." *International Peacekeeping* 2, no. 1 (spring): 1–100.

Lewer, N., and S. Schofield. 1997. "Non-Lethal Weapons for UN Military Operations." *International Peacekeeping* 4, no. 3 (autumn): 71–93.

Lie, T. 1954. *In the Cause of Peace: Seven Years with the United Nations.* New York: Macmillan.

Liu, F. T. 1992. *United Nations Peacekeeping and the Non-Use of Force.* Boulder, CO, and London: Lynne Rienner.

Louise, C. 1997. "MINUGUA's Peacebuilding Mandate in Western Guatemala." *International Peacekeeping* 4, no. 2 (summer): 50–73.

Luard, E. 1972. "The Civil War in the Congo." In *The International Regulation of Civil Wars,* edited by E. Luard. New York: New York University Press.

Lund, M. 1997. "Preventive Diplomacy for Macedonia, 1992–1996: Containment Becomes Nation-Building." In *Preventive Diplomacy in the Post–Cold War World: Opportunities Missed, Opportunities Seized, and Lessons Learned,* edited by B. Jentleson. New York: Rowman and Littlefield.

Macdonald, O. A. K. 1997. "Peacekeeping Lessons Learned: An Irish Perspective." *International Peacekeeping* 4, no. 3 (autumn): 94–103.

MacInnis, J. A. 1996. "Peacekeeping and International Humanitarian Law." *International Peacekeeping* 3, no. 3 (autumn): 92–97.

Mackenzie, L. 1993. "Military Realities of UN Peacekeeping Operations." *The RUSI Journal* 138, no. 1 (winter): 21–24.

———. 1994. *Peacekeeper: The Road to Sarajevo.* Toronto: HarperCollins.

Mackinlay, J. 1989. *The Peacekeepers: An Assessment of Peacekeeping Operations at the Arab-Israeli Interface.* London and Boston, MA: Unwin Hyman.

————. 1990. "The Commonwealth Monitoring Force in Zimbabwe/Rhodesia, 1979–1980." In *Humanitarian Emergencies and Military Help in Africa*, edited by T. G. Weiss. New York: St. Martin's Press.

————. 1998. "War Lords." *Royal United Services Institute Journal* (April): 24–32.

————, ed. 1996. *A Guide to Peace Support Operations.* Providence, RI: Thomas J. Watson Jr. Institute for International Studies, Brown University.

Mackinlay, J., and J. Chopra. 1992. "Second Generation Multinational Operations." *The Washington Quarterly* (summer): 113–131.

Mackinlay, J., and R. Kent. 1997. "A New Approach to Complex Emergencies." *International Peacekeeping* 4, no. 4 (winter): 31–49.

Macrae, J., A. Zwi, and M. Duffield. 1994. *War and Hunger: Rethinking International Responses to Complex Emergencies.* London: Zed Books/Save the Children.

Makinda, S. M. 1993. "Seeking Peace from Chaos: Humanitarian Intervention in Somalia." International Peace Academy Occasional Paper Series. Boulder, CO: Lynne Rienner.

Malaquias, A. 1996. "The UN in Mozambique and Angola: Lessons Learned." *International Peacekeeping* 3, no. 2 (summer): 87–103.

Maloney, S. M. 1997. "Operation *Bolster:* Canada and the EC Monitor Mission in Former Yugoslavia, 1991–92." *International Peacekeeping* 4, no. 1 (spring): 26–50.

Matanle, E. 1995. "The UN Security Council: Prospects for Reform." RIIA Discussion Papers, no. 62. London: Royal Institute of International Affairs.

May, R., and G. Cleaver. 1997. "African Peacekeeping: Still Dependent?" *International Peacekeeping* 4, no. 2 (summer): 1–21.

May, R., and S. Massey. 1998. "The OAU Interventions in Chad: Mission Impossible or Mission Evaded?" *International Peacekeeping* 5, no. 1 (spring): 46–65.

Mays, T. M. 1996. *Historical Dictionary of Multinational Peacekeeping.* Lanham, MD: Scarecrow Press.

Mazarr, M., D. M. Snider, and J. A. Blackwell Jr. 1992. *Desert Storm.* Boulder, CO: Westview Press.

McCoubrey, H. 1995. *International Organizations and Civil Wars.* Aldershot, England, and Brookfield, VT: Dartmouth.

McCoubrey, H., and N. D White. 1996. *The Blue Helmets: Legal Regulation of United Nations Military Operations.* Aldershot, England: Dartmouth.

McDermott, A. 1994. "Peacekeeping Operations: Funding Problems and Solutions." In *Peacekeeping and the Challenge of Civil Conflict Resolution*, edited by D. A. Charters. Fredericton: Centre for Conflict Studies, University of New Brunswick.

McNutty, M. 1997. "France's Role in Rwanda and External Military Intervention: A Double Discrediting." *International Peacekeeping* 4, no. 3 (autumn): 24–44.

Miall, H., O. Ramsbotham, and T. Woodhouse. Forthcoming. *Contemporary Conflict Resolution.* Cambridge: Polity Press.

Minear, L. 1994. "Humanitarian Action in the Former Yugoslavia: The U.N.'s Role, 1991–1993." Thomas J. Watson Jr. Institute for International Studies Occasional Papers, no. 18. Providence, RI: Brown University.

Minear, L., and T. G. Weiss. 1993. *A Handbook for Practitioners: Humanitarian Action in Times of War.* Boulder, CO, and London: Lynne Rienner.

————. 1995. *Mercy under Fire: War and the Global Humanitarian Community.* Oxford and Boulder, CO: Westview Press.

Minear, L., T. G. Weiss, and K. M. Campbell. 1991. "Humanitarianism and War: Learning the Lessons from Recent Armed Conflicts." Thomas J. Watson Jr. Institute of International Studies Occasional Papers, no. 8. Providence, RI: Brown University.

Morris, J. 1995. "Force and Democracy: UN/US Intervention in Haiti." *International Peacekeeping* 2, no. 3 (autumn): 391–412.

Morrison, A. 1994. "A Standing United Nations Military Force: Future Prospects." In *Peacekeeping and the Challenge of Civil Conflict Resolution*, edited by D. A. Charters. Fredericton: Centre for Conflict Studies, University of New Brunswick.

Moskos, C. C. 1976. *Peace Soldiers: The Sociology of a United Nations Military Force.* Chicago: University of Chicago Press.

Moxon-Browne, E., ed. 1998. *A Future for Peacekeeping?* London: Macmillan.

Murphy, R. 1998. "Ireland, the United Nations, and Peacekeeping Operations." *International Peacekeeping* 5, no. 1 (spring): 22–45.

Nassif, R. 1988. *U Thant in New York, 1961–1971: A Portrait of the Third UN Secretary-General.* London: Hurst.

Netherlands Institute of International Relations. 1994. *Case-Studies in Second Generation UN Peacekeeping.* Clingendael, Netherlands: Netherlands Institute of International Relations.

Norden, D. L. 1995. "Keeping the Peace, Outside and In: Argentina's UN Missions." *International Peacekeeping* 2, no. 3 (autumn): 330–349.

Nordic Committee for Military United Nations Matters (NORDSAMFN). 1993. *Nordic/UN Standby Forces.* Helsingfors, Denmark: NORDSAMFM.

Nordic UN Tactical Manual. 1992. 2 vols. Jyvaskyla, Finland: Gumerus Kirjapaino Oy.

O'Ballance, E. 1989. *The Cyanide War: Tamil Insurrection in Sri Lanka, 1973–88.* London: Brassey's.

O'Brien, K. A. 1994. "Regional Security in Southern Africa: South Africa's National Perspective." *International Peacekeeping* 3, no. 3 (autumn): 52–76.

Ofuatey-Kodjoe, W. 1994. "Regional Organizations and the Resolution of Internal Conflict: The ECOWAS Intervention in Liberia." *International Peacekeeping* 1, no. 3 (autumn): 261–302.

Olonisakin, F. 1996. "UN Co-operation with Regional Organizations in Peacekeeping: The Experience of ECOMOG and UNOMIL in Liberia." *International Peacekeeping,* vol. 3, no. 3 (autumn): 33–51.

Olsson, F. 1996. "Stress Management in Emergency Situations." *International Peacekeeping* 3, no. 3 (autumn): 98–110.

Omaar, R., and A. de Waal. 1993. *Somalia: Human Rights Abuses by the United Nations Forces.* London: African Rights.

Organization for African Unity. 1993. "Declaration of Heads of State and Government on the Establishment, within the OAU, of a Mechanism for Conflict Prevention, Management, and Resolution." In *Resolving Conflicts in Africa: Implementation Options,* edited by A. Ababa. Addis Ababa: OAU.

Outram, Q. 1997. "'It's Terminal Either Way': An Analysis of Armed Conflict in Liberia, 1989–1996." *Review of African Political Economy* 73: 355–371.

Owen, D. 1995. *Balkan Odyssey.* New York: Harcourt, Brace.

Parsons, A. 1995. *From Cold War to Hot Peace: UN Interventions, 1947–1995.* London: Penguin Books.

Pearson, G. A. H. 1983. "Canadian Attitudes toward Peacekeeping." In *Peacekeeping: Appraisals and Proposals,* edited by H. Wiseman. New York: Pergamon Press.

Pearson Peacekeeping Center. 1996. *Peacekeeping and International Relations* 25, no. 3 (May/June).

Peck, C. 1998. *Sustainable Peace: The Role of the UN and Regional Organizations in Preventing Conflict.* Lanham, MD: Rowman and Littlefield.

Pelcovits, N. A. 1975. "UN Peacekeeping and the 1973 Arab-Israeli Conflict." *Orbis* 19 (spring): 146–165.

———. 1993. *The Long Armistice: UN Peacekeeping and the Arab-Israeli Conflict, 1948–1960.* Boulder, CO: Westview Press.

Pérez de Cuéllar, J. 1988. "The Role of the UN Secretary-General." In *United Nations, Divided World: The UN's Roles in International Relations,* edited by A. Roberts and B. Kingsbury. Oxford: Clarendon Press.

Poole, J. B., and R. Guthrie. 1996. "Verification 1996: Arms Control, Peacekeeping, and the Environment." Boulder, CO, and Oxford: Westview Press.

Powell, C. L. 1994. "U. S. Forces: Challenges Ahead." *Foreign Affairs* 71, no. 5 (winter): 32–45.

Prunier, G. 1995. *The Rwanda Crisis: History of a Genocide 1959–1994.* London: Hunt and Co.

Pugh, M. C. 1995. "The Challenge of Peacebuilding: The Disaster Relief Model." Plymouth International Papers, no. 3. Plymouth, England: University of Plymouth.

———, ed. 1994. *Maritime Security and Peacekeeping: A Framework for United Nations Operations.* Manchester, England, and New York: Manchester University Press.

———, ed. 1996. "The UN, Peace, and Force." *International Peacekeeping* 3, no. 4 (winter), special issue.

Quandt, W. B. 1977. *Decade of Decisions: American Policy toward the Arab-Israeli Conflict.* Berkeley and Los Angeles: University of California Press.

Rabinovich, I. 1985. *The War in Lebanon, 1970–1985.* Ithaca, NY: Cornell University Press.

Raevsky, A., and I. N. Vorobbev. 1994. "Russian Approaches to Peacekeeping Operations." UNIDIR Research Papers, no. 28. New York: United Nations Institute for Disarmament Research.

Ramsbotham, A., O. Ramsbotham, and T. Woodhouse. 1994– . "Peacekeeping Mission Digests." *International Peacekeeping.* Quarterly from spring 1994.

Ramsbotham, D. 1995. *The Changing Nature of Intervention: The Role of UN Peacekeeping.* Conflict Studies, no. 282. London: Research Institute for the Study of Conflict and Terrorism.

Ramsbotham, O., and T. Woodhouse. 1996a. "'Terra Incognita: Here Be Dragons.' Peacekeeping and Conflict Resolution in Contemporary Conflict: Some Relationships Considered." INCORE Paper. Northern Ireland: University of Ulster.

———. 1996b. *Humanitarian Intervention in Contemporary Conflict.* Cambridge: Blackwell.

Rana, S. 1995. "Small Arms and Intra-State Conflicts." Research Paper no. 34. New York: United Nations Institute for Disarmament Research. March.

Ratner, S. R. 1997. *The New UN Peacekeeping: Building Peace in Lands of Conflict after the Cold War.* London: Macmillan.

Reed, P. L. J., M. Vaccaro, and W. J. Durch. 1995. *Handbook on United Nations Peace Operations.* Washington, DC: Henry L. Stimson Center.

Renner, M. 1993. "Critical Juncture: The Future of Peacekeeping." Worldwatch Papers, no. 114. Washington, DC: Worldwatch Institute.

Rikhye, I. J. 1984. *The Theory and Practice of Peacekeeping.* London: Hurst.

———. 1992. *Strengthening UN Peacekeeping: New Challenges and Proposals.* Washington, DC: United States Institute of Peace.

Rikhye, I. J., M. N. Harbottle, and B. Egge. 1974. *The Thin Blue Line: International Peacekeeping and Its Future.* New Haven, CT: Yale University Press.

Rikhye, I. J., and K. Skjelsbaek, eds. 1991. *The United Nations and Peacekeeping: Results, Limitations, and Prospects. The Lessons of 40 Years of Experience.* London: Macmillan.

Rogers, A. P. V. 1996. *Law on the Battlefield.* Manchester, England: Manchester University Press.

Rogers, P., and Dando, M. 1992. *A Violent Peace: Global Security after the Cold War.* London: Brassey's.

Rose, M. 1998. *Fighting for Peace.* London: Harvill Press.

Rosende, R., and D. Beltrand. 1997. "The International Commission for Support and Verification (CIAV)–Organization of American States (OAS) Mission In Nicaragua, 1990–96." *International Peacekeeping* 4, no. 1 (spring): 149–151.

Ruggie, J. G. 1994. "The New US Peacekeeping Doctrine." *Washington Quarterly* (autumn): 175–184.

Sahnoun, M. 1994. *Somalia: The Missed Opportunities.* Washington, DC: United States Institute of Peace Press.

Saikal, A. 1996. "The UN and Afghanistan: A Case of Failed Peacemaking Intervention." *International Peacekeeping* 3, no. 1 (spring): 19–34.

Sandoz, Y. 1997. "The International Committee of the Red Cross and the Law of Armed Conflict Today." *International Peacekeeping.* 4, no. 4: 86–99.

Schear, J. A. 1995. "Beyond Traditional Peacekeeping: The Case of Cambodia." In *Beyond Traditional Peacekeeping,* edited by D. C. F. Daniel and B. C. Hayes. London: Macmillan.

Schirch, L. 1995. *Keeping the Peace: Exploring Civilian Alternatives in Conflict Prevention.* Research Reports, no. 18. Uppsala, Sweden: Life and Peace Institute.

Schultz, K. 1994. *Building Peace from the Ground Up: About People and the UN in a War Zone in Croatia.*

TFF Conflict-Mitigation Reports, no. 5. Lund, Sweden: Transnational Foundation for Peace and Future Research.

Sesay, A. 1994. "Peacekeeping by Regional Organizations: The OAU and ECOWAS Peacekeeping Forces in Comparative Perspective." In *Peacekeeping and the Challenge of Civil Conflict Resolution,* edited by D. A. Charters. Fredericton: Centre for Conflict Studies, University of New Brunswick.

Shashenkov, M. 1994. "Russian Peacekeeping in the 'Near Abroad.'" *Survival* (autumn): 46–69.

Shear, J. 1996. "Bosnia's Post-Dayton Traumas." *Foreign Policy* 104 (fall): 87–101.

Sherry, G. 1996. "Afghanistan and the Limits of UN Mediation: A Response to Saikal. Saikal's Reply." *International Peacekeeping* 3, no. 1 (spring): 35–37.

Shope, V. C. 1994. *Peacekeeping: A Selected Bibliography.* Carlisle Barracks, PA: U.S. Army War College Library.

Siekmann, R. C. R. 1989. *Basic Documents on United Nations and Related Peacekeeping Forces: With an Appendix on UN Military Observer Missions.* 2nd enlarged ed. Dordrecht, Netherlands: Martinus Nijhoff.

———. 1991. *National Contingents in United Nations Peacekeeping Forces.* Dordrecht, Netherlands, and Boston, MA: Martinus Nijhoff.

———. 1993. "The Financing of UN Peacekeeping Operations." *Internationale Spectator,* November.

Skold, N. 1996. *United Nations Peacekeeping after the Suez War. UNEF I: The Swedish Involvement.* New York: St. Martin's Press.

Slim, H. 1996. "The Stretcher and the Drum: Civil-Military Relations in Peace Support Operations." *International Peacekeeping* 3, no. 2 (summer): 123–139.

Smith, C. D. 1996. *Palestine and the Arab-Israeli Conflict.* New York: St Martin's Press.

Smith, H. 1994. "Intelligence and UN Peacekeeping." *Survival (*autumn): 174–192.

———, ed. 1990. *Australia and Peacekeeping.* Canberra: Australian Defence Studies Centre, University of New South Wales, Australian Defence Forces Academy.

———, ed. 1993. *Peacekeeping: Challenges for the Future.* Canberra: Australian Defense Studies Centre, Australian Defence Force Academy.

Smith, M. A. 1995. "At Arm's Length: NATO and the UN in the Cold War Era." *International Peacekeeping* 2, no. 1 (spring): 56–73.

Smith, M. L., and D. M. Jones. 1997. "ASEAN, Asian Values, and Southeast Asian Security in the New World Order." *Contemporary Security Policy* 18, no. 3 (December): 126–156.

Snow, D. M. 1993. *Peacekeeping, Peacemaking, and Peace-Enforcement: The US Role in the New International Order.* Carlisle Barracks, PA: U.S. Army War College.

Srivastava, P. 1969. *UN and Peaceful Co-existence: The Role of the United Nations in Peaceful Co-existence as Conceived and Promoted by Its Secretary-General.* Delhi: Universal.

Stanley, W., and D. Holiday. 1997. "Peace Mission Strategy and Domestic Actors: UN Mediation, Verification, and Institution-Building in El Salvador." *International Peacekeeping* 4, no. 2 (summer): 22–48.

Stedman, S. J. 1990. *Peacemaking in Civil War: International Mediation in Zimbabwe, 1974–1980.* Boulder, CO: Lynne Rienner.

———. 1995. "Alchemy for a New World Order: Overselling 'Preventive Diplomacy.'" *Foreign Affairs* 74, no. 3 (May/June): 14–20.

Steele, D. B. 1998. "Securing Peace for Humanitarian Aid." *International Peacekeeping* 5, no. 1 (spring): 66–88.

Stewart, R. 1993. *Broken Lives: A Personal View of the Bosnian Conflict.* London: HarperCollins.

Stjernfelt, B. 1992. *The Sinai Peace Front: U.N. Peacekeeping Operations in the Middle East, 1973–1980.* London: Hurst; New York: St. Martin's Press.

Tercinet, J. 1998. "Europe and United Nations Peacekeeping." In *Peacekeeping and Peacemaking: Towards Effective Intervention in Post–Cold War Conflicts,* edited by T. Woodhouse, R. Bruce, and M. Dando. London: Macmillan.

Thakur, R. C. 1987. *International Peacekeeping in Lebanon: United Nations Authority and Multinational Force.* Westview Special Studies in Peace, Conflict, and Conflict Resolution. Boulder, CO: Westview Press.

Thakur, R. C., and C. A. Thayer, eds. 1995. *A Crisis of Expectations: UN Peacekeeping in the 1990s.* Boulder, CO: Westview Press.

Thant, U. 1978. *View from the UN: The Memoirs of U Thant.* New York: Doubleday.

Thornberry, C. 1990. *The UNTAG Experience in Namibia: First Phase.* Johannesburg: South African Institute of International Affairs.

———. 1995. *Peacekeeping, Peacemaking, and Human Rights.* Coleraine, England: INCORE.

Touval, S. 1985. *The Peacebrokers: Mediators in the Arab-Israeli Conflict, 1948–1979.* Princeton: Princeton University Press.

Traynor, J. 1988. *International Peacekeeping, 1918–1986.* Basingstoke, England: Macmillan Education.

United Kingdom. Ministry of Defence. 1997. *Peace Support Operations.* Joint Warfare Publication 3.01. Ministry of Defence.

United Nations. 1963. *The United Nations in West New Guinea.* New York: United Nations.

———. 1995. *The United Nations and El Salvador, 1990–1995.* New York: United Nations Department of Public Information.

———. 1996. *The Blue Helmets: A Review of United Nations Peacekeeping.* 3rd ed. New York: United Nations Department of Public Information.

United Nations Department of Peacekeeping Operations (UNDPKO). http://www.un.org/depts/dpko/training.

United Nations Department of Public Information (UNDPI). 1996. *The United Nations and Somalia 1992–1996.* New York: United Nations.

UNHCR. 1997. *The State of the World's Refugees.* Oxford: Oxford University Press.

UNICEF. 1996. *The State of the World's Children: Children and War.* New York and Geneva: UNICEF.

UNIDIR. 1995. *Managing Arms in Peace Processes.* Geneva: UNIDIR.

U.S. Army. 1994. *Field Manual 100-23: Peace Operations.* Washington, DC: Department of the Army.

U.S. Congress. House of Representatives Committee on Foreign Affairs. 1966. *The Cost of World Peacekeeping.* Report by B. O'Hara and P. H. B. Frelinghuysen, members of the U.S. Delegation to the 20th session of the U.N. General Assembly, September 21 to December 21, 1965, pursuant to H. Res. 84. U.S. 89th Cong., 2nd sess. Report 1404. Washington, DC: GPO.

U.S. Congress. House of Representatives Committee on Foreign Affairs. Subcommittee on Africa. 1994. *Peacekeeping and Conflict Resolution in Africa:* Hearing before the Subcommittee on Africa of the Committee on Foreign Affairs, House of Representatives. 103rd Cong., 1st sess., March 31, 1993. Washington, DC: GPO.

U.S. Congress. Senate Committee on Foreign Relations. 1993. *Reform of United Nations Peacekeeping Operations: A Mandate for Change.* Staff report. Washington, DC: GPO.

Urquhart, B. E. 1972. *Hammarskjöld.* New York: Alfred A. Knopf.

———. 1980. "United Nations Peacekeeping in the Middle East." *World Today* 36, no. 3: 88–93.

———. 1987. *A Life in Peace and War.* New York: Harper and Row.

———. 1992. "The United Nations System and the Future." *International Affairs* 68, no. 2: 225–231.

van der Merwe, H. 1989. *Pursuing Justice and Peace in South Africa.* London and New York: Routledge and Kegan Paul.

Vassall-Adams, G. 1994. *Rwanda: An Agenda for International Action.* Oxford: OXFAM.

Verrier, A. 1981. *International Peacekeeping: United Nations Forces in a Troubled World.* Harmondsworth, England: Penguin.

———. 1994. "Peacekeeping or Peacemaking? The Commonwealth Monitoring Force, Southern Rhodesia-Zimbabwe, 1979–1980." *International Peacekeeping* 1, no. 4 (winter): 440–461.

Vierruci, L. 1995. "The Role of the Western European Union in the Maintenance of International Peace and Security." *International Peacekeeping* 2, no. 3 (autumn): 309–329.

Vogt, M. A., and E. E. Ekoko, eds. 1993. *Nigeria in International Peacekeeping, 1960–1992.* Oxford: Malthouse.

Waldheim, K. 1985. *In the Eye of the Storm: A Memoir.* London: Weidenfeld and Nicolson.

Walters, F. P. 1960. *A History of the League of Nations.* London: Oxford University Press.

Weiss, T. G. 1993. "New Challenges for UN Military Operations: Implementing an Agenda for Peace." *Washington Quarterly* 16, no. 1 (winter): 51–66.

———. 1995. *The United Nations and Civil Wars.* Boulder, CO: Lynne Rienner.

———, ed. 1990a. *Humanitarian Emergencies and Military Help in Africa.* Issues in Peacekeeping and Peacemaking. Houndmills, Basingstoke, Hampshire: Macmillan in Association with the International Peace Academy.

———, ed. 1990b. *The United Nations in Conflict Management: American, Soviet, and Third World Views.* New York: International Peace Academy.

White, N. D. 1993. *Keeping the Peace: The United Nations and the Maintenance of International Peace and Security.* Manchester, England, and New York: Manchester University Press.

Whitman, J., and D. Pocock, eds. 1996. *After Rwanda: The Co-ordination of United Nations Humanitarian Asssistance.* London: Macmillan.

Who's Who 1998. London and New York: St. Martin's Press.

Willett, S. 1995. "Ostriches, Wise Old Elephants, and Economic Reconstruction in Mozambique." *International Peacekeeping* 2, no. 1 (spring): 34–55.

Wiseman, H., ed. 1983. *Peace-Keeping: Appraisals and Proposals.* New York: Pergamon Press.

Woodhouse, T. 1996. "Ethnicity, Conflict Resolution, and Post–Cold War Security." In *Issues in Peace Research 1995–96,* edited by L. Broadhead. Bradford, England: Department of Peace Studies, University of Bradford.

———. 1998. "Peacebuilding from Below." *World Encyclopaedia of Peace.* Oxford and Seoul: Pergamon Press.

Woodhouse, T., R. Bruce, and M. Dando, eds. 1998. *Peacekeeping and Peacemaking: Towards Effective Intervention in Post Cold War Conflicts.* London: Macmillan.

Woodward, S. L. 1995. *Balkan Tragedy: Chaos and Dissolution after the Cold War.* Washington, DC: Brookings Institution.

Zacher, M. W. 1979. *International Conflicts and Collective Security, 1946–1977: The United Nations, Organization of American States, Organization of African Unity, and Arab League.* New York: Praeger.

Zartman, I. W., ed. 1995. *Elusive Peace: Negotiating an End to Civil Wars.* Washington, DC: Brookings Institute.

Zhang, Y. 1996. "China and UN Peacekeeping: From Condemnation to Participation." *International Peacekeeping* 3, no. 3 (autumn): 1–15.

Zoubir, Y. H., and D. Volman, eds. 1993. *International Dimensions of the Western Sahara Conflict.* Westport, CT: Praeger.

Abdullah (king of Jordan), 152
Abdullojonov, Abdumalik, 242
Aberderahman, S. Aberderahman, 287
Abidjan Accord, 220
Abkhazia, 98–100, 204, 207
Abu Rudeis, 267
Abuja Agreement, 144–145
Accra Agreement, 144, 145
Acheson Plan, 296
Act of Dominican Reconciliation, 77
Aden, 303
Adeniji, Oluyemi, 36
Adoula, Cyril, 54, 55, 56
Advance electoral planning unit, 29
Advisory Committee on Administrative
        and Budgetary Questions, 92
Afghanistan, 200, 242, 268–270
Africa
    non-governmental organizations in,
        176
    OAU-UN cooperation and, 204
    participation in UN missions, 249
    peacekeeping training programs in,
        79, 246
    refugees, returnees, and displaced
        persons in, 203(table)
    See also Organization of African
        Unity
"Africa fatigue," 215
African National Congress, 229
Agenda for Peace, An (Boutros-Ghali),
        1–2
    on conflict prevention, 47–48
    on humanitarian interventions, 114
    on peace enforcement, xxii–xxiii, 198
    post–Cold War era peacekeeping
        and, 21, 45, 197
    on postconflict reconstruction, 200,
        201
Ahmed bin Yahya, 303
Ahn, Choung-Jun, 275
Ahtisaari, Martti, 2, 168, 170, 171
Aid convoys, in Bosnia, 281
Aidid, Hussein, 228
Aidid, Mohammed Farah, 195, 222–223,
        224, 226, 227, 295
Air exclusion zones. See No-fly zones
Air support, 2–3
    in Bosnia, 18, 180, 283
    New Zealand and, 173
    in Operation Desert Storm, 104, 272
    United States and, 294
Airborne Warning and Control System,
        180
Ajello, Aldo, 161
Akashi, Yasushi, 3–4, 25, 28, 31, 149, 278
Akazu, 210

Akosombo Agreements, 144, 145
Al Ahram Iktisadi (journal), 21
Al-Badr, Mohammed, 303
Albania, 4–5
    Greek conflict and, 102
    Italian peacekeeping and, 122
    Macedonia and, 149
    naval peacekeeping forces and, 172,
        173
    peacekeepers in, xxiii
    UNPROFOR III and, 285
Albanians
    in Kosovo, 276
    in Macedonia, 149–150, 285
Algeria, 156, 188, 217–218
Ali Mahdi Mohammed, 222, 223, 227,
        228
All Ceylon Buddhist Congress, 234
Allied Command Europe Rapid
        Reaction Corps, 75
Al-Rodan, Eid Kamel, 278
Alvor Agreements, 6
Amal movement, 135
Amin Dada, Idi, 113, 188
Amnesty, in Namibia, 170–171
Amsterdam Treaty, 90
Andropov, Yuri, 269
Anglo-French Peacekeeping Initiative,
        95
Angola, xvi, 5–10, 167, 168, 201
Angola Peace Accords. See Bicesse
        Accords
Annan, Kofi, 10–11
    on African military coups, 188
    on the future of peacekeeping,
        xxiii–xxiv
    on human rights, 111
    on Sierra Leone, 220
    Somalia and, 227

Index

    on the Special Committee on
        Peacekeeping Operations, 287
    UN reforms and, 255, 257
    in UNPREDEP, 149
Anstee, Margaret Joan, 8, 9, 10, 11, 301
Aouzou Strip, 257–258
Arab Deterrent Force, 129, 133
Arab League. See League of Arab States
Arab League Force, 129, 133
Arab-Israeli conflict. See Middle East
        conflict
Arafat, Yasser, 132, 133
Aragona, Giancarlo, 191
Arbitration, 154
Area of limitation, 259, 261
Area of separation, 259, 261
Argentina, 184
    Contadora Support Group and, 57
    naval peacekeeping forces, 173
    participation in UN missions, 249,
        250
    peacekeeping training workshops
        and, 245
    White Helmets proposal and, 300
Argentinean Peacekeeping Academy,
        246
Arias, Oscar, 184
Aristide, Jean-Bertrand, 107, 109
Armed Forces of Liberia, 139, 140, 143,
        144
Armée National Congolasie, 51, 56
Armée Nationale pour un Kampuchea
        Indépendent, 27, 30
Armenia, 46, 192
Armistice Demarcation Lines, 264, 290,
        291
Arms control, 11–12
    OSCE on, 192
    treaties, 190, 191

UN Department of Political Affairs and, 255
Arms embargoes
   against Haiti, 108
   against Liberia, 140
   against Rwanda, 213, 214
   against Somalia, 223
   against Yugoslavia, 277
   See also Economic sanctions
Arms trade, 12, 271
Army Peacekeeping Training Institute (U.S.), 246
Army Rangers (U.S.), 226
Arnault, Jean, 104
Ar-Rashid, Harun, 100
Arusha Agreements, 210, 211, 212
ASEAN. *See* Association of Southeast Asian Nations
ASEAN Regional Forum, 14
Asharaf clan, 221
Asia, refugees, returnees, and displaced persons in, 203(table)
Assad, Hafiz al-, 132, 136
Association of Southeast Asian Nations (ASEAN), 13–14, 249
Aswan Dam, 261
Atlantic Charter, 251
Atrocities. *See* Ethnic cleansing; Human rights abuses; Massacres
Australia, 14–15, 246, 247
Australian Defence Force Peacekeeping Center, 246
Austria, 207, 246, 247, 259
Austrian Study Center for Peace and Conflict Resolution, 247
Austrian Training Center for Peacekeeping Operations, 246
Auxiliary Transitory Police (El Salvador), 84
Azerbaijan, 46

Bab el Mandeb Strait, 267
Baghdad Pact, 261
Bahamuddin, Mazlan, 258
Baidoa, 223
Baidoa Humanitarian Relief Sector, 14
Baker, James, III, 158
Balaguer, Joaquín, 77
Balkans. *See* Albania; Bosnia and Herzegovina; Croatia; Greece; Kosovo; Macedonia; Serbia; UNPROFOR; UNSCOB; Yugoslavian conflict
Ballistic missiles, Iraq and, 121
Baluba federations, 51
Bamako, 140
Banana, Canaan, 141

Bandaranaike, Sirimavo, 231, 236
Bangladesh, 173, 249, 274, 275
Bangui Agreements, 35
Baranja, 58
Barre, Muhammad Siyad, 220, 222
Barrera, Antonio Imbert, 76
Barrios de Chamorro, Violeta. *See* Chamorro, Violeta Barrios de
Basic Agreement on the Region of Eastern Slavonia, Baranja, and Western Sirmium, 60, 61, 284
Basic Law, German, 100, 101
"Baskets," 189–190
Bazin, Mark, 107
Beattie, Clayton, 48
Begin, Menachem, 21, 133
Beirut, 131, 134, 135, 136–138, 292–293
Belarus, 46
Belgian Congo. *See* Congo
Belgium, Rwanda and, 209, 210, 213, 215
Benadir clan, 221
Berbera, 224
Berisha, Sali, 4
Bernadotte, Folke, 289, 290
Bethlehem, 125
Beye, Alioune Blondin, 8, 9
Bicesse Accords, 7, 9, 10
Bihać, 217, 282, 283, 284
Bildt, Carl, 19, 20, 277, 284
Biological weapons, Iraq and, 121
Bishkek Summit, 46
Bizimungu, Pasteur, 212
Blue Helmets, 17, 44
Blue Helmets, The, xi, 17
Booh-Booh, Jacques-Roger, 212
Bosch, Juan, 76
Bosnia and Herzegovina, 17–21, 278
   air power and, 3, 283
   Croatia and, 58, 283
   European Community Monitoring Mission and, 88
   German peacekeeping and, 101
   NATO and, xxiii, 176, 180, 217, 283
   no-fly zones and, 176
   population of, 276
   postconflict resolution and, 201
   UN safe areas in, 217
   UNCRO and, 60
   United Nations Human Rights Center and, 251
   UNPF and, 59
   UNPROFOR and, xvi–xvii, 280–284
   Vance-Owen Peace Plan and, 277
   See also Yugoslavian conflict
Bosnia-Croat Federation, 284
Bota, Liviu, 100

Botswana, 249
Bougainville, 196
Bougainville Interim Government, 196
Bougainville Revolutionary Army, 196
Boutros-Ghali, Boutros, 21, 197
   contacts with NATO, 180
   El Salvador and, 84
   on humanitarian interventions, 114
   on Mozambique, 160
   on peace enforcement, xxii–xxiii, 198
   on postconflict reconstruction, 200, 201
   Rwanda and, 212, 213, 214
   on Somalia, 195, 223
   on South Africa, 229
   on standby forces, 288
   on Tajikistan, 242
   on UN cooperation with regional organizations, 204
   UNMOP and, 60
   UNPROFOR II and, 280, 281, 282
   on UNTAES, 62
   See also Agenda for Peace, An
Brahimi, Lakhdar, 144
Brazil, 57, 184
Bresque, Homero Vaz, 86
Brezhnev, Leonid, 269
Brioni Talks, 88
British peacekeeping, xxii, xxiv, 21–23, 49. *See also* Commonwealth, The; Great Britain
Broken Lives (Stewart), 238
Broody, Reed, 86
Broz, Josip, 276
Brundtland Commission, 217
Budapest Summits, for CSCE, 191
Buddhism, Sri Lanka and, 231, 234
Buffer zones
   compared to demilitarized zones, 73
   in Cyprus, 69–70
   in Iraq-Kuwait war, 272
   in Macedonia-Serbia, 150
   in southern Lebanon, 133–135
   UNEF II and, 267
   in Yom Kippur War, 259
Bulgaria, 102
Bunche, Ralph, 23, 296
Burkard, Alfredo Cristiani. *See* Cristiani Burkard, Alfredo
Burkina Faso, 35, 144
Burundi, 209, 211, 214
Bush, George, 4, 185

Cable News Network, 118
Cabral, Donald Reid, 76
Cairo Agreement, 132, 133

Cairo Center for African Crisis Solving, 204
Cairo Centre for Training on Conflict Resolution and Peacekeeping in Africa, 79, 246
Calderón Sol, Armando, 85
Cambodia, 25–32
    ASEAN Regional Forum and, 14
    behavior of peacekeepers in, 44
    Canadian peacekeepers in, 33
    criticism of UN personnel in, xxii
    New Zealand peacekeepers and, 173
    postconflict resolution and, 201
    UNTAC and, xvii. *See also* UNTAC
Cambodian People's Armed Forces, 26, 30, 31
Cambodian People's Party, 30, 32
Cameroon, 209
Camp David Accords, 166
Campesinos, 175
Canada, 32–34
    International Commission for Supervision and Control and, 119
    Lester Pearson and, 199
    participation in UN missions, 247, 259
    peacekeeping training programs in, 247
Cantonment
    of Cambodian forces, 29, 30, 31
    in Mozambique, 163
    See also Demobilization
Caputo, Dante, 107
Cardenas, Emilio, 287
Carnegie Commission on Preventing Deadly Conflict, 193, 296, 297
Carrington, Peter, 89, 277, 281
Carter, Jimmy
    Bosnian crisis and, 283
    Cyrus Vance and, 297
    Haiti and, 108
    Lebanon and, 133
    Nicaragua and, 183
Cease-fires, 35
    in Bosnia, 281, 283
    in Cyprus, 66, 69, 70
    in El Salvador, 84
    in Indo-Pakistan conflict, 274
    interposition and, 120
    in Iran-Iraq War, 270, 271
    in Liberia, 139, 140, 145
    military observers and, 154
    in Mozambique, 160, 161, 162
    in Somalia, 224
    in southern Lebanon, 134
    in Sri Lanka, 234, 236
    in Suez Canal crisis, 262, 264

    in Tajikistan, 242, 243
    in West New Guinea, 116
    in Western Sahara, 157, 158
    in Yom Kippur War, 258, 259, 261, 266
    in Yugoslav conflict, 279, 280
Cedras, Raoul, 107, 109
Center for Disarmament Affairs, 257
Center for Human Rights (Yugoslavia), 276
Center for International Peacebuilding, 110
Central African Republic, 35–36
Central America, 57, 250. *See also* ONUCA
Central Revolutionary Council (Liberia), 143, 144
Ceylon, 230. *See also* Sri Lanka
Chad, 35, 188, 257–258
Chain of command, 36–37
    in observation missions, 37–38
Chamorro, Violeta Barrios de, 185, 186
Chamoun, Camille, 130, 132
Chand, Prem, 172
Charter of the United Nations, 37
Chechnya, 192
Chehab, Fouad, 132
Chemical weapons, Iraq and, 121
Chief military observer (CMO), 37–38
Child soldiers, 38–40
    in Liberia, 145
    in Mozambique, 159, 163
Childers, Erskine, 40
Chile, 249
China, 40–41
    Korean War and, 127
    Security Council and, 252, 253
    Special Committee on Peacekeeping Operations and, 287
    United Nations history and, 252
Chissano, Joaquim, 160, 163, 165
Chopra, Jarat, 218
Choung-Jun Ahn, 275
Christian Democratic Party (El Salvador), 81
CINCSOUTH (Commander in chief southern command), 18, 19
CIS. *See* Commonwealth of Independent States
Civil wars
    in Angola, 6–10
    in El Salvador, 82–83, 84
    in Liberia, 138–146
    in Nicaragua, 183–184
    noncombatants and, 43
    in Rwanda, 210–212, 213
    in Somalia, 222–223

    third-party interventions and, 285–286
    in Yugoslavia, 58–59, 61, 276–286
    See also Internal conflicts
Civilian casualties
    in Croatia, 278
    in Lebanon, 135, 136, 137
    in Liberia, 138, 139
    modern concepts of war and, 49
    in modern conflicts, numbers of, 49
    in Mozambique, 159
    in Operation Desert Storm, 104–105
    in Rwanda, 208, 210–211, 213
    in Sarajevo, 283
    in Somalia, 220, 222, 223, 226
Civilian peacekeeping forces, 41–42
    in contemporary peacekeeping, xv
    training programs for, 122–123, 244–247
    White Helmets and, 300
    women in, 301
Civilian police, 42–43
    in contemporary peacekeeping, xv
    in El Salvador, 84, 86
    Haitian, 109, 110
    Somalian, 224
    in UNTAC, 30, 32
    women in, 300
    See also CIVPOL; Secret police
Civilian Police Support Group in Croatia, 42–43
Civilian-military operations centers, 155
Civilians, in conflict zones, 43. *See also* Civilian casualties
CIVPOL (United Nations Civilian Police), 42–43
    in Cyprus, 67, 69
    demilitarized zones and, 73
    in first-generation peacekeeping, 94
    intelligence support for, 118
    Irish police in, 122
    in Mozambique, 160, 161, 163, 164, 165
    in Namibia, 170, 171
    in Rwanda, 213
    United Nations Civilian Police Support Group, 63
    See also Civilian police
Clans, in Somalia, 221–222
Clerides, Glafcos, 67
Clinton, Bill
    Bosnia and, 17
    Haiti and, 108
    Kosovo and, 4
    Presidential Decision Directive on U.S. peacekeeping, 295
    Somalia and, 227

CMO. *See* Chief military observer
CNN (Cable News Network), 118
Coalition forces. *See* Operation Desert Storm; Persian Gulf War
Coalition Government of Democratic Kampuchea, 27
Coalition pour la Défence de la République (Rwanda), 211
Codes of conduct, 43–44
of OSCE, 191
See also Rules of engagement
Cold War, 44–45
Congo and, 51–52, 56–57
Contadora group and, 57
first-generation peacekeeping in, xi–xiii, 93–94
Greek conflict and, 102
humanitarian interventions and, 113
Korean War and, 127
Lebanese conflicts and, 32, 131
Military Staff Committee and, 154
NATO and, 180
Nordic peacekeepers and, 179
Security Council and, 253
Suez Canal crisis and, 261, 262
U Thant and, 244
UN intelligence gathering in, 117
UNEF II and, 266, 267–268
Yom Kippur War and, 266
Colombia, 57, 184
Colombo, 234, 236
COMIFOR (Commander in theater of IFOR), 18, 19
Comision nacional de los Cascos Blancos, 300
Command and control. *See* Chain of command
Command and control warfare, xxv
Commission on Global Governance, 199
Commission on Human Rights, 276–277
Commission on Indonesia, 94
Committee of 34. *See* United Nations Special Committee on Peacekeeping Operations
Committee on Humanitarian Responses, 155
Common foreign and security policy (European Union), 89, 90
Commonwealth, The, 45–46. *See also* British peacekeeping; Great Britain
Commonwealth Monitoring Force, 45–46
Commonwealth Observer Group, 45
Commonwealth of Independent States (CIS), 46

CSCE and, 191, 192
in Georgia, xxiii, 99–100
Russian peacekeeping and, 207–208
in Tajikistan, xxiii, 242, 243–244
UN missions and, 204
Communist Party
in El Salvador, 82 (*see also* Frente Farabundo Martí para la Liberación Nacional)
Greek, 102
in Tajikistan, 241–242
Community Sant' Egidio, 4
Community-based organizations, 176. *See also* Nongovernmental organizations
"Compassion fatigue," 215
Complex emergencies, 46–47, 255
Conference for National Reconciliation in Somalia, 226
Conference of Ambassadors, 301
Conference on Security and Cooperation in Europe (CSCE), 189–191
Nagorno-Karabakh and, 192
Partnership for Peace and, 197
in Slovenia, 88
Tajikistan and, 242
See also Organization for Security and Cooperation in Europe
Conflict Data Project, 50
Conflict management, 188
Conflict prevention, 47–48, 188–189. *See also* Preventive diplomacy
Conflict Prevention Center, 190
Conflict resolution, xxv, 48–49
cease-fires and, 35
in Nicaragua, 174–175
peace support operations and, xxv
training programs, 247
Conflict zones
civilians in, 43
See also War(s)
Conflicts
major armed, defined, 50
major regional, 294
patterns and occurrences of, 49–50
See also Total war concept; War(s)
Congo, xii–xiii, 50–57
Contadora Group, 57, 184
Contadora Support Group, 57, 184
Contras, xvi, 183, 184, 185
Convention on the Privileges and Immunities of the United Nations, 238
Convention on the Rights of the Child, 38
Conventional Armed Forces, 190, 191

Convergencia Democrática (El Salvador), 85
Convoys. *See* Aid convoys
Cordovez, Diego, 71, 269
Costa del Sol Declaration, 57
Costa Rica, 184
Costs of peacekeeping, 57–58, 59(table)
Cot, Jean, 95, 278
Côte d'Ivoire, 140, 144
Cotonou Peace Agreement, 141, 144, 145
Council for a Livable World Education Fund, 302
Council of Europe, 149
Council of the League of Arab States, 129
Counterinsurgencies
Great Britain and, 21–22
in Namibia, 170
Cristiani Burkard, Alfredo, 82
Croatia, 58–63, 192, 277–280
alliance with Bosnia and Herzegovina, 283
CIVPOL in, 43
European Community Monitoring Mission and, 88
European Union and, 89
Implementation Force troops in, 19
peace agreement with Federal Republic of Yugoslavia, 284
population of, 276
UNPROFOR and, xvi, 278–280
See also Yugoslavian conflict
Croatian Nationalist Party, 58
Cuba
Angola and, 6, 7, 167, 168
Western Sahara and, 156
Cuíto Cuanavale, battle of, 168
Culture, peacekeeping forces and, 63–65
Cyprus, xiii, 65–71, 200
Czech Republic, 250
Czechoslovakia, 261

D'Abuisson, Roberto, 82
Dallaire, Romeo, 33, 212
Damascus, 292
DANFOR, 179
Danish International Brigade, 75, 179
Danish Reaction Brigade, 75
Darod clan, 221, 222
Databases. *See* Peacekeeping Training Courses Database
Dayton Peace Agreement, xxiii, 17, 18, 19, 20, 61, 89, 180, 191, 277, 284
De Facto Forces, 134, 135
de Klerk, F. W., 229
de Vergara, Evergisto Arturo, 71
Death squads, in El Salvador, 82

Declaration of Cancun about Central American Peace, 57
Defense Department, U.S., peacekeeping training programs, 155, 246–247
Delta Force commandos (U.S.), 226
Demilitarized zones (DMZs), 73, 75
    military observers and, 154
    in Rwanda, 212, 213
    in Yemen, 74(map)
    in Yom Kippur War, 259, 261
Demobilization
    in Eastern Slavonia, 61, 62
    in El Salvador, 85, 86
    in Liberia, 143–144
    in Mozambique, 160, 161, 163
    in Namibia, 170
    in Nicaragua, 185–186, 186
    See also Cantonment; Disarmament
Democratic Revolutionary Front (El Salvador), 81
Democratic Turnhalle Alliance, 171
Denktash, Rauf, 65, 67
Denmark, 75, 178, 179, 245, 246
Deñó, Francisco Caamaño, 76
der Stoel, Max van, 191
Desert Storm. See Operation Desert Storm
Developing countries, participation in UN missions, 248–249
DHA. See United Nations Department of Humanitarian Affairs
Dharmapala, 231
Dhlakama, Afonso, 160, 163, 165
Digil clan, 221
Diplomacy. See Humanitarian diplomacy; Preventive diplomacy
Dir clan, 221
Disarmament, 11, 12–13
    in Bosnia, 19
    of Cambodian forces, 30, 31
    in Central African Republic, 35
    Department of Political Affairs and, 257
    in Liberia, 143–144
    in Somalia, 226
    in Sri Lanka, 234, 235
    See also Cantonment; Demobilization
Disaster response programs
    Red Cross code of conduct, 43–44
    See also Natural disasters
Displaced persons, 203
    in Liberia, 138, 139, 143, 144
    in Mozambique, 159
    in Rwanda, 208, 210, 211, 214
    UNHCR and, 251
    from Yugoslav crisis, 276

Disraeli, Benjamin, 65
Dixit, J. N., 232
Djibouti, 221
DMZs. See Demilitarized zones
Dniester Republic, 208
Doe, Samuel, 138
Dominican Republic, 76–77, 189, 294
DOMREP (Representative of the Secretary-General in the Dominican Republic), xiii, 76–77, 93
dos Santos, José Eduardo, 6, 7, 8, 9
DPKO. See United Nations Department of Peacekeeping Operations
Duarte, José Napoléon, 81, 82
Dumbarton Oaks, 252
Dunant, Henry, 112
Durao Barroso, Jose, 7
Dushanbe, 242
Dutch East Indies, 15
Duvalier, Claude, 107
Duvalier, François, 107

East Bengal, 274
East Pakistan, 274
Eastern Slavonia, 59, 60, 61–63
ECMM. See European Community Monitoring Mission
ECOMOG. See Military Observer Group of the Economic Organization of West African States
Economic Organization of West African States (ECOWAS)
    Liberia and, 138, 140, 141, 144, 145
    Sierra Leone and, 220
    UNOMIL and, xvii
    See also Military Observer Group of the Economic Organization of West African States
Economic sanctions
    Security Council and, 253
    on Serbia-Montenegro, 191, 280
    UN Charter and, 37
    See also Arms embargoes; Embargoes
ECOWAS. See Economic Organization of West African States
Eelam National Democratic Liberation Front (ENDLF), 234–235, 236, 237
Eelam Peoples Revolutionary Liberation Front (ERPLF), 234–235, 236, 237
Egypt, xii, 79
    Armistice Agreement with Israel, 290, 291
    in League of Arab States, 129

Multinational Force and Observers and, 165–166
    participation in UN missions, 249
    peacekeeping training and, 245, 246
    rapprochement with Israel, 21
    Six-Day War and, 265
    Suez Canal crisis and, 261–264
    UNEF I and, 262–265, 291
    UNEF II and, 165–166, 266–268
    UNTSO observer groups and, 292
    U.S. Sinai Missions and, 295
    Yemen, 303, 304
    Yom Kippur War and, 165, 265–266
    See also Middle East conflict; United Arab Republic
Egyptian-Israeli Peace Treaty, 295
El Salvador, 79–87
    CIVPOL in, 43
    Nicaragua and, 183, 184, 185
    ONUCA and, xvi
    postconflict resolution and, 201
Elections
    in Cambodia, 25, 29, 31–32
    in Eastern Slavonia, 62
    in El Salvador, 82, 85
    in Haiti, 107, 109
    in Liberia, 143
    in Mozambique, 160, 161–163, 164–165
    in Namibia, 170, 171
    in Nicaragua, 185
    in South Africa, 229
    in Sri Lanka, 236
    in Tajikistan, 242
    in Western Sahara, 156159
Electronic warfare, xxv
Eliasson, Jan, 87
Elisabethville, 56
Embargoes
    against Haiti, 107, 108
    See also Arms embargoes; Economic sanctions
Emergency Relief Coordinator, 155, 255
Empowerment, peace building from below and, 198
"Enclave, the," 134
ENDLF. See Eelam National Democratic Liberation Front
Engström, Juha, 149, 278, 285
Enosis, 65
Equipment, for peacekeeping forces, 87–88. See also Logistics
Eritrea, 88
ERPLF. See Eelam Peoples Revolutionary Liberation Front
Espiell, Hector Gros, 156

Index

Esquipulas Agreements I and II, 57, 83, 184, 185, 186
Estonia, 192
Ethiopia, 88, 221, 222
Ethnic cleansing, 47
   in Georgia, 98
   in Yugoslavian conflict, 276, 278, 279, 281
   See also Human rights abuses
Eurocorps, 89, 299
EUROFOR, 299
EUROMARFOR, 299
Europe
   financing of peacekeeping by, 248
   participation in UNPROFOR, 248
   refugees, returnees, and displaced persons in, 203(table)
European Community, Yugoslav crisis and, 277, 278, 281
European Community Monitoring Mission (ECMM), 88–89
European Community's Conference on Yugoslavia, 277, 281
European Community's Humanitarian Office, 211
European Political Cooperation, 89
European Union, 89–90, 229, 239

Fact-Finding Declaration, 117
Fact-finding missions, 253
Factional conflicts, 50
Faisal (king of Saudi Arabia), 266
Faisal I (king of Iraq), 152
Falklands-Malvinas conflict, 73, 120
Fallmann, Walter, 63
Famine, in Somalia, 223, 224
Fanning, Steven, 172
FAO. *See* Food and Agriculture Organization
Farabundo Martí, Augustin, 82
Fedayeen, 291. *See also* Palestine Liberation Organization (PLO)
Federal Republic of Yugoslavia, 279
   Macedonia and, 149, 150
   peace agreement with Croatia, 284
   UNPROFOR III and, 285
   See also Yugoslavian conflict
Feissel, Gustave, 71
Ferrera Gomes, Pericles, 7
Field Administration and Logistics Division, 146
Field Manual on Wider Peacekeeping, xxii, 22, 49
Fiji, 247
Financing of peacekeeping, 91–92, 247–248
Finland, 92–93

Martti Ahtisaari and, 2
participation in UN missions, 247, 259
peace enforcement missions and, 179
peacekeeping training programs and, 246
Russian peacekeeping and, 207
standby forces and, 178
training programs of, 179
First U.S. Marine Expeditionary Force, 178
First-generation peacekeeping, 93–94
   China and, 41
   history of, xi–xiii
   interposition and, 120
   UN Charter and, 37
Fitzgerald, Peter, 17
FMLN. *See* Frente Farabundo Martí para la Liberación Nacional
Fonseca, Gulf of, 173
Food and Agriculture Organization (FAO), 155
   in Somalia, 228
   World Food Program and, 252
Force. *See also* Militaries; Military peacekeeping forces; Peace enforcement
   in British peacekeeping doctrine, 22
   in second-generation peacekeeping, 219
   in Somalia, 224–227
   U.S. peacekeeping doctrine and, 294
   used by ONUC, 54–56
Force commanders, 94
   chain of command, 36–37
Force Mobile Reserve, 94
Ford Foundation, on UN peacekeeping funding, 92
Former Yugoslavia. *See* Yugoslavia
France, 94–95
   Cambodia and, 26
   Eurocorps and, 89
   Lebanon and, 130, 133, 134, 135, 137, 138
   Middle East and, 151, 152
   peacekeepers in MINURCA, 35
   Rwanda and, 213
   Security Council and, 252, 253
   Somalia and, 221
   Suez Canal crisis and, 261–262, 264
FRELIMO. *See* Frente del Liberaçao do Mozambique
Frente del Liberaçao do Mozambique (FRELIMO), 160, 165
Frente Farabundo Martí para la Liberación Nacional (FMLN), 81–82, 83, 84, 85, 183, 184, 185

Frente Nacional de Libertaçao de Angola, 6
From Cold War to Hot Peace (Parsons), 196
Front Uni National pour un Cambodge Indépendent, Neutre, Pacifique, et Cooperatif (FUNCINPEC), 27, 28, 32
FUNCINPEC. *See* Front Uni National pour un Cambodge Indépendent, Neutre, Pacifique, et Cooperatif

Gabon, 35
Gadhafi, Muammar al-, 188
Galbraith, Peter, 284
Gali, 99, 100
Gamasakhurdia, Zviad, 98
Gambari, Ibrahim, 287
Gambia, 139
Gandhi, Rajiv, 232–233, 235, 236, 237, 238
Garcia-Sayán, Diego, 86
Garuba, Chris Abutu, 9
Gaza Strip, 290, 291
Gaza, UNEF I and, 262, 264, 265
Gemayel, Bashir, 137
General Agreement on the Establishment of Peace and National Accord in Tajikistan, 243
General Armistice Agreements (Israeli-Arab), 290–291, 292
General Assembly (United Nations), 252–253
   in financing peacekeeping, 91, 92
   Special Committee on Peacekeeping Operations and, 287
   Uniting for Peace resolution, 296
General Framework Agreement for Peace (on Bosnia). *See* Dayton Peace Agreement
General Peace Agreement (Mozambique), 160–161, 162, 163
Generals for Peace and Disarmament, 110
Geneva Accords (on Afghanistan), 269
Geneva Conventions, 97
   on child soldiers, 38
   on demilitarized zones, 73
   on humanitarian assistance, 112
   International Committee of the Red Cross/Red Crescent and, 120
   on noncombatants, 43
Genocide
   Bosnian crisis and, 284
   in Rwanda, 208, 210–211, 213
   See also Ethnic cleansing; Human rights abuses

Georgia, 98–100, 192
CIS and, xxiii, 46
Russian peacekeeping and, 207, 208
UNOMIG and CIS cooperation in, 204
German Basic Law, 100, 101
Germany, 100–101
Eurocorps and, 89
League of Nations and, 130
UNIIMOG and, 271
Yugoslavia and, 278
Gersony Report, 159
Ghana
Liberia and, 139, 140, 144
participation in UN missions, 247, 249
Gligorov, Kiro, 149
Golan Heights, xii, 258–261, 291, 292
Good Offices Commission, 15
Goodwill visits, 254
Gorazde, 217, 281, 282, 283, 284
Gorbachev, Mikhail, 168, 184, 190, 269
Gordon-Somers, Trevor, 141
Gore, Al, 59
Governors Island Agreement, 108
Grassroots organizations, 176. See also
Nongovernmental organizations
Great Britain
Commonwealth and, 45–46
Cyprus and, 65, 66, 67, 69
Greek conflict and, 102
India-Pakistan conflict and, 273–274
Jordan and, 132
Middle East and, 151–153
naval peacekeeping forces, 172
Palestine and, 286, 289
peacekeeping doctrine in, xxii, xxiv, 21–23, 49
peacekeeping training programs in, 246
Security Council and, 252, 253
Somalia and, 221
Suez Canal crisis and, 261–262, 264
United Nations history and, 252
Yemen and, 303
Great Lakes Region (Africa), 218. See
also Burundi; Rwanda
Greece, xii, 101–103
Cyprus and, 65, 66, 67, 69
Macedonia and, 285
Greek Cypriot Paramilitary
Organization, 65
Greek Cypriots, 65–67, 69–71
Green line (Cyprus), 66, 137
Grenada, 189
Ground Self-Defence Force (Japan), 125

Groupement des Observateurs
Militaries Neutres. See Neutral
Military Observers Group
Guatemala, 103–104, 184
Guerrilla warfare
noncombatants and, 43
See also Insurgencies
Guinea, 139, 144
Guinea-Bissau, 140, 188
Gulf Wars, 104–105. See also Iran-Iraq
War; Persian Gulf War
Gunaratna, Rohan, 236
Gyani, P. S., 67

Habyarimana, Juvenal, 209, 210, 211
Haddad, Saad, 134, 135
Hague, The, 97
Haile Selassie, 88
Haiti, 107–109
Canadian peacekeepers and, 33
naval peacekeeping forces and, 172, 173
UN joint operations in, 204
UNMIH and, xvii–xviii
Haitian National Police, 109
Hameed, A. C. S., 237
Hammarskjöld, Dag, 110
Congo and, 52, 55
death of, 55
Nobel Peace Prize, 175–176
principles of peacekeeping and, xi, 32–33, 37, 48, 93–94
on standby forces, 178
UNEF I and, 262, 264, 265
Hanset, Willy, 63
Harbottle, Eirwen and Michael, 110
Harff, H., 101
Hassan II (king of Morocco), 157
Hawiye clan, 221, 222, 223
Helsinki Final Act, 189, 190
Helsinki II Summit, 190–191
Heng Samrin, 26
Hernández Martínez, Maximiliano, 81
Herzegovina. See Bosnia and
Herzegovina
Hezbollah, 135
Hieberg, M., 64–65
High Commission on National
Minorities, 48, 191
High-intensity conflicts, 50
Hirose, Yukinari, 287
Holbrooke, Richard, 17
Honduras
Contras and, 183, 184, 185
El Salvador and, 81
Horn of Africa, 221. See also Somalia
Host countries, 110–111

Hostages, in Bosnia, 283
Houphouet-Boigny, Félix, 140
Höynck, Wilhelm, 191
Huambo massacre, 8
Hull, Cordell, 175
Human rights, 111–112
Human rights abuses
in Angola, 8, 9
in El Salvador, 81, 82, 83
in Georgia, 98
in Guatemala, 103, 104
in Haiti, 107, 109
in Mozambique, 159
by police forces, 43
in Rwanda, 208, 210–211, 213
in Sri Lanka, 235
by UN personnel, xxii
in Yugoslavia, 276, 281. See also
Ethnic cleansing
Human Rights Field Operation,
Rwanda, 111, 213–214
Human rights missions
in Cambodia, 29–30
in El Salvador, 84, 86–87
in Nicaragua, 174–175
OSCE and, 190
in Rwanda, 111, 213–214
in Yugoslavia, 276–277
See also United Nations Human
Rights Commission; Universal
Declaration of Human Rights
Human Rights Watch, 242, 282
Humanitarian assistance, 112
in Bosnia and Herzegovina, 280, 281
in internal peacekeeping, 119
in Iraq, 105, 121
in Lebanon, 136
in Liberia, 144, 145
in Mozambique, 160, 162, 164
non-governmental organizations
and, 176
in Somalia, 223, 224
as target of violence, 47
in Yugoslavia, 277
Humanitarian diplomacy, 95
Humanitarian Early Warning System,
256(box)
Humanitarian interventions, 47,
113–114
Humanitarian law, 97
Humanitarian organizations. See
International Committee of the
Red Cross/Red Crescent
"Humanitarian war" (Somalia), 195
Hun Sen, 26, 32
Hungary, 119
Hurd, Douglas, 195

Husayn ibn 'Ali. *See* Hussein (Sharif of Mecca)

Husayn ibn Talal. *See* Hussein (king of Jordan)

Hussein (king of Jordan), 132

Hussein, Saddam, 113, 121

Hussein (Sharif of Mecca), 152

Hutu people, 208–212, 213

ICRC. *See* International Committee of the Red Cross/Red Crescent (ICRC)

Identification Commission (Morocco), 157, 158

Identity conflicts, 50

IFOR. *See* Implementation Force

Ileo, Joseph, 54

IMF. *See* International Monetary Fund

Immediate Reaction Force, 179, 181

Implementation Force (IFOR)
  deployment of, 17, 18–20, 181, 284
  German peacekeepers in, 101
  number of troops in, xxiii
  Partnership for Peace and, 197
  postconflict resolution and, 201

Independent Commission on International Humanitarian Issues, 193

Independent Democratic Serb Party, 62

Independent Electoral Commission (South Africa), 229

Independent National Patriotic Front of Liberia, 140

India, 115
  Indian Peacekeeping Force, 230, 234–238
  Indo-Pakistani conflict, xii, 244, 273–275
  Indo-Sri Lankan Agreement, 232–234
  participation in UN missions, 247, 249
  peacekeeping training workshops and, 245
  Russian peacekeeping and, 207
  United Nations debt to, 58

Indian Air Force, 234

Indian Peacekeeping Force (IPKF), 115, 230, 234–238

"Indigenous empowerment," 198

Indonesia, 116–117, 119

Indo-Pakistani conflict, xii, 244, 273–275

Indo-Sri Lankan Agreement, 232–234

Ingo, 209

Initiative on Conflict Resolution and Ethnicity, 247, 302

Institute for East-West Security Studies, 81

Insurgencies, 218
  child soldiers and, 38–40
  in Sri Lanka. *See* Janatha Vimukht Peramuna
  See also Guerrilla warfare

Integrated Regional Information Network, 256(box)

Intelligence processing, DPKO and, 256

Intelligence services, Indian, 232, 236, 237–238

Intelligence support, 117–118

Inter-Action, 155

Inter-Africa Mission to Monitor the Implementation of the Bangui Agreements. *See* MISAB

Inter-African Force, 188

Interagency Standing Committee, 155

Interahamwe, 210, 211

Inter-American Peace Force, 76, 77, 189

Interdisciplinary Research Program on Causes of Human Rights Violations, 49

Intergovernmental organizations, xv

Interim Government of National Unity (Liberia), 139, 140

Intermediate-Range Nuclear Forces, 190

Internal conflicts, 118–119
  CSCE on, 190–191
  interposition and, 120
  in Mozambique, 159
  Organization of African Unity on, 187–188
  refugees and, 49
  second-generation peacekeeping and, 218–219
  types of, 50
  in Yugoslavia, 58–59, 61, 276–286
  See also Civil wars

Internally displaced persons, 203, 251. *See also* Displaced persons

International Association of Peacekeeping Training Centers, 247, 302

International Association of Permanent Representative to the United Nations, 81

International Atomic Energy Agency, 121

International Brigade (Denmark), 75, 179

International Civilian Peacekeeping and Peace Building Training Program, 247

International Commission for Supervision and Control (Vietnam War), 119

International Commission for Support and Verification (Nicaragua), 174–175, 184

International Committee of the Red Cross/Red Crescent (ICRC), 155
  code of conduct, 43–44
  in contemporary peacekeeping, xv
  on humanitarian assistance, 112
  international humanitarian law and, 120
  Nobel Peace Prize and, 175
  refugees and, 203
  Rwanda and, 211
  in Somalia, 223, 226, 228
  UNEF II and, 267

International Conference on the Former Yugoslavia, 193, 277, 281, 285, 297

International Council for Voluntary Agencies, 155

International Court of Justice
  Aouzou Strip controversy and, 257
  Nicaraguan-Honduran conflict and, 185

International humanitarian law, 97
  on humanitarian assistance, 112
  ICRC and, 120
  Rwanda and, 213

International Index of Human Suffering, 159

International Monetary Fund (IMF)
  Bosnia and, 17
  Liberia and, 139
  Rwanda and, 209

International NGO Consortium, 155

International nongovernmental organizations, 176. *See also* Nongovernmental organizations

International Organization for Migration, 155, 252

International Peace Academy, 81, 205, 247

International Refugee Organization, 251

International Relations and Security Network, 302

International War Crimes Tribunals, 97
  for the Former Yugoslavia, 277, 284
  for Rwanda, 213

Internationalization, 120
  of Jerusalem, 125–126, 286, 289

Internet, 256(box), 301–302

Interposition, 120

Interstate Defence and Security Conference (Africa), 246, 305

Interstate wars, decline in, 50

IPKF. *See* Indian Peacekeeping Force

Iran, 104, 135, 259, 268–269. *See also* Iran-Iraq War

Iran-Contra scandal, 270
Iran-Iraq War, 104, 270–272, 299
Iraq, 121
    Great Britain and, 151, 152
    humanitarian interventions in, 113
    in League of Arab States, 129
    naval peacekeeping forces and, 173
    no-fly zones in, 176
    Operation Provide Comfort and,
        206–207
    safe havens and, 217
    weapons of mass destruction and,
        272
    See also Iran-Iraq War; Kurds;
        Persian Gulf War
Ireland, 121–122, 246, 247
Irish Defense Forces, 121–122
Irish peacekeeping, 121–122
Iskandarov, Akbarsho, 242
Islam. See Shia Muslims; Sunni Muslims
Israel
    conflicts in southern Lebanon,
        132–138
    conflicts with Palestinians, 132–138,
        146, 264–265
    conflicts with Syria, 291–292
    first-generation peacekeeping and,
        xii
    General Armistice Agreements and,
        290–291
    Multinational Force and Observers
        and, 165–166
    rapprochement with Egypt, 21
    seizure of Golan Heights, Sinai, West
        Bank, 291
    Six-Day War and, 132, 259, 265
    Suez Canal crisis and, 261   264
    UNDOF and, 259–261
    UNEF I and, 262–265
    UNEF II and, 165–166, 266–268
    UNTSO and, 289–293
    War of Independence, 132
    Yom Kippur War and, 165, 258–259,
        265–266
    See also Jerusalem; Middle East
        conflict
Israeli Defence Force, in southern
        Lebanon, 133, 134, 135–136,
        137–138
Israeli War of Independence, 132
Israeli-Palestinian conflict, 264–265
    Lebanon and, 132–138
    Trygve Lie and, 146
Issaq clan, 221, 222
Italy, 122–123
    Albania and, 4
    Lebanon and, 137, 138

peacekeeping training programs in,
        247
    Somalia and, 221
Izetbegovic, Alija, 284
Izydorczyk, Boleslaw, 244

Jaffna, 73, 232, 235
James, Alan, 119, 301
Jammu, 273. See also Kashmir
Janatha Vimukht Peramuna, 230, 231,
        233, 234, 236, 237
Janvier, Bernard, 149, 278
Japan, 125
Japanese Self Defence Force, 125
Jawaharlal Nehru Award, 200
Jayewardene, J. R., 232, 233, 235, 236
Jerusalem, 120, 125–126, 286, 289, 290
JNA. See Yugoslav's People's Army
Johnson, Lyndon, 76
Johnson, Prince, 140
Johnson, Roosevelt, 143
Joint Commission for the Formation of
        the Armed Forces (Angola), 7, 9
Joint Deployable Intelligence Support
        System (U.S.), 118, 256
Joint Forces Handbook for Peace
        Operations, 122
Joint International Civilian Mission in
        Haiti. See MICIVIH
Joint Political-Military Commission
        (Angola), 7, 8
Joint Readiness Training Center, 155
Jordan
    Armistice Agreement with Israel,
        290, 291
    Great Britain and, 132
    Jerusalem and, 126, 290
    participation in UN missions, 249
    PLO in, 264
    UNTSO in, 292
    See also Middle East conflict
Joshi, Subhash, 220
Joulwan, 18
Juba, 226

Kabbah, Ahmed Tejan, 220
Kabul, 268
Kagame, Paul, 212
Kaifu, Toshiki, 125
Kampuchea, 26. See also Cambodia
Kanyarengwe, Alexis, 210, 211
Karachi Agreement, 274, 275
Karadzic, Radovan, 284
Karim, Ataul, 28
Karmal, Babrak, 268
Karsgaard, David, 287
Kasavubu, Joseph, 51, 52, 54, 55, 56

Kashmir, xii, 173, 273–274, 275
Katanga, 51, 54–56
Kayibanda, Gregoire, 209
Kazakhstan, 46
Keeping the Peace, 21, 22
Kenya, 188, 221, 249
Khan, S. M., 212
Khieu Samphan, 26, 27, 28
Khmer People's National Liberation
        Front, 27, 32
Khmer Rouge, 26, 29, 30
Khmer Rouge Party of Democratic
        Kampuchea (PDK), 27, 28, 30, 31
Khomeini, Ayatollah Ruholla, 270, 271
Khrushchev, Nikita, 52, 110
Kibeho, 214
Kiev Agreement on Collective Security
        Forces, 46
Kigali, 208, 210, 212–213
Kigeri IV, 209
Kiichi Miyazawa, 125
Kijevo, 278
Kinshasa. See Léopoldville
Kisangani. See Stanleyville
Kismayu, 223, 224, 226
Kissinger, Henry, 259, 266, 267
Kitona Accord, 55
Kittani, Ismat, 224
"Kiwi Company," 174
Klein, Jacques Paul, 62, 63
Koevoet counterinsurgents, 170
Kolwezi, 56
Konrote, Jioje Konouse, 136
Korean War, 40, 95, 127, 146, 296
Kosovo, 4, 5, 192, 276
Kouchner, Bernard, 95
Kouyaté, Lansana, 144
KPNL Armed Forces, 27, 30
Krahn people, 139, 143
Krajina, 58, 59, 60, 278, 279, 280
Kromah, Alhaji, 143
Krulak, Charles, 178
Kumar, Shiva, 212
Kurds, 105, 113, 121, 206–207, 217
Kuwait, 104–105, 129. See also Persian
        Gulf War
Kyrgyzstan, 46

Lamb, Christopher, 177
Lancaster House Agreement, 45
Land mines
    in Angola, 8
    in Bosnia, 19
    in Cambodia, 28, 29, 33
    disarmament and, 13
    in Mozambique, 160, 165
    See also Mine clearing

Lapresle, Bertrand de, 278
Latin America
    participation in UN missions, 249
    refugees, returnees, and displaced
        persons in, 203(table)
Latvia, 192
Laws of war, 97
    on child soldiers, 38
    on humanitarian assistance, 112
League of Arab States, 129–130, 133,
    217, 223
League of Nations, 130
    history of, 252
    Namibia and, 167
    peacekeeping activities of, xi
    refugees and, 251
Lebanon, xii, 130–138
    Armistice Agreement with Israel,
        290, 291
    attack on U.S. Marines in, 294
    League of Arab States forces in,
        129–130
    PLO raids into Israel, 292
    UNTSO observer groups and,
        292–293
    women peacekeepers in, 300
    See also Middle East conflict
Lederach, John Paul, 198
Léopoldville, 51, 54
Lessons Learned Unit, xxiii, 254
Lester B. Pearson International
        Peacekeeping Training Center,
        199, 247, 301
Liberation Tigers of Tamil Eelam
        (LTTE), 230, 231–232, 233–238
Liberia, xxiii, 138–146, 204
Liberian National Conference, 144
Liberian National Transitional
        Government, 141, 143, 144
Liberian Peace Council, 140, 143
Libya, 156, 188, 257–258
Lidimo, L., 163
Lie, Trygve, 110, 146, 296
Lieber code, 97
Lincoln Agreement, 196
LINK program, 155
Lisbon Summit (OSCE), 191–192
Litani River, 133, 135
Lithuania, 130
Lofa Defence Force, 143, 144
Logistics, 146–147
    naval peacekeeping forces and, 172,
        173
    United Nations Logistics Base,
        Brindisi, 123
*Logistics Manual for Out of Area
    Operations,* 122

Lomé, 140
Lon Nol, 26
London Peace Implementation
    Conference, 19, 20
Lopez, Joseph, 18–19
López Pintor, Rafael, 86
Loridan, Jean-Michel, 28
Low-intensity conflicts, 49–50
LTTE. *See* Liberation Tigers of Tamil
    Eelam
Lubowski, Anton, 171
Lumumba, Patrice, 51, 52, 54, 187
Lundula, Victor, 51
Lusaka Protocol, 8–9

Maastricht Treaty, 89
Macedonia, 149–150, 192
    independence declared, 278
    population of, 276
    preventive deployment in, 2, 4. *See
        also* UNPREDEP
    UNPROFOR III and, xvii, 284–285
    U.S. peacekeepers in, 294
    See also Yugoslavian conflict
Mackenzie, Lewis, 150, 186
Mackinlay, John, xxii, 150–151, 218, 219
Magnaña, Alvaro, 82
Mahkamov, Qahhor, 241
Major armed conflicts, defined, 50
Major regional conflicts, 294
Makarios III, 65, 66
Malaysia, 249
Malaysian Peacekeeping Training
    Center, 14
Mali, 35, 139
Malval, Robert, 108
Managua Agreements, 185, 186
Mandates, 151
    Security Council and, 253
Mandela, Nelson, 9, 229
Mandingo people, 139, 143
*Manual for Peacekeeping Operations and
    Humanitarian Missions,* 122
Marine boundary disputes, 173
Maritime forces. *See* Naval peacekeeping
Maronite Christians, 132
Marrack, Goulding, 101
Martí, Augustin Farabundo. *See*
    Farabundo Martí, Augustin
Massacres
    in Angola, 8
    in El Salvador, 81
    in Rwanda, 208, 210–211, 213
    See also Ethnic cleansing; Human
        rights abuses
Matanza, 81
Matuszewski, Zbigniew, 287

Mauritania, 156
Mechanism for Conflict Prevention,
    Management, and Resolution,
    188, 189
Médecins sans Frontières, 95
Mediation. *See also* Conflict resolution
    military observers and, 154
Medical aid
    Norwegian peacekeepers and, 180
    Pakistani peacekeepers and, 195
    peacekeeping missions and, 153
Meir, Golda, 266, 267
"Memorandum for Peace through the
    United Nations" (Lie), 146
Memorandum of Understanding
    (Yugoslavian conflict), 88
Menderes, Adnan, 65
Menem, Carlos, 300
Merrem, Gerd, 243, 244
Mexico, 57, 184
Mexico City Agreement, 83
MICIVIH (Joint International Civilian
    Mission in Haiti), xvii, 41, 107,
    109, 111, 204, 251
Microdisarmament, 12–13
Middle East conflict, 151–153
    Camp David Accords, 166
    Canadian peacekeepers and, 33
    demilitarized zones and, 73, 74(map)
    European Union and, 89
    first-generation peacekeeping and,
        xii
    General Armistice Agreements and,
        290–291
    Israeli seizure of Golan Heights,
        Sinai, West Bank, 291
    Israeli War of Independence, 132
    Israeli-Egyptian rapprochement, 21
    Israeli-Palestinian conflicts,
        132–138, 264–265
    Israeli-Syrian conflict, 291–292
    Jerusalem and, 125–126
    in Lebanon, 130–138
    Multinational Force and Observers,
        165–166
    Ralph Bunche and, 23
    Six-Day War, 132–138, 244, 259, 265
    Trygve, Lie and, 146
    U Thant and, 244
    UNDOF and, 258–261
    UNEF I and, 262–265
    UNEF II and, 266–268
    UNTSO and, 289–293
    Yom Kippur War, 165, 258–259,
        265–266, 292
    See also Suez Canal Crisis
Mierlo, Hans van, 198

Militaries
  child soldiers and, 38–40
  See also Total war concept; War(s)
Military exclusion zones, in Bosnia, 283
Military expenditures, compared to
  peacekeeping costs, 58, 59(table)
Military information offices, 118. *See
  also* Intelligence support
Military intelligence. *See* Intelligence
  services; Intelligence support
Military medicine, 153. *See also* Medical
  aid
Military Observer Group of the
  Economic Organization of West
  African States (ECOMOG), xvii,
  xxiii, 139–141, 143, 144, 145. *See
  also* Economic Organization of
  West African States
Military observer missions, 153–154
  chief military observer and, 37–38
  financing of, 91
  New Zealand peacekeepers and, 173
  See also individual Observer missions
Military Observers in Beirut, 95
Military operations other than war
  (MOOTW), xix, 294
Military peacekeeping forces
  code of conduct, 44
  in contemporary peacekeeping, xv
  cultural studies of, 64–65
  demilitarized zones and, 73
  in Eastern Slavonia, 61
  force commanders, 94
  humanitarian missions and, 113,
    154–155
  in Mozambique, 161
  training programs, 244–247
  UN chain of command, 36–37
  UNTAC and, 29, 31, 32
  women in, 300
  See also Peace enforcement
Military Staff Committee (MSC), 36,
  154, 198, 219
Military-humanitarian relations,
  154–155
Milosevic, Slobodan, 4, 276, 283, 284
Mine clearing, New Zealand and, 173
Minear, L., 120
Minor armed conflicts, defined, 50
Minorities at Risk Project, 50
MINPONUH (United Nations Civilian
  Police Mission in Haiti), 43
MINUGUA (Mision de los Naciones
  Unidas en Guatemala), 41,
  103–104, 111, 251
MINURCA (United Nations Mission in
  the Central African Republic), 35

MINURSO (United Nations Mission for
  the Referendum in Western
  Sahara), xvi, 95, 119, 156–159,
  300
MINUSAL (United Nations Mission in
  El Salvador), 86
Mirotvorcheskie voiska, 207
MISAB (Inter-Africa Mission to
  Monitor the Implementation of
  the Bangui Agreements), 35
Mision de los Naciones Unidas en
  Guatemala. *See* MINUGUA
Mission mandates, 151
Mission Planning Service, 256
Mixed Armistice Commissions,
  290–291, 293
Miyazawa, Kiichi, 125
Mladic, Ratko, 284
Mobutu, Joseph, 51, 54, 56
Mogadishu, 195, 221, 222, 223, 224,
  226–227, 295
Moldova, 46, 192, 207, 208
Monrovia, 139, 140, 141
Montenegro, 191, 276, 279, 280
MONUA (United Nations Observer
  Mission in Angola), 9
MOOTW. *See* Military operations other
  than war
Morocco, 156–159
Moscow Declaration, 252
Moscow Protocol, 243
Moskos, C. C., 64
Mostar, 283
Mouvement National Congolaise, 51
Mouvement Révolutionnaire National
  pour le Développement, 210, 211
Movimento Nacional Revolucionario (El
  Salvador), 85
Movimento Popular de Libertaçao de
  Angola, 6, 7, 8, 167
Moxon-Browne, Edward, 301
Mozambican Defence Force, 160, 161,
  163
Mozambique, 159–165
  behavior of peacekeepers in, 44
  LINK program, 155
  New Zealand peacekeepers and, 173
  ONUMOZ and, xvii
  postconflict resolution and, 201
MPLA. *See* Movimento Popular de
  Libertaçao de Angola
MSC. *See* Military Staff Committee
Mujahideen, 268, 269
Multiculturalism, in contemporary
  peacekeeping, xvi
Multidimensional peacekeeping
  operations, xvi–xix, 41, 180, 218.

  See also Second-generation
    peacekeeping
Multilateralism, xv
Multinational Force and Observers
  (MFO), 165–166
  Canadian peacekeepers in, 33
  French peacekeepers in, 95
  naval support, 172
  U.S. peacekeepers in, 292, 294
  U.S. Sinai Field Mission and, 295
Multinational forces
  cultural interactions and, 64–65
  in Haiti, 108–109
  in Lebanon, 95, 136–138
  naval support, 172
  Organization of American States
    and, 189
  UNMIH and, xvii
Multinational UN Standby Forces High
  Readiness Brigade, 75
Multinationalism, in contemporary
  peacekeeping, xvi
Musa Sadr, Imam, 132
Museveni, Yoweri Kaguta, 210
Muslims. *See* Shia Muslims; Sunni
  Muslims
Mwami, 209

Nabiev, Rahmon, 242
NACC. *See* North Atlantic Cooperation
  Council
Nagorno-Karabakh, 191, 192, 204
Nambiar, Satish, 115, 278
Namibia, xvi, 167–172
  Angola and, 6, 7
  Martti Ahtisaari and, 2
  New Zealand peacekeepers and, 173
  postconflict resolution and, 201
Namibia Accords, 168
Nasser, Gamal, 115, 130, 262, 265
National Army of Democratic
  Kampuchea, 27, 30, 31
National Civil Police (El Salvador), 84,
  85
National Council for the Defense of
  Human Rights (El Salvador), 84
National Elections Commission
  (Mozambique), 161, 162, 164, 165
National Liberation Front (Greece), 102
National Patriotic Front of Liberia, 138,
  139–140, 141, 143, 144
Nationalist Republican Alliance (El
  Salvador), 83, 85
NATO. *See* North Atlantic Treaty
  Organization
Natural disasters
  coordination of relief efforts, 155

humanitarian interventions and, 113
UN Department of Humanitarian
Affairs and, 255
See also Disaster response programs
Naval peacekeeping, 172–173, 299
NBC weapons, Iraq and, 121
Negotiation. *See* Conflict resolution
Nepal, 247
Netherlands, 116
Neto, Agostinho, 6
Neutral Military Observers Group
(NMOG), 188, 210, 212, 213
Neutrality, Russian peacekeeping and,
208
New Zealand, 173–174, 247
News agencies, intelligence and, 118
Ngonhamo, M., 163
Nicaragua, 83, 174–175, 183–187
Nicosia, 66
Nigeria, 188
Aouzou Strip controversy and, 257
Liberia and, 139, 140, 143, 144
participation in UN missions, 249,
250
Nimeiri, Gaafar, 188
NMOG. *See* Neutral Military Observers
Group
Nobel, Alfred, 175
Nobel Peace Prize, 175–176
Javier Pérez de Cuéllar, 200
Lester Pearson, 33, 199
Ralph Bunche, 23
UNICEF, 252
No-fly zones, 105, 113, 176, 217, 282
Noncombatants. *See* Civilian casualties;
Civilians, in conflict zones
Nongovernmental organizations
(NGOs), 176–177
conflict prevention and, 48
in contemporary peacekeeping, xv,
41
military peacekeeping forces and,
154, 155
in Mozambique, 162, 164
Norwegian Emergency Preparedness
Systems and, 181
peace building from below and, 198
Red Cross code of conduct, 43–44
Rwanda and, 211
in Somalia, 223, 226, 228
South Africa and, 229
UN Department of Humanitarian
Affairs and, 255
World Food Program and, 252
Nonintervention principles
humanitarian interventions and, 114
Javier Pérez de Cuéllar on, 200

Organization of African Unity and,
187–188
Nonlethal weapons, 177–178, 179(box)
NORBATT I, 179
Nordic Committee for Military United
Nations Matters, 178, 246
Nordic countries, 178–179, 246
Nörgaard, Carl, 171, 172
NORSTAFF, 180
North America, refugees, returnees, and
displaced persons in, 203(table)
North Atlantic Cooperation Council
(NACC), 18, 19, 197
North Atlantic Treaty Organization
(NATO), 180
in Bosnia and Herzegovina, xxiii, 17,
18–20, 176, 217, 283 (*see also*
Implementation Force;
Stabilization Force)
Cold War and, 45
CSCE and, 191, 192
Cyprus and, 65, 66
Denmark and, 75
Finland and, 93
Germany and, 100, 101
Immediate Reaction Forces and, 179,
181
intelligence sharing and, 118
Michael Harbottle and, 110
naval peacekeeping forces and, 172,
173
Partnership for Peace and, 197
Robert Stewart and, 238
UNPROFOR and, 204
North Korea, 127
Northeastern Provincial Council (Sri
Lanka), 234, 236, 237
Norting, 175
Norway, 175, 178, 179, 246, 247
Norwegian Emergency Preparedness
Systems, 181
Norwegian peacekeeping, 181
Norwegian Resource Bank for
Democracy and Human Rights,
181
Ntaryamira, Cyprien, 211
Nuclear weapons, Iraq and, 121
Nuremberg law, 97
Nuri, Sayed Abdullo, 243
Nyakyi, Anthony, 141
Nyerere, Julius, 113, 188
Nyiginya, 209

Oakley, Robert, 224
OAS. *See* Organization of American
States
Obasanjo, Olesegun, 188

Observation Detachment Damascus,
292
Observation Group Beirut, 292–293
Observer Group Egypt, 292
Observer Group Golan, 292
Observer Group Lebanon, 292
Observer missions. *See* Military
observer missions
Oceania, refugees, returnees, and
displaced persons in, 203(table)
Office of the High Representative, 17, 20,
21
Office of the Secretary-General in
Afghanistan and Pakistan. *See*
OSGAP
Ogaden, 221, 222
Oil embargoes, 108
Okelo, Francis, 220
Olaf Palme Prize, 200
Olcto, Henry, 231
On-line journalism, 302
ONUC (United Nations Operation in the
Congo), xii–xiii, 52–57
effects on Organization of African
Unity, 187
Hammarskjöld and, 110
Indian peacekeepers in, 115
Irish peacekeepers in, 121
Military Information Branch in,
118
Pakistani peacekeepers in, 195
Swedish peacekeepers in, 239
UNTEA and, 117
UNTSO and, 293
ONUCA (United Nations Observer
Group in Central America), xvi,
84, 173, 184–187, 293
ONUMOZ (United Nations Operation in
Mozambique), xvii, 160, 161–165,
201, 293
ONUSAL (United Nations Observer
Mission in El Salvador), 186
civilian peacekeepers in, 41
deployment of, 80(map), 83–87
France and, 94
human rights and, 111, 251
overview of, xvi
postconflict resolution and, 201
ONUVEH (United Nations Observer
Group for the Verification of
Elections in Haiti), 94, 107, 293
ONUVEN (United Nations Observation
Mission for the Verification of
Elections in Nicaragua), 184
ONUVER (United Nations Observer
Mission for the Verification of
Elections in Eritrea), 88

OOTW. *See* Operations other than war
Opande, Daniel, 141
Operation Alba, 4, 122
Operation Desert Storm, 3, 104–105, 272. *See also* Persian Gulf War
Operation Grandslam, 56
Operation Joint Endeavor, 18
Operation Liberation, 232
Operation Morthor, 55
Operation Pawan, 235
Operation Provide Comfort, 105, 113, 206–207
Operation Rum Punch, 54–55
Operation Southern Watch, 105
Operation Tourquoise, 95, 213
Operation United Shield, 178, 179(box)
Operation Viraja, 236
Operation Virat, 236
Operational security, xxv
Operations, 294
Operations other than war (OOTW), xix, 294
Organization for Security and Cooperation in Europe (OSCE), 189–192
　Albania and, 4
　Bosnia and, 20
　conflict prevention and, 48
　Denmark and, 75
　Macedonia and, 149
　Partnership for Peace and, 197
　Russian peacekeeping and, 207
　Swedish peacekeepers and, 239
　in Tajikistan, 243
　United Nations and, 204
　United Nations Human Rights Center and, 251
　UNPROFOR III and, 285
　Western European Union and, 299
　See also Conference on Security and Cooperation in Europe
Organization of African Unity (OAU), 187–189
　Aouzou Strip controversy and, 257
　Cairo Center for African Crisis Solving, 204
　Cairo Center for Training on Conflict Resolution and Peacekeeping in Africa and, 79
　Egypt and, 166
　Liberia and, 139, 144
　Mohammed Sahnoun and, 217, 218
　Morocco and, 156
　Rwanda and, 210
　Somalia and, 223
　South Africa and, 229
　UN missions and, 204

Organization of American States (OAS), 189
　Contadora Group and, 57
　Dominican Republic and, 76, 77
　El Salvador and, 81
　Haiti and, 107
　Nicaragua and, 174–175
　United Nations and, 204
　UNMIH and, 204
Organization of East Caribbean States, 189
Organization of the Islamic Conference, 223
OSCE. *See* Organization for Security and Cooperation in Europe
OSGAP (Office of the Secretary-General in Afghanistan and Pakistan), 269
Osijek, 276
Ossetia, 46
Ottoman Empire, 151, 152
Owen, David, 193, 277
Oxfam, 176

"Painting a country blue," 195
Pakistan, 195–196
　Afghan conflict and, 268–269
　Indo-Pakistani conflict, xii, 244, 273–275
　naval peacekeeping forces and, 172
　New Zealand peacekeepers and, 173
　peacekeepers in Somalia, 224, 226
　United Nations debt to, 58
Palestine, xii, 151, 152, 289
　Israeli-Palestinian conflict, 132–138, 146, 264–265
　Jerusalem and, 125–126
　Ralph Bunche and, 23
　UNSCOP and, 286
　See also Middle East conflict; Palestine Liberation Organization
Palestine Liberation Organization (PLO), 132–138, 264–265, 292
Panama, 57, 184
Panama Canal, 184
Panguan copper mine, 196
Panmunjom, 127
Papua New Guinea, 196
Pardo, Victor Suanzes, 86
Paris Accords (on Vietnam War), 119
Paris Agreements (on Cambodia), 25, 27, 28, 29
Parson, Anthony, 196
Partition Plan (for Palestine), 286, 290
Partnership for Peace Program, 93, 179, 197, 246
Patassé, Ange-Félix, 35
Patriotic Front (Zimbabwe), 45, 46

PDK. *See* Khmer Rouge Party of Democratic Kampuchea
Peace and Human Rights Commissions (Nicaragua), 174–175
Peace building
　from below, 197–198
　Boutros-Ghali on, 1, 2, 197
　defined, xx
　in Nicaragua, 174–175
　in second-generation peacekeeping, 219
　See also Postconflict reconstruction
Peace enforcement, 198–199
　in British peacekeeping doctrine, 22
　consent and, xxii
　defined, xxi
　Nordic forces and, 179
　ONUC operations and, 54–56
　Organization of East Caribbean States and, 189
　in peace support operations, xxiv–xxv
　Russian peacekeeping and, 207
　second-generation peacekeeping and, 218–219
　in Somalia, xiii, 224–227
　in Sri Lanka, 234–238
　UN Charter and, 37
　UNPROFOR and, xvii
Peace enforcement units, xxii–xxiii
Peace Operations, 294
Peace operations, xix. *See also* Peace Support Operations
Peace Support Operations, 22–23
Peace Support Operations (PSOs)
　air power and, 2
　in British peacekeeping doctrine, 22
　defined, xix–xx
　Italian categorization of, 122
　NATO on, 180
　nonlethal weapons in, 177–178
　operational techniques in, xxv
　peace enforcement and, xxiv–xxv
　second-generation peacekeeping and, 218
　UNPROFOR experience and, 286
　U.S. peacekeeping doctrine and, 294
Peaceful stable situations, 49
Peacekeepers
　codes of conduct, 43–44
　rules of engagement, 206–207
　training of. *See* Training programs
　violence against, 47, 195, 283
Peacekeeper's Handbook (Harbottle), 110
Peacekeeping
　An Agenda for Peace on, 1–2

arms control and, 12
Cold War and, 45
conflict resolution theory and, 48–49
contemporary debate on, xxii–xxiii
costs of, 57–58, 59(table)
cultural interactions and, 63–65
definition of terms in, xix–xxi
definitions of, xx, xxii, 1, 22, 93
disarmament and, 12
effects of World War I on, 301
equipment, supply of, 87–88. *See also* Logistics
financing of, 91–92
first generation, xi–xiii, 37, 41, 93–94
future of, xxiii–xxv
Hammarskjöld-Pearson principles of, xi, 32–33, 37, 48, 93–94, 110
history of, xi–xix
host countries and, 110–111
intelligence support and, 117–118
internal, types of, 119
interposition and, 120
logistics and, 146–147
military medicine and, 153
mission mandates and, 151
multidimensional, xvi–xix, 218
naval forces and, 172–173
peace building from below and, 197–198
post–Cold War, characteristics of, xiii–xix. *See also* Second-generation peacekeeping
regional organizations and, 204–205
rules of engagement, 206–207
self-sufficiency of forces, 147
status of forces agreement, 238
UN Charter and, 37
women in, 300–301
Peacekeeping Operations Law (Japan), 125
Peacekeeping Reserve Fund, 92
Peacekeeping Training Courses Database, 245
Peacemaking
An Agenda for Peace on, 1
defined, xx
Pearson, Lester, 199
Nobel Peace Prize, 175
principles of peacekeeping and, xi, 32–33, 48, 93–94, 110
Suez Canal crisis and, 178
UNEF I and, 265, 296
Pedauye, Antonio, 17
Penny-packets, 173
People's Democratic Party of Afghanistan, 268

People's Liberation Army of Namibia, 167
Peoples Liberation Organization of Tamil Eelam, 235
People's Republic of China. *See* China
People's war concept, child soldiers and, 39
Pérez de Cuéllar, Javier, 200
Afghan conflict and, 269
El Salvador and, 83
on humanitarian interventions, 114
Office for the Collection of Research Information and, 256
on ONUCA, 185
Western Sahara and, 156
Persian Gulf, naval peacekeeping forces in, 173
Persian Gulf War (Iraq-Kuwait), 104–105, 217
effects on Iran-Iraq conflict, 271
humanitarian interventions in, 113
Japan and, 125
logistics and, 147
no-fly zones and, 176
UNIKOM and, 272–273
Western European Union and, 299
See also Operation Desert Storm; Operation Provide Comfort
Peru, 57, 184, 200, 259
Perumal, Annamalai, 236
Petersburg Tasks, 90, 299
Pink zones, 88, 279, 280
Plan for National Reconciliation (Congo), 55–56
Planning cells, 299
Pol Pot, 26, 27
Poland, 119, 130, 259, 266
Police. *See* Civilian police; Secret police
POLISARIO. *See* Popular Front for the Liberation of Saguiet el Hamr and Rio de Oro
Political crises, 49
Political tension situations, 49
Popular Front for the Liberation of Saguiet el Hamr and Rio de Oro (POLISARIO), 156–158
Port Said, 262
Portugal, 5–6, 7
Postconflict peace building. *See* Postconflict reconstruction
Postconflict reconstruction, 200–201
An Agenda for Peace on, 1, 2
demilitarized zones and, 75
disarmament and, 12, 13
landmines and, 13
See also Peace building
POWs. *See* Prisoners of war

Prabhakaran, V., 232, 233–234, 235, 236
Premadasa, Ranasinghe, 232, 235, 236–237
Presidential Decision Directive 25, xxii, 295
Preval, Rene, 109
Preventive deployment, 2, 75. *See also* UNPREDEP
Preventive diplomacy, xxi, 1, 2. *See also* Conflict prevention
Prevlaka, 60–61
"Principles for a Peaceful Settlement in South-West Africa," 168
Prison camps, in Yugoslavia, 281, 282
Prisoners of war (POWs)
children as, 39
in Yugoslavia, 281, 282
Private voluntary organizations. *See* Nongovernmental organizations
Procedure for the Establishment of a Firm and Lasting Peace in Central America, 57
Procurement. *See* Logistics
Program for Institutional Support (Nicaragua), 174–175
Program for Observation and Verification (Nicaragua), 174
Program of Correspondence Instruction in Peacekeeping Operations, 245–246
Project on Peacekeeping Policy, 302
Protectorates, 120. *See also* Internationalization
Psychological operations, xxv
Punjab, 274
Purwadi, General, 63

Qaddafi, Muammar. *See* Gadhafi, Muammar al-
Qana, 135
Quainoo, Arnold, 139
Quarantine, 119
Quellet, Jean, 199
Queseda Goméz, Agustín, 186

Radio-Television Libre des Milles Collines, 211
Rahanweyne clan, 221
Rahmonov, Imomali, 242, 243
Ramachandran, M. G., 232
Ranariddh, Norodom, 27, 32
Rapid response forces
Allied Command Europe Rapid Reaction Corps, 75
in Bosnia, 284
Canadian peacekeeping doctrine and, 34

Danish Reaction Brigade, 75
Finland and, 93
Immediate Reaction Force, 180, 181
proposals for, 198–199
Rawlings, Jerry, 144
Reagan, Ronald, 6, 183, 184
Red Cross/Red Crescent. *See*
International Committee of the
Red Cross/Red Crescent
Red line (Lebanon), 133
Reer Hamar clan, 221
Refugee camps, Rwandan, 214
Refugee law, humanitarian assistance
and, 113
Refugees, 203
Afghan, 269
Angolan, 8
Cambodian, 30
in Georgia, 100
internal conflicts and, 49
Liberian, 145
Mozambican, 159, 164
Namibian, 171
Rwandan, 208, 209, 210, 211, 212,
214
Somalian, 220, 222
Sri Lankan, 232, 237
from Yugoslav crisis, 61, 276, 277, 278
See also UNHCR
Regional organizations, 204–205
Regional training programs, 246
Reintegration Support Scheme
(Mozambique), 164
Relief Web, 256(box), 302
RENMAO. *See* Resistancia Nacional
Mocambicana
*Report of the Secretary-General on the
Work of the Organization,* 204
Representative of the Secretary-General
in the Dominican Republic. *See*
DOMREP
Republika Srpska, 284
Republika Srpska Krajina, 58
Research and Intelligence Wing (Indian
intelligence), 232, 236, 237–238
Resettlement
of Mozambican refugees, 164
of Namibian refugees, 171
of Rwandan refugees, 210, 213, 214
Resistancia Nacional Mocambicana
(RENAMO), 159, 160, 161, 162,
163, 164, 165
Returnees, 203. *See also* Refugees;
Resettlement
Revolutionary conflicts, 50
Revolutionary United Front (Sierra
Leone), 220

Rhodesia, 45–46, 172
Rikhye, Indar Jit, 205
Rivera, Julio, 81
Riyadh Summit, 129, 133
Riza, Iqbal, 17
Roberto, Holden, 6
Rodrigues da Silva, L. G., 162
Rodriguez, Jose, 104
Romero, Carlos Humberto, 81
Romero, Oscar Arnulfo, 81–82
Rose, Michael, 206
Royal Navy, 172
Rugo, 209
Rules of engagement, 178, 206–207. *See
also* Codes of conduct
Russia
Georgia and, 98, 99, 100
Security Council and, 252, 253
United Nations debt, 58
See also Commonwealth of
Independent States
Russian peacekeeping, 207–208,
243–244
Russians, in Tajikistan, 241
Rwanda, 208–215
France and, 95
New Zealand peacekeepers and, 173,
174
nongovernmental organizations and,
176
Organization of African Unity and,
188
Rwandese Patriotic Front, 210, 212, 214

Saar International Force, 130
Saassa, 258
Sabra, 137
Sadat, Anwar, 21, 266
Safe areas, 217, 282–283
Safe havens, 105, 113, 121, 217
Saharan Arab Democratic Republic, 156
Sahnoun, Mohammed, 217–218, 223,
224
Sahrawi people, 156, 157
Salam, Mohammed Abdus, 162
San Isidro Declaration, 185
San José Agreement, 83
Sanctions. *See* Economic sanctions
Sanderson, John M., 14, 28, 31
Sandinista Front for National
Liberation, 183, 185, 186
Sandinista Popular Army, 174
Sandjak, 192
Sarajevo, 18, 217, 280–281, 282, 283, 284
Sarajevo On-line project, 302
Saudi Arabia, 129, 156, 303–304
Save the Children, 176

Savimbi, Jonas, 6, 7, 8, 9
Sawyer, Amos, 139, 140
Schoups, Jozef, 63
Scuola Superiore Di Studi Universitari E
Perferzionamento S. Anna, 247
SEATO. *See* Southeast Treaty
Organization
Second Generation Multinational
Operations, 151
Second-generation peacekeeping,
218–219, 286
Secret police, in Mozambique, 161
Secretariat, 254
Secretary-General, 253–254
in UN chain of command, 36
Security. *See* Operational security
Security Council, 253
An Agenda for Peace
recommendations, 1–2
Cold War and, 45
in financing peacekeeping, 91, 92
India and, 115
peacekeeping mission mandates
and, 151
permanent members, 252
secretary-general and, 254
in UN chain of command, 36
UN Charter and, 37
Security zones
in Nicaragua, 185
in Rwanda, 213
in southern Lebanon, 135, 136
See also Buffer zones; Demilitarized
zones; Safe areas; Safe havens
Self-defense. *See* Rules of engagement
Self-determination
in internal peacekeeping, 119
in West New Guinea, 117
See also Elections
Senegal, 140, 188, 247, 249
Serbia
Croatia and, 58, 59, 61, 278–280
European Union and, 89
Federal Republic of Yugoslavia and,
279
Macedonia and, 150
population of, 276
sanctions against, 191, 280
UN safe areas and, 217
WEU and UN cooperation in, 204
See also Yugoslavian conflict
Serbian Autonomous Region, 278
Serbian Republic of Krajina, 58
Serbs, in Croatia, 58, 59, 60, 61, 62
SFOR. *See* Stabilization force
Shaba. *See* Katanga
Shabra refugee camp, 292

SHAPE. *See* Supreme Headquarters Allied Powers in Europe
Sharm al-Sheikh, 262, 264
Sharma'arke, Abdirashid, 222
Shatila refugee camp, 137, 292
Shevardnadze, Eduard, 98, 99
Shia Muslims, 121
  in Iraq, 105, 113
  in Lebanon, 130, 132, 135
SHIR-BRIG. *See* Standby Forces High Readiness Brigade
Shultz, George, 294
Sibanda, Phillip, 9, 305
Sierra Leone, 139, 144, 220
Sihanouk, Norodom, 26, 27, 28, 29, 31, 32
Sinai, 291, 292
Sinai Field Mission, 166, 267, 295
Sinai Support Mission, 295
Singh, Sir Hari, 273
Singh, V. P., 237
Single European Act, 89
Sinhalese. *See* Tamil-Sinhalese conflict
Situation Center (DPKO), xxiii, 117–118, 256, 287
Six-Day War, 132–138, 244, 259, 265
Slavonia, 58, 278, 279
Slovenia, 88, 276, 278
Small arms
  microdisarmament and, 12–13
  See also Weapons
Smith, Leighton, 18
Smith, Rupert, 278, 283
Sokalski, Henryk, 149
Somali National Alliance, 222–223, 226–227
Somali National Front, 222, 223
Somali National Movement, 222, 223
Somali Salvation Democratic Front, 222
Somalia, 220–228
  Australian forces in, 14–15
  criticism of UN personnel in, xxii, 44
  German peacekeepers in, 101
  "humanitarian war" in, 195
  Indian peacekeepers in, 115
  infiltration of UN forces in, 117
  International NGO Consortium in, 155
  Mohammed Sahnoun and, 218
  naval peacekeeping forces and, 172, 173
  New Zealand peacekeepers and, 173, 174
  Pakistani peacekeepers in, 195
  peace enforcement and, xiii, xxi
  UNOSOM and, xvii. *See also* UNOSOM

U.S. forces in, 295
  use of nonlethal weapons in, 178, 179(box)
  women peacekeepers in, 300
Somalia Intervention Web page, 302
Somaliland, 221, 223
Somoza dynasty, 183
Son Sann, 27
South Africa, 228–229
  Angola and, 6–7, 9
  Commonwealth Mission to, 46
  Mozambique and, 159, 160, 165
  Namibia and, 167, 168, 170, 171, 172
South African Defence Force, 168, 170
South Korea, 127
South Lebanon Army, 135
South Ossetia, 46, 207
South Pacific Peacekeeping Force, 196
South West Africa People's Organization (SWAPO), 167, 168, 170, 171, 172
South West Africa Police, 170, 171
South West Africa Territorial Force, 170
Southeast Asian Nuclear Weapon-Free Zone, 13
Southeast Treaty Organization (SEATO), 13
Southern African region, 305
Soviet Union
  Afghanistan and, 268–270
  Angola and, 6, 7, 167, 168
  Cold War and, 45
  Congo and, 51, 52
  Cyprus and, 67
  Greek conflict and, 102
  Indonesia and, 116
  Lebanon and, 131, 133, 138
  Namibia and, 167, 168
  Nicaragua and, 183
  Somalia and, 222
  Suez Canal crisis and, 261, 262
  Tajikistan and, 241
  U Thant and, 244
  UNEF II and, 166, 266, 267–268
  United Nations history and, 252
  Yemen and, 303
  Yom Kippur War and, 265, 266
Spain, 156, 250
Special Committee on Peacekeeping Operations, 253
Special representative of the secretary-general (SRSG), 230, 253
  in Angola, 8, 9, 10
  in Cambodia, 28, 29, 31
  coordination of military-humanitarian activities, 155
  in Liberia, 140–141
  Mohammed Sahnoun, 218

in Morocco, 156
  in Mozambique, 161, 162, 163
  in Namibia, 167, 168, 170, 171
  Ralph Bunche, 23
  in Rwanda, 212
  in Sierra Leone, 220
  in Somalia, 223, 224
  in UN chain of command, 36
  to UNPREDEP, 149
  Yasushi Akashi, 3
  in Yugoslavia, 278
Srebrenica, 217, 282, 284
Sri Lanka, 73, 230–238
Sri Lanka Freedom Party, 235, 236
Sri Lanka Muslim Congress, 236
Sri Lankan Armed Forces, 232, 233, 236, 237
Srpska, 284
Stabilization Force (SFOR), xxiii, 17, 20–21, 180, 201
Standby forces
  An Agenda for Peace on, 2
  Denmark and, 75
  Finland and, 93
  France and, 95
  High Readiness Brigade, 288–289
  Norwegian, 181
  in second-generation peacekeeping, 219
  Swedish, 239
Standby Forces High Readiness Brigade (SHIR-BRIG), 288–289
Standby resources, 146–147
Standing forces
  proposals for, 198–199, 289
  in second-generation peacekeeping, 219
Stanleyville, 51
START. *See* Strategic Arms Reduction Talks
State Department, U.S., 155
State of Cambodia, 26, 27, 28, 30
Status of Forces Agreement, 153, 238
Stewart, Robert, 238
Stoltenberg, Thorvald, 277, 278, 283, 284
Strategic Arms Reduction Talks (START), 190
Stress, 153
Structural adjustment programs, Rwanda and, 209
Suanzes Pardo, Victor, 186
Sudan, 151
Suez, Gulf of, naval peacekeeping forces, 173
Suez Canal
  UNEF II and, 267
  Yom Kippur War and, 265

Suez Canal Company, 261
Suez Canal crisis, 178, 261–265, 291
    Lester Pearson and, 199
    origin of Blue Helmets and, 17
    UNEF I and, xi, xii
    Uniting for Peace resolution and, 296
Sukarno, 116
Sunni Muslims
    in Lebanon, 132, 137
    in Somalia, 221
Supervisory and Monitoring
        Commission (Mozambique), 160,
        161
Supplement to An Agenda for Peace
        (Boutros-Ghali), 201, 204
Supreme Headquarters Allied Powers in
        Europe (SHAPE), 180
Supreme National Council (of
        Cambodia), 27–28, 29, 32
Suttner, Bertha von, 175
SWAPO. *See* South West Africa People's
        Organization
Swayer, Amos, 139
Sweden, 238–239
    participation in UN missions, 247,
        249
    peace enforcement missions and, 179
    peacekeeping training programs in,
        246
    Russian peacekeeping and, 207
    standby forces and, 178
    training programs of, 179
Swedish Armed Forces International
        Center, 239
Swedish peacekeeping, 238–239
Symbolic Arab Security Force, 129
Synthetic Aperture Radar, 118
Syria, xii
    Armistice Agreement with Israel,
        290, 291
    border conflicts with Israel, 291–292
    in League of Arab States, 129, 130
    Lebanon and, 129, 130, 131,
        132–133, 135, 136, 137, 138
    PLO in, 264
    Six-Day War and, 265
    UNDOF and, 259–261
    Yom Kippur War and, 165, 258–259,
        265
    See also Middle East conflict; United
        Arab Republic

Tajikistan, 241–244
    CIS and, xxiii, 46
    OSCE and, 192
    Russian peacekeeping and, 207, 208
    UNMOT and CIS cooperation in, 204

Talha, Mahmoud, 141
Tamil Eelam, 231, 232, 233, 234
Tamil Eelam Liberation Organization,
        235, 236
Tamil Nadu, 230, 232, 236, 238
Tamil National Army, 237
Tamil United Liberation Front, 231
Tamil-Sinhalese conflict, 230–234
"Tanker War," 1984–1988, 173
Tanzania, 113, 143, 209, 210
Tarvainen, Esa Kalervo, 273
Tashkent Protocol on Collective
        Peacekeeping Forces, 46
Taylor, Charles, 138, 139–140
Taylor, Tamba, 144
Tehran Agreement, 242
Tela Accord, 174, 185
Territorial integrity, Organization of
        African Unity and, 187–188
Terrorism, in Sri Lanka, 232
Texier, Philippe, 86
Thailand, 249
Thant, U, 55, 56, 244, 265, 303
Thatcher, Margaret, 196
Theodhoros, Ayios, 66
Thileepan, Dharmalingam, 235
Third World countries, participation in
        UN missions, 248–249
Tiberias, Lake, 291
Tilakaratna, Bernard, 237
Tiran, Strait of, 172, 291
Tito. *See* Broz, Josip
Togo, 139, 140
Tolber, William, 139
Toshiki Kaifu, 125
Total war concept
    child soldiers and, 39
    noncombatants and, 47
    violence against peacekeepers, 47,
        195, 283
Tousignant, Guy, 212
*Toward a Rapid Reaction Capability for
        the United Nations Report,* 34
Traditional peacekeeping. *See* First-
        generation peacekeeping
Training assistance teams, 245
Training Program for Civilian Personnel
        of Peacekeeping/Humanitarian
        Operations, 122–123
*Training Programme for Peace
        Operations,* 122
Training programs, 244–247
    Cairo Center for Training on Conflict
        Resolution and Peacekeeping in
        Africa, 79
    in Ireland, 122
    in Italy, 122–123

Joint Readiness Training Center, 155
Lester B. Pearson International
        Peacekeeping Training Center,
        199
    Nordic, 179
    in Russia, 208
    in Zimbabwe, 305
Transitional National Council
        (Somalia), 226
Transjordan, 129, 151, 152. *See also*
        Jordan
Treaty of Friendship and Good
        Neighbors, 257
Trieste, 120
Trincomalee, 232, 233, 234, 235
Troop-contributing countries, 247–250
    intelligence sharing and, 117
    See also individual countries
Truce Commission for Palestine, 286
Truces
    military observers and, 154
    See also Cease-fires
Truman Doctrine, 102
Trustee Councilship, 125
Tshombe, Moise, 51, 54, 55, 56, 110
Tubman, William, 139
Tudjman, Franjo, 58, 59, 61, 276, 284
Tunisia, 249
Turkey, Cyprus and, 65, 66, 67, 69
Turkish Cypriots, 65–67, 69–71
Turkish Republic of Northern Cyprus,
        67
Turkmenistan, 46
Turnhalle initiative, 167
Tutsi people, 208–212, 213
Tuzla, 217, 282
Twa people, 208, 209
Twagiramungu, Faustin, 212
Tyre, 133

Uganda, 113, 143, 209, 210, 212
Ukraine, 46, 192, 249
"UN line," 150
UN Peacekeeping Training Manua, 245
UNAMIC (United Nations Advance
        Mission in Cambodia), 14, 25,
        28
UNAMIR (United Nations Assistance
        Mission in Rwanda), 212–215
    Canadian peacekeepers and, 33
    Norwegian peacekeepers in, 181
    OAU and, 212–215
    overview of, xviii
    standby forces and, 289
    Zimbabwean peacekeepers in, 305
UNASOG (United Nations Aouzou Strip
        Observer Group), 257–258

UNAVEM I-III (United Nations Angola Verification Mission), 7–10
overview of, xvi
postconflict resolution and, 201
training assistance teams and, 245
UNTSO and, 293
Zimbabwean peacekeepers in, 305
UNCED (United Nations Conference on Environment and Development), 217
UNCI (United Nations Commission for Indonesia), 15
UNCIP (United Nations Commission for India and Pakistan), xii, 274
UNCIVPOL. See CIVPOL
UNCRO (United Nations Confidence Restoration Organization in Croatia), 59–60, 280
UNDAC (United Nations Disaster Assessment and Coordination Teams), 155
UNDOF (United Nations Disengagement Observer Force), 258–261
Canadian peacekeepers and, 33
Chinese peacekeepers in, 41
deployment of, xii, 93, 292
Kurt Waldheim and, 299
UNTSO and, 293
women peacekeepers in, 300
UNDP (United Nations Development Program), 251
Interagency Standing Committee and, 155
in Mozambique, 162
in Somalia, 228
volunteers and, 300
UNDPKO. See United Nations Department of Peacekeeping Operations
UNEF I (United Nations Emergency Force I), 261–265
Cold War and, 45
conflict resolution theory and, 48
costs and financing of, 52, 54, 91
in first-generation peacekeeping, xi, xii, 93
Hammarskjöld peacekeeping principles and, xi, 32–34, 37, 110
host country principles and, 111
Indian peacekeepers in, 115
Lester Pearson and, 199
Lewis MacKenzie and, 150
Nordic forces in, 179
Uniting for Peace resolution and, 296
UNTEA and, 117
UNTSO and, 293

withdrawal of, 291
UNEF II (United Nations Emergency Force II), 265–268
costs and financing of, 52, 54, 92
deployment of, 292
in first-generation peacekeeping, xiii
Irish peacekeepers in, 121
Kurt Waldheim and, 299
Multinational Force and Observers and, 165–166
U Thant and, 244
UNDOF and, 259, 261
UNTSO and, 293
U.S. Sinai Support Mission and, 295
UNESCO (United Nations Educational, Scientific, and Cultural Organization), 205
UNFICYP (United Nations Peacekeeping Force in Cyprus)
civilian police in, 42
cultural studies of, 64
deployment of, 67–71
in first-generation peacekeeping, 93
Irish peacekeepers in, 121
Kurt Waldheim and, 299
Lester Pearson and, 199
Lewis MacKenzie and, 150
mandate of, xiii, 66
UN civilian police in, 94
UNEF II and, 266
UNGCI (United Nations Guards Contingent in Iraq), 121, 217
UNGOMAP (United Nations Good Offices Mission in Afghanistan and Pakistan), 119, 268–270, 293
UNHCR (United Nations High Commissioner for Refugees), 203, 251
creation of office, 111
Eastern Slavonia and, 61
on humanitarian assistance, 112
Interagency Standing Committee and, 155
on Mozambique, 164
Namibia and, 171, 172
New Zealand and, 174
nongovernmental organizations and, 41, 176–177
Rwanda and, 211, 214
Somalia and, 228
Yugoslavia and, 277
Uniao Democratica (Mozambique), 165
Uniao Nacional para a Independência Total de Angola (UNITA), 6, 7, 8, 9, 160
UNICEF (United Nations Children's Fund), 155, 164, 228, 251–252

Unidad Revolucionaria Nacional Guatemalteca, 103
Unified Task Force (UNITAF), 195, 224, 256, 295, 305
UNIFIL (United Nations Interim Force in Lebanon)
cultural study of, 64–65
deployment of, 133–136, 292
in first-generation peacekeeping, 93
Force Mobile Reserve in, 94
France and, 95
Ireland's training program and, 246
Irish peacekeepers in, 121
Kurt Waldheim and, 299
League of Arab States on, 130
mission of, 119
Norwegian peacekeepers in, 181
UNTSO and, 293
UNIIMOG (United Nations Iran-Iraq Military Observer Group), 104, 270–272
UNTSO and, 293
UNIKOM (United Nations Iraq-Kuwait Observation Mission), 94, 272–273, 293
Unimna, Edward, 8
Union Minière du Haut Katanga, 51, 52
Unión Nacional Opositora, 185
UNIPOM (United Nations India-Pakistan Observation Mission), xiii, 93, 244, 274–275
UNIPTF (United Nations International Police Task Force), 17–18
UNITA. See Uniao Nacional para a Independência Total de Angola
UNITAF. See Unified Task Force
UNITAR (United Nations Institute for Training and Research), 245–246, 301
United Arab Republic, 131, 303, 304
United Liberation Movement for Democracy in Liberia, 140, 141, 143, 144
United National Party (Sri Lanka), 234, 236
United Nations
agencies of, 251–252
An Agenda for Peace recommendations, 1–2
chain of command, 36–37
CSCE and, 192
definition of peacekeeping, 93
financing of peacekeeping operations, 52, 54, 91–92
general budget of, 91
history of, 251
history of peacekeeping in, xi–xix

intelligence gathering and, 117–118
Javier Pérez de Cuéllar and, 200
NATO and, 180
Nobel Peace Prize to, 176
Organization of African Unity and,
    187, 188–189
Organization of American States
    and, 189
organizational structure, xxi–xii,
    252–257
peace building from below and, 198
peace enforcement and, 198
peacekeeping operations, xiv(map),
    xxiv(table)
postconflict resolution and, 200–201
regional organizations and,
    204–205
World Wide Web and, 301–302
See also United Nations Charter
United Nations Advance Mission in
    Cambodia. See UNAMIC
United Nations Angola Verification
    Mission I-III. See UNAVEM I-III
United Nations Aouzou Strip Observer
    Group. See UNASOG
United Nations Assistance Mission in
    Rwanda. See UNAMIR
United Nations Center for Disarmament
    Affairs, 257
United Nations Charter, 37
    drafting of, 252
    on non-governmental organizations,
        175
    Organization of African Unity and,
        187
    peacekeeping operations and, xi
    Preamble to, 254(box)
    status of forces agreement and, 238
United Nations Children's Fund. See
    UNICEF
United Nations Civilian Police. See
    CIVPOL
United Nations Civilian Police Mission
    in Haiti. See MINPONUH
United Nations Civilian Police Support
    Group, 63
United Nations Commission for India
    and Pakistan. See UNCIP
United Nations Conference on
    Environment and Development.
    See UNCED
United Nations Conference on
    Humanitarian Assistance to
    Somalia, 226
United Nations Confidence Restoration
    Organization in Croatia. See
    UNCRO

United Nations Department for
    Disarmament and Arms
    Regulation, 257
United Nations Department of
    Administration and
    Management, xxi, 255
United Nations Department of
    Humanitarian Affairs (DHA)
    establishment of, 112, 113
    Jan Eliasson and, 81
    in military-humanitarian relations,
        155
    in Mozambique, 165
    reform of, 254
    responsibilities of, xxi, 113–114, 255
    White Helmets and, 300
    World Wide Web and, 256(box), 301
United Nations Department of
    Peacekeeping Operations
    (DPKO/UNDPKO), 255–256
    code of conduct, 44
    peacekeeping equipment needs and,
        87
    reform of, 287
    responsibilities of, xxi
    Rwanda and, 214
    Situation Room, xxiii, 117–118
    training programs and, 245
    UN Secretariat and, 254
    World Wide Web and, 301–302
United Nations Department of Political
    Affairs, xxi, 256
United Nations Development Program.
    See UNDP
United Nations Disaster Assessment
    and Coordination Teams. See
    UNDAC
United Nations Disaster Management
    Team, 155, 212
United Nations Disengagement
    Observer Force. See UNDOF
United Nations Emergency Forces, in
    Gaza and Sinai, 199, 205
United Nations Good Offices Mission in
    Afghanistan and Pakistan. See
    UNGOMAP
United Nations guardianship. See
    Internationalization;
    Protectorates
United Nations Guards Contingent in
    Iraq. See UNGCI
United Nations High Commissioner for
    Refugees. See UNHCR
United Nations Human Rights Center,
    251
United Nations Human Rights
    Commission, 251

United Nations Humanitarian
    Assistance Coordination Unit, 8
United Nations India-Pakistan
    Observation Mission. See
    UNIPOM
United Nations Institute for Training
    and Research. See UNITAR
United Nations Interim Force in
    Lebanon. See UNIFIL
United Nations International Children's
    Emergency Fund. See UNICEF
United Nations International Police Task
    Force. See UNIPTF
United Nations Iran-Iraq Military
    Observer Group. See UNIIMOG
United Nations Iraq-Kuwait
    Observation Mission. See
    UNIKOM
United Nations Legion, proposals for,
    198–199, 289
United Nations Liaison Office in Beirut.
    See UNLOB
United Nations Logistics Base, Brindisi,
    123
United Nations Medical Support Unit,
    153
United Nations Military Observer Group
    in India and Pakistan. See
    UNMOGIP
United Nations Mission for the
    Referendum in Western Sahara.
    See MINURSO
United Nations Mission in Bosnia and
    Herzegovina. See UNMIBH
United Nations Mission in El Salvador.
    See MINUSAL
United Nations Mission in Haiti. See
    UNMIH
United Nations Mission in Rwanda. See
    UNAMIR
United Nations Mission in the Central
    African Republic. See
    MINURCA
United Nations Mission of Observers in
    Prevlaka. See UNMOP
United Nations Mission of Observers in
    Tajikistan. See UNMOT
United Nations Mission to Central
    America. See UNOMCA
United Nations Observation Group in
    Lebanon. See UNOGIL
United Nations Observation Mission for
    the Verification of Elections in
    Nicaragua. See ONUVEN
United Nations Observer Group for the
    Verification of Elections in Haiti.
    See ONUVEH

United Nations Observer Mission for the Verification of Elections in Eritrea. *See* ONUVER
United Nations Observer Mission in Angola. *See* MONUA
United Nations Observer Group in Central America. *See* ONUCA
United Nations Observer Mission in El Salvador. *See* ONUSAL
United Nations Observer Mission in Georgia. *See* UNOMIG
United Nations Observer Mission in Sierra Leone. *See* UNOMSIL
United Nations Observer Mission in Uganda/Rwanda. *See* UNOMUR
United Nations Observer Mission to South Africa. *See* UNOMSA
United Nations Office for Humanitarian Assistance Coordination. *See* UNOHAC
United Nations Office for the Collection of Research Information, 256
United Nations Office for the Coordination of Humanitarian Affairs, 253–254, 256(box)
United Nations Operation in Mozambique. *See* ONUMOZ
United Nations Operation in Somalia. *See* UNOSOM
United Nations Palestine Commission, 286
United Nations Partition Plan, 286, 290
United Nations Peace Forces. *See* UNPF
United Nations Peace Forces Headquarters. *See* UNPF-HQ
United Nations Peacekeeping Force in Cyprus. *See* UNFICYP
United Nations Peacekeeping Forces, Nobel Peace Prize, 176
United Nations Preventive Deployment Force Macedonia. *See* UNPREDEP
United Nations Protected Areas. *See* UNPAs
United Nations Relief and Rehabilitation Administration, 251
United Nations Relief Works Agency for Palestinian Refugees. *See* UNRWA
United Nations Rwanda Emergency Office. *See* UNREO
United Nations Special Commission. *See* UNSCOM
United Nations Special Committee on Palestine. *See* UNSCOP
United Nations Special Committee on Peacekeeping Operations, 40, 287–288

United Nations Special Committee on the Balkans. *See* UNSCOB
United Nations Special Coordinator's Office. *See* UNSCOL
United Nations Standby Arrangements System. *See* UNSAS
United Nations Standby Forces. *See* Standby forces; UNSAS
United Nations Support Mission for Haiti. *See* UNSMIH
United Nations Training School Ireland. *See* UNTSI
United Nations Transitional Administration for Eastern Slovenia, Baranja, and Western Sirmium. *See* UNTAES
United Nations Transitional Assistance Group. *See* UNTAG
United Nations Transitional Authority in Cambodia. *See* UNTAC
United Nations Truce Supervision Organization. *See* UNTSO
United Nations Verification Mission in Guatemala. *See* MINUGUA
United Nations Volunteer Force, proposals for, 199
United Nations Volunteers (UNVs), 252
  in Cambodia, 29, 31
  White Helmets and, 300
United Nations Yemen Observer Mission. *See* UNYOM
United Somali Congress, 222, 223, 227
United States
  Afghan conflict and, 268, 269
  Angola and, 5, 6, 7, 8
  Cold War and, 45
  Congo and, 51, 54
  coordination of military-humanitarian efforts and, 155
  Dominican Republic and, 76–77
  El Salvador and, 82, 83
  Greek conflict and, 102
  Grenada invasion, 189
  Haiti and, 109
  Indonesia and, 116
  intelligence sharing and, 118
  Iran-Contra scandal, 270
  Iran-Iraq conflict and, 270, 271
  Kosovo and, 4
  League of Nations and, 130
  Lebanon and, 131–132, 133, 136, 137, 138
  Liberia and, 138, 139
  logistic support and, 147
  Multinational Force and Observers and, 166
  Namibia and, 168

  naval peacekeeping forces and, 172, 173
  Nicaragua and, 183, 184, 185
  nonlethal weapons and, 177, 178, 179(box)
  peacekeeping training programs in, 246–247
  refugees and, 203
  rules of engagement and, 206–207
  Rwanda and, 211
  Security Council and, 252, 253
  Somalia and, 195, 222, 224, 226–227, 228
  Sri Lanka and, 232
  Suez Canal crisis and, 261, 262
  UNEF I and, 262, 264
  UNEF II and, 267
  United Nations debt, 58
  United Nations history and, 252
  United Nations peacekeeping and, funding of, 92, 248
  United Nations volunteer force and, 199
  Western Sahara and, 156
  women peacekeepers and, 300
  Yemen and, 303
  Yom Kippur War and, 265, 266
  Yugoslav crisis and, 17, 277, 283
  See also North America; Persian Gulf War; United States peacekeeping
United States Agency for International Development, 155
United States Information Agency, 232
United States Institute for Peace, 247, 302
United States Joint Task Force (Somalia), 228
United States peacekeeping, 293–295
  conflict resolution and, 49
  Presidential Decision Directive 25, xxii
United States Sinai Field Mission, 166, 267, 295
United States Sinai Support Mission, 295
United Tajik Opposition, 242, 243
Uniting for Peace resolution, 52, 296
Universal Declaration of Human Rights, 111, 112, 187
UNAMIR (United Nations Mission in Rwanda), xviii
UNLOB (United Nations Liaison Office in Beirut), 292
UNMIBH (United Nations Mission in Bosnia and Herzegovina), 17, 60

UNMIH (United Nations Mission in Haiti), xvii–xviii, 108–110, 204, 245

UNMOGIP (United Nations Military Observer Group in India and Pakistan), xii, 38, 173, 273–274, 275

UNMOP (United Nations Mission of Observers in Prevlaka), 18, 60–61

UNMOT (United Nations Mission of Observers in Tajikistan), 204, 242–244

UNOGIL (United Nations Observation Group in Lebanon), xiii, 93, 121, 131–132, 293

UNOHAC (United Nations Office for Humanitarian Assistance Coordination), 162, 165

UNOMCA (United Nations Mission to Central America), 150

UNOMIG (United Nations Observer Mission in Georgia), 98–100, 204, 207

UNOMIL (United Nations Observer Mission in Liberia), xvii, 138, 141–146, 204

UNOMSA (United Nations Observer Mission to South Africa), 229

UNOMSIL (United Nations Observer Mission in Sierra Leone), 220

UNOMUR (United Nations Observer Mission in Uganda/Rwanda), 212, 213

UNOSOM (United Nations Operation in Somalia), xvii

UNOSOM I (United Nations Operation in Somalia I), 119, 223–224

UNOSOM II (United Nations Operation in Somalia II), 224–228
  DPKO Situation Center and, 256
  German peacekeepers in, 101
  Irish peacekeepers in, 122
  New Zealand peacekeepers in, 174
  Pakistani peacekeepers in, 195
  U.S. forces in, 295
  use of nonlethal weapons in, 178, 179(box)
  Zimbabwean peacekeepers in, 305

UNPAs (United Nations Protected Areas)
  in Croatia, 58–59, 278–279, 280
  France and, 95

UNPF (United Nations Peace Forces), 59, 60, 61

UNPF-HQ (United Nations Peace Forces Headquarters), 149, 280

UNPREDEP (United Nations Preventive Deployment Force Macedonia)
  conflict prevention and, 48, 119
  deployment of, 4, 149–150
  Finnish peacekeepers and, 93
  overview of, xvii
  in UNPF, 60
  UNPROFOR III and, xvii, 280, 285

UNPROFOR (United Nations Protection Force in Former Yugoslavia)
  air support and, 18
  in Bosnia and Herzegovina, xvi–xvii, 280–284
  conflict profile, 276–278
  cooperation with NATO, 204
  criticism of, 285–286
  in Croatia, xvi, 59, 60, 278–280
  Danish peacekeeping forces in, 75
  deployment of, 278–286
  European participation in, 248
  expense of, 285
  extension of mandate, 17
  France and, 95
  Indian peacekeepers in, 115
  Lewis MacKenzie and, 150
  in Macedonia, xvii, 284–285. See also UNPREDEP
  Michael Rose and, 206
  NATO and, 180, 204
  Norwegian peacekeepers in, 181
  overview of, xvi–xvii
  Robert Stewart and, 238
  Russian peacekeepers in, 207
  Swedish peacekeepers in, 239
  UN safe areas and, 217
  UNTSO and, 293

UNPROFOR I (United Nations Protection Force in Former Yugoslavia I), xvi, 278–280

UNPROFOR II (United Nations Protection Force in Former Yugoslavia II), xvi–xvii, 280–284

UNPROFOR III (United Nations Protection Force in Former Yugoslavia III), xvii, 150, 284–285

UNREO (United Nations Rwanda Emergency Office), 212, 213

UNRWA (United Nations Relief Works Agency for Palestinian Refugees), 264

UNSAS (United Nations Standby Arrangements System), xxiii, 122, 147, 178, 288–289

UNSCOB (United Nations Special Committee on the Balkans), xii, 94, 102–103

UNSCOL (United Nations Special Coordinator's Office), 140

UNSCOM (United Nations Special Commission), 121

UNSCOP (United Nations Special Committee on Palestine), 286, 289

UNSF (United Nations Security Force in West Guinea), xiii, 93, 116–117, 195. See also UNTEA/UNSF

UNSMIH (United Nations Support Mission for Haiti), xvii, 109

UNTAC (United Nations Transitional Authority in Cambodia), 28–32
  Australia and, 14
  Chinese peacekeepers in, 41
  civilian police in, 42
  components of, 27
  France and, 95
  human rights and, 111, 251
  Japanese peacekeepers in, 125
  naval peacekeeping forces and, 172, 173
  overview of, xvii, 25
  postconflict resolution and, 119, 201

UNTAES (United Nations Transitional Administration for Eastern Slovenia, Baranja, and Western Sirmium), 60, 61–63, 245

UNTAG (United Nations Transitional Assistance Group), xvi, 41, 93, 101, 201, 250

UNTATs. See Training assistance teams

UNTEA (United Nations Temporary Executive Authority), xiii, 93, 116–117, 172. See also UNTEA/UNSF

UNTEA/UNSF, 91, 93

UNTSI (United Nations Training School Ireland), 122, 246

UNTSO (United Nations Truce Supervision Organization), 151
  deployment of, 289–293
  in first-generation peacekeeping, xii, 38
  France and, 94
  Italian peacekeepers in, 122
  naval support, 172
  overview of, xii
  in Palestine, 286
  in southern Lebanon, 133–134
  UNEF II and, 266, 267
  UNTEA and, 117
  U.S. peacekeepers in, 294
  U.S. Sinai Field Mission and, 295

UNYOM (United Nations Yemen Observation Mission)
  demilitarized zone, 74(map)
  deployment of, 303–304
  financing of, 91

in first-generation peacekeeping, xiii, 93
Pakistani peacekeepers in, 195
UNTSO and, 293
Urquhart, Brian, xi, 40, 92, 199, 218–219, 296
Uruguay, 57, 184
Uwilingiyimana, Agathe, 211
Uzbekistan, 46, 241

Vadamarachi, 232
Vaddukodai Resolution, 231
Vance, Cyrus, 276, 277, 297
Vance-Owen Peace Plan, 277
Venezuela, 57, 184
Vietnam, Cambodia and, 14, 26
Vietnam War, 119, 294
Vilna International Force, 130
Violent political conflicts, 49
Voice of America, 232
Voiska po podderzhanivu mira, 207
Vojvodina, 192, 276
Voter registration
in Mozambique, 164
in Namibia, 171
in Western Sahara, 157–158
Vranitzky, Franz, 4
Vukovar, 276, 278

Wahlgren, Lars-Eric, 278
Waldheim, Kurt, 167, 266, 270, 299
Wallensteen, Peter, 50
Walvis Bay, 167
War(s)
child soldiers in, 38–40
defined, xxi
interstate, decline in, 50
laws of, 38, 97, 112
nonlethal weapons in, 177–178
See also Civil wars; Conflict zones; Conflicts; Internal conflicts; Total war concept
War criminals, 97. *See also* International War Crimes Tribunals
Warsaw Pact countries
Cold War and, 45
Lebanon and, 133
Partnership for Peace and, 197
War-Torn Societies Project, 218
Weapons
arms control, 11–12
arms trade, 12
child soldiers and, 39

disarmament, 11, 12–13
of mass destruction, Iraqi, 272
Weinberger, Caspar, 294
Weinberger Doctrine, 294
Weiss, T. G., 120
West Bank, 291
West Irian. *See* West New Guinea
West New Guinea, 116–117, 172
West Pakistan, 274
Western European Union (WEU), 299
CSCE and, 191, 192
France and, 95
Germany and, 101
naval peacekeeping and, 173
United Nations and, 204
Western Sahara, 156–159
Western Sirmium. *See* Eastern Slavonia
Western Slavonia, 59, 60
Western Srem, 58
WEU. *See* Western European Union
WFP. *See* World Food Program
White Helmets, 300
WHO. *See* World Health Organization
Wider peacekeeping, xxii, 22–23, 218. *See also* Second-generation peacekeeping
Wijeratne, Ranjan, 237
Wijeweera, Rohan, 237
Windhoek, 167
Wiseman, H., 94
Woerner, Manfred, 180
Women
in peacekeeping, 300–301
in Rwanda, 208
World Bank, 164, 209
World Commission on Environment and Development, 217
World Court. *See* International Court of Justice
World Federation of United Nations Associations, 40
World Food Program (WFP), 155, 164, 177, 211, 228, 252
World Health Organization (WHO), 155, 177, 228, 252
World Military and Social Expenditures, 49
World War I
effects on peacekeeping, 301
Middle East and, 151, 152
World War II, United Nations history and, 252
World Wide Web, 256(box), 301–302

Wranker, Bo Lennart, 149, 285

Yamoussoukro Accords, 140, 141
Yasushi Akashi. *See* Akashi, Yasushi
Yemen, 74(map), 129, 303–304
Yom Kippur War, 165, 258–259, 265–266, 292
Yugoslavian conflict, 276–286
Canadian peacekeepers and, 33
Cyrus Vance and, 297
Danish peacekeepers and, 75
Dayton Peace Agreement, 18, 19, 20, 61, 89, 191, 277
ethnic cleansing and, 47
European Community Monitoring Mission and, 88–89
European Union and, 89
German peacekeeping and, 101
Greek conflict and, 102
International Committee of the Red Cross/Red Crescent in, 120
Martti Ahtisaari and, 2
NATO and, 178–179
naval peacekeeping forces and, 172, 173
nongovernmental organizations and, 176
UN cooperation with regional organizations and, 204
UNPROFOR and, xvi–xvii, 278–286
U.S. peacekeeping in, 294
Western European Union and, 299
See also Bosnia and Herzegovina; Croatia; Federal Republic of Yugoslavia; Macedonia; Serbia
Yugoslav's People's Army (JNA)
in Croatia, 278, 279
in Slovenia, 88
Yukinari Hirose, 287

Zagreb Resolution, 97
Zaire, 188, 209, 214
Zambia, 188, 246
Zamora, Rubén, 85
Zepa, 217, 282, 284
Zimbabwe, 45–46, 227, 246, 249, 305
Zimbabwe Defence Force, 305
Zimbabwe Staff College, 246
Zimbabwean-Danish Government Agreement, 305
Zinni, Anthony, 178
Zone of Peace, Neutrality, and Freedom, 13F